ECONOMETRICS

Economics Handbook Series

Anderson: *National Income Theory and Its Price Theoretic Foundations*
Atkinson and Stiglitz: *Lectures on Public Economics*
Carlson: *Economic Security in the United States*
Chacholiades: *International Monetary Theory and Policy*
Chacholiades: *International Trade Theory and Policy*
Chow: *Econometrics*
Gapinski: *Macroeconomic Theory: Statics, Dynamics, and Policy*
Hansen: *A Survey of General Equilibrium Systems*
Hansen: *The American Economy*
Harris: *The Economics of Harvard*
Harris: *Monetary Theory*
Harrod: *The British Economy*
Henderson and Quandt: *Microeconomic Theory: A Mathematical Approach*
Herrick and Kindleberger: *Economic Development*
Hirsch: *The Economics of State and Local Government*
Hirsch: *Urban Economic Analysis*
Jones: *An Introduction to Modern Theories of Economic Growth*
Kendrick: *Stochastic Control for Economic Models*
Maddala: *Econometrics*
Ott, Ott, and Yoo: *Macroeconomic Theory*
Quirk and Saposnik: *Introduction to General Equilibrium Theory and Welfare Economics*
Taylor: *A History of Economic Thought*
Theil, Boot, and Kloek: *Operations Research and Quantitative Economics*
Walton and McKersie: *A Behavioral Theory of Labor Negotiations*

ECONOMETRICS

Gregory C. Chow

Professor of Economics
Princeton University

McGraw-Hill Book Company

New York St. Louis San Francisco Auckland Bogotá Hamburg
Johannesburg London Madrid Mexico Montreal New Delhi
Panama Paris São Paulo Singapore Sydney Tokyo Toronto

This book was set in Times Roman by Santype-Byrd.
The editors were Peter J. Dougherty and Scott Amerman;
the production supervisor was Leroy A. Young.
Halliday Lithograph Corporation was printer and binder.

ECONOMETRICS

1234567890 HALHAL 89876543

ISBN 0-07-010847-1

Library of Congress Cataloging in Publication Data

Chow, Gregory C., date
    Econometrics.

    (Economics Handbook Series)
    Includes bibliographies and index.
    1. Econometrics. I. Title.
HB139.C483   1983   330′.028   82-20903
ISBN 0-07-010847-1

TO THOSE WHO TAUGHT ME ECONOMETRICS:

Milton Friedman
Arnold C. Harberger
Clifford Hildreth
Hendrik S. Houthakker
Tjalling C. Koopmans
William H. Kruskal
Jacob Marschak
L. Jimmie Savage
W. Allen Wallis

CONTENTS

Preface   xi

Chapter 1 Simple Linear Regression   1

1.1   What Is Econometrics?   1
1.2   Model of Simple Linear Regression   3
1.3   Point Estimation   4
1.4   Testing Hypotheses and Interval Estimation   6
1.5   Use of Matrix Notation   7
*1.6   The Multivariate Normal Distribution and Two Regressions   8
1.7   Errors in Observations   14
*1.8   Convergence in Probability   16
*1.9   Central Limit Theorems   18
1.10   The Cramer-Rao Inequality   22
*1.11 Asymptotic Distribution of Maximum-Likelihood Estimators   25
1.12   Estimating the Quantity of, and Demand for, Computers   27

Chapter 2 Multiple Linear Regression   38

2.1   The Model of Multiple Linear Regression   38
2.2   Least-Squares Estimation for β and σ^2 39
*2.3   Geometric Interpretation of the Least-Squares Regression   41
2.4   Testing Hypotheses about β and σ^2 43
2.5   Demand for Automobiles: Theory   47
2.6   Demand for Automobiles: Statistical Findings, 1921–1953   53
2.7   Testing the General Linear Hypothesis   58
2.8   Testing Equality between Sets of Regression Coefficients   60
2.9   Forecasting   62
2.10   Testing the Stability of Automobile Demand Functions   64

* Starred sections may be omitted without loss of continuity; see Preface.

2.11 Use of Statistical Demand Functions for Long-Run Forecasting 65
2.12 Partial Correlation Coefficients 69
*2.13 Asymptotic Distribution of the Least-Squares Estimator b 72

Chapter 3 Topics in Regression Analysis 77

3.1 Method of Generalized Least Squares 77
*3.2 Asymptotic Distribution of the GLS Estimator 81
3.3 Analysis of Regression Residuals 84
3.4 Robust Estimators 88
*3.5 Bayesian Estimation 90
3.6 Non-Bayesian Use of Extraneous Information 96
3.7 Multicollinearity without Other Information 98
3.8 Distributed Lags 102
3.9 Errors in Observations 105
3.10 Method of Instrumental Variables 107

Chapter 4 Simultaneous Equations: Model and Identification 111

4.1 Model of Linear Simultaneous Stochastic Equations 111
4.2 Two Problems Associated with the Simultaneous-Equation Model 114
4.3 Conditions for Identifying a Structural Equation 117
*4.4 Identification of a Set of Structural Parameters 122
4.5 Formulation of a Macroeconometric Model 126
4.6 Some Statistical Considerations for the Model 132
4.7 Empirical Results from the Model 137
4.8 Goodness of Fit and Forecasting Value of the Model 141
4.9 Relative Importance of Various Factors in Income Determination 144
4.10 Final Form of a Linear Dynamic Model 145

Chapter 5 Estimation of Linear Simultaneous Equations 153

5.1 Method of Two-Stage Least Squares 153
*5.2 Method of Limited-Information Maximum Likelihood 157
5.3 The k-Class Estimator 164
5.4 Method of Three-Stage Least Squares 167
*5.5 Method of Full-Information Maximum Likelihood 170
5.6 Method of Instrumental Variables 175
*5.7 Treatment of Identities and Linear Restrictions 177
*5.8 FIML with Autoregressive Residuals 178
5.9 Choice of Estimators 180
5.10 Estimation of the Reduced Form 182

Chapter 6 Time-Series Analysis 188

6.1 Time-Series Models 188
6.2 Dynamic Properties of Time Series 190
6.3 Autocovariance Matrix of a Linear Model 192
6.4 Spectral-Density Matrix of a Linear Model 196
*6.5 Decomposition of Time Series into Periodic Components 200

6.6   Note on the Estimation of Spectral Densities   204
*6.7   Estimation of ARMA Models   207
6.8   Box-Jenkins Techniques   211
*6.9   Definition and Tests of Causality   212

Chapter 7   Nonlinear Models   220

7.1   Introduction   220
7.2   Method of GLS or Minimum Distance   222
7.3   Nonlinear Regression   228
7.4   Method of Maximum Likelihood   230
7.5   Numerical Methods of Maximization   232
*7.6   FIML for Nonlinear Simultaneous Equations   235
7.7   Method of Instrumental Variables   240
*7.8   Nonlinear Two- and Three-Stage Least Squares   243
*7.9   Models of Markets in Disequilibrium   244
7.10   Dynamic Properties of Nonlinear Simultaneous Equations   248

Chapter 8   Discrete and Limited Dependent Variables   253

8.1   Introduction   253
8.2   Probit Analysis   254
8.3   Logit Analysis   255
*8.4   Utility Theory for Discrete-Choice Models   257
8.5   Maximum-Likelihood Estimation of Multinomial Logit Models   260
*8.6   Nested Logit Models   263
8.7   Limited Dependent Variables   265
*8.8   The E-M Algorithm   268
8.9   Truncated Sample   271

Chapter 9   Criteria for Model Selection   277

9.1   Introduction   277
9.2   A Method for Selecting Nonnested Regression Models   278
9.3   Some Tests of Nonnested Hypotheses   284
9.4   Lagrangian Multiplier and Related Tests   286
9.5   The C_p Criterion   291
9.6   The Information Criterion   293
9.7   The Posterior-Probability Criterion   300
9.8   Comparison of the Posterior-Probability and Information Criteria   302
*9.9   Estimation of the Information Criterion for Simultaneous-Equation Models   305
9.10   Should a Linear Econometric Model Be Decomposed or Aggregated?   309
9.11   Tests and Analysis of Model Specifications   313

Chapter 10   Models of Time-Varying Coefficients   320

10.1   Introduction   320
10.2   Derivation of $\beta_{t|s}$ by Recursive Regression of β_t on $y_1, \ldots, y_s$ 321

10.3 Derivations of $\beta_{t|s}$ by Regression of $y_1, \ldots, y_s$ on $x_1, \ldots, x_s$ 326
10.4 Maximum-Likelihood Estimation of σ^2, V, and M 327
*10.5 System of Linear Regressions with Time-Varying Coefficients   330
*10.6 System of Linear Simultaneous Equations   333
*10.7 System of Nonlinear Simultaneous Equations   337
10.8 Model with Stationary Coefficients   338
*10.9 Identifiability of Parameters   340
10.10 Testing Constancy of Regression Coefficients   342
10.11 The Estimation of Seasonal Components in Economic Time Series   345

Chapter 11   Models under Rational Expectations   351

11.1 The Assumption of Rational Expectations   351
11.2 The Problem of Multiple Solutions   353
11.3 Solution to Linear Expectations Models   356
*11.4 The Solution of Blanchard and Kahn   362
11.5 Estimation of Linear Models without Expectations of
Future Variables   364
11.6 Estimation of Linear Models with Future Expectations   366

Chapter 12   Models of Optimizing Agents   373

12.1 Introduction and Preview   373
12.2 Deriving an Optimal Feedback Control Equation   377
*12.3 Method of Maximum Likelihood   380
12.4 Method of Two-Stage Least Squares   385
12.5 Two Economic Examples   386
12.6 Alternative Derivation of the Optimal Rule   390
12.7 Explicit Solution for the Optimal Rule   392
12.8 The Assumptions of Optimization Models   394
12.9 Model of a Dynamic Game   395
*12.10 Policy Evaluation and Optimization under Rational Expectations   396
*12.11 Estimation of a Dynamic Game Model with a Dominant Player   400
*12.12 Estimation of a Dynamic Game Model under Nash Equilibrium   401

Tables   405
Index   419

PREFACE

Since the 1970s, the development of econometrics has been so rapid that it has become difficult to find a textbook that treats the new topics and provides an updated perspective of the field. This text is intended to fill this need.

Most existing texts cover only the topics of Chaps. 1 to 5, the topics of Chaps. 6 to 12 being covered only infrequently. In order to incorporate new developments in a text, as it has been done in field after field for several decades, one must emphasize the basic ideas that underlie the subject. I believe from my teaching experience in Princeton that it is possible to cover the topics of seven chapters in about the same time and with the same effort on the part of students as previously spent in covering the topics of the first five chapters alone. This requires omitting nonessential details in, and improving the exposition of, previous material, as well as exposing the threads that connect all the material, old and new. After the new material has been integrated, the reader will gain a more up-to-date perspective of the subject.

This book is intended mainly for graduate students, although as the curriculum is constantly being upgraded, more and more advanced undergraduates will find the less theoretical parts readable. It assumes familiarity with the basic techniques of statistical inference and some exposure to matrix algebra. Naturally, more preparation in these two areas will make this text easier to read and simpler to comprehend. Chapter 1 can be used to test the reader's preparation. A reader with the minimum required preparation should find Secs. 1.1 to 1.5 easily comprehensible but may find the later starred sections difficult. In this case, I would recommend studying the nonstarred sections of Chap. 2 before returning to the more theoretical starred sections of Chap. 1. In fact, *an applications-*

oriented reader may skip the starred sections or read only the results therein without going through the proofs.

As another means of accommodating students with different backgrounds in statistics and mathematics, I have chosen to weave the required background material into the body of the text rather than presenting appendixes, which are usually dry and formal. This approach has the advantages of motivating the material and helping the student learn it while using it. Material that is used more often will be more firmly absorbed, as it should be.

The level of abstraction at which to present econometrics is a matter of taste. This book has interwoven empirical material to show students how empirical investigations in econometrics are conducted and to motivate the theoretical material. Some readers would prefer more empirical material than is actually presented and some less. Some would prefer having less theorem proving and others would prefer having more and at a higher level of mathematical abstraction. The level selected reflects the author's opinion concerning what the first-year graduate student in economics should be trained to do in the field of econometrics.

Although this text has a broader coverage than existing texts, it cannot possibly cover all important topics, as a textbook is not an encyclopedia. The selection of topics is also a matter of taste. Given the selection of topics, the choice of the tools and concepts to be presented within each topic has been guided by two criteria: the usefulness of the methods in applied work and the usefulness of the theoretical ideas in the further development of econometric methods. For example, the t test is useful in applied work, and the idea of maximum likelihood is useful for developing new estimators. Once the basic tools have been mastered, the student can apply them to study and solve new problems not covered in this text.

How this book should be used depends on the preparation of the students. As mentioned above, the starred sections can be omitted by applications-oriented readers. For the students of applied econometrics who have not had the material in Secs. 1.6 to 1.11, a one-semester course may cover Chaps. 1 to 5, omitting most of the proofs in the starred sections. For the students of theoretical econometrics who have not had the material in Secs. 1.6 to 1.11, a one-semester course may include Chaps. 1 to 5, covering the above sections, and Secs. 2.13, 3.2, and 3.3 *after* the nonstarred sections of Chaps. 1 to 3 have been studied. Less time will be devoted to the empirical studies. Students having had one semester of statistical methods including the materials of Secs. 1.6 to 1.11 may take up additional topics from Chaps. 6, 7, or 9. Chapters 6 to 12 can serve as a text for a second semester in econometrics.

I am indebted to the students at Princeton who helped me learn the material in this text, some using drafts of various chapters and offering comments, including George Mailath, Loretta Mester, and In-Koo Cho, who have also helped prepare the index. Thanks are due to Takeshi Amemiya and John B. Taylor who read Chap. 11, and to David Brownstone who read Chap. 8, and to Adrian

Pagan and Gary Skoog who read many chapters and provided useful comments. It is impossible to express sufficient gratitude to my colleague Richard Quandt, who read the entire manuscript and made many useful suggestions for improvement. Pia Ellen has typed drafts of the manuscript with remarkable efficiency and good spirit. Without her help, the book would not have been completed. I would like to thank all the publishers for granting permission to reprint material written by me and published by them. References are given in the text. Results of research supported by the National Science Foundation through several grants find their way into many sections in this book, especially in Chaps. 7 and 9 to 12.

Gregory C. Chow

ONE

SIMPLE LINEAR REGRESSION

1.1 WHAT IS ECONOMETRICS?

Econometrics is the art and science of using statistical methods for the measurement of economic relations. In the practice of econometrics, economic theory, institutional information, and other assumptions are relied upon to formulate a statistical model, or a set of statistical hypotheses, to explain the phenomena in question. Econometric methods are used to estimate the parameters of the model, to test hypotheses concerning them, and to generate forecasts from the model. The formulation of an econometric model is an art, just as using knowledge of architecture to design a building is an art. A good econometrician uses sound judgment to bring the relevant knowledge in economics to bear in formulating a useful model. The most important variables are selected while the nonessential ones are discarded. The crucial relationships are formulated and incorporated in the model. Care is taken to ensure that the statistical data used actually correspond to the variables to be measured according to theoretical considerations.

Given a set of requirements in the construction of a building, two good architects will come up with two different designs. Both may serve the purposes well. Similarly, given the same objectives, two econometricians are not likely to come up with two identical models, but both may capture the essential elements of the problem sufficiently to be useful. Good econometric models, like good architectural designs, can serve as prototypes to be followed in future investigations. The art of formulating a good econometric model is difficult to learn. One needs a solid command of the tools of economic analysis and sound judgment to select the essential variables of the problem. In a Walrasian system of general equilibrium all economic variables are related, but only a subset of variables will be selected in a particular investigation. One can read the best econometric studies to see how they were done, in the same way that an architect reads the best designs or an artist studies masterpieces of art. Finally, one can practice building one's own models and thus learn by doing.

This book is devoted mainly to an easier aspect of the practice of econometrics, namely, the study of some of the statistical methods most useful for drawing inferences from an econometric model. Knowledge of econometric methods is essential, though by no means sufficient, for the construction of good econometric models, as we have just pointed out. Our presentation presumes that the reader is familiar with the basic ideas of statistical inference. To review some of the basic ideas and to indicate the level of preparation suitable for reading this book, we shall introduce the required tools of statistics in this chapter and apply them to the model of simple linear regression as a warmup exercise. Most of the techniques presented later in this book can be viewed as generalizations, extensions, or modifications of this simple model.

At the beginning of an econometric investigation, an econometrician needs to know clearly what economic phenomena are to be explained, what important factors will contribute to the explanation, how these factors should be measured, what quantitative relationships exist, how such relations can be estimated or tested, and what conclusions can be drawn from the investigation. Consider the example of studying the demand for apples in the United States. The annual consumption of apples through time may be selected as the phenomenon to be explained. The important factors explaining the demand for apples may be the price of apples and income of the consumer. One may choose the per capita annual consumption of apples (in pounds) as the dependent variable. The price of apples per pound, deflated by a consumer price index, and per capita disposable income, also deflated by a consumer price index, may serve as the explanatory variables. The logarithm of per capita apple consumption may be assumed to be a linear function of the log of relative price, the log of per capita real disposable income, and a normally distributed random disturbance summarizing the combined effects of omitted factors. Time-series data may be used to estimate this linear relation. The coefficients of log price and log income will be interpreted respectively as the price and income elasticities of demand for apples. One objective of the investigation may be to estimate these demand elasticities. Another may be to test the hypotheses that both elasticities are less than 1 in absolute value. A third may be to use the estimated relation to forecast the demand for apples 5 years from now.

In the above illustration, many issues will have to be resolved by the econometrician. For example, is deflation of total apple consumption by total population in the United States sufficient to account for the effects of demographic factors on apple consumption? Is the age distribution relevant? Is mean income sufficient to explain apple consumption without taking the distribution of income into account? Is the relationship approximately linear in the logarithms of the variables? Does one have to account for the effects of lagged incomes on consumption? Is it useful to combine cross-section data with time-series data to estimate the price and income elasticities? Does the coefficient of log price in the postulated linear relation measure solely the price elasticity of demand, rather than the elasticity of supply? Is it necessary to formulate a supply equation for apples and estimate a system of two equations simultaneously?

The study of demand for apples is an easy econometric problem, and yet all these issues and others must be resolved. Consider the more difficult problem of studying the demand for computers in the United States. Just the measurement of the dependent variable requires some serious thought. Since there are large and small computers, or computers with different computing powers and capabilities, how is the total quantity of computers to be measured? Since the quality of the computers, however measured, has improved so rapidly through time, how should the effect of this rapid technological change be incorporated in a study of the demand for computers? Related to the measurement of the quantity of computers is the problem of measuring the price per unit of computers. If the quantity of computers can be measured appropriately, one will know what 1 unit of computers is and the price per unit can be determined accordingly. These problems are only illustrative of the issues an econometrician faces in the formulation of an econometric model. Other issues have been stated at the beginning of the paragraph before last. The problem of the demand for computers is considered in Sec. 1.12. The issues in formulating an econometric model cannot be systematically discussed in this book but will be illustrated by case studies cited in Chaps. 1, 2, and 4. Before embarking on a statistical analysis, the econometrician should have resolved all these issues and planned ahead, deciding how conclusions should be drawn before performing the statistical computations. Having made these introductory remarks, we begin by describing the model of simple linear regression.

1.2 MODEL OF SIMPLE LINEAR REGRESSION

Let y_i denote the ith observation of the dependent variable and x_i denote the associated explanatory variable. A simple linear regression model can be written as

$$y_i = \alpha + \beta x_i + \epsilon_i \qquad i = 1, \ldots, n \tag{1}$$

where the residual or disturbance terms ϵ_i are assumed to be normal and independent, each having mean zero and variance σ^2. The observations on x_i are treated as fixed numbers, except when specified otherwise, as in Secs. 1.6, 1.7, and 3.8. That is, a probability distribution for x_i is not postulated. The parameters of this model are α, β, and σ^2. The mean of the random variable y_i is $\alpha + \beta x_i$, as we observe by taking the mathematical expectations (or means) of both sides of (1). The mean is thus a linear function of x; the mean is called a *regression function*. As an example, consider n families selected from Princeton, New Jersey. Let y_i denote the logarithm of the quantity of apples consumed by the ith family during a given period and x_i denote the logarithm of its income during the same period. The mean of y_i can be assumed to be a linear function of x_i. Given x_i, that is, for families having log income equal to x_i, the distribution of log apple consumption is assumed to be normal, having mean $\alpha + \beta x_i$ and standard deviation σ.

In classical statistics the two main problems are to estimate the unknown parameters, α, β, and σ^2 in this case, and to test hypotheses concerning them. These topics will be discussed in turn.

1.3 POINT ESTIMATION

Let point estimates of the parameters α and β be denoted respectively by a and b. Other methods will be presented in due course, but first we discuss a popular method for finding these estimates, namely, the method of least squares. In this method one chooses the values of a and b which minimize the sum of squares of the deviations of y_i from the estimated regression line $a + bx_i$, that is,

$$\sum_{i=1}^{n} [y_i - (a + bx_i)]^2$$

Setting to zero the derivative of this sum with respect to a, we obtain

$$a = \frac{\sum_{i=1}^{n} y_i - b \sum_{i=1}^{n} x_i}{n} \equiv \bar{y} - b\bar{x} \tag{2}$$

Substituting $\bar{y} - b\bar{x}$ for a in this sum and setting to zero its derivative with respect to b, we obtain

$$b = \left[\sum_i x_i(x_i - \bar{x}) \right]^{-1} \sum_i x_i(y_i - \bar{y})$$

$$= \left[\sum_i (x_i - \bar{x})^2 \right]^{-1} \sum_i (x_i - \bar{x})(y_i - \bar{y}) \tag{3}$$

where we have used $\sum_i \bar{x}(x_i - \bar{x}) = 0$ and $\sum_i \bar{x}(y_i - \bar{y}) = 0$. Equations (2) and (3) are the *normal equations* for computing the estimates a and b.

To decide whether these formulas or *estimators* are good we consider their sampling distributions. As seen from (2) and (3), the estimators a and b are functions of the random variables $y_1, \ldots, y_n$ and therefore random variables themselves. The term *estimates* refers to the particular numbers representing a and b which we obtain by using a particular sample $(y_1, \ldots, y_n)$. The term *estimators* refers to possible numbers a and b which we could obtain by (hypothetically) drawing repeated samples of $(y_1, \ldots, y_n)$ given the values of $x_1, \ldots, x_n$. An estimator is a random variable; an estimate is a number which is computed by using the data for one particular sample. To evaluate the mean and variance of the distribution of b or of the random variable b we substitute $\alpha + \beta x_i + \epsilon_i$ for y_i in (3) and write b as a function of ϵ_i

$$b = \left[\sum_i (x_i - \bar{x})^2 \right]^{-1} \left[\sum_i (x_i - \bar{x})y_i \right]$$

$$= \left[\sum_i (x_i - \bar{x})^2 \right]^{-1} \left[\sum_i (x_i - \bar{x})(\alpha + \beta x_i + \epsilon_i) \right]$$

$$= \left[\sum_i (x_i - \bar{x})x_i \right]^{-1} \left[\sum_i (x_i - \bar{x})\beta x_i + \sum_i (x_i - \bar{x})\epsilon_i \right]$$

$$= \beta + \left[\sum_i (x_i - \bar{x})^2 \right]^{-1} \left[\sum_i (x_i - \bar{x})\epsilon_i \right] \tag{4}$$

The mean of the random variable b is obtained by taking the mathematical expectation of (4) yielding

$$E[b] = E[\beta] + \left[\sum_i (x_i - \bar{x})^2 \right]^{-1} \left[\sum_i (x_i - \bar{x})E\epsilon_i \right] = \beta \tag{5}$$

where we have treated $\sum_i (x_i - \bar{x})^2$ as a constant and taken the expectation of the sum $\sum_i (x_i - \bar{x})\epsilon_i$ as the sum $\sum_i E[(x_i - \bar{x})\epsilon_i]$ of the expectations, each $E\epsilon_i$ being zero by assumption. Since $E[b] = \beta$, b is an *unbiased estimator* of β.

To find the variance of b we use (4) and (5) to evaluate

$$\text{Var } b \equiv E[(b - Eb)^2] = E\left\{ \left[\sum_i (x_i - \bar{x})^2 \right]^{-1} \left[\sum_i (x_i - \bar{x})\epsilon_i \right] \right\}^2$$

$$= \left[\sum_i (x_i - \bar{x})^2 \right]^{-2} E\left[\sum_i (x_i - \bar{x})\epsilon_i \right]^2$$

$$= \left[\sum_i (x_i - \bar{x})^2 \right]^{-2} \sum_i (x_i - \bar{x})^2 E\epsilon_i^2 = \left[\sum_i (x_i - \bar{x})^2 \right]^{-1} \sigma^2 \tag{6}$$

where the third line has used the assumption that $E\epsilon_i \epsilon_j = 0$ for $i \neq j$. Thus the variance of the sampling distribution of b is directly proportional to the variance σ^2 of the regression residuals ϵ_i and inversely proportional to the variance of the explanatory variable. Having more variations in x permits a tighter estimate of b.

Note from the first line of (4) that b is a linear function of $y_1, \ldots, y_n$ and is called a *linear* estimator. It is an *unbiased* estimator of β, as shown by (5). In fact, among all linear, unbiased estimators, b has the *smallest variance*, as will be proved in Chap. 2. Thus, the least-squares estimator b is said to be *best linear unbiased*. We leave the evaluation of the mean and variance of the distribution of the estimator a as exercises.

A frequently used point estimate of σ^2 is

$$s^2 = (n - 2)^{-1} \sum_{i=1}^n (y_i - a - bx_i)^2 \tag{7}$$

It will be shown in Chap. 2 that $(n - 2)s^2/\sigma^2$ or $\sum_{i=1}^n (y_i - a - bx_i)^2/\sigma^2$ is distributed as χ^2 with $n - 2$ degrees of freedom. Since a $\chi^2(n - 2)$ distribution has a mean equal to $n - 2$, the mean of s^2/σ^2 is 1, or the mean of s^2 is σ^2. In other words, s^2 is an unbiased estimator for σ^2. However, the mean-squared error $E(s^2 - \sigma^2)^2$ can be improved by replacing the denominator $n - 2$ by $n - 1$. This would produce a biased estimator, whose expectation is smaller than σ^2, but the variance of the estimator would also be reduced, leading to a smaller mean-squared error. The estimator s^2 is often used because it is convenient to use standard tables for the χ^2 distribution for its sampling distribution.

1.4 TESTING HYPOTHESES AND INTERVAL ESTIMATION

From (4) we observe that $b - \beta$ is a linear combination of $\epsilon_1, \ldots, \epsilon_n$. Therefore, if the ϵ_i are normal, the linear combination $b - \beta$ will also be normal. Even if ϵ_i are not normal but have a finite variance, the linear combination $b - \beta$ will have a distribution which approaches the normal distribution as the sample size n increases, according to the central limit theorem, discussed in Sec. 1.9. From (6) we obtain the variances of b. Hence

$$\frac{b - \beta}{\left[\sum_i (x_i - \bar{x})^2\right]^{-1/2}\sigma} \tag{8}$$

has a standard normal distribution. If σ^2 is known, the statistic (8) can be used to test hypotheses concerning β. Let the null hypothesis be $\beta = \beta_0$ and the alternative hypothesis be $\beta \neq \beta_0$. Let the level of significance be 5 percent. Under the null hypothesis, the probability that the statistic (8) with $\beta = \beta_0$ will be larger than 1.96 or smaller than -1.96 is .05. If this statistic as computed from our sample turns out to exceed 1.96 in absolute value, the null hypothesis $\beta = \beta_0$ will be rejected. If the alternative hypothesis is one-sided, say $\beta < \beta_0$, the null hypothesis will be rejected when the statistic (8) is smaller than -1.64 since the probability for a standard normal random variable to be smaller than this value is .05.

To construct a symmetric interval estimate or confidence interval for β with a confidence coefficient of .95 we use inequalities

$$-1.96 < \frac{b - \beta}{\left[\sum_i (x_i - \bar{x})^2\right]^{-1/2}\sigma} < 1.96$$

implying

$$b + 1.96\left[\sum_i (x_i - \bar{x})^2\right]^{-1/2}\sigma > \beta > b - 1.96\left[\sum_i (x_i - \bar{x})^2\right]^{-1/2}\sigma \tag{9}$$

To test the null hypothesis that $\sigma^2 = \sigma_0^2$ we use the fact that under the null hypothesis $(n - 2)s^2/\sigma_0^2$ has a $\chi^2(n - 2)$ distribution. If this statistic exceeds an upper critical value C_U or falls below a lower critical value C_L according to the $\chi^2(n - 2)$ distribution, the null hypothesis will be rejected. Similarly a confidence interval for σ^2 can be constructed by using

$$C_L < \frac{(n - 2)s^2}{\sigma^2} < C_U$$

implying

$$\frac{(n - 2)s^2}{C_L} > \sigma^2 > \frac{(n - 2)s^2}{C_U}$$

To test the null hypothesis $\beta = \beta_0$ when σ^2 is unknown we use the statistic

$$\frac{b - \beta_0}{\left[\sum_i (x_i - \bar{x})^2\right]^{-1/2}s} \tag{10}$$

which is the ratio of (8) to s/σ. The numerator (8) is standard normal. The denominator s/σ is the square root of a $\chi^2(n-2)$ variable divided by the degrees of freedom $(n-2)$. As will be shown in Chap. 2, the numerator and the denominator are statistically independent. Therefore, the ratio (10) will have Student's t distribution with $n-2$ degrees of freedom. Hypothesis testing and interval estimation for β can be performed using the $t(n-2)$ distribution for the statistic (10). For example, the .025 upper-tail critical values for $t(10)$ and $t(20)$ are respectively 2.228 and 2.086, compared with 1.960 for the standard normal statistic. A $\chi^2(m)$ variable is the sum of squares of m independent standard normal variables. If $\chi^2(m)$ and $\chi^2(n)$ are independent, the ratio of $\chi^2(m)/m$ to $\chi^2(n)/n$ has an $F(m, n)$ distribution. An $F(1, n)$ variable is the square of a $t(n)$ variable. Tables for the normal, χ^2, t, and F distributions are provided at the end of this book.

1.5 USE OF MATRIX NOTATION

In order to study the model of multiple linear regression, where the mean of y is a linear function of several explanatory variables, it is convenient to use matrix notation. Let the model (1) be written as

$$y_i = \beta_1 x_{i1} + \beta_2 x_{i2} + \epsilon_i \qquad i = 1, \dots, n \qquad (11)$$

where we write the original α as β_1 and the original β as β_2, and let the ith observation of the first independent variable x_{i1} be equal to 1 identically so that its coefficient β_1 is the intercept. Denote by y, x_1, x_2, and ϵ, respectively, the column vectors of n observations on the dependent variable, the first and the second explanatory variables, and the random disturbance, namely,

$$y = \begin{bmatrix} y_1 \\ y_2 \\ \vdots \\ y_n \end{bmatrix} \quad x_1 = \begin{bmatrix} x_{11} \\ x_{21} \\ \vdots \\ x_{n1} \end{bmatrix} \quad x_2 = \begin{bmatrix} x_{12} \\ x_{22} \\ \vdots \\ x_{n2} \end{bmatrix} \quad \epsilon = \begin{bmatrix} \epsilon_1 \\ \epsilon_2 \\ \vdots \\ \epsilon_n \end{bmatrix}$$

We can write the n observations of the model (11) as

$$y = \beta_1 x_1 + \beta_2 x_2 + \epsilon \qquad (12)$$

The vector y equals the sum of three vectors, $\beta_1 x_1$, $\beta_2 x_2$, and ϵ. When a scalar β_1 multiplies a vector x_1, each element of x_1 is multiplied by the scalar to form a vector $\beta_1 x_1$ as the product. When the three vectors $\beta_1 x_1$, $\beta_2 x_2$, and ϵ are added, their corresponding elements are added to form the elements of the sum, which in our case equals the vector y. The equality sign in (12) signifies that each element of y equals the corresponding element of the vector on the right, obtained as the sum of the three vectors.

The inner product of a row vector and a column vector is the sum of the products of their corresponding elements. For example, let x_1' be the row vector $[x_{11} \quad x_{21} \quad \cdots \quad x_{n1}]$ obtained by taking the transpose (indicated by a prime) of the column vector x_1, and let x_2 be the column vector as defined above. The inner product $x'_1 x_2$ equals $\sum_{i=1}^{n} x_{i1} x_{i2}$. An $m \times n$ matrix A is a rectangular array of m rows and n columns. If A is an $m \times n$ matrix with a_{ij} as its element in the ith row and jth column and B is an $n \times p$ matrix with b_{ij} as its ijth element, the product AB is an $m \times p$ matrix whose ijth element is the inner product of the ith row of A and the jth column of B. Let the product AB be denoted by the matrix C with c_{ij} as its ijth element. Then $c_{ij} = \sum_{k=1}^{n} a_{ik} b_{kj}$. Naturally, two matrices are equal if and only if their corresponding elements are equal; a scalar multiplies a matrix by multiplying all its elements to form a product matrix.

Now let X be an $n \times 2$ matrix with x_{ij} as its elements; x_{ij} is the ith observation on the jth explanatory variable, $j = 1, 2$. Let β be the column vector, or the 2×1 matrix, with β_1 and β_2 as its elements. Using the above notation, we can write (12) as

$$
\begin{bmatrix} y_1 \\ y_2 \\ \vdots \\ y_n \end{bmatrix} = \begin{bmatrix} x_{11} & x_{12} \\ x_{21} & x_{22} \\ \vdots & \vdots \\ x_{n1} & x_{n2} \end{bmatrix} \begin{bmatrix} \beta_1 \\ \beta_2 \end{bmatrix} + \begin{bmatrix} \epsilon_1 \\ \epsilon_2 \\ \vdots \\ \epsilon_n \end{bmatrix} \tag{13}
$$

or more compactly as

$$
y = X\beta + \epsilon \tag{14}
$$

Matrix notation will be used in Chap. 2 to study the model of multiple linear regression having several explanatory variables.

★1.6 THE MULTIVARIATE NORMAL DISTRIBUTION AND TWO REGRESSIONS†

We have treated the simple regression model by assuming that the observations on the explanatory variable are fixed numbers, and not generated by a random process. Alternatively, one could view both variables y and x as random, satisfying some joint-distribution function. A useful model for the joint distribution of a set of p random variables $y_1, y_2, \ldots, y_p$ is the multivariate normal distribution. For example, if y_1 denotes the height of the father, y_2 denotes the height of the first son, and y_3 denotes the height of the second son of a family selected at random from a certain human population, the vector (y_1, y_2, y_3) of random variables will have a multivariate normal distribution. We denote the multivariate normal density function for a random vector y by $N(\mu, \Sigma)$, where μ is the vector of the means of the component random variables and Σ is the covariance matrix, with its ijth element equal to $\sigma_{ij} = \text{Cov}(y_i, y_j) = E(y_i - \mu_i)(y_j - \mu_j)$.

The multivariate normal density function of a random vector y of p components takes the form

$$
f(y \mid \mu, \Sigma) = (2\pi)^{-p/2} |\Sigma|^{-1/2} \exp\left[-\tfrac{1}{2}(y - \mu)'\Sigma^{-1}(y - \mu) \right] \tag{15}
$$

† See the Preface on skipping the sections marked by ★.

Strictly speaking, we should have denoted the random vector by Y, leaving y for the particular value which Y may take. The probability density at y is given by the above density function f which has only two parameters, μ and Σ. The $p \times p$ covariance matrix Σ has an inverse Σ^{-1}, which satisfies $\Sigma^{-1}\Sigma = I$ and $\Sigma\Sigma^{-1} = I$, where I is the $p \times p$ identity matrix with ones on the diagonal and zeros elsewhere. When I multiplies any matrix on the left or on the right, the matrix remains unchanged; that is, $IA = A$ and $BI = B$ for any A and B; $|\Sigma|$ denotes the determinant of the matrix Σ; $(y - \mu)'\Sigma^{-1}(y - \mu)$ is a quadratic form in the variables $y - \mu$; it is a quadratic function of the elements of $y - \mu$, being equal to $\sum_i \sum_j \sigma^{ij}(y_i - \mu_i)(y_j - \mu_j)$, where σ^{ij} denotes the ijth element of Σ^{-1} and $y_i - \mu_i$ is the ith element of the vector $y - \mu$. For $p = 1$, the vectors y and μ become scalars, and the covariance matrix Σ becomes the variance σ^2. Equation (15) is reduced to the familiar univariate normal density function.

In order to study the relations between subsets of random variables which are distributed according to a multivariate normal distribution, we decompose the random vector y into two subvectors y_1 and y_2, consisting respectively of p_1 and p_2 elements, with $p_1 + p_2 = p$. Accordingly we decompose the mean vector μ into μ_1 and μ_2 and partition the covariance matrix as

$$\Sigma = \begin{bmatrix} \Sigma_{11} & \Sigma_{12} \\ \Sigma_{21} & \Sigma_{22} \end{bmatrix} \tag{16}$$

where Σ_{11} is the $p_1 \times p_1$ covariance matrix of the random vector y_1, Σ_{22} is the $p_2 \times p_2$ covariance matrix of the random vector y_2, and

$$\Sigma_{12} = E(y_1 - \mu_1)(y_2 - \mu_2)' \tag{17}$$

The expectation E of the $p_1 \times p_2$ matrix $(y_1 - \mu_1)(y_2 - \mu_2)'$ is defined as the matrix whose ijth element is the expectation of the ijth element of $(y_1 - \mu_1)(y_2 - \mu_2)'$. Note that $\Sigma_{21} = \Sigma_{12}'$.

Given the joint density (15) of two random vectors y_1 and y_2, one may be interested in the marginal density $f_2(y_2)$ of y_2 and the conditional density $g(y_1 | y_2)$ of y_1 given y_2. The *marginal density* $f_2(y_2)$ is obtained by integrating out the vector $y_1 = (y_{11}, y_{12}, \ldots, y_{1p_1})$ from the joint density; i.e.,

$$f_2(y_2) = \int_{-\infty}^{\infty} f(y_1, y_2)\, dy_1 \tag{18}$$

where for briefness we have written dy_1 for $dy_{11}\, dy_{12} \ldots dy_{1p_1}$ and $\int_{-\infty}^{\infty}$ for $\int_{-\infty}^{\infty} \cdots \int_{-\infty}^{\infty}$. The *conditional density* $g(y_2 | y_2)$ is, by definition,

$$g(y_1 | y_2) = \frac{f(y_1, y_2)}{f_2(y_2)} \tag{19}$$

We now factor $f(y_1, y_2)$ and write it as the product of $g(y_1 | y_2)$ and $f_2(y_2)$. Let Σ^{-1} be denoted by R,

$$\Sigma^{-1} \equiv R = \begin{bmatrix} R_{11} & R_{12} \\ R_{21} & R_{22} \end{bmatrix} \tag{20}$$

where R_{11} is $p_1 \times p_1$, and R_{22} is $p_2 \times p_2$, and $R_{21} = R'_{12}$. Since Σ is a symmetric matrix, with $\sigma_{ij} = \sigma_{ji}$, its inverse R is also symmetric. The exponent of (15) can be written as $-\frac{1}{2}$ times

$$
[y'_1 - \mu'_1 \quad y'_2 - \mu'_2] \begin{bmatrix} R_{11} & R_{12} \\ R_{21} & R_{22} \end{bmatrix} \begin{bmatrix} y_1 - \mu_1 \\ y_2 - \mu_2 \end{bmatrix}
$$

$$
= (y_1 - \mu_1)'R_{11}(y_1 - \mu_1) + 2(y_1 - \mu_1)'R_{12}(y_2 - \mu_2) + (y_2 - \mu_2)'R_{22}(y_2 - \mu_2)
$$

$$
\tag{21}
$$

since the scalar $(y_2 - \mu_2)'R_{21}(y_1 - \mu_1)$ equals its transpose $(y_1 - \mu_1)'R'_{21}(y_2 - \mu_2)$, where the rule $(ABC)' = C'B'A'$ is used and $R'_{21} = R_{12}$.

To factor out $g(y_1 | y_2)$ from $f(y_1, y_2)$, leaving a function $f_2(y_2)$ of y_2 alone, we need to collect terms involving y_1. This requires completing the square for y_1 in (21), namely, writing (21) as

$$
(y_1 - \mu_1^*)'R^*(y_1 - \mu_1^*) = y'_1 R^* y_1 - 2y'_1 R^* \mu_1^* + \mu_1^{*'} R^* \mu_1^*
$$

plus terms not involving y_1, for some vector μ_1^* and some matrix R^*. To this end, we expand (21) and collect terms in y_1

$$
y'_1 R_{11} y_1 - 2y'_1 R_{11} \mu_1 + \mu'_1 R_{11} \mu_1 + 2y'_1 R_{12}(y_2 - \mu_2)
$$

$$
- 2\mu'_1 R_{12}(y_2 - \mu_2) + (y_2 - \mu_2)'R_{22}(y_2 - \mu_2)
$$

$$
= y'_1 R_{11} y_1 - 2y'_1 R_{11}[\mu_1 - R_{11}^{-1} R_{12}(y_2 - \mu_2)]
$$

$$
+ [\mu_1 - R_{11}^{-1} R_{12}(y_2 - \mu_2)]' R_{11}[\mu_1 - R_{11}^{-1} R_{12}(y_2 - \mu_2)]
$$

$$
- [\mu_1 - R_{11}^{-1} R_{12}(y_2 - \mu_2)]' R_{11}[\mu_1 - R_{11}^{-1} R_{12}(y_2 - \mu_2)] + \mu'_1 R_{11} \mu_1
$$

$$
- 2\mu'_1 R_{12}(y_2 - \mu_2) + (y_2 - \mu_2)'R_{22}(y_2 - \mu_2)
$$

$$
= y'_1 R_{11} y_1 - 2y'_1 R_{11} \mu_1^* + \mu_1^{*'} R_{11} \mu_1^* + (y_2 - \mu_2)'(R_{22} - R'_{12} R_{11}^{-1} R_{12})(y_2 - \mu_2)
$$

$$
\tag{22}
$$

where
$$
\mu_1^* = \mu_1 - R_{11}^{-1} R_{12}(y_2 - \mu_2) \tag{23}
$$

The sum of the first three terms after the last equals sign of (22) can be written as

$$
(y_1 - \mu_1^*)'R_{11}(y_1 - \mu_1^*)
$$

and we have completed the sum of squares for y_1.

To form the conditional density $g(y_1 | y_2)$ we need to find the appropriate normalization constant to associate with $\exp\left[-\frac{1}{2}(y_1 - \mu_1^*)'R_{11}(y_1 - \mu_1^*)\right]$. From the definition (15) of a multivariate normal density function as applied to the vector y_1 we observe that

$$
\int_{-\infty}^{\infty} (2\pi)^{-p_1/2} |R_{11}^{-1}|^{-1/2} \exp\left[-\frac{1}{2}(y_1 - \mu_1^*)'R_{11}(y_1 - \mu_1^*)\right] dy_1 = 1 \tag{24}
$$

by the definition of a multivariate density function. Therefore, the joint density (15) for y_1 and y_2 should be written as the product of the above integrand and a function of y_2. Using the last line of (22), we rewrite the joint density (15) as

$$f(y_1, y_2) = (2\pi)^{-p/2}|\Sigma|^{-1/2}\exp\{-\tfrac{1}{2}[(y_1 - \mu_1^*)'R_{11}(y_1 - \mu_1^*)$$
$$+ (y_2 - \mu_2)'(R_{22} - R_{21}R_{11}^{-1}R_{12})(y_2 - \mu_2)]\}$$
$$= (2\pi)^{-p_1/2}|R_{11}^{-1}|^{-1/2}\exp[-\tfrac{1}{2}(y_1 - \mu_1^*)'R_{11}(y_1 - \mu_1^*)]$$
$$\cdot (2\pi)^{-p_2/2}|R_{11}^{-1}|^{1/2}|\Sigma|^{-1/2}\exp[-\tfrac{1}{2}(y_2 - \mu_2)'$$
$$\cdot (R_{22} - R_{21}R_{11}^{-1}R_{12})(y_2 - \mu_2)]$$
$$= g(y_1|y_2)f_2(y_2) \tag{25}$$

In (25) we have written the joint density $f(y_1, y_2)$ as the product of the conditional density $g(y_1|y_2)$ and the marginal density $f_2(y_2)$. If we integrate (25) with respect to y_1, the result is the marginal density $f_2(y_2)$ by virtue of the fact that integral (24) equals 1.

Our remaining task is to express the densities $g(y_1|y_2)$ and $f_2(y_2)$ in terms of the elements of the covariance matrix Σ rather than the elements R_{ij} of its inverse R. This task is accomplished by using the algebraic relations between the partitioned matrix Σ of (16) and its partitioned inverse R of (20). By definition,

$$\begin{bmatrix} \Sigma_{11} & \Sigma_{12} \\ \Sigma_{21} & \Sigma_{22} \end{bmatrix}\begin{bmatrix} R_{11} & R_{12} \\ R_{21} & R_{22} \end{bmatrix} = \begin{bmatrix} I & 0 \\ 0 & I \end{bmatrix}$$

which implies the following four equations,

$$\Sigma_{11}R_{11} + \Sigma_{12}R_{21} = I \qquad \Sigma_{21}R_{11} + \Sigma_{22}R_{21} = 0$$
$$\Sigma_{11}R_{12} + \Sigma_{12}R_{22} = 0 \qquad \Sigma_{21}R_{12} + \Sigma_{22}R_{22} = I \tag{26}$$

To solve the first two of Eqs. (26) for R_{11} and R_{21} we premultiply the second equation by Σ_{22}^{-1} to get

$$\Sigma_{22}^{-1}\Sigma_{21}R_{11} + \Sigma_{22}^{-1}\Sigma_{22}R_{21} = \Sigma_{22}^{-1}\Sigma_{21}R_{11} + R_{21} = 0$$

Substituting this result for R_{21} in the first equation gives

$$\Sigma_{11}R_{11} - \Sigma_{12}\Sigma_{22}^{-1}\Sigma_{21}R_{11} = I$$

Postmultiplying by R_{11}^{-1} yields

$$\Sigma_{11} - \Sigma_{12}\Sigma_{22}^{-1}\Sigma_{21} = R_{11}^{-1} \tag{27}$$

If we transpose the result for R_{21}, we have

$$R_{21}' = -(\Sigma_{22}^{-1}\Sigma_{21}R_{11})' = -R_{11}'\Sigma_{21}'\Sigma_{22}^{-1} = -R_{11}\Sigma_{12}\Sigma_{22}^{-1}$$

because R_{11} and Σ_{22}^{-1} are symmetric and $\Sigma_{21}' = \Sigma_{12}$. Premultiplying by R_{11}^{-1} and noting that $R_{21}' = R_{12}$ yields

$$R_{11}^{-1}R_{12} = -\Sigma_{12}\Sigma_{22}^{-1} \tag{28}$$

Using (28), we can rewrite (23) as

$$\mu_1^* = \mu_1 + \Sigma_{12}\Sigma_{22}^{-1}(y_2 - \mu_2) \tag{29}$$

Relations (27) and (29) can be substituted into the conditional density function $g(y_1 | y_2)$ in (25) to give

$$g(y_1 | y_2) = (2\pi)^{-p_1/2} |\Sigma_{11} - \Sigma_{12}\Sigma_{22}^{-1}\Sigma_{21}|^{-1/2}$$
$$\exp\left[-\tfrac{1}{2}(y_1 - \mu_1^*)'(\Sigma_{11} - \Sigma_{12}\Sigma_{22}^{-1}\Sigma_{21})^{-1}(y_1 - \mu_1^*)\right] \quad (30)$$

To summarize, *if y_1 and y_2 are $p_1 \times 1$ and $p_2 \times 1$ vectors having a joint normal density with means μ_1 and μ_2 and covariance matrix (16), the conditional density $g(y_1 | y_2)$ of y_1 given y_2 is also normal, with mean μ_1^* given by (29) and covariance matrix given by (27).*

The conditional mean vector μ_1^* of y_1 given y_2 (or the regression function) is a linear function of y_2, according to (29). The first element of μ_1^*, say, equals the first element of μ_1 plus the inner product of the first row of the matrix $\Sigma_{12}\Sigma_{22}^{-1}$ and the column vector $y_2 - \mu_2$. *Hence the first row of $\Sigma_{12}\Sigma_{22}^{-1}$ is a set of regression coefficients in the regression of the first variable of y_1 on the variables y_2. The matrix $\Sigma_{12}\Sigma_{22}^{-1}$ is a matrix of regression coefficients;* its ith row is a set of regression coefficients in the regression of the ith variable of y_1 on the variables y_2.

In the special case when both p_1 and p_2 equal 1 or when both y_1 and y_2 are scalar random variables, the assumption that y_1 and y_2 are jointly normal implies that the regression of y_1 given y_2 is a linear function of y_2. By interchanging the subscripts 1 and 2 in (30) we know that the conditional density of y_2 given y_1 is also normal and that the regression of y_2 on y_1 is linear. If the variances and covariance of the joint distribution are σ_{11}, σ_{22}, and σ_{12}, respectively, the slope of the regression of y_1 on y_2 is $\Sigma_{12}\Sigma_{22}^{-1} = \sigma_{12}/\sigma_{22}$ whereas the slope of the regression of y_2 on y_1 is $\Sigma_{21}\Sigma_{11}^{-1} = \sigma_{12}/\sigma_{11}$. These two regression lines are different. In a two-dimensional diagram with y_1 measured on the vertical axis and y_2 on the horizontal axis, the slope of the first regression is σ_{12}/σ_{22}, whereas the slope of the second regression is dy_1/dy_2 or $(\sigma_{12}/\sigma_{11})^{-1} = \sigma_{11}/\sigma_{12}$. Because the square of the correlation coefficient cannot be greater than 1, i.e.,

$$\frac{\sigma_{12}^2}{\sigma_{11}\sigma_{22}} = \frac{\sigma_{12}}{\sigma_{11}}\frac{\sigma_{12}}{\sigma_{22}} \leq 1 \quad (31)$$

the product of the two regression coefficients is not greater than 1. Taking absolute values, we have

$$\left|\frac{\sigma_{12}}{\sigma_{11}}\right| \cdot \left|\frac{\sigma_{12}}{\sigma_{22}}\right| \leq 1 \quad \text{or} \quad \left|\frac{\sigma_{12}}{\sigma_{22}}\right| \leq \left|\frac{\sigma_{11}}{\sigma_{12}}\right|$$

This means that the slope σ_{12}/σ_{22} of the regression of y_1 on y_2 is smaller in absolute value than the slope σ_{11}/σ_{12} of the regression of y_2 on y_1 in the two-dimensional diagram except when the correlation between the two variables is perfect, in which case the two slopes are equal. Geometrically, the first regression line is flatter than the second regression line.

The conditional density (30) further specifies that the covariance matrix of y_1 given y_2 is $\Sigma_{11} - \Sigma_{12}\Sigma_{22}^{-1}\Sigma_{21}$, to be contrasted with the covariance matrix Σ_{11} of y_1 without the conditioning of y_2. For example, if y_1 denotes the height of the father and y_2 the height of the first son, the variance of y_1 may be 8.1 square inches but the variance of the father's height with the son's height fixed may be

3.2 square inches. Note that the conditional covariance matrix of y_1 given y_2 is constant and not a function of y_2. When y_1 is a scalar, this means that the variance of y_1 given y_2 is a constant. It is the variance σ^2 of y_1 around the linear regression on y_2.

A brief comment should be made about the marginal density $f_2(y_2)$ of y_2 implicit in (25). Using the second and the fourth of Eqs. (26), one can solve for Σ_{21} and Σ_{22}, obtaining

$$\Sigma_{22}^{-1} = R_{22} - R_{21}R_{11}^{-1}R_{12} \tag{32}$$

(see Prob. 3). Note the symmetry between (32) and (27). To rewrite the normalization constant for $f_2(y_2)$ we apply the following theorem on determinants. The determinant of a matrix partitioned as in (16) can be factored as

$$|\Sigma| = \begin{vmatrix} \Sigma_{11} & \Sigma_{12} \\ \Sigma_{21} & \Sigma_{22} \end{vmatrix} = |\Sigma_{11}| \cdot |\Sigma_{22} - \Sigma_{21}\Sigma_{11}^{-1}\Sigma_{12}|$$

$$= |\Sigma_{22}| \cdot |\Sigma_{11} - \Sigma_{12}\Sigma_{22}^{-1}\Sigma_{21}|$$

$$= |\Sigma_{22}| \cdot |R_{11}^{-1}| \tag{33}$$

where the last equality is due to (27). Substituting (32) and (33) into the marginal density $f_2(y_2)$ given in (25), we have

$$f_2(y_2) = (2\pi)^{-p2/2}|\Sigma_{22}|^{-1/2}\exp\left[-\tfrac{1}{2}(y_2 - \mu_2)'\Sigma_{22}^{-1}(y_2 - \mu_2)\right] \tag{34}$$

Thus if y_1 and y_2 are jointly normal with density (15), *the marginal density of y_2 is normal with mean μ_2 and covariance matrix Σ_{22}.* By symmetry, the marginal density of y_1 is normal with mean μ_1 and covariance matrix Σ_{11}.

The multivariate normal density function has been presented to provide a model for the joint distribution of two random vectors y_1 and y_2. It has the property that the conditional distribution of y_1 given y_2 is normal, its mean being a linear function of y_2 and its (conditional) covariance matrix being a constant, independent of the value of y_2. When y_1 is a scalar, this means that the regression of y_1 on y_2 is linear with a constant variance σ^2 and that the distribution of y_1 given y_2 is normal. These are the assumptions made for the simple linear regression model of this chapter. Of course, a bivariate normal model for both y and x implies the linear regression model but is not implied by it. One can adopt the assumption, as we did in Sec. 1.2, that the values of x are fixed numbers without postulating a probabilistic model for the generation of x. On that assumption, we have derived the sampling distribution of the least-squares estimators for the coefficients of the regression equation. Alternatively, one could adopt a bivariate normal model for both x and y, thus treating x as random also. In this case, one could still consider statistical inferences conditioned on the given set of values for x which the sample happens to have generated.

The bivariate normal model also brings home the existence of two regression lines. The regression of y on x is different from the regression of x on y. In the xy diagram the first regression line is flatter than the second. Thus the regression equation used to predict the father's height y given the son's height x is different from the regression equation used to predict the son's height from the father's height. In the father-son example, the slope of each regression line, or the derivative of the mean of the dependent variable with respect to the explanatory variable, is less than unity since the line is flatter than the 45° line through the origin. This fact has an interesting implication. If the explanatory variable, say the father's height, is above average, the expected value of his son's height, the dependent variable, is smaller than the father's height. Similarly, if the father's height is below average, the expected value of the son's height is greater than the father's height. This implication is valid if the joint distribution of the heights remains constant through time. In other words, tall and short fathers tend to have sons whose heights are closer to the average, but people's heights do not tend to shrink toward the middle, i.e., to have a reduced variance through time. The reason for predicting the son's height to be shorter than the height of a very tall father is that factors other than the father's height help determine the son's height. Given an unusually tall father, chances are that the other factors will not be equally favorable to produce a son of equal stature. This does not mean that the heights of people are getting closer to the average through time.

1.7 ERRORS IN OBSERVATIONS

In a simple linear regression model if the explanatory variable is measured with an error which is independently distributed, the slope of the regression line will be reduced in absolute value.

Let y and x have a bivariate normal distribution with means μ_1 and μ_2 and covariance matrix $\Sigma = (\sigma_{ij})$. Let y be measured with a random error e_1 and x be measured with a random error e_2. Let the joint distribution of e_1 and e_2 be bivariate normal with means zero and variances v_1 and v_2, the covariance of e_1 and e_2 being zero. Let e_1 and e_2 be independent of y and x. The measured variables are $y^* = y + e_1$ and $x^* = x + e_2$. The random vector of measured variables

$$\begin{bmatrix} y^* \\ x^* \end{bmatrix} = \begin{bmatrix} y \\ x \end{bmatrix} + \begin{bmatrix} e_1 \\ e_2 \end{bmatrix}$$

has mean equal to

$$E\begin{bmatrix} y^* \\ x^* \end{bmatrix} = E\begin{bmatrix} y \\ x \end{bmatrix} + E\begin{bmatrix} e_1 \\ e_2 \end{bmatrix} = \begin{bmatrix} \mu_1 \\ \mu_2 \end{bmatrix}$$

and covariance matrix equal to

$$\begin{aligned}
\mathrm{Cov}\begin{bmatrix} y^* \\ x^* \end{bmatrix} &= E\left\{ \left[\begin{bmatrix} y \\ x \end{bmatrix} - \begin{bmatrix} \mu_1 \\ \mu_2 \end{bmatrix} + \begin{bmatrix} e_1 \\ e_2 \end{bmatrix} \right] \left[\begin{bmatrix} y \\ x \end{bmatrix} - \begin{bmatrix} \mu_1 \\ \mu_2 \end{bmatrix} + \begin{bmatrix} e_1 \\ e_2 \end{bmatrix} \right] \right\} \\
&= E\left\{ \left[\begin{bmatrix} y \\ x \end{bmatrix} - \begin{bmatrix} \mu_1 \\ \mu_2 \end{bmatrix} \right] \left[\begin{bmatrix} y \\ x \end{bmatrix} - \begin{bmatrix} \mu_1 \\ \mu_2 \end{bmatrix} \right]' \right\} + E\left\{ \begin{bmatrix} e_1 \\ e_2 \end{bmatrix} \begin{bmatrix} e_1 \\ e_2 \end{bmatrix} \right\} \\
&= \begin{bmatrix} \sigma_{11} & \sigma_{12} \\ \sigma_{21} & \sigma_{22} \end{bmatrix} + \begin{bmatrix} v_1 & 0 \\ 0 & v_2 \end{bmatrix}
\end{aligned} \tag{35}$$

where we have used the assumption that the vector (e_1, e_2) is uncorrelated with the vector (y, x). Because the vector (y^*, x^*) is a linear combination (in fact a sum) of normal vectors, it is also normal.

By (29), the regression of y on x is linear with a coefficient equal to

$$\beta = \frac{\sigma_{12}}{\sigma_{22}} \tag{36}$$

The regression of y^* on x^* is also linear, with a coefficient equal to the ratio of the covariance between y^* and x^* to the variance of x^*. By (35), this regression coefficient is

$$\beta^* = (\text{Var } x^*)^{-1} \text{Cov } (y^*, x^*) = (\sigma_{22} + v_2)^{-1}\sigma_{12} = (\sigma_{22} + v_2)^{-1}\sigma_{22}\beta$$

$$= (\sigma_{22} + v_2)^{-1}(\sigma_{22} + v_2 - v_2)\beta = \beta - (\sigma_{22} + v_2)^{-1}v_2\beta \tag{37}$$

From (37) we observe that the coefficient β^* of the regression of the measured y^* on the measured x^* is smaller in absolute value than the coefficient of the regression of y on x. Note that the variance v_1 of the error in measuring the dependent variable y does not affect the regression slope. It contributes to the residual variance of the regression of y^* on x^* (see Prob. 4).

A simple linear regression model with measurement errors in both the dependent and the explanatory variables forms the basis of the well-known theory of the consumption function of Friedman (1957), in which y and x represent permanent consumption and permanent income, respectively. It is assumed that the regression of y on x is linear and homogeneous with slope β. That is, consumers, on the average, consume a fraction β of their income irrespective of the size of income. This assumption is different from that made in the *General Theory* of Keynes (1936) which asserts that the fraction of income consumed decreases as income increases. Friedman was led to his hypothesis partly by observing the fact that the ratio of consumption to income had remained roughly constant for long periods in the history of the United States and had not declined when per capita income increased, as Keynes' assumption implies. However, Friedman's hypothesis appears to be inconsistent with family budget studies, which show that, at a given time, high-income families tend to consume proportionally less than low-income families.

Friedman reconciles the cross-section regression of family consumption on family income, which has a positive intercept and a smaller slope, with the time-series regression of aggregate consumption on aggregate income over long periods, which has a zero intercept and a larger slope, by suggesting that both the consumption and income variables are measured with errors. The measured consumption expenditures and income are respectively $y^* = y + e_1$ and $x^* = x + e_2$, where the errors e_1 and e_2 represent the transitory components of consumption and income respectively and are assumed to be distributed independently of y and x. The existence of transitory income e_2 in family budget data leads to a smaller slope than β in the estimated consumption function using cross-section data. When a consumption function is estimated using aggregate time-series data, there are also measurement errors in both variables, or transitory components of aggregate consumption and aggregate income. The variances of these transitory components, relative to the variances of the permanent components, may be different from those of transitory components in cross-section data. Therefore, the reduction of the estimated slope in the consumption function may be different in the two cases. Furthermore, as the sample period of a time-series study is extended, the variance of the explanatory variable (income) increases relative to the variance of the error or the transitory component. By formula (37), therefore, the longer the sample period, the closer the estimated slope of the consumption function to its true value β according to Friedman's theory.

$\star$ 1.8 CONVERGENCE IN PROBABILITY

In the remainder of this chapter we study further the sampling distribution of the least-squares estimator of the slope of a simple linear regression function. In Sec. 1.3 we showed that the least-squares estimator b is an unbiased estimator of the parameter β. In Sec. 1.4 we pointed out that if the residuals ϵ_i are normal, the sampling distribution of b is also normal and that even if the ϵ_i are not normal but have finite variances, the sampling distribution of b will be approximately normal by the central limit theorem. We now drop the assumption that the ϵ_i are normal and study the distribution of b as the sample size n increases. Will the random variable b get very close to β, with a very high probability, as n increases? Under what conditions will the sampling distribution of b be very close to a normal distribution as the sample size n increases? These are the two key questions. In more technical language, will b_n, the least-squared estimator based on n observations, converge in probability to β? When will b_n converge in distribution to a normal distribution? The material of Secs. 1.8 to 1.11 is technical, being concerned mainly with theorem proving. Readers may wish to skip the details or to postpone studying these sections until some applied material in Chap. 2 has been covered.

A sequence of random variables $x_1, x_2, \ldots, x_n$ is said to *converge in probability* to a constant c if, for any positive ϵ however small,

$$\lim_{n \to \infty} P(|x_n - c| < \epsilon) = 1 \tag{38}$$

By the definition of limit, $\lim_{n \to \infty} P = 1$ means that, for any positive δ however small, the probability P will differ from 1 by less than δ when n is larger than some number $N(\delta)$. The definition (38) for convergence in probability can be stated thus: x_n converges in probability to c if one is extremely sure (with probability higher than $1 - \delta$) that x_n will be extremely close to c (deviating from c by less than ϵ) for sufficiently large n. One can write equivalently

$$\operatorname*{plim}_{n \to \infty} x_n = c \tag{39}$$

and assert that the probability limit of x_n equals c, or x_n *converges in probability* to c. There is a stronger form of convergence which we point out in passing but do not pursue in this chapter. One says that x_n *converges with probability 1* (or *converges almost surely*) to c if

$$P\left(\lim_{n \to \infty} x_n = c\right) = 1 \qquad (40)$$

This means that the event $\lim_{n \to \infty} x_n = c$ occurs with probability 1. For example, if $\bar{x}_n$ is the mean of a random sample of n observations from a distribution with mean μ and variance σ^2, $\bar{x}_n$ converges to μ with probability 1. It is also true that $\bar{x}_n$ converges *in probability* to μ, as we shall presently show.

A useful fact concerning the probability limit is that if $f(\cdot)$ is a continuous function, $\text{plim} f(x_n) = f(\text{plim } x_n)$. The following lemma can often be used to prove convergence in probability.

Lemma 1.1 $\text{plim}_{n \to \infty} x_n = c$ if (*i*) $\lim_{n \to \infty} Ex_n = c$ and (ii) $\lim_{n \to \infty} \text{Var } x_n = 0$.

PROOF Chebyshev's inequality states that if the random variable x has mean μ and standard deviation σ,

$$P(|x - \mu| \geq k\sigma) \leq \frac{1}{k^2}$$

or equivalently $\qquad P(|x - \mu| < k\sigma) > 1 - \frac{1}{k^2}$

The conclusion of the lemma is that for ϵ and δ, however small,

$$P(|x_n - c| < \epsilon) > 1 - \delta$$

We let $1/k^2 = \delta$ and apply Chebyshev's inequality to yield

$$P[|x_n - Ex_n| < \delta^{-1/2}(\text{Var } x_n)^{1/2}] > 1 - \delta$$

Assumption (i) states that for any ϵ_1, however small, $|Ex_n - c| < \epsilon_1$ for sufficiently large n. Assumption (ii) states that for any positive λ, however small, $|\text{Var } x_n| < \lambda$ or $(\text{Var } x_n)^{1/2} < \lambda^{1/2}$ for sufficiently large n. We use the inequality

$$|x_n - c| \leq |x_n - Ex_n| + |Ex_n - c|$$

and assumption (i) to conclude that for any ϵ_1 and sufficiently large n

$$|x_n - c| < |x_n - Ex_n| + \epsilon_1$$

If $|x_n - Ex_n| < \delta^{-1/2}(\text{Var } x_n)^{1/2}$, we have, using assumption (ii),

$$|x_n - c| < \delta^{-1/2}(\text{Var } x_n)^{1/2} + \epsilon_1 \leq \delta^{-1/2}\lambda^{1/2} + \epsilon_1$$

for any ϵ_1 and λ and sufficiently large n. For any given ϵ and δ, we can always choose ϵ_1 and λ to make $\delta^{-1/2}\lambda^{1/2} + \epsilon_1 = \epsilon$. Thus $|x_n - c| < \epsilon$ whenever $|x_n - Ex_n| < \delta^{-1/2}(\text{Var } x_n)^{1/2}$ under assumptions (i) and (ii). The latter event has probability greater than $1 - \delta$, implying

$$P(|x_n - c| < \epsilon) > 1 - \delta$$

Applying Lemma 1.1, one can easily show that the mean $\bar{x}_n$ of a sample of n observations from a population with mean μ and variance σ^2 converges in probability to μ. Since $E\bar{x}_n = \mu$ and Var $\bar{x}_n = \sigma^2/n$, implying conditions (i) and (ii) of the lemma, respectively, $\bar{x}_n$ converges in probability to μ. This result can be generalized to a situation where each observation x_i has its own mean or expectation μ_i and variance σ_i^2. The conclusion desired is that *the sample mean* $\sum_{i=1}^n x_i/n$ *converge in probability to the mean* $\sum_{i=1}^n \mu_i/n$ *of the expectations.* In other words, the sample mean $\bar{y} = \sum_i y_i/n$ of random variables $y_i = x_i - \mu_i$ converges in probability to zero. Since $E\bar{y} = 0$, assumption (i) of the lemma is satisfied. If the y_i are independent, Var $\bar{y} = \left(\sum_{i=1}^n \sigma_i^2\right)/n^2$. Therefore, as long as lim $\left(\sum_{i=1}^n \sigma_i^2\right)/n^2 = 0$, which the mathematician refers to as $\left(\sum_{i=1}^n \sigma_i^2\right) = o(n^2)$, assumption (ii) is also satisfied, and the conclusion follows. We have just proved a version of the *weak law of large numbers*, which states that the mean of the sample converges in probability to the mean of the expectations as the sample size increases.

In statistics, the concept of convergence in probability is used to define *consistency* of a sequence of estimators. A sequence of estimators is said to be *consistent* if it converges in probability to the parameter to be estimated. We have just shown that, under the conditions of independent observations and $\sum_{i=1}^n \sigma_i^2 = o(n^2)$, the sample mean is a consistent estimator.

Along similar lines, let us consider the consistency of the least-squares estimator b of the slope β in a simple linear regression.

Theorem 1.1 If the residuals ϵ_i are independently and identically distributed with mean zero and variance σ^2, and if $\sum_{i=1}^n (x_i - \bar{x})^2$ approaches infinity as n increases, the least-squares estimator b is consistent.

PROOF Under the assumption that each ϵ_i has zero mean, (4) implies that $Eb = \beta$, satisfying assumption (i) of Lemma 1.1. Var $b = \left[\sum_i (x_i - \bar{x})^2\right]^{-1}\sigma^2$ by (6). It approaches zero as n increases if $\sum_{i=1}^n (x_i - \bar{x})^2$ approaches infinity, satisfying assumption (ii) of Lemma 1.1.

In Theorem 1.1 we have dropped the assumption that the ϵ_i are normal but retained the assumption that they are identically distributed with variance σ^2. The theorem still holds if the variances σ_i^2 of ϵ_i are different but are bounded, say below K (see Prob. 8). One observes that the condition $\sum_{i=1}^n (x_i - \bar{x})^2 \to \infty$ is satisfied if the sample variance of the x's approaches a limit Q (see Prob. 9).

$\star$1.9 CENTRAL LIMIT THEOREMS

To say that b is consistent (more precisely that the sequence of estimators b_n is consistent) is not saying very much. We would like to study the distribution of b

in large samples, which requires studying the distribution function for a sequence x_n of random variables as n increases. In a variety of situations such a distribution can be approximated by a normal distribution.

A sequence of random variables $x_1, x_2, \ldots, x_n$, having (cumulative) distribution functions $F_1(\cdot), F_2(\cdot), \ldots, F_n(\cdot)$, *converges in distribution* to a random variable x with distribution function $F(\cdot)$, or simply to the distribution function $F(\cdot)$, if $\lim_{n \to \infty} F_n(z) = F(z)$ for all continuity points of $F(\cdot)$. The sequence of random variables $x_1, x_2, \ldots, x_n$ is said to have $F(\cdot)$ as the limiting distribution. If x_i has density function $f_i(\cdot)$ $(i = 1, \ldots, n)$ and x has density function $f(\cdot)$, convergence in distribution to x or to $f(\cdot)$ means, for every a, b with $a \leq b$, that

$$\lim_{n \to \infty} P(a \leq x_n \leq b) = \int_a^b f(s) \, ds$$

We are mainly interested in studying convergence to a normal distribution. A useful tool for proving convergence in distribution is the characteristic function.

The *characteristic function* of a random variable x is defined as

$$\phi_x(t) \equiv Ee^{itx} = E\left[1 + itx + \frac{1}{2} (it)^2 x^2 + \frac{1}{3!} (it)^3 x^3 + \cdots \right]$$

$$= 1 + it(Ex) - \frac{1}{2} t^2 (Ex^2) - \frac{i}{3!} t^3 (Ex^3) + \cdots \quad (41)$$

where E denotes expectation, $i = \sqrt{-1}$, and we have expanded e^{itx} in an infinite series. If we differentiate $\phi_x(t)$ with respect to t, the kth derivative evaluated at $t = 0$ equals $i^k(Ex^k)$. There are several important facts about the characteristic function.

1. The characteristic function uniquely determines the distribution.
2. If a sequence ϕ_n of characteristic functions converges to a characteristic function ϕ, then the corresponding sequence of distribution functions converges to the distribution function determined by ϕ.
3. If x_1 and x_2 are independent and have characteristic functions ϕ_1 and ϕ_2, respectively, the characteristic function for $x_1 + x_2$ is $\phi_1\phi_2$.
4. If $\phi(t)$ is the characteristic function for x, $\phi(t/k)$ is the characteristic function for x/k.

The characteristic function of a random vector x is similarly defined as

$$\phi_x(t) = E(e^{it'x})$$

where t is a vector of the same dimension as x. The above four important facts apply equally to the vector case. Let us find the characteristic function of a k-variate normal vector x with mean μ and covariance matrix Σ

$$\phi_x(t) = E(e^{it'x}) = \int_{-\infty}^{\infty} (2\pi)^{-k/2} |\Sigma|^{-1/2} \exp\left[-\tfrac{1}{2}(z - \mu)'\Sigma^{-1}(z - \mu) + iz't \right] dz \quad (42)$$

To integrate, we complete the square for z in the exponent of the integrand as in

(22), yielding

$$\phi_x(t) = \exp\left(i\mu't - \tfrac{1}{2}t'\Sigma t\right) \tag{43}$$

as the characteristic function of a multivariate normal vector (see Prob. 10). The characteristic function of a standard normal variable is therefore

$$\phi_x(t) = e^{-t^2/2} \tag{44}$$

To prove that a sequence x_n converges in distribution to the standard normal distribution, one need only show that the corresponding sequence ϕ_n of characteristic functions converges to (44). This method is used to prove the following central limit theorem.

Theorem 1.2 Let $x_1, x_2, \ldots, x_n$ be independent and have identical distributions with mean μ and variance σ^2, and let $\bar{x}_n$ be the sample mean. Then $\sqrt{n}(\bar{x}_n - \mu)/\sigma$ converges in distribution to a standard normal distribution.

PROOF Let $\phi(t)$ be the characteristic function of each $x_i - \mu = y$, say. The first two derivatives of $\phi(t)$ are

$$\phi'(t) = E\frac{d}{dt}e^{ity} = E(iye^{ity})$$

and $\qquad \phi''(t) = E(iy)^2 e^{ity} = -Ey^2 e^{ity}$

Because $e^{ity} = \cos ty + i\sin ty$ is bounded and the expectations Ey and Ey^2 exist, these derivatives exist and can be shown to be continuous. Using the fact that if a function $\phi(t)$ has a continuous mth derivative in some neighborhood of 0 then

$$\phi(t) = \phi(0) + \phi'(0)t + \frac{\phi''(0)}{2}t^2 + \cdots + \frac{\phi^{(m)}(0)}{m!}t^m + o(t^m)$$

we can write the characteristic function of y as

$$\phi(t) = 1 + i(Ey)t - \frac{Ey^2}{2}t^2 + o(t^2) = 1 - \frac{\sigma^2 t^2}{2} + o(t^2)$$

The characteristic function of $(x_i - \mu)/\sigma\sqrt{n}$, by property 4, is

$$\phi\left(\frac{t}{\sigma\sqrt{n}}\right) = 1 - \frac{t^2}{2n} + o\left(\frac{t^2}{n}\right)$$

where we recall that $z = o(x)$ means $z/x \to 0$ and $z = o(t^2/n)$ if and only if $z = o(t^2/\sigma^2 n)$ for any nonzero constant σ^2.

The random variable of interest is the sum of n independent terms

$$\sum_{i=1}^{n}\frac{x_i - \mu}{\sigma\sqrt{n}} = \sqrt{n}\sum_{i=1}^{n}\frac{x_i - \mu}{n\sigma} = \frac{\sqrt{n}(\bar{x}_n - \mu)}{\sigma}$$

This sum, by property 3, has a characteristic function

$$\phi_n(t) = \left[1 - \frac{t^2}{2n} + o\left(\frac{t^2}{n}\right) \right]^n$$

or, on taking natural logarithms,

$$\ln \phi_n(t) = n \ln \left[1 - \frac{t^2}{2n} + o(n^{-1}) \right] \rightarrow \frac{-t^2}{2}$$

using the expansion of $\ln (1 + z)$ for small z. Therefore, $\phi_n(t)$ approaches $e^{-t^2/2}$ as n approaches infinity.

The assumption of Theorem 1.2 that each x_i has the same variance σ^2 can be relaxed. We state without proof the following central limit theorem.

Theorem 1.3: Lindeberg-Feller Central Limit Theorem Let $x_1, x_2, \ldots, x_n$ be independent, and let x_i have density function f_i with mean zero and variance v_i. A necessary and sufficient condition for $\sum_{i=1}^{n} x_i/(\mathrm{Var} \sum_i x_i)^{1/2}$ to have a standard normal limiting distribution is that

$$\lim_{n \to \infty} \max_{k \le n} \frac{1}{v_k} \int_{|z| \ge tS_n} z^2 f_k(z) \, dz = 0 \qquad \begin{array}{l} \text{for every } t > 0 \\ \text{where } S_n = \left(\mathrm{Var} \sum_{i=1}^{n} x_i \right)^{1/2} \end{array} \qquad (45)$$

Condition (45) guarantees that each random variable x_k will have a variance v_k which is extremely small compared with the variance S_n^2 of the sum $\sum_{i=1}^{n} x_i$. If S_n is extremely large compared with the standard deviation of each x_k, the integral in (45) will be extremely small compared with the variance v_k (see Prob. 17). The Lindeberg condition (45) requires that $S_n^2 \to \infty$. S_n^2 is the sum of variances which are positive and is thus monotone-increasing. It either approaches infinity or is bounded. If $S_n^2 \le B$ for all n, we can choose t to make

$$\int_{|z| \ge tS_n} z^2 f_1(z) \, dz > \frac{v_1}{2}$$

and the maximum in (45) will be greater than $\frac{1}{2}$ for all n, contradicting the condition. If each x_i has the same variance $v_i = \sigma^2$, the sum $S_n^2 = n\sigma^2$ approaches infinity and so does the product tS_n for any positive t. The integral in (45) approaches zero for each k. Theorem 1.3 implies Theorem 1.2. Condition (45) was used by Lindeberg in 1922 to prove a central limit theorem. In 1935 Feller showed that it is a necessary and sufficient condition for the central limit theorem when $x_1, \ldots, x_n$ are independent. Feller (1966, pp. 256–257) contains a proof; see also Prob. 17.

Let us apply Theorem 1.3 to a study of the distribution of the least-squares estimate b of the slope β in a simple linear regression. Assume that ϵ_i are independent and identically (but not necessarily normally) distributed having density function f with mean zero and variance σ^2. By (4), the distribution of $b - \beta$ is determined by the distribution of the sum

$$\sum_{i=1}^{n} (x_i - \bar{x})\epsilon_i \equiv \sum_{i=1}^{n} z_i \tag{46}$$

The variance of z_i is $(x_i - \bar{x})^2 \sigma^2$. The variance of the sum (46) is

$$S_n^2 = \operatorname{Var} \sum_{i=1}^{n} z_i = \sigma^2 \sum_{i=1}^{n} (x_i - \bar{x})^2$$

The Lindeberg condition states that for any $k \le n$ and $t > 0$

$$\lim_{n \to \infty} \frac{1}{(x_k - \bar{x})^2 \sigma^2} \int_{|s| \ge tS_n/(x_k - \bar{x})} (x_k - \bar{x})^2 s^2 f(s) \, ds = \lim_{n \to \infty} \frac{1}{\sigma^2} \int_{|s| \ge tS_n/(x_k - \bar{x})} s^2 f(s) \, ds = 0$$

where we have changed the variable from $z_k = (x_k - \bar{x})\epsilon_k$ to ϵ_k. This condition holds if

$$\frac{S_n}{x_k - \bar{x}} = \sigma \sqrt{\sum_{i=1}^{n} \frac{(x_i - \bar{x})^2}{(x_k - \bar{x})^2}} \to \infty \qquad \text{for } k \le n$$

or if

$$\sum_{i=1}^{n} \frac{(x_i - \bar{x})^2}{(x_k - \bar{x})^2} \to \infty \tag{47}$$

Thus (47) is a sufficient condition for the least-squares estimator b to converge in distribution to a normal distribution. An equivalent statement is that b is *asymptotically normal*.

★1.10 THE CRAMER-RAO INEQUALITY

In Secs. 1.8 and 1.9 two properties of an estimator were studied, consistency and asymptotic normality. Another interesting property is *efficiency*, which is concerned with the size of the variance. An estimator is said to be *efficient* if it is unbiased and if its variance is the smallest possible. To prove the latter, one can use the Cramer-Rao inequality, which provides a lower bound for the variance.

To derive the Cramer-Rao inequality, consider a sample $x = (x_1, \ldots, x_n)$ of n observations on a random vector. Let $L(x; \theta)$ be the joint density of x given the parameter vector θ. If x is treated as given, $L(x; \theta)$ is the likelihood function with θ as the argument. Because all density functions integrate to 1, we have

$$\int_{-\infty}^{\infty} L(x; \theta) \, dx = 1$$

In this derivation we assume that the limits of integration of $L(x; \theta)$ over x are independent of θ and the derivatives can be taken under the integral sign. Differentiating both sides of this equation with respect to the vector θ and assuming the validity of differentiation under the integral sign, we obtain

$$\int_{-\infty}^{\infty} \frac{\partial L(x, \theta)}{\partial \theta} \, dx = 0$$

where the derivative $\partial L/\partial \theta$ denotes a column vector whose ith element is $\partial L/\partial \theta_i$ and the integral is a vector of the corresponding integrals which is set equal to the zero vector. Since

$$\frac{\partial \log L}{\partial \theta_i} = L^{-1} \frac{\partial L}{\partial \theta_i}$$

the above implies

$$\int_{-\infty}^{\infty} \frac{\partial \log L}{\partial \theta} L(x, \theta) \, dx \equiv E \frac{\partial \log L}{\partial \theta} = 0 \tag{48}$$

where $(\partial \log L)/\partial \theta$ is a vector of random variables if the argument x is treated as random and $L(x, \theta)$ is the density function of x. Equation (48) says that the expectation of $(\partial \log L)/\partial \theta$ is zero.

The vector (48) can be differentiated with respect to the row vector θ' to form a matrix whose ijth element is the derivative of the ith element of (48) with respect to the jth element of θ' or to θ_j. Again, differentiating under the integral sign yields

$$\int_{-\infty}^{\infty} \frac{\partial^2 \log L}{\partial \theta \, \partial \theta'} L(x, \theta) \, dx + \int_{-\infty}^{\infty} \frac{\partial \log L}{\partial \theta} \frac{\partial L}{\partial \theta'} \, dx = 0$$

or $\qquad \displaystyle\int_{-\infty}^{\infty} \frac{\partial \log L}{\partial \theta} \frac{\partial \log L}{\partial \theta'} L(x, \theta) \, dx = -E \frac{\partial^2 \log L}{\partial \theta \, \partial \theta'} \equiv R(\theta) \tag{49}$

The ijth element of the matrix $(\partial^2 \log L)/(\partial \theta \, \partial \theta')$ is the second partial derivative of $\log L$ with respect to θ_i and θ_j. The negative of the expectation of this matrix, defined by $R(\theta)$, is *Fisher's information matrix*. Equation (49) asserts that Fisher's information matrix equals the covariance matrix of the vector $(\partial \log L)/\partial \theta$, which has mean zero by (48).

An estimator for θ must be some (vector) function $g(x)$ of the observations $x = (x_1, \ldots, x_n)$. Assume the estimator $g(x)$ to be unbiased,

$$E[g(x)] = \int_{\infty}^{\infty} g(x)L(x; \theta) \, dx = \theta \tag{50}$$

Differentiation of (50) with respect to the row vector θ' gives

$$\int_{-\infty}^{\infty} g(x) \frac{\partial \log L}{\partial \theta'} L(x; \theta) \, dx = E\left[g(x) \frac{\partial \log L}{\partial \theta'} \right] = I \tag{51}$$

where $g(x)$ is a column vector and $(\partial \log L)/\partial \theta'$ is a row vector having mean zero. Consider the covariance matrix of the vector consisting of both $g(x)$ and $(\partial \log L)/\partial \theta$

$$\text{Cov} \begin{bmatrix} g(x) \\ \dfrac{\partial \log L}{\partial \theta} \end{bmatrix} = \begin{bmatrix} \text{Cov } g(x) & I \\ I & R(\theta) \end{bmatrix}$$

where both (49) and (50) have been used. Since a covariance matrix is positive semidefinite, i.e., for any nonzero vector z, $z'(\text{Cov})\,z \geq 0$, we have

$$[z' \quad -z'R^{-1}(\theta)]\begin{bmatrix} \text{Cov } g(x) & I \\ I & R(\theta) \end{bmatrix}\begin{bmatrix} z \\ -R^{-1}(\theta)z \end{bmatrix}$$

$$= z'[\text{Cov } g(x) - R^{-1}(\theta)]z \geq 0 \quad (52)$$

which is known as the *Cramer-Rao inequality*. It asserts that the covariance matrix of an unbiased estimator $g(x)$ cannot be smaller than the inverse of Fisher's information matrix, in the sense that the covariance matrix minus the inverse of the information matrix is a positive semidefinite matrix.

To apply this inequality to studying the efficiency of the least-squares estimator b, let us find the information matrix of the parameters α and β. The likelihood function for the simple regression model is

$$L = (2\pi)^{-n/2}\sigma^{-n} \exp -\frac{1}{2}\sum_{i=1}^{n} \frac{(y_i - \alpha - \beta x_i)^2}{\sigma^2} \quad (53)$$

and the log likelihood is

$$\log L = -\tfrac{1}{2}n \log 2\pi - \tfrac{1}{2}n \log \sigma^2 - \frac{1}{2}\sum_{i=1}^{n} \frac{(y_i - \alpha - \beta x_i)^2}{\sigma^2} \quad (54)$$

The information matrix is

$$-E\begin{bmatrix} \dfrac{\partial^2 \log L}{\partial \alpha^2} & \dfrac{\partial^2 \log L}{\partial \alpha\, \partial \beta} \\ \dfrac{\partial^2 \log L}{\partial \beta\, \partial \alpha} & \dfrac{\partial^2 \log L}{\partial \beta^2} \end{bmatrix} = -E\begin{bmatrix} -\dfrac{n}{\sigma^2} & -\dfrac{\Sigma x_i}{\sigma^2} \\ -\dfrac{\Sigma x_i}{\sigma^2} & -\dfrac{\Sigma_i x_i^2}{\sigma^2} \end{bmatrix} = \frac{1}{\sigma^2}\begin{bmatrix} n & \Sigma x_i \\ \Sigma x_i & \Sigma x_i^2 \end{bmatrix} \quad (55)$$

The inverse of the information matrix is

$$R^{-1} = \frac{\sigma^2}{n\sum_i x_i^2 - (\sum_i x_i)^2}\begin{bmatrix} \Sigma x_i^2 & -\Sigma x_i \\ -\Sigma x_i & n \end{bmatrix} \quad (56)$$

Therefore, by the Cramer-Rao inequality, the variance of an unbiased estimator of β cannot be smaller than

$$\frac{n\sigma^2}{n\sum_i x_i^2 - (\sum_i x_i)^2} = \frac{\sigma^2}{\sum_i (x_i - \bar{x})^2}$$

Since the least-squares estimator b is unbiased and its variance is precisely this quantity, it is *efficient*. In other words, under the assumption that the ϵ_i are normal, b is *best unbiased*; among all the unbiased estimators it has the smallest variance possible. We pointed out in Sec. 1.3 and will prove in Chap. 2 that b is best *linear* unbiased. Now, using the Cramer-Rao inequality, we are making a stronger statement by dropping the word "linear." We no longer have to restrict ourselves to linear estimators when we say that the estimator b is best unbiased. However, we have used the assumption that the ϵ_i are normal, whereas this assumption is not required to assert best linear unbiasedness.

⋆1.11 ASYMPTOTIC DISTRIBUTION OF MAXIMUM-LIKELIHOOD ESTIMATORS

We have studied the distribution of b in a variety of ways. In small samples we have shown that b is normal and is best unbiased or efficient under the assumption that the residuals are independent and normally and identically distributed. b is best linear unbiased if we drop the normality assumption in the above statement but still assume that the variances of ϵ_i are identical. In large samples we have shown that b is consistent under the assumption $\sum_i (x_i - \bar{x})^2 \to \infty$ and that b is asymptotically normal under condition (47). When we deal with more complicated econometric models, it would be useful to say that certain estimators are consistent, asymptotically normal, and/or asymptotically efficient in the sense that their limiting distribution has the smallest covariance matrix possible. In fact, under certain fairly general assumptions, the method of maximum likelihood yields estimators which have all three of these properties.

Theorem 1.4 Let $x = (x_1, \ldots, x_n)$ be n independent and identically distributed random vectors, each having a density function $f(\cdot; \theta)$ with θ as the parameter vector of m elements. Assume:

(i) The first two derivatives of $f(z, \theta)$ with respect to θ exist and are continuous for all z and for all θ in a set A containing the true parameter value θ_0 as an interior point.

(ii) The limits of integration for the likelihood function $L(x; \theta) = \Pi_i f(x_i; \theta)$ over x are independent of θ, and derivatives can be taken under the integral sign, so that the conditions for the Cramer-Rao inequality hold.

(iii) The covariance matrix of $[\partial \log f(x_i; \theta_0)]/\partial \theta$ is positive definite and bounded.

(iv) The third derivatives of $\log f(z; \theta)$ with respect to θ are bounded for all z and for all θ in A.

Under assumptions (i) to (iii) the likelihood equation

$$\frac{n^{-1} \partial \log L(x; \theta)}{\partial \theta} = 0$$

has a root $\hat{\theta}_n$ which is consistent. Under the additional assumption (iv) this root is asymptotically normal and asymptotically efficient.

PROOF To prove consistency we observe that, by (48), (49), and assumption (iii), $n^{-1} E[\log L(x; \theta)]$ has a zero vector of first derivatives and a negative-definite matrix of second derivatives and therefore reaches a maximum at $\theta = \theta_0$, where θ_0 is the true parameter value and the expectation E is evaluated using θ_0. That is, for a vector $\delta > 0$

$$n^{-1} E_{\theta_0}[\log L(x; \theta_0)] > n^{-1} E_{\theta_0}[\log L(x; \theta_0 \pm \delta)] \tag{57}$$

By the law of large numbers, the corresponding sample averages satisfy the relation

$$\frac{1}{n}\sum_{i=1}^{n}\log f(x_i;\theta_0) > \frac{1}{n}\sum_{i=1}^{n}\log f(x_i;\theta_0 \pm \delta) \tag{58}$$

with probability greater than $1 - \epsilon$ for any ϵ however small and for sufficiently large n (see Prob. 15). With this high probability, the function $n^{-1}\sum_i \log f(x_i;\theta)$ will be greater at $\theta = \theta_0$ than at $\theta = \theta_0 \pm \delta$. Whenever this happens, this function will have a local maximum within $\theta_0 \pm \delta$ because the function is continuous in $\theta_0 \pm \delta$ by assumption (i). In other words, with probability higher than $1 - \epsilon$, a root $\hat\theta$ of the likelihood equation $[n^{-1} \, \partial \log L(x;\theta)]/\partial\theta = 0$ will be within $\theta_0 \pm \delta$. This proves that a root of the likelihood equation is consistent, and not that the (global) maximum of the likelihood function is consistent. The latter statement follows if $n^{-1}E[\log L(Y,\theta)]$ has a global maximum at $\theta = \theta_0$, that is, (57) holds for all δ, which has been shown by Wald (1949) using further assumptions.

To derive the asymptotic distribution of the consistent root $\hat\theta$ of the likelihood equation, we expand $[n^{-1} \, \partial \log L(x;\hat\theta)]/\partial\theta$ about θ_0 to get

$$n^{-1}\frac{\partial \log L(x;\theta_0)}{\partial\theta} + n^{-1}\frac{\partial^2 \log L(x;\theta_0)}{\partial\theta\,\partial\theta'}(\hat\theta - \theta_0)$$

$$+ \frac{1}{2}\begin{bmatrix} (\hat\theta - \theta_0)'B_1(\hat\theta - \theta_0) \\ \vdots \\ (\hat\theta - \theta_0)'B_m(\hat\theta - \theta_0) \end{bmatrix}$$

$$= n^{-1}\frac{\partial \log L(x;\theta_0)}{\partial\theta}$$

$$+ \left\{ n^{-1}\frac{\partial^2 \log L(x;\theta_0)}{\partial\theta\,\partial\theta'} + \frac{1}{2}\begin{bmatrix} (\hat\theta - \theta_0)'B_1 \\ \vdots \\ (\hat\theta - \theta_0)'B_m \end{bmatrix} \right\}(\hat\theta - \theta_0)$$

$$= n^{-1}\frac{\partial \log L(x;\theta_0)}{\partial\theta}$$

$$+ \left[n^{-1}\frac{\partial^2 \log L(x;\theta_0)}{\partial\theta\,\partial\theta'} + o(1) \right](\hat\theta - \theta_0) = 0 \tag{59}$$

where $\qquad B_i = n^{-1}\dfrac{\partial^3 \log L(x;\theta^*)}{\partial\theta\,\partial\theta'\,\partial\theta_i} \qquad \begin{array}{l} i = 1,\ldots,m \\ \theta_0 \le \theta^* \le \hat\theta \end{array}$

By assumption (iv), each B_i is bounded. Together with the consistency of $\hat\theta$, this implies that plim $(\hat\theta - \theta_0)'B_i = 0$. We denote by $o(z)$ a function f such that $\lim (f/z) = 0$. Thus $o(1)$ is used to denote a function f such that $\lim f = 0$. Here we use $o(1)$ to denote a function which has zero as its probability limit.

The solution of (59) is

$$\sqrt{n}(\hat{\theta} - \theta_0) = -\left[n^{-1}\frac{\partial^2 \log L}{\partial \theta \, \partial \theta} + o(1)\right]^{-1} n^{-1/2}\frac{\partial \log L(x; \theta_0)}{\partial \theta} \quad (60)$$

We need to multiply $\hat{\theta} - \theta_0$ by $\sqrt{n}$ to study its limiting distribution because $\hat{\theta} - \theta_0$ itself converges in probability to zero. On the other hand, the covariance matrix of $\sqrt{n}(\hat{\theta} - \theta_0)$ will neither shrink nor expand as n increases.

The last term of (60)

$$\frac{\partial \log L(x; \theta_0)}{\partial \theta} = \sum_{i=1}^{n} \frac{\partial \log f(x_i; \theta_0)}{\partial \theta}$$

is a sum of independent and identically distributed random vectors, each having mean zero by (48) and covariance matrix R_1 by (49), which is the information matrix based on one observation. By the multivariate version of Theorem 1.2, which is the result of Prob. 16, $(n^{-1/2} \, \partial \log L)/\partial \theta$ converges in distribution to a multivariate normal distribution with mean zero and covariance matrix R_1. By the law of large numbers, the term in brackets in (60)

$$n^{-1}\frac{\partial^2 \log L}{\partial \theta \, \partial \theta'} + o(1) = n^{-1}\sum_{i=1}^{n}\frac{\partial f^2(x_i; \theta_0)}{\partial \theta \, \partial \theta'} + o(1)$$

converges in probability to the expectation $-R_1$. The negative of its inverse, being a continuous (matrix) function of the original matrix, converges in probability to R_1^{-1}. We now use the following fact. *If a sequence $\{Y_n\}$ of random vectors converges in distribution to Y, and if the sequence $\{A_n\}$ of random matrices converges in probability to A, then $\{A Y_n\}$ converges in distribution to $A Y$.* Being the product of two terms on the right-hand side of (60), $\sqrt{n}(\hat{\theta} - \theta_0)$ thus converges in distribution to a normal vector with covariance matrix $R_1^{-1}R_1 R_1^{-1'} = R_1^{-1}$. The covariance matrix R_1^{-1} is the minimum by the Cramer-Rao inequality. Note that the covariance matrix of $\hat{\theta}$ itself is approximated by $n^{-1}R_1^{-1}$ or $(nR_1)^{-1}$, as the information matrix based on all n observations is nR_1 by virtue of

$$-E\frac{\partial^2 \log L}{\partial \theta \, \partial \theta'} = -\sum_{i=1}^{n} E\frac{\partial^2 \log f(x_i; \theta_0)}{\partial \theta \, \partial \theta'} = nR_1$$

When the covariance matrix of its limiting distribution reaches the Cramer-Rao bound, the estimator is said to be *asymptotically efficient*.

1.12 ESTIMATING THE QUANTITY OF, AND DEMAND FOR, COMPUTERS

To introduce the subject of multiple linear regression through an example and to answer a question raised in Sec. 1.1 in the discussion of formulating an econometric model, we use part of a study of the demand for computers. Although the reader may be unfamiliar with some of the technical material it includes, the need to understand such material provides a motivation for studying Chaps. 2 and 3. One learns little from reading only material that is perfectly comprehensible.†

To what extent has the use of electronic computers grown in the United States since 1955? What can explain the rate of growth?

We propose to measure different computers by the monthly rentals which would have been charged if the models had been introduced in the year 1960. This method of measurement requires first establishing a relationship between rental and the computer's basic characteristics for 1960 models and then applying the relationship to estimate what each computer would have cost if it had been introduced in 1960. By this method, the stock of general-purpose digital computers has grown from an estimated 1960 rental of about $370,000 per month at the end of 1954 to about $194 million at the end of 1965. An average annual rate of growth of 78 percent would have accomplished this.

To explain this tremendous growth, one has to isolate the natural growth which would have prevailed had there been no technological change from the growth induced by technological change. In other words, two elements account for the increase in the use of computers. First, it takes time for a new product to reach an equilibrium level even without quality change. Second, in the meantime, the quality of the product is improving, so that the equilibrium level is being continuously raised. An explanation ought to combine these two elements and assess their roles in the growth process.

For natural growth, two differential equations have been popular. They are the differential equations generating the Gompertz curve and the logistic curve. For reasons of empirical validity as well as analytical convenience, we have chosen the former, but a test of the latter will also be presented.

A simple way of incorporating the effect of technological change into the natural growth process is to assume that the equilibrium level, which the growth curve approaches, is a function of price, given quality. A price index can be constructed once the quantity of each computer is established, by its hypothetical 1960 rental as previously indicated. An average of the ratios of rentals to quantities, for models introduced in a period, would serve as a price index for the period.

Our price index, deflated by the GNP deflator, shows an annual average rate of reduction of 20 percent between 1954 and 1965. If the price elasticity of demand for equilibrium stock of computers is 1.3, say, price reduction alone would account for a 34 percent annual growth, out of a total of 78 percent observed.

The remainder of this section develops more fully the ideas sketched above, provides measurements of the use of computers and of their prices, and attempts to explain the growth of computers in the United States between 1955 and 1965. The theory will be formulated first; then the construction of quantity and price

† The balance of the section is modified from Chow (1967) by permission.

indexes will be described; statistical analyses of the time-series data will be performed, and some conclusions will be drawn.

Theory

To describe the process of natural growth of a new product it is often assumed that the rate of growth depends on two factors. First, the quantity of existing stock y_t asserts a positive influence, partly rationalized by the idea that the more the product has been accepted, the more prospective buyers have come in contact with and learned about the product. Second, the difference or ratio between the equilibrium level y^* ultimately to be reached and the existing level y_t also asserts a positive influence. Although the existing stock y_t has a positive effect on the rate of growth, as it shows the extent of the awareness of the product, the closer it comes to the equilibrium level y^*, the smaller the number of prospective buyers remaining.

One formulation of the growth process incorporating these two factors is

$$\frac{dy}{dt} = \alpha y(\log y^* - \log y) \tag{61}$$

or

$$\frac{d \log y}{dt} = \alpha(\log y^* - \log y)$$

The solution of the differential equation (61) yields the Gompertz curve. Another formulation is

$$\frac{dy}{dt} = \gamma y(y^* - y) \tag{62}$$

or

$$\frac{d \log y}{dt} = \gamma(y^* - y)$$

the solution of which is the logistic curve. Both formulations assume that the two factors affecting the rate of growth enter multiplicatively. Hence they become hypotheses explaining the percentage rate of growth. According to (61), the percentage rate of growth is a linear decreasing function of log y. According to (62), the percentage growth is a linear decreasing function of y. Thus, in a later stage of the growth process, or for a large value of y, any given increment in y will dampen the rate of growth more for the logistic hypothesis than for the Gompertz hypothesis. In other words, in the later stages, the Gompertz rate of growth is more nearly constant than the logistic rate of growth.

A further observation on the difference between these two growth curves is in terms of the stage at which the maximum rate of growth is reached. Setting the derivative of (61) with respect to y equal to zero leads to $y = e^{-1}y^* = .37y^*$. Setting the derivative of (62) equal to zero leads to $y = .5y^*$. Hence, the maximum rate of growth is reached when the stock is about 37 percent of its equilibrium level by the Gompertz curve and when the stock is 50 percent of equilibrium by the logistic curve. Since the rate of growth given by Eq. (62) is the same for y equal to $.5y^* + k$ or to $.5y^* - k$, the logistic curve is symmetrical. On the other hand, the Gompertz curve attains its maximum rate of growth at an earlier stage than the logistic curve and maintains a more nearly constant rate of growth later on.

There are two a priori reasons for choosing the Gompertz differential equation (61). According to a study of the growth of television sets in the United Kingdom by Bain (1964), the growth curve is not symmetric, as the logistic would imply; the growth rate is higher at an early stage and declines gradually in later stages. Although the Gompertz curve possesses this characteristic, Bain rejected it because it is too rigid, implying the maximum rate of growth to be at 37 percent of equilibrium. We have no reason to reject the Gompertz in favor of the equally rigid logistic curve. In fact, rigidity is the price we must pay for choosing an equation with only one parameter.

The second reason for preferring the Gompertz differential equation is analytical convenience. We shall approximate the derivative of $\log y$ by its difference $\log y_t - \log y_{t-1}$ and the existing stock y by y_{t-1}. Equation (61) will then become

$$\log y_t - \log y_{t-1} = \alpha(\log y^* - \log y_{t-1}) \tag{63}$$

If the equilibrium stock y^* is assumed to be a function of certain variables with constant elasticities, the right-hand side of (63) will be a linear function of the logarithms of these variables and of $\log y_{t-1}$. Unless we assume y^* to be a linear function of these variables, a similar transformation of (62) would be nonlinear and more difficult to analyze statistically.

Equation (63), with $\log y^*$ replaced by a linear function of the logarithms of certain variables affecting the equilibrium level, is familiar in econometrics. One wonders why this model has scarcely been applied, if at all, to the study of a new product. In another occasion Chow (1965) pointed out the need to integrate the growth process with the comparative static theory of demand in the study of a new product. Why not let his model provide such an integration?

By the comparative static theory of the demand for input, two of the most important determinants are relative price p_t and the output x_t of the firms employing the input. In the case of a durable good, the quantity of the input used can be measured by the stock. Assuming constant elasticities, one can determine the equilibrium stock y^* by

$$\log y_t^* = \beta_0 - \beta_1 \log p_t + \beta_2 \log x_t \tag{64}$$

Substituting (64) for $\log y^*$ in (63) gives

$$\log y_t - \log y_{t-1} = \alpha\beta_0 - \alpha\beta_1 \log p_t + \alpha\beta_2 \log x_t - \alpha \log y_{t-1} \tag{65}$$

For any new product one can think of, the price always declined, and the output of the industries employing the product (if it is an input) or the income of the consumers (if it is a consumer good) always increased. It is only by allowing for the price and output effects explicitly that one can isolate the process of natural growth.

Measurement of Quantity and Price of Computers

We assume that all general-purpose digital computers can be grouped into one commodity. The quantity of a computer is measured by an estimate of what its monthly rental would have been if it had been introduced in 1960. To form such an estimate we first establish a relationship between rental and the computer's basic characteristics for models introduced in 1960.

Three characteristics are chosen to establish the required relationship: multiplication time, memory size, and access time. Multiplication time is the average time in microseconds required to get and complete the multiplication instruction. It should have a negative effect on rental. (Addition time was also considered but was found to be a slightly inferior variable.) Memory size, in thousands of binary digits or equivalents, is the product of the number of words in the main memory (in thousands) and the number of binary digits per word, with a decimal digit counting as four and an octal digit counting as three binary digits. It should assert a positive influence on rental. Access time is the average time required to retrieve information from the memory. Its effect on rental should be negative.

It is recognized that the hardware of a computer has many other characteristics and that the characteristics of software support may be important. As far as the omitted characteristics of the hardware are concerned, it is assumed that they are highly correlated with the three characteristics included, so that our estimate of the hypothetical 1960 rental will not be too inaccurate. Insofar as software has been improving through time, its omission may be more serious. The only defense for this omission is to include software improvement as part of the adjustments allowed in reaching long-run equilibrium in our model.

The relationship between rental and the above-mentioned characteristics for models introduced in the same year is assumed to be linear in the logarithms of all variables. Our quantity index will be independent of the base year (the year chosen to establish this relationship) if the coefficients in the linear function are the same for different years. The intercept is expected to decline through time because the price of computers with the same characteristics has been declining. To examine how similar the coefficients are for different years we have computed a regression for each year from 1955 to 1965. For each year, beginning in 1960, the number of new computer models introduced during the year is at least 10. For each year up to 1959 the number of new models is less than 10, and we have included models introduced in the preceding year. The main source of data on rental and computer characteristics is the three surveys by Weik (1955, 1961, 1964). A supplementary source is the June issues of *Computers and Automation*, in which a Buyers Guide contains the relevant information. From October 1962 on, *Computers and Automation* has included a monthly computer census, in which data on average monthly rental can be found. We have relied on Weik's surveys as much as possible because they provide rental figures corresponding to different memory sizes available for the same computer model whereas *Computers and Automation* has only an average rental and a range for memory sizes.

The estimated coefficients (with standard errors in parentheses) of the regressions of rental on the three characteristics, all variables in logarithms, are presented in Table 1.1. Judging from the 11 cross-section regressions for the individual years, memory size has a larger coefficient (in absolute value) than either access time or multiplication time. Three of the coefficients of multiplication time and one coefficient of access time have wrong signs, though they are small fractions of their standard errors. While the standard errors are large for many coefficients, as a result of the high correlations between the three explanatory variables and of the small sample sizes, the orders of magnitude of the three coefficients do not appear to have changed drastically through time. Note also that the intercept tends to be smaller for later years, but its decline is far from uniform.

We have decided to pool the data from 1960 on, assuming unchanging

Table 1.1 Relationship between rental and computer characteristics
All variables in logarithms

Year	Multi-plication time	Memory size	Access time	Intercept	R^2	s^2	No. obser-vations
1955	.0108 (.1021)	.4297 (.1530)	−.2895 (.0618)	2.027	.947	.0461	9
1956	−.0505 (.1911)	.4495 (.1624)	−.1991 (.1076)	1.675	.890	.2081	11
1957	.0549 (.1596)	.5651 (.1481)	−.2187 (.0807)	.140	.941	.1476	10
1958	−.0171 (.0891)	.5311 (.0697)	−.1617 (.0565)	.542	.976	.0972	10
1959	−.2116 (.0366)	.3562 (.0395)	−.1270 (.0337)	2.489	.993	.0360	10
1960	−.1523 (.1009)	.4234 (.1797)	−.1208 (.0783)	1.205	.943	.1924	10
1961	−.0615 (.0729)	−.5507 (.1078)	.1755 (.0519)	.005	.944	.1159	12
1962	.0786 (.1411)	.8264 (.1525)	−.2571 (.1167)	−2.404	.916	.2414	11
1963	−.0675 (.0690)	.5750 (.0732)	−.0412 (.1228)	−.801	.951	.0794	15
1964	−.1486 (.0525)	.6867 (.0754)	.0412 (.1048)	−1.590	.895	.0978	18
1965	−.0411 (.0779)	.5778 (.0821)	−.1465 (.0999)	−1.354	.877	.2518	16
1960–1965	−.0654 (.0284)	.5793 (.0354)	−.1406 (.0293)	−.1045	.908	.1476	82
	$-.1398d_{61}$ (.1665)	$-.4891d_{62}$ (.1738)	$-5938d_{63}$ (.1661)	$-.9248d_{64}$ (.1663)	$-1.163d_{65}$ (.166)		

coefficients but introducing a dummy variable d_t for each year beginning 1961 to allow for change in the intercept. The estimated regression is presented at the bottom of Table 1.1. All three coefficients are highly significant, in spite of the strong correlations between the explanatory variables. The proportional effects of multiplication time, memory size, and access time on rental are about -7, 58, and -14 percent, respectively. The coefficient of the dummy variable is decreasing uniformly, reflecting the price decline.

To test the null hypothesis that the three coefficients have remained the same from 1960 to 1965 one would compute the sum of squares A of the residuals in the pooled regression, with 73 degrees of freedom, and the sum of squares B of the residuals in the six individual regressions, with 58 degrees of freedom. Under the null hypothesis, together with the assumption that the residuals in the individual regressions are normally distributed with the same variance, the ratio of $(A - B)/15$ to $B/58$ would be distributed as the F distribution with 15 and 58 degrees of freedom. From our calculations, A is 10.77 and B is 9.04. The F statistic is only .74, strongly supporting the null hypothesis. Therefore, we shall use the coefficients obtained by the pooled regression, with $-.1045$ as the intercept for 1960, in the estimation of the hypothetical 1960 rental for each computer model. The quantity index so constructed is independent of the base year chosen, at least from 1960 to 1965; it would hardly be affected even if a year in the 1950s were chosen as the base year, in view of the temporal stability of the coefficients in Table 1.1.

The computer models included in our quantity index are those listed in the monthly computer census of *Computers and Automation*; they are United States–made general-purpose digital computers only and exclude certain small models that are not internally programmed, notably IBM 604, 607 to 610, and CPC. The author has used IBM data, where available, on the number of IBM (domestic) installations as of December each year. For installation figures of other models, he has relied on *Computers and Automation* and the *Automatic Data Processing Newsletter*, published by the Diebold Group, Inc. The quantity index, in thousands of dollars of estimated 1960 monthly rental, is presented in Table 1.2.

To measure the price per fixed quantity for each computer model, one simply takes the ratio of its rental to its quantity, the latter being measured by its hypothetical 1960 rental as described. To obtain a price index number for a given year, one can average the prices over all models currently introduced. Some weighted average was considered, but it was not easy to decide on the weights. An obvious possibility would be to use the quantity (measured in our sense) of the installations as of December of each year, but this weight would depend too much on the date when the model was first introduced. In principle, one could use the quantity as of a fixed period after the first installation, but such quantity data are difficult to obtain. Furthermore, a weighted mean, when the weights are highly uneven, is subject to much larger sampling error than an unweighted mean, something we can ill afford in view of the sizable errors in estimating price and the small numbers of observations revealed in the individual regressions of Table 1.1.

Another alternative to the simple arithmetic mean is the geometric mean. In fact, the logarithm of the geometric mean from 1961 on has already been calculated in Table 1.1; it is the coefficient of the dummy variable for the corresponding year. We have constructed the geometric mean price index for the entire sample period and have found the results to be virtually identical with those obtained by employing the simple arithmetic mean presented in Table 1.2. Note, incidentally, that while the geometric mean equals 1 for the base year 1960, the arithmetic mean is slightly above 1.

Now that we have explained and presented the quantity and price indexes, the magnitudes of their errors should be noted. After examining installation figures from different sources, the author would not be too surprised to find an error, in our aggregate quantity index, to be as large as 10 percent for some year after 1956 or as large as 15 percent for an earlier year. Of course, if our sources consistently over- or underestimate the installation figures by the same percentage, it does not matter for our analyses of the proportional rate of growth, but we cannot be sure of this.

As far as the price index is concerned, assuming that the error of observation on actual rental is unbiased, one can get an upper bound on its standard error by noting the standard errors of the logarithms of the geometric mean index, i.e., of the coefficients of the dummy variables in the pooled regression of Table 1.1. A standard error of .17 means that the percentage error of the geometric mean is approximately 18 percent. This estimate of the standard error is too high for our purpose, because it has included the variations of the price-quantity ratios for the same year due to different firms' pricing policies. Conceptually our index is the (population) mean of the prices (per fixed quantity) of the models introduced in a given year. The variations in these prices alone should not produce an error in our index.

Table 1.2 Quantity, price, and related data on the demand for computers

Year	Quantity (thousands of dollars of 1960 rentals)	$\dfrac{\text{Quantity}_t}{\text{Quantity}_{t-1}}$	Absolute price index	GNP deflator	GNP (billions of 1958 dollars)
1954	370.26		3.2554	.896	
1955	991.67	2.678	2.9610	.909	438.0
1956	2,389.9	2.410	2.5336	.940	446.1
1957	5,087.6	2.129	2.3168	.975	452.5
1958	8,362.0	1.644	2.0342	1.000	447.3
1959	12,549	1.501	1.5884	1.016	475.9
1960	19,072	1.520	1.0716	1.033	487.8
1961	38,264	2.006	.9042	1.046	497.3
1962	64,349	1.682	.6873	1.057	530.0
1963	95,815	1.489	.5712	1.071	550.0
1964	136,845	1.428	.4186	1.089	577.6
1965	194,136	1.419	.3416	1.109	614.4

Statistical Analyses

With the quantity and price indexes at our disposal, we would like to raise three empirical questions. First, without explicitly accounting for the change in equilibrium stock, is the growth pattern closer to the Gompertz hypothesis or to the logistic hypothesis? Second, do the data support the notion of a moving equilibrium, due mainly to the drastic price reduction, and, if so, how large is the price elasticity of equilibrium demand? Third, can we measure the output effect on equilibrium stock?

The answer to the first question is obvious from the data. A plot of the logarithm of the ratio y_t/y_{t-1} (a ratio exhibited in Table 1.2) against log y_{t-1} is much closer to a linear function, as the Gompertz hypothesis implies, than against y_{t-1}, as the logistic hypothesis would imply. If we were to insist on a linear relation between log (y_t/y_{t-1}) and y_{t-1}, we would have to stop in 1959. Unless we are willing to use two models, one for initial growth and another based on the theory of comparative statics, there seems to be no way of maintaining the logistic hypothesis. But it is precisely the purpose of this study to integrate both elements into one model.

To answer the second question, pursuing the Gompertz hypothesis further, we examine the partial effects of price on log (y_t/y_{t-1}), given log y_{t-1}. This amounts to performing a regression of log (y_t/y_{t-1}) on both log p_t and log y_{t-1}. The price variable p_t used is the relative price, obtained by deflating our absolute price index by the GNP deflator. The result of the regression, using 11 annual observations from 1955 to 1965, is

$$\log \frac{y_t}{y_{t-1}} = - \underset{(.1726)}{.3637} \log p_t - \underset{(.0739)}{.2526} \log y_{t-1} + 2.950$$

$$R^2 = .834 \qquad s^2 = .0104$$

(66)

The coefficient of log p is negative, as expected. The ratio of the estimated coefficient to its standard error is -2.107. The null hypothesis of no price effect, against the one-sided alternative hypothesis of a negative price effect, would be rejected at the 5 percent level, where the critical value of the t ratio is -1.860, but would not be rejected at the 2.5 percent level, where the critical t value is -2.306. Since there are only 8 degrees of freedom, the power of the t test is low. Under this circumstance, the rejection of the null hypothesis tends to give strong support for the negative price effect. The Durbin-Watson statistic is 1.77, consistent with no serial correlation in the regression residuals.

A point estimate of the price elasticity of demand for equilibrium stock can be obtained as the ratio of the two coefficients in Eq. (66). It is 1.44. Partly because of our small sample size and the high correlation between the two explanatory variables, the standard error of the price coefficient is large, being almost half of the coefficient itself. However, the ratio between the two coefficients is subject to smaller error than the former coefficient by itself because the two coefficients are positively correlated. A 60 percent confidence interval for the ratio is $1.379 \pm .274$, and an 80 percent confidence interval is $1.326 \pm .382$.† The parameter α of the Gompertz difference equation is about .253, with a standard error of .074.

As matters of historical fact, we have found the stock of computers growing by more than 100 percent annually between 1954 and 1957 and by more than 40 percent annually between 1962 and 1965, averaging to about 78 percent from 1954 to 1965. During the same period the relative price of computers has declined by 20 percent annually, on the average. On the theoretical side, we have found that the Gompertz difference equation, modified by a moving equilibrium due to the comparative statics of price change, can explain the rate of growth for this new commodity and is much better than the logistic difference equation. The price elasticity of equilibrium demand is somewhat over 1, the growth parameter of the Gompertz difference equation is about .25, but no output elasticity has been successfully estimated.

PROBLEMS

1. Show that the estimator a of the intercept of a simple linear regression equation is unbiased, under the assumptions of Sec. 1.2.

2. Derive the variance of the estimator a of the intercept of a simple linear regression equation.

3. Derive Eq. (32).

4. Find the regression function of y^* on x^* and the residual variance of y^* around this regression function, in the model of Sec. 1.7, where y and x are jointly normal and their errors of measurement e_1 and e_2 are also jointly normal and independent, $y^* = y + e_1$ and $x^* = x + e_2$ being the variables measured with errors.

5. In Friedman's theory of the consumption function, how is the intercept affected (*a*) when income is measured with an independent error and (*b*) when consumption is measured with an independent error?

6. If y_1 and y_2 are random vectors which have a multivariate normal distribution, show that y_1 and y_2 are statistically independent if and only if they are uncorrelated, i.e., if $E(y_1 - \mu_1)(y_2 - \mu_2)' = \Sigma_{12} = 0$.

7. Using characteristic functions, show that if y_1 and y_2 are normal random vectors of the same dimension, a linear combination $A_1 y_1 + A_2 y_2$ is also normal.

8. Show that the conclusion of Theorem 1.1 remains valid if the residuals ϵ_i have variances σ_i^2.

---

† To obtain an interval estimate of the ratio between two regression coefficients b_1 and b_2, form the linear combination $b_1 - zb_2$, where z is yet to be determined. This linear combination has a variance equal to Var $b_1 + z^2$ Var $b_2 - 2z$ Cov (b_1, b_2), which, as estimated by our data, is $.02979 + .005463z^2 - .02484z$. If z is the true ratio, this linear combination would have mean zero. The probability is 60 percent that the sample value of this linear combination is within .889 times its standard deviation, where .889 is obtained from the t table. Thus

$$(.3637 - .2526z)^2 < (.889)^2(.02979 + .005463z^2 - .02484z)$$

with probability .60. Treating the above as a quadratic equation of z, we find $z = 1.379 \pm .274$. Replacing .889 by 1.397, we obtain an 80 percent confidence interval for z, namely, $1.326 \pm .382$. This method is described in Fisher (1950, pp. 143–144).

9. Provide an economic application in which the explanatory variable x_i satisfies $\sum_{i=1}^{n} (x_i - \bar{x})^2 \to \infty$, but $\sum_{i=1}^{n} (x_i - \bar{x})^2/n$ does not have a limit.

10. Show that the characteristic function for a multivariate normal random vector x is given by (43).

11. Under the assumptions of Sec. 1.2, show that $\sum_{i=1}^{n} (y_i - a - bx_i)^2/n$ is a consistent estimate for σ^2, given that $\sum_{i=1}^{n} (y_i - a - bx_i)^2/\sigma^2$ has a $\chi^2(n-2)$ distribution.

12. Is the least-squares estimator a of the intercept of a simple normal linear regression function best unbiased? Prove your assertion.

13. Find the maximum-likelihood estimators for the three parameters α, β, and σ^2 in a simple normal linear regression model.

14. Find the information matrix for the three parameters α, β, and σ^2 in a simple normal linear regression model.

15. If the sequences $\{y_n\}$ and $\{z_n\}$ converge in probability to the constants b and c, respectively, show that the sequence $\{y_n - z_n\}$ converges in probability to $b - c$.

16. Prove the multivariate version of Theorem 1.2; i.e., show that if x_i are independent and identically distributed random vectors each with mean μ and covariance matrix Σ, the sum $n^{-1/2} \sum_{i=1}^{n} (x_i - \mu)$ converges in distribution to a multivariate normal distribution with mean zero and covariance matrix Σ.

17. Show that the Lindeberg condition (45) is equivalent to

$$\lim_{n \to \infty} \frac{1}{S_n^2} \sum_{k=1}^{n} \int_{|z| \geq tS_n} z^2 f_k(z) \, dz = 0$$

REFERENCES

Bain, A. D. (1964): *The Growth of Television Ownership in the United Kingdom: A Lognormal Model*, Cambridge University Press, Cambridge.

Chow, G. C. (1965): "Review of *The Growth of Television Ownership in the United Kingdom since the War: A Lognormal Model* by A. D. Bain," *Econometrica*, **33**:657–659.

———— (1967): "Technological Change and the Demand for Computers," *Am. Econ. Rev.*, **57**: 1118–1130.

Cramer, H. (1946): *Mathematical Method of Statistics*, Princeton University Press, Princeton, N.J.

Feller, W. (1966): *An Introduction to Probability Theory and Its Applications*, vol. II, Wiley, New York.

Fisher, R. A. (1950): *Statistical Methods for Research Workers*, 11th ed., Hafner, New York.

Friedman, M. (1957): *A Theory of the Consumption Function*, Princeton University Press, Princeton, N.J.

Keynes, J. M. (1936): *The General Theory of Employment, Interest and Money*, Harcourt Brace Jovanovich, New York.

Munroe, M. E. (1951): *Theory of Probability*, McGraw-Hill, New York.

Rao, C. R. (1973): *Linear Statistical Inference and Its Applications*, Wiley, New York.

Wald, A. (1949): "Note on the Consistency of the Maximum-Likelihood Estimate," *Ann. Math. Statis.*, **50**: 595–601.

Weik, M. H., Jr. (1955, 1961, and 1964): *Survey of Domestic Electronic Digital Computing Systems*, Ballistic Research Laboratories Reports 971, 1115, and 1227, Aberdeen Proving Ground, Md.

MULTIPLE LINEAR REGRESSION

2.1 THE MODEL OF MULTIPLE LINEAR REGRESSION

In contrast with the simple linear regression model, the model of multiple linear regression explains the dependent variable y_i in the ith observation by a linear function of k explanatory variables $x_{i1}, x_{i2}, \ldots, x_{ik}$ plus a random term ϵ_i, which is normal with mean zero and variance σ^2 and independent of ϵ_j ($j \neq i$). A sample of n observations generated by this model can be written as

$$
\begin{aligned}
y_1 &= x_{11}\beta_1 + x_{12}\beta_2 + \cdots + x_{1k}\beta_k + \epsilon_1 \\
y_2 &= x_{21}\beta_1 + x_{22}\beta_2 + \cdots + x_{2k}\beta_k + \epsilon_2 \\
&\quad \cdots\cdots\cdots\cdots\cdots\cdots\cdots\cdots\cdots\cdots\cdots\cdots\cdots \\
y_n &= x_{n1}\beta_1 + x_{n2}\beta_2 + \cdots + x_{nk}\beta_k + \epsilon_n
\end{aligned}
\tag{1}
$$

or, using matrix notation,

$$
\begin{bmatrix} y_1 \\ y_2 \\ \cdot \\ y_n \end{bmatrix} = \begin{bmatrix} x_{11} & x_{12} & \cdots & x_{1k} \\ x_{21} & x_{22} & \cdots & x_{2k} \\ & \cdots\cdots\cdots\cdots\cdots & \\ x_{n1} & x_{n2} & \cdots & x_{nk} \end{bmatrix} \begin{bmatrix} \beta_1 \\ \beta_2 \\ \cdot \\ \beta_k \end{bmatrix} + \begin{bmatrix} \epsilon_1 \\ \epsilon_2 \\ \cdot \\ \epsilon_n \end{bmatrix}
\tag{2}
$$

or, more compactly as

$$
y = X\beta + \epsilon
\tag{3}
$$

where the $n \times 1$ vector y, the $n \times k$ matrix X, the $k \times 1$ vector β, and the $n \times 1$ vector ϵ are defined by the corresponding expressions in (2). The elements of the X matrix are treated as fixed numbers except when otherwise specified.

The covariance matrix of the random vector ϵ is, with prime denoting transpose,

$$
\text{Cov } \epsilon = E[\epsilon\epsilon'] = \begin{bmatrix} E\epsilon_1^2 & E\epsilon_1\epsilon_2 & \cdots & E\epsilon_1\epsilon_n \\ E\epsilon_2\epsilon_1 & E\epsilon_2^2 & \cdots & E\epsilon_2\epsilon_n \\ \cdots\cdots\cdots\cdots\cdots\cdots\cdots \\ E\epsilon_n\epsilon_1 & E\epsilon_n\epsilon_2 & \cdots & E\epsilon_n^2 \end{bmatrix} = \begin{bmatrix} \sigma^2 & 0 & \cdots & 0 \\ 0 & \sigma^2 & \cdots & 0 \\ & & \cdots & \\ 0 & 0 & \cdots & \sigma^2 \end{bmatrix} = \sigma^2 I_n
$$

(4)

where I_n is an $n \times n$ identity matrix. If the first explanatory variable x_{i1} is set equal to 1, the first coefficient β_1 will become the intercept. The parameters of this model are β and σ^2.

2.2 LEAST-SQUARES ESTIMATION FOR β AND σ^2

By the method of least squares, the point estimate b of the vector β of regression coefficients minimizes

$$
\sum_{i=1}^{n} (y_i - x_{i1}b_1 - x_{i2}b_2 - \cdots - x_{ik}b_k)^2 = (y - Xb)'(y - Xb)
$$

$$
= y'y - 2b'X'y + b'X'Xb \tag{5}
$$

Review the differentiation rules

$$
\frac{\partial b'a}{\partial b} = a \qquad \frac{\partial(b'Ab)}{\partial b} = Ab + A'b \tag{6}
$$

where b and a are column vectors, A is a square matrix, and the derivative $\partial f/\partial b$ of a scalar function f with respect to a vector b is defined as the vector of the derivatives of f with respect to the elements of b. We minimize (5) by setting its (vector) derivative with respect to b equal to (vector) zero,

$$
-2X'y + 2X'Xb = 0
$$

yielding

$$
b = (X'X)^{-1}X'y \tag{7}
$$

For the inverse of the $k \times k$ matrix $X'X$ to exist, matrix X must have rank k.

To find the mean vector and the covariance matrix for the sampling distribution of the random vector b we first substitute $X\beta + \epsilon$ for y in (7) to obtain

$$
b = (X'X)^{-1}X'(X\beta + \epsilon) = (X'X)^{-1}X'X\beta + (X'X)^{-1}X'\epsilon
$$

$$
= \beta + (X'X)^{-1}X'\epsilon \tag{8}
$$

The mean of b is obtained by taking expectation of (8), giving

$$
E[b] = \beta + (X'X)^{-1}X'(E\epsilon) = \beta \tag{9}
$$

which shows that b is an unbiased estimator of β.

The covariance matrix of b is, again using (8),

$$\text{Cov } b = E[(b - Eb)(b - Eb)'] = E[(X'X)^{-1}X'\epsilon\epsilon'X(X'X)^{-1}]$$
$$= (X'X)^{-1}X'(E\epsilon\epsilon')X(X'X)^{-1} = (X'X)^{-1}X'X(X'X)^{-1}\sigma^2$$
$$= (X'X)^{-1}\sigma^2 \tag{10}$$

where we have recalled that $E\epsilon\epsilon' = I\sigma^2$. This covariance matrix is the product of the residual variance σ^2 and the inverse of $X'X$.

Theorem 2.1: Gauss-Markov theorem In model (3), assuming that $E\epsilon = 0$ and $E\epsilon\epsilon' = I\sigma^2$, the least-squares estimator b is best linear unbiased.

PROOF Consider any linear estimator Ay, where A is a $k \times n$ matrix of constants. For Ay to be unbiased

$$E(Ay) = E[A(X\beta + \epsilon)] = AX\beta = \beta$$

implying that $AX = I$. The covariance matrix of a linear unbiased estimator Ay is thus

$$E(Ay - \beta)(Ay - \beta)' = E(AX\beta + A\epsilon - \beta)(AX\beta + A\epsilon - \beta)'$$
$$= E(A\epsilon\epsilon'A') = AA'\sigma^2$$

Since A can always be written as $(X'X)^{-1}X' + B$, which actually defines B, the unbiasedness condition requires that

$$[(X'X)^{-1}X' + B]X = I + BX = I$$

or $BX = 0$. On substitution of $(X'X)^{-1}X' + B$ for A the covariance matrix of Ay is

$$\text{Cov } (Ay) = [(X'X)^{-1}X' + B][X(X'X)^{-1} + B']\sigma^2$$
$$= [(X'X)^{-1} + (X'X)^{-1}X'B' + BX(X'X)^{-1} + BB']\sigma^2$$
$$= [(X'X)^{-1} + BB']\sigma^2 \tag{11}$$

where we have used the unbiasedness condition $BX = 0$. Since BB' is positive definite unless B is a matrix of zeros, the covariance matrix of Ay is larger than the covariance matrix $(X'X)^{-1}\sigma^2$ of the least-squares estimator unless $A = (X'X)^{-1}X'$ or Ay is the least-squares estimator itself.

The word "best" in the theorem means that the covariance matrix of any other linear unbiased estimator exceeds the covariance matrix of the least-squares estimator by a positive-definite matrix. Note that in the above proof we have used the assumption that $E\epsilon\epsilon' = I\sigma^2$ but not the assumption that ϵ_i are normal.

The vector of residuals from the least-squares regression is

$$e = y - Xb = X\beta + \epsilon - X[\beta + (X'X)^{-1}X'\epsilon] = [I_n - X(X'X)^{-1}X']\epsilon \tag{12}$$

An unbiased estimator for σ^2 is

$$s^2 = (n - k)^{-1} e'e \tag{13}$$

To show that s^2 is unbiased we evaluate the expectation of $e'e$ using (12),

$$
\begin{aligned}
Ee'e &= E\{\epsilon'[I_n - X(X'X)^{-1}X'][I_n - X(X'X)^{-1}X']\epsilon\} \\
&= E\{\epsilon'[I - X(X'X)^{-1}X']\epsilon\} = E\{\mathrm{tr}(\epsilon'[I - X(X'X)^{-1}X']\epsilon)\} \\
&= E\{\mathrm{tr}[I - X(X'X)^{-1}X']\epsilon\epsilon'\} = \mathrm{tr}\{[I_n - X(X'X)^{-1}X']E\epsilon\epsilon'\} \\
&= \sigma^2[\mathrm{tr}\ I_n - \mathrm{tr}\ (X'X)^{-1}X'X] = \sigma^2(n - k) \tag{14}
\end{aligned}
$$

where $\mathrm{tr}M$ stands for the trace, or sum of the diagonal elements, of a square matrix M and we have used the fact $\mathrm{tr}\ (AB) = \mathrm{tr}\ (BA)$, A and B not necessarily square.

★2.3 GEOMETRIC INTERPRETATION OF THE LEAST-SQUARES REGRESSION

Let the vector y represent a point in an n-dimensional vector space. The estimate of y using the least-squares estimate b is Xb, and the vector of residuals is $e = y - Xb$. Thus y is viewed as the sum of two components, the explained part Xb and the residual or unexplained part e.

Let X be written as $(x_1, x_2, \ldots, x_k)$, where the jth column x_j represents n observations on the jth explanatory variable. Each vector x_j also represents a point in an n-dimensional vector space. Xb is a linear combination of the k vectors $x_1, x_2, \ldots, x_k$, since

$$Xb = x_1b_1 + x_2b_2 + \cdots + x_kb_k$$

where b_j is the jth regression coefficient obtained by the method of least squares. A linear combination of the vectors $x_1, x_2, \ldots, x_k$ is also a vector or a point in the n-dimensional space. To visualize the situation, consider the case $n = 3$, $k = 2$, $b_1 = 1.2$, and $b_2 = .5$. We have

$$
Xb = \begin{bmatrix} x_{11} \\ x_{21} \\ x_{31} \end{bmatrix}(1.2) + \begin{bmatrix} x_{12} \\ x_{22} \\ x_{32} \end{bmatrix}(.5) = \begin{bmatrix} 1.2x_{11} + .5x_{12} \\ 1.2x_{21} + .5x_{22} \\ 1.2x_{31} + .5x_{32} \end{bmatrix}
$$

In this case one can actually draw two points in a three-dimensional space to represent the vectors x_1 and x_2 and a third point to represent $Xb = 1.2x_1 - .5x_2$. When n is greater than 3, the same geometric intuition carries over, as given by Fig. 2.1. As the regression coefficients b_1 and b_2 change, the linear combination $Xb = x_1b_1 + x_2b_2$ will also change. All possible linear combinations of x_1, $x_2, \ldots, x_k$ or all possible points $x_1b_1 + x_2b_2 + \cdots + x_kb_k$ form a subspace of dimension k. This subspace is said to be spanned by the basis vectors $x_1, \ldots, x_k$.

In Fig. 2.1 the subspace is of dimension 2; part of this subspace is encircled. Of course, all points in this subspace are also points in the n-dimensional vector space where the vectors y and $e = y - Xb$ belong.

An important property of the least-squares estimate b is that the residual vector e is uncorrelated with the explanatory variables. The vector of covariances between e and the k explanatory variables is, by (12),

$$(x_1, \ldots, x_k)'e = X'[I - X(X'X)^{-1}X']\epsilon = (X' - X')\epsilon = 0$$

Since e is uncorrelated with each x_j, it is also uncorrelated with the linear combination Xb of all x_j ($j = 1, \ldots, k$). That is, $(Xb)'e = b'X'e = 0$. Geometrically, when we minimize the sum of squares $(y - Xb)'(y - Xb) = e'e$ with respect to b, we are minimizing the squared length of the vector $y - Xb$. In other words, we are finding the shortest (squared) distance from the vector y to a point Xb in the subspace spanned by $x_1, \ldots, x_k$; see Fig. 2.1. Xb is the orthogonal (perpendicular) projection of y onto the subspace spanned by $x_1, \ldots, x_k$. The residual vector $e = y - Xb$ has just been shown to be uncorrelated with Xb, or $(Xb)'e = 0$. We now show that $(Xb)'e = 0$ means that e is orthogonal to Xb.

Geometrically, to measure the degree of linear association between a vector y and a vector x we first project y onto the space spanned by x; that is, we find a scalar b to minimize

$$(y - xb)'(y - xb)$$

yielding $b = (x'x)^{-1}x'y$. The square of the cosine of the angle θ between y and xb is, by definition,

$$\cos^2 \theta = \frac{b'x'xb}{y'y} = \frac{y'x(x'x)^{-1}x'x(x'x)^{-1}xy}{y'y} = \frac{y'x(x'x)^{-1}x'y}{y'y} \tag{15}$$

If $xb = y$, or x explains y completely, $\cos^2 \theta = 1$. Since it is the ratio of the sum of squares of the elements of xb to the sum of squares of the elements of y, $\cos^2 \theta$ is the squared correlation coefficient between y and x.

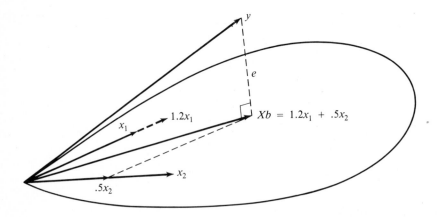

Figure 2.1 Geometry of least-squares regression.

If the two vectors y and x are orthogonal, the angle θ is $90°$ or $\cos^2 \theta = 0$. By (15), $\cos^2 \theta = 0$ if and only if $x'y = 0$. Therefore, two vectors y and x are orthogonal if and only if $x'y = 0$.

The above demonstration for $\cos^2 \theta$ remains valid for measuring the degree of linear association between a vector y and a set of k vectors $(x_1, \ldots, x_k) = X$. We need only replace the vector x by the matrix X for (15) to be the squared multiple correlation coefficient (also called the *coefficient of determination*) between y and $X = (x_1, \ldots, x_k)$; it is the squared correlation coefficient between the vectors y and Xb. Thus the method of least squares decomposes y into two orthogonal components, Xb and e. The coefficient of determination is the ratio between the squared length of Xb and the squared length of y. It is the proportion of the sum of squares of y explained by the x's.

It is often more meaningful to measure the proportion of the variance of y explained by the x's. This would eliminate the contribution of the constant term toward explaining $\sum_{i=1}^{n} y_i^2$. To this end, we write the estimated regression equation, with $x_{i1} = 1$, as

$$y_i = b_1 + b_2 x_{i2} + \cdots + b_k x_{ik} + e_i$$
$$= \bar{y} + b_2 (x_{i2} - \bar{x}_2) + \cdots + b_k (x_{ik} - \bar{x}_k) + e_i \tag{16}$$

since the intercept b_1 satisfies

$$b_1 = \bar{y} - b_2 \bar{x}_2 - \cdots - b_k \bar{x}_k$$

Define y^* and X^* as deviations of y and X from their respective means and b^* as $(b_2, \ldots, b_k)'$. The coefficient of determination is defined as $b^{*'}X^{*'}X^*b^*/y^{*'}y^*$ or

$$R^2 = \frac{\sum_{i=1}^{n} [b_2 (x_{i2} - \bar{x}_2) + \cdots + b_k (x_{ik} - \bar{x}_k)]^2}{\sum_{i=1}^{n} (y_i - \bar{y})^2} \tag{17}$$

Note that $R^2 = 1 - (\sum_i e_i^2)/\sum_i (y_i - \bar{y})^2$. Given the same variance $(\sum_i e_i^2)/n$ for e_i, R^2 will be increased if the variance $\sum_i (y_i - \bar{y})^2/n$ of y_i is increased, for example, by having more variations in the explanatory variables.

2.4 TESTING HYPOTHESES ABOUT β AND σ^2

From (8) we observe that $b - \beta$ is a linear function of $\epsilon_1, \ldots, \epsilon_n$ and therefore has a k-variate normal distribution if $\epsilon_1, \ldots, \epsilon_n$ are normal. The covariance matrix of b is $(X'X)^{-1}\sigma^2$. We can use this normal distribution to test hypotheses about, and form the confidence interval for, β if σ^2 is known. In practice σ^2 is not known and is often estimated by $s^2 = e'e/(n - k)$. We shall show that $e'e/\sigma^2$ has a $\chi^2 (n - k)$ distribution. Thus we shall be concerned with the distribution of

$$e'e = \epsilon'[I - X(X'X)^{-1}X']\epsilon$$

The matrix $M = I - X(X'X)^{-1}X'$, satisfies $MM = M$ and is thus an *idempotent matrix*. We shall *diagonalize* M, that is, write it as $CD_\lambda C'$, where D_λ is a diagonal matrix.

To review the algebra, consider an $n \times n$ matrix A. If $\lambda_1, \ldots, \lambda_n$ are its characteristic roots (eigenvalues) and $c_1, \ldots, c_n$ are the corresponding (column) characteristic vectors (eigenvectors), by definition, $Ac_i = \lambda_i c_i$ $(i = 1, \ldots, n)$, or

$$A(c_1, \ldots, c_n) = (\lambda_1 c_1, \ldots, \lambda_n c_n) = (c_1, \ldots, c_n)D_\lambda$$

where D_λ is a diagonal matrix with $\lambda_1, \ldots, \lambda_n$ on the diagonal. Let $C = (c_1, \ldots, c_n)$ be the matrix whose columns are the (right) characteristic vectors of A. We thus have

$$AC = CD_\lambda$$

When C^{-1} exists, we postmultiply by C^{-1} to yield

$$A = CD_\lambda C^{-1} \tag{18}$$

This diagonalization could have been achieved by considering the (row) characteristic vectors b_i, which satisfy $b_i A = \lambda_i b_i$ $(i = 1, \ldots, n)$, or

$$\begin{bmatrix} b_1 \\ \vdots \\ b_n \end{bmatrix} A = BA = D_\lambda B$$

yielding

$$A = B^{-1} D_\lambda B \tag{19}$$

If A is symmetric, $Ac_i = \lambda_i c_i$ can be transposed to give $c_i' A' = c_i' A = \lambda_i c_i'$. Thus the transpose of the column (right) characteristic vector c_i is the corresponding row (left) characteristic vector b_i. With B replaced by C', (19) becomes

$$A = C'^{-1} D_\lambda C' \tag{20}$$

Comparing (18) and (20), we find for a symmetric A that $C' = C^{-1}$, implying $C'C = I$ and $CC' = I$. C is said to be an *orthogonal matrix*: $C'C = I$ means that each column of C is orthogonal to (uncorrelated with) any other column; $CC' = I$ means that each row of C is orthogonal to any other row, and each row or column of C has length 1.

We now diagonalize M using (20). Since M is symmetric, we have $C' = C^{-1}$ or $C'^{-1} = (C^{-1})^{-1} = C$, and thus

$$M = CD_\lambda C' \tag{21}$$

Since M is idempotent, we have

$$CD_\lambda C' = M = MM = CD_\lambda C' CD_\lambda C' = CD_\lambda D_\lambda C' = CD_\lambda^2 C'$$

or $D_\lambda = D_\lambda^2$, implying $\lambda_i = \lambda_i^2$ $(i = 1, \ldots, n)$. This can happen only if λ_i is either 0 or 1. Hence, the roots of an idempotent matrix are either 0 or 1. The trace of M is

$$\text{tr } M = \text{tr } (CD_\lambda C') = \text{tr } (D_\lambda C'C) = \text{tr } D_\lambda$$

which is equal to the number of nonzero (unity) roots of M. But the trace of M is also equal to $n - k$, as shown in (14). The number of unity roots of M is therefore $n - k$. Let them be the first $n - k$ diagonal elements of D_λ.

Finally, the statistic of interest can be written as

$$e'e = \epsilon'M\epsilon = \epsilon'CD_\lambda C'\epsilon \equiv \eta'D_\lambda\eta = [\eta_1' \quad \eta_2']D_\lambda\begin{bmatrix}\eta_1\\\eta_2\end{bmatrix} = \eta_1'\eta_1 \tag{22}$$

where we have defined η as $C'\epsilon$ and η_1 as a subvector consisting of its first $n - k$ elements. Since ϵ is normal, $\eta = C'\epsilon$ is also (multivariate) normal. The covariance matrix of η is

$$E\eta\eta' = E(C'\epsilon\epsilon'C) = C'C\sigma^2 = I_n\sigma^2$$

This implies that the $n - k$ elements of the subvector η_1 are normal and un-correlated, each having variance σ^2. The sum of squares $\eta_1'\eta_1$ of these $n - k$ elements, divided by σ^2, is therefore distributed as $\chi^2(n - k)$. Hence we conclude that $e'e/\sigma^2$ or $(n - k)s^2/\sigma^2$ has a $\chi^2(n - k)$ distribution. This distribution can be used to test hypotheses about, and construct a confidence interval for, σ^2.

To test hypotheses about β when σ^2 is unknown we exploit the important fact that the residual vector e and the least-squares estimator b are uncorrelated (and also independent because both are normal). That is, $E[(b - \beta)e'] = 0$. To demonstrate this fact, we use (8) and (12) to write

$$
\begin{aligned}
E[(b - \beta)e' &= E\{(X'X)^{-1}X'\epsilon\epsilon'[I - X(X'X)^{-1}X']\}\\
&= (X'X)^{-1}X'(E\epsilon\epsilon')[I - X(X'X)^{-1}X']\\
&= (X'X)^{-1}X'[I - X(X'X)^{-1}X']\sigma^2\\
&= [(X'X)^{-1}X' - (X'X)^{-1}X'X(X'X)^{-1}X']\sigma^2\\
&= 0 \tag{23}
\end{aligned}
$$

First consider testing the null hypothesis that one coefficient β_i equals some given β_{i0}. Denote the matrix $(X'X)^{-1}$ by $C = (c_{ij})$, not to be confused with the matrix C defined in (18). From (8) and the remark at the beginning of this section we know that $b_i - \beta_{i0}$ is normal with mean zero and variance $c_{ii}\sigma^2$ under the null hypothesis $\beta_i = \beta_{i0}$. The ratio

$$\frac{(b_i - \beta_{i0})/\sqrt{c_{ii}}\,\sigma}{s/\sigma} = \frac{b_i - \beta_{i0}}{\sqrt{c_{ii}}\,s} \tag{24}$$

is a ratio between a unit normal random variable and the square root of a χ^2 $(n - k)$ variable divided by its number of degrees of freedom. Since the numer-ator and denominator are independent, as shown by (23), this ratio has a $t(n - k)$ distribution. The t test based on (24) is the most commonly used test in regression analysis because the null hypothesis $\beta_i = \beta_{i0}$ is frequently encountered in practice. If one rejects the null hypothesis $\beta_i = 0$, one concludes that the variable x_i is statistically significant in the explanation of y. If one accepts this null hypothesis, the x_i variable is considered statistically insignificant and may be omitted from the regression equation. The t ratio (24) is formed by dividing $b_i - \beta_{i0}$ by its standard deviation $\sqrt{c_{ii}}\,s$ estimated from the sample, where $\sqrt{c_{ii}}\,\sigma$ is its true (population) standard deviation; $\sqrt{c_{ii}}\,s$ is called the standard error of the regression coefficient b_i.

Next consider testing the null hypothesis that a given linear combination $r_1\beta_1 + r_2\beta_2$ of regression coefficients equals a given constant r_0. Under the null hypothesis, the random variable $r_1 b_1 + r_2 b_2$ will have mean $r_1\beta_1 + r_2\beta_2 = r_0$. Its variance is

$$\text{Var}\,(r_1 b_1 + r_2 b_2) = \text{Var}\,r_1 b_1 + \text{Var}\,r_2 b_2 + 2\,\text{Cov}\,(r_1 b_1, r_2 b_2)$$
$$= r_1^2\,\text{Var}\,b_1 + r_2^2\,\text{Var}\,b_2 + 2 r_1 r_2\,\text{Cov}\,(b_1, b_2)$$
$$= (r_1^2 c_{11} + r_2^2 c_{22} + 2 r_1 r_2 c_{12})\sigma^2$$

Again, the ratio

$$\frac{r_1 b_1 + r_2 b_2 - r_0}{(r_1^2 c_{11} + r_2^2 c_{22} + 2 r_1 r_2 c_{12})^{1/2} s} \tag{25}$$

is a ratio between a standard normal random variable and the square root of an independent $\chi^2(n-k)$ variable divided by its number of degrees of freedom, the denominator being s/σ. It therefore has a $t(n-k)$ distribution, which can be used to test the null hypothesis $r_1\beta_1 + r_2\beta_2 = r_0$.

The above test of one linear restriction can be generalized to a set of m linear restrictions. Let R be an $m \times k$ matrix and r be an $m \times 1$ vector. The m linear restrictions can be written as $R\beta = r$. Under the null hypothesis Rb will be m-variate normal having a mean vector

$$E(Rb) = R(Eb) = R\beta = r$$

and a covariance matrix

$$\text{Cov}\,(Rb) = E[R(b-\beta)(b-\beta)'R'] = RE(b-\beta)(b-\beta)'R' = R(X'X)^{-1}R'\sigma^2$$

If an m-variate normal random vector z has mean zero and covariance matrix V, the quadratic form $z'V^{-1}z$ will have a $\chi^2(m)$ distribution. This can be seen by writing $V^{-1} = P'DP$ as in (21), with $PP' = I$ and D written as $D^{1/2}D^{1/2}$, and observing that

$$\text{Cov}\,(D^{1/2}Pz) = E(D^{1/2}Pzz'P'D^{1/2}) = D^{1/2}P(Ez'z)P'D^{1/2} = D^{1/2}PVP'D^{1/2}$$
$$= D^{1/2}P(P'DP)^{-1}P'D^{1/2} = D^{1/2}PP'D^{-1}PP'D = D^{1/2}D^{-1}D^{1/2}$$
$$= I$$

Thus the m elements of the vector $D^{1/2}Pz$ are uncorrelated, each having zero mean and unit variance. The sum of squares of these elements, or

$$(D^{1/2}Pz)'(D^{1/2}Pz) = z'P'DPz = z'V^{-1}z$$

will have a $\chi^2(m)$ distribution, which is to be proved.

Returning to testing the null hypothesis $R\beta = r$, we can use the statistic

$$\frac{(Rb-r)'[\text{Cov}\,(Rb)]^{-1}(Rb-r) = (Rb-r)'[R(X'X)^{-1}R']^{-1}(Rb-r)}{\sigma^2}$$

which will have a $\chi^2(m)$ distribution. If σ^2 is not known, we form the ratio of this $\chi^2(m)$ variable divided by m to an independent $\chi^2(n - k)$ variable $(n - k) s^2/\sigma^2$ divided by $n - k$, namely,

$$(Rb - r)'[R(X'X)^{-1}R']^{-1} \frac{Rb - r}{ms^2} \tag{26}$$

The statistic (26) will have an $F(m, n - k)$ distribution. It should be observed that when $m = 1$, and when the restriction is

$$Rb = [r_1 \quad r_2 \quad 0 \cdots 0] \begin{bmatrix} b_1 \\ b_2 \\ \vdots \\ b_k \end{bmatrix} = r_0$$

the $F(1, n - k)$ statistic (26) reduces to the square of the t statistic (25).

2.5 DEMAND FOR AUTOMOBILES: THEORY

Before presenting more statistical theory of the multiple regression model, it may be useful to provide some economic applications of this model, using the author's study on demand for automobiles in the United States (1957, 1960a), covering the period from 1921 to 1953. This section gives the basic theory, and the following section discusses some empirical findings using regression analysis.†

Long-Run Demand for Automobile Stock

A salient feature of the demand for consumer durables in general, and for automobiles in particular, is that annual purchase is only a part of the total stock available for the satisfaction of wants. Purchase is made primarily to fill the gap between the quantity of total stock desired and the quantity of old stock remaining from the preceding period. In order to explain the demand for purchase, therefore, the demand for desired stock will be first explained. By "desired stock" is meant that level of ownership which actual ownership will approach in the course of time, given that the determining variables remain unchanged.

A difficulty immediately presents itself in obtaining an empirical definition of the stock of automobiles. There are old and new cars and, in any model year, expensive and cheap cars. The wide range of prices for which different makes and ages of cars sell at any one time is itself evidence that the buying public does not consider them all to be equivalent.

In this study the stock of cars was expressed in terms of new-car equivalents, older cars being considered as equivalent to half a new car if their price was half that of new cars, etc. The weights used in converting old cars into new-car equivalents were the relative prices of cars of different ages in 1937. The relative

---

† The rest of this section and Sec. 2.6 are modified from Chow (1960a, pp. 149–162) by permission.

price structure of cars according to age changed remarkably little over the period of the study. The prices of various ages of cars in any one year was approximated very well by the assumption of a constant percentage rate of depreciation, which is between 22 and 24 percent for 19 of the 33 years considered, between 21 and 25 percent for 25 of the 33 years, and in no case less than 19 or more than 30 percent.† The 1937 rate of depreciation was 23 percent—the median rate for the whole period. Thus we did not have to be concerned with the common index-number problems of changing or unrepresentative weights.

Much misunderstanding of the automobile market has come from the tendency to "count cars." The evidence just cited is strong that the market does not consider all cars to be equivalent and that its preferences among cars of different ages are remarkably stable over time. This evidence suggests that it is much more meaningful to talk in terms of, say, 25 million new-car equivalents than in terms of 55 million cars on the road.

One point should be noted, however. Since our stock data were expressed in terms of new-car equivalents, they do not contain any adjustment for the secular improvement in the quality of automobiles. Had such an adjustment been made, the series on automobile stocks and on new purchases would have shown a greater secular increase, and the series on relative price would have shown a lower secular increase or, more probably, a secular decline. Instead of becoming involved in the difficult task of making a quality adjustment directly in the data, the alternative course was pursued of including a trend variable as an additional "test variable" in the estimation of the income and price elasticities of demand, net of trendwise movements in the variables, and accordingly "adjusted" for any trendwise change in quality [see Eq. (31) below].

The price data themselves were based on used-car price quotations in newspaper advertisements. New-car prices were not used because during the period of the study the relationships between list prices and actual prices paid by purchasers varied greatly. For our purpose the new-car price was the price in the used-car market of cars of the current model year. Our series of prices based on used-car quotations is closely similar to the price series of the National Automobile Dealers Association as far back as 1934, but it appears to be more accurate than series derived from other sources for the period prior to 1934.

The stock of automobiles, expressed in terms of the relative prices of cars of different ages, does not necessarily indicate the service yield obtained in any given year. The service yield is measured by the price consumers are paying for the use of their cars for a year, i.e., by the amount by which their cars depreciate plus the interest forgone by holding their capital in the form of cars. When automobiles depreciate at a constant annual rate, the price paid for the use of the stock of cars for a year is proportional to the value of the stock itself. For the years considered in this study, it has hovered in the neighborhood of 30 percent of the value of the

---

† These percentage rates of depreciation can be derived from the average prices of automobiles, classified by age, found in Chow (1957, pp. 102–103).

stock.† We shall here neglect the relatively small variations which occurred in this fraction and treat "consumption" of automobile services as strictly proportional to the stock, and we shall use *demand for stock* and *consumption demand* interchangeably.

The desired stock of automobiles is taken to depend principally on relative price and real income. Let the desired stock of automobiles $\dot{X}_{jt}$ of the jth consumer in year t be a linear function of the relative price of automobiles to the jth consumer and his real income in year t

$$\dot{X}_{jt} = a_{jt} + b_{jt}\,P_{jt} + c_{jt}\,I_{jt}$$

where the intercept a_{jt} is affected both by the taste of the jth individual and by the variables not taken into account, especially the relative prices of complements and substitutes, at year t. For a given year t, there will be a frequency distribution of each of the five variables, a_{jt}, b_{jt}, P_{jt}, c_{jt}, and I_{jt}, for the group of individuals. Their means are denoted, respectively, by a_t, b_t, P_t, c_t, and I_t. Taking expectations over j on both sides of the above equation, we have $\dot{X}_t = a_t + E(b_{jt}\,P_{jt}) + E(c_{jt}\,I_{jt})$. Under the assumption that b_{jt} and P_{jt} are statistically independent and that c_{jt} and I_{jt} are also statistically independent, the mean demand for desired stock becomes

$$\dot{X}_t = a_t + b_t\,P_t + c_t\,I_t$$

It is further assumed that the mean effects of price and income, namely, b_t and c_t, remain constant through time; thus the t subscripts for these two coefficients can be dropped. We propose to break up a_t into two parts, the average for the period of study a and a random element u_t which summarizes the combined effect of the variables left out. The mean demand for desired stock can now be written as a linear function of mean price and mean income with coefficients independent of time

$$\dot{X}_t = a + bP_t + cI_t + u_t$$

Note that we have avoided the problem of changes in the distribution of income by the assumption that c_{jt} is statistically independent of I_{jt}. This assumption implies that the mean of the product of these two variables is the product of their means. A similar aggregation procedure can be applied to demand functions linear in the logarithms of the variables.

We decide to work with a per capita demand function rather than a per family demand function because of the apparent weaknesses of the latter. Assume that both families A and B have the same income and that A has only half as many members as B. Assume also that the other variables affecting demand are

† The price paid for the use of a car may be defined to include license fees, gasoline, oil, tire, and repair costs, in addition to interest and depreciation; but it need not be so defined. Under our more restricted definition, license, gasoline, etc., are considered as complementary products, whose prices, relative to the general price level, are assumed in our empirical analysis to have moved in a fashion not highly correlated with the relative price of cars.

identical for the two families. If a per family demand function is employed, A and B should have the same desired automobile ownership. On the other hand, according to a per capita demand function, B's per capita income is only half of A's, and B's per capita demand will be less than one-half of, or B's family demand will be less than, A's, given that income elasticity is higher than unity. The implication of the per capita demand function seems closer to the truth insofar as family B tends to spend more on food and clothing for its members. The same point can be extended to the whole economy. Assuming both national income and the number of families to remain the same, we would predict the same demand for automobile ownership using a per family demand function irrespective of any increase in population. Assuming both national income and population to remain unchanged, we would, using the same demand function with income elasticity higher than unity, predict a *decline* in automobile ownership to follow an *increase* in the number of families; when the number of families increases, income per family declines and demand per family declines proportionally more. These considerations suggest a per capita demand function for desired stock to be the better alternative.

Demand for Annual Purchase under Assumption of Instantaneous Adjustment

We have proposed to explain the desired stock of automobiles (in equivalent units) per capita by the relative price P of automobiles and real income per capita I. If the desired stock were achieved all the time, purchase per capita during a year would simply be the difference between desired stock per capita at the end of the year and the depreciated old stock per capita from the preceding year. The latter will be assumed to be a fraction k of the per capita stock 1 year earlier. Not only is k the result mostly of annual depreciation but also it takes into account the effects of scrappage and of the change in population, since it is the ratio of old stock per capita at the end of the year to the entire per capita stock at the beginning of the year. However, numerically, k has been very close to .75 because the effect of scrappage has been slight compared with the effect of depreciation measured by price decline and because the ratio of year-end population to beginning-of-year population has been practically 1.

Purchase of an automobile by a consumer can take the form of trading in a used car for a newer one. Annual purchase of the economy is the sum of individual purchases and, after aggregation, will equal the number of new cars bought during the year provided that there is no net inflow from, or outflow to, the stocks in the hands of the dealers. Let new purchase per capita in year t be X_t^1, desired stock per capita at the end of year t be $\dot{X}_t$, and total stock per capita at the end of year $t - 1$ be X_{t-1}. Under the assumption that automobile stock is instantaneously adjusted to its desired level as governed by price and income, annual purchase per capita will be

$$X_t^1 = \dot{X}_t(P_t, I_t, u_t) - kX_{t-1}$$

where u_t, as we have defined it, is a combination of all variables other than price and income that affect the demand for desired stock. This demand function can alternatively be written as

$$X_t^1 = (\dot{X}_t - X_{t-1}) + (1 - k)X_{t-1}$$

breaking up annual purchase into two parts. The first, $\dot{X}_t - X_{t-1}$, is the demand for desired change in stock during the year; the second, $(1 - k)X_{t-1}$, is the demand for replacement of old stock.

When existing stock is adjusted to the desired level instantaneously, the time path of annual purchase generated by a single and permanent shift in the demand for desired stock is illustrated by the following example. This example will be simplified by the assumption of a constant population so that we may refer to either per capita demand or total demand of the economy. Here the rate of depreciation (including scrappage) is taken to be .25. Start with year 1, when total stock is 100 and purchase is 25. Let desired stock in year 2 be shifted to 110. Such a shift requires the purchase of 35 (25 for replacement and 10 to meet the desired change in stock). In the third year, with desired stock still at 110 and depreciated stock from the second year at .75 (110) = 82.5, purchase will be 27.5. An annual purchase of 27.5 will be continued as long as desired stock remains at 110. Two points regarding the effect of a shift in desired ownership on the demand for purchase are illustrated by this example. In the short run, or the second year in our example, a 10 percent change in desired stock can generate a 40 percent change in purchase, an increase of 10 units in purchase from the original 25 units. However, in the long run when equilibrium is again reached, the percentage change in purchase (2.5 units of the original 25 units) will be the same as the percentage change in desired stock. Thus the short-run elasticities of demand for purchase will be 4 times as high as the long-run elasticities of demand for desired ownership under the assumptions that adjustment is instantaneous and that the annual rate of depreciation is 25 percent. On the other hand, the long-run elasticities of demand for purchase will be the same as the long-run elasticities of demand for desired ownership.

Demand for Annual Purchase with Time Lag

In the above numerical example annual purchases show a time path of 25, 35, 27.5, 27.5, ... in successive years as a result of a 10 percent shift in desired stock. This path showing a sharp jump in the year of the shift and a large drop in the year immediately afterward may appear unreasonable. Why does the adjustment of existing stock to the desired level have to be accomplished in 1 year? As a matter of fact, there are reasons to the contrary, the most important one being the cost of buying and selling automobiles. If this model of individual consumers were valid, they would be observed to buy and sell automobiles frequently in response to any changes in price and income. With a positive cost of transaction, individuals may not change their automobile stock at once even if it is somewhat different from their desired ownership. In the aggregate only a fraction c of the desired change in ownership will be assumed to take place in 1 year, and our theory of demand for purchase will be modified accordingly.

Our previous demand function is

$$X_t^1 = \dot{X}_t(P_t, I_t, u_t) - kX_{t-1}$$

which can also be separated into demand for change in stock and demand for replacement

$$X_t^1 = [\dot{X}_t(P_t, I_t, u_t) - X_{t-1}] + (1 - k)X_{t-1}$$

If only a fraction c of the desired change in ownership is made during the year, the demand function becomes

$$X_t^1 = c[\dot{X}_t(P_t, I_t, u_t) - X_{t-1}] + (1 - k)X_{t-1}$$

The adjustment coefficient c is applied to the desired change in stock $\dot{X}_t - X_{t-1}$ rather than the entire purchase $\dot{X}_t - kX_{t-1}$ required to bring existing stock to the desired level, because the latter model would imply an amount purchased in year t, or $c(\dot{X}_t - kX_{t-1})$, insufficient to keep the stock in equilibrium at the end of the year, even if it had been in equilibrium in the beginning of the year. Under our scheme of adjustment purchase will consist of the entire replacement $(1 - k)X_{t-1}$ when there is no desire to change the stock during year t.

By way of a numerical example, we can illustrate the time path of annual purchase resulting from a single shift in desired stock. A rate of depreciation of .25 and an adjustment coefficient of .5 due to time lag will be assumed. Again in year 1, total stock is 100 and purchase is 25. Let desired stock be shifted to 110 in year 2. The movements of the relevant variables can be summarized:

			Year		
	1	2	3	4 $\cdots$	∞
Desired stock		110	110	110	110
Change in stock		5	2.5	1.25	0
Actual stock	100	105	107.5	108.75	110
Replacement		25	26.25	26.875	27.5
Purchase	25	30	28.75	28.125	27.5

Replacement is 25 percent of actual stock at the end of the preceding year. Purchase can be calculated as the sum of replacement and the change in stock during the year.

Two points concerning the relationship between the elasticities of demand for desired stock and the elasticities of demand for annual purchase are again illustrated by the above example. In the short run, i.e., the year when desired stock is changed, purchase will be changed by 5 units, or 20 percent, as a result of the 10 percent change in desired stock. After the incomplete adjustment of existing stock to its desired level is allowed for, the short-run elasticities of demand for purchase are only twice as large as the corresponding elasticities of demand for desired stock. In the long run, purchase will settle down to 27.5 units, or 10 percent higher than the original amount. The long-run elasticities of demand for purchase are thus identical with the corresponding elasticities of demand for desired stock.

2.6 DEMAND FOR AUTOMOBILES: STATISTICAL FINDINGS, 1921–1953

This section reports on some of the statistical demand functions for automobile stock and for annual purchase in the United States estimated from time-series observations for the period 1921–1953 with the theoretical framework set forth above. A more detailed discussion of these functions, as well as demand functions based on alternative hypotheses, can be found in Chow (1957). The ones chosen here are believed to be more promising for reasons already stated in that reference. They will be confronted with additional observations not available at the time of their estimation and will be used to provide predictions of automobile demand in the long run and in the short run.

We are interested in explaining two variables, automobile stock X_t (in equivalent units) per capita at the end of the year and purchase of new automobiles X_t^1 per capita during the year. The desired level of the former is assumed to be a function of the relative price of automobiles P_t and per capita real income I_t. The latter requires for its explanation another variable, per capita stock at the end of the previous year X_{t-1}. Table 2.1 presents observations on these variables. In brief, they are measured as follows.

Variable X_t is a weighted sum of registrations of passenger automobiles in various age groups at the end of year t divided by population. The weights are proportional to the average prices of automobiles of different ages at the end of 1937, a 1-year-old car (purchased during year t) counting as 1 unit. Since ownership per capita has been somewhere between .04 and .13 equivalent unit, X_t is recorded in hundredths of a unit, ranging between 4 and 13.

X_t^1 is the number of new automobiles purchased in year t divided by population, also in hundredths of a unit.

P_t is a price index of automobiles constructed with the stocks at the end of 1937 as weights divided by the GNP deflator of the U.S. Department of Commerce, set equal to 100 for 1937. The prices of automobiles, classified by age, have been obtained from newspaper advertisements at the end of year t.

I_{dt} is per capita disposable personal income of the Department of Commerce divided by the GNP deflator, in 1937 dollars.

I_{et} is real "expected income" or "permanent income" per capita in 1937 dollars, used by Friedman, (1957) defined as a weighted average of past real disposable incomes per capita.

Long-Run Demand for Automobile Stock

Desired stock per capita has been assumed to be a function of the relative price of automobiles as a group, real income per capita, and other variables whose effects are summarized by the variable u_t. It has been pointed out that desired stock may not always be realized because of the time lag in adjustment. However,

Table 2.1 Automobile stocks, annuals purchase, and their determinants, 1921–1953 (Chow, 1957)

Year	Automobile stock per capita X_t	New purchase per capita X_t^1	Relative price of automobiles P_t	Real disposable income per capita I_{dt}	Real expected income per capita I_{et}
1920	4.677				
1921	4.805	1.354	120.9	407.8	475.2
1922	5.426	1.887	111.2	460.4	474.4
1923	6.888	2.988	100.6	509.2	493.3
1924	7.849	2.776	90.9	509.3	506.6
1925	8.418	2.806	81.7	525.6	515.1
1926	8.928	2.974	92.6	532.3	528.9
1927	8.774	2.273	105.6	543.3	540.3
1928	9.130	2.817	91.0	545.1	544.8
1929	9.698	3.311	95.1	572.6	563.0
1930	9.092	2.153	85.9	525.2	559.3
1931	8.106	1.533	102.4	498.2	546.3
1932	6.915	.878	107.9	417.4	511.0
1933	6.340	1.214	95.6	394.3	483.8
1934	6.172	1.524	107.0	421.4	476.0
1935	6.530	2.250	105.2	475.2	484.8
1936	7.515	2.741	109.3	525.6	511.3
1937	8.343	2.719	100.0	551.2	532.8
1938	7.786	1.505	109.3	511.0	534.1
1939	7.719	2.079	104.9	547.9	547.8
1940	8.221	2.622	97.1	578.8	567.5
1941	9.178	2.797	120.1	642.7	611.6
1942	7.420		119.0	719.1	623.9
1943	5.790		204.7	741.6	636.6
1944	4.457		356.3	798.0	649.4
1945	3.513		449.3	787.2	662.5
1946	4.057		338.6	743.2	707.9
1947	5.291	2.198	263.4	696.4	717.4
1948	6.101	2.381	236.2	721.2	727.1
1949	8.076	3.243	159.7	696.7	730.2
1950	10.256	4.170	161.8	745.8	751.2
1951	11.463	3.278	161.2	743.9	762.8
1952	11.194	2.648	169.6	753.7	773.8
1953	12.057	3.594	152.4	772.3	787.7

incomplete adjustment is much more important for the study of annual purchase than for the study of automobile ownership. As first approximations, demand functions for desired stock are applied to explain actual stock directly. Any differences between the two are assumed to be absorbed by the residual u_t.

We shall first present the statistical demand functions for desired stock per capita in linear form. They are to serve as the fundamental relationships from which demand functions for annual purchase will be derived. These functions, both for stock and for purchase, are estimated by the method of least squares from 28 annual observations in the period 1921–1953, excluding the years 1942–1946. Standard errors of the regression coefficients are given in parentheses. The two measures of income employed are real disposable personal income per capita of the Department of Commerce and real expected income per capita used by Friedman to explain total consumption through time. They have been denoted by I_{dt} and I_{et}, respectively.

$$\dot{X}_t = 1.1666 \quad - 0.039544 P_t + 0.020827 I_{dt} \qquad \begin{matrix} R^2 = 0.850 \\ s = 0.738 \end{matrix} \qquad (27)$$
$$\underset{(0.004522)}{} \qquad \underset{(0.001749)}{}$$

$$\dot{X}_t = -0.7247 - 0.048802 P_t + 0.025487 I_{et} \qquad \begin{matrix} R^2 = 0.895 \\ s = 0.618 \end{matrix} \qquad (28)$$
$$\underset{(0.004201)}{} \qquad \underset{(0.001747)}{}$$

Price and income have accounted for a significant portion of the variance of automobile stock. According to the demand function using disposable income, price elasticity at mean price 122.8 and mean per capita stock 8.081 is -0.601; income elasticity at mean income 565.2 and mean stock is 1.46. According to the demand function using expected income, price elasticity at mean price and mean stock is -0.742; income elasticity at mean expected income 580.6 and mean stock is 1.83. Expected income, which has been found by Friedman to be more closely associated with total consumption than disposable income, has also turned out to be a better variable for the explanation of automobile stock from the comparison of the multiple correlation coefficients in the above demand functions. If disposable income is interpreted as expected income measured with an error, we can account for the lower income elasticity estimated from the former. The coefficient of an explanatory variable in a multiple regression will become smaller when the variable is subject to error. Error in one explanatory variable will also affect the coefficient of another variable. This may also account for the difference between the coefficients of price in the above demand functions.

For comparison with these results concerning price and income elasticities of demand for automobile stock, demand functions with different functional form, a different dependent variable, and different observations were estimated. Linear demand functions in the logarithms of the variables are now assumed. The logarithm of price is treated as the dependent variable. The years 1942–1946 are included, giving a total of 33 annual observations. Using disposable income, we have

$$\ln P_t = -3.2247 - .9014 \ln X_t + 1.5564 \ln I_{dt} \qquad \begin{matrix} R^2 = .898 \\ s = .146 \end{matrix} \qquad (29)$$
$$\underset{(.0876)}{} \qquad \underset{(.1210)}{}$$

The solution of (29) for $\ln X_t$ is

$$\ln X_t = -3.5774 - 1.1094 \ln P_t + 1.7266 \ln I_{dt}$$

Using expected income, we have

$$\ln P_t = -6.6077 - 1.0528 \ln X_t + 2.1336 \ln I_{et} \qquad \begin{array}{l} R^2 = .948 \\ s = .104 \end{array} \qquad (30)$$
$${\scriptstyle(.0632)}{\scriptstyle(.1133)}$$

The solution of (30) for $\ln X_t$ is

$$\ln X_t = -6.2763 - 0.9498 \ln P_t + 2.0266 \ln I_{et}$$

Elasticities with respect to disposable income and expected income are now, respectively, 1.73 and 2.03, compared with 1.46 and 1.83 obtained from the linear demand functions. The new estimates of price elasticity, -1.11 and $-.950$, are somewhat higher than the previous estimates $-.601$ and $-.742$. The two sets of estimates are different partly because there are two regressions between stock and price after the effect of income is netted out. A partial regression of stock on price will give a lower price elasticity than the corresponding partial regression of price on stock. It should be pointed out that the war years are included in estimating the demand functions of constant elasticities. Only when the ratios between the variables observed do not change violently will the linear demand functions give elasticities similar to those given by the demand functions linear in logarithms. In 1945, to take the extreme case, the ratio of price to stock was 449.3 to 3.513, or 127.9, much higher than the ratio 15.20 between mean price and mean stock for the 28 years included in the linear regressions. Therefore, in 1945, the price elasticity according to (28) would be -6.24. Insofar as the observations in the war period are consistent with the demand functions of constant elasticities, they are not consistent with the linear demand functions.

A more rigorous test can be performed in order to choose between disposable income and expected income for inclusion in a demand function for automobile stock. Hotelling (1940) has shown that the partial correlation coefficients between the same dependent variable and two alternative explanatory variables can be compared by Student's t distribution. The t ratio for comparing the partial correlation between $\ln P_t$ and $\ln I_{dt}$, given $\ln X_t$, and the partial correlation between $\ln P_t$ and $\ln I_{et}$ is 2.079 with 29 degrees of freedom. The null hypothesis that these two partial correlations are the same would be rejected at the 2.5 percent level, against the alternative hypothesis that the latter is higher. A trend variable t, which begins at 1 for 1921 and increases by 1 in each successive year, is added to the demand function (30) but fails to yield any significant improvement

$$\ln P_t = -5.8538 - 1.0480 \ln X_t + 2.0074 \ln I_{et} + .002383t \qquad (31)$$
$${\scriptstyle(.0645)}{\scriptstyle(.2563)}\phantom{\ln I_{et} + }{\scriptstyle(.004325)}$$

Our findings so far seem to justify the conclusion that price and income alone have traced a large part of the variations in automobile stock. Expected income has turned out to be a better variable for explaining automobile consumption than disposable income. Income elasticity is probably somewhere between 1.4 and 2.0. Price elasticity probably ranges between $-.6$ and -1.0.

Demand for Annual Purchase with Time Lag

Using the linear demand functions for automobile stock (27) and (28) as the basic relationships, we shall attempt to explain annual purchase of automobiles. As pointed out in the theoretical section, demand for purchase per capita is related to the demand for desired stock per capita in the following way

$$X_t^1 = c[\dot{X}_t(P_t, I_t, u_t) - X_{t-1}] + (1 - k)X_{t-1}$$
$$= c\dot{X}_t(P_t, I_t, u_t) + (1 - k - c)X_{t-1}$$

Besides price and income which determine the demand for desired stock, ownership at the beginning of the year will influence purchase during the year.

The statistical results, first estimated in conjunction with disposable income and then with expected income, from the same 28 observations as in the linear demand functions for desired stock are

$$X_t^1 = .07791 - .020127P_t + .011699I_{dt} - .23104X_{t-1} \qquad (32)$$
$$\underset{(.002648)}{\qquad} \underset{(.001070)}{\qquad} \underset{(.04719)}{\qquad}$$

$$R^2 = .858 \qquad s = .308$$

$$X_t^1 = -.39966 - .025936P_t + .014307I_{et} - .29709\ X_{t-1} \qquad (33)$$
$$\underset{(.005939)}{\qquad} \underset{(.002583)}{\qquad} \underset{(.09549)}{\qquad}$$

$$R^2 = .628 \qquad s = .499$$

Price and income elasticities of demand for stocks of automobiles can be derived from the results presented above. The coefficient of purchase with respect to price [$-.02$ in (32)] is equal to the partial derivative of desired stock with respect to price multiplied by the adjustment coefficient c. To obtain the elasticity of desired stock with respect to price, divide ($-.02$) by the estimated adjustment coefficient times mean stock and multiply the result by mean price. The estimated adjustment coefficient c is obtained from the coefficient of X_{t-1}, which is an estimate of $1 - k - c$. Recall that k is known to be very close to .75.

According to (32), then, the price elasticity of demand for stock is $-.63$, the income elasticity 1.70, and the adjustment coefficient .48. These elasticity estimates compare with $-.60$ and 1.46, obtained from Eq. (27) which also used disposable income but assumed full rather than partial adjustment.

According to (33), the price elasticity of demand for stock is $-.72$, the income elasticity 1.88, and the adjustment coefficient .55. The elasticity estimates here are very close to the figures $-.74$ and 1.83 obtained in the comparable full adjustment equation, (28).

It is interesting to compare the relative performances of the disposable and expected-income variables in the partial-adjustment model just presented with their relative performances in the full-adjustment model presented earlier. The disposable-income variable accounts for considerably more of the variation in purchases than the expected-income variable. Yet expected income performs better than disposable income in explaining variations in the stock of automobiles on the road.

These results can be interpreted in at least two ways. First, we can view the expected-income variable as playing part of the role of the adjustment coefficient. When complete adjustment of stock is assumed, the disposable-income formulation has no way of taking into account a slow approach of stocks to a new equilibrium level, while the expected-income formulation does, because the income variable itself only changes in each year by a fraction of the distance between its recent level and the new level of disposable income. Once partial adjustment is permitted, the adjustment coefficient itself accounts for the slow approach of stocks to their new level. On this interpretation the disposable-income formulation is the correct one, and the expected-income variable performs better in explaining variations in stocks only because the averaging procedure built into it acts as a partial surrogate for the adjustment mechanism.

On the second interpretation expected and unexpected income are allowed to play separate roles. Unexpected income is defined as $I_{dt} - I_{et}$. Equation (34) represents an attempt to explore this interpretation. The model on which it is based is

$$X_t^1 = a' + b'P_t + c'I_{et} + d'X_{t-1} + e'(I_{dt} - I_{et})$$

or

$$X_t^1 = a' + b'P_t + (c' - e')I_{et} + d'X_{t-1} + e'I_{dt}$$

$$X_t^1 = .14400 - \underset{(.003903)}{.018857}P_t - \underset{(.0003018)}{.001357}\,I_{et} - \underset{(.061547)}{.21378}\,X_{t-1} + \underset{(.002026)}{.012467}I_{dt} \quad (34)$$

$$R^2 = .859 \qquad s = .314$$

According to this regression, the coefficient c' of expected income is $.0125 - .0014 = .0111$ while the coefficient e' of unexpected income is $.0125$. Since the responsiveness of purchases to unexpected income is virtually the same as to expected income, this interpretation is not operationally distinguishable from the disposable-income formulation presented earlier.

2.7 TESTING THE GENERAL LINEAR HYPOTHESIS

In Sec. 2.4 an F statistic (26) was presented to test the null hypothesis $R\beta = r$. This section gives a different approach to deriving the same test for a set of m linear restrictions $R\beta = r$ on the regression coefficients β. The basic idea is the following. Let b be the least-squares estimate of β without imposing the restrictions and b^* be the least-squares estimate of β subject to the restriction $Rb^* = r$. The sum of squares of the residuals $y - Xb^*$ will be larger than the sum of squares of the residuals $y - Xb$. Decompose $y - Xb^*$ into two components

$$y - Xb^* = (y - Xb) + (Xb - Xb^*) \quad (35)$$

If $(y - Xb^*)'(y - Xb^*)$ is much larger than $(y - Xb)'(y - Xb)$, this means that the restriction $Rb^* = r$ on b^* makes the fit of the regression equation much poorer and therefore it should be rejected.

Premultiplying (35) by its transpose, we obtain the important relation

$$\underset{A}{(y - Xb^*)'(y - Xb^*)} = \underset{B}{(y - Xb)'(y - Xb)} + \underset{D}{(Xb - Xb^*)'(Xb - Xb^*)} \quad (36)$$

as the cross product vanishes

$$(y - Xb)'(Xb - Xb^*) = e'X(b - b^*) = 0 \tag{37}$$

because $e'X = 0$. The increase in the sum of squares due to the restriction is measured by the difference $D = (Xb - Xb^*)'(Xb - Xb^*)$ between A and B in (36). The sum of squares $B = e'e$ divided by σ^2 has a $\chi^2(n - k)$ distribution. The sum of squares D divided by σ^2 will be shown to have a $\chi^2(m)$ distribution. The two terms are independent by (37). Therefore

$$\frac{(Xb - Xb^*)'(Xb - Xb^*)/m}{e'e/(n - k)} = \frac{D}{ms^2} = \frac{A - B}{ms^2} \tag{38}$$

will have an $F(m, n - k)$ distribution. The F statistic (38) can be used to test the null hypothesis $R\beta = r$, and is identical with (26).

To prove the equality between (26) and (38) let us find the least-squares estimate b^* of β subject to the restriction $Rb^* = r$. This is done by forming the lagrangian expression

$$L = \tfrac{1}{2}(y - Xb^*)'(y - Xb^*) + \lambda'(Rb^* - r)$$

where λ is a vector of m langrangian multipliers. Differentiating L yields

$$\frac{\partial L}{\partial b^*} = -X'(y - Xb^*) + R'\lambda = 0$$

$$\frac{\partial L}{\partial \lambda} = Rb^* - r = 0$$

Premultiplying the first equation by $R(X'X)^{-1}$ gives

$$-R(X'X)^{-1}X'(y - Xb^*) + R(X'X)^{-1}R'\lambda = 0$$

which can be solved for λ

$$\lambda = [R(X'X)^{-1}R']^{-1}[R(X'X)^{-1}X'y - R(X'X)^{-1}X'Xb^*]$$
$$= [R(X'X)^{-1}R']^{-1}(Rb - r) \tag{39}$$

where $Rb^* = r$ was used. Substituting this result for λ in the first equation gives

$$-X'y + X'Xb^* + R'[R(X'X)^{-1}R']^{-1}(Rb - r) = 0$$

which can be solved for b^*

$$b^* = (X'X)^{-1}X'y - (X'X)^{-1}R'[R(X'X)^{-1}R']^{-1}(Rb - r)$$
$$= b - (X'X)^{-1}R'[R(X'X)^{-1}R']^{-1}(Rb - r) \tag{40}$$

Having obtained b^* in (40), we can easily show that (38) is identical with (26). By (40), the term D in (38) is

$$D = (b - b^*)'X'X(b - b^*)$$
$$= \{(X'X)^{-1}R'[R(X'X)^{-1}R']^{-1}(Rb - r)\}'X'X\{(X'X)^{-1}R'[R(X'X)^{-1}R']^{-1}(Rb - r)\}$$
$$= (Rb - r)'[R(X'X)^{-1}R']^{-1}R(X'X)^{-1}R'[R(X'X)^{-1}R']^{-1}(Rb - r)$$
$$= (Rb - r)'[R(X'X)^{-1}R']^{-1}(Rb - r)$$

which is identical with the numerator of (26). In connection with (26) this term D, divided by σ^2, was shown to have a $\chi^2(m)$ distribution. This justifies the construction of (38) as an F statistic for testing $R\beta = r$.

The construction of (38) is based on decomposing the residuals e^* of the restricted regression

$$e^* \equiv y - Xb^* = e + X(b - b^*) \tag{35}$$

The corresponding decomposition of the sum of squares or variance is

$$e^{*\prime}e^* = e'e + (b - b^*)'X'X(b - b^*) = B + D \tag{36}$$

The F ratio (38) is formed by comparing D/m with $B/(n - k)$. This approach is known as the analysis of variance, since the variance or sum of squares of the residuals of the restricted regression is analyzed in (36). It is a powerful approach for testing linear restrictions on the coefficients of a linear regression model. It provides an alternative interpretation of the test statistic (26) based on the distribution of the vector Rb, which has mean r and covariance matrix $R(X'X)^{-1}R'\sigma^2$ under the null hypothesis $R\beta = r$.

One application of the analysis of variance deserves special emphasis. It is to test the restriction $\beta_i = 0$. The R matrix is a row vector $(0 \ \cdots \ 1 \ \cdots \ 0)$ which has all zeros (imposing no restrictions on the β's) except a 1 in the ith position. The r vector is the scalar 0. In (28), $A = e^{*\prime}e^*$ is the sum of squares of the residuals in the regression with this restriction imposed, i.e., the regression with the ith explanatory variable omitted. $B = e'e$ is the sum of squares of the residuals in the regression including the ith explanatory variable. To test the null hypothesis H_0: $\beta_i = 0$ we compare $D = A - B$ with B using the F ratio (38). In other words, we decide to reject $\beta_i = 0$ or to include x_i in the regression if it significantly reduces the sum of squares of the regression residuals, the reduction being measured by $e^{*\prime}e^* - e'e = D$. Since the F test based on (38) is equivalent to the test (26) based on the distribution of $Rb - r$ (or $b_i - 0$ in this case) and the latter test reduces to the t test of (24), we can interpret the t test for $\beta_i = 0$ as testing whether the regression residuals are significantly reduced by the inclusion of x_i, using the analysis of variance.

2.8 TESTING EQUALITY BETWEEN SETS OF REGRESSION COEFFICIENTS

Another important application of the analysis of variance is testing the equality between subsets of coefficients in two or more linear regressions. Let there be two regressions, representing observations in two countries for a cross-section study or in two different periods for a time-series study. One may ask whether the behavior in the two countries or in the two different periods differs by testing the null hypothesis that the regression coefficients (or a subset of them) are equal for the two samples. In a time-series study the question amounts to testing whether economic behavior remains constant through time.

Let the two samples of n_1 and n_2 observations be represented by

$$y_1 = X_1\beta_1 + \epsilon_1 \quad \text{and} \quad y_2 = X_2\beta_2 + \epsilon_2$$

where y_1 is $n_1 \times 1$, X_1 is $n_1 \times k$, etc. Let the null hypothesis be $H_0 : \beta_1 = \beta_2$. In the framework of testing linear restrictions $R\beta = r$, we write the model as

$$\begin{bmatrix} y_1 \\ y_2 \end{bmatrix} = \begin{bmatrix} X_1 & 0 \\ 0 & X_2 \end{bmatrix} \begin{bmatrix} \beta_1 \\ \beta_2 \end{bmatrix} + \begin{bmatrix} \epsilon_1 \\ \epsilon_2 \end{bmatrix} \tag{41}$$

and the k restrictions as

$$R\beta = \begin{bmatrix} I & -I \end{bmatrix} \begin{bmatrix} \beta_1 \\ \beta_2 \end{bmatrix} = 0$$

The sum of squares $A = e^{*\prime}e^*$ is obtained by regressing the $n_1 + n_2$ observations of y on X_1 and X_2, assuming that $\beta_1 = \beta_2$. It has $n_1 + n_2 - k$ degrees of freedom. The sum of squares $B = e'e$ is obtained by the regression model (41), with $n_1 + n_2 - 2k$ degrees of freedom. The null hypothesis $\beta_1 = \beta_2$ is tested by using

$$\frac{(A - B)/k}{B/(n_1 + n_2 - 2k)} = F(k, n_1 + n_2 - 2k) \tag{42}$$

If β_i $(i = 1, 2)$ is decomposed into subvectors γ_i and δ_i, consisting of k_1 and k_2 elements, respectively, and we are interested in testing $H_0 : \gamma_1 = \gamma_2$, the model can be written as

$$\begin{bmatrix} y_1 \\ y_2 \end{bmatrix} = \begin{bmatrix} Z_1 & 0 & W_1 & 0 \\ 0 & Z_2 & 0 & W_2 \end{bmatrix} \begin{bmatrix} \gamma_1 \\ \gamma_2 \\ \delta_1 \\ \delta_2 \end{bmatrix} + \begin{bmatrix} \epsilon_1 \\ \epsilon_2 \end{bmatrix} \tag{43}$$

and the k_1 restrictions as

$$R\beta = \begin{bmatrix} I & -I & 0 & 0 \end{bmatrix} \begin{bmatrix} \gamma_1 \\ \gamma_2 \\ \delta_1 \\ \delta_2 \end{bmatrix}$$

The sum of squares $A = e^{*\prime}e^*$ is obtained by the regression model

$$\begin{bmatrix} y_1 \\ y_2 \end{bmatrix} = \begin{bmatrix} Z_1 & W_1 & 0 \\ Z_2 & 0 & W_2 \end{bmatrix} \begin{bmatrix} \gamma \\ \delta_1 \\ \delta_2 \end{bmatrix} + \begin{bmatrix} \epsilon_1 \\ \epsilon_2 \end{bmatrix}$$

which imposes the restriction $\gamma_1 = \gamma_2 = \gamma$. It has $n_1 + n_2 - k_1 - 2k_2$ degrees of freedom. The sum of squares $B = e'e$ is again based on model (43), having $n_1 + n_2 - 2k_1 - 2k_2$ degrees of freedom. The test statistic, with $k = k_1 + k_2$, is

$$\frac{(A - B)/k_1}{B/(n_1 + n_2 - 2k)} = F(k_1, n_1 + n_2 - 2k) \tag{44}$$

The generalization of the test (44) to more than two regressions is straightforward (see Prob. 6).

Often the explanatory variables W consist of dummy variables. As a special case, W_1 is a column of n_1 ones for the first sample, and W_2 is a column of n_2 ones for the second sample. In this case we are interested in testing whether all coefficients except the intercept are the same for the two samples. For example, people living in a city may demand fewer automobiles than those living in the suburbs in a cross-section study but may have the same income and price elasticities of demand.

Dummy variables can be used to represent other factors which are either present or absent. For example, in a time-series study using monthly data, they form a matrix of 12 columns; each column has ones corresponding to observations in a particular month and zeros elsewhere. When we introduce 12 seasonal dummy variables, we should not include another column of ones for the intercept. This column equals the sum of the other 12 columns and makes the columns of the matrix of explanatory variables linearly dependent. The matrix $X'X$ cannot be inverted. In other words, since there is a constant term for every month in the regression, there is really no need for another overall constant term. For example, if one believes that the seasonal effects may differ between the North and the South because of climate, one can introduce two sets of seasonal dummy variables W_1 and W_2 for the North and the South separately. The other economic variables may have similar effects on the dependent variable. At least, this is a hypothesis which can be tested by the F ratio (44).

2.9 FORECASTING

Having estimated a regression model using a sample of n_1 observations y_1, one may wish to use the estimated regression coefficient b_1 to forecast n_2 new observations associated with explanatory variables X_2. We shall be concerned with constructing a point forecast and an interval forecast.

The model for the n_2 observations is

$$y_2 = X_2 \beta_2 + \epsilon_2 \tag{45}$$

For a point forecast, we use the least-squares predictor based on b_1

$$X_2 b_1 = X_2 (X_1' X_1)^{-1} X_1' y_1 \tag{46}$$

This predictor is a linear function of y_1. It is easily seen to be an unbiased predictor for y_2 if $\beta_2 = \beta_1$, since

$$E X_2 b_1 = X_2 E b_1 = X_2 \beta_1 = E y_2$$

In fact, among all linear, unbiased predictors, it has the smallest covariance matrix for the forecasting error (see Prob. 7).

To construct an interval forecast we consider the vector of forecast errors

$$d = y_2 - X_2 b_1 = X_2 \beta_2 - X_2 \beta_1 + \epsilon_2 - X_2 (X_1' X_1)^{-1} X_1' \epsilon_1$$

The expectation of d is $X_2 \beta_2 - X_2 \beta_1$. The covariance matrix of d, with $E\epsilon_1 \epsilon_2' = 0$, is

$$
\begin{aligned}
\text{Cov } d &= E[\epsilon_2 - X_2 (X_1' X_1)^{-1} X_1' \epsilon_1][\epsilon_2 - X_2 (X_1' X_1)^{-1} X_1' \epsilon_1]' \\
&= E\epsilon_2 \epsilon_2' + E[X_2 (X_1' X_1)^{-1} X_1' \epsilon_1 \epsilon_1' X_1 (X_1' X_1)^{-1} X_2'] \\
&= I\sigma^2 + X_2 (X_1' X_1)^{-1} X_2' \sigma^2
\end{aligned}
$$

When $n_2 = 1$, y_2 and d become scalars and X_2 becomes a row vector. The variance of d is

$$\text{Var } d = [1 + X_2(X_1'X_1)^{-1}X_2']\sigma^2$$

An interval forecast for y_2 can be constructed from the statistic

$$\frac{y_2 - X_2 b_1}{[1 + X_2(X_1'X_1)^{-1}X_2']^{1/2}s_1} \equiv \frac{y_2 - X_2 b_1}{s_d}$$

where $s_1^2 = (y_1 - X_1 b_1)'(y_1 - X_1 b_1)/(n_1 - k)$. This statistic is distributed as $t(n_1 - k)$ if $\beta_2 = \beta_1$. If we denote by $t_{.05}$ that value which is exceeded by this statistic with probability .05, we can assert with probability .90 that

$$-t_{.05}\, s_d < y_2 - X_2 b_1 < t_{.05}\, s_d$$

The symmetric prediction interval for y_2 with .90 confidence is

$$X_2 b_1 - t_{.05}\, s_d < y_2 < X_2 b_1 + t_{.05}\, s_d$$

When $n_2 > 1$, we can use the statistic

$$\frac{d'(\text{Cov } d)^{-1}d}{n_2 s_1^2} = (y_2 - X_2 b_1)'[I + X_2(X_1'X_1)^{-1}X_2']^{-1}\frac{y_2 - X_2 b_1}{n_2 s_1^2} \qquad (47)$$

which has an $F(n_2, n_1 - k)$ distribution if $\beta_2 = \beta_1$. This statistic is a quadratic function in y_2 and can be employed to construct the confidence ellipsoid for y_2, using the inequality

$$F_{.95}\, n_2 s_1^2 < (y_2 - X_2 b_1)'[I + X_2(X_1'X_1)^{-1}X_2']^{-1}(y_2 - X_2 b_2) < F_{.05}\, n_2 s_1^2$$

The statistic (47) can also be used to test the hypothesis $\beta_2 = \beta_1$. If the vector $y_2 - X_2 b_1$ of forecast errors is large, as measured by its covariance matrix, one would reject the hypothesis that the n_2 new observations y_2 came from the same regression model as y_1.

When $n_2 > k$, we have suggested the statistic (42) to test the hypothesis $\beta_2 = \beta_1$. This statistic requires computing two separate regressions using the model (41) to get the residual e for $B = e'e$, whereas (47) does not require two regressions (see Prob. 8).

When $n_2 \leq k$, although we cannot compute the second regression in the model (41), we can assert that the residual e_2 of the second regression is a zero vector. Thus, in the analysis of variance,

$$B = e'e = e_1'e_1 = (y_1 - X_1 b_1)'(y_1 - X_1 b_1)$$

with $n_1 - k$ degrees of freedom. We have no problem in computing e^* from the regression with $n_1 + n_2$ observations under the assumption $\beta_2 = \beta_1$. The sum of squares $A = e^{*'}e^*$ has $n_1 + n_2 - k$ degrees of freedom, as before. To test the hypothesis $\beta_2 = \beta_1$ we use the statistic

$$\frac{(e^{*'}e^* - e_1'e_1)/n_2}{e_1'e_1/(n_1 - k)} = \frac{e^{*'}e^* - e_1'e_1}{n_2 s_1^2} \qquad (48)$$

which has an $F(n_2, n_1 - k)$ distribution. In fact this test statistic based on the analysis of variance is identical with the test statistic (47) based on the distribution of the vector d of prediction errors (see Prob. 9).

2.10 TESTING THE STABILITY OF AUTOMOBILE DEMAND FUNCTIONS

As applications of the tests (42) and (48) we consider the stability of the demand functions (28) and (32) reported in Sec. 2.6. The first is a statistical demand function for automobile ownership computed from observations of 33 years from 1921 to 1953

$$\dot{X}_t = -.7247 - .048802P_t + .025487I_{et} \quad \begin{array}{l} R^2 = .895 \\ s = .618 \end{array} \quad (49)$$
$$\quad\quad\quad (.004201) \quad (.001747)$$

The second is a statistical demand function for new purchase computed from observations of 28 years, from 1921 to 1953 but excluding 1942 to 1946

$$X_t^1 = .07791 - .020127P_t + .011699I_{dt} - .23104X_{t-1} \quad \begin{array}{l} R^2 = .858 \\ s = .308 \end{array} \quad (50)$$
$$\quad\quad\quad (.002648) \quad (.001070) \quad (.04719)$$

The new data for the years 1954–1957, which became available after the above two demand functions had been estimated, are given in Table 2.2. Using the four additional observations, we would like to test whether these demand functions remained stable over time. Since four observations are sufficient for computing a separate regression of the form (49), test (42) was used. To determine the stability of (50), test (48) was used. The follow-up study is described more thoroughly in Chow (1960a). Before presenting the analysis of variance (42) for the demand function (49), we exhibit here the estimated values of the dependent variable together with the deviations of the observed values from the estimated values:

Table 2.2 Automobile stock, annual purchase, and their determinants, 1954–1957 (Chow, 1960a)

Year	Automobile stock per capita X_t	New purchase per capita X_t^1	Relative price of automobiles P_t	Real disposable income per capita I_{dt}	Real expected income per capita† I_{et}
1953	12.057				
1954	12.052	3.408	141.3	769.6	795.9
1955	13.072	4.338	141.3	793.3	808.8
1956	13.430	3.543	141.5	805.2	822.3
1957	13.462	3.496	151.1	798.0	828.8

† Permanent income I_{et} is a weighted mean of $I_{dt}, I_{d(t-1)}, \ldots, I_{d(t-8)}$, with weights .34403, .23526, .16089, .11003, .07524, .05146, .03518, .02406, and .01646.

X_t	1954	1955	1956	1957
Estimated from (49)	12.665	12.993	13.328	13.025
Observed minus estimated	−.613	.079	.102	.437

The residuals of the observed values from the estimated values are very small compared with the standard error of .618. They do not indicate any shifts in the pattern of demand for automobile ownership during the 4 years 1954 to 1957. For testing the demand function (49) the sum of squares A is 10.1155, and B is 9.6130. The ratio $F(3, 26)$ is therefore .45. In order to interpret the new observations as coming from a different structure at the 5 percent level of significance, F would have to be at least 2.98. Our impression from examining the four deviations that there was no change in structure is strongly confirmed.

The following is a comparison of the estimated and observed values of the dependent variable of the demand function (50):

X_t^1	1954	1955	1956	1957
Estimated from (50)	3.452	3.730	3.630	3.270
Observed minus estimated	−.044	.608	−.087	.226

Again, inspection of the residuals reveals that they are not large relative to 0.308, the standard error of estimate for (50). The year 1955 is an exception, where we find the residual to be twice as large as the standard error. To apply test (48) we compute the sum of squares A of the 32 deviations from the regression including the four new observations, with $32 - 4 = 28$ degrees of freedom. A turns out to be 2.6444 numerically. The sum of squares B of the 28 deviations from the regression of the original set of observations turns out to be 2.2818, with 24 degrees of freedom. According to (48), the F ratio is the ratio of $(A - B)/4$ to $B/24$, or .95 numerically. Therefore, we accept the null hypothesis that automobile purchases in the years 1954 to 1957 were governed by the same relationship as before.

2.11 USE OF STATISTICAL DEMAND FUNCTIONS FOR LONG-RUN FORECASTING[†]

Although the main purpose of the statistical analysis presented above has been to ascertain the extent to which the prevalent theoretical framework of consumer demand, modified to take account of the problem of existing stock, can explain past variations in automobile ownership and automobile sales, a possible by-product of such an analysis is its usefulness for predicting sales in the future. In this section we shall reflect on the implications of our findings on automobile

[†] This section is based on the research work of the author in 1958 and is reprinted with modifications from Chow (1960a, pp. 169–174), by permission.

demand in the long run and in the short run. Looking ahead 10 years from now, we may wish to foresee the magnitudes of the forces governing automobile purchase. Is the market now saturated in the sense that annual purchases in the future will not be any higher than the present level? If not, at what level will the demand in 1968 be? On the other hand, looking 1 year ahead, we may wish to form an idea of the total purchase of automobiles. These questions are by no means easy to answer. It is our hope to bring a few of the important factors to bear and to suggest some partial answers to them.

At the outset it is well to point out the limiting assumptions on which our partial answers will be based. First of all, the demand relationships we have estimated will be assumed to hold in the future, at least until 1968. Second, as it has been pointed out, the primary interest in our statistical analysis has been the estimation of the effects of a few variables that are considered important in the economic theory of demand. Only their effects on automobile sales will be considered. Whatever predictions we make are predictions of the partial effects of these variables while the combined effect of all other variables is held constant. Third, all we have estimated are statistical demand functions. Accordingly, only the shifts in the demand curves will be examined. The quantity demanded, whether stock or purchase, cannot be specified without an additional assumption concerning the supply of automobiles.

Our first task is to make a forecast of automobile demand in 1968. Long-run demand for automobile purchase will be derived from long-run demand for automobile stock. The short-run factors such as time lag do not concern us here, since our present purpose is to get a rough order of magnitude of the demand 10 years from now rather than to predict the fluctuations in demand from year to year. With this in mind, we can regard the desired stock as being actually fulfilled and make no distinction between actual stock and desired stock. A forecast will first be worked out on a per capita basis and then translated into the total number of automobiles.

Given the per capita demands for desired stock at the end of two consecutive years in the future $\dot{X}_t$ and $\dot{X}_{t-1}$, a long-run forecast of per capita demand for purchase in year t can be regarded as $\dot{X}_t - k\dot{X}_{t-1}$. Alternatively, this relationship can be written as

$$X_t^1 = (\dot{X}_t - \dot{X}_{t-1}) + (1 - k)\dot{X}_{t-1}$$

A long-run forecast of demand for purchase is thus broken into two parts, the change in desired stock during the year $\dot{X}_t - \dot{X}_{t-1}$ and the demand for replacing the stock at the beginning of the year $(1 - k)\dot{X}_{t-1}$. For predicting the sales of automobiles in 1968, therefore, calculations of the change in desired stock during 1968 and of the replacement of the stock at the end of 1967 have to be made.

A few comments on replacement sales are in order at this point to make clear our position on the question of possible saturation in automobile sales. Saturation is understood to be the state of affairs in which existing ownership is sufficient to satisfy demand in the near future, so that annual purchase will be declining or at least will not be increasing, There has been some conjecture that the automobile market is already saturated in 1958. However, our analysis seems to point to the contrary. Since one used car is not a perfect substitute for a new car and since the annual rate of depreciation is close to 25 percent, roughly a quarter of the existing automobile stock needs to be replaced just to keep the ownership level from falling. In other words, the replacement demand is around a quarter of the number of automobiles (in new-car equivalent units) being used currently. At the end of 1957 there were 23.0 million units of automobiles registered. A quarter of this stock, or 5.75 million units, would be needed annually for replacement alone even if per capita income and population were to remain unchanged. Expected increases in per capita income and in population will raise annual demand above 5.75 million in a manner to be described presently.

To estimate replacement demand in 1968, we first need an estimate of the demand for desired stock at the end of 1967. The latter in turn requires estimates of per capita income and population in 1967. As we have concluded previously, the measure of income appropriate for determination of desired stock is expected income. It is beyond our scope to dwell on elaborate forecasts of income and population. We shall simply project past trends of these two variables into the future and investigate into the effects of these variables, so projected, on the demand for automobiles. From 1921 to 1957, real expected income per capita was growing at an annual average rate of 1.5 percent; from 1946 to 1957 it was growing at an average rate of 1.4 percent. For projecting expected income from 1957 on, 1.4 percent will be used. Compounded continuously for 10 years, this rate amounts to a 15 percent growth from the expected income per capita in 1957. The result of this projection is 953 for the expected income in 1967. Since the end of World War II, population in the United States has been rising at an annual average rate of 1.7 percent. Using this rate for projecting population from 1957, we obtain 203 million as the estimated population in 1967.

Let us see how the projected growth of expected income affects our demand curves for desired stock per capita. The forecasts are based on the demand functions

$$\dot{X}_t = -.7482 - .048800P_t + .025526I_{et} \tag{49'}$$

$$\ln P_t = -6.4998 - 1.0600 \ln X_t + 2.1187 \ln I_{et} \tag{30'}$$

which are similar to equations (49) and (30) except that the four additional observations of Table 2.2 were included in estimating them. From these demand functions we derive the relationships between desired stock and price, given an expected income of 828.8 as it was in 1957,

$$\dot{X}_t = 20.408 - 0.048800P_t \tag{49a}$$

and

$$\ln \dot{X}_t = 7.300 - 0.9434 \ln P_t \tag{30a}$$

Given an expected income of 953 as projected for 1967, these demand curves become

$$\dot{X}_t = 23.578 - 0.048800P_t \tag{49b}$$

$$\ln \dot{X}_t = 7.579 - 0.9434 \ln P_t \tag{30b}$$

By comparing the two pairs of intercepts we find that the growth of income alone will increase the per capita demand for desired stock by an absolute amount of

23.578 − 20.408 = 3.170 (hundredths of an equivalent unit) according to (49a, b) and by a factor of $e^{(7.579-7.300)}$ or 1.322 according to (30a, b).

What do the above indicated shifts in the per capita demand curves mean in terms of per capita demand for desired stock in 1967, total demand for desired stock in 1967, and total demand for replacement in 1968? It would be more revealing to deal with the quantities demanded rather than the demand curves in all cases. Merely for the sake of expressing our results in terms of the quantities demanded, the price in 1957 will be used in the following calculations. Assuming the price index to be 151.1 as it was in 1957, we proceed first to calculate the desired stocks per capita in 1967 from (49b) and (30b). The corresponding estimates of total desired stock can be obtained, given our projected population of 203 million. One-quarter of total desired stock at the end of 1967 will constitute our forecast of replacement demand in 1968:

	Desired stock per capita (hundredths)			Total desired stock, End of 1967 (millions)	Replacement demand, 1968 (millions)
Eq.	End of 1957	Eq.	End of 1967		
(49a)	13.03	(49b)	16.20	32.9	8.2
(30a)	13.01	(30b)	17.20	34.9	8.7

Predictions based on both (49′) and (30′) are exhibited here for comparison. Equation (49′) is a regression with per capita stock as the dependent variable, whereas (30′) is a regression of the logarithm of relative price. But both calculations show that the projected increases in per capita income and in population would be enough to raise replacement sales to over 8 million in 1968 if the relative price of automobiles were to remain unchanged.

To arrive at the demand for purchase in 1968, the demand due to the change in desired stock should be added to replacement demand. Under the same assumption of constant price, desired stock per capita will be changed from 16.20 to 16.54 during the year 1968 according to (49′) as per capita income is expected to rise by 1.4 percent. This increase of .34 in desired stock per capita, when multiplied by the projected population in 1968, is converted to .7 million automobiles as the increase in total desired stock. The sum of .7 million and the 8.2 million for replacement is the complete estimate of demand for purchase in 1968 according to (49′). Similar calculations based upon function (30′) are shown here also:

Eq.	Desired stock per capita, end of 1968 (hundredths)	Change in desired stock per capita during 1968 (hundredths)	Change in total stock during 1968 (millions)	Demand for purchase during 1968 (millions)
(49′)	16.54	.34	.7	8.9
(30′)	17.68	.48	1.0	9.7

It should be emphasized that the estimates of 8.9 million and 9.7 million are not forecasts of actual automobile sales in 1968, but are intended to indicate effects of the projected increases in per capita income and population on the demand for automobiles under the arbitrary assumption that relative price of automobiles is to remain constant.

Another way to indicate the shift of total demand for purchase resulting from the projected increases in per capita income and population is by the rise in price which would be necessary to keep total purchase in 1968 at the same level as in 1957. Here we are concerned with automobile purchases as governed by the long-run factors in these 2 years. Therefore, we can rephrase our question: How much does the price rise need to be in order to keep total *desired* stock at the end of 1968 the same as total *desired* stock at the end of 1957? If total stock is prevented from growing, purchase will consist entirely of replacement. Purchases in these 2 years are considered equal if the desired stocks are equal. According to (49′), per capita desired stock is 13.03 in 1957. In order to keep total desired stock in 1968 the same as in 1957, when population increases from 171.1 to 206.4 million, per capita desired stock in 1968 has to be reduced to 10.80. The price index required to achieve this level of per capita stock, under the assumption that expected income increases to 966.4 in 1968, is 269, which can easily be verified by substitutions into (49′). Similar substitutions into (30′) give a price index of 255. Thus the growth in per capita income and population would be sufficient to raise the relative price of automobiles by some 70 percent in the next 10 years if total automobile stock were not adjusted upward. Such a price would be close to one prevailing at the end of 1947, as given in Table 2.1.

Our views on the long-run prospects of automobile sales can be summed up briefly. Expected income and population, if they are to grow at the same rate as in the last decade, will increase the total demand for automobiles significantly. In 1968 the number of automobiles demanded would be in the neighborhood of 9 million if the relative price of automobiles were not to move up at all; price would have to move up to the level which prevailed at the end of 1947 in order to keep total demand from exceeding the present demand. In reaching these conclusions, the author has not been oblivious of the hazards of long-run forecasting in economics, but no better alternative has occurred to him than the application of the measures of price and income effects from past observations. (See Prob. 16.)

2.12 PARTIAL CORRELATION COEFFICIENTS

The square of the correlation coefficient between two variables y and x is defined as

$$r_{yx}^2 = \frac{\text{Cov}^2(y, x)}{\text{Var } y \text{ Var } x} = \frac{b \text{ Cov }(y, x)}{\text{Var } y} = \frac{\text{Var }(a + bx)}{\text{Var } y} \tag{51}$$

where $a + bx = \hat{y}$ is the estimated value of y by the least-squares regression line and $\text{Var }(a + bx) = b^2 \text{ Var } x$. It can be interpreted as the proportion of the variance of y that is explained by the regression function; it is the ratio of Var $\hat{y}$ to Var y.

Similarly, the square of the multiple correlation coefficient between y and a set of k variables $x_1, \ldots, x_k$ (with $x_1 = 1$) is defined as

$$R^2 = \frac{\text{Var } \hat{y}}{\text{Var } y} = \frac{b_1 \text{ Cov } (y, x_1) + \cdots + b_k \text{ Cov } (y, x_k)}{\text{Var } y} \tag{52}$$

where $\hat{y} = b_1 x_1 + \cdots + b_k x_k$ is the estimated value of y by the least-squares regression equation and the second equality sign of (52) is left as an exercise (Prob. 3). Note that Cov $(y, x_1) = 0$ for $x_1 = 1$.

The partial correlation coefficient between y and x_k with $x_1, \ldots, x_{k-1}$ held fixed is defined as the correlation coefficient between the residual of the regression of y on $x_1, \ldots, x_{k-1}$ and the residual of the regression of x_k on $x_1, \ldots, x_{k-1}$. It measures the degree of linear association between y and x_k holding the values of $x_1, \ldots, x_{k-1}$ constant, or eliminating their effects by employing the residuals of the regressions of y and of x_k on these variables.

It will be useful to examine the relation of the partial correlation coefficient between y and x_k to the regression coefficient b_k. First we shall give an interpretation of b_k. Let y_* be the residual of the regression of y on $x_1, \ldots, x_{k-1}$ and x_{k*} be the residual of the regression of x_k on $x_1, \ldots, x_{k-1}$; b_k is the coefficient of the regression of y_* on x_{k*}. To prove this statement, the vector b and the matrix $X = [X_* \quad x_k]$ are partitioned.

$$b = \begin{bmatrix} b_* \\ b_k \end{bmatrix} = (X'X)^{-1}X'y = \begin{bmatrix} X'_* X_* & X'_* x_k \\ x'_k X_* & x'_k x_k \end{bmatrix}^{-1} \begin{bmatrix} X'_* y \\ x'_k y \end{bmatrix} \tag{53}$$

Using Eqs. (27) and (28) of Chap. 1, we can write $(X'X)^{-1}$ as

$$(X'X)^{-1} = \begin{bmatrix} [X'_* X_* - X'_* x_k(x'_k x_k)^{-1}x'_k X_*]^{-1} & -(X'_* X_*)^{-1}X'_* x_k(x'_{k*} x_{k*})^{-1} \\ -(x'_{k*} x_{k*})^{-1}x'_k X_*(X'_* X_*)^{-1} & (x'_{k*} x_{k*})^{-1} \end{bmatrix}$$

$$\tag{54}$$

where

$$x'_{k*} x_{k*} = x'_k x_k - x'_k X_*(X'_* X_*)^{-1}X'_* x_k \tag{55}$$

The regression coefficient b_k is therefore

$$b_k = (x'_{k*} x_{k*})^{-1}[-x'_k X_*(X'_* X_*)^{-1}X'_* y + x'_k y]$$

$$= (x'_{k*} x_{k*})^{-1}(x'_k y_*) = (x'_{k*} x_{k*})^{-1}(x'_{k*} y_*) \tag{56}$$

where the last equality sign is due to the fact that $x_k = x_{k*} + \hat{x}_k$ and y_* is uncorrelated with $\hat{x}_k$, which is a linear combination of the columns of X_*. Equation (56) is the statement to be proved (see Prob. 10). All coefficients of a multiple regression can therefore be interpreted as partial regression coefficients, in the sense that they are coefficients in a regression of residuals on residuals. Both the dependent and the explanatory variables are residuals of regressions on a given set of other explanatory variables.

The partial correlation coefficient between y and x_k, given $x_1, \ldots, x_{k-1}$, is the correlation coefficient between y_* and x_{k*}

$$r_{yxk*} = \frac{\text{Cov}(y_*, x_{k*})}{\sqrt{\text{Var } y_* \text{ Var } x_{k*}}} = \frac{x'_{k*} y_*}{\sqrt{(y'_* y_*)(x'_{k*} x_{k*})}} = b_k \left(\frac{\text{Var } x_{k*}}{\text{Var } y_*}\right)^{1/2} \tag{57}$$

where both y_* and x_{k*} have zero mean. The partial correlation is related to the multiple correlation R between y and all k x's and to the multiple correlation R_* between y and the first $k-1$ x's as follows. By the use of (54) for $(X'X)^{-1}$ and

$$[X'_* X_* - X'_* x_k(x'_k x_k)^{-1}x'_k X_*]^{-1}$$
$$= (X'_* X_*)^{-1} + (X'_* X_*)^{-1}X'_* x_k(x'_{k*} x_{k*})^{-1}x'_k X_*(X'_* X_*)^{-1} \tag{58}$$

which can be verified as an exercise (Prob. 11), the sum of squared residuals from the first regression, with $X = (X_* \quad x_k)$ and $\hat{x}_k$ denoting $X_*(X'_* X_*)^{-1}X'_* x_k$, is

$$y'[I - X(X'X)^{-1}X']y$$

$$= y'[I - X_*(X'_* X_*)^{-1}X'_* - \hat{x}_k(x'_{k*} x_{k*})^{-1}\hat{x}'_k + \hat{x}_k(x'_{k*} x_{k*})^{-1}x'_k$$
$$+ x_k(x'_{k*} x_{k*})^{-1}\hat{x}'_k - x_k(x'_{k*} x_{k*})^{-1}x'_k]y$$

$$= y'[I - X_*(X'_* X_*)^{-1}X'_*]y - y'[I - X_*(X'_* X_*)^{-1}X'_*]$$
$$\cdot x_k(x'_{k*} x_{k*})^{-1}x'_k[I - X_*(X'_* X_*)^{-1}X'_*]y$$

$$= y'_* y_* - y'_* x_k(x'_{k*} x_{k*})^{-1}x'_k y_* = y'_* y_* - b_k^2(x'_{k*} x_{k*})$$

$$= y'_* y_*(1 - r_{yxk*}^2) \tag{59}$$

where the last two equality signs have used (56) and (57). In words, the sum of squared residuals in the regression of y on k x's equals the sum of squared residuals in the regression on the first $k-1$ x's times a fraction which is 1 minus the squared partial correlation between y and x_k. Equation (59) is equivalent to

$$1 - R^2 = (1 - R_*^2)(1 - r_{yxk*}^2) \tag{60}$$

which relates the partial correlation to the two multiple correlations.

To test the significance of a partial correlation coefficient, one can use the t test for the significance of the corresponding regression coefficient since the partial correlation is a monotone function of the t statistic. Using (54), (57) or $b_k(x'_{k*} x_{k*})^{1/2} = r_{yxk*}(y'_* y_*)^{1/2}$, and (59), we write the t statistic as

$$t = \frac{b_k}{\sqrt{(x'_{k*} x_{k*})^{-1}s^2}} = r_{yxk*}(y'_* y_*)^{1/2}(n-k)^{1/2}\{y'[I - X(X'X)^{-1}X']y\}^{-1/2}$$

$$= r_{yxk*}(1 - r_{yxk*}^2)^{-1/2}(n-k)^{1/2} \tag{61}$$

which is a monotone-increasing function of the partial correlation coefficient. It has been assumed in the above analysis that the values of the explanatory variable are fixed, and not random, as in the standard model of multiple linear regression.

*2.13 ASYMPTOTIC DISTRIBUTION OF THE LEAST-SQUARES ESTIMATOR b

We have shown that if the residuals ϵ_i are normal, the distribution of the least-squares estimator b, which is a linear function of the ϵ's, will also be normal. By the Gauss-Markov Theorem 2.1, even if the ϵ_i are not normal but each has a variance σ^2, the least-squares estimator b is best linear unbiased. Several questions concerning the distribution of b may be asked. If the ϵ_i are normal and identically distributed, is b best unbiased or efficient; i.e., can we omit the word "linear" in Theorem 2.1? If the ϵ_i are identically distributed but not necessarily normal, is b consistent? When will b be asymptotically normal? These questions were answered in Chap. 1 for the slope b in the simple linear regression model.

To show that b is efficient one can find the information matrix and apply the Cramer-Rao inequality. The log-likelihood function is

$$\log L(y; \beta, \sigma^2) = -\tfrac{1}{2}n \log 2\pi - \tfrac{1}{2}n \log \sigma^2 - \frac{\tfrac{1}{2}(y - X\beta)'(y - X\beta)}{\sigma^2} \qquad (62)$$

and its second partial with respect to β is $-X'X/\sigma^2$. The information matrix is $-E(-X'X/\sigma^2) = X'X/\sigma^2$. Since b is unbiased and its covariance matrix is $(X'X)^{-1}\sigma^2$, it is efficient under the normality assumption (see Prob. 12).

Concerning the consistency of b, we examine the two conditions of Lemma 1.1. First, $Eb = \beta$, satisfying the first condition. Second, $\text{Cov } b = (X'X)^{-1}\sigma^2$. As long as the diagonal elements of $(X'X)^{-1}$ have zero limits, the second condition is satisfied and b is consistent. A sufficient condition is that the matrix $(1/n) X'X$ of second moments of the explanatory variables approach a positive-definite matrix. This means that $[(1/n)X'X]^{-1} = n(X'X)^{-1}$ approaches a positive-definite matrix or $(X'X)^{-1}$ approaches a zero matrix.

To study the asymptotic normality of b we use (8) to write

$$\sqrt{n}(b - \beta) = \sqrt{n}(X'X)^{-1}X'\epsilon = \left(\frac{1}{n} X'X\right)^{-1} n^{-1/2} X'\epsilon \qquad (63)$$

and consider the distribution of the vector

$$n^{-1/2} X'\epsilon = n^{-1/2}(x_1\epsilon_1 + x_2\epsilon_2 + \cdots + x_n\epsilon_n) \qquad (64)$$

where x_j is the jth column of X', or a column vector consisting of the jth observation on the explanatory variables. As in the proof of Theorem 1.2, the characteristic function $\phi_j(t)$ of the vector $n^{-1/2}x_j\epsilon_j = z_j$ can be expanded in a Taylor series up to the term $E(t'z_j)^2$

$$\phi_j(t) = Ee^{it'z_j} = 1 + iE(t'z_j) + \frac{i^2}{2!} E(t'z_j z_j' t) + o[E(t'z_j)^2]$$

$$= 1 - \tfrac{1}{2}t'x_j x_j' t\sigma^2 n^{-1} + o(t'x_j x_j' t\sigma^2 n^{-1}) \qquad (65)$$

We assume that each element of x_j is bounded, so that $x_j x_j'$ is bounded. Therefore, the last term of (65) is $o(n^{-1})$. The characteristic function of the sum (54) is the product

$$\prod_{j=1}^{n} [1 - \tfrac{1}{2}t'x_j x_j' t\sigma^2 n^{-1} + o(n^{-1})]$$

The logarithm of this characteristic function is

$$\sum_{j=1}^{n} \log\left[1 - \tfrac{1}{2}t'x_j x_j' t\sigma^2 n^{-1} + o(n^{-1})\right] = \sum_{j=1}^{n}\left[-\tfrac{1}{2}t'x_j x_j' t\sigma^2 n^{-1} + o(n^{-1})\right]$$

$$= -\tfrac{1}{2}t'(n^{-1}X'X)t\sigma^2 + o(1)$$

If we make the assumption that $n^{-1}X'X$ approaches a positive-definite matrix Q as the limit, then the above expression approaches $-\tfrac{1}{2}t'Qt\sigma^2$. This is the logarithm of the characteristic function for a normal vector with mean zero and covariance matrix $Q\sigma^2$. Therefore, (64) has a limiting distribution which is normal with mean zero and covariance matrix $Q\sigma^2$.

Under the assumption that $n^{-1}X'X \to Q$ and the elements of X are bounded, (63) converges in distribution to Q^{-1} times a normal vector with mean zero and covariance matrix $Q\sigma^2$. Hence $\sqrt{n}(b - \beta)$ has a normal limiting distribution with mean zero and covariance matrix $Q^{-1}(Q\sigma^2)Q^{-1'} = Q^{-1}\sigma^2$. For a discussion of the asymptotic distribution of b under more general conditions, see Anderson (1971, pp. 23–25).

Under the same assumption $n^{-1}X'X \to Q$, the estimated residual variance s^2 is a consistent estimator of σ^2. To prove consistency, let us consider

$$\frac{n-k}{n}s^2 = n^{-1}y'[I - X(X'X)^{-1}X']y = n^{-1}\epsilon'[I - X(X'X)^{-1}X']\epsilon$$

and its probability limit

$$\operatorname*{plim}_{n\to\infty}\left(\frac{n-k}{n}s^2\right) = \operatorname{plim} n^{-1}\epsilon'\epsilon - \operatorname{plim} n^{-1}\epsilon'X \operatorname{plim}(n^{-1}X'X)^{-1} \operatorname{plim} n^{-1}X'\epsilon$$

(66)

On the right-hand side of (66), $\operatorname{plim} n^{-1}\epsilon'\epsilon = \sigma^2$ on account of the law of large numbers; $\operatorname{plim} n^{-1}X'\epsilon = 0$ because $En^{-1}X'\epsilon = 0$ and

$$\operatorname{Cov}(n^{-1}X'\epsilon) = En^{-2}X'\epsilon\epsilon'X = n^{-2}X'X\sigma^2$$

implying $\lim \operatorname{Cov}(n^{-1}X'\epsilon) = 0$ under the assumption that $\lim n^{-1}X'X = Q$. The consistency of $(n-k)s^2/n$ and of s^2 is proved by evaluating the right-hand side of (66) term by term.

PROBLEMS

1. Using a multiple-regression model with two explanatory variables, the first equal to 1 always, derive the least-squares estimates of the two regression coefficients and show that they agree with the estimates of the intercept and the slope given in Chap. 1.

2. Using the model of Prob. 1, provide t tests for the two null hypotheses $\beta_1 = 0$ and $\beta_2 = 0$. Compare the second with the t test for the slope given in Chap. 1.

3. Show that the numerator of the correlation coefficient R as defined by (17) equals

$$b_2 \sum_{i=1}^{n}(x_{i2} - \bar{x}_2)y_i + \cdots + b_k \sum_{i=1}^{n}(x_{ik} - \bar{x}_k)y_i$$

4. Show explicitly that the analysis-of-variance test using (38) for the hypothesis $\beta_i = 0$ is equivalent to the t test of (24).

5. For the regression model (29) how can one construct an interval estimate for the income elasticity of demand for automobile stock with a 90 percent confidence coefficient? Note that the point estimate of income elasticity, 1.7266, is the ratio of the coefficient b_3 (1.5564) to the coefficient $-b_2$ (.9014) in the regression equation (29). To find a confidence interval for the ratio $r = -\beta_3/\beta_2$ consider the linear combination $z = b_2 r + b_3$. The expectation of z is $\beta_2 r + \beta_3 = 0$. Find an estimate s_z of the standard deviation of z. Thus, with .90 probability z will lie between c and $-c$, where c is a constant to be found from the t distribution. Given $P(-c < b_2 r + b_3 < c) = .90$, we can find a .90 confidence interval for r. This method was given by Fisher (1950, pp. 142–144).

6. Generalize the F test of (44) to q regressions, where $q > 2$.

7. Show that the least-squares predictor (46) gives the minimum covariance matrix for the forecast error vector among all unbiased predictors which are linear functions of y. Write a linear predictor as $[X_2(X_1'X_1)^{-1}X_1' + B]y_1$.

8. Explain why the statistic (42) is better than the statistic (47) for testing the null hypothesis $\beta_2 = \beta_1$ if the number of observations n_2 in the second example exceeds the number of regression coefficients k.

9. (Chow, 1960b.) Show that when $n_2 < k$, the statistic (48) based on the analysis of variance is identical with the statistic (47) based on the distribution of the vector of forecasting errors for testing the hypothesis $\beta_1 = \beta_2$.

10. In a regression of y on $x_1, \ldots, x_k$, let b_* be the vector consisting of the first $k - 1$ regression coefficients. Interpret b_* as the coefficients of a regression on $k - 1$ explanatory variables. What is the dependent variable and what are the explanatory variables in this regression? Prove your assertions.

11. Verify relation (58) using definition (55).

12. Using the information matrix of β and σ^2 jointly, discuss the efficiency of b and s^2.

13. Let $e = y - Xb$ be the vector of estimated regression residuals. Under the assumption $n^{-1}X'X \to Q$, show that the vector $e - \epsilon$ converges in probability to a zero vector. Find the covariance matrix of $e - \epsilon$ and show that the variance of each element $e_i - \epsilon_i$ converges to zero.

14. Using the data in Tables 2.1 and 2.2 for the demand for automobiles from 1921 to 1957 and omitting 1942 to 1946,

(*a*) Estimate the linear demand function explaining new purchase per capita by relative price, disposable income per capita, and lagged stock per capita.

(*b*) Estimate the price and income elasticities of demand at the mean of the regression. Test the null hypothesis that the price elasticity (in absolute value) is equal to the income elasticity against the alternative hypothesis that it is smaller, using (i) the covariance matrix of the coefficient estimates and (ii) analysis of variance.

(*c*) Form an 80 percent confidence interval for the ratio of price elasticity to income elasticity, both evaluated at the mean of the regression.

(*d*) By considering a quadratic form of prediction errors test the hypothesis that the last four observations came from the same regression model as the previous observations.

(*e*) Test the hypothesis that in the last 4 years the coefficient of the price variable alone remained the same as it was in previous years.

15. The first column in the table gives the price y of a computer disk, the second its size x_1, and the third the time x_2 required to transfer a fixed number of data from the disk (the third variable being inversely proportional to speed).

(*a*) Regress y on x_1, x_2, and a dummy variable representing the year.

(*b*) Do the same regression except for imposing a zero intercept in the regression for the first year.

(*c*) Compare the coefficients of x_2 in parts (*a*) and (*b*) and explain the difference. What conclusions can you draw concerning the relation between speed and the price of computer disk?

16. Find the necessary statistical data to check the accuracy of the 10-year-ahead forecast of automobile sales in the United States in 1968 described at the end of Sec. 2.11. Discuss the results.

Year	Price y	Size x_1	Time x_2	Year	Price y	Size x_1	Time x_2
1965	53.6	7.25	.114	1968	33.2	2.7	.099
	79.9	14.5	.114		55.5	5.4	.099
	106.2	21.75	.114		36.4	5.4	.114
	132.5	29	.114		61.9	10.8	.114
	158.8	36.25	.114		51.9	7.25	.114
	185.1	43.5	.114		77.4	14.5	.114
	211.4	50.75	.114		102.9	21.75	.114
	237.7	58	.114		128.4	29	.114
					153.9	36.25	.114
1966	33.2	2.7	.099		179.4	43.5	.114
	55.5	5.4	.099		204.9	50.75	.114
	36.4	5.4	.114		230.4	58	.114
	61.9	10.8	.114		244.4	233.6	.101
	51.9	7.25	.114		87.4	16.2	.114
	77.4	14.5	.114				
	102.9	21.75	.114	1969	90.2	29.2	.086
	128.4	29	.114		108.4	58.4	.086
	153.9	36.25	.114		132.5	87.6	.086
	179.4	43.5	.114		146.7	116.8	.086
	204.9	50.75	.114		170.8	146	.086
	230.4	58	.114		188.3	175.2	.086
					212.4	204.4	.086
1967	33.2	2.7	.099		226.6	233.6	.086
	55.5	5.4	.099		32.2	2.7	.099
	36.4	5.4	.114		53.8	5.4	.099
	61.9	10.8	.114		35.3	5.4	.114
	51.9	7.25	.114		60	10.8	.114
	77.4	14.5	.114		50.3	7.25	.114
	102.9	21.75	.114		75	14.5	.114
	128.4	29	.114				
	153.9	36.25	.114				
	179.4	43.5	.114				
	204.9	50.75	.114				
	230.4	58	.114				
	244.4	233.6	.101				

REFERENCES

Anderson, T. W. (1971): *The Statistical Analysis of Time Series*, Wiley, New York.

Chow, G. C. (1957): *Demand for Automobiles in the United States: A Study in Consumer Durables*, North-Holland, Amsterdam.

——— (1960a): "Statistical Demand Functions for Automobiles and Their Use for Forecasting," in A. C. Harberger (ed.), *The Demand for Durable Goods*, University of Chicago Press, Chicago.

——— (1960b): "Tests of Equality between Sets of Coefficients in Two Linear Regressions," *Econometrica*, **28**: 591–605.

Fisher, R. A. (1950): *Statistical Methods for Research Workers*, 11th ed., Hafner, New York.

Friedman, M. (1957): *A Theory of the Consumption Function*, Princeton University Press, Princeton, N.J.

Hotelling, H. (1940): "The Selection of Variates for Use in Prediction with Some Comments on the General Problem of Nuisance Parameters," *Ann. Math. Statist.* **11**: 271–283.

Intriligator, M. D. (1978): *Econometric Models, Techniques, and Applications*, Prentice-Hall, Englewood Cliffs, N.J.

Johnston, J. (1972): *Econometric Methods*, 2d ed. McGraw-Hill, New York.

Maddala, G. S. (1977): *Econometrics*, McGraw-Hill, New York.

Malinvaud, E. (1970): *Statistical Methods of Econometrics*, North-Holland, Amsterdam.

Theil, H. (1971): *Principles of Econometrics*, Wiley, New York.

THREE

TOPICS IN REGRESSION ANALYSIS

3.1 METHOD OF GENERALIZED LEAST SQUARES

In practical applications of regression analysis the basic assumptions made in Sec. 2.1 concerning ϵ and X in the regression model are often not satisfied. We therefore relax the assumptions concerning ϵ and X in turn and introduce statistical methods to deal with the new situations. Some topics are treated here more briefly than in other texts because when the basic ideas are understood, the reader can easily study the topics independently. It is not necessary to cover all the topics before studying Chap. 4.

First, we relax the assumption that the ϵ_i are independent and have identical variances. The simplest case to examine is when the covariance matrix of the vector ϵ of n residuals is known. The model is

$$y = X\beta + \epsilon \qquad \begin{matrix} E\epsilon = 0 \\ E\epsilon\epsilon' = V\sigma^2 \end{matrix} \qquad (1)$$

where V^{-1} is assumed to exist and σ^2 is a scalar. If we scale the matrix V to make tr $V = n$ (tr V being the trace, or the sum of the diagonal elements, of V), then the average of the diagonal elements of $V\sigma^2$ is σ^2; σ^2 is the average of the variances of the residuals. For $V = I$ model (1) reduces to the standard linear regression model.

Let (1) be premultiplied by an $n \times n$ matrix P

$$Py = PX\beta + P\epsilon \qquad (2)$$

This can be interpreted as a regression model with Py as a vector of dependent variables, PX as a matrix of k new explanatory variables, and $P\epsilon$ as a vector of residuals. The covariance matrix of $P\epsilon$ is

$$EP\epsilon\epsilon'P = PVP'\sigma^2 \tag{3}$$

Therefore, if P is chosen so as to make $PVP' = I$, (2) becomes a standard regression model and the least-squares estimator of β will have its optimal properties as discussed in Chap. 2. The matrix P should satisfy

$$V = P^{-1}P'^{-1} \quad \text{or} \quad V^{-1} = (P^{-1}P'^{-1})^{-1} = P'P \tag{4}$$

V^{-1} is symmetric positive definite because V is assumed to be. Let B be an $n \times n$ matrix whose columns are the characteristic vectors of V^{-1}

$$V^{-1}B = BD \quad \text{or} \quad V^{-1} = BDB' = BD^{1/2}D^{1/2}B' \tag{5}$$

where D is a diagonal matrix consisting of the characteristic roots of V^{-1} and $B' = B^{-1}$. Thus if we let

$$P = D^{1/2}B' \tag{6}$$

we shall have $P'P = V^{-1}$, satisfying condition (4).

The method of least squares can be applied to model (2) to yield

$$\hat{\beta} = [(PX)'(PX)]^{-1}(PX)'(Py) = (X'P'PX)^{-1}X'P'Py$$
$$= (X'V^{-1}X)^{-1}X'V^{-1}y \tag{7}$$

which is Aitken's generalized least-squares (GLS) estimator of vector β in regression model (1). The covariance matrix of $\hat{\beta}$ is $(X'V^{-1}X)^{-1}\sigma^2$. The GLS estimator is best linear unbiased since it is the least-squares estimator of the standard linear regression model (2) involving the transformed variables Py, PX, and $P\epsilon$. If ϵ is normal, the GLS estimator will be best unbiased, as can be shown by applying the Cramer-Rao inequality. We can also apply the statistical tests developed for the least-squares estimator b in Chap. 2 by using the transformed variables Py and PX (see Probs. 1 to 3). When $P \neq I$, the least-squares estimator $b = (X'X)^{-1}X'y$ is still linear unbiased but its covariance matrix will be larger than that of the GLS estimator. Following are three examples of model (1) with a special structure for the matrix V to which the method of GLS can be applied.

Example 1 This is a multiple linear regression model where the residuals ϵ_i are independent but have different variances σ_i^2. Thus V is a diagonal matrix. In statistical terminology, the assumption of homoscedasticity (equal variances) in the standard regression model is replaced by the assumption of *heteroscedasticity* (unequal variances). It might be reasonable to assume that the standard deviation of ϵ_i is proportional to the mean of y_i, that is,

$$\sigma_i = c(\beta_1 x_{i1} + \beta_2 x_{i2} + \cdots + \beta_k x_{ik}) \tag{8}$$

If σ_i^2 are known, the covariance matrix $E\epsilon\epsilon' = V\sigma^2$ is a known diagonal matrix with σ_i^2 along the diagonal. The method of GLS can be applied to estimate β. If

σ_i^2 are not known, one can apply the method of least squares to obtain consistent estimators of $\beta_1, \ldots, \beta_k$ and thus consistent estimates of σ_i^2 using (8), except for a factor of proportionality. These estimates can be used to compute an approximate GLS estimate of β.

Example 2 This example results from the assumption that the residual ϵ_i obey a first-order autoregressive model

$$\epsilon_i = a\epsilon_{i-1} + u_i \tag{9}$$

where the u_i are independent, each having variance v. When the variables of a linear regression model are time-series observations, (9) is often a reasonable model for its residual because the residual, which summarizes the combined effect of omitted explanatory variables, can be serially correlated and (9) is the simplest model to represent serial correlation. To find the elements of the matrix $V\sigma^2$ one must evaluate $E\epsilon_i\epsilon_{i-k}$ ($k \geq 0$). By repeated substitutions for the explanatory variable on the right-hand side of (9) we write

$$\epsilon_i = u_i + au_{i-1} + a^2 u_{i-2} + \cdots + a^k u_{i-k} + a^{k+1} u_{i-k-1} + \cdots \tag{10}$$

Using (10) for ϵ_i and a similar expression for ϵ_{i-k}, given $Eu_i u_j = 0$ for $i \neq j$, we have

$$E\epsilon_i\epsilon_{i-k} = E(a^k u_{i-k}^2 + a^{k+2} u_{i-k-1}^2 + a^{k+4} u_{i-k-2}^2 + \cdots)$$
$$= a^k v(1 + a^2 + a^4 + \cdots) \tag{11}$$

Under the necessary and sufficient condition $|a| < 1$, (11) becomes

$$E\epsilon_i\epsilon_{i-k} = \frac{a^k v}{1 - a^2} \equiv \gamma_k \qquad k \geq 0 \tag{12}$$

This is the *autocovariance function* for ϵ_i; it gives the covariance between ϵ_i and ϵ_{i-k} as a function of the lag k. Under the assumption $|a| < 1$, the autocovariance function γ_k is a function of k and not of i; in this case the time series ϵ_i is said to be *covariance-stationary*. The autocovariance function has the property $\gamma_k = \gamma_{-k}$. Setting $k = 0$ in (12), we have the variance

$$E\epsilon_i^2 = \gamma_0 = \frac{v}{1 - a^2} \tag{13}$$

The *autocorrelation function* for a covariance-stationary time series ϵ_i is

$$\rho_k = \frac{\text{Cov}(\epsilon_i, \epsilon_{i-k})}{\sqrt{\text{Var}\,\epsilon_i\,\text{Var}\,\epsilon_k}} = \frac{\gamma_k}{\gamma_0} \tag{14}$$

For model (9), $\rho_k = a^k = \rho_{-k}$ for $k \geq 0$.

To construct the matrix V for model (1), we know that if the residual ϵ_i is covariance-stationary, the diagonal elements of V are equal; they are equal to 1 by the normalization rule $\text{tr}\,V = n$. Therefore, the ijth element of V is γ_{i-j}/γ_0 or

$\rho_{i-j} = a^{i-j}$ for $i - j \geq 0$. If we know the coefficient a of model (9), the matrix V is known,

$$V = \begin{bmatrix} 1 & a & a^2 & \cdots & a^{n-1} \\ a & 1 & a & \cdots & a^{n-2} \\ & & \cdots & & \\ a^{n-1} & a^{n-2} & a^{n-3} & \cdots & 1 \end{bmatrix} \tag{15}$$

The method of GLS can be applied to estimate β in model (1). If a is unknown, one can apply least squares to estimate β by b. The residuals ϵ_i can be estimated by

$$e_i = y_i - b_1 x_{i1} - \cdots - b_k x_{ik}$$

Then e_i will be regressed on e_{i-1} to obtain the least-squares estimate $\hat{a}$ of a. One can use $\hat{a}$ for a in (15) to compute an approximate GLS estimator of β in model (1).

In the above procedure, b is a consistent estimator of β under fairly weak conditions (see Prob. 5). In fact $\hat{a} = \sum_{i=1}^{n} e_i e_{i-1} / \sum_i e_{i-1}^2$, where we let $e_0 = 0$, is a consistent estimator of a. To prove this assertion, we first observe that regressing ϵ_i on ϵ_{i-1} will yield a consistent estimate of a, that is,

$$\operatorname*{plim}_{n \to \infty} \frac{\sum_{i=1}^{n} \epsilon_i \epsilon_{i-1}}{\sum_{i=1}^{n} \epsilon_{i-1}^2} = \frac{\operatorname{plim} \sum_i \epsilon_i \epsilon_{i-1}}{\operatorname{plim} \sum_i \epsilon_{i-1}^2} = \frac{E \epsilon_i \epsilon_{i-1}}{E \epsilon_i^2} = \frac{\gamma_1}{\gamma_0} = a \tag{16}$$

Because the ϵ_i are not independent, one cannot simply apply the law of large numbers to state that the sample moments $n^{-1} \sum_i \epsilon_i \epsilon_{i-1}$ and $n^{-1} \sum_i \epsilon_{i-1}^2$ converge in probability to the population moments. A proof of the validity of this statement, which justifies the second equality sign of (16), is left as an exercise (Prob. 6).

Second, we shall prove that $\operatorname{plim} \left(n^{-1} \sum_i e_i e_{i-1} \right) = \operatorname{plim} \left(n^{-1} \sum_i \epsilon_i \epsilon_{i-1} \right)$. Let B be an $n \times n$ matrix whose first row consists of all zeros and whose ith row consists of a 1 in the $(i-1)$th position and 0's elsewhere, for $i \geq 2$. Thus $B\epsilon$ is a vector consisting of $0, \epsilon_1, \epsilon_2, \ldots, \epsilon_{n-1}$. In the proof the initial ϵ_0 is set equal to zero because one observation does not affect the results. We write $n^{-1} \sum_i e_i e_{i-1}$ as

$$n^{-1} e' B e = n^{-1} \epsilon'[I - X(X'X)^{-1}X'] B[I - X(X'X)^{-1}X']\epsilon$$
$$= n^{-1} \epsilon' B \epsilon - n^{-1} \epsilon' X(X'X)^{-1}X' B \epsilon - n^{-1} \epsilon' B X(X'X)^{-1}X'\epsilon$$
$$+ n^{-1} \epsilon' X(X'X)^{-1}X' B X(X'X)^{-1}X'\epsilon \tag{17}$$

Following the proof of the consistency of s^2 at the end of Sec. 2.13, one can show that the last three terms of (17) have zero as their probability limits. Therefore the probability limit of (17) equals the probability limit of the first term, which is γ_1 by (16). Similarly, $\operatorname{plim} \left(n^{-1} \sum_i e_i^2 \right) = \operatorname{plim} \left(n^{-1} \sum_i \epsilon_i^2 \right)$, and the consistency of $\hat{a}$ is proved.

Example 3 Consider the model consisting of a system of seemingly unrelated regression equations introduced by Zellner (1962). Let there be a set of m regression models, and let n observations on model j be represented by

$$y_j = X_j \beta_j + \epsilon_j \qquad E\epsilon_j \epsilon_j' = \sigma_j^2 I \tag{18}$$

where y_j is $n \times 1$, X_j is $n \times k_j$, and β_j is $k_j \times 1$. These equations can be stacked to form a combined regression model

$$\begin{bmatrix} y_1 \\ y_2 \\ \vdots \\ y_m \end{bmatrix} = \begin{bmatrix} X_1 & 0 & \cdots & 0 \\ 0 & X_2 & \cdots & 0 \\ & & \ddots & \\ 0 & 0 & \cdots & X_m \end{bmatrix} \begin{bmatrix} \beta_1 \\ \beta_2 \\ \vdots \\ \beta_m \end{bmatrix} + \begin{bmatrix} \epsilon_1 \\ \epsilon_2 \\ \vdots \\ \epsilon_m \end{bmatrix} \tag{19}$$

Assume that the residuals in different regression equations are correlated, with $E\epsilon_i \epsilon_j' = \sigma_{ij} I$ ($\sigma_{ii} \equiv \sigma_i^2$). In practice this will be the case when the set of m dependent variables is affected by some common factors not explicitly included in the explanatory variables. The covariance matrix of the residual vector of (19) is then

$$\sigma^2 V = \begin{bmatrix} \sigma_{11} I & \sigma_{12} I & \cdots & \sigma_{1m} I \\ \sigma_{12} I & \sigma_{22} I & \cdots & \sigma_{2m} I \\ & & \cdots & \\ \sigma_{1m} I & \sigma_{2m} I & \cdots & \sigma_{mm} I \end{bmatrix} = \Sigma \otimes I \tag{20}$$

where $\Sigma = (\sigma_{ij})$ and $\otimes$ denotes the Kronecker product, an operation defined by (20).

   If Σ is known, (20) can be used to form a GLS estimator for $\beta_1, \ldots, \beta_m$ which is best linear unbiased. If least squares is applied to each equation separately, the covariance matrix for $b_1, \ldots, b_m$ is larger than that of the above GLS estimator, on account of the optimum property of the latter. If Σ is unknown, the vectors e_i of residuals from the least-squares regressions can be used to form consistent estimates $n^{-1} e_i' e_j$ of σ_{ij}. Hence the covariance matrix (20) can be consistently estimated to form an approximate GLS estimator for $\beta_1, \ldots, \beta_m$.

★ 3.2 ASYMPTOTIC DISTRIBUTION OF THE GLS ESTIMATOR

In the three examples of the last section some consistent estimate of V in model (1) was substituted for V in the GLS formula to form an approximate GLS estimator. How do such approximations affect the sampling distributions of the estimators? Let us consider the asymptotic distribution of the GLS estimator for β in model (1) when ϵ is not necessarily normal.

   Consider first the case of known V. Model (1) is identical with model (2) after a transformation of variables. By treating the new variables Py, PX, and $P\epsilon$ in model (2) one can apply the results of Sec. 2.13 to the distribution of the GLS estimator of model (1). It was shown there that for a standard multiple regression model if the elements of the residual vector are independent and have identical variances σ^2, and if the explanatory variables satisfy $n^{-1}X'X \to Q$, where Q is positive definite, the least-squares LS estimator b will be asymptotically normal, the covariance matrix of the limiting distribution of $\sqrt{n}(b - \beta)$ being $Q^{-1}\sigma^2$. This result can be applied directly to the present case. For model (1), if the elements of $P\epsilon$ are independent and if

$$n^{-1}(PX)'PX = n^{-1}X'V^{-1}X \to Q \tag{21}$$

the GLS estimator

$$\hat{\beta} = (X'V^{-1}X)^{-1}X'V^{-1}y$$

is asymptotically normal, the covariance matrix of the limiting distribution of $\sqrt{n}(\hat{\beta} - \beta)$ being $Q^{-1}\sigma^2$. The proof is found in Sec. 2.13, where the variable X is now replaced by PX and the variable ϵ by $P\epsilon$.

If V is unknown and some consistent estimate $\hat{V}$ replaces V in $\hat{\beta}$, consistency meaning that each element of the expanding $n \times n$ matrix V is estimated consistently, the asymptotic distribution of the approximate GLS estimator

$$\hat{\beta}_n = (X'\hat{V}^{-1}X)^{-1}X'\hat{V}^{-1}y \tag{22}$$

can be investigated by using the following theorem.

Theorem 3.1 $\hat{\beta}_n$ has the same limiting distribution as $\hat{\beta}$ if

(i) plim $n^{-1}X'(\hat{V}^{-1} - V^{-1})X = 0$

and

(ii) plim $n^{-1/2}X'(\hat{V}^{-1} - V^{-1})\epsilon = 0$

PROOF We consider the limiting distributions of

$$\sqrt{n}(\hat{\beta} - \beta) = (n^{-1}X'V^{-1}X)^{-1}n^{-1/2}X'V^{-1}\epsilon$$

and $\qquad \sqrt{n}(\hat{\beta}_n - \beta) = (n^{-1}X'\hat{V}^{-1}X)^{-1}n^{-1/2}X'\hat{V}^{-1}\epsilon$

The difference between these two sequences of random vectors is $\sqrt{n}(\hat{\beta}_n - \hat{\beta})$. The probability limit of this difference is zero if assumptions (i) and (ii) hold. The theorem is proved by appealing to the rule that if the difference between two sequences has zero as the probability limit and if one sequence has a limiting distribution, the other sequence will have the same limiting distribution.

Let us apply Theorem 3.1 to study the asymptotic distribution of the approximate GLS estimator for the coefficient vector in the model of seemingly unrelated regressions, following Theil (1971). The covariance matrix $\Sigma = (\sigma_{ij})$ in this model is estimated by

$$S = (s_{ij}) = (n^{-1}e_i'e_j) \tag{23}$$

where $\qquad e_i = y_i - X_i(X_i'X_i)^{-1}X_i'y_i = [I - X_i(X_i'X_i)^{-1}X_i']\epsilon_i$

Following the proof of the consistency of s_{ii} at the end of Sec. 2.13, one can prove the consistency of s_{ij} $(i \neq j)$ (see Prob. 7). Matrix V is estimated by $\hat{V} = S \otimes I$. To check condition (i) of the theorem, we examine the ijth submatrix of $n^{-1}X'(\hat{V}^{-1} - V^{-1})X$, which can be written as

$$(s^{ij} - \sigma^{ij})n^{-1}X_i'X_j$$

where s^{ij} is the ijth element of S^{-1} and we have used the rule $(S \otimes A)^{-1} = S^{-1} \otimes A^{-1}$. The probability limit of this submatrix is zero since plim $(s^{ij} - \sigma^{ij}) = 0$ and lim $n^{-1}X_i'X_j$ is assumed to exist.

To check condition (ii) of the theorem, we examine the ith subvector of $n^{-1/2}X'(\hat{V}^{-1} - V^{-1})\epsilon$, which can be written as

$$n^{-1/2} \sum_{j=1}^{m} (s^{ij} - \sigma^{ij})X_i'\epsilon_j$$

The probability limit of this subvector is zero since plim $(s^{ij} - \sigma^{ij}) = 0$ and the vector $n^{-1/2}X_i'\epsilon_j$ has a limiting normal distribution by the argument of Sec. 2.13. Hence the approximate GLS estimator has the same limiting distribution as the GLS estimator for the model of seemingly unrelated regressions. This result was originally shown by Zellner (1962) using a different proof.

For the regression model with first-order autoregressive residuals, the matrix $V = (P'P)^{-1}$ was given by (15). One can easily check that in this case

$$V^{-1} = P'P = \frac{1}{1-a^2} \begin{bmatrix} 1 & -a & 0 & \cdots & 0 & 0 \\ -a & 1+a^2 & -a & & 0 & 0 \\ 0 & -a & 1+a^2 & & 0 & 0 \\ & & & \ddots & & \\ 0 & 0 & 0 & \cdots & 1+a^2 & -a \\ 0 & 0 & 0 & \cdots & -a & 1 \end{bmatrix} \quad (24)$$

and $\qquad P = (1-a^2)^{-1/2} \begin{bmatrix} \sqrt{1-a^2} & 0 & 0 & \cdots & 0 & 0 \\ -a & 1 & 0 & \cdots & 0 & 0 \\ 0 & -a & 1 & \cdots & 0 & 0 \\ & & & \ddots & & \\ 0 & 0 & 0 & \cdots & 1 & 0 \\ 0 & 0 & 0 & \cdots & -a & 1 \end{bmatrix} \quad (25)$

If the transformation P is applied to the data y and X, the ith element of the vector Py is $y_i - ay_{i-1}$ and the ith observation of the jth transformed explanatory variable is $x_{ij} - ax_{i-1,j}$, except for the first observation, which will be ignored in a discussion of the limiting distribution of the approximate GLS estimator. We showed in Sec. 3.1 that $\hat{a} = \left(\sum_i e_i e_{i-1}\right)/\left(\sum_i e_{i-1}^2\right)$ is a consistent estimator of a, where e_i are the least-squares residuals.

Condition (i) of Theorem 3.1 will be fulfilled if each element of $n^{-1}X'\hat{V}^{-1}X$ or

$$(n - 1)^{-1} \sum_{i=2}^{n} (x_{ij} - \hat{a}x_{i-1,j})(x_{im} - \hat{a}x_{i-1,m}) \qquad j, m = 1, \ldots, k$$

has the same probability limit as the corresponding expression with $\hat{a}$ replaced by a. This is the case if $(n - 1)^{-1} \sum_i x_{ij} x_{i-1,m}$ and $(n - 1)^{-1} \sum_i x_{ij} x_{im}$ approach finite limits for all $j, m = 1, \ldots, k$ as n increases. Condition (ii) is fulfilled since, for $j = 1, \ldots, m$, each element of $n^{-1/2}X'(\hat{V}^{-1} - V^{-1})\epsilon$ or

$$(n - 1)^{-1/2} \sum_{i=2}^{n} [(x_{ij} - \hat{a}x_{i-1,j})(\epsilon_i - \hat{a}\epsilon_{i-1}) - (x_{ij} - ax_{i-1,j})(\epsilon_i - a\epsilon_{i-1})] \quad (26)$$

can be shown to have zero as its probability limit (see Prob. 8). Hence the approximate GLS estimator has the same asymptotic distribution as the GLS estimator for a regression model with first-order autoregressive residuals. This approximate GLS estimator is sometimes called a feasible GLS estimator.

★3.3 ANALYSIS OF REGRESSION RESIDUALS

After a regression equation has been estimated, nothing is more important than a careful analysis of the estimated residuals. Such an analysis helps detect possible defects of the model and may suggest an improved respecification. For example, an important explanatory variable may be omitted. If the residuals are plotted against this variable and an obvious association is observed, this variable can be added as an additional explanatory variable. In regressions involving time-series data, one such variable is time itself. If the residuals show a trend, a time trend can be added; however, a trend variable is often found to be statistically significant because it is correlated with some omitted economic variables. It would be preferable to uncover those variables and include them in the regression instead. As another possibility, the residuals may be seen to be serially correlated. If so, some autoregressive process may be introduced to explain them. As a third possibility, the residuals may be far from normal, and some method of estimating the regression equation other than least squares may be appropriate, as discussed in Sec. 3.4. When plotted against the regression function (or the estimated value of y), the residuals can signify the existence of heteroscedasticity if the variance of y is related to its mean. When plotted against one explanatory variable, they may reveal a nonlinear relationship between the dependent variable and that explanatory variable. More importantly, one or two observations of that explanatory variable could account for a significant t ratio; these observations might be outliers or recording errors. In the diagram, most observations might scatter randomly, with one or two points very far from the scatter, which can account for a significant partial relation between y_i and x_{ij}. Seeing such a relation, the econometrician might choose to omit these observations or use a more robust method of estimation, as discussed in Sec. 3.4.

To test for first-order serial correlation of the regression residuals e_i the statistic proposed by Durbin and Watson (1950, 1951) can be used. It is defined as

$$d = \frac{\sum_{i=1}^{n-1} (e_{i+1} - e_i)^2}{\sum_{i=1}^{n} e_i^2} \tag{27}$$

If successive residuals are positively correlated, the numerator of d will tend to be small, compared with when they are uncorrelated. In the latter case, the numerator

$$\sum_{i=1}^{n-1} (e_{i+1} - e_i)^2 = \sum_{i=1}^{n-1} e_{i+1}^2 + \sum_{i=1}^{n-1} e_i^2 - 2 \sum_{i=1}^{n-1} e_{i+1} e_i$$

should be, on the average, approximately twice the denominator $\sum_{i=1}^{n} e_i^2$, since the cross-product term has zero expectation. A value of the Durbin-Watson statistic near 2 therefore suggests the absence of serial correlation. A much smaller value would suggest positive serial correlation, while a much larger value would suggest negative serial correlation. However, the distribution of d under the null hypothesis of no serial correlation depends on the nature of the explanatory variables and cannot be tabulated independently. Durbin and Watson (1950) have given bounds to the distribution. Given the level of significance, if d turns out to be smaller than d_L as tabulated, reject the null hypothesis of no positive serial correlation. If d is larger than d_U, accept the null hypothesis. If d falls between d_L and d_U, the test is inconclusive. Nerlove and Wallis (1966) point out that if lagged dependent variables appear in the regression, the statistic d tends toward 2 and thus the test has low power [see part (b) of Prob. 10]. To remedy this, Durbin (1970a) suggests using

$$h = \left(1 - \frac{d}{2}\right) \sqrt{\frac{n}{1 - n\hat{V}(b_1)}}$$

where $\hat{V}(b_1)$ is the estimate of the variance of the coefficient of y_{t-1} given by least-squares analysis, and testing h as a standard normal deviate. Generalizations to testing for higher-order serial correlations have been treated by Wallis (1972) and Godfrey (1978).

To test for heteroscedasticity Goldfeld and Quandt (1965) have suggested partitioning the n observations into two groups with n_1 and n_2 observations, respectively, and estimating separate regressions for the two groups. The sum of squared residuals of the ith group ($i = 1, 2$) divided by the true residual variance σ_i^2 will be distributed as $\chi^2(n_i - k)$. The ratio of the two sums of squares each divided by its number of degrees of freedom will therefore be distributed as $F(n_1 - k, n_2 - k)$ under the null hypothesis that the residual variances of the two groups are equal. When n is even, one can let $n_1 = n_2 = \frac{1}{2}n$. When n is odd, one can omit the middle observation and let $n_1 = n_2 = \frac{1}{2}(n - 1)$. If one suspects that the variance is an increasing function of certain explanatory variables or of the mean of y, the observations can be divided accordingly.

To detect possible violation of the normality assumption, the residuals can be tabulated in a histogram. The observed frequencies O_i in different intervals can be compared with the expected frequencies E_i from a normal distribution with mean zero and variance s^2. Let there be m intervals. The statistic $\sum_{i=1}^{m} (O_i - E_i)^2/E_i$ will be distributed asymptotically as $\chi^2(m - 1)$ as the sample size n increases. A simpler alternative is to plot the empirical cumulative distribution of the residuals on normal-probability paper and examine visually whether the points form an approximately straight line. White and MacDonald (1980) have examined various tests of normality of regression residuals, some based on the third and fourth moments of the empirical distribution of the residuals. Sometimes the normality assumption is violated because of the existence of extreme observations, a few observations lying along the tails of the distribution. In such situations, methods other than least squares should be used to fit the regression, as discussed in Sec. 3.4.

In the above discussion it has been taken for granted that the residuals to be used in various tests are the residuals from an equation estimated by the method of least squares. The least-squares residual vector e is best linear unbiased, in the sense of having the smallest covariance matrix for $e - \epsilon$ among the linear estimators Cy which satisfy $E(Cy - \epsilon) = 0$. To show this, consider the restriction imposed upon a linear unbiased estimator

$$E(Cy) = EC(X\beta + \epsilon) = CX\beta = 0$$

The implication is that

$$CX = 0 \qquad (28)$$

Given (28), the linear unbiased estimator can be written equivalently as

$$Cy = C\epsilon = Ce \qquad (29)$$

since $y = X\beta + \epsilon = Xb + e$.

For the least-squares residual vector e, $C = I - X(X'X)^{-1}X' \equiv M$, and the covariance matrix of the estimation error $e - \epsilon$ is

$$\text{Cov}\,(e - \epsilon) = \text{Cov}\,(M\epsilon - \epsilon) = E(M - I)\epsilon\epsilon'(M - I)$$

$$= (MM - M - M + I)\sigma^2 = (I - M)\sigma^2 = X(X'X)^{-1}X'\sigma^2 \qquad (30)$$

Any linear unbiased estimator can be written as $(M + B)y = (M + B)\epsilon$ on account of (29). The covariance matrix of its estimation error is

$$\text{Cov}\,[(M + B)\epsilon - \epsilon] = \text{Cov}\,[B - X(X'X)^{-1}X']\epsilon$$

$$= [B - X(X'X)^{-1}X'][B' - X(X'X)^{-1}X']\sigma^2$$

$$= BB'\sigma^2 + X(X'X)^{-1}X'\sigma^2 \qquad (31)$$

where the last equality sign has made use of $BX = 0$, which is a consequence of $(M + B)X = 0$ and $MX = 0$. The difference between (31) and (30) is a positive-definite matrix $BB'\sigma^2$ unless $B = 0$.

★ Theil's BLUS Residuals

Although the least-squares residual vector e is best linear unbiased, its covariance matrix

$$Eee' = EM\epsilon\epsilon'M = M\sigma^2 \tag{32}$$

is not of the form I times a scalar (called a *scalar matrix*) as assumed for the vector ϵ. To ensure this, Theil (1971, chap. 5) proposed an estimator of ϵ which is best linear unbiased and has a scalar covariance matrix (BLUS). In order for a linear unbiased estimator $Cy = C\epsilon = Ce$ to have a scalar covariance matrix

$$\text{Cov } C\epsilon = EC\epsilon\epsilon'C' = CC'\sigma^2$$

one must impose an additional restriction

$$CC' = I \tag{33}$$

The restriction (28), with X having k columns, is a set of k linear restrictions on the columns of C. Therefore, the rank of C cannot exceed $n - k$. We thus let C be an $(n - k) \times n$ matrix and Cy be an estimator of only $n - k$ components of ϵ. Accordingly Theil partitions the standard regression model as

$$\begin{bmatrix} y_0 \\ y_1 \end{bmatrix} = \begin{bmatrix} X_0 \\ X_1 \end{bmatrix} \beta + \begin{bmatrix} \epsilon_0 \\ \epsilon_1 \end{bmatrix} = \begin{bmatrix} X_0 \\ X_1 \end{bmatrix} b + \begin{bmatrix} e_0 \\ e_1 \end{bmatrix} \tag{34}$$

where X_0 is a nonsingular $k \times k$ matrix and X_1 is an $(n - k) \times k$ matrix. The linear estimator can be written as

$$Ce = C_0 e_0 + C_1 e_1 \tag{35}$$

C_1 being $(n - k) \times (n - k)$. Using $X_0' e_0 + X_1' e_1 = 0$, we have

$$e_0 = -(X_1 X_0^{-1})'e_1 = -Z'e_1$$

where $Z = X_1 X_0^{-1}$. Then using $C_0 X_0 + C_1 X_1 = 0$, we have

$$C_0 = -C_1 X_1 X_0^{-1} = -C_1 Z$$

Thus (35) becomes

$$Ce = (-C_1 Z)(-Z'e_1) + C_1 e_1 = C_1(I + ZZ')e_1 \tag{36}$$

The constraint (33) for a scalar covariance matrix yields

$$C_0 C_0' + C_1 C_1' = C_1 ZZ'C_1' + C_1 C_1' = C_1(I + ZZ')C_1' = I \tag{37}$$

The linear estimator is alternatively written as

$$C_0 \epsilon_0 + C_1 \epsilon_1 = -C_1 Z\epsilon_0 + C_1 \epsilon_1 \tag{38}$$

The vector of errors in using (38) to estimate ϵ_1 has a covariance matrix

$$\text{Cov } [-C_1 Z\epsilon_0 + (C_1 - I)\epsilon_1] = \sigma^2[C_1(I + ZZ')C_1' + I - C_1 - C_1'] \tag{39}$$

To find the matrix C_1 in the estimator (36) which minimizes the trace of (39), adopting Theil's definition of "best," subject to the constraint (37) for a scalar covariance matrix, Chow (1976) proposed forming the Lagrangian expression

$$L = \text{tr}\,[C_1(I + ZZ')C_1' + I - C_1 - C_1'] - \text{tr}\,N[C_1(I + ZZ')C_1' - I] \quad (40)$$

where N is a symmetric $(n - k) \times (n - k)$ matrix of Lagrange multipliers, and differentiating with respect to C_1. Using the differentiation rule $[\partial\,\text{tr}\,(AB)]/\partial A = B'$, we have

$$\frac{\partial L}{\partial C_1} = 2C_1(I + ZZ') - 2I - 2NC_1(I + ZZ') = 0 \quad (41)$$

To solve Eqs. (41) and (37) for the two unknowns C_1 and N we postmultiply (41) by C_1' and use (37) to obtain

$$N = I - C_1' \quad (42)$$

Substituting (42) for N in (41) gives

$$C_1'C_1(I + ZZ') = I \quad (43)$$

Since C_1 is symmetric because N in (42) is symmetric, (43) implies that $C_1^2 = (I + ZZ')^{-1}$ or

$$C_1 = (I + ZZ')^{-1/2} \quad (44)$$

which is the solution.

Theil has written the solution in the form of $C_1 = PDP'$, where P is a matrix consisting of the characteristic vectors of $I + ZZ'$ corresponding to the roots d_i^{-2} and D is diagonal with elements d_i so that $I + ZZ' = PD^{-2}P'$; see Theil (1971) for further treatment of this topic. Note that in testing for serial correlation in small samples the use of the BLUS residuals has been found by Abrahamse and Koerts (1969) to involve some loss of power compared with the Durbin-Watson test employing least-squares residuals. On the other hand, a BLUS residual vector can be used to test the disturbances for normality, homoscedasticity, and linearity in one or more explanatory variables.

3.4 ROBUST ESTIMATORS

If the distributions of the residuals ϵ_i have much thicker tails than the normal distribution, the method of least squares can be improved upon. Minimizing the sum of *squares* of the observed residuals gives lots of weight to large deviations, positive or negative, according to the squares of these deviations. It may be better, for example, to minimize the sum of the *absolute values* of the observed residuals in estimating the regression coefficients. When the distribution of the residuals is long-tailed, this estimator will have a smaller variance than the least-squares estimator. According to the Gauss-Markov theorem, the method of least squares is best linear unbiased if the ϵ_i are identically and independently distributed with variance σ^2. It may happen that the variance of ϵ_i does not exist. Even when the conditions of the Gauss-Markov theorem prevail, it applies only to linear estimators, and the estimator obtained by minimizing the sum of absolute deviations is not linear in y. If ϵ_i are normal, the least-squares estimator is best unbiased, as shown by using the Cramer-Rao inequality. This is not necessarily true if ϵ_i are not normal.

Since the regression function is the mean of y, the problem of estimating a regression function is reduced to the problem of estimating a mean, in the special case when the matrix X consists of a column of 1s. A robust method is one that provides an estimator with good sampling properties under a variety of conditions for the parent population, although it may not be quite as good as least squares for a truly normal population. Robust estimation of the mean has been the subject of study by Andrews et al. (1972). In fact, for some skewed distributions, the population mean may not be as useful for measuring central tendency as some other parameters, e.g., the median. To estimate the mean one can use the method of least squares, which yields the sample mean, or one can minimize the sum of absolute deviations, or one can use other robust estimators which avoid giving too much weight to extreme observations. A robust estimator is defined by specifying the weight it gives to extreme observations. A robust weighting scheme useful for estimating the mean can be applied to the weighting of residuals and thus to the estimation of regression coefficients.

One way to reduce the weight given to large residuals is to formulate the problem as one of weighted regression. For example, to minimize the sum of the absolute values of the residuals e_i is to minimize the sum $\sum_i e_i^2/|e_i|$. The weight w_i to be applied to e_i in the weighted-regression problem is simply $|e_i|^{-1/2}$. Although the weight depends on the value of e_i itself, one may choose to iterate by using a previous value of e_i in the weight for the weighted regression in the current iteration. This method breaks down if a previous value of e_i is zero, in which case one may choose to replace it by a small number. In finding alternative weighting functions one important idea, due to Huber (1964), is to replace e_i^2 in the function $\sum_i e_i^2$ to be minimized in the method of least squares by some function $\rho(e_i)$.

Denote the derivative of $\rho(e_i)$ by $\psi(e_i)$. Several of these ψ functions have been suggested. For example, Huber (1964) originally suggested

$$\psi(e; k) = \begin{cases} -k & e < -k \\ e & -k < e < k \\ k & e > k \end{cases}$$

where k may be a certain multiple of a robust measure of dispersion of e_i. Robust measures of dispersion include the interquartile range and the median absolute deviation. Integrating the above ψ function, one finds the weighting function

$$\rho(e; k) = \begin{cases} -ke & e < -k \\ \frac{1}{2}e^2 & -k < e < k \\ ke & e > k \end{cases}$$

When $k = \infty$, the method employing the above weighting function is the method of least squares; when k is very small, it is the method of least absolute residuals. See Andrews et al. (1972, pp. 11–16, 41–44) for suggestions of other ψ functions. Numerous Monte Carlo and analytical studies have been conducted to investigate the sampling distributions of various robust estimators.

The objective of using a robust estimator is to reduce the influence of extreme observations on the estimated regression. A related subject is the search for methods of detecting influential observations and outliers in a regression analysis. Some of the extreme observations may be deleted. The influences of each observation on the regression coefficients, the t statistics, the estimated values of y, and the regression residuals can be ascertained by omitting the observation in question. The influences of a set of observations can also be investigated; see Belsley, Kuh, and Welsch (1980).

★3.5 BAYESIAN ESTIMATION

We now turn from the problems of ill-behaved residuals to the problems connected with poor data on the explanatory variables. If the k columns of the X matrix are linearly dependent, in the sense that one column can be expressed as a linear combination of other columns, the rank of the matrix $X'X$ is less than k. The formula $(X'X)^{-1}X'y$ for b cannot be evaluated because $(X'X)^{-1}$ does not exist. If the columns of X are not exactly linearly dependent but nearly so, the determinant of $X'X$ is nearly zero and the matrix $(X'X)^{-1}$ will have very large diagonal elements. The variances of the least-squares estimators of the regression coefficients will be very large, making the estimates almost useless. One remedy for this situation is to introduce prior information concerning the regression coefficients. Bayesian methods provide one approach to introducing prior information on unknown parameters.

Although the systematic use of prior information is an important Bayesian trait, some orthodox Bayesian statisticians may object to the way Bayesian statistics is introduced in this text. To them, Bayesian methods are not merely a set of tools which can be selected from among other useful tools; since in their view there is only one correct way of doing statistics, the Bayesian way, Bayesian logic should be discussed in the first chapter of any text. From the basic Bayesian logic all statistical methods should follow. It was a significant accomplishment for Savage (1954) to lay the foundations of statistics in Bayesian terms. Savage starts with a set of seven postulates of rational human behavior under uncertainty and deduces from them a theory of statistical decision. Among others, he interprets the probability of an event as a personal degree of belief rather than as a relative frequency in the long run (however defined) or as a logical necessity, although a believer of the frequency view of probability may accept Bayesian methods. For the philosophically inclined, it is certainly satisfying to be able to answer questions on the foundations of probability and statistics. Like a physicist who talks physics without dwelling on the philosophy of science or the justification of inductive inference, the author of this text has chosen not to dwell on foundations but to present useful tools. The usefulness of the tools will ultimately be judged by how frequently they are used by practitioners. The definition of usefulness is admittedly somewhat subjective because the frequency of use is not only a historical frequency but a projected frequency of future use. It is in this spirit that Bayesian methods are introduced here. Interested readers should consult Zellner (1971) for an introduction to Bayesian methods in econometrics.

Bayesian inference concerning a vector θ of parameters makes use of the Bayes theorem

$$p(\theta \mid y) = \frac{p(y, \theta)}{p(y)} = \frac{p(y \mid \theta)p(\theta)}{\int p(y, \theta)\, d\theta} \propto p(y \mid \theta)p(\theta) \tag{45}$$

where p stands for probability density function and $p(y \mid \theta)$ is the likelihood function for θ if the data y are treated as given. $p(\theta)$ is the *prior density* of θ, which summarizes the knowledge the statistician had of θ before observing y. $p(\theta \mid y)$ is the *posterior density* of θ given the data y. The posterior density summarizes the statistician's knowledge of θ after y has been observed. It combines the information about θ from the likelihood function and the prior density. In fact, it is proportional to (indicated by the $\propto$ sign) the product of the likelihood and the prior density. The factor of proportionality is the inverse of $p(y)$, which is not a function of θ but is obtained by integrating $p(y \mid \theta)p(\theta)$ with respect to θ.

The essential steps of Bayesian inference about θ are to specify the prior density and to analyze the product of the likelihood and the prior density. (Here we assume the statistical model, and hence the likelihood function, to be given. Bayesian and non-Bayesian methods for selecting one of several models will be discussed in Chap. 9.) For example, a point estimate of θ is obtained from a measure of central tendency of the posterior distribution of θ. A confidence region is obtained by taking a region in θ space which has the highest probability according to the posterior distribution of θ. The main distinction of the Bayesian approach is the introduction of the prior density, since all statisticians extract information from the likelihood function. How to choose the prior density is an important question in Bayesian inference. If a previous statistical study is available, the posterior density from that study can serve as the prior density in the new study. Otherwise, the statistician or user must make a judicious choice. In practice, the form of the prior density is often chosen according to mathematical convenience. Given a likelihood function, a mathematically convenient prior density function is such that their product will have the same mathematical form as the prior density itself. If this is the case, the posterior density can serve as the prior density of the next investigation.

Let us illustrate with a mathematically convenient prior density for the vector β of a normal linear regression model with known σ^2. The likelihood function, with constants omitted, is

$$\exp\left[\frac{-(y - X\beta)'(y - X\beta)}{2\sigma^2}\right] = \exp\left[\frac{-(y - Xb)'(y - Xb) - (\beta - b)'X'X(\beta - b)}{2\sigma^2}\right]$$

$$\tag{46}$$

where $b = (X'X)^{-1}X'y$ and we have decomposed $y - X\beta$ into $y - Xb$ and $Xb - X\beta$ so that the sum of squares $(y - X\beta)'(y - X\beta)$ is made up of two components, the cross-product term being zero. The motivation is to be able to write the exponent of (46) as a quadratic form in $\beta - b$ plus another term, i.e., to complete the square for β, anticipating that (46) will become a part of a normal posterior density of β. Without being multiplied by a prior density of β, (46) is already a normal density function of β with mean b and covariance matrix $(X'X)^{-1}\sigma^2$ provided that the normalization constant is chosen to make the integral with respect to β equal to 1.

It is convenient to choose a prior density for β which is normal, since then the product of the prior density and the likelihood will also be normal after the terms in the exponents have been regrouped. Let the prior density of β be normal with mean b_0 and covariance matrix V_0. The product of this prior density and the likelihood (46) will have an exponent equal to $-\frac{1}{2}$ times

$$\frac{(\beta - b)'X'X(\beta - b)}{\sigma^2} + (\beta - b_0)'V_0^{-1}(\beta - b_0)$$

$$= \beta'(X'X\sigma^{-2})\beta - 2\beta'(X'X\sigma^{-2})b + b'(X'X\sigma^{-2})b$$
$$+ \beta'V_0^{-1}\beta - 2\beta'V_0^{-1}b_0 + b_0'V_0^{-1}b_0$$

$$= \beta'(X'X\sigma^{-2} + V_0^{-1})\beta - 2\beta'(X'X\sigma^{-2}b + V_0^{-1}b_0)$$
$$+ b'(X'X\sigma^{-2})b + b_0'V_0^{-1}b_0$$

$$= (\beta - b_1)'(X'X\sigma^{-2} + V_0^{-1})(\beta - b_1) + \text{terms not involving } \beta \quad (47)$$

where $\quad b_1 = (X'X\sigma^{-2} + V_0^{-1})^{-1}(X'X\sigma^{-2}b + V_0^{-1}b_0) \quad (48)$

In (47) we have completed the square in β. From the last line of (47) we conclude that the posterior density of β is normal with mean b_1 given by (48) and covariance matrix $(X'X\sigma^2 + V_0^{-1})^{-1}$ because $-\frac{1}{2}$ times the last line of (47) is the exponent of such a normal density function. Note that the mean b_1 of the posterior density function of β is a matrix-weighted average of b and b_0, the weights being the inverses of their covariance matrices.

Thus through the use of information outside the sample, in the form of a prior density function for β, one succeeds in solving the problem of the near singularity of the $X'X$ matrix. In Eq. (48) it is the matrix $\sigma^{-2}X'X + V_0^{-1}$ that has to be inverted to find the mean b_1 of the posterior density for β to serve as its point estimate. It should be noted that although the normal distribution is used in both Bayesian and non-Bayesian inferences concerning β, the interpretations are different in the two cases. In the Bayesian case, β is treated as a random variable and the statistician's knowledge about it is contained in the posterior density function. In the non-Bayesian case, β is treated as fixed though unknown, and the sampling distribution of b is used for inferences. It is not incidental that we discuss Bayesian methods after robust methods. The contrast between the two schools is interesting. The Bayesian takes pride in imposing more information in a specified manner than the classical statistician. The data analyst using robust methods tries to get away with fewer assumptions by inventing techniques that would work reasonably well under a variety of circumstances. If we imagine the classical statistician as standing somewhere near the middle of the road, we can view the Bayesian, who introduces more rules to the game, as being on the left and the data analyst, who abandons some of the classical assumptions, as standing on the right, where "left" and "right" of course have no political connotations.

In a normal linear regression model with known σ^2, the likelihood function for β is normal. If a normal prior density of β is used, the resulting posterior density will also be normal. Let us consider the problem of estimating β and $r \equiv 1/\sigma^2$ jointly. The mathematical manipulations in Bayesian inference are often simplified by considering the inverse of the variance—or of the covariance matrix as the case may be. The inverse of the covariance matrix is known as the *precision matrix*, with larger values on the diagonal showing increasing precision. For example, if we had used precision matrices instead of covariance matrices in (48), b_1 would simply be called a weighted average of b and b_0, which is much simpler to say than "inverses of the sum of inverses."

The likelihood function of β and r from a normal regression model is, by (46),

$$(2\pi)^{-n/2} r^{n/2} \exp\left[\frac{-(n-k)s^2 r}{2}\right] \exp\left[\frac{-(\beta - b)'X'X(\beta - b)r}{2}\right] \tag{49}$$

where $(n - k)s^2$ equals $(y - Xb)'(y - Xb)$. Let us construct a joint density of β and r from (49) as the product of a conditional density $g(\beta|r)$ and a marginal density for r. The last term of (49) can serve as a normal conditional density of β, given r, which has mean b and covariance matrix $(X'X)^{-1}/r$, or precision matrix $X'Xr$. Its normalization constant is $(2\pi)^{-k/2}|X'Xr|^{1/2}$. Incorporating this normalization constant into $g(\beta|r)$, we can write (49) as

$$(2\pi)^{-(n-k)/2}|X'X|^{-1/2} r^{(n-k)/2} \exp\left[\frac{-(n-k)s^2 r}{2}\right] g(\beta|r) \tag{50}$$

where
$$g(\beta|r) = (2\pi)^{-k/2}|X'X|^{1/2} r^{k/2} \exp\left[\frac{-(\beta - b)'(X'Xr)(\beta - b)}{2}\right] \tag{51}$$

Recalling that the gamma density for a random variable x with parameters α and θ is

$$f(x|\alpha, \theta) = \frac{\theta^{\alpha+1}}{\alpha!} x^\alpha e^{-\theta x} \qquad x > 0 \tag{52}$$

we observe that the remaining part of (50) is a gamma density function for r with parameters $\alpha = (n - k)/2$ and $\theta = (n - k)s^2/2$, except for the normalization constant. For mathematical convenience we shall specify a prior density for β and r as the product of normal and gamma densities

$$p(\beta, r) = \frac{\theta_0^{\alpha_0+1}}{\alpha_0!} r^{\alpha_0} \exp\left(-\theta_0 r\right)(2\pi)^{-k/2}|R_0|^{1/2} r^{k/2}$$

$$\exp\left[\frac{-(\beta - b_0)'(R_0 r)(\beta - b_0)}{2}\right] \tag{53}$$

The product of (50) and (53), which constitutes the posterior density, is also a product of a normal density for β given r and a gamma density for r. The conditional normal density is the product of the normal parts of (50) and (53)

$$g_1(\beta \mid r; y, X) = (2\pi)^{-k/2} \mid X'X + R_0 \mid^{1/2} r^{k/2}$$

$$\exp \left[\frac{-(\beta - b_1)'(X'Xr + R_0 r)(\beta - b_1)}{2} \right] \quad (54)$$

where, by (48), $b_1 = (X'X + R_0)^{-1}(X'Xb + R_0 b_0)$ (55)

The gamma density is

$$f_1(r \mid y, X) = \frac{\theta_1^{\alpha_1 + 1}}{\alpha_1 !} \, r^{\alpha_1} \exp(-\theta_1 r) \quad (56)$$

where, on collecting appropriate exponents in (50) and (53) and noting the extra $r^{k/2}$ term coming from (53), we have

$$\alpha_1 = \frac{n}{2} + \alpha_0 \qquad \theta_1 = \frac{(n-k)s^2}{2} + \theta_0 \quad (57)$$

The posterior density of β and r, which is the product of (54) and (56), has the same form as (53).

The density (53) is known as a normal-gamma density for β and r. It is called a *natural conjugate prior density* for the likelihood of β and r in a normal linear regression model. The term is suggestive. When a natural conjugate prior density is multiplied by the likelihood, the product, which constitutes the posterior density except for the normalization constant, will have the same form as the prior density. Thus a natural conjugate prior density reproduces itself through successive new samples.

While the posterior density $f_1(r \mid y, X)g_1(\beta \mid r; y, X)$ contains all the information concerning β and r, one may be interested in the posterior density for β alone. This is accomplished by integrating the joint posterior density with respect to r, noting that the integral of (52) is one.

$$\int_0^\infty p(\beta, r \mid y, X) \, dr$$

$$= \int_0^\infty f_1(r \mid y, X)g_1(\beta \mid r; y, X) \, dr$$

$$= c \int_0^\infty r^{\alpha_1} \exp(-\theta_1 r) r^{k/2} \exp \left[\frac{-(\beta - b_1)'(X'X + R_0)(\beta - b_1)r}{2} \right] dr$$

$$= c \frac{(\alpha_1 + k/2)!}{[\theta_1 + (\beta - b_1)'(X'X + R_0)(\beta - b_1)/2]^{\alpha_1 + 1 + k/2}}$$

where $c = \dfrac{\theta_1^{\alpha_1 + 1}}{\alpha_1 !} (2\pi)^{-k/2} \mid X'X + R_0 \mid^{1/2}$

Regrouping terms and simplifying, we can write the above marginal posterior density for β as

$$p(\beta \mid y, X) = \int_0^\infty p(\beta, r \mid y, X) \, dr$$

$$= \frac{(\alpha_1 + k/2)! \, |(X'X + R_0)/2\theta_1|^{1/2}}{\pi^{k/2}\alpha_1! [1 + (\beta - b_1)'(X'X + R_0)(\beta - b_1)/2\theta_1]^{\alpha_1 + 1 + k/2}} \quad (58)$$

The density (58) is a k-variate t distribution for β with parameters b_1, $H = (X'X + R_0)/2\theta_1$, and α_1. The mean of this distribution is b_1. Its covariance matrix, for $\alpha_1 > 0$, can be shown to be $H^{-1}/2\alpha_1$. The symbol $\alpha!$ stands for $\Gamma(\alpha + 1)$, and the gamma function $\Gamma(\alpha + 1)$ can be evaluated as the integral of $\theta^{\alpha+1}x^\alpha e^{-\theta x}$ over $x > 0$.

Like the multivariate normal density function discussed in Sec. 1.6, the multivariate t density has the property that both the conditional and marginal densities are t densities. Let z have a k-variate t density with parameters μ, H, and $\upsilon = 2(\alpha_1 + 1)$, and let z be decomposed into z_1 and z_2 with k_1 and k_2 elements, respectively. The joint density of z_1 and z_2 is

$$f(z_1, z_2) = \frac{\Gamma[(\upsilon + k)/2]}{\pi^{k/2}\Gamma[\upsilon/2]} |H|^{1/2}[1 + (z - \mu)'H(z - \mu)]^{-(\upsilon+k)/2} \quad (59)$$

Partitioning the matrix H and following the derivation of Eqs. (20) to (23) of Chap. 1, we can write

$$(z - \mu)'H(z - \mu) = (z_1 - \mu_1^*)'H_{11}(z_1 - \mu_1^*) + (z_2 - \mu_2)'H_{22}^*(z_2 - \mu_2)$$

where $\quad \mu_1^* = \mu_1 - H_{11}^{-1}H_{12}(z_2 - \mu_2) \qquad H_{22}^* = H_{22} - H_{21}H_{11}^{-1}H_{12}$

This decomposition permits us to write

$$1 + (z - \mu)'H(z - \mu) = 1 + Q_1 + Q_2 = (1 + Q_2)[1 + Q_1/(1 + Q_2)]$$

and then to factor the joint density (59) as

$$f(z_1, z_2) = \frac{\Gamma[(\upsilon + k_2)/2]}{\pi^{k_2/2}\Gamma(\upsilon/2)} |H_{22}^*|^{1/2}[1 + (z_2 - \mu_2)'H_{22}^*(z_2 - \mu_2)]^{-(\upsilon+k_2)/2}$$

$$\cdot \frac{\Gamma\left(\dfrac{k + \upsilon}{2}\right)[1 + (z_2 - \mu_2)'H_{22}^*(z_2 - \mu_2)]^{-k_1/2}|H_{11}|^{1/2}}{\pi^{k_1/2}\Gamma\left(\dfrac{\upsilon + k_2}{2}\right)\left\{1 + \dfrac{(z_1 - \mu_1^*)'H_{11}(z_1 - \mu_1^*)}{1 + (z_2 - \mu_2)'H_{22}^*(z_2 - \mu_2)}\right\}^{(\upsilon+k)/2}}$$

$$= f_2(z_2)g(z_1 \mid z_2) \quad (60)$$

where we have used the fact that $|H| = H_{11} \cdot |H_{22}^*|$. Thus both the marginal density $f_2(z_2)$ and the conditional density $g(z_1 \mid z_2)$ are multivariate t densities. For $k_2 = 1$, $f_2(z_2)$ reduces to the univariate t density with $\upsilon + 1$ degrees of freedom.

Instead of using the prior density (53), which is an *informative prior density* of β and r, one can choose a *diffuse prior density* to represent the lack of prior information concerning β and r

$$p(\beta, r) = p(r)p(\beta) \propto r^{-1} \tag{61}$$

The prior density $p(\beta)$ is very flat and is not a function of β. The prior density of log r, r being always positive, is also assumed to be very flat and proportional to a constant. After a change of variable from log r to r, using the jacobian $r^{-1} = (d \log r)/dr$, we find the prior density of r proportional to r^{-1}, as in (61). Although the density (61) is improper because one cannot find a constant to make its integral equal to 1, one can still find a posterior density as the product of (61) and (50), yielding

$$p(\beta, r \mid y, X) = (2\pi)^{-k/2} \mid X'X \mid^{1/2} r^{k/2} \exp \left[\frac{-(\beta - b)'(X'Xr)(\beta - b)}{2} \right]$$

$$\frac{\theta_1^{\alpha_1 + 1}}{\alpha_1!} r^{\alpha_1} \exp(-\theta_1 r) \tag{62}$$

where b is the least-squares estimate of β

$$\alpha_1 = \frac{n}{2} - 1 \quad \text{and} \quad \theta_1 = \frac{(n-k)s^2}{2}$$

and the normalization constants are chosen to complete a normal-gamma density. The marginal density of β is multivariate t as given by (58), with $R_0 = 0$, $b_1 = b$, and $2\theta_1 = (n-k)s^2$. Although the Bayesian ends up with the t distribution for inference on the coefficient vector β as the classical statistician does, again the interpretation is different. The Bayesian provides a posterior density for β, taking b as given, whereas the classicist treats b as a random variable and is concerned with the distribution of b, assuming β to be fixed though unknown. This section in no way exhausts the subject of Bayesian regression analysis, but it serves to explain and illustrate Bayesian methods.

3.6 NON-BAYESIAN USE OF EXTRANEOUS INFORMATION

Besides the sample (y, X) one may have other information concerning the coefficient vector β. For example, if (y, X) represents n times-series observations on the per capita demand for a commodity as explained by relative price and per capita real income, and the price and income series are highly correlated, there may be cross-section data on the demand by a family as related to its income and family size. The family budget data can be converted into demand per person and income per person in the family. The data can be arranged thus

$$\begin{bmatrix} y_1 \\ \cdot \\ y_n \\ y_{n+1} \\ \cdot \\ y_{n+m} \end{bmatrix} = \begin{bmatrix} 1 & 0 & x_{13} & x_{14} \\ \cdot & \cdot & \cdot & \cdot \\ 1 & 0 & x_{n3} & x_{n4} \\ 0 & 1 & 0 & x_{n+1,4} \\ \cdot & \cdot & \cdot & \cdot \\ 0 & 1 & 0 & x_{n+m,4} \end{bmatrix} \begin{bmatrix} \beta_1 \\ \beta_2 \\ \beta_3 \\ \beta_4 \end{bmatrix} + \begin{bmatrix} \epsilon_1 \\ \cdot \\ \epsilon_n \\ \eta_1 \\ \cdot \\ \eta_m \end{bmatrix} \tag{63}$$

where the first n observations are from the time series and the last m observations are from the cross section; x_{13} stands for relative price, which is assumed to be the same for all families in the cross-section data; and x_{14} stands for income per person. The ϵ_i and η_i are assumed to be independent and identically distributed with variance σ^2 and σ_0^2, respectively.

Rewrite (63) as

$$\begin{bmatrix} y \\ z \end{bmatrix} = \begin{bmatrix} X \\ W \end{bmatrix} \beta + \begin{bmatrix} \epsilon \\ \eta \end{bmatrix} \tag{64}$$

Applying GLS to (64) yields

$$\begin{aligned} \hat{\beta} &= (\sigma^{-2}X'X + \sigma_0^{-2}W'W)^{-1}(\sigma^{-2}X'y + \sigma_0^{-2}W'z) \\ &= (\sigma^{-2}X'X + \sigma_0^{-2}W'W)^{-1}(\sigma^{-2}X'Xb + \sigma_0^{-2}W'Wb_0) \end{aligned} \tag{65}$$

where the second line gives an interpretation of the GLS estimate as a weighted average of the least-squares estimates b and b_0 from the two samples. It is formally identical to the Bayesian estimator (55) of the last section if R_0 is set equal to $(\sigma/\sigma_0)^2 W'W$, although the interpretation is different. In practice, when σ^2 and σ_0^2 are unknown, they can be replaced by the least-squares estimates from the respective samples.

As a historical note, the estimation of regression coefficients by applying GLS to two sets of sample observations dates back at least to Durbin (1953). Later Theil and Goldberger (1961) suggested that the "second sample" may be based on some prior notion of the investigator. In the notation of (64), z need not be a vector of actual observations of the dependent variable; instead it is the expected value of $W\beta$ in the mind of the econometrician, where the matrix W is itself specified a priori. For example, W may simply be the identity matrix. The variances of η are assumed to be known. They reflect the variations of $W\beta$ from the best guess z. Such a combination of prior information with the sample is called *mixed estimation*. Obviously, the covariance matrices of ϵ and η may be changed to $V\sigma^2$ and $V_0\sigma_0^2$ and the estimator (65) modified accordingly.

When $X'X$ may be nearly singular but no other information is explicitly specified, another estimator of β is available. It is the *ridge* estimator, proposed by Hoerl (1962),

$$\hat{\beta}(k) = (X'X + kI)^{-1}X'y = (X'X + kI)^{-1}X'Xb = [I + k(X'X)^{-1}]^{-1}b \tag{66}$$

By letting $(\sigma/\sigma_0)^2 = k$ and $b_0 = 0$ in (65) we can give a GLS or a Bayesian interpretation to the ridge estimator. The covariance matrix from the extra information or the prior density, as the case may be, is assumed to be diagonal in (66). The question is how to choose k for this ridge estimator without using information other than the sample information. Numerous suggestions have been proposed. A Monte Carlo study by Lin and Kmenta (1982) has found that the ridge estimators, based on various k, do outperform the least-squares very substantially when the degree of collinearity among the X's is medium or high, whether the loss criterion is mean-square error, mean absolute error, or maximum absolute error. A formula for k which works quite well and is easy to compute, as reported in the above reference, is the one suggested by Hoerl, Kennard, and Baldwin (1975)

$$k = \frac{ps^2}{b'b}$$

where p denotes the number of explanatory variables and s^2 and b are defined as usual. The above formula appeals to the fact that the value of k that minimizes $E[\hat{\beta}(k) - \beta]'[\hat{\beta}(k) - \beta]$ is $p\sigma^2/\beta'\beta$ when $X'X = I$. The proof of this fact is left as an exercise (see Prob. 9).

One explanation for the reported superiority of the ridge estimator over the least-squares estimator when $X'X$ is nearly singular is that the ridge estimator is a weighted average of the least-squares estimator and the zero vector. In Monte Carlo experiments the true values of the regression coefficients are usually assumed to be near zero. Therefore, when the diagonal elements of $X'X$ are very large and the least-squares estimates b vary considerably, it is a good strategy to take an average of b and the zero vector. For example, in the experiment of Lin and Kmenta (1982) the values of the true coefficients lie mostly between 0 and 6.0, with one maximum coefficient equal 11.83. Considering all the real numbers, these numbers lie within an extremely small range near zero. Therefore zero is not a bad guess. Similarly, in econometric studies, the econometrician must have specified the units for the variables in such a way that a regression coefficient of 10,000 or larger is extremely unlikely, or the units would have been changed. If the standard error of an estimated coefficient obtained from $(X'X)^{-1}\sigma^2$ is extremely large, one has almost no information about the true coefficient from the sample data; why not take the average of the least-squares estimate and zero? In other words, the estimator (66) implicitly incorporates information outside the sample, namely, the fact that in performing Monte Carlo studies or in specifying econometric relations econometricians almost always make the true coefficients not very far from zero.

3.7 MULTICOLLINEARITY WITHOUT OTHER INFORMATION

The approaches just suggested for dealing with the situation where the matrix $X'X$ is nearly singular all rely on the use of extra information, explicitly or implicitly. What happens if one does not have outside information? In practice, one should always try one's best to obtain more information. Data in econometrics do not come freely. Effort, ingenuity, and care are required to obtain good information. Therefore, the existence of information depends on the econometrician. We should rephrase our question to read: What is the best that can be done with poor data?

In the extreme case when $X'X$ is singular, there is nothing that one can do in estimating some coefficients. Singularity of $X'X$ occurs when the k columns of X are linearly dependent. For example, if the first column x_1 equals 3 times the second column x_2,

$$\beta_1 x_1 + \beta_2 x_2 = \beta_1 x_1 + \beta_2 x_2 + \theta(x_1 - 3x_2)$$

$$= (\beta_1 + \theta)x_1 + (\beta_2 - 3\theta)x_2 = (3\beta_1 + \beta_2)x_2$$

The coefficients β_1 and β_2 cannot be identified. If β_1 and β_2 give a good fit, $\beta_1 + \theta$ and $\beta_2 - 3\theta$ will fit just as well, since the value of latter regression is identical with the former regression. However $3\beta_1 + \beta_2$ can be estimated if the rank of $[x_2 \quad x_3 \quad \cdots \quad x_k]$ is $k - 1$. We simply drop x_1 as an explanatory variable and regress y on the remaining x's. The coefficients $\beta_3, \ldots, \beta_k$ can be estimated but nothing can be done to estimate β_1 and β_2 separately.

It may be of interest to characterize what coefficients or linear combinations of coefficients can or cannot be estimated when $X'X$ is singular. One way to do this is to use the characteristic roots and vectors of $X'X$. Let

$$X'X = PDP'$$

where D is a diagonal matrix consisting of the characteristic roots λ_i of $X'X$ arranged in decreasing order and P is a matrix whose columns are the characteristic vectors, with $PP' = P'P = I$. Using the matrix P, we can rewrite the regression model as

$$y = X\beta + \epsilon = (XP)(P'\beta) + \epsilon \equiv Z\alpha + \epsilon$$

where $Z = XP$ is the matrix of the new explanatory variables and $\alpha = P'\beta$ is the new coefficient vector. The cross-product matrix of the z's is

$$Z'Z = P'X'XP = D$$

The new variables Z are known as the *principal components* of X. The ith column $z_i = Xp_i$ of Z is a linear combination of the columns of X using the ith characteristic vector p_i as weights.

If the rank of X is $k - m$, there are m zero roots or $\lambda_i = 0$ $(i = k - m + 1, \ldots, k)$. The corresponding columns of P satisfy $(X'X)p_i = 0$, implying $Xp_i = 0$; otherwise $p_i' X'Xp_i \neq 0$, contradicting $(X'X)p_i = 0$. Thus the last m principal components are zero. The last m coefficients of α disappear from the regression function $Z\alpha$ and cannot be estimated. The first $k - m$ coefficients of α can be estimated. Decompose α into α_a and α_b, the latter having m elements. Similarly, let $P = [P_a \quad P_b]$ and $Z = [Z_a \quad Z_b]$, with $Z_b = 0$. To estimate α_a we use the regression

$$y = Z_a \alpha_a + Z_b \alpha_b + \epsilon = Z_a \alpha_a + \epsilon \tag{67}$$

and apply least squares to obtain $\hat{\alpha}_a$.

To estimate β using principal components, we use the relation $\alpha = P'\beta$ or $P\alpha = \beta$. An estimate of β can be obtained as $P\hat{\alpha}$ once an estimate $\hat{\alpha}$ of α has been found. When m roots of $X'X$ are zero, we estimate only the first $k - m$ elements α_a of α. The estimate of β is

$$\hat{\beta} = P\hat{\alpha} = P_a \hat{\alpha}_a + P_b \hat{\alpha}_b \tag{68}$$

Therefore, a linear combination $w'\beta$ can be estimated if and only if

$$w'\beta = w'P_a\alpha_a + w'P_b\alpha_b \tag{69}$$

can be obtained from $w'P_a\alpha_a$ alone, i.e., if and only if $w'P_b = 0$. To test whether β_i can be estimated we test whether $w'P_b = 0$, where w is a vector of zeros except for a unity in the ith position. The use of principal components thus provides an answer to the question whether a given linear combination $w'\beta$ of β can be estimated. It also provides a method of estimation for the estimable linear combinations. If a certain linear combination $w'\beta$ is not estimable, using the formula $w'\beta = w'P_a\hat{\alpha}_a$ is inappropriate since it ignores the unknown component $w'P_b\alpha_b$, where $w'P_b \neq 0$. Let $w'_1\beta$ and $w'_2\beta$ be two estimable functions. Their covariance is

$$\text{Cov}(w'_1\hat{\beta}, w'_2\hat{\beta}) = \text{Cov}(w'_1P_a\hat{\alpha}_a, w'_2P_a\hat{\alpha}_a) = w'_1P_a(Z'_aZ_a)^{-1}P'_aw_2\sigma^2$$

$$= w'_1P_aD_a^{-1}P'_aw_2\sigma^2 \tag{70}$$

where D_a is a diagonal matrix consisting of the $k - m$ nonzero roots of $X'X$.

The above method of estimating β using the principal components of $X'X$ can be presented in terms of the generalized inverse of $X'X$. For a symmetric matrix A the *generalized inverse* is defined as

$$A^+ = P_aD_a^{-1}P'_a \tag{71}$$

where D_a is a diagonal matrix consisting of the nonzero roots of A and P_a is a matrix consisting of the corresponding right characteristic vectors. If A is nonsingular, all roots are nonzero and $A^+ = A^{-1}$. For a regression model, if $X'X$ is singular, the least-squares estimate of β is

$$\beta^* = (X'X)^+X'y = P_aD_a^{-1}P'_aX'y \tag{72}$$

where $X'X$ replaces matrix A in (71). If we ignore $P_b\alpha_b$ in (68), the estimate $\hat{\beta}$ becomes

$$\hat{\beta} = P_a\hat{\alpha}_a = P_a(Z'_aZ_a)^{-1}Z'_ay = P_aD_a^{-1}(XP_a)'y \tag{73}$$

which is identical with (72). Note that if a certain element β_i of β is not estimable, the above formula for $\hat{\beta}_i$ is not reliable. Consider the example where $X'X$ is diagonal with the last diagonal element equal to zero. This occurs when the last explanatory variable, when measured from the mean, equals zero or its variance equals zero. The last row of $(X'X)^+$ will be zero, making the last element $\hat{\beta}_k$ of $\hat{\beta}$ equal to zero. The estimated equation $X\hat{\beta}$ will fit the data as well as any other linear regression function, but $\hat{\beta}_k = 0$ is certainly not a reliable estimate of β_k since other values of $\hat{\beta}_k$ will do as well.

Let us now turn to the case when $X'X$ is not singular but nearly so. Without defining precisely what "nearly" means, let us simply say that the problem of collinearity among the explanatory variables occurs when the econometrician finds some diagonal elements of $(X'X)^{-1}s^2$ so large that the interval estimates of the corresponding coefficients become useless. One ad hoc estimation procedure is to use the regression of y on principal components.

When $X'X$ is nearly singular, some of its roots are nearly zero. Let us rescale the x's to make $\sum_i x_{ij} = 0$ and $\sum_i x_{ij}^2 = 1$ or make $X'X$ a matrix of correlations of the x's, the intercept being eliminated from the regression. After rescaling, it is still somewhat arbitrary to decide which roots are nearly zero. Hence the following procedure is somewhat ad hoc. Let m of the smallest roots be treated as zero roots. Accordingly, the last m principal components $z_i = Xp_i$ are treated as zero. Only the first $k - m$ principal components are used as explanatory variables to estimate the first $k - m$ coefficients α_a of α by least squares, resulting in $\hat{\alpha}_a$ with $k - m$ elements. The estimate of β is $\hat{\beta} = P_a \hat{\alpha}_a$, where P_a consists of the first $k - m$ columns of P. We have observed that this method is valid only if the last term of (68) can be ignored. This is true whether $X'X$ is singular or nearly so. In the latter case, the method of principal components helps one concentrate the information in $X'X$ on the estimation of the estimable linear combinations of β, leaving the estimation of the nearly unestimable ones unsolved. For a more precise definition of "nearly" singular and related topics concerning multicollinearity, see Silvey (1969) and Belsley, Kuh, and Welsch (1980). The literature on multicollinearity is quite extensive but, ingenuity aside, one cannot expect to get something from nothing.

To milk the last ounce of information from the sample one can consider using an estimator proposed by Stein (1956). The Stein estimator dominates least squares if the loss function is $(\hat{\beta} - \beta)'X'X(\hat{\beta} - \beta)$. Consider first the problem of estimating k means $\mu_1, \ldots, \mu_k$ in the model

$$y_i = \mu_i + \epsilon_i \qquad i = 1, 2, \ldots, k$$

where ϵ_i are independently and normally distributed with mean zero and variance σ^2. The least-squares estimator $\hat{\mu}_i$ of μ_i is simply y_i itself, or $\hat{\mu} = y$ is the least squares estimator of μ in vector notation. If $k \geq 3$, the Stein estimator

$$\mu^* = \left[1 - \frac{(k - 2)\sigma^2}{y'y} \right] y \tag{74}$$

dominates $\hat{\mu}$ in the sense of $E(\mu^* - \mu)'(\mu^* - \mu) < E(\hat{\mu} - \mu)'(\hat{\mu} - \mu)$ for all μ. This result does not contradict the Markov theorem on least squares because μ^* is neither linear nor unbiased.

To apply the Stein estimator to the standard normal regression model, write $X'X = PDP'$, where D is a diagonal matrix consisting of the characteristic roots of $X'X$ and $PP' = I = P'P$. Let $C = n^{1/2}PD^{-1/2}$, so that $C'X'XC = nI$. Write the linear model as

$$y = XCC^{-1}\beta + \epsilon = W\alpha + \epsilon$$

where $W = XC$ and $\alpha = C^{-1}\beta$. Premultiply by W' to obtain

$$W'y = C'X'XC\alpha + W'\epsilon = n\alpha + u$$

where $u = W'\epsilon$ is normal with mean zero and covariance matrix $W'W\sigma^2 = n\sigma^2 I$. Dividing by n, we have the model

$$n^{-1}W'y = \alpha + n^{-1}u$$

which is identical with the model of k means, the variance of each residual being $n^{-1}\sigma^2$. The Stein estimator (74) becomes

$$\alpha^* = \left[1 - \frac{(k-2)n\sigma^2}{y'WW'y}\right]n^{-1}W'y$$

compared with the least-squares estimate $\hat{\alpha} = n^{-1}W'y$. In terms of the original coefficients β, the Stein estimator is

$$\beta^* = C\alpha^* = \left[1 - \frac{(k-2)n\sigma^2}{y'XCC'X'y}\right]C\hat{\alpha} = \left[1 - \frac{(k-2)\sigma^2}{y'X(X'X)^{-1}X'y}\right]b \qquad (75)$$

This estimator dominates the least-squares estimator b if the expected loss function, or *risk function*, is

$$E(\alpha^* - \alpha)'(\alpha^* - \alpha) = E(\beta^* - \beta)'C^{-1'}C^{-1}(\beta^* - \beta) = n^{-1}E(\beta^* - \beta)'X'X(\beta^* - \beta)$$

By giving up linearity and unbiasedness one can do better than using least squares according to the loss function $(\beta^* - \beta)'X'X(\beta^* - \beta)$.

3.8 DISTRIBUTED LAGS

One important econometric problem in which the ill conditioning of the X matrix shows up is the estimation of the lagged effects of an explanatory variable distributed over many time periods. With the subscript t denoting time period, we may have a model

$$y_t = \alpha + \sum_{j=0}^{k} \beta_j x_{t-j} + \epsilon_t \qquad (76)$$

describing the effects of the current and past x's on y. The number k of lagged x's included may be finite or infinite. Even if k is finite but fairly large, it would be difficult to obtain accurate estimates of the coefficients β_j because the explanatory variables are likely to be highly correlated. The matrix $X'X$ is likely to be nearly singular. Therefore some restrictions must be imposed on the β_j. Several approaches to imposing restrictions on β_j will be discussed in this section.

One simple assumption is that β_j declines geometrically

$$\beta_j = \lambda^j \beta_0 \qquad (77)$$

This assumption reduces the set of β_j to only two parameters, β_0 and λ. To estimate the model (76) subject to this restriction, Koyck (1954) has suggested subtracting an equation for λy_{t-1} from (76) to yield

$$y_t = \lambda y_{t-1} + (1-\lambda)\alpha + \beta_0 x_t + (\epsilon_t - \lambda\epsilon_{t-1}) \qquad (78)$$

Such a Koyck transform would introduce a lagged dependent variable y_{t-1} into the equation and change the residual to $\epsilon_t - \lambda\epsilon_{t-1}$. If ϵ_t is uncorrelated with ϵ_{t-1}, one finds y_{t-1} to be correlated with the new residual $\epsilon_t - \lambda\epsilon_{t-1}$, since

$$E[y_{t-1}(\epsilon_t - \lambda\epsilon_{t-1})] = E[\epsilon_{t-1}(\epsilon_t - \lambda\epsilon_{t-1})] = -\lambda\sigma^2$$

Two basic assumptions of the regression model are now violated. The explanatory variables are no longer fixed. The residual is correlated with the explanatory variable. If the explanatory variables are stochastic but uncorrelated with the residual, that is, plim $n^{-1}X'\epsilon = 0$, the least-squares estimator b is still consistent if plim $n^{-1}X'X = Q$ because

$$b = \beta + (n^{-1}X'X)^{-1}n^{-1}X'\epsilon$$

and $$\text{plim } b = \beta + \text{plim } (n^{-1}X'X)^{-1} \text{plim } n^{-1}X'\epsilon = \beta$$

where plim $n^{-1}X'\epsilon = 0$ by assumption. On the other hand, if $Ex_{ij}\epsilon_i \neq 0$ for the ith observation, $n^{-1}\sum_i x_{ij}\epsilon_i$ will not converge in probability to zero, or plim $n^{-1}X'\epsilon \neq 0$, and b will not be consistent. Thus regression of y_t on y_{t-1} and x_t in (78) will not yield consistent estimates of the regression coefficients *unless* the residual $u_t = \epsilon_t - \lambda\epsilon_{t-1}$ is uncorrelated with y_{t-1} (see Prob. 10).

Let us consider the estimation of the model

$$y_t = \gamma_0 + \gamma_1 y_{t-1} + \gamma_2 x_t + u_t \tag{79}$$

which is of the same form as (78) if the residual u_t equals $\epsilon_t - \lambda\epsilon_{t-1}$. The method of estimation differs according to the specification of u_t. First, u_t may be assumed to be independent and identically distributed, and the method of least squares will yield consistent estimates of the coefficients. Such a model may be derived from a *stock-adjustment* model as used by Chow (1957) and reported in Chap. 2 to describe the demand for automobiles. In such a model desired stock y_t^* is a linear function of x_t and a serially independent residual, and actual change $y_t - y_{t-1}$ is assumed to equal a fraction α of $y_t^* - y_{t-1}$, so that y_t becomes a linear function of y_t, x_t, and a serially independent residual.

Second, u_t may be assumed to be $\epsilon_t - \lambda\epsilon_{t-1}$, where ϵ_t are independently and identically distributed. Such a model can be derived from an *adaptive-expectations* model in which y_t is assumed to be a linear function of the expectation x_t^e of x_t and a residual ϵ_t, and the expectation x_t is formed by

$$x_t^e - x_{t-1}^e = \theta(x_t - x_{t-1}^e) \tag{80}$$

which after repeated substitutions for the lagged x_{t-k}^e implies

$$x_t^e = \theta x_t + (1 - \theta)\theta x_{t-1} + (1 - \theta)^2\theta x_{t-2} + \cdots = \theta \sum_{j=0}^{\infty} (1 - \theta)^j x_{t-j} \tag{81}$$

The lag structure (81) has the form (77), with $\theta = \beta_0$ and $1 - \theta = \lambda$. The adaptive-expectations model will have the form (76) with geometrically declining coefficients and can be converted into form (79) with $u_t = \epsilon_t - \lambda\epsilon_{t-1}$.

When $u_t = \epsilon_t - \lambda\epsilon_{t-1}$, model (79) cannot be consistently estimated by the method of least squares. If the ϵ_t are independent and normal, each having a variance σ^2, the log-likelihood function for (79) is derived from

$$-n \log \sigma - \frac{1}{2} \sum_{t=1}^{n} \epsilon_t^2 = -n \log \sigma - \frac{1}{2} \sum_{t=1}^{n} (y_t - \gamma_0 - \gamma_1 y_{t-1} - \gamma_2 x_t + \lambda\epsilon_{t-1})^2$$

where $$\lambda\epsilon_{t-1} = \lambda(y_{t-1} - \gamma_0 - \gamma_1 y_{t-2} - \gamma_2 x_{t-1} + \lambda\epsilon_{t-2})$$

and a similar expression holds for $\lambda \epsilon_{t-2}$, etc. One can appreciate that the problem of maximizing the likelihood function of a model involving a moving-average residual such as $u_t = \epsilon_t - \lambda \epsilon_{t-1}$ is quite complicated. This problem will be treated in Chap. 6, where we study time-series models of a more general form than (79), as represented by *autoregressive moving-average* processes. Autoregressive models include one or more lagged y's; moving-average models include ϵ_t and one or more lagged ϵ's; both y_t and ϵ_t may be vectors.

The lag structure of (79) can be generalized in different ways. One useful structure is the *rational distributed lag*, studied by Jorgenson (1966). The dynamic relation between y and x is assumed to be

$$\alpha_0 y_t + \alpha_1 y_{t-1} + \cdots + \alpha_p y_{t-p} = \beta_0 x_t + \beta_1 x_{t-1} + \cdots + \beta_q x_{t-q} + u_t \quad (82)$$

Letting L denote the lag operator, with $Ly_t = y_{t-1}$, $L^2 y_t = y_{t-2}$, etc., we can write this relation as

$$(\alpha_0 + \alpha_1 L^1 + \cdots + \alpha_p L^p)y_t = (\beta_0 + \beta_1 L^1 + \cdots + \beta_q L^q)x_t + u_t$$

or
$$\alpha(L)y_t = \beta(L)x_t + u_t \quad (83)$$

where we have let $\alpha(L)$ and $\beta(L)$ denote the polynomials in the lag operator L given in the line above. Note that the operator L can be treated as a variable, since it obeys the rules of algebra, and can be factored, multiplied, etc. When $p = 1$ and $q = 0$, the rational distributed lag structure reduces to the lag structure of (79). Again, if u_t are serially independent, the method of least squares can be applied. If u_t follows a moving-average process with normal residuals, the method of maximum likelihood can be applied, as discussed more thoroughly in Chap 6. Also see Prob. 12.

Let us return to model (76) and assume k to be finite. To impose restrictions on β_j one can follow Almon (1965) by assuming that β_j is a low-order polynomial in j,

$$\beta_j = \gamma_0 + \gamma_1 j + \cdots + \gamma_q j^q \quad (84)$$

The relation between the vector of coefficients in (76) and the vector of coefficients in the polynomial (84) is

$$
\begin{bmatrix} \beta_0 \\ \beta_1 \\ \beta_2 \\ \\ \beta_k \end{bmatrix}
=
\begin{bmatrix}
1 & 0 & 0 & \cdots & 0 \\
1 & 1 & 1 & \cdots & 1 \\
1 & 2 & 2^2 & \cdots & 2^q \\
& & \cdots & & \\
1 & k & k^2 & \cdots & k^q
\end{bmatrix}
\begin{bmatrix} \gamma_0 \\ \gamma_1 \\ \gamma_2 \\ \cdot \\ \gamma_q \end{bmatrix}
$$

or
$$\beta = A\gamma \quad (85)$$

The model (76) can be rewritten as

$$y = X\beta + \epsilon = XA\gamma + \epsilon = Z\gamma + \epsilon \quad (86)$$

The large number of unknown coefficients in β is converted into a small number of coefficients in γ, with the matrix X replaced by an $n \times (q + 1)$ matrix $Z = XA$ of new explanatory variables. Least squares can be applied to the transformed model (86) to estimate γ by $\hat{\gamma}$ say, and β can be estimated by $A\hat{\gamma}$. If one wishes to impose a restriction such as $\beta_8 = 0$, it amounts to a linear restriction

$$\beta_8 = \gamma_0 + 8\gamma_1 + 8^2\gamma_2 + \cdots + 8^q\gamma_q = 0$$

on γ, and standard methods can be applied to estimate γ subject to such a restriction or to test the restriction itself.

The polynomial restriction (85) on β can be generalized to form a stochastic restriction equivalent to the smoothness prior restriction suggested by Shiller (1973). First solve (85) for γ as a function of β. Consider (85) as a regression model with β as observations on the dependent variable, γ as regression coefficients, and 0 as residuals. The least-squares estimate of γ will permit the dependent variable to be explained completely, i.e.,

$$\beta - A(A'A)^{-1}A'\beta = [I - A(A'A)^{-1}A']\beta = 0$$

Instead of using the above restriction, which is equivalent to (85), one may use the stochastic restriction

$$R\beta = v_0$$

where $R = I - A(A'A)^{-1}A'$ and the covariance matrix of v_0 is assumed to be $I\sigma_0^2$. To estimate β, Taylor (1975) points out that one can combine this restriction with the original model (76) to form

$$\begin{bmatrix} y \\ 0 \end{bmatrix} = \begin{bmatrix} X \\ R \end{bmatrix} \beta + \begin{bmatrix} \epsilon \\ v_0 \end{bmatrix}$$

GLS can be applied to estimate β, as discussed in Sec. 3.6. The literature on distributed lags is extensive. Only a few selected approaches are covered in this section.

3.9 ERRORS IN OBSERVATIONS

In Sec. 1.7 it was pointed out that if the explanatory variable is measured with an error in a simple regression model, the least-squares estimate of the slope will not be consistent because the model with x subject to error has a population slope which is smaller in absolute value than the slope of the original regression on x. We would like to generalize the discussion to the model of multiple linear regression and present one consistent method for estimating the regression coefficients.

Lindley (1947) has shown that in a linear regression model if the vector ψ of independent errors in measuring the explanatory variables x is k-variate normal, the regression of y on $x^* = x + \psi$ is linear, if and only if x is itself k-variate normal. Let $X^* = X + \Psi$ be an $n \times k$ matrix of explanatory variables measured with errors. We assume that $E(\Psi) = 0$, $n^{-1}E(\Psi'\Psi) = Q_\psi$, plim $n^{-1}\Psi'X = 0$, plim

$n^{-1}\Psi'y = 0$, and plim $n^{-1}\Psi'\epsilon = 0$. The least-squares estimator can be written

$$b = (X^{*\prime}X^*)^{-1}X^*y = (n^{-1}X^{*\prime}X^*)^{-1}n^{-1}X^{*\prime}X\beta + (n^{-1}X^{*\prime}X^*)^{-1}n^{-1}X^{*\prime}\epsilon \quad (87)$$

Under the assumptions that plim $n^{-1}X'X = Q$ and plim $n^{-1}X'\epsilon = 0$ we can easily evaluate the probability limit of b by (87) as

$$\plim_{n\to\infty} b = (Q + Q_\psi)^{-1}Q\beta = (Q + Q_\psi)^{-1}(Q + Q_\psi - Q_\psi)\beta = \beta - (Q + Q_\psi)^{-1}Q_\psi\beta$$

$$(88)$$

Thus the least-squares estimator b is not consistent. In the above analysis, the matrix X may be regarded either as fixed or random. If X is fixed, we assume that lim $n^{-1}X'X = Q$ which implies plim $n^{-1}X'X = Q$. Formula (88) remains unchanged if the dependent variable is also measured with an error, being equal to $y^* = y + \delta$, *provided* that plim $n^{-1}\Psi'\delta = 0$ and plim $n^{-1}X'\delta = 0$. With y^* replacing y in (87), a term $(n^{-1}X^{*\prime}X^*)^{-1}n^{-1}X^{*\prime}\delta$ will be added to its right-hand side. The probability limit of this term is zero under the two assumptions concerning the error δ. Equation (88) generalizes Eq. (37) of Chap. 1.

It may be of interest to consider the case when only one explanatory variable, say x_k, is measured with an error, so that Q_ψ is a matrix of zeros except for the last diagonal element, which equals σ_ψ^2. We can partition $(Q + Q_\psi)^{-1}$ as

$$(Q + Q_\psi)^{-1} = \begin{bmatrix} N & p \\ p' & q \end{bmatrix}$$

where p is a column vector and q is a scalar. From the algebra of the partitioned inverse, including a result analogous to Eq. (27) of Chap. 1, one can show that q^{-1} equals the residual variance in the regression of x_k^* on $x_1, \ldots, x_{k-1}$. The coefficient vector α of this regression is the same as the corresponding coefficient vector in the regression of x_k on $x_1, \ldots, x_{k-1}$ since the error in x_k^* is independent. The residual variance in this regression is the sum of the residual variance σ_k^2 of the latter regression and σ_ψ^2. That is,

$$q = (\sigma_k^2 + \sigma_\psi^2)^{-1}$$

From the partitioned inverse we also know that

$$p = -q\alpha$$

Equation (88) then becomes

$$\plim_{n\to\infty} (b - \beta) = -\begin{bmatrix} N & -q\alpha \\ -q\alpha' & q \end{bmatrix}\begin{bmatrix} 0 & 0 \\ 0 & \sigma_\psi^2 \end{bmatrix}\beta = \frac{\sigma_\psi^2\beta_k}{\sigma_k^2 + \sigma_\psi^2}\begin{bmatrix} \alpha \\ -1 \end{bmatrix} \quad (89)$$

When x_k is measured with an independent error having variance σ_ψ^2, Eq. (89) shows how the probability limit of the least-squares estimator b differs from the true β. The probability limit of b_k is smaller than β_k in absolute value, the difference being $-\sigma_\psi^2\beta_k/(\sigma_k^2 + \sigma_\psi^2)$, where σ_k^2 is the residual variance in the regression of x_k on $x_1, \ldots, x_{k-1}$. This result generalizes Eq. (37) of Chap. 1 for the simple linear regression model. The error in x_k^* also affects the least-squares estimator of the first $k - 1$ coefficients. The probability limit of this vector differs from the true coefficients by $\sigma_\psi^2 \beta_k / (\sigma_k^2 + \sigma_\psi^2)$ times the vector α of coefficients in the regression of x_k on $x_1, \ldots, x_{k-1}$. An application of (89) to the demand function for automobiles when the income variable is subject to measurement error can be found in Chow (1957), as reported in equations (27) and (28) of Chap. 2 and the discussion following.

3.10 METHOD OF INSTRUMENTAL VARIABLES

The inconsistency of the least-squares estimator b given by (87) can be viewed in another way. Write the model as

$$y = X\beta + \epsilon = X^*\beta + (\epsilon - \Psi\beta) \tag{90}$$

The explanatory variables X^* are correlated with the residuals $\epsilon - \Psi\beta$ since

$$\text{plim } n^{-1} X^{*\prime}(\epsilon - \Psi\beta) = -\text{plim } n^{-1}(X + \Psi)'\Psi\beta = -Q_\psi \beta$$

Therefore, the least-squares estimator is inconsistent. A consistent estimator can be obtained by the use of *instrumental variables*, a method suggested by Reiersøl (1945) and Geary (1949), and discussed by Sargan (1958).

Given a model

$$y = X\beta + \epsilon \tag{91}$$

where X may be stochastic or fixed, with plim $n^{-1} X'\epsilon \neq 0$, let the $n \times k$ matrix of *instrumental variables* W satisfy

$$\text{plim } n^{-1} W'X = P$$

where P is nonsingular, and let $n^{-1/2} W'\epsilon$ converge in distribution to a k-variate normal distribution with mean zero and convariance matrix Φ. Then the *instrumental-variable estimator*

$$\hat{\beta} = (W'X)^{-1} W'y \tag{92}$$

is consistent, and the limiting distribution of $n^{-1/2}(\hat{\beta} - \beta)$ is normal with mean zero and covariance matrix $P^{-1} \Phi P'^{-1}$. The proof of this statement is left as an exercise (Probs. 11 and 12). For the model (90) with X^* as explanatory variables, if a matrix W of instrumental variables can be found which has the two required properties, one can find a consistent estimator of β.

The method of instrumental variables is very important in econometrics. In Chaps. 5 and 7 there will be applications of this method to the estimation of linear and nonlinear simultaneous equations. The reader will learn more about this method through applications. Its basic theory is very simple, as described in the last paragraph. Doing Probs. 11 and 12 is essential for understanding the theory.

PROBLEMS

1. Show directly that the GLS estimator $\hat{\beta}$ of β in model (1) is best linear unbiased by considering a linear estimator of the form

$$[(X'V^{-1}X)^{-1}X'V^{-1} + B]y$$

2. Find an unbiased estimator for σ^2 in model (1) which corresponds to s^2 in the standard linear regression model, assuming V to be known. How is the hypothesis $\sigma^2 = \sigma_0^2$ to be tested?

3. Develop a test for the null hypothesis $\beta_2 = 1.6\beta_3$ in model (1). How can a 95 percent confidence interval for the ratio β_2/β_3 be constructed?

4. Show that the least-squares estimator b applied to model (1) is linear unbiased. Find its covariance matrix.

5. State a set of sufficient conditions under which the least-squares estimator b applied to model (1) will be consistent by considering the covariance matrix of b.

6. For the first-order autoregressive model (9), show that, for any $k \geq 0$, the sample moment $n^{-1}\sum_{i=1}^{n} \epsilon_i \epsilon_{i-k}$ converges in probability to the population moment given by (12). In your proof, replace the operation $E(\cdot)$ in the first line of (11) by the operation $n^{-1}\sum_{i=1}^{n}(\cdot)$.

7. In the model consisting of a set of m regressions, prove the consistency of the estimator s_{ij} defined by (23) for the covariance σ_{ij} of the residuals of the ith and jth regressions.

8. Show that if $\hat{a}$ is a consistent estimator of a, (26) has probability limit zero.

9. Show that $k = p\sigma^2/\beta'\beta$ minimizes $E[\hat{\beta}(k) - \beta]'[\hat{\beta}(k) - \beta]$ if $X'X = I$ and X has p columns, where $\hat{\beta}(k)$ is defined by (66).

10. Consider the model $y_t = \beta y_{t-1} + u_t$, with $u_t = au_{t-1} + \epsilon_t$, where ϵ_t are independent and identically distributed with mean zero and variance σ^2.

    (a) Find the probability limit of the least-squares estimator of β.

    (b) Let b be the least-squares estimator of β. Let d be the Durbin-Watson statistic computed by using the least-squares residuals $\hat{u}_t = y_t - by_{t-1}$. Show that

$$\text{plim } d = 2\left(1 - a\frac{\beta^2 + \beta a}{1 + \beta a}\right)$$

Let d^* be the Durbin-Watson statistic computed by using the residuals $u_t^* = y_t - \hat{\beta}y_{t-1}$, where $\hat{\beta}$ is a consistent estimator of β. Show that

$$\text{plim } d^* = 2(1 - a)$$

(This model illustrates that when a lagged dependent variable is used as an explanatory variable, the Durbin-Watson statistic d computed from least-squared residuals tends toward 2 since $\beta^2 < 1$.)

11. Under the assumption that plim $n^{-1}W'X = P$ and that the limiting distribution of $n^{-1/2}W'\epsilon$ is normal with mean zero and covariance matrix Φ, show that the instrumental-variable estimator (92) is consistent and that the limiting distribution of $n^{-1/2}(\hat{\beta} - \beta)$ is normal with mean zero and covariance matrix $P^{-1}\Phi P'^{-1}$.

12. For the distributed-lag model (79), assuming that $u_t = \epsilon_t - \lambda\epsilon_{t-1}$, where ϵ_t are serially independent each with mean zero and variance σ^2, can x_t and x_{t-1} serve as instrumental variables? Explain. Derive the asymptotic distribution of this instrumental-variable estimator.

13. (Chow and Lin, 1971, 1976.) Let $3n$ monthly observations satisfy the regression model

$$y = X\beta + \epsilon \qquad E\epsilon\epsilon' = V$$

The n quarterly observations which are obtained by summing the monthly observations satisfy

$$y_* = Cy = CX\beta + C\epsilon = X_*\beta + \epsilon_*$$

where C is the appropriate $n \times 3n$ matrix. Assuming that monthly observations on X are observed but monthly observations on y are not, the problem is to estimate y.

(a) Show that a linear unbiased estimator $\hat{y} = Ay_*$ of y which has the minimum tr $E(\hat{y} - y)$ $(\hat{y} - y)'$ is

$$\hat{y} = X_* \hat{\beta} + (V_{\ell *} V_{**}^{-1}) \hat{\epsilon}_*$$

where
$$\hat{\beta} = (X'_* V_{**}^{-1} X_*)^{-1} X'_* V_{**}^{-1} y_* \qquad V_{**} = E\epsilon_* \epsilon'_*$$

$$V_{\ell *} = E\epsilon\epsilon'_* \qquad \text{and} \qquad \hat{\epsilon}_* = y_* - X_* \hat{\beta}$$

Note that

$$E(\hat{y} - y)(\hat{y} - y)' = AV_{**} A' - AV_{*\ell} - V_{\ell *} A' + V$$

and that unbiasedness implies $AX_* - X = 0$.

(b) Provide a practical method for implementing the estimator $\hat{y}$ under the assumption that $\epsilon_t = a\epsilon_{t-1} + u_t$, where u_t is serially uncorrelated, each having variance σ^2.

14. Let the third column of the matrix X of explanatory variables in (63) be changed by replacing the m zeros by m p's, where p is the price observed in the cross-section sample. How will the least-squares estimates b_1, b_2, b_3, and b_4 be affected? How will s^2 be affected? Explain your answers.

REFERENCES

Abrahamse, A. P. J., and J. Koerts (1969): "A Comparison between the Power of the Durbin-Watson Test and the Power of the BLUS Test," *J. Am. Statist. Assoc.*, **64**: 938–952.

Almon, S. (1965): "The Distributed Lag between Capital Appropriations and Expenditures," *Econometrica*, **33**: 178–196.

Andrews, D. F., et al. (1972): *Robust Estimates of Location*, Princeton University Press, Princeton, N.J.

Belsley, D. A., E. Kuh, and R. E. Welsch (1980): *Regression Diagnostics*, Wiley, New York.

Chow, G. C. (1957), *Demand for Automobiles in the United States: A Study in Consumer Durables*, North-Holland, Amsterdam.

——— (1976): "A Note on the Derivation of Theil's BLUS Residuals," *Econometrica*, **44**: 609–610.

——— and A. Lin (1971): "Best Linear Unbiased Interpolation, Distribution, and Extrapolation of Time Series by Related Series," *Rev. Econ. and Statist.*, **53**: 372–375.

——— and ——— (1976): "Best Linear Unbiased Estimation of Missing Observations in an Economic Time Series," *J. Am. Statist. Assoc.*, **71**: 719–721.

Dhrymes, P. (1981): *Distributed Lags: Problems of Estimation and Formulation*, North-Holland, Amsterdam.

Durbin, J. (1953): "A Note on Regression When There Is Extraneous Information about One of the Coefficients," *J. Am. Statist. Assoc.*, **48**: 799–808.

——— (1970a): "Testing for Serial Correlation in Least-Squares Regression When Some of the Regressors Are Lagged Dependent Variables," *Econometrica*, **38**: 410–421.

——— (1970b): "An Alternative to the Bounds Test for Testing for Serial Correlation in Least-Squares Regression," *Econometrica*, **38**: 422–429.

——— and G. S. Watson (1950): "Testing for Serial Correlation in Least Squares Regression, I, " *Biometrika*, **37**: 409–428.

——— and ——— (1951): "Testing for Serial Correlation in Least Squares Regression, II," *Biometrika*, **38**: 159–178.

Geary, R. (1949): "Determination of Linear Relations between Systematic Parts of Variables with Errors of Observation the Variances of Which are Unknown," *Econometrica*, **17**: 30–58.

Godfrey, G. L. (1978), "Testing for Higher-Order Serial Correlation in Regression Equations When the Regressors Include Lagged Dependent Variables," *Econometrica*, **46**: 1303–1310.

Goldfeld, S. M., and R. E. Quandt (1965): "Some Tests for Homoscedasticity," *J. Am. Statist. Assoc.*, **60**: 539–547.

Hoerl, A. E. (1962): "Application of Ridge Analysis to Regression Problems," *Chem. Eng. Progr.* **58**: 54–59.

—— R. W. Kennard, and K. F. Baldwin (1975): "Ridge Regression: Some Simulation," *Commun. Statist.* **4**: 105–123.

Huber, P. J. (1964): "Robust Estimation of a Location Parameter," *Ann. Math. Statist.*, **35**: 73–101.

Jorgenson, D. W. (1966): "Rational Distributed Lag Functions," *Econometrica*, **34**: 135–149.

Koyck, L. M. (1954): *Distributed Lags and Investment Analysis*, North-Holland, Amsterdam.

Lin, K., and J. Kmenta (1982): "Ridge Regression under Alternative Loss Criteria," *Rev. Econ. and Statist.*, **64**: 488–494.

Lindley, D. V. (1947): "Regression Lines and the Linear Functional Relationship," *Suppl. J. R. Statist. Soc.*, 218–244.

Nerlove, M. (1958): *Distributed Lags and Demand Analysis*, U.S. Department of Agriculture, Washington.

—— and K. F. Wallis (1966): "Use of the Durbin-Watson Statistic in Inappropriate Situations," *Econometrica*, **34**: 235–238.

Raiffa, H., and R. Schlaifer (1961): *Applied Statistical Decision Theory*, Harvard Business School, Boston.

Reiersøl, O. (1945): "Confluence Analysis by Means of Instrumental Sets of Variables," *Arkiv Math., Astron. Fys.*, **32**: 1–119.

Sargan, J. D. (1958): "The Estimation of Economic Relationships Using Instrumental Variables," *Econometrica*, **26**: 393–415.

Savage, L. J. (1954): *The Foundations of Statistics*, Wiley, New York.

Schmidt, P. (1976): *Econometrics*, Dekker, New York.

Shiller, R. J. (1973): "A Distributed-Lag Estimator Derived from Smoothness Priors," *Econometrica*, **41**: 775–788.

Silvey, S. D. (1969): "Multicollinearity and Imprecise Estimation," *J. R. Statist. Soc.*, **B35**: 67–75.

Stein, C. M. (1956): "Inadmissibility of the Usual Estimator of the Mean of a Multivariate Normal Distribution," *Proc. 3d Berkeley Symp. Math. Statis. Probab.*, 197–206.

Taylor, W. E. (1974), "Smoothness Priors and Stochastic Prior Restrictions in Distributed Lag Estimation," *Int. Econ. Rev.*, **15**: 803–804.

Theil, H. (1971): *Principles of Econometrics*, Wiley, New York.

—— and A. S. Goldberger (1961): "On Pure and Mixed Statistical Estimation in Economics," *Int. Econ. Rev.*, **2**: 65–78.

Wallis, K. F. (1972), "Testing for Fourth-Order Autocorrelation in Quarterly Regression Equations," *Econometrica*, **40**: 617–636.

White, H. and G. M. MacDonald (1980), "Some Large-Sample Tests for Nonnormality in the Linear Regression Model," *J. Am. Statist. Assoc.*, **75**: 16–28.

Zellner, A. (1962): "An Efficient Method of Estimating Seemingly Unrelated Regressions and Tests for Aggregation Bias," *J. Am. Statist. Assoc.*, **57**: 348–368.

—— (1971): *An Introduction to Bayesian Inference in Econometrics*, Wiley, New York.

FOUR

SIMULTANEOUS EQUATIONS: MODEL AND IDENTIFICATION

4.1 MODEL OF LINEAR SIMULTANEOUS STOCHASTIC EQUATIONS

One of the most important models in econometrics is the model of simultaneous stochastic equations. Its importance is due to the fact that both in micro- and macroeconomics economic variables are often thought of as being determined jointly by a system of interdependent relations rather than individually one by one. Consider two examples.

Example 1 In a partial equilibrium model of demand and supply for a commodity, let y_{t1} denote the quantity of the commodity demanded or supplied in period t (assumed to be equal in equilibrium) and let y_{t2} denote the price of the commodity in period t. One can postulate a demand equation and a supply equation for a consumer good to be, respectively,

$$-y_{t1} + \beta_{12} y_{t2} + \gamma_{11} x_{t1} + \gamma_{12} x_{t2} + 0 = \epsilon_{t1} \tag{1}$$

$$\beta_{21} y_{t1} - y_{t2} + \gamma_{21} x_{t1} + 0 + \gamma_{23} x_{t3} = \epsilon_{t2} \tag{2}$$

where y_{t1} is per capita demand in period t; y_{t2} is price per unit in period t; x_{t1} is a dummy variable equal to 1 identically, so that γ_{11} and γ_{21} are the intercepts; x_{t2} is income per capita in period t; x_{t3} is an index of the price of the materials used in producing the commodity; and ϵ_{t1} and ϵ_{t2} are assumed to be serially independent and jointly normal, with mean zero and covariance matrix Σ. Given a random drawing from the bivariate normal distribution for ϵ_{t1} and ϵ_{t2}, the quantity y_{t1} and the price y_{t2} are determined by solving the simultaneous equations (1) and (2), reflecting the fact that quantity and price are determined jointly by the intersection of the demand and supply equations.

Example 2 Consider a simplified macroeconomic model for the determination of aggregate consumption expenditures C_t and aggregate output Y_t in a closed economy with private investment expenditures I_t and government expenditures G_t treated as given. Consumption expenditures are assumed to be a linear function of after-tax income $(1 - \tau)Y_t$, where τ is the tax rate, and of lagged consumption expenditures. The model consists of a consumption function and an identity for the GNP

$$C_t = \beta_1(1 - \tau)Y_t + \beta_2 C_{t-1} + \epsilon_t \tag{3}$$

$$Y_t = C_t + I_t + G_t \tag{4}$$

Given a random drawing from the distribution for ϵ_t, consumption C_t and aggregate product Y_t are jointly determined by solving Eqs. (3) and (4), with C_{t-1}, I_t, and G_t treated as given constants. Algebraically, the solutions for C_t and Y_t are

$$C_t = \frac{\beta_1^*}{1 - \beta_1^*} I_t + \frac{\beta_1^*}{1 - \beta_1^*} G_t + \frac{\beta_2}{1 - \beta_1^*} C_{t-1} + \frac{1}{1 - \beta_1^*} \epsilon_t \tag{5}$$

$$Y_t = \frac{1}{1 - \beta_1^*} I_t + \frac{1}{1 - \beta_1^*} G_t + \frac{\beta_2}{1 - \beta_1^*} C_{t-1} + \frac{1}{1 - \beta_1^*} \epsilon_t \tag{6}$$

where $\beta_1^* = \beta_1(1 - \tau)$.

Using these two examples, we can define a few terms. The variables y_{ti} which the system of simultaneous equations will determine are called *dependent variables* or *endogenous variables*. The number of endogenous variables should equal the number of simultaneous equations which determine them. The variables which are determined outside of the system and which help determine the endogenous variables in the system but are not jointly determined with them are called *exogenous variables*. They correspond to the explanatory variables or independent variables in a linear regression model. The distribution of the random variables ϵ_{ti} should be independent of the exogenous variables. Although the lagged endogenous variables, such as C_{t-1} in (3), are determined by the system and the exogenous variables in the past, their values are taken as given for the purpose of determining the values of the current endogenous variables y_{ti} in period t. The exogenous variables together with the lagged endogenous variables form a set of *predetermined variables* in the system.

A *model* of simultaneous stochastic equations consists of a system of simultaneous equations where random disturbances occur. An example is the system (1) and (2). If the equations are linear and the disturbances are additive, as in (1) and (2), the model is *linear*. A model specifies the forms of the equations and of the probability distributions of the random disturbances, leaving the values of the parameters unspecified. A *structure* is a model with the numerical values of the parameters specified. The equations of a structure are referred to as *structural equations*. When the structural equations are solved for the endogenous variables, the solution is called the *reduced form*. In the example of Eqs. (3) and (4), the *reduced form* consists of Eqs. (5) and (6). Each *reduced-form equation* expresses one endogenous variable as a function of the predetermined variables and of the random disturbances ϵ_{ti}. While one structural equation may (and frequently does) include several endogenous variables, one reduced-form equation includes and explains only one endogenous variable.

In Chaps. 4 and 5 we shall be concerned only with models of *linear* simultaneous equations, leaving the treatment of *nonlinear* simultaneous equations to Chap. 7. We write a model of G linear simultaneous stochastic equations with K predetermined variables as

$$
\begin{aligned}
\beta_{11}y_{t1} + \beta_{12}y_{t2} + \cdots + \beta_{1G}y_{tG} + \gamma_{11}x_{t1} + \cdots + \gamma_{1K}x_{tK} &= \epsilon_{t1} \\
\beta_{21}y_{t1} + \beta_{22}y_{t2} + \cdots + \beta_{2G}y_{tG} + \gamma_{21}x_{t1} + \cdots + \gamma_{2K}x_{tK} &= \epsilon_{t2} \\
&\cdots\cdots\cdots\cdots\cdots\cdots\cdots\cdots\cdots\cdots\cdots\cdots\cdots \\
\beta_{G1}y_{t1} + \beta_{G2}y_{t2} + \cdots + \beta_{GG}y_{tG} + \gamma_{G1}x_{t1} + \cdots + \gamma_{GK}x_{tK} &= \epsilon_{tG}
\end{aligned}
\tag{7}
$$

where β_{ij} is the coefficient of the jth endogenous variable in the ith structural equation; γ_{ij} is the coefficient of the jth predetermined variable in the ith equation; β_{ii} is usually set equal to -1 for normalization so that y_{ti} becomes the variable on the left-hand side in the ith equation; and $\epsilon_{t1}, \ldots, \epsilon_{tG}$ are assumed to be serially independent and G-variate normal with mean zero and covariance matrix $\Sigma = (\sigma_{ij})$. Denoting by $y_{t.}$ the column vector consisting of $y_{t1}, \ldots, y_{tG}$, by $x_{t.}$ the column vector consisting of $x_{t1}, \ldots, x_{tK}$, and by $\epsilon_{t.}$ the column vector consisting of $\epsilon_{t1}, \ldots, \epsilon_{tG}$, we can write the structural equations (7) as

$$
By_{t.} + \Gamma x_{t.} = \epsilon_{t.}
\tag{8}
$$

The reduced-form equations are obtained by solving the structural equations for $y_{t.}$

$$
y_{t.} = -B^{-1}\Gamma x_{t.} + B^{-1}\epsilon_{t.} \equiv \Pi x_{t.} + v_{t.}
\tag{9}
$$

where we have defined $\Pi = -B^{-1}\Gamma$ as the matrix of reduced-form coefficients and $v_{t.} = B^{-1}\epsilon_{t.}$ as the residual vector of the reduced-form equations, with $Ev_{t.}v_{t.}' = B^{-1}\Sigma B^{-1'} = \Omega$. The parameters of the structure consist of three matrices

$$
(B, \Gamma, \Sigma)
\tag{10}
$$

whereas the parameters of the reduced form are

$$
(\Pi, \Omega)
\tag{11}
$$

The two sets of parameters are related by

$$
\Pi = -B^{-1}\Gamma \qquad \Omega = B^{-1}\Sigma B^{-1'}
\tag{12}
$$

Since the structural equations must be solved to explain the endogenous variables through the reduced form, the econometrician must assume that B^{-1} exists.

The model of simultaneous stochastic equations was first proposed by Haavelmo (1943, 1944) in two classic papers, although Tinbergen (1939) had already constructed a system of equations to explain the United States economy under the auspices of the League of Nations. Haavelmo's classic papers emphasize two major points. First, a system of simultaneous stochastic equations is a suitable model for many economic applications. Second, one has to formulate a stochastic model in order to test economic theory and estimate economic relations using statistical data. A nonstochastic model is almost always contradicted by statistical observations; economic hypotheses must be embedded in a stochastic model in order to be tested and estimated statistically. The Cowles Commission of the University of Chicago, under the successive directorship of J. Marschak and T. C. Koopmans, performed basic research in simultaneous stochastic equations in the late 1940s and early 1950s. Koopmans (1950) and Hood and Koopmans (1953) summarized a major portion of this research work. Since the middle 1950s, the model of simultaneous equations has gained wide acceptance in economic research.

4.2 TWO PROBLEMS ASSOCIATED WITH THE SIMULTANEOUS-EQUATION MODEL

For an econometrician wishing to use the model of simultaneous equations there are two major problems to be resolved. First is the problem of *identification*. After a model has been specified in the form of the structural equations (8), it is capable of explaining the relations between the endogenous variables and the predetermined variables through the reduced form (9) which can be observed. Let there be a sample of n observations $(y_t., x_t.)$ $(t = 1, \ldots, n)$, which can be used to estimate the parameters Π and Ω of the reduced form. Is it possible to infer from (Π, Ω) the structural parameters (B, Γ, Σ)? This is the problem of *identification*. We discuss the identification problem informally in this section, leaving a more formal discussion to Secs. 4.3 and 4.4. Second, given that a certain subset of the structural parameters can be identified, how should they be estimated using the observations available? This is the problem of *estimation*. We also comment briefly on the estimation problem in this section, leaving a more systematic treatment to Chap. 5.

To appreciate the problem of identification, let us consider a modified version of the example consisting of Eqs. (1) and (2), with $\gamma_{12} = 0$ and $\gamma_{23} = 0$. The model thus consists of a demand equation relating quantity and price and a supply equation relating the same two variables. Let observations on y_{t1}, y_{t2}, and $x_{t1} = 1$ be available for $t = 1, \ldots, n$. Is it possible to estimate the coefficients β_{12}, β_{21}, γ_{11}, and γ_{21}? The answer is no, however large the sample size n may be. This result is intuitively obvious. If both the demand and the supply equations consist of the same set of variables, after estimating an equation relating these variables, how is it possible to decide whether one has estimated a demand equation or a supply equation or perhaps even a linear combination of the two equations? The parameters are *unidentifiable* in the sense that different sets of parameter values will generate the same observations.

If the above example is modified to make $\gamma_{12} \neq 0$, so that income x_{t2} will shift the demand curve but γ_{23} remains zero (or x_{t3} has not changed during the sample period so that $\gamma_{23} x_{t3}$ becomes a constant to be absorbed in the intercept γ_{21} in the supply equation), we can imagine that the demand curve has shifted and the supply curve has been traced out in the sample. Thus the parameters of the supply equation are identifiable, but the parameters of the demand equation are not. Similarly, if $\gamma_{12} = 0$ but $\gamma_{23} \neq 0$, the shifts of the supply curve during the sample period, due to changes in the price x_{t3} of the materials used in production, will help trace out the demand curve. In this example, the parameters of the demand curve are identifiable, but the parameters of the supply function are not. Historically the problem of identification was recognized by Working (1927) in a classic paper. He pointed out that one cannot in general identify a demand or a supply curve simply by observing data on price and quantity and that if the demand curve has shifted but not the supply curve, the data will help identify the supply curve.

An important conclusion of the above examples is that the parameters of a system of simultaneous equations cannot be identified if all equations contain the same set (or almost the same set) of variables; the parameters of one equation can be identified if it excludes certain variables in the system so that movements of these variables will shift the other equations, thus tracing out the equation in question. In order to build a system of simultaneous equations of which the parameters can be identified, an econometrician must impose a priori restrictions on the parameters. These restrictions often take the form of requiring certain coefficients in a structural equation to be zero. In order to make the parameters in different equations identifiable, the econometrician can specify different sets of variables in different equations so that they will be distinguishable.

Having specified an equation which is identifiable, which means that the parameters in the equation are identifiable, the econometrician faces the problem of estimating the parameters in this equation. An important point to note is that the method of least squares will not yield consistent estimates of the parameters. In Eq. (1) if we regress y_{t1} on y_{t2}, x_{t1} and x_{t2}, the coefficients will not be consistently estimated because y_{t2} is correlated with all residuals $\epsilon_{t.}$ in a simultaneous system, as can be seen by the reduced form (9), where each y_{ti} is a linear function of $x_{t.}$ and of $\epsilon_{t.}$. Methods other than ordinary least squares (OLS) have to be devised in order to obtain consistent estimates of the structural parameters.

One such method is two-stage least squares. By this method, in the first stage, least squares is applied to estimate the coefficients Π in the reduced-form equations (9). That is, each y_{ti} is regressed on $x_{t.}$, yielding an estimate of the ith row of Π. Having thus obtained the estimate $\hat{\Pi}$ of Π, we form the vector of estimated endogenous variable $\hat{y}_{t.} = \hat{\Pi} x_{t.}$ using the regression equations. Note that $\hat{y}_{t.}$, being a linear function of $x_{t.}$, is uncorrelated with the estimated residual $\hat{v}_{t.} = y_{t.} - \hat{y}_{t.}$ as a property of the method of least squares; $\hat{y}_{t.}$ is also uncorrelated with the true residual $v_{t.}$ in the limit. In the second stage, the ith structural equation is estimated by regressing y_{ti} on the other $\hat{y}_{tj}$ included in the equation and on the selected predetermined variables x_{tj}. That is, the other endogenous variables are replaced by their estimated values from the first stage, and a regression is performed using these estimated values instead of the observed values of the endogenous variables. The estimates of the structural coefficients are consistent because the explanatory variables $\hat{y}_{tj}$ are no longer correlated with the residual ϵ_{ti} in the limit.

Now that the problem of providing consistent estimates of the structural parameters has been recognized and one method for solving the problem described, it may be asked why one needs to estimate the structural parameters in the first place. To provide forecasts of the endogenous variables generated by a structure of simultaneous equations knowledge of the reduced-form equations (9) will suffice if there are no changes in the structure. In this case, one can simply estimate (9) by least squares and use $\hat{\Pi}x_{t.}^p$, where $x_{t.}^p$ is the projected value for the vector of predetermined variables, to forecast the endogenous variables. However, if the structural parameters change because of policy changes, the reduced-form parameters will also change. One can no longer employ the estimate $\hat{\Pi}$ of the reduced-form parameters from a historical sample to forecast future values of the endogenous variables after the policy changes. For example, in the model of Eqs. (3) and (4), if the tax rate τ is changed, the parameter $\beta_1^* = \beta_1(1 - \tau)$ will be changed. The parameters of the reduced-form equations (5) and (6) will be changed accordingly. If these latter parameters are estimated by applying least squares to the reduced form without knowledge of the structure, one does not know how they should be changed after the policy changes. On the other hand, if the structural parameters β_1^* and thus β_1 are consistently estimated under the old regime with tax rate $\tau = \tau_0$, the parameters $\beta_1^* = \beta_1(1 - \tau_1)$ under a new tax rate $\tau = \tau_1$ can easily be ascertained and the reduced-form parameters can be revised accordingly for the purpose of forecasting and assessing the economic effects of the tax change. Marschak (1953) provides an excellent discussion of this point, illustrating by a microeconomic example why knowledge of the structural parameters is necessary for forecasting and evaluating the impact of policy changes.

An important distinction often made between economics and most natural sciences is that controlled experiments are in many situations costly in economics. Economists frequently have to rely on observations generated by history rather than by experiments they have designed. For example, an experimental approach to measuring the macroeconomic effects of a specified change in the income tax rates would be to change the rates and observe the consequences while removing the possible effects of other variables by regression analysis. But such an experiment would be too costly and perhaps politically infeasible. By postulating a model and estimating the structural parameters using historical data alone, the economist can infer what the effects of the new tax rates would be without actually having tried them. This methodology is illustrated by the discussion of the last paragraph. It is remarkable that by using structural equations the economist can predict the effects of policy changes without relying on controlled experiments.

4.3 CONDITIONS FOR IDENTIFYING A STRUCTURAL EQUATION

Returning to a discussion of the identification problem, in this section we consider conditions for the identification of the parameters of one structural equation. One basic idea is that for a set of structural parameters to be identifiable they must be uniquely determined if the reduced-form parameters are known. The parameters of the reduced form (9) can be consistently estimated by the method of least squares. If certain parameters of the structure can be inferred uniquely from the reduced-form parameters through the relation $B\Pi = -\Gamma$, they are identifiable. If two or more sets of values for the structural parameters (B, Γ) are consistent with the same Π, they are not identifiable. These structures, which imply the same reduced form, are said to be observationally equivalent. A structure is identified if there exists no other observationally equivalent structure.

We define two structures to be *observationally equivalent* if they generate the same probability distribution for the endogenous variables given the predetermined variables. From the reduced form (9), we know that the conditional distribution of y_t given x_t is normal, with mean Πx_t and covariance matrix $\Omega = B^{-1}\Sigma B^{-1\prime}$. Since the reduced form specifies the conditional distribution of y_t given x_t, we say that two structures are observationally equivalent if they imply the same reduced form. Similarly, a set of structural parameters is identifiable if and only if no other set of parameter values can yield the same reduced form.

To investigate the conditions for the identifiability of the parameters of one structural equation, one may ask under what conditions the parameters of this equation can be inferred uniquely from the parameters of the reduced form through the relation $B\Pi = -\Gamma$. Without loss, we consider the first structural equation since by rearrangement any equation can be renamed the first. The coefficients of the first equation are the elements of the first row of $[B \ \Gamma]$. Let $\beta_{11} = -1$ by normalization, and let G_1 endogenous variables and K_1 predetermined variables be included in the first equation. The coefficients of the first equation can be written as $[-1 \ \beta' \ 0 \ \gamma' \ 0]$, where the two zeros are respectively the coefficients of the $G - G_1$ endogenous variables and the $K - K_1$ predetermined variables excluded from the first structural equation. The excluded variables can always be arranged to be the last.

The relation between the coefficients of the first structural equation and the reduced-form coefficients Π is given by the first row of $B\Pi = -\Gamma$,

$$[-1 \ \ \beta' \ \ 0] \begin{bmatrix} \Pi_{11} & \Pi_{12} \\ \Pi_{21} & \Pi_{22} \end{bmatrix} = -[\gamma' \ \ 0] \tag{13}$$

where the matrix Π has been partitioned, Π_{11} and Π_{12} having G_1 rows, Π_{21} and Π_{22} having $G - G_1$ rows, Π_{11} and Π_{21} having K_1 columns, and Π_{12} and Π_{22} having $K - K_1$ columns. Expression (13) consists of two sets of equations,

$$[-1 \ \ \beta']\Pi_{11} = -\gamma' \tag{14}$$

and

$$[-1 \ \ \beta']\Pi_{12} = 0 \tag{15}$$

If β can be identified, γ can always be identified by using (14). The question then is under what conditions β can be identified by relation (15) given Π_{12}.

Equation (15) is a set of $K - K_1$ linear equations (corresponding to the $K - K_1$ columns of Π_{12}) in the $G_1 - 1$ unknowns which are elements of the vector β. A *necessary and sufficient condition* for a unique solution for β (and thus for the identification of the first structural equation) is that the *rank of the matrix* Π_{12} *be* $G_1 - 1$, that is, be equal to the number of unknown coefficients of the endogenous variables included in the first structural equation. This is known as the *rank condition* for identification of a structural equation.

A *necessary condition* for a unique solution for β, and thus for the identification of the first structural equation, is that the number $K - K_1$ of equations be no smaller than the number $G_1 - 1$ of unknowns in β. This is known as the *order condition* for identification of a structural equation

$$K - K_1 \geq G_1 - 1 \tag{16}$$

There are different ways to remember the order condition. The number of excluded predetermined variables in the structural equation should be no less than the number of included endogenous variables minus 1 (of the number of unknown coefficients of the included endogenous variables). Alternatively, with $G - G_1$ added to both sides of (16), we have

$$G - G_1 + K - K_1 \geq G - 1 \tag{17}$$

or the number of excluded (endogenous and exogenous) variables in the equation should be no less than the number of simultaneous equations in the model minus 1. In other words, the number of excluded variables in each structural equation should be no less than the total number of endogenous variables minus 1 for the structure to be identifiable. This is a more precise statement of the requirement, hinted at in Sec. 4.2, that different structural equations should contain different sets of variables in order for the structure to be identifiable. A third way to express condition (16) is to add K_1 on both sides, yielding

$$K \geq G_1 + K_1 - 1$$

which asserts that the number of predetermined variables in the system can be no less than the number of unknown coefficients in the equation to be identified.

If the necessary condition (16) or (17) is not met, the structural equation is *underidentified* or *not identifiable*. If the equality sign holds in (16) or (17), the structural equation is *just identified* or *exactly identified*. There are exactly as many linear equations in (15) as unknowns, the elements of Π_{12} being the given coefficients for determining the unknown elements of β. When the inequality sign holds in (16) or (17), the number of equations or the number of columns of Π_{12}, $K - K_1$, is larger than the number of unknowns in β, $G_1 - 1$. The structural equation is said to be *overidentified*. A structural equation is identified if it is either just identified or overidentified. In the model consisting of Eqs. (1) and (2), the first equation has one excluded predetermined variable, and the number of included endogenous variables minus 1 is also 1. By (16), this equation is just identified. Alternatively, the first equation has one excluded (predetermined or endogenous) variable, and the total number of endogenous variables in the system minus 1 is also 1. By (17), this equation is just identified. Similarly, Eq. (2) is just identified.

We have derived the rank condition and the order condition for identifying one structural equation by using the relation $B\Pi = -\Gamma$. While the order condition is easy to apply, the rank condition is more difficult because Π_{12} is a nonlinear function of β and it is hard to ascertain its rank by inspection. It therefore would be desirable to develop conditions for identification via the structural coefficients. One approach is to employ the definition of two observationally equivalent structures and derive algebraic conditions which they are required to satisfy. If the specification of the first structural equation is such that only two identical structural equations can be observationally equivalent, the equation is identified.

Theorem 4.1 Two linear structures (B, Γ, ϵ) and $(B^*, \Gamma^*, \epsilon^*)$ are observationally equivalent if and only if they are connected by a nonsingular transformation F; that is $(B^*, \Gamma^*, \epsilon^*) = F(B, \Gamma, \epsilon)$, and $\Sigma^* = F\Sigma F'$.

PROOF If the first structure is

$$By_{t.} + \Gamma x_{t.} = \epsilon_{t.}$$

and the second structure is

$$FBy_{t.} + F\Gamma x_{t.} = F\epsilon_{t.}$$

their reduced forms are identical, both being $y_{t.} = -B^{-1}\Gamma x_{t.} + B^{-1}\epsilon_{t.}$; hence they are observationally equivalent. If the two structures are observationally equivalent, their reduced-form parameters are identical,

$$\Pi = \Pi^* \qquad \text{and} \qquad \Omega = \Omega^*$$

implying that $B^{-1}\Gamma = B^{*-1}\Gamma^*$ or $(B^*B^{-1})\Gamma = \Gamma^*$ and $(B^*B^{-1})B = B^*$. Letting $F = B^*B^{-1}$, we have $\Gamma^* = F\Gamma$ and $B^* = FB$. Multiplying the first structure by F and using these results, we obtain

$$F\epsilon_{t.} = FBy_{t.} + F\Gamma x_{t.} = B^*y_{t.} + \Gamma^*x_{t.} = \epsilon^*_{t.}$$

implying $\epsilon^*_{t.} = F\epsilon_{t.}$. Hence the two structures are connected by a nonsingular transformation $F = B^*B^{-1}$, and the proof is complete.

Again, let the coefficients of the first structural equation be $[-1 \quad \beta'_1 \quad 0 \quad \gamma'_1 \quad 0]$, the first zero having $G - G_1$ elements and the second having $K - K_1$ elements, and let the structural coefficients be partitioned as

$$[B \quad \Gamma] = \begin{bmatrix} -1 & \beta'_1 & 0 & \gamma'_1 & 0 \\ B_0 & B_1 & B_2 & \Gamma_1 & \Gamma_2 \end{bmatrix} \tag{18}$$

where B_0 is a $(G-1) \times 1$ column vector of coefficients in B below the coefficient $\beta_{11} = -1$, B_1 is a $(G_1 - 1) \times (G_1 - 1)$ matrix of coefficients in B below the row vector β_1', etc. If the first equation is to be identifiable, any observationally equivalent structure with coefficients $[B^* \quad \Gamma^*]$ must have identical coefficients on the first row. By the above theorem, this means that the first row of the matrix F connecting the two structures with

$$[B^* \quad \Gamma^*] = F[B \quad \Gamma] \tag{19}$$

must be the unit row vector $[1 \quad 0 \quad \cdots \quad 0]$. For then, the first row of any observationally equivalent structure $[B^* \quad \Gamma^*]$ must be equal to the first row of $[B \quad \Gamma]$.

The question is whether the imposition of two zero vectors in the row $[-1 \quad \beta_1' \quad 0 \quad \gamma_1' \quad 0]$ will force the first row of F to be $[1 \quad 0 \quad \cdots \quad 0]$. Write the first row of F as $[f_{11} \quad \cdots \quad f_{1G}]$. The requirement that the first row of $[B^* \quad \Gamma^*]$ have zeros in the same places as the first row of $[B \quad \Gamma]$ implies, by (18) and (19),

$$[f_{11} \quad f_{12} \quad \cdots \quad f_{1G}]\begin{bmatrix} 0 & 0 \\ B_2 & \Gamma_2 \end{bmatrix} = [0 \quad 0] \tag{20}$$

If and only if the rank of $[B_2 \quad \Gamma_2]$ is $G - 1$ will the vector $[f_{12} \quad \cdots \quad f_{1G}]$ be zero. If we also normalize $\beta_{11}^* = -1$ for the observationally equivalent structure, by (19),

$$\beta_{11}^* = -1 = [f_{11} \quad f_{12} \quad \cdots \quad f_{1G}]\begin{bmatrix} -1 \\ B_0 \end{bmatrix}$$

$[f_{12} \quad \cdots \quad f_{1G}] = 0$ implies $f_{11} = 1$. Hence, a necessary and sufficient condition for any observationally equivalent structure to have the same first equation, i.e., for the first equation to be identifiable, is that the rank of $[B_2 \quad \Gamma_2]$ be $G - 1$.

To apply this rank condition for identifying any structural equation we form the matrix $[B_2 \quad \Gamma_2]$. This is done by collecting all the columns of the $[B \quad \Gamma]$ matrix which correspond to the zero coefficients of the structural equation in question. The matrix $[B_2 \quad \Gamma_2]$ has $G - 1$ rows and $(G - G_1) + (K - K_1)$ columns. We then inspect this matrix and see whether its rank is $G - 1$.

For the rank of $[B_2 \quad \Gamma_2]$ to be $G - 1$, the number of columns must be at least $G - 1$. Thus

$$(G - G_1) + (K - K_1) \geq G - 1$$

is a necessary condition for the identifiability of the first equation. This is the same order condition (17) we derived by using the reduced-form coefficients Π_{12} in Eq. (15).

Applying the rank condition for $[B_2 \quad \Gamma_2]$ to study the identifiability of Eq. (1) in the system of Eqs. (1) and (2), we find that this matrix is simply γ_{23}, which corresponds to the only zero coefficient in the first equation. Since the rank of γ_{23} is 1, or equal to the number of equations G minus 1, the first equation is identified. Note that the rank condition for $[B_2 \quad \Gamma_2]$ just applied is a necessary and sufficient condition. We now know that the first equation is identified. The order condition (16) and (17), ascertained by counting the number of zero coefficients, is a necessary condition but not a sufficient condition for identification.

The above discussion is confined to imposing zero restrictions on the coefficients of the first structural equation, but it can easily be extended to deal with linear restrictions. Let the first row of $[B \quad \Gamma]$ be denoted by α'_1. A set of R linear restrictions on α_1 can be written as

$$\alpha'_1 \phi = d'$$

where ϕ is a $(G + K) \times R$ matrix and d' is a row vector of R elements. For example, the restrictions $\beta_{11} = -1, \beta_{12} = 2\beta_{13}$, and $\beta_{14} = 5$ can be written as

$$[\beta_{11} \quad \beta_{12} \quad \cdots \quad \beta_{1G} \quad \gamma_{11} \quad \gamma_{12} \quad \cdots, \quad \gamma_{1G}] \begin{bmatrix} 1 & 0 & 0 \\ 0 & 1 & 0 \\ 0 & -2 & 0 \\ 0 & 0 & 1 \\ 0 & 0 & 0 \\ & \cdot \cdot \cdot \cdot & \\ 0 & 0 & 0 \end{bmatrix} = [-1 \quad 0 \quad 5]$$

A main result of the identification of one structural equation whose coefficients are subject to linear restrictions is contained in the following theorem.

Theorem 4.2 Let the coefficients α_1 of the first structural equation be subject to R linear restrictions (including the normalization restriction $\beta_{11} = -1$) of the form $\alpha'_1 \phi_1 = d'_1$. The first equation is identified if and only if the rank of $[B \quad \Gamma]\phi_1$ equals G.

PROOF We wish to show that the coefficients α^*_1 of an observationally equivalent structure must equal α_1 by showing that the first row of the matrix F for transforming $[B \quad \Gamma]$ into $[B^* \quad \Gamma^*]$ must be $[1 \quad 0 \quad \cdots \quad 0]$. The first row of $[B^* \quad \Gamma^*]$ is

$$\alpha^{*'}_1 = [f_{11} \quad f_{12} \quad \cdots \quad f_{1G}][B \quad \Gamma]$$

Since α^*_1 must satisfy the same linear restrictions as α_1, we have

$$\alpha^{*'}_1 \phi_1 = [f_{11} \quad f_{12} \quad \cdots \quad f_{1G}][B \quad \Gamma]\phi_1 = d'_1$$

$[B \quad \Gamma]\phi_1$ is a $G \times R$ matrix. The above is a set of R linear equations in the G unknowns, $f_{11}, \ldots, f_{1G}$, with the columns of $[B \quad \Gamma]\phi_1$ as coefficients. We know that $[f_{11} \quad \cdots \quad f_{1G}] = [1, \quad 0 \quad \cdots \quad 0]$ is a solution because in this case $\alpha^*_1 = \alpha_1$ will satisfy the restriction $\alpha^{*'}_1 \phi_1 = d'_1$. This solution is unique, or the first equation is identified, if and only if the rank of $[B \quad \Gamma]\phi_1$ equals G. This proof applies to the ith equation by replacing $[f_{11}, \quad \ldots, \quad f_{1G}]$ by $[f_{i1}, \ldots, f_{iG}]$ which should equal $[0, \quad \ldots, \quad 1, \quad \ldots, \quad 0]$ with 1 in the ith position.

The reader can easily check that when the restrictions take the form of imposing $G - G_1$ zeros on the coefficients of the endogenous variables and $K - K_1$ zeros on the coefficients of the predetermined variables, the rank condition of Theorem 4.2 reduces to the rank of $[B_2 \quad \Gamma_2]$ being $G - 1$.

*4.4 IDENTIFICATION OF A SET OF STRUCTURAL PARAMETERS

One can extend the discussion of identification of structural parameters via the reduced-form parameters to cover linear restrictions on parameters in different structural equations. One can also study the identification of a subset of structural parameters. This topic was studied by Richmond (1974). The subject matter of this section beyond Theorem 4.3 is specialized and may be omitted without loss of continuity.

To begin the discussion, let us restate the rank condition for identifying the first structural equation by rewriting the relation between the structural parameters and the reduced-form parameters as

$$B\Pi + \Gamma = 0$$

the first row of which is

$$\beta'_1\Pi + \gamma'_1 = 0$$

or

$$[\beta'_1 \quad \gamma'_1]\begin{bmatrix} \Pi \\ I \end{bmatrix} = 0 \tag{21}$$

which is a set of K linear equations with the $G + K$ unknowns in $[\beta'_1 \quad \gamma'_1]$. There are not enough equations to determine the unknowns. Let the restrictions $[\beta'_1 \quad \gamma'_1]\phi_1 = d'_1$ be imposed. We then combine (21) with the restrictions to yield

$$[\beta'_1 \quad \gamma'_1]\begin{bmatrix} \Pi \\ I \end{bmatrix} \phi_1 = [0 \quad d'_1] \tag{22}$$

which is used to prove the following theorem.

Theorem 4.3 Let the coefficients of the first equation be subject to $[\beta'_1 \quad \gamma'_1]\phi_1 = d'_1$. The solution for $[\beta'_1 \quad \gamma'_1]$ from the reduced form is unique, or the first equation is identified, if and only if the rank of

$$\begin{bmatrix} \Pi \\ I_K \end{bmatrix} \phi_1 \tag{23}$$

is $G + K$.

This treatment for one structural equation can be extended to cover all G structural equations by stacking up equations of the form (21) for all G equations,

$$[\beta'_1 \quad \cdots \quad \beta'_G \quad \gamma'_1 \quad \cdots \quad \gamma'_G]\begin{bmatrix} \Pi & 0 & \cdots & 0 \\ 0 & \Pi & \cdots & 0 \\ & & \ddots & \\ 0 & 0 & \cdots & \Pi \\ I & 0 & \cdots & 0 \\ 0 & I & \cdots & 0 \\ & & \ddots & \\ 0 & 0 & \cdots & I \end{bmatrix} = [0 \quad 0 \quad \cdots \quad 0] \tag{24}$$

or, more compactly,
$$[\beta' \quad \gamma'] \begin{bmatrix} I_G \otimes \Pi \\ I_{GK} \end{bmatrix} = 0 \qquad (25)$$

Let the vector $\delta' = [\beta' \quad \gamma']$ of structural coefficients satisfy the restriction $\delta'\Phi = d'$. Combining the restriction with (25), we have

$$\delta' \begin{bmatrix} I_G \otimes \Pi \\ I_{GK} \end{bmatrix} \Phi = [0 \quad d'] \qquad (26)$$

which is used to prove the following theorem.

Theorem 4.4 Let the structural coefficients $\delta' = [\beta' \quad \gamma']$ satisfy $\delta'\Phi = d$. The solution for δ' is unique, or the entire system of structural equations is identified, if and only if the rank of

$$\begin{bmatrix} I_G \otimes \Pi \\ I_{GK} \end{bmatrix} \Phi \qquad (27)$$

is $G(G + K)$, which is the number of unknown elements in δ. This is a straightforward extension of Theorem 4.3.

To extend Theorem 4.2 to all structural equations, we follow its proof by using the relations between the coefficients $[\beta_i^{*\prime} \quad \gamma_i^{*\prime}]$ of an observationally equivalent structure and the coefficients $[B \quad \Gamma]$ of the structure to be identified

$$[\beta_i^{*\prime} \quad \gamma_i^{*\prime}] = [f_{i1} \quad f_{i2} \quad \cdots \quad f_{iG}][B \quad \Gamma]$$

and the fact that both sets of coefficients must satisfy $\delta'\Phi = d'$

$$[\beta_1^{*\prime} \quad \cdots \quad \beta_G^{*\prime} \quad \gamma_1^{*\prime} \quad \cdots \quad \gamma_G^{*\prime}]\Phi = d'$$

$$= [f_{11} \quad \cdots \quad f_{1G} \quad f_{21} \quad \cdots \quad f_{2G} \quad \cdots] \begin{bmatrix} B & 0 & \cdots & 0 & \Gamma & 0 & \cdots & 0 \\ 0 & B & \cdots & 0 & 0 & \Gamma & \cdots & 0 \\ & & \ddots & & & & \ddots & \\ 0 & 0 & \cdots & B & 0 & 0 & \cdots & \Gamma \end{bmatrix} \Phi \quad (28)$$

Treating (28) as a system of linear equations in the unknowns $f_{i,j}(i, j = 1, \ldots, G)$, we know that a solution is $f_{ij} = 0$ for $i \neq j$ and $f_{ii} = 1$ because $\delta' = [\beta_1' \quad \beta_2' \quad \cdots \quad \gamma_1' \quad \gamma_2' \quad \cdots]$ satisfies the restriction $\delta'\Phi = d'$. This solution is unique if the rank of the product of the last two matrices in (28) equals the number G^2 of unknowns. This proves the following theorem.

Theorem 4.5 Let the structural coefficients $\delta' = [\beta' \quad \gamma']$ satisfy $\delta'\Phi = d'$. The entire system of structural equations is identified if and only if the rank of

$$
\begin{bmatrix}
B & 0 & \cdots & 0 & \Gamma & 0 & \cdots & 0 \\
0 & B & \cdots & 0 & 0 & \Gamma & \cdots & 0 \\
 & & \ddots & & & & \ddots & \\
0 & 0 & \cdots & B & 0 & 0 & \cdots & \Gamma
\end{bmatrix}\Phi
$$

is G^2. This is an extension of Theorem 4.2.

We now proceed to study the identifiability of a linear combination $\xi'\delta$ of the elements of δ. The identifiability of a single coefficient in δ is treated by letting ξ be a vector of zeros except for the element corresponding to this coefficient, which is set equal to 1. We know that every parameter vector δ has to satisfy (26), rewritten as $\delta'W = b'$. If the rank of W is $G(G + K)$, all elements of δ are identified according to Theorem 4.4. If the rank of W is smaller, we ask whether a linear combination $\delta'\xi$ is identified by the restriction $\delta'W = b'$. To answer this question we use an algebraic result from Gale (1960, p. 41): either (i) a set of linear equations $Wx = \xi$ has a solution for x or (ii) there exists a vector c such that $c'W = 0$ and $c'\xi = 1$, but not both. If $Wx = \xi$, then $c'Wx = c'\xi$ and therefore (ii) cannot hold. It is harder to show that if (ii) does not hold, (i) must hold.

Theorem 4.6 The linear combination $\delta'\xi$ is identified by $\delta'W = b'$ if and only if there exists η such that $W\eta = \xi$, that is, if the rank of $[W \quad \xi]$ equals the rank of W (since ξ is a linear combination of the columns of W), where δ' satisfies the restriction $\delta'\Phi = d'$ and

$$
W = \begin{bmatrix} I_G \otimes \Pi \\ \\ I_{GK} \end{bmatrix}\Phi
$$

PROOF If there exists η such that $W\eta = \xi$, then for any δ satisfying $\delta'W = b'$, the linear combination $\delta'\xi$ equals $\delta'W\eta = b'\eta$, which is a constant independent of δ. Therefore, $\delta'\xi$ is identified.

If $\delta'\xi$ is unique for each δ satisfying $\delta'W = b'$, we let δ^* satisfy $\delta^{*'}W = b'$. Then for any c satisfying $c'W = 0$, $(\delta^* + c)'W = b'$. Since both $(\delta^* + c)$ and δ^* satisfy the required restrictions, we have $(\delta^* + c)'\xi = \delta^{*'}\xi$ by the uniqueness assumption. This implies $c'\xi = 0$. Hence, the equations $c'W = 0$ and $c'\xi = 1$ have no solution. This rules out situation (ii) of the algebraic result cited, leaving situation (i): there exists a solution η satisfying $W\eta = \xi$.

To apply Theorem 4.6 to determine the identifiability of the jth parameter in δ, we let ξ be a unit vector with all zeros except the jth element, which is unity. Theorem 4.6 asserts that the jth parameter is identifiable if and only if W has the same rank as $[W \ \xi]$, or, in this case, the rank of W is unchanged when its jth row is deleted.

To apply Theorem 4.6 to determine the identifiability of all the coefficients in the first structural equation which are subject to the restriction $[\beta_1' \quad \delta_1']\phi_1 = d_1'$ the relevant part of the W matrix becomes

$$\begin{bmatrix} \Pi \\ I_K \end{bmatrix} \phi_1$$

This matrix has $G + K$ rows. The vector ξ for forming a linear combination is a column vector with $G + K$ elements. The unit vector ξ for identifying the coefficient β_{1j} has unity for its jth element; the unit vector ξ for identifying the coefficient γ_{1j} has unity for its $(G + j)$th element. When all these unit vectors are appended on the right of the above matrix, its rank should be unchanged if the first equation is to be identified. This is true if and only if the matrix has full rank, which is $G + K$. This result agrees with Theorem 4.3.

As an illustration, consider the identifiability of γ_{13} in Eq. (1) of the model consisting of Eqs. (1) and (2). Originally, we assumed $\gamma_{13} = 0$, but now we are dropping that assumption. Without further restrictions, the first equation is not identified. We now impose the restriction $\gamma_{13} = 2\gamma_{21}$ in addition to $\beta_{11} = -1$, $\beta_{22} = -1$, and $\gamma_{22} = 0$. Incorporating these four restrictions in the columns of Φ, we exhibit the $[W \quad \xi]$ matrix.

$$[W \quad \xi] = \begin{bmatrix}
\pi_{11} & \pi_{12} & \pi_{13} & 0 & 0 & 0 & 1 & 0 & 0 & 0 & 0 \\
\pi_{21} & \pi_{22} & \pi_{23} & 0 & 0 & 0 & 0 & 0 & 0 & 0 & 0 \\
0 & 0 & 0 & \pi_{11} & \pi_{12} & \pi_{13} & 0 & 0 & 0 & 0 & 0 \\
0 & 0 & 0 & \pi_{21} & \pi_{22} & \pi_{23} & 0 & 0 & 1 & 0 & 0 \\
1 & 0 & 0 & 0 & 0 & 0 & 0 & 0 & 0 & 0 & 0 \\
0 & 1 & 0 & 0 & 0 & 0 & 0 & 0 & 0 & 0 & 0 \\
0 & 0 & 1 & 0 & 0 & 0 & 0 & 1 & 0 & 0 & 1 \\
0 & 0 & 0 & 1 & 0 & 0 & 0 & -2 & 0 & 0 & 0 \\
0 & 0 & 0 & 0 & 1 & 0 & 0 & 0 & 0 & 1 & 0 \\
0 & 0 & 0 & 0 & 0 & 1 & 0 & 0 & 0 & 0 & 0
\end{bmatrix} \quad (29)$$

Note that the 10×10 matrix W has rank 10. Therefore, the rank is unchanged after the last column ξ is appended. By theorem 4.6, γ_{13} is identified. If the restriction $\gamma_{13} = 2\gamma_{21}$ were absent, the eighth column of W would disappear and W would be a 10×9 matrix with rank 9. Adding the last column ξ would raise its rank to 10, signifying that the coefficient γ_{13} is not identifiable.

The literature on identification is quite extensive, and the above discussion serves only as an introduction. For an excellent survey, see Hsiao (1981). An important point conveyed in the discussion of identification is that without a priori restrictions imposed by economic theory it would be impossible to estimate economic relationships, which are highly interdependent. In fact, Liu (1960) went so far as to argue that economic relations are not identifiable because the world is so interdependent as to have almost all variables appearing in every equation, thus violating the necessary condition for identification. More recently, Sims (1980) has echoed Liu's point and advocated building time-series models (discussed in Chap. 6) rather than models of simultaneous structural equations. One can reply to Liu by pointing out that economic relations are indeed distinct. The demand equation is determined by a different set of variables from the supply equation, and the investment equation from the consumption function, etc. A more technical reply will be presented in Chap. 9 when we discuss statistical criteria for choosing between alternative models for the measurement of economic relations.

The remaining sections of this chapter are largely devoted to a report on a simple macroeconomic model of the United States in order to bring out some important applications of the model of simultaneous stochastic equations.

4.5 FORMULATION OF A MACROECONOMETRIC MODEL

The report was an attempt to study statistically the multiplier, the accelerator, and the liquidity-preference relations in macroeconomics and the extent to which they alone can explain and predict national income in the United States. It may be considered as a partial statistical appendix to such classic papers in macroeconomics as those by Hicks (1937), Modigliani (1944), and Samuelson (1939).†

To test statistically the hypotheses of Keynes' *General Theory* (1936), the post-Keynesian formulations, and the acceleration principle, some modifications to the formulations of Hicks (1937) and Modigliani (1944) are unavoidable since they are essentially static in nature and, as such, not identifiable; i.e., they fail to include sufficiently different sets of variables in different equations. Fortunately, by introducing simple distributed lags one can specify an adjustment process toward equilibrium, supply enough distinct variables in different equations to ensure identification, and keep the model as close as possible to macroeconomic theory.

The Consumption Function

The following simple distributed lag consumption function, relating equilibrium consumption $\dot{C}$ to current income Y, is consistent with two major post-Keynesian findings on consumption, namely, that aggregate consumption can be explained and that its response to current income is small

$$\dot{C}_t = a_0 + a_1 Y_t \tag{30}$$

Assuming a fraction β_1 of $\dot{C}_t - C_{t-1}$ to be realized we have

$$C_t - C_{t-1} = \beta_1(\dot{C}_t - C_{t-1}) = \beta_1(a_0 + a_1 Y_t - C_{t-1}) \tag{31}$$

implying $\qquad C_t = \beta_1 a_0 + \beta_1 a_1 Y_t + (1 - \beta_1)C_{t-1} \tag{32}$

To avoid high serial correlation in (32) we shall test

$$\Delta C_t = \beta_1 a_1 \, \Delta Y_t + (1 - \beta_1) \, \Delta C_{t-1} \tag{33}$$

† The balance of this section to the end of Sec. 4.9 is modified from Chow (1967) by permission.

The effect of the stock of money on consumption, M_t in Eq. (32) or ΔM_t in Eq. (33), will also be tested.

Concerning the treatment of consumer durables, should the variable C be the stock in existence or the amount purchased? The answer depends partly on our hypothesis about consumer behavior and partly on the choice between statistical approximations. It may be reasonable to hypothesize that (32) or (33) describes consumption (measured by stock in case of durables) rather than consumer expenditures. As a matter of statistical approximation, Eqs. (32) or (33) can be applied to the purchase of new durables if their durability is short. The less durable a commodity, the better the approximation in treating it as a perishable. In our model, we choose to deal with an aggregate of consumer durables. Whether this aggregate belongs to Eq. (33) or behaves more like an investment (flow) equation (to be derived below from assumptions about desired stock) is essentially a statistical question.

The Investment Function

The investment decision may be complicated, but we shall simply modify the static theory of the firm by a stock-flow transformation and by lags. Let the equilibrium demand for a capital good $\dot{K}_t$ be a linear function of the firm's output Y' and the relative price p of its service, and let β_2 be the adjustment coefficient. Analogous to (32) is

$$K_t = \beta_2 b_0 + \beta_2 b_1 Y'_t + \beta_2 b_2 p_t + (1 - \beta_2)K_{t-1} \tag{34}$$

A serious statistical difficulty in using Eq. (34) is the lack of accurate data on capital stock. Taking its first difference or obtaining an equation for net investment $I''_t = K_t - K_{t-1}$ does not avoid this difficulty, but taking the difference $K_t - (1 - d)K_{t-1}$, where d is the percentage rate of depreciation, will yield cross investment I_t

$$I_t = \beta_2 b_1 [Y'_t - (1 - d)Y'_{t-1}] + \beta_2 b_2 [p_t - (1 - d)p_{t-1}] + (1 - \beta_2)I_{t-1}$$
$$+ \text{const} \tag{35}$$

Equation (35) shows the acceleration principle by relating investment to the change in output $Y'_t - (1 - d)Y'_t$. It implies statistically that if both Y'_t and Y'_{t-1} appear as explanatory variables for gross investment, the coefficient of Y'_{t-1} should be approximately equal to the negative of the coefficient of Y'_t.

The rate of interest R affects investment through the price effect, i.e., through the relation $p = P(d + R)$, where P is the price of the capital stock. This simple relation implies that the interest elasticity of demand equals a fraction $R/(d + R)$ of the price elasticity of demand, since a 1 percent change in R will result in an $R/(d + R)$ percent change in p

$$\frac{\partial \log p}{\partial \log R} = \frac{\partial \log (d + R)}{\partial \log R} = \frac{R}{d + R}$$

If $R = .05$, this fraction will be .20 for $d = .20$. It will be .50 for $d = .05$. Thus, except for the very durable among durable goods, say those with depreciation lower than .10, the interest elasticity is a small fraction, say lower than one-third, of the price elasticity of demand. Our theoretical analysis suggests that the interest elasticity for most durable goods is small (smaller for the less durable) and that the investment functions with interest as an explanatory variable should be classified according to the durabilities of the commodities.

In our macroeconomic model we shall ignore the effects of relative prices and assume constant rates of depreciation, leaving R to be the only variable affecting p. In Eq. (35) p will be replaced by R (without introducing a new symbol for the coefficient b_2). Furthermore, we shall use the same national product variable Y in the consumption function for the aggregate product variable Y' in the aggregate gross investment function. Thus,

$$I_t = \beta_2 b_1 [Y_t - (1 - d)Y_{t-1}] + \beta_2 b_2 [R_t - (1 - d)R_{t-1}] + (1 - \beta_2)I_{t-1}$$

$$+ \text{const} \tag{36}$$

Two theoretical complications may arise in our formulation of the investment function (36). First, we have implicitly assumed that the capital market is near enough to being perfect for the cost to a firm of using the service of a capital good to be simply its equivalent rental. In a perfect capital market, the rent would be equal to $p = P(d + R)$. If the capital market is highly imperfect, the firm will find it much more economical to purchase a capital good than to rent it and the quantity of a capital good it can purchase will be restricted by the amount of liquid assets available. To some extent, the availability of liquid assets is measured by the rate of interest. However, liquid funds may simply be "unavailable" to the firm; i.e., the effective rate of interest on the firm's borrowing may be much higher than any observed rate. This would make the amount of liquid assets available an important constraint on the firm's ability to purchase capital goods. In our empirical investigation this possibility will be examined by introducing ΔM into Eq. (36).

Second, the lag structure that has been assumed may be considered too simple for the demand for capital goods. Since K_t denotes the actual quantity of capital goods and I_t denotes investment actually realized, there is the possibility that the change $K_t - K_{t-1}$ may depend on decisions to fill the gap between desired and actual stocks made more than one period (year) ago. Instead of the simple lag one might assume, for example,

$$K_t - K_{t-1} = \beta_{21}(\dot{K}_t - K_{t-1}) + \beta_{22}(\dot{K}_{t-1} - K_{t-2}) \tag{37}$$

implying an equation for K_t. Then, $K_t - (1 - d)K_{t-1}$ will be

$$I_t = \beta_{21} b_1 [Y_t - (1 - d)Y_{t-1}] + \beta_{21} b_2 [R_t - (1 - d)R_{t-1}] + (1 - \beta_{21})I_{t-1}$$

$$+ \beta_{22} b_1 [Y_{t-1} - (1 - d)Y_{t-2}]$$

$$+ \beta_{22} b_2 [R_{t-1} - (1 - d)R_{t-2}] - \beta_{22} I_{t-2}$$

$$+ \text{const} \tag{38}$$

Thus, the lag structure (37) requires, as explanatory variables for investment, one more period of observations on income change, interest change, and lagged investment. In the empirical section, we shall first employ the sample structure (36), bearing in mind the possible complication (38).

The Demand for Money

The derivation of our demand function for money will parallel the development of our consumption function, Eqs. (30) to (33), yielding

$$\Delta M_t = \beta_3 e_1 \, \Delta Y_t + \beta_3 e_2 \, \Delta R_t + (1 - \beta_3) \, \Delta M_{t-1} \tag{39}$$

where β_3 is the adjustment coefficient. As in the case of investment, the demand for money may involve more complicated issues than our simple derivation of (39) seems to suggest. Some of these issues have been discussed in Chow (1966). Without going further into these issues, we merely report that the final form of a demand function consistent with United States annual data from 1897 to 1958 can be first-differenced to yield (39). The rationalization for this final form may be more involved than indicated here; however, in view of our present objective of setting forth a macroeconomic model, short of embarking on a major project on each equation, we have chosen the simplest and most direct set of assumptions to justify the aggregate equations to be tested.

The Model as a Whole

To build a macro model from the three major equations (33), (36), and (39) we have to decide what statistical series to use to measure the aggregative variables and what phenomena in real life to ignore for the purpose of examining the role of the three selected relations alone in determining national income. Consider the identity

$$\text{GNP} = C + I + G + E$$

with consumption, gross investment, government purchases, and net exports over imports as four components. First, we omit net exports E from our analysis and treat GNP as if it had only three components, $C + I + G$.

It seems reasonable to assume that the income variable appearing in our three demand equations should be net national product $C + I^n + G$ minus government taxes net of transfers T. For the consumption function, such an income variable would differ from the more widely adopted disposable personal income mainly by the inclusion of undistributed corporate profits. Whether undistributed corporate profits should be included in the income variable affecting aggregate demand is an open question. However, the income variable Y, which we actually use, is $C + I + G - T$ rather than $C + I^n + G - T$. Gross investment is used instead of net investment because the data on capital consumption allowances are admittedly poor and because the change in the cross-income variable is approximately proportional to the change in the net-income variable.

From the definition of our income variable

$$Y = C + I + G - T \tag{40}$$

and from our treatment of net exports over imports, undistributed corporate profits, and capital consumption allowances, the strategy of building our model seems apparent. We prefer combining or omitting certain components of GNP in our equations to introducing additional equations whenever we believe that such aggregation is justified as a first approximation. This strategy differs from the practice of some recent econometric models, where additional equations are introduced for components of GNP without much recourse to theory. The difference in strategy is due partly to our aim of testing macroeconomic theory per se and partly to our unwillingness to introduce equations of which our theoretical knowledge is weak, as they may contaminate other equations while using up degrees of freedom.

So far, our model consisting of Eqs. (33), (36), (39) and the identity (40) has not specified the role of government. In our model, government purchases G will be treated as exogenous. Taxes minus transfers T will be treated as endogenous

$$T = g(C + I + G) + g_0 \tag{41}$$

If we denote private aggregate demand $C + I$ by Y_1, the first difference of the income variable entering into Eqs. (33), (36), and (39) will be, by (40) and (41),

$$\Delta Y = (1 - g)(\Delta Y_1 + \Delta G) \tag{42}$$

In our statistical investigation, we have occasion to separate the two components, $(1 - g)\,\Delta Y_1$ and $(1 - g)\,\Delta G$, of ΔY and study their relative multiplier effects. Since major changes in tax rates occurred during our period of study, in particular in 1943 and 1964, we have to allow for a change in our economic structure in the estimation of its parameters. The same method employed in estimating a changing structure will also be used to assess the effects of the change of tax rates in 1964.

Simple assumptions have been made in order to evaluate the effects of fiscal policies through government expenditures G and the marginal tax rate g. How about monetary policies? Our model is very crude—possibly too crude—in this regard, since the stock of money M will be treated as exogenous. We have made this assumption not so much because a large body of the macroeconomic literature has done so as because we consider the present study to be an intermediate step toward an understanding of the role of monetary factors in economic life. If the stock of money is found to be very important, the monetary sector will be investigated in greater detail.

One further issue to be cleared up before the formulation of our model is complete is whether the above equations explaining aggregate consumption and investment expenditures should be interpreted in real terms or in money terms and, if the former, how nominal expenditures are to be explained. For those who believe that these equations refer to variables in nominal terms nothing further need be said. For them, our model is meant to explain consumption and investment in current dollars, leaving open the decomposition of changes of expenditures into changes in physical units and changes in the price level.

For others, including the author, who believe that considerations in real terms do enter into the behavioral relations specified above, some form of price deflation would be necessary. As our model is not intended to explain relative prices, only the general price level P_t will be used. The relation between a variable, say consumption, in real terms C_t^r and the variable in nominal terms C_t is simply

$$C_t = P_t C_t^r, \quad \text{or} \quad \Delta C_t \simeq P_t \, \Delta C_t^r + \Delta P_t \, C_t^r$$

Since the second term is small compared with the first, i.e., the ratio of $\Delta P_t / P_t$ to $\Delta C_t^r / C_t^r$ is small, and since our model does not explain ΔP_t, we shall approximate ΔC_t by the first term and, in fact, by $P_{t-1} \, \Delta C_t^r$. If our consumption and investment functions are designed for variables in real terms, such as $\Delta C_t^r = \Delta C_t / P_{t-1}$, equations relating nominal variables can be obtained after multiplication by P_{t-1} and will have the same form as the previous equations except that they will have P_{t-1} as an additional variable. Note that the consumption function specified by (33) does not include an intercept, but the possibility of a trend would require an intercept. Note also that we purposely did not mention deflation of the demand function for money. The justification, discussed more thoroughly in Chow (1966), is that the income elasticity of demand is unity so that a double-log demand function in nominal variables is valid, and the linear function is considered as an approximation to it. In short, for the consumption and investment functions, we shall use a linear deflation device by introducing P_{t-1} as an additional (predetermined) variable.

In summary, our model consists of the following equations (with some simplifications in writing the coefficients):

$$\Delta C_t = a_1 \, \Delta Y_t + a_2 \, \Delta C_{t-1} + a_3 \, \Delta M_t + a_4 \, P_{t-1} \tag{43}$$

$$\Delta I_t = b_1 \, \Delta Y_t + b_1' \, Y_{t-1} + b_2 \, \Delta R_t + b_2' \, R_{t-1} + b_3 \, I_{t-1} + b_4 \, \Delta M_t + b_5 \, P_{t-1} \tag{44}$$

$$\Delta M_t = e_1 \, \Delta Y_t + e_2 \, \Delta R_t + e_3 \, \Delta M_{t-1} \tag{45}$$

$$\Delta Y_t = (1 - g)(\Delta Y_{1t} + \Delta G_t) \tag{46}$$

$$\Delta Y_{1t} = \Delta C_t + \Delta I_t \tag{47}$$

We have chosen to write out the two terms ΔY_t and Y_{t-1}, rather than Y_t and $(1 - d)Y_{t-1}$, in the investment function partly to facilitate interpreting the statistical results regarding our formulation of the accelerations hypothesis. According to our formulation, the coefficient of Y_{t-1} should be the rate of depreciation d times the coefficient of ΔY_t when these two variables are used. The coefficient of Y_{t-1} is minus $(1 - d)$ times the coefficient of Y_t, as Eq. (36) was originally written. In Eq. (44) I_{t-1} has been subtracted from both sides, with ΔI_t replacing I_t as the dependent variable. This requires reinterpretation of the coefficient b_3 and of the multiple correlation coefficient of this equation, the latter being expected to be lower than for I_t. Note also that ΔM_t is included in both Eqs. (43) and (44) to allow for the possibility that it may affect consumption or investment directly.

Our model of five equations (43) to (47) explains the five dependent variables ΔC_t, ΔY_t, ΔI_t, ΔR_t, and ΔY_{1t}. Equation (47) is an identity. Equation (46), though not an identity, will be treated as given since g is to be estimated from outside information. We are thus left with three structural equations to estimate. Note, however, that the consumption and investment equations may be broken up according to the durability of the goods concerned, as pointed out in the theoretical discussions above, so that there may be more than three structural equations in our statistical analyses. This and other statistical questions will be discussed in the following section.

4.6 SOME STATISTICAL CONSIDERATIONS FOR THE MODEL

Possible Disaggregation of Consumption and Investment Functions

It has been pointed out that total consumption expenditures might be broken up into two dependent variables, nondurables plus services, and durables. Of course, further disaggregation such as separating services from nondurable goods, and so forth, would be possible but would not be consistent with the objective of our study. If the behavioral assumptions made in Eq. (33) apply to consumption expenditures rather than consumption per se, one may not wish to treat consumer durables separately. If the assumptions made in Eq. (33) apply to the quantities consumed, i.e., consumption of services from total stock in the case of durables, one can introduce an equation for the expenditures on consumer durables separately. Such an equation can be derived from Eq. (30), treating C_t as the stock of durables. Instead of taking the difference $C_t - C_{t-1}$ for net investment in consumer durables as in (33), we take the difference $C_t - (1 - d)C_{t-1}$ for gross investment or expenditures on durables as in (36). The resulting function C'_t explaining expenditures will be

$$C'_t = C_t - (1 - d)C_{t-1} = \beta_1 a_1 [Y_t - (1 - d)Y_{t-1}] + (1 - \beta_1)C'_{t-1} \qquad (48)$$

It will have the same form as our gross-investment function (36).

Even if we interpret the assumptions about consumer behavior as applying to the amount consumed rather than the amount purchased, Eq. (33), with C measuring expenditures, may still be a good approximation to reality. By Eq. (48), the change in expenditures would be

$$\Delta C'_t = \beta a_1 \Delta Y_t - \beta a_1 (1 - d) \Delta Y_{t-1} + (1 - \beta) \Delta C'_{t-1} \qquad (49)$$

The only difference between this equation and Eq. (33) applied to expenditures is the term involving ΔY_{t-1}. The coefficient of ΔY_{t-1} will be small when the rate of depreciation d is large. Some consumer durables have annual depreciation rates much less than 1, for example, approximately .25 for automobiles. However, many consumer durables so classified by the U.S. Department of Commerce have large annual depreciation rates. It would be a better approximation to group them in Eq. (33) with a zero coefficient for ΔY_{t-1} than in Eq. (49) together with other durables with much smaller rates of depreciation. The ideal treatment of consumer durables, under the constraint that only one equation be introduced, would be to find an optimal grouping of some durables with short lives to be included in Eq. (33) and other durables with longer lives to be included in Eq. (48). Short of such a regrouping, it may be as well to treat all consumer expenditures by Eq. (33). This we do first, in our statistical analyses, bearing in mind that Eq. (48) may be introduced for consumer durables separately if the aggregation of all consumer expenditures in (33) fails to be a good approximation.

As far as investment expenditures are concerned, we have pointed out that the interest elasticity varies according to the rate of depreciation. There are three components of gross investment in the Department of Commerce classification, namely, new construction, producers' durable equipment, and change in business inventories. The rate of depreciation for construction is in the neighborhood of the rate of interest, so that $R/(d + R)$ being approximately one-half, the interest elasticity is about half of the price elasticity. Producers' durable equipment is a horse of a very different color. Going through the list of items included in it, one finds very few whose rates of depreciation are as low as .20. Even for $d = .20$ and $R = .05$ the interest elasticity would be about $.05/.25$, or one-fifth of price elasticity. Therefore, we are led to treat new construction and producer durables separately.

There are three possible treatments for the change in inventories. The first is to combine it with producers' durable equipment, with misgivings partly because it is not a gross concept as gross investment in producer durables and partly because the statistical entity called change in business inventories is constructed by accounting rather than economic concepts. The second is to treat it separately, thus making a total of three investment equations. If the same functional form as (36) is employed, a similar misgiving as in the first alternative may arise. The third is to exclude inventory change in our definition of GNP (and Y), as net exports E have been excluded. In our statistical analysis, we shall first combine inventory changes with producer durables, bearing in mind the other two possibilities if our first attempt fails.

Treatment of Change in Tax Rate

During the period of observations used to estimate the parameters of our model, 1929–1963, there was at least one major change in the tax rate g, occurring in 1943. This change affected the parameters and necessitated a statistical procedure for estimating the changing parameters. Furthermore, to assess the effect of the reduction in g that occurred in 1964 it would also be necessary to evaluate the effect of g on the parameters.

It is quite straightforward to set forth algebraically the dependence of our structural and reduced-form parameters on the tax rate g. In doing so, we shall use a structure of only three behavioral equations, observing that the relations so derived can easily be generalized to deal with possible disaggregation of the consumption or investment functions. When $h(\Delta Y_{1t} + \Delta G_t)$ is substituted for ΔY_t, using Eq. (46) and denoting $1 - g$ by h, the three structural equations become

$$\Delta C_t = a_1 h\, \Delta Y_{1t} + a_1^* h\, \Delta G_t + a_2\, \Delta C_{t-1} + a_3\, \Delta M_t + a_4\, P_{t-1} \qquad (50)$$

$$\Delta I_t = b_1 h\, \Delta Y_{1t} + b_1^* h\, \Delta G_t + b_1'\, Y_{t-1} + b_2\, \Delta R_t + b_2'\, R_{t-1} + b_3\, I_{t-1}$$
$$+ b_4\, \Delta M_t + b_5\, P_{t-1} \quad (51)$$

$$\Delta R_t = c_1 h\, \Delta Y_{1t} + c_1^* h\, \Delta G_t + c_2\, \Delta M_t + c_3\, \Delta M_{t-1} \qquad (52)$$

where we have distinguished a_1^*, b_1^*, and c_1^* from a_1, b_1, and c_1 to allow for the possibility that government expenditures may have different multiplier effects from private expenditures and we have solved Eq. (45) for the dependent variable ΔR_t to obtain Eq. (52). Thus, the proportion of income after tax $h = 1 - g$ is a multiplicative factor in the coefficients of ΔY_{1t} and ΔG_t in all three structural equations.

How h enters into the coefficients of the reduced form can also be derived in a straightforward manner. The reduced-form equation for ΔY_{1t} can be obtained by first combining Eqs. (50) and (51), using the identity $\Delta C_t + \Delta I_t = \Delta Y_{1t}$, and then substituting for ΔR_t, using Eq. (52) and rearranging terms

$$\Delta Y_{1t} = \frac{1}{1 - h(a_1 + b_1 + b_2 c_1)}\, [a_2\, \Delta C_{t-1} + b_3\, I_{t-1} + b_1'\, Y_{t-1} + b_2'\, R_{t-1}$$
$$+ h(a_1^* + b_1^* + b_2 c_1^*)\, \Delta G_t + (a_3 + b_4 + b_2 c_2)\, \Delta M_t$$
$$+ b_2 c_3\, \Delta M_{t-1} + (a_4 + b_5)P_{t-1}] \qquad (53)$$

This reduced-form equation shows that h affects the multiplicative factor $1/[1 - h(a_1 + b_1 + b_2 c_1)]$ as applied to all coefficients alike and also affects the coefficient of ΔG_t in particular. If (53) is substituted for ΔY_{1t} in the structural equations (50) to (52), reduced-form equations for ΔC_t, ΔI_t, and ΔR_t will result; they will not be shown here.

Equation (53) justifies a simple method of estimation using time-series data when tax rate changed from g_1 in period 1 to g_2 in period 2. Let

$$k_1 = \frac{1 - h_1(a_1 + b_1 + b_2 c_1)}{1 - h_2(a_1 + b_1 + b_2 c_1)}$$

To estimate the reduced-form coefficients as of the second (standard) period, we simply multiply the dependent variable ΔY_{1t} by k_1 and one predetermined variable ΔG_t by h_1/h_2 for the first period. The estimated values of the dependent variable for the first period in stage one of two-stage least squares, for example, are estimates of $k_1\, \Delta Y_{1t}$. If the coefficients as of the second period are again chosen as standard, structural equations (50) to (52) require that the estimates ΔY_{1t}^* for the first period be multiplied by h_1/h_2. No further changes in the data on ΔG_t are required since it was already multiplied by h_1/h_2. Therefore, *after the reduced form has been estimated by changing the data on ΔY_{1t} and ΔG_t as previously indicated, the standard set of structural coefficients can be estimated by multiplying the estimated dependent variable for the first period by the factor $h_1/h_2 k_1$.*

In our model only the reduced-form equation for ΔY_{1t} has to be estimated in the first stage of the method of two-stage least squares. Although another dependent variable, ΔR_t, appears in the investment equation (51), we can estimate the structural equation (52) first to obtain estimated values of ΔR_t, which can then be applied to Eq. (51) in the second stage. Our method, as described, assumes knowledge of the various factors by which the data on ΔY_{1t} and ΔG_t are multiplied. In practice, we shall use extraneous information to estimate the tax rates g_1 and g_2. Insofar as the factor k_1 depends also on the structural parameters a_1, b_1, b_2, and c_1, we shall make some crude estimates of them for insertion into k_1 in order to apply the above estimation procedure. One could iterate until the estimates of these parameters turn out to be close to the values put in for k_1.

Once the reduced-form coefficients in (53) are estimated as of period 2, one can obtain a forecasting equation valid for period 3, say, when the tax rate is changed to g_3. We multiply the coefficients as of period 2 by

$$\frac{1 - h_2(a_1 + b_1 + b_2 c_1)}{1 - h_3(a_1 + b_1 + b_2 c_1)}$$

and the coefficient of ΔG_t, in addition, by h_3/h_2. This case illustrates the point so well discussed by Marschak (1953), i.e., the necessity of estimating the parameters of the structural equations even for the purpose of forecasting. It is also an example of the changes in the multipliers resulting from a structural change so much discussed in the literature of macroeconomics.

A Summary of Statistical Hypotheses

The hypotheses contained in the three-equation model (50) to (52) that are fairly widely accepted are concerned with:

H1. The signs of various coefficients, except H4 and H5 below
H2. The ratio (depending on the rate of depreciation) of the coefficients of Y_t and of Y_{t-1}, or the ratio of the coefficients of ΔY_t and Y_{t-1}, in the investment function
H3. Government expenditures having the same multiplying effects on consumption and investment as private expenditures.

The hypotheses contained in the three-equation model that are somewhat questionable relate to

H4. The additional effect of the stock of money on consumption, given income
H5. The additional effect of the change in money stock on investment, given the rate of interest.

Other areas which we would like to explore, not necessarily restricted to a three-equation model, include

H6. The difference in the interest effects on new construction and on gross investment in producers' durable equipment
H7. The possibility of treating expenditures on consumer durables as part of consumer expenditures in one aggregative consumption function

Table 4.1 Symbols, definitions, and sources

Symbol	Definition	Source
C_1	Personal consumption expenditures on nondurable goods and services in millions of current dollars	1
C_2	Personal consumption expenditures on durable goods	1
C	Total personal consumption expenditures, $C_1 + C_2$	
I_{11}	Gross private domestic investment in producers' durable equipment in millions of current dollars	1
I_{12}	Change in business inventories	1
I_1	$I_{11} + I_{12}$	
I_2	New construction	1
I	Total gross private domestic investment, $I_1 + I_2$	
Y_1	$C + I$	
G	Government purchases of goods and services, in millions of current dollars	1
$T - G$	Government surplus or deficit ($-$) on income and product account	2
Y	$Y_1 + G - T$	
M	Currency and demand deposits adjusted in the middle of the year, in millions of current dollars	3
P	GNP deflator (1954 = 100)	4
R_a	Yield of 20-year corporate bonds	5
R_b	Yield of 5-year corporate bonds	5
R_c	Bank rate on short-term business loans	6

SOURCE KEY:

1. 1926–1946 from *U.S. Income and Output*, U.S. Department of Commerce, Office of Business Economics, 1958, pp. 118–119; 1947–1963 from *Survey of Current Business*, July 1964, p. 8.
2. 1929–1945 from *National Income, 1954 Edition: A Supplement to the Survey of Current Business*, pp. 164–165; 1946–1955 from *U.S. Income and Output*, p. 188; 1956–1958, equal to federal government surplus, *Survey of Current Business*, July 1962, p. 16, plus state and local government surplus, ibid., p. 17; 1959–1963, equal to federal surplus, *Survey of Current Business*, July 1964, p. 18, plus state and local surplus, ibid., p. 19.
3. 1929–1957 from *Historical Statistics of the United States: Colonial Times to 1957*, U.S. Bureau of the Census, 1960, Series 267, p. 646; 1958–1963 from *Federal Reserve Bulletin*, various issues.
4. 1929–1946 from *U.S. Income and Output*, p. 222; 1947–1963 from *Survey of Current Business*, July 1964, p. 10.
5. 1929–1957 from *Historical Statistics of the United States: Colonial Times to 1957*, p. 657; 1958–1963 from *Statistical Abstract*, 1964, p. 472, annual percentage rate multiplied by 10,000 in our calculations.
6. 1929–1957 from *Historical Statistics of the United States: Colonial Times to 1957*, Series X-322, p. 655; 1958–1963 from *Federal Reserve Bulletin*, March issues.

H8. The possibility of combining inventory change with investment in producer durables in one equation

H9. The extent of money illusion in the aggregate demand functions and the possibility of applying our model to nominal values of all variables without using the linear deflation device

H10. The relative importance of the behavioral characteristics of our private economy (including the effect of private expenditures on consumption, the effect of its change on investment, etc.) and of government policies (G_t and M_t) in the determination of national income

H11. The relative importance of deterministic versus random factors in the explanation of cyclical patterns of national income fluctuations.

Major problems in macroeconomics which the present study does not cover include, among others,

1. The determination of price level
2. The mechanism of the supply of money, when money is not treated as exogenous
3. The effects on the rate of interest of the demands for other assets than money.

Sources of Data

National income data are taken from the U.S. Department of Commerce. Money data are taken from the *Federal Reserve Bulletin*. The period of observations on the dependent variables is annually from 1931 to 1940 and from 1948 to 1963, providing 26 observations. A list of symbols, their definitions, and sources is given in Table 4.1.

4.7 EMPIRICAL RESULTS FROM THE MODEL

The graphic method was first used to estimate g_1 and g_2. Annual data on $C + I + G$ and on T were plotted on a scatter diagram, for the years 1929 to 1963. Two lines were drawn free hand to approximate the relationships before and after 1943, respectively. Their slopes are $g_1 = .11$, and $g_2 = .21$. The ratio h_1/h_2 to be used to adjust the prewar data is therefore $.89/.79$ to 1.12658. After five iterations to estimate the structural coefficients of Eqs. (i) to (iv) in Table 4.2 by the method of two-stage least squares modified to deal with the tax change it was found that $a_1 + b_1 + b_2 c_1$ is approximately .88. The factor k_1 is thus .711286. This value will be used for all calculations presented below, without further iterations. If consumption (or investment) is separated into many components, the coefficient a_1 (or b_1) will be the sum of the income effects on these components. In the formula for k_1 this sum will replace a_1. Therefore, the same value of k_1 should be applicable to different versions of our model with varying degrees of disaggregation.

Table 4.2 Coefficients of four structural equations

Eq.	ΔY_1^*	ΔR_a^*	ΔC_{-1}	$I_{1,-1}$	$I_{2,-1}$	Y_{-1}	ΔM	ΔM_{-1}	ΔG	P_{-1}	Constant	DW	R_2
(i) ΔC	.308 (.094)		.194 (.130)				.408 (.410)		.078 (.159)	87.7 (46.4)	−4797	2.26	.850
(ii) ΔI_1	.278 (.084)	.123 (.489)		−.672 (.300)		.010 (.035)			.161 (.192)	152 (193)	−5703	1.87	.683
(iii) ΔI_2	.106 (.021)	−.166 (.147)			−.457 (.207)	.033 (.027)			−.061 (.046)	104 (51)	−6060	2.10	.773
(iv) ΔR_a	.111 (.062)						−.739 (.305)	.318 (.248)	.187 (.114)		−973	2.54	.336
(v) ΔM	.150	−1.35						.430	.253		−1316		
(vi) ΔI_1	.281 (.082)			−.663 (.291)		.009 (.033)			.168 (.186)	159 (187)	−6125	1.91	.682
(vii) ΔI_2	.105 (.021)	−.220 (.144)			−.510 (.207)	.041 (.027)				92.8 (51.3)	−5996	2.14	.752

The main set of estimates to be presented belongs to a four-equation model with one consumption function, two investment functions (producer durables combined with inventory change and new construction), and one money demand function and with no direct effect of money on investment. Eight predetermined variables were used to estimate ΔY_1^* in the first stage. They are ΔC_{t-1}, $I_{1,t-1}$, $I_{2,t-1}$, Y_{t-1}, ΔM_t, ΔM_{t-1}, ΔG_t, and P_{t-1}. Recall that our gross investment function captures the accelerations principle by using ΔY_t and Y_{t-1} as income variables and ΔR_t and R_{t-1} as interest variables. The coefficients of Y_{t-1} and R_{t-1} are expected to be the rate of depreciation d times the coefficients of ΔY_t and ΔR_t, respectively. An explanatory variable Y_{t-1} was used in the investment functions to test this formulation of the acceleration principle. R_{t-1} was omitted because its coefficient is a samll fraction d of the already small coefficient of ΔR_t. R_{t-1} had been used in an early stage but was found to be insignificant. In Table 4.2 numbers in parentheses denote standard errors of the coefficients, and the last two columns give the squared multiple correlation coefficient and the Durbin-Watson statistic for first-order serial correlation.

Judging Eqs. (i) to (iv) in Table 4.2 against the hypotheses (H1), one must conclude that the signs have all turned out to be as expected except for the coefficient of interest in the investment function (ii), which is insignificant anyway (being one-quarter of its standard error). The estimated consumption function shows a marginal propensity (highly significant) of .308 with respect to current income and an adjustment coefficient (somewhat inaccurate) of $1 - .194 = .806$. A noteworthy feature of these results is the strong confirmation of our formulation of the acceleration principle (H2). The coefficients of lagged income in both investment functions are small fractions of the coefficients of the change in income; i.e., they are opposite in sign but approximately equal in magnitude to the coefficients of current income. In principle, the ratio of the coefficient of Y_{-1} to the coefficient of ΔY_1^* is an estimate of the annual rate of depreciation, but the point estimates of the coefficients of lagged income in our two investment functions are subject to large errors. The stronger interest effect on construction than on producer durables is in agreement with our hypothesis (H6). In fact, the interest effect on the latter turns out to be insignificant. The larger adjustment coefficient, .672, for producer durables than that, .457, for construction appears reasonable, but these estimates contain fairly sizable errors.

In regard to the demand for money we have found positive effects of income and of lagged money stock and a negative effect of the rate of interest. The estimated equation (iv) was solved for ΔM to yield Eq. (v) for easier reading. When Eq. (v) is compared with a demand-for-money equation obtained by applying least squares directly to explain the dependent variable M, without using first differences (Chow, 1966), the coefficients of income and of lagged money stock are found to be similar but the coefficient of the interest rate, -1.35, turns out to be much larger (in absolute value). This difference can be attributed to the fact that the slope of the regression of M on R is smaller than the slope of the line obtained by regressing R on M. One should note the small squared multiple correlation coefficient, .336, for Eq. (iv). While our demand function for money can explain a large fraction of the variance of money, it can explain only a small fraction of the variance of the rate of interest. As Ralph Turvey (1965, p. 460) reminds us,

> If we reverse the demand function for money, we deduce that, ceteris paribus, a change in the quantity of money will alter interest rates. But there are also demand functions for short-term and long-term paper. By the same token, therefore, a change in the quantities of these assets will also alter interest rates. Thus knowledge of the demand function for money, though necessary, is not sufficient to explain interest rates.

Determination of the rate of interest by simply inverting the demand function for money is probably one of the weakest links in macroeconomic theory.

The coefficients of P_{-1}, relative to their standard errors, suggest that, on the question of money illusion (H9), the use of some deflation device is helpful in constructing macroeconomic demand relationships. One might dispute the degree of money illusion, but one should not overlook the possibility that consumption and investment decisions may be made by considerations in physical terms. Our present concern is less with measuring the degree of money illusion than with allowing for the above possibility in testing a set of macroeconomic hypotheses.

Concerning the role of government expenditures, it is generally assumed (H3) that G should be added to $C + I$ as a part of aggregate demand. However, our calculations show that this assumption may not be valid. The coefficient of ΔG is smaller than the coefficient of ΔY_1 in all three components of demand [Eqs. (i) to (iii)], being (insignificantly) negative in the last case. While one might rationalize these coefficients by pointing out the possibly nonpermanent (i.e., undependable for forming future expectations) nature of government expenditures, we are prepared to present our results merely as a vote for skepticism and as a suggestion that G may be given a smaller weight than $C + I$ as a component of effective demand.

The coefficient of money in the consumption function is about the size of its standard error. It is consistent with the hypothesis (H4) that the stock of money has a positive effect on consumption, given income. However, we have found that, via the rate of interest, the effect of money on investment is small. First, there is the weak link between money and interest. Second, the interest effect on durables with relatively short lives is insignificant, and the interest effect on construction is not very strong. This statement remains valid, and so do the other results presented in Eqs. (i) to (iv), when interest rates R_b and R_c replace R_a in our calculations. We have also tested the direct effect of money on investment (H5) by adding ΔM to Eqs. (ii) and (iii). While the other features of these equations remain about the same, the coefficients of $\Delta R_a{}^*$ and ΔM (and their standard errors) are, respectively, 1.11 (1.67) and .926 (1.494) in the equation for ΔI_1 and $-.070$ (.293) and .095 (.250) in the equation for ΔI_2. These coefficients certainly do not speak for an important effect of money on investment expenditures. An economist whose a priori estimates of the effects of money are high may conclude that our results are consistent with positive (however small) influences of money on consumption and investment. On the other hand, our theoretical discussion has suggested a small interest effect on investment (except for the very durable, perhaps) and the absence of the direct effect of money (except when the capital market is highly imperfect).

There is the possibility, pointed out in Sec. 4.5, that the lag structure of investment may be more complicated than that given in Eq. (36). The more complicated structure (38) was tested…[test results and a table omitted]. There is insufficient evidence in favor of choosing the structure (38) in preference to (36).

We studied separately the expenditures on consumer durables (H7) according to Eq. (48) and found expected signs and magnitudes for all coefficients. When inventory change (H8) was separated from I_1, the coefficients also behaved as expected. However, the gains in disaggregation did not justify inclusion of either equation in the model. Space does not permit presentation of results using real (1954) values (omitting P_{t-1}), but they support all stated conclusions.

As an overall evaluation, one must conclude that the very aggregative model of Table 4.2 has stood up very well against the data of the United States from the 1930s to the 1960s. Not only have the signs of all coefficients turned out as expected, but the fractions of the variances of annual changes in consumption and investment expenditures that are explained by the respective equations are quite large. Note that I_{t-1} has been subtracted from both sides of the original investment function to yield a function explaining the first difference of investment. The multiple correlations for levels of investment are even higher than those shown for changes in investment. Investment expenditures have been found to depend heavily on the changes in income, thus being no more exogenous than consumption expenditures. The Durbin-Watson statistics are all close to 2, indicating that most serial correlations in the residuals have been eliminated by taking first differences. When the levels of the variables were used instead, the Durbin-Watson statistics ranged between .5 and 1.2, approximately.

4.8 GOODNESS OF FIT AND FORECASTING VALUE OF THE MODEL

For the purpose of explaining and predicting national income, the reduced-form equation for ΔY_1 will be used. This is the restricted reduced-form equation, obtained by solving the estimated structural equations, rather than the unrestricted equation, by regressing ΔY_1 freely on the predetermined variables. Since the coefficient of $\Delta R_a{}^*$ in Eq. (ii) and the coefficient of ΔG in Eq. (iii) both have the wrong sign and are highly insignificant, they are assumed to be zero, and Eqs. (ii) and (iii) have been recomputed to yield Eqs. (vi) and (vii) in Table 4.2. Equations (i), (iv), (vi), and (vii) are used to compute the restricted reduced-form equation for ΔY_1.

Following the well-known discussion of Hicks (1937), we first obtain an IS curve [Eq. (viii) in Table 4.3] relating income, interest, and the predetermined variables by combining equations (i), (vi), and (vii). The LL curve [Eq. (ix)] is simply Eq. (iv), now solved for ΔY_1 as a function of ΔR and the predetermined

Table 4.3 Derivation of reduced-form equation through IS and LL equations

Coefficients of	ΔR_a	ΔC_{-1}	$I_{1,-1}$	$I_{2,-1}$	Y_{-1}	ΔM	ΔM_{-1}	ΔG	P_{-1}	Const.
(viii) IS ΔY_1	−.7171	.6323	−2.162	−1.664	.1631	1.331		.8046	1106	−55,195
(ix) LL ΔY_1	9.017					6.663	−2.866	−1.688		8770
(x) R ΔY_1		.5857	−2.002	−1.541	.1511	1.724	−.2112	.6210	1025	−50,479
Data										
1964		18,200	35,400	46,600	457,000	6187	4622	6000	118.5	
1965		24,300	38,800	48,900	487,000	6669	6187	5000	120.7	
1966		28,700	45,000	51,000	524,000	7000	6669	6000	122.7	

variables. Using these two equations to eliminate ΔR, one arrives at the restricted reduced-form equation (x).

When the restricted reduced-form equation (x) is used to explain the actual changes in private expenditures ΔY_1 for the periods 1931–1940 and 1948–1953, the square of the correlation coefficient is .69 and the standard error is approximately 8 billion current dollars. Our model thus explains about 70 percent of the variance of ΔY_1. It is significant to note that a standard error of 8 billion dollars in explaining national income is not large even compared with econometric models consisting of many more equations.

In Table 4.4 the values of ΔY_1 computed from the restricted reduced form are compared with the actual values (in billions of dollars). For the 10 observations from 1931 to 1940, the actual figures shown are $k_1 = .711286$ times ΔY_1, and the predetermined variable for the changes in government expenditures is $h_1/h_2 = 1.12658$ times ΔG, since the standard set of coefficients of Eq. (x) given in Table 4.3 is valid for the period 1948–1963. The model is able to trace the declines in income during the three depression years and in 1938. For 1949, it shows a down turn but overestimates the level of income by some 11 billion dollars. It would have predicted practically no increase in income in 1957, while the actual annual figures indicate no change in 1958. In this connection, one must note the limitation of an annual model in explaining the timing of minor recessions.

Besides examining the goodness of fit, it is interesting to evaluate the predictive value of the reduced-form equation for the years 1964, 1965, and 1966, not included in the estimation of its parameters. The data on the predetermined variables for these years are shown in Table 4.3. The figures for 1966 are guesses

Table 4.4 Goodness of fit of reduced-form equation (x)

Year	ΔY_1 Actual	ΔY_1 Estimated	Year	ΔY_1 Actual	ΔY_1 Estimated
1931	−10.23	−6.24	1953	13.35	17.26
1932	−11.83	−9.72	1954	3.91	10.61
1933	−1.73	−5.81	1955	33.89	24.69
1934	4.98	3.62	1956	16.50	5.79
1935	5.54	10.82	1957	14.01	1.41
1936	6.01	5.91	1958	−1.45	11.29
1937	5.68	.02	1959	36.42	36.31
1938	−5.48	−7.89	1960	13.72	3.83
1939	3.97	4.22	1961	6.12	22.05
1940	5.80	4.94	1962	29.77	26.17
1948	24.53	20.14	1963	21.08	19.87
1949	−7.26	4.18	1964	30.00	21.43
1950	30.80	21.93	1965		21.32
1951	21.16	16.68	1966		16.98
1952	3.50	14.69			

made after inspecting the data for the first quarter of 1965, which is the last set of data available at the time of writing (July 1965). Using the coefficients of Eq. (x) *without adjustment for the change in income tax rates that occurred in* 1964, one obtains the values of estimated ΔY_1 given in Table 4.4.

By how much should the estimates of ΔY_1 be raised because of the tax reduction? It was indicated in Sec. 4.6 that the estimate should be multiplied by the factor

$$\frac{1 - h_2(a_1 + b_1 + b_2 c_1)}{1 - h_3(a_1 + b_1 + b_2 c_1)}$$

and that, in addition, the coefficient of ΔG should be multiplied by h_3/h_2. The latter adjustment is minor. We shall not go into any elaborate method of estimating the marginal tax rate after 1964 since this can be a project in itself. To get a rough estimate of the effect of the 1964 tax reduction via our model it is sufficient to try some reasonable guesses on g_3. If g_3 is .18, compared with $g_2 = .21$, the above factor will be

$$\frac{1 - .79(.88)}{1 - .82(.88)} = 1.095$$

It will be 1.131 for $g_3 = .17$ and 1.061 for $g = .19$. It seems reasonable to increase the estimates of ΔY_1 given in Table 4.4 by about 10 percent for the years 1964, 1965, and 1966.

Regardless of the accuracy of our guess for g_3, one can reasonably conclude that our forecast for 1964 is quite close. We are also predicting two more prosperous years, 1965 and 1966, with the rate of increase perhaps a little lower in 1966 than in 1965. How good our forecasts for these years are, only time will tell.

4.9 RELATIVE IMPORTANCE OF VARIOUS FACTORS IN INCOME DETERMINATION

Since the effect of the rate of interest on investment expenditures and the direct effect of money on the same are small, the reduced-form equation [x] in Table 4.3 is nearly the same as the IS curve [Eq. (viii)] alone. With ΔY_1 plotted along the y axis and ΔR along the x axis, the IS curve is practically flat and the LL curve [Eq. (ix)] nearly vertical. Thus, the expenditure sector is much more important than the monetary sector in determining aggregate demand. The multiplier and the accelerator are more important than liquidity preference.

The effect of money amounts to 1.7 dollars of ΔY_1 per dollar of ΔM and $- 0.2$ dollar of ΔY_1 per dollar of ΔM_{t-1}. During the 26 years included in our sample, the standard deviation of ΔM was 2.7 billion dollars. To prevent the fall in Y_1 of 10 billion dollars in 1931 (in a structure equivalent to the postwar period), it would have taken an increase of $10/1.7 = 5.9$ billion in money stock, compared with its actual figure. Since ΔM was -1.6 in 1931, the net increase required would have been 4.3 billion. The effectiveness of monetary policy depends also on whether such large changes in money stock can be achieved by the government authorities, a question beyond the scope of this text.

While the coefficient of ΔM in Eq. (x) is 1.7, the coefficient of ΔG is only .62. Thus, a dollar increase of government expenditures has a much smaller effect on private expenditures than a dollar increase in money stock. (In the unrestricted reduced-form equation for ΔY_1, the coefficient of ΔM is 1.3 and the coefficient of ΔG is .76.) We have pointed out that ΔG has smaller coefficients than $\Delta(C + I)$ in the consumption and investment functions and that our results question the generally accepted treatment of government expenditures on an equal footing with private expenditures in macroeconomics. Our calculations show that while the multiplier of ΔM is not large, the multiplier of ΔG is even smaller, being slightly over one-third the former. The multiplier is here defined for private expenditures Y_1 only. The multiplier of ΔG for GNP would be $1 + .62$, similar to the money multiplier.

Having suggested two main qualifications to the "extreme Keynesian" expenditure model, namely, the dependence of investment on income and the small weight given to government expenditures, we wish to emphasize the limitation of using a demand function for money alone for the determination of national income. As the LL curve in Table 4.3 is much less important than the IS curve in the derivation of the reduced-form equation (x), it would be highly misleading to use the demand-for-money equation alone to explain or predict ΔY_1. The coefficient of ΔM in this equation is 6.7, but the partial derivative of ΔY_1 with respect to ΔM in Eq. (x) is only 1.7.

A major limitation of this study is that, because annual data are used to cover both the prewar and postwar periods, the precise lag structures of the equations cannot be ascertained. This limitation applies in particular to our test of the more complicated lag structure (38) for investment and to the use of the reduced-form equation (x) for the purpose of forecasting the timing of a recession. Our major finding is that macroeconomics is useful, the multiplier and the accelerator being more important than liquidity preference. The multiplier stems not only from the dependence of consumption expenditures on income but also from the dependence of investment expenditures on the change in income. Our formulation of the acceleration principle has come out beautifully, supporting the consensus of recent studies of investment on a micro level. While the stock of money is not so important as the advocates of a modern version of the quantity theory of money would claim, government expenditures have an even smaller multiplying effect on private expenditures, dollar for dollar, than money stock.

4.10 FINAL FORM OF A LINEAR DYNAMIC MODEL

To make explicit the dynamic nature of the model and to distinguish the truly exogenous variables z_t from the lagged endogenous variables, both being included in the predetermined variables x_t, we rewrite model (8) as

$$By_{t.} + \Gamma_1 y_{t-1.} + \cdots + \Gamma_p y_{t-p} + \Gamma_0 z_{t.} + \cdots + \Gamma_{p+r} z_{t-r.} = \epsilon_{t.} \tag{54}$$

The reduced form of (54), with the dots omitted from subscripts when there is no ambiguity, is

$$
\begin{aligned}
y_t &= -B^{-1}(\Gamma_1 y_{t-1} + \cdots + \Gamma_p y_{t-p} + \Gamma_0 z_t + \cdots + \Gamma_{p+r} z_{t-r}) + B^{-1}\epsilon_t \\
&= \Pi_1 y_{t-1} + \cdots + \Pi_p y_{t-p} + \Pi_0 z_t + \cdots + \Pi_{p+r} z_{t-r} + v_t
\end{aligned} \tag{55}
$$

To examine the dynamic properties of the model, we rewrite (55) as a first-order system involving only the current z_t

$$
\begin{bmatrix}
y_t \\
y_{t-1} \\
\cdot \\
y_{t-p+1} \\
z_t \\
z_{t-1} \\
\cdot \\
z_{t-r+}
\end{bmatrix}
=
\begin{bmatrix}
\Pi_1 & \Pi_2 & \cdots & \Pi_{p-1} & \Pi_p & \Pi_{p+1} & \cdots & \Pi_{p+r} \\
I & 0 & \cdots & 0 & 0 & 0 & \cdots & 0 \\
\hline
0 & 0 & \cdots & I & 0 & 0 & \cdots & 0 \\
0 & 0 & \cdots & 0 & 0 & 0 & \cdots & 0 \\
0 & 0 & \cdots & 0 & 0 & I & & 0 \\
\hline
0 & 0 & \cdots & 0 & 0 & 0 & \cdots I & 0
\end{bmatrix}
\begin{bmatrix}
y_{t-1} \\
y_{t-2} \\
\cdot \\
y_{t-p} \\
z_{t-1} \\
z_{t-2} \\
\cdot \\
z_{t-r}
\end{bmatrix}
+
\begin{bmatrix}
\Pi_0 \\
0 \\
\cdot \\
0 \\
I \\
0 \\
\cdot \\
0
\end{bmatrix}
z_t
+
\begin{bmatrix}
v_t \\
0 \\
\cdot \\
0 \\
0 \\
0 \\
\cdot \\
0
\end{bmatrix}
$$

$$\tag{56}$$

or more compactly as

$$y_t^* = \Pi_1^* y_{t-1}^* + \Pi_0^* z_t + v_t^* \tag{57}$$

Hence any reduced form can be rewritten to include only the lagged endogenous variables of the first order and only the current exogenous variables. To study the effects of current and past z_{t-k} on y_t we eliminate the lagged endogenous variables from (57) by repeated substitutions

$$
\begin{aligned}
y_t^* &= \Pi_0^* z_t + v_t^* + \Pi_1^*(\Pi_0^* z_{t-1} + v_{t-1}^* + \Pi_1^* y_{t-2}^*) \\
&= \Pi_0^* z_t + \Pi_1^* \Pi_0^* z_{t-1} + \Pi_1^{*2} \Pi_0^* z_{t-2} + \cdots + \Pi_1^{*t-1} \Pi_0^* z_1 + v_t^* \\
&\quad + \Pi_1^* v_{t-1}^* + \cdots + \Pi_1^{*t-1} v_1^* + \Pi_1^{*t} y_0^*
\end{aligned} \tag{58}
$$

where the initial condition y_0^* is assumed given.

In order for y_t^* given by (58) not to explode, we require that Π_1^{*t} approach a zero matrix as t approaches infinity. Let Π_1^* defined in (56) be written as

$$\Pi_1^* = BDB^{-1} \tag{59}$$

where D is a diagonal matrix consisting of the characteristic roots of Π_1^* and B is a matrix whose columns are the right characteristic vectors of Π_1^*. Since $\Pi_1^{*t} = BD^t B^{-1}$, this matrix approaches a zero matrix if and only if all the roots of Π_1^*

are less than 1 in absolute value. Let Π_1^* be partitioned as

$$\Pi_1^* = \begin{bmatrix} A_{11} & A_{12} \\ 0 & A_{22} \end{bmatrix} \qquad A_{11} = \begin{bmatrix} \Pi_1 & \Pi_2 & \cdots & \Pi_p \\ I & 0 & \cdots & 0 \\ \hdotsfor{4} \\ 0 & \cdots & I & 0 \end{bmatrix} \tag{60}$$

The characteristic roots λ_i of Π_1^* are obtained by solving $|\Pi_1^* - \lambda I| = 0$ or

$$|A_{11} - \lambda I| \cdot |A_{22} - \lambda I| = 0$$

The roots of $|A_{22} - \lambda I| = 0$ are zero because

$$|A_{22} - \lambda I| = \begin{vmatrix} -\lambda I & & & \mathbf{0} \\ I & -\lambda I & & \\ & & \ddots & \\ 0 & 0 & I & -\lambda I \end{vmatrix} = |\lambda I|^r$$

Therefore, the characteristic roots of Π_1^* are less than 1 in absolute value if and only if the roots of the matrix A_{11} as defined by (60) are less than 1 in absolute value.

Equation (58) is called the *final form* of the model (57). It explains y_t by the current and lagged values of the exogenous variables, the lagged endogenous variables in the *reduced form* having been eliminated by repeated substitutions. The coefficients of the final form give various multipliers. The first submatrix Π_0 of Π_0^* consists of *impact multipliers*, which measure the effects of current z_t on y_t. The first row (submatrix) of $\Pi_1^*\Pi_0^*$ gives the *delayed multipliers* of one period, which measure the effects of z_{t-1} on y_t. Similarly, the first row of $\Pi_1^{*k}\Pi_0^*$ gives the delayed multipliers of k periods, which measure the effects of z_{t-k} on y_t. *Short-run* or *intermediate-run multipliers* of k periods are obtained from the first row of the sum

$$\sum_{j=0}^{k-1} \Pi_1^{*j} \Pi_0^*$$

Also called *interim multipliers*, they measure the effects on y_t of unit changes in z_t lasting from period $t - k + 1$ to the current period t. The *total* or *long-run multipliers* are obtained from the infinite sum

$$\sum_{j=0}^{\infty} \Pi_1^{*j}\Pi_0^* \tag{61}$$

These long-run multipliers exist if and only if the characteristic roots of Π_1^* are less than 1 in absolute value (see Prob. 8).

The condition that all characteristic roots of Π_1^* be less than 1 in absolute value is important. It is a necessary and sufficient condition for the model (58) not to explode, as the last term $\Pi_1^{*t}y_0$ of (58) will explode or not depending on whether Π_1^{*t} has a limit as t increases. It is also a necessary and sufficient condition for the long-run multipliers (61) to be finite. Furthermore, if we assume the second moments of the exogenous variables z_t to exist, it is a necessary and sufficient condition for the second moments of y_t^* in (57) to have finite probability limits. The last result is stated in the following theorem.

Theorem 4.7 Assume the second moments of z_t to exist, i.e.,

$$\lim_{n \to \infty} (n - r)^{-1} \sum_{t=r+1}^{n} z_t z_{t-r}' = Q_r \qquad \text{for all } r$$

Then a necessary and sufficient condition for $\text{plim}_{n \to \infty} n^{-1} \sum_{t=1}^{n} y_t^* y_t^{*'}$ to exist in model (57) is for the roots of Π_1^* or of A_{11} as defined by (60) to be less than 1 in absolute value.

PROOF With $\Pi_1^* \Pi_1^*$ denoted by Π_1^{*2}, etc., use (58) to write

$$y_t^* y_t^{*'} = (\Pi_0^* z_t + \Pi_1^* \Pi_0^* z_{t-1} + \Pi_1^{*2} \Pi_0^* z_{t-2} + \cdots + v_t^* + \Pi_1^* v_{t-1}^*$$
$$+ \cdots + \Pi_1^{*'} y_0)(z_t' \Pi_0^{*'} + z_{t-1}' \Pi_0^{*'} \Pi_1^{*'} + z_{t-2}' \Pi_0^{*'} \Pi_1^{*'2}$$
$$+ \cdots + v_t^{*'} + v_{t-1}^{*'} \Pi_1^{*'} + \cdots + y_0' \Pi_1^{*''})$$

Consider first the products involving the z's only. They can be grouped into products of terms with the same time subscript, with time subscripts differing by 1, differing by -1, differing by 2, etc. The probability limit of the sum of products having the same time subscript is, by the use of (59) for Π_1^* and with C_0 denoting $\Pi_0^* Q_0 \Pi_0^{*'}$,

$$\Pi_0^* Q_0 \Pi_0^{*'} + \Pi_1^* \Pi_0^* Q_0 \Pi_0^{*'} \Pi_1^{*'} + \Pi_1^{*2} \Pi_0^* Q_0 \Pi_0^{*'} \Pi_1^{*'2} + \cdots$$
$$= BB^{-1} C_0 BB^{-1} + BDB^{-1} C_0 BDB^{-1} + BD^2 B^{-1} C_0 BD^2 B^{-1} + \cdots$$
$$\equiv B(G_0 + DG_0 D + D^2 G_0 D^2 + \cdots)B^{-1}$$
$$= B[g_{0,ij}(1 + \lambda_i \lambda_j + \lambda_i^2 \lambda_j^2 + \cdots)]B^{-1} = B\left[\frac{g_{0,ij}}{1 - \lambda_i \lambda_j}\right]B^{-1}$$

where we have let $G_0 = B^{-1} C_0 B = (g_{0,ij})$ and have observed that the infinite geometric series converges if and only if all the roots λ_i of Π_1^* are less than 1 in absolute value.

The probability limit of the sum of products with time subscripts differing by 1, with C_1 denoting $\Pi_0^* Q_1 \Pi_0^{*'}$, is

$$\Pi_0^* Q_1 \Pi_0^* \Pi_1^{*'} + \Pi_1^* \Pi_0^* Q_1 \Pi_0^{*'} \Pi_1^{*'2} + \Pi_1^{*2} \Pi_0^* Q_1 \Pi_0^{*'} \Pi_1^{*'3} + \cdots$$
$$= BB^{-1} C_1 BDB^{-1} + BDB^{-1} C_1 BD^2 B^{-1} + BD^2 B^{-1} C_1 BD^3 B^{-1} + \cdots$$
$$\equiv B(G_1 + DG_1 D + DG_1 D^2 + \cdots)DB^{-1} = B\left[\frac{g_{1,ij}}{1 - \lambda_i \lambda_j}\right]DB^{-1}$$

where we have let $G_1 = B^{-1} C_1 B = (g_{1,ij})$. Similarly, the probability limit of the sum of products with time subscripts differing by r is

$$B\left[\frac{g_{r,\,ij}}{1 - \lambda_i \lambda_j}\right] D^r B^{-1} \tag{62}$$

with $G_r = B^{-1}C_r B = (g_{r,\,ij})$ and $C_r = \Pi_0^* Q_r \Pi_0^{*'}$. Since Q_r exists for all r by assumption, C_r and thus G_r are bounded. Hence the sum of the terms of the form (62) over r is finite if and only if the sum $\sum_r D^r$ is finite, i.e., if and only if all roots of Π_1^* are less than 1 in absolute value. We have shown that the sum of all products involving the z's in $y_t^* y_t^{*'}$ has a finite probability limit.

Next consider the probability limit of the sum of products involving the v's. Since the v's are independent and have zero mean, the sum of products of v_t^* and terms involving the z's, y_0, and v_{t-k}^* ($k \neq 0$) all have probability limit zero. We are left with

$$\operatorname*{plim}_{n \to \infty} n^{-1}\left(\sum_t v_t^* v_t^{*'} + \Pi_1^* \sum_t v_{t-1}^* v_{t-1}^{*'} \Pi_1^{*'} + \Pi_1^{*2} \sum_t v_{t-2}^* v_{t-2}^{*'} \Pi_1^{*'2} + \cdots\right)$$

The probability limit of each $n^{-1}\sum_t v_t^* v_t^{*'}$ is $\Omega^* = E(v_t^* v_t^{*'})$ by the law of large numbers. By writing $\Pi_1^* = BDB^{-1}$ it is easy to show, as in the preceding two paragraphs, that the sum

$$\Omega^* + \Pi_1^* \Omega^* \Pi_1^{*'} + \Pi_1^{*2} \Omega^* \Pi_1^{*'2} + \cdots$$

converges if and only if all roots of Π_1^* are less than 1 in absolute value.

Third, we consider

$$\operatorname*{plim}_{n \to \infty} n^{-1} \sum_t \Pi_1^{*'} y_0 (z_{t-k}' \Pi_0^* + z_{t-k-1}' \Pi_0^* \Pi_1^{*'} + z_{t-k-2}' \Pi_0^{*'} \Pi_1^{*'2} + \cdots) \tag{63}$$

Since the terms $y_0 z_{t-k-j}' \Pi_0^*$ ($j = 0, 1, \ldots$) are bounded, the sum

$$\sum_t \Pi_1^{*'}(y_0 z_{t-k-j}' \Pi_0^*) \qquad j = 0, 1, \ldots$$

exists if the roots of Π_1^* are less than 1 in absolute value, as can be easily seen by writing $\Pi_1^{*'} = BD^t B^{-1}$ and noting that

$$\sum_t \Pi_1^{*'} = B(I + D + D^2 + \cdots)B^{-1} = B(I - D)^{-1}B^{-1}$$

Hence $$\operatorname*{plim}_{n \to \infty} n^{-1} \sum_t \Pi_1^{*'}(y_0 z_{t-k-j}' \Pi_0^*) = 0$$

and (63) is zero.

Finally, consider

$$\sum_t \Pi_1^{*'} y_0 y_0' \Pi_1^{*''} = \sum_t BD^t B^{-1} y_0 y_0' B'^{-1} D^t B$$

$$= B \sum_t [D^t(B^{-1} y_0 y_0' B'^{-1})D^t] B'$$

which is finite if and only if the roots of Π_1^* are less than 1 in absolute value. Hence the probability limit of n^{-1} times the above sum is zero.

Corollary 1 Under the assumption of Theorem 4.7 a necessary and sufficient condition for $\text{plim}_{n \to \infty} (n - k)^{-1} \sum_{t=k+1}^{n} y_t^* y_{t-k}^{*\prime}$ to exist in model (57) is for the roots of Π_1^*, or of A_{11} defined by (60), to be less than 1 in absolute value.

PROOF For $k = 1$, by (57),

$$\text{plim } n^{-1} \sum_t y_t^* y_{t-1}^{*\prime}$$

$$= \text{plim } n^{-1} \sum_t (\Pi_1^* y_{t-1}^* + \Pi_0^* z_t + v_t^*) y_{t-1}^{*\prime}$$

$$= \Pi_1^* (\text{plim } n^{-1} \sum_t y_{t-1}^* y_{t-1}^{*\prime}) + \Pi_0^* (\text{plim } n^{-1} \sum_t z_t y_{t-1}^{*\prime})$$

$$+ \text{plim } n^{-1} \sum_t v_t^* y_{t-1}^{*\prime}$$

The first term is finite by Theorem 4.7. The second term can be shown to be finite by considering the product of z_t and

$$y_{t-1}^{*\prime} = z_{t-1}' \Pi_0^{*\prime} + z_{t-2}' \Pi_0^{*\prime} \Pi_1^{*\prime} + \cdots + v_{t-1}^{*\prime} + v_{t-2}^{*\prime} \Pi_1^{*\prime} + \cdots + y_0' \Pi_1^{*\prime-1}$$

The third term can be shown to be zero by considering the product of v_t^* and $y_{t-1}^{*\prime}$ given above. Assuming the result to be true for $k = m$, by writing

$$\text{plim } n^{-1} \sum_t y_t^* y_{t-(m+1)}^{*\prime}$$

$$= \text{plim } n^{-1} \sum_t (\Pi_1^* y_{t-1}^* + \Pi_0^* z_t + v_t^*) y_{t-(m+1)}^{*\prime}$$

$$= \Pi_1^* (\text{plim } n^{-1} \sum_t y_{t-1}^* y_{t-1-m}^{*\prime}) + \Pi_0^* (\text{plim } n^{-1} \sum_t z_t y_{t-1-m}^{*\prime})$$

$$+ \text{plim } n^{-1} \sum_t v_t^* y_{t-1-m}^{*\prime}$$

one easily sees that the first term is finite by assumption while the second is finite and the third term is zero.

Corollary 2 For all r assume

$$\text{plim}_{n \to \infty} (n - r)^{-1} \sum_{t=r+1}^{n} z_t z_{t-r}' = Q_r$$

and

$$\text{plim}_{n \to \infty} (n - r)^{-1} \sum_{t=r+1}^{n} z_t v_{t-r}^{*\prime} = 0$$

A necessary and sufficient condition for $\text{plim}_{n \to \infty} (n - k)^{-1} \sum_{t=k+1}^{n} y_t^* y_{t-k}^{*\prime}$ to exist in model (57) is for all the roots of A_{11} as defined in (60) to be less than 1 in absolute value.

The proof of Corollary 2 is identical with that of Theorem 4.7, where we were taking only probability limits. In econometrics, if the exogenous variables z_t are regarded not as fixed but as being generated by some random process independent of ϵ_t and thus of $v_t = B^{-1}\epsilon_t$, Corollary 2 will be useful.

PROBLEMS

1. Consider the model consisting of Eqs. (1) and (2). If $\gamma_{12} = 0$, explain why each of the two equations is underidentified, just identified, or overidentified. If $\gamma_{14}\,x_{t4}$ is added to the first equation, with $\gamma_{12} \neq 0$, explain why each of the two equations is underidentified, just identified, or overidentified.

2. In the model consisting of Eqs. (1) and (2), assuming $\gamma_{12} = 0$, study the identifiability of each structural equation using the rank of $[B_2 \quad \Gamma_2]$ as defined in Eq. (18).

3. Study the identifiability of each equation in the structure

$$-y_{t1} + \beta_{12}\,y_{t2} \qquad\qquad + \gamma_{11}\,x_{t1} \qquad\qquad + \gamma_{13}\,x_{t3} = \epsilon_{t1}$$

$$\beta_{21}\,y_{t1} - y_{t2} + \beta_{23}y_{t3} + \gamma_{21}\,x_{t1} + \gamma_{22}\,x_{t2} \qquad\qquad = \epsilon_{t2}$$

$$\beta_{32}\,y_{t2} - \qquad y_{t3} + \gamma_{31}\,x_{t1} \qquad\qquad = \epsilon_{t3}$$

using the order condition and the rank condition on $[B_2 \quad \Gamma_2]$ of Eq. (18) successively.

4. Consider the model consisting of Eqs. (i), (iv), (vi), and (vii) in Table 4.2 and the relevant identities.

(*a*) Explain why each of these equations is underidentified, just identified, or overidentified.

(*b*) Study the identifiability of each of the structural equations using the rank of $[B_2 \quad \Gamma_2]$ defined in Eq. (18).

5. Provide an example of a model in which the first structural equation satisfies the order condition for identification but fails to satisfy the rank condition on the matrix $[B_2 \quad \Gamma_2]$ defined in Eq. (18).

6. In the model consisting of Eqs. (1) and (2), assuming $\gamma_{12} = 0$

(*a*) study the identifiability of each structural equation using (i) Theorem 4.2 and (ii) Theorem 4.3.

(*b*) Determine whether the entire set of structural coefficients is identified using (i) Theorem 4.4 and (ii) Theorem 4.5.

(*c*) Study the identifiability of each structural parameter using Theorem 4.6.

7. Repeat part (*c*) of Prob. 6 assuming $\gamma_{13} = 0$.

8. Show that the matrix of long-run multipliers $\sum_{j=0}^{\infty} \Pi_1^{*j}\Pi_0$ converges to a finite limit if and only if the characteristic roots of Π_1^* are less than 1 in absolute value.

9. Theil and Boot (1962) tried to obtain the various multipliers by transforming the reduced form (55) into a first-order system as follows:

$$
\begin{bmatrix} y_t \\ y_{t-1} \\ \cdot \\ y_{t-p+1} \end{bmatrix}
=
\begin{bmatrix} \Pi_1 & \Pi_2 & \cdots & \Pi_p \\ I & 0 & \cdots & 0 \\ & & \cdot & \\ 0 & 0 & I & 0 \end{bmatrix}
\begin{bmatrix} y_{t-1} \\ y_{t-2} \\ \cdot \\ y_{t-p} \end{bmatrix}
+ [\Pi_0 \quad \cdots \quad \Pi_{p+r}]
\begin{bmatrix} z_t \\ \vdots \\ z_{t-r} \end{bmatrix}
+
\begin{bmatrix} v_t \\ 0 \\ \cdot \\ 0 \end{bmatrix}
$$

or, more compactly, as

$$y_t^* = \Pi_1^* y_{t-1}^* + \Pi_0^* z_t^* + v_t^*$$

which can be converted into a final form similar to (58). They claimed (on p. 147) that the first row (submatrix) of the matrix $\Pi_1^{*k}\Pi_0^*$ would give the k-period delayed multipliers measuring the effects of z_{t-k} on y_t. Explain why this claim is incorrect.

10. For the model given by Eqs. (i), (iv), (vi), and (vii) of Table 4.2 (*a*) write out all matrices and explain clearly all steps required to compute the delayed multipliers of M_{t-2} and G_{t-2} on C_t, I_{1t}, I_{2t}, and R_t and (*b*) compute the above multipliers.

REFERENCES

Chow, G. C. (1966): "On the Long-Run and Short-Run Demand for Money," *J. Polit. Econ.* **74**: 111–131.
——— (1967): "Multiplier, Accelerator and Liquidity Preference in the Determination of National Income in the United States," *Rev. Econ. Statist.*, **49**: 1–15.
Dhrymes, P. (1978): *Introductory Econometrics*, Springer-Verlag, New York.
Fisher, F. M. (1966): *The Identification Problem in Econometrics*, McGraw-Hill, New York.
Gale, D. (1960): *The Theory of Linear Economic Models*, McGraw-Hill, New York.
Haavelmo, T. (1943): "The Statistical Implications of a System of Simultaneous Equations," *Econometrica*, **11**: 1–12.
——— (1944): "The Probability Approach to Econometrics," *Econometrica, Suppl.*
Hicks, J. R. (1937): "Mr. Keynes and the 'Classics': A Suggested Interpretation," *Econometrica*, **5**: 147–159.
Hood, W. C., and T. C. Koopmans (eds.) (1953): *Studies in Econometric Methods*, Wiley, New York.
Hsiao, C. (1981): "Identification," *Univ. Toronto Inst. Policy Anal., Working Pap.* 8103.
Intriligator, M. D. (1978): *Econometric Models, Techniques, and Applications*, Prentice-Hall, Englewood Cliffs, N.J.
Johnston, J. (1972): *Econometric Methods*, 2d ed., McGraw-Hill, New York.
Keynes, J. M. (1936): *The General Theory of Employment, Interest and Money*, Harcourt Brace Jovanovich, New York.
Koopmans, T. C. (ed.) (1950): *Statistical Inference in Dynamic Economic Models*, Wiley, New York.
——— and W. C. Hood (1953): "The Estimation of Simultaneous Linear Economic Relationships," chap. VI in W. C. Hood and T. C. Koopmans (eds.), *Studies in Econometric Methods*, Wiley, New York.
Liu, T. C. (1960): "Underidentification, Structural Estimation and Forecasting," *Econometrica*, **28**: 855–865.
Maddala, G. S. (1977): *Econometrics*, McGraw-Hill, New York.
Malinvaud, E. (1966): *Statistical Methods of Econometrics*, North-Holland, Amsterdam.
Marschak, J. (1953): "Econometric Measurements for Policy and Prediction," chap. I in W. C. Hood and T. C. Koopmans (eds.), *Studies in Econometric Methods*, Wiley, New York.
Modigliani, F. (1944): "Liquidity Preference and the Theory of Interest and Money," *Econometrica*, **12**: 45–88.
Richmond, J. (1974): "Identifiability in Linear Models," *Econometrica*, **42**, 731–736.
Rothenberg, T. J. (1971): "Identification in Parametric Models," *Econometrica*, **39**: 577–592.
Samuelson, P. A. (1939): "Interactions between the Multiplier Analysis and the Principle of Acceleration," *Rev. Econ. Statist.* **21**: 75–78.
Sims, C. A. (1980): "Macroeconomics and Reality," *Econometrica*, **48**: 1–48.
Theil, H. (1970): *Principles of Econometrics*, Wiley, New York.
——— and J. Boot (1962): "The Final Form of Econometric Equation Systems," *Rev. Int. Statist. Inst.* 146–147.
Tinbergen, (1939): *Statistical Testing of Business-Cycle Theories*, League of Nations, Geneva.
Turvey, R. (1965): "On the Demand for Money," *Econometrica*, **33**: 459–460.
Working, E. J. (1927): "What Do Statistical 'Demand Curves' Show?" *Q. J. Econ.*, **41**: 212–235.

ESTIMATION OF LINEAR
SIMULTANEOUS EQUATIONS

5.1 METHOD OF TWO-STAGE LEAST SQUARES

This chapter is concerned with methods for estimating the parameters of linear simultaneous equations. The methods proposed are mainly applications of the principles of least squares, maximum likelihood, and instrumental variables. The estimators can be classified into two types, called *full information* when the entire system is specified and estimated simultaneously and *limited information* when a subset of equations is specified and estimated, but the remaining equations are not completely specified. Only asymptotic distributions of the estimators will be derived. Although exact distributions of certain estimators in finite samples have been investigated, either by Monte Carlo or analytical methods, useful results are limited. We begin by studying limited-information methods, to be followed by full-information methods.

The model is as given by Eq. (54) of Chap. 4, namely,

$$By_{t.} + \Gamma_1 y_{t-1.} + \cdots + \Gamma_p y_{t-p.} + \Gamma_0 z_{t.} + \cdots + \Gamma_{p+r} z_{t-r.} = \epsilon_{t.} \tag{1}$$

where z_t is a vector of exogenous variables, $E\epsilon_{t.} = 0$, $E\epsilon_{t.}\epsilon_{t.}' = \Sigma$, and $E\epsilon_{t.}\epsilon_{t-k.}' = 0$ for $k \neq 0$. Its reduced form is

$$y_{t.} = \Pi_1 y_{t-1.} + \cdots + \Pi_p y_{t-p.} + \Pi_0 z_{t.} + \cdots + \Pi_{p+r} z_{t-r.} + v_{t.} \tag{2}$$

Denote by x_t the vector of predetermined variables, including $y_{t-1}, \ldots, y_{t-p}$, $z_t, \ldots, z_{t-r}$, by Γ the matrix $[\Gamma_1 \quad \cdots \quad \Gamma_{p+r}]$ of structural coefficients of x_t, and by Π the matrix $[\Pi_1 \quad \cdots \quad \Pi_{p+r}]$ of reduced-form coefficients. Equations (1) and (2) are written respectively as

$$By_{t.} + \Gamma x_{t.} = \epsilon_{t.} \tag{3}$$

and

$$y_{t.} = -B^{-1}\Gamma x_{t.} + B^{-1}\epsilon_{t.} = \Pi x_{t.} + v_{t.} \tag{4}$$

For the purpose of estimation, let n observations be available. Denote by Y' a $G \times n$ matrix whose tth column is $y_{t.}$ $(t = 1, \ldots, n)$, by X' a $K \times n$ matrix whose tth column is $x_{t.}$, and by E' a $G \times n$ matrix whose tth column is $\epsilon_{t.}$. The n observations of the model (3) can be written as

$$BY' + \Gamma X' = E' \tag{5}$$

and its reduced form is

$$Y' = \Pi X' + B^{-1}E' = \Pi X' + V' \tag{6}$$

We let X be an $n \times k$ matrix to be consistent with the notation used in regression analysis. Unfortunately, in regression analysis the coefficients are usually denoted by a *column* vector, whereas in simultaneous equations the ith *row* of $[B \quad \Gamma]$ denotes the coefficients of the ith structural equation. If we decide to use a column vector for the unknown coefficients in each equation for the discussion of estimation methods, we must transpose Eq. (5) to get

$$YB' + X\Gamma' = E \tag{7}$$

and write the ith equation, or the ith column of (7), as

$$Y\bar{\beta}_i + X\bar{\gamma}_i = \epsilon_i \tag{8}$$

where $\bar{\beta}_i$ and $\bar{\gamma}_i$ denote the ith columns of B' and Γ', respectively, and ϵ_i denotes the ith column of E, to be distinguished from $\epsilon_{t.}$, which is the transpose of the tth row of E. Whereas $\epsilon_{t.}$ in (1) and (3) denotes a column vector of G correlated residuals of different equations in period t, ϵ_i in (8) denotes a column vector of n independent residuals of the ith equation over n periods. To study the identification problem and the dynamic properties of an econometric model it is necessary to consider $\epsilon_{t.}$ and $y_{t.}$ as column vectors of G variables in period t. To study estimation problems it is convenient and conventional to let the ith column of E, Y, and X represent n observations of one variable, denoted by ϵ_i, y_i, and x_i, respectively.

Consider a limited-information method of estimation for the ith structural equation (8). Among the a priori restrictions imposed to ensure identification, many elements of $\bar{\beta}_i$ and $\bar{\gamma}_i$ are known to be zero and the corresponding columns of Y and X can be omitted from (8). If one further adopts the normalization convention $\beta_{ii} = -1$, one can write (8) as

$$-y_i + Y_i\beta_i + X_i\gamma_i = \epsilon_i \tag{9}$$

where y_i is the ith column of Y, consisting of n observations on the ith endogenous variable; Y_i consists of $G_i - 1$ columns of n observations on the other $G_i - 1$

endogenous variables included in equation i; X_i consists of K_i columns of n observations on the K_i predetermined variables included in equation i; and β_i and γ_i denote the column vectors of the corresponding structural coefficients, to be distinguished from $\bar{\beta}_i$ and $\bar{\gamma}_i$ in (8), which include the zero coefficients. Letting

$$W_i = [Y_i \quad X_i] \quad \text{and} \quad \delta_i = \begin{bmatrix} \beta_i \\ \gamma_i \end{bmatrix} \tag{10}$$

we write (9) as

$$y_i = [Y_i \quad X_i]\begin{bmatrix} \beta_i \\ \gamma_i \end{bmatrix} + \epsilon_i = W_i\delta_i + \epsilon_i \tag{11}$$

The method of least squares as applied to (11) will not yield a consistent estimator of δ_i because plim $n^{-1}Y_i'\epsilon_i$ is not zero. Postmultiplying the reduced-form (6) by ϵ_i, we find

$$Y'\epsilon_i = \Pi X'\epsilon_i + B^{-1}E'\epsilon_i$$

and observe that plim $n^{-1}E'\epsilon_i$ equals the ith column of Σ. The endogenous variables Y_i on the right-hand side of (11) are correlated with the residual ϵ_i because they are determined by the reduced form (6), in which the ith column of the residual V is $B^{-1}\epsilon_i$. Let Π_i be a $(G_i - 1) \times K$ matrix whose rows are the coefficients of the $G_i - 1$ reduced-form equations explaining Y_i'. Thus the corresponding rows of (6) can be written as

$$Y_i' = \Pi_i X' + V_i' \tag{12}$$

where V_i' results from selecting the corresponding $G_i - 1$ rows from V'.

To get rid of the correlations between ϵ_i and the explanatory variables in (11) one can replace Y_i by

$$\hat{Y}_i = X\hat{\Pi}_i' = X(X'X)^{-1}X'Y_i \tag{13}$$

where $\hat{\Pi}_i$ is the least-squares estimate of Π_i in (12), and perform a regression of y_i on $\hat{Y}_i$ and X_i to estimate δ_i in (11). This is the two-stage least-squares (2SLS) method. In the first stage $\hat{\Pi}_i$ and $\hat{Y}_i = X\hat{\Pi}_i'$ are estimated by applying least squares to the reduced-form equations for Y_i. In the second stage, least squares is applied to estimate the structural coefficients δ_i in (11) by using

$$\hat{W}_i = [\hat{Y}_i \quad X_i] = [X(X'X)^{-1}X'Y_i \quad X_i] = X(X'X)^{-1}X'W_i$$

as explanatory variables. Thus the 2SLS estimator of δ_i is

$$d_i = (\hat{W}_i'\hat{W}_i)^{-1}\hat{W}_i'y_i = [W_i'X(X'X)^{-1}X'W_i]^{-1}W_i'X(X'X)^{-1}X'y_i \tag{14}$$

The method of 2SLS was proposed independently by Theil (1953) and Basmann (1957).

Two other interpretations of the 2SLS method are revealing. First, it is an application of the method of generalized least squares. Let Eq. (11) be premultiplied by X' to yield

$$X'y_i = X'W_i\delta_i + X'\epsilon_i \tag{15}$$

The covariance matrix of the residual $X'\epsilon_i$ is $X'X\sigma_{ii}$. Treating $X'y_i$ as a vector of dependent variables and $X'W_i$ as a matrix of explanatory variables, one can apply GLS to (15) and obtain the 2SLS estimator given by (14). Before the premultiplication by X', the residual ϵ_i in (11) is correlated with the explanatory variable W_i, leading to the inconsistency of the least-squares estimator applied to (11). After (11) has been premultiplied by X' and GLS applied to (15), the expression $n^{-1}W_i'\epsilon_i$ in the least-squares estimator is replaced by $n^{-1}W_i'X(X'X)^{-1}X'\epsilon_i$, which will be seen below to have probability limit zero, thus avoiding the problem of inconsistency.

Second, the 2SLS method can be interpreted as an application of the method of instrumental variables. The matrix of instruments for W_i is $\hat{W}_i = X(X'X)^{-1}X'W_i$, namely, the matrix of the estimated values of W_i by a least-squares regression of W_i on all the predetermined variables X. From Sec. 3.9 and as shown below, if plim $n^{-1}\hat{W}_i'W$ exists and if plim $n^{-1}\hat{W}_i'\epsilon_i = 0$, the instrumental-variable estimator

$$d_i = (\hat{W}_i'W_i)^{-1}\hat{W}_i'y_i$$

for the coefficient vector δ_i in (11) will be consistent.

To study the consistency of the 2SLS estimator we write

$$
\begin{aligned}
d_i &= (\hat{W}_i'W_i)^{-1}\hat{W}_i'(W_i\delta_i + \epsilon_i) \\
&= \delta_i + [(n^{-1}W_i'X)(n^{-1}X'X)^{-1}(n^{-1}X'W_i)]^{-1} \\
&\quad \cdot (n^{-1}W_i'X)(n^{-1}X'X)^{-1}n^{-1}X'\epsilon_i \\
&\equiv \delta_i + G_i n^{-1}X'\epsilon_i
\end{aligned}
\tag{16}
$$

We make the assumption of Theorem 4.7, namely, that $\lim (n-k)^{-1}\sum_{t=k+1}^{n} z_t z_{t-k}'$ exists for all k, where z_t is the vector of exogenous variables in model (1). Theorem 4.7 then states that a necessary and sufficient condition for plim $n^{-1}\sum y_t^* y_t^{*'}$ to exist is that all the characteristic roots of the matrix A as defined by Eq. (60) of Chap. 4 be less than 1 in absolute value, where y_t^* includes the vectors $y_t, y_{t-1}, \ldots, y_{t-p}, z_t, z_{t-1}, \ldots, z_{t-r}$. The matrix X includes the variables $y_{t-1}, \ldots, y_{t-p}, z_t, \ldots, z_{t-r}$. The matrix W_i consists of variables selected from y_t^* which are included in the ith equation. If we assume the above necessary and sufficient condition to hold, the matrices $n^{-1}W_i'X$ and $n^{-1}X'X$ will have probability limits. Since plim $n^{-1}X'\epsilon_i = 0$ by assumption, taking probability limits of both sides of (16) will show

$$\text{plim } d_i = \delta_i + (\text{plim } G_i)(\text{plim } n^{-1}X'\epsilon_i) = \delta_i$$

or the consistency of the 2SLS estimator d_i.

To study the asymptotic distribution of the 2SLS estimator we consider

$$\sqrt{n}(d_i - \delta_i) = G_i n^{-1/2}X'\epsilon_i$$

If $n^{-1/2}X'\epsilon_i$ has a limiting normal distribution with mean zero, and if plim G_i exists, then $\sqrt{n}(d_i - \delta_i)$ will also have a limiting normal distribution with mean zero. The covariance matrix of the former limiting distribution is

$$\text{plim } n^{-1}X'X\sigma_{ii.} = Q\sigma_{ii.}$$

The covariance matrix of $\sqrt{n}(d_i - \delta_i)$ is therefore

$$(\text{plim } G_i)(\text{plim } n^{-1}X'X)(\text{plim } G_i)'\sigma_{ii} = \text{plim } (n^{-1}\hat{W}_i' W_i)\sigma_{ii} \qquad (17)$$

where G_i is defined in (16) and the right-hand side results after some cancellations. The above derivation assumes that $n^{-1/2}X'\epsilon_i$ has a limiting normal distribution. If X is fixed, each element of the column vector $n^{-1/2}X'\epsilon_i$ is a linear combination of n independent random variables. One can appeal to the Lindeberg-Feller central limit theorem for the normality of its limiting distribution. However, in our case X may include lagged endogenous variables, and therefore the elements in each row of X' or each column of X are not statistically independent. Each element of $n^{-1/2}X'\epsilon_i$ becomes a linear combination of n statistically dependent random variables. One can no longer appeal to the Lindeberg-Feller central limit theorem which covers sums of independent random variables. It is more involved to prove that the limiting distribution of $n^{-1/2}X'\epsilon_i$ is normal under the assumption of Theorem 4.7. One approach is to treat a lagged endogenous variable in X as a weighted average of past random disturbances, as we did in the proof of Theorem 4.7, and consider the sum of the products of ϵ_{ti} and this average. For a derivation of the central limit theorem governing the sum of such statistically dependent random variables, see Anderson (1971, pp. 198–199).

★5.2 METHOD OF LIMITED-INFORMATION MAXIMUM LIKELIHOOD

The method of maximum likelihood can be applied to estimate one structural equation, say the first, without loss. Equation (9), for $i = 1$, can now be rewritten as

$$[y_1 \quad Y_1]\begin{bmatrix} -1 \\ \beta_1 \end{bmatrix} + X_1\gamma_1 = Y_1^0\beta_1^0 + X_1\gamma_1 = \epsilon_1 \qquad (18)$$

where Y_1^0 is an $n \times G_1$ matrix of observations on all the G_1 endogenous variables included in the first equation; X_1 is an $n \times K_1$ matrix of observations on the K_1 predetermined variables included in the first equation; and the vector β_1^0 includes the coefficient of y_1. The likelihood function for model (18) is based on the likelihood of the model explaining Y_1^0, that is, of the reduced form for Y_1^0

$$Y_1^{0'} = \Pi_{11}X_1' + \Pi_{12}X_1^{*'} + V_1' \qquad (19)$$

where Π_{11} is $G_1 \times K_1$, Π_{12} is $G_1 \times (K - K_1)$, and $[X_1 \quad X_1^*] = X$. Assuming the ith column v_i. of V_1' to be G_1-variate normal with mean zero and covariance matrix Ω_1, we write its probability density function as

$$p(v_{i.}) = (2\pi)^{-G_1/2} |\Omega_1|^{-1/2} \exp\left(-\tfrac{1}{2} v'_{i.} \Omega_1^{-1} v_{i.}\right)$$

If the n columns of $V'_1 = [v_{1.} \quad v_{2.} \quad \dots \quad v_{n.}]$ are statistically independent, their joint density function is

$$p(V'_1) = (2\pi)^{-nG_1/2} |\Omega_1|^{-n/2} \exp\left(-\frac{1}{2} \sum_{i=1}^{n} v'_{i.} \Omega_1^{-1} v_{i.}\right)$$

$$= (2\pi)^{-nG_1/2} |\Omega_1|^{-n/2} \exp\left[-\tfrac{1}{2} \operatorname{tr}\left(\Omega_1^{-1} V'_1 V_1\right)\right] \tag{20}$$

where the exponent has been rewritten on account of

$$\sum_{i=1}^{n} \operatorname{tr}\left(v'_{i.} \Omega_1^{-1} v_{i.}\right) = \sum_{i=1}^{n} \operatorname{tr}\left(\Omega_1^{-1} v_{i.} v'_{i.}\right) = \operatorname{tr}\left(\Omega_1^{-1} \sum_{i=1}^{n} v_{i.} v'_{i.}\right)$$

Treating Π_{11}, Π_{12}, and Ω_1 as unknown parameters, we obtain the likelihood function of Y_1^0 by using (19) to substitute Y_1^0 for V_1 in (20)

$$p(Y_1^{0'}) = (2\pi)^{-nG_1/2} |\Omega_1|^{-n/2} \exp\left\{-\tfrac{1}{2} \operatorname{tr}\left[\Omega_1^{-1}(Y_1^{0'} - \Pi_{11}X'_1 - \Pi_{12}X_1^{*'})\right.\right.$$
$$\left.\left.\cdot (Y_1^0 - X_1\Pi'_{11} - X_1^*\Pi'_{12})\right]\right\} \tag{21}$$

This step amounts to the change of variables from V_1 to Y_1^0. The jacobian to be used in the transformation is the absolute value of the determinant of the matrix of the partial derivatives of the variables in V_1 with respect to the variables in Y_1^0. This matrix is an identity matrix according to (20). Therefore, the jacobian is simply 1 in this change of variables.

Equation (21) is the likelihood function for the model (19) explaining Y_1^0, but our interest is in the model (18) explaining a linear combination $Y_1^0 \beta_1^0$ of the columns of Y_1^0. If we transpose (19) and postmultiply by β_1^0, we obtain

$$Y_1^0 \beta_1^0 = X_1 \Pi'_{11} \beta_1^0 + X_1^* \Pi'_{12} \beta_1^0 + V_1 \beta_1^0 = -X_1 \gamma_1 + \epsilon_1 \tag{22}$$

where

$$\Pi'_{11} \beta_1^0 = -\gamma_1 \tag{23}$$

and

$$\Pi'_{12} \beta_1^0 = 0 \tag{24}$$

which are respectively Eqs. (14) and (15) of Chap. 4 as derived from the relation $B\Pi = -\Gamma$. Equation (22) agrees with the model (18) we wish to estimate. The unknown parameters are now Π_{11}, Π_{12}, β_1^0, γ_1, and Ω_1. The likelihood function is (21), subject to the constraint (24). The constraint (23) does not affect the likelihood function to be maximized; in fact, it provides an estimate of γ_1 once Π_{11} and β_1^0 have been estimated.

The log-likelihood function (21) can be maximized subject to (24) by the use of the Lagrangian expression

$$L = -\frac{n}{2} \log |\Omega_1| - \tfrac{1}{2} \operatorname{tr}\left[\Omega_1^{-1}(Y_1^{0'} - \Pi_{11}X'_1 - \Pi_{12}X_1^{*'})\right.$$
$$\left.\cdot (Y_1^0 - X_1\Pi'_{11} - X_1^*\Pi'_{12})\right] + \lambda' \Pi'_{12} \beta_1^0 \tag{25}$$

where λ is a vector of $K - K_1$ Lagrange multipliers. We first differentiate L with respect to Ω_1^{-1}, using the rules $(\partial \log |A|)/\partial A = A'^{-1}$ and $[\partial \text{ tr } (AB)]/\partial A = B'$ and noting that $|\Omega_1^{-1}| = |\Omega_1|^{-1}$. When Ω_1^{-1} is symmetric, the derivative of $\log |\Omega_1^{-1}|$ with respect to an off-diagonal element of Ω_1^{-1} equals *twice* the corresponding element of Ω_1; the derivative of tr $(\Omega_1^{-1}B)$ with respect to an off-diagonal element of Ω_1^{-1} equals *twice* the corresponding element of B'. The equation below combines the derivatives of L with respect to the diagonal elements of Ω_1^{-1} with *half* the derivatives with respect to the off-diagonal elements.

$$\frac{n}{2}\Omega_1 - \tfrac{1}{2}(Y_1^{0\prime} - \Pi_{11}X_1' - \Pi_{12}X^{*\prime})(Y_1^0 - X_1\Pi_{11}' - X_1^*\Pi_{12}') = 0$$

As expected, the solution for Ω_1 is

$$\hat{\Omega}_1 = n^{-1}(Y_1^{0\prime} - \hat{\Pi}_{11}X_1' - \hat{\Pi}_{12}X_1^{*\prime})(Y_1^0 - X_1\hat{\Pi}_{11}' - X_1^*\hat{\Pi}_{12}') \qquad (26)$$

where the hats denote maximum-likelihood estimates. Substitution of (26) for Ω_1 in (25) gives

$$L^* = -\frac{n}{2}\log |n^{-1}(Y_1^{0\prime} - \Pi_{11}X_1' - \Pi_{12}X_1^{*\prime})(Y_1^0 - X_1\Pi_{11}' - X_1^*\Pi_{12}')|$$
$$+ \lambda'\Pi_{12}'\beta_1^0 \quad (27)$$

where Π_{11} and Π_{12} (without hats) are treated as variables in the maximization problem and we have omitted the constant $-\tfrac{1}{2}$ tr $(n\hat{\Omega}_1^{-1}\hat{\Omega}_1) = -nG_1/2$. The problem is to maximize L^* with respect to Π_{11}, Π_{12}, β_1^0, and λ.

To facilitate the differentiation of L^*, let $\hat{\Omega}_1 = (\hat{\omega}_{ij})$, where, by (26),

$$\hat{\omega}_{ij} = n^{-1}(y_i - X_1\pi_{i1} - X_1^*\pi_{i2})'(y_j - X_1\pi_{j1} - X_1^*\pi_{j2}) \qquad (28)$$

in which π_{i1} denotes the *i*th column of Π_{11}' and π_{i2} denotes the *i*th column of Π_{12}'. The partial derivative of L^* with respect to π_{k1} is

$$\frac{\partial L^*}{\partial \pi_{k1}} = -\frac{n}{2}\sum_i \sum_j \frac{\partial \log |\hat{\Omega}_1|}{\partial \hat{\omega}_{ij}} \frac{\partial \hat{\omega}_{ij}}{\partial \pi_{k1}}$$

Since

$$\frac{\partial \hat{\omega}_{ij}}{\partial \pi_{k1}} = \begin{cases} 0 & \text{if } k \neq i, j \\ -n^{-1}X_1'(y_j - X_1\pi_{j1} - X_1^*\pi_{j2}) & \text{if } k = i \\ -n^{-1}X_1'(y_i - X_1\pi_{i1} - X_1^*\pi_{i2}) & \text{if } k = j \end{cases}$$

we have

$$\frac{\partial L^*}{\partial \pi_{k1}} = \sum_j \hat{\omega}^{kj}X_1'(y_j - X_1\pi_{j1} - X_1^*\pi_{j2}) = X_1'(Y_1^0 - X_1\Pi_{11}' - X_1^*\Pi_{12}')\hat{\omega}^k \qquad (29)$$

where $\hat{\omega}^{kj}$ is the kjth element and $\hat{\omega}^k$ is the kth column of $\hat{\Omega}_1^{-1}$. Collecting the columns $\pi_{11} \ldots \pi_{G11}$ of Π'_{11}, we obtain the derivative of L^* with respect to the matrix Π'_{11}

$$\frac{\partial L^*}{\partial \Pi'_{11}} = X'_1(Y_1^0 - X_1\Pi'_{11} - X_1^*\Pi'_{12})\hat{\Omega}_1^{-1} = 0 \tag{30}$$

After postmultiplication by $\hat{\Omega}_1$, (30) can be solved for Π'_{11}

$$\hat{\Pi}'_{11} = (X'_1X_1)^{-1}X'_1(Y_1^0 - X_1^*\hat{\Pi}'_{12}) \tag{31}$$

Given (30) and $\lambda'\Pi'_{12}\beta_1^0 = \text{tr}(\Pi'_{12}\beta_1^0\lambda')$, the differentiation of L^* with respect to Π'_{12} is straightforward

$$\frac{\partial L^*}{\partial \Pi'_{12}} = X_1^{*\prime}(Y_1^0 - X_1\Pi'_{11} - X^*\Pi'_{12})\hat{\Omega}_1^{-1} + \lambda\beta_1^{0\prime} = 0 \tag{32}$$

Substituting (31) for Π'_{11} in (32) and letting

$$M_1 = I - X_1(X'_1X_1)^{-1}X'_1 \tag{33}$$

give

$$X_1^{*\prime}M_1(Y_1^0 - X_1^*\Pi'_{12})\hat{\Omega}_1^{-1} + \lambda\beta_1^{0\prime} = 0 \tag{34}$$

Differentiation with respect to β_1^0 yields

$$\frac{\partial L^*}{\partial \beta_1^0} = \Pi_{12}\lambda = 0 \tag{35}$$

and differentiation with respect to λ gives (24). Solving (34), (35), and (24) for the three unknowns Π'_{12}, β_1^0, and λ gives the limited-information maximum-likelihood (LIML) estimates for all the parameters. Note that $\hat{\Omega}_1$ is a function of $\hat{\Pi}_{11}$ and $\hat{\Pi}_{12}$ by (26) and $\hat{\Pi}_{11}$ is a function of $\hat{\Pi}_{12}$ by (31).

Postmultiplying (34) by $\hat{\Omega}_1\beta_1^0$ and using (24) lead to

$$X_1^{*\prime}M_1Y_1^0\beta_1^0 + \lambda\beta_1^{0\prime}\hat{\Omega}_1\beta_1^0 = 0$$

which implies
$$\hat{\lambda} = -(\beta_1^{0\prime}\hat{\Omega}_1\beta_1^0)^{-1}X_1^{*\prime}M_1Y_1^0\beta_1^0 \tag{36}$$

Substitution of (36) for λ in (34) and (35) yields, respectively,

$$X_1^{*\prime}M_1(Y_1^0 - X_1^*\Pi'_{12}) - (\beta_1^{0\prime}\hat{\Omega}_1\beta_1^0)^{-1}X_1^{*\prime}M_1Y_1^0\beta_1^0\beta_1^{0\prime}\hat{\Omega}_1 = 0 \tag{37}$$

and
$$\Pi_{12}X_1^{*\prime}M_1Y_1^0\beta_1^0 = 0 \tag{38}$$

We are left with two equations, (37) and (38), for the two unknowns, Π_{12} and β_1^0. Premultiplying (37) by $(X_1^{*\prime}M_1X_1^*)^{-1}$ gives

$$\hat{\Pi}'_{12} = (X_1^{*\prime}M_1X_1^*)^{-1}X_1^{*\prime}M_1Y_1^0[I - (\beta_1^{0\prime}\hat{\Omega}_1\beta_1^0)^{-1}\beta_1^0\beta_1^{0\prime}\hat{\Omega}_1] \tag{39}$$

Since $\hat{\Omega}_1$ is a function of $\hat{\Pi}_{12}$, (39) is not an explicit solution of Π_{12} in terms of β_1^0. Substituting (39) for Π_{12} in (38) gives

$$[I - (\beta_1^{0\prime}\hat{\Omega}_1\beta_1^0)^{-1}\hat{\Omega}_1\beta_1^0\beta_1^{0\prime}]Y_1^{0\prime}M_1X_1^*(X_1^{*\prime}M_1X_1^*)^{-1}X_1^{*\prime}M_1Y_1^0\beta_1^0 = 0 \tag{40}$$

We are still left with two unknowns β_1^0 and $\hat{\Omega}_1$, the latter being a function of Π_{12}. To obtain a solution for β_1^0 using (40) it is necessary to express $\hat{\Omega}_1$ as a function of β_1^0. Unfortunately this last step is somewhat tedious, for $\hat{\Omega}_1$ is a function of Π_{12} and, by (39), Π_{12} is a fairly complicated function of $\hat{\Omega}_1$ and β_1^0.

If one cares to go through the derivations, one can start by using (31) and (39) to write

$$Y_1^0 - X_1\Pi_{11}' - X_1^*\Pi_{12}' = M_1(Y_1^0 - X_1^*\Pi_{12}')$$
$$= M_1 Y_1^0 - M_1 X_1^*(X_1^{*\prime}M_1 X_1^*)^{-1}X_1^{*\prime}M_1 Y_1^0$$
$$\cdot [I - (\beta_1^{0\prime}\hat{\Omega}_1\beta_1^0)^{-1}\beta_1^0\beta_1^{0\prime}\hat{\Omega}_1] \tag{41}$$

Using the partitioned inverse

$$[X'X]^{-1} = \begin{bmatrix} X_1'X_1 & X_1'X_1^* \\ X_1^{*\prime}X_1 & X_1^{*\prime}X_1^* \end{bmatrix}^{-1} = \begin{bmatrix} \mathbb{A} & \mathbb{B} \\ \mathbb{C} & \mathbb{D} \end{bmatrix} \tag{42}$$

where $\mathbb{A} = (X_1'X_1)^{-1} + (X_1'X_1)^{-1}X_1'X_1^*(X_1^{*\prime}M_1 X_1^*)^{-1}X_1^{*\prime}X_1(X_1'X_1)^{-1}$

$\mathbb{B} = -(X_1'X_1)^{-1}X_1'X_1^*(X_1^{*\prime}M_1 X_1^*)^{-1}$

$\mathbb{C} = -(X_1^{*\prime}M_1 X_1^*)^{-1}X_1^{*\prime}X_1(X_1'X_1)^{-1}$

$\mathbb{D} = (X_1^{*\prime}M_1 X_1^*)^{-1}$

one obtains

$$X(X'X)^{-1}X' = X_1(X_1'X_1)^{-1}X_1' + M_1 X_1^*(X_1^{*\prime}M_1 X_1^*)^{-1}X_1^{*\prime}M_1$$

or $$M_1 - M = M_1 X_1^*(X_1^{*\prime}M_1 X_1^*)^{-1}X_1^{*\prime}M_1$$

where $M = I - X(X'X)^{-1}X'$. Substitution into (41) gives

$$Y_1^0 - X_1\Pi_{11}' + X_1^*\Pi_{12}' = MY_1^0 + (\beta_1^{0\prime}\hat{\Omega}_1\beta_1^0)^{-1}(M_1 - M)Y_1^0\beta_1^0\beta_1^{0\prime}\hat{\Omega}_1 \tag{43}$$

Equations (26) and (43) imply

$$\hat{\Omega}_1 = n^{-1}Y_1^{0\prime}MY_1^0 + \frac{\beta_1^{0\prime}Y_1^{0\prime}(M_1 - M)Y_1^0\beta_1^0}{n(\beta_1^{0\prime}\hat{\Omega}_1\beta_1^0)^2}\hat{\Omega}_1\beta_1^0\beta_1^{0\prime}\hat{\Omega}_1 \tag{44}$$

where we have used $M(M_1 - M) = 0$ because $MX_1 = 0$ or $MM_1 = M$.

Postmultiplying (44) by β_1^0 and solving the resulting equation for $\hat{\Omega}_1\beta_1^0$ give

$$\hat{\Omega}_1\beta_1^0 = n^{-1}(1 - \alpha)^{-1}Y_1^{0\prime}MY_1^0\beta_1^0 \tag{45}$$

where $$\alpha = \frac{\beta_1^{0\prime}Y_1^{0\prime}(M_1 - M)Y_1^0\beta_1^0}{n(\beta_1^{0\prime}\hat{\Omega}_1\beta_1^0)} \geq 0$$

Premultiplying (45) by $\beta_1^{0\prime}$ yields

$$\beta_1^{0\prime}\hat{\Omega}_1\beta_1^0 = n^{-1}(1 - \alpha)^{-1}\beta_1^{0\prime}Y_1^{0\prime}MY_1^0\beta_1^0 \tag{46}$$

When (44) is pre- and postmultiplied by β_1^0 directly, the result is

$$\beta_1^{0\prime}\hat{\Omega}_1\beta_1^0 = n^{-1}\beta_1^{0\prime}Y_1^{0\prime}M_1 Y_1^0\beta_1^0 \tag{47}$$

These two equations provide a solution for $1 - \alpha$

$$1 - \alpha = \frac{\beta_1^{0\prime} Y_1^{0\prime} M Y_1^0 \beta_1^0}{\beta_1^{0\prime} Y_1^{0\prime} M_1 Y_1^0 \beta_1^0} \tag{48}$$

Finally, using (45) and (46), we can eliminate $\hat{\Omega}_1$ from (40) to obtain

$$[I - (\beta_1^{0\prime} Y_1^{0\prime} M Y_1^0 \beta_1^0)^{-1} Y_1^{0\prime} M Y_1^0 \beta_1^0 \beta_1^{0\prime}] Y_1^{0\prime} (M_1 - M) Y_1^0 \beta_1^0$$

$$= Y_1^{0\prime}(M_1 - M) Y_1^0 \beta_1^0 - \frac{\alpha}{1 - \alpha} Y_1^{0\prime} M Y_1^0 \beta_1^0$$

$$= \left(Y_1^{0\prime} M_1 Y_1^0 - \frac{1}{1 - \alpha} Y_1^{0\prime} M Y_1^0 \right) \beta_1^0 = 0 \tag{49}$$

To solve (49) for a nonzero β_1^0 the last matrix in parentheses must be singular; i.e., its determinant must be zero. Letting $(1 - \alpha)^{-1} = \mu$, we solve the determinant equation

$$| Y_1^{0\prime} M_1 Y_1^0 - \mu Y_1^{0\prime} M Y_1^0 | = 0 \tag{50}$$

for μ. Given μ, (49) is solved for β_1^0.

An analytical solution for β_1^0 can be obtained as follows. Let

$$Q' Y_1^{0\prime} M Y_1^0 Q = D_\lambda \qquad Q'Q = I$$

where the columns of Q are the characteristic vectors and the diagonal elements of D_λ are the characteristic roots of $Y_1^{0\prime} M Y_1^0$. Also let

$$Q_1' D_\lambda^{-1/2} Q' Y_1^{0\prime} M_1 Y_1^0 Q D_\lambda^{-1/2} Q_1 = D_\mu \qquad Q_1'Q_1 = I$$

where the columns of Q_1 are the characteristic vectors and the diagonal elements of D_μ are the characteristic roots of $D_\lambda^{-1/2} Q' Y_1^{0\prime} M_1 Y_1^0 Q D_\lambda^{-1/2}$. The matrix $B = Q D_\lambda^{-1/2} Q_1$ has the properties

$$B' Y_1^{0\prime} M_1 Y_1^0 B = D_\mu \qquad B' Y_1^{0\prime} M Y_1^0 B = Q_1' D_\lambda^{-1/2} D_\lambda D_\lambda^{-1/2} Q_1 = I \tag{51}$$

which after premultiplication by B'^{-1}, imply,

$$Y_1^{0\prime} M_1 Y_1^0 B = B'^{-1} D_\mu = Y_1^{0\prime} M Y_1^0 B D_\mu$$

If b_i is the ith column of B and μ_i is the ith diagonal element of D_μ, the last equation is equivalent to

$$Y_1^{0\prime} M_1 Y_1^0 b_i = \mu_i Y_1^{0\prime} M Y_1^0 b_i$$

and $\beta_1^0 = b_i$ is a solution to Eq. (49), with $(1 - \alpha)^{-1} = \mu_i$. The root μ_i is thus a solution to the determinantal equation (50). Surely an analytical solution of (49) is simply to let β_1^0 be a characteristic vector of the matrix $(Y_1^{0\prime} M Y_1^0)^{-1} Y_1^{0\prime} M_1 Y_1^0$, but such a solution method does not automatically yield the second property of (51), which will be needed to determine which characteristic vector to use. Also, the method of diagonalizing two symmetric matrices simultaneously as in (51) is of interest in itself.

To decide on which root of (50) to use, we examine which will maximize the likelihood function (27), or minimize $|\hat{\Omega}_1|$. Using (45) and (46), we rewrite (44) as

$$\hat{\Omega}_1 = n^{-1}Y_1^{0\prime}MY_1^0 + n^{-1}\alpha(1-\alpha)^{-1}(\beta_1^{0\prime}Y_1^{0\prime}MY_1^0\beta_1^0)^{-1}Y_1^{0\prime}MY_1^0\beta_1^0\beta_1^{0\prime}Y_1^{0\prime}MY_1^0 \quad (52)$$

Since (49) determines β_1^0 up to a multiplicative constant, one can normalize β_1^0 by letting $\beta_1^{0\prime}Y_1^{0\prime}MY_1^0\beta_1^0 = 1$. Equation (52) thus becomes, with $\mu = (1-\alpha)^{-1}$,

$$n\hat{\Omega}_1 = Y_1^{0\prime}MY_1^0 + (\mu-1)Y_1^{0\prime}MY_1^0\beta_1^0(\beta_1^{0\prime}Y_1^{0\prime}MY_1^0) \quad (53)$$

If β_1^0 is the ith column b_i of B satisfying (51), we can pre- and postmultiply (53) by B' and B to obtain

$$nB'\hat{\Omega}_1 B = I + (\mu_i - 1)e_i e_i'$$

where e_i is the ith column of the identity matrix $I = B'Y_1^{0\prime}MY_1^0B$. The matrix $e_i e_i'$ has all zero elements except the ith diagonal element, which is 1. The right-hand side of the above equation is an identity matrix, except for the ith diagonal element, which is μ_i. Its determinant is μ_i, or

$$\mu_i = |nB'\hat{\Omega}_1 B| = |n\hat{\Omega}_1| \cdot |B'| \cdot |B| = |n\hat{\Omega}_1| \cdot |Y_1^{0\prime}MY_1^0|^{-1} \quad (54)$$

where the last equality sign is due to (51). Since $|n\hat{\Omega}_1|$ is to be minimized, the smallest root μ_i of Eq. (50) will be used.

The above derivation of LIML is admittedly lengthy and tedious for inclusion in a textbook, and cannot be justified by the practical importance alone of LIML; however, the methods used are of sufficient importance for students interested in theoretical econometrics, and some of the results will be used in our derivation of the method of full-information maximum likelihood. The LIML method was proposed by Anderson and Rubin (1949) when there was no 2SLS and we knew much less about the computation of full-information maximum-likelihood estimates, in terms of both algorithms and computer facilities. A teacher of econometrics should have the option of deciding how much of the proof of LIML to include in the course. The above derivation could be studied carefully up to a certain point, such as Eq. (38), where we are left with two equations for the two unknowns Π_{12} and β_1^0.

One interpretation of LIML is intuitively appealing. The endogenous variables Y_1^0 appearing in the first equation are explained by the reduced-form equations

$$Y_1^0 = X_1\Pi_{11}' + X_1^*\Pi_{12}' + V_1$$

The first structural equation is an economic hypothesis about a linear combination $Y_1^0\beta_1^0$ of the variables Y_1^0

$$Y_1^0\beta_1^0 = X_1\Pi_{11}'\beta_1^0 + X_1^*\Pi_{12}'\beta_1^0 + V_1\beta_1^0 = -X_1\gamma_1 + \epsilon_1$$

which specifies that $\Pi_{12}'\beta_1^0 = 0$ or that X_1^* does not explain the linear combination. If so, it seems reasonable to choose as our estimate that value of β_1^0 which makes the sum of squares of the residuals

$$Y_1^0\beta_1^0 - X_1\Pi_{11}'\beta_1^0$$

small compared with the residuals

$$Y_1^0\beta_1^0 - X_1\Pi'_{11}\beta_1^0 - X_1^*\Pi'_{12}\beta_1^0$$

If Π'_{11} in the first set of residuals is replaced by its least-squares estimate $(X'_1X_1)^{-1}X'Y_1^0$, and if Π_{11} and Π_{12} in the second set of residuals are replaced by $(X'X)^{-1}X'Y_1^0$, where $X = (X_1 \quad X_1^*)$, we shall be minimizing the ratio

$$\mu = \frac{\beta_1^{0\prime}Y_1^{0\prime}M_1Y_1^0\beta_1^0}{\beta_1^{0\prime}Y_1^{0\prime}MY_1^0\beta_1^0}$$

Differentiation with respect to β_1^0 gives

$$2(\beta_1^{0\prime}Y_1^{0\prime}MY_1^0\beta_1^0)^{-1}Y_1^{0\prime}M_1Y_1^0\beta_1^0 - 2(\beta_1^{0\prime}Y_1^{0\prime}MY_1^0\beta_1^0)^{-2}$$

$$\cdot (\beta_1^{0\prime}Y_1^{0\prime}M_1Y_1^0\beta_1^0)Y_1^{0\prime}MY_1^0\beta_1^0 = 0$$

or
$$(Y_1^{0\prime}M_1Y_1^0 - \mu Y_1^{0\prime}MY_1^0)\beta_1^0 = 0 \tag{49}$$

which is the equation defining the LIML estimator. Hence the LIML estimator is sometimes called a *least variance ratio* estimator. Another exposition of the LIML estimator appears in Sec. 5.3.

To test the identification restriction $\Pi'_{12}\beta_1^0 = 0$ on the first structural equation Anderson and Rubin (1950) proposed using the statistic $n(\mu - 1)$, which has $\chi^2(K - K_1 - G_1 + 1)$ as its limiting distribution under the null hypothesis $\Pi'_{12}\beta_1^0 = 0$. The matrix Π'_{12} is $(K - K_1) \times G_1$. Identification requires $K - K_1 - G_1 + 1 \geq 0$. For exact identification, the $K - K_1$ equations of $\Pi'_{12}\beta_1^0 = 0$ are just sufficient to determine the $G_1 - 1$ unknowns. If the $K - K_1$ predetermined variables excluded from the first equation are really important and Π'_{12} is a matrix of coefficients of these variables, the numerator of μ, which excludes these variables, will tend to be large. Therefore a large χ^2 statistic should lead one to reject the null hypothesis. Basmann (1960), after discovering through Monte Carlo experiments that the χ^2 distribution is a poor approximation to the distribution of $n(\mu - 1)$ in small samples, proposed the statistic

$$\frac{(y_1 - Y_1\hat{\beta}_1)'(M_1 - M)(y_1 - Y_1\hat{\beta}_1)}{(y_1 - Y_1\hat{\beta}_1)'M(y_1 - Y_1\hat{\beta}_1)} \frac{n - K}{K - K_1 - G_1 + 1}$$

where $\hat{\beta}_1$ is the 2SLS estimate of β_1. This statistic is distributed approximately as $F(K - K_1 - G_1 + 1, n - K)$ under the null hypothesis. Note that passing the test does not mean that the first equation is correctly specified, since the test is concerned only with the excluded predetermined variables. The equation may be misspecified because of erroneous exclusion or inclusion of endogenous variables.

5.3 THE k-CLASS ESTIMATOR

The k-class estimator suggested by Theil (1958) includes both 2SLS and LIML as special cases. To estimate the coefficient vector of the first structural equation

$$y_1 = Y_1\beta_1 + X_1\gamma_1 + \epsilon_1$$

the k-class estimator is obtained by solving

$$\begin{bmatrix} Y_1'Y_1 - k\hat{V}_1'\hat{V}_1 & Y_1'X_1 \\ X_1'Y_1 & X_1'X_1 \end{bmatrix} \begin{bmatrix} \hat{\beta}_1(k) \\ \hat{\gamma}_1(k) \end{bmatrix} = \begin{bmatrix} Y_1' - k\hat{V}_1' \\ X_1' \end{bmatrix} y_1 \tag{55}$$

where $\hat{V}_1 = MY_1$ is an $n \times (G_1 - 1)$ matrix of estimated residuals in the least-squares regression of Y_1 on X. One can easily see that if $k = 1$, the solution of (55) gives the 2SLS estimator, since

$$\hat{Y}_1 = X(X'X)^{-1}X'Y_1 = Y_1 - \hat{V}_1$$

and $$\hat{Y}_1'\hat{Y}_1 = Y_1'Y_1 - Y_1'\hat{V}_1 - \hat{V}_1'Y_1 + \hat{V}_1'\hat{V}_1 = Y_1'Y_1 - \hat{V}_1'\hat{V}_1$$

because $$\hat{Y}_1'\hat{V}_1 = 0 \quad \text{and} \quad Y_1'\hat{V}_1 = \hat{V}_1'\hat{V}_1$$

It is convenient to consider the solution of (55) in two steps. First, solve the second of Eqs. (55)

$$X_1'Y_1\hat{\beta}_1(k) + X_1'X_1\hat{\gamma}_1(k) = X_1'y_1$$

for $\hat{\gamma}_1(k)$ in terms of $\hat{\beta}_1(k)$ to obtain

$$\hat{\gamma}_1(k) = (X_1'X_1)^{-1}X_1'[y_1 - Y_1\hat{\beta}_1(k)] \tag{56}$$

Second, substitute (56) for $\hat{\gamma}_1(k)$ in the first of Eqs. (55)

$$(Y_1'Y_1 - kY_1'MY_1)\hat{\beta}_1(k) + Y_1'X_1(X_1'X_1)^{-1}X_1'[y_1 - Y_1\hat{\beta}_1(k)] = (Y_1' - kY_1'M)y_1$$

and solve for $\hat{\beta}_1(k)$ in the resulting equation

$$(Y_1'M_1Y_1 - kY_1'MY_1)\hat{\beta}_1(k) = Y_1'(M_1 - kM)y_1 \tag{57}$$

One can easily see that when $k = \mu$, (57) is identical with Eqs. (49) defining the LIML estimator for β_1. If we normalize β_1^0 in (49) by letting $\beta_{11} = -1$ and recall $Y_1^0 = [y_1 \quad Y_1]$, we can write (49) as

$$[y_1 \quad Y_1]'(M_1 - \mu M)[y_1 \quad Y_1]\begin{bmatrix} -1 \\ \beta_1 \end{bmatrix} = \begin{bmatrix} y_1'(M_1 - \mu M)(-y_1 + Y_1\beta_1) \\ Y_1'(M_1 - \mu M)(-y_1 + Y_1\beta_1) \end{bmatrix} = \begin{bmatrix} 0 \\ 0 \end{bmatrix} \tag{58}$$

The second of Eqs. (58) is identical with (57) when $k = \mu$. Therefore the LIML estimator is a k-class estimator when $k = \mu$, where μ is the minimum of the ratio of $\beta_1^{0'}Y_1^0M_1Y_1^0\beta_1^0$ to $\beta_1^{0'}Y_1^0MY_1^0\beta_1^0$ obtained by choosing the minimum root of the determinantal equation (50). Given $\hat{\beta}_1$, the estimate of $\hat{\gamma}_1$ is given by (56).

One characteristic of the LIML estimator as a k-class estimator can be noted. The LIML estimator of β_1^0 is the only member of the k class that satisfies all G_1 equations in (49) or (58). All other members fail to satisfy one of the G_1 equations. In other words, all other estimators in the k class are obtained by converting the nonlinear problem of finding the smallest root μ of (50) and the corresponding vector β_1^0 satisfying (49) or (58) into a linear problem. The linear problem is to let $\mu = k$, ignore one of the G_1 equations, and solve the remaining $G_1 - 1$ equations for the $G_1 - 1$ unknowns in β_1^0, one coefficient being normalized to -1. Note that the first of Eqs. (58) is not satisfied if μ is replaced by k, which is not a root of

Eq. (50). By definition only the roots of (50) will make all G_1 equations of (58) hold simultaneously. After solving all G_1 equations in (49) to obtain the LIML estimate of β_1^0, one can still normalize by letting $\hat{\beta}_{11} = -1$ and have the first of Eqs. (58) satisfied. However, the limiting distributions of all k-class estimators are the same, provided $\text{plim}_{n \to \infty} (k - 1) = 0$.

Theorem 5.1 Provided $\text{plim}_{n \to \infty} (k - 1) = 0$, all k-class estimators are consistent and have the same limiting distribution.

PROOF We use (57) to write

$$\hat{\beta}_1(k) = [Y_1'(M_1 - kM)Y_1]^{-1} Y_1'(M_1 - kM)(Y_1\beta_1 + X_1\gamma_1 + \epsilon_1)$$

$$= \beta_1 + [Y_1'(M_1 - kM)Y_1]^{-1} Y_1'(M_1 - kM)\epsilon_1$$

where we have noted that $M_1 X_1 = 0$ and $MX_1 = 0$. Consider the limiting distribution of

$$\sqrt{n}[\hat{\beta}_1(k) - \beta_1] = [n^{-1} Y_1'(M_1 - kM)Y_1]^{-1} n^{-1/2} Y_1'(M_1 - kM)\epsilon_1$$

If $\text{plim}\,(k - 1) = 0$,

$$\text{plim}\,[n^{-1} Y_1'(M_1 - kM)Y_1]^{-1} = \text{plim}\,[n^{-1} Y_1'(M_1 - M)Y_1]^{-1}$$

and $n^{-1/2} Y_1'(M_1 - kM)\epsilon_1$ will have the same limiting distribution as $n^{-1/2} Y_1'(M_1 - M)\epsilon_1$ since their difference $(1 - k)n^{-1/2} Y_1' M\epsilon_1$ converges in probability to zero. The vector $\sqrt{n}[\hat{\beta}_1(k) - \beta_1]$ therefore converges in distribution to

$$\text{plim}\,[n^{-1} Y_1'(M_1 - M)Y_1]^{-1} n^{-1/2} Y_1'(M_1 - M)\epsilon_1$$

which has precisely the limiting distribution of $\sqrt{n}[\hat{\beta}_1(1) - \beta_1]$ for the 2SLS estimator $\hat{\beta}_1(1)$. Given that $\sqrt{n}[\hat{\beta}_1(k) - \beta_1]$ converges in distribution to a normal distribution with zero mean and a finite covariance matrix, $\hat{\beta}_1(k) - \beta_1$ itself, being the above random vector divided by $\sqrt{n}$, will converge in probability to zero. Thus $\hat{\beta}_1(k)$ is consistent.

Using (56), we write

$$\hat{\gamma}_1(k) - \hat{\gamma}_1(1) = (n^{-1} X_1' X_1)^{-1} (n^{-1} X_1' Y_1)[\hat{\beta}_1(1) - \hat{\beta}_1(k)]$$

Since the probability limits of both $n^{-1} X_1' X_1$ and $n^{-1} X_1' Y_1$ exist under the assumptions of Theorem 4.7 and $\text{plim}\,[\hat{\beta}_1(1) - \hat{\beta}(k)] = 0$, as we have just shown, the difference $\hat{\gamma}_1(k) - \hat{\gamma}_1(1)$ converges in probability to zero and $\hat{\gamma}_1(k)$ has the same limiting distribution as $\hat{\gamma}_1(1)$.

One theoretical point should be mentioned. The fact that, under the assumption $\text{plim}\,(k - 1) = 0$, the k-class estimator has the same normal limiting distribution as 2SLS does not tell us much about the distribution of this class of estimators in finite samples. For example, the second moment of the exact sampling distribution of $\hat{\beta}(k)$ may not exist in some cases. The moments of a limiting distribution are different from the limits of the moments of the exact distribution as n increases. For example, let $y_n = x + z/n$, where x is normal and z has a Cauchy distribution of which the first moment does not even exist. The first moment of y_n therefore does not exist. However, since the difference z/n between y_n and x converges in probability to zero, the limiting distribution of y_n is the same as that of x, which is normal. For exact sampling distributions of the k-class estimators in special cases see Richardson (1968).

5.4 METHOD OF THREE-STAGE LEAST SQUARES

We now turn to a discussion of full-information estimators, which require the specification of all structural equations in the system. When a limited-information method is applied to estimate the coefficients δ_i of the ith structural equation, one must specify the variables y_i, Y_i, and X_i in that equation and the other predetermined variables X_i^* in the system. One need not specify which variables enter the other structural equations individually. When a full-information method is applied, all structural equations have to be specified, and their parameters are estimated simultaneously. We shall consider application of the methods of least squares, maximum likelihood, and instrumental variables to the estimation of the entire system of structural equations.

The method of three-stage least squares (3SLS), proposed by Zellner and Theil (1962), adds one more stage to 2SLS in estimating the coefficients of all structural equations simultaneously. Let 2SLS be applied to each equation

$$y_i = Y_i \beta_i + X_i \gamma_i + \epsilon_i = W_i \delta_i + \epsilon_i$$

to obtain the estimate d_i of δ_i and the corresponding estimate of σ_{ij}

$$s_{ij} = n^{-1}(y_i - W_i d_i)'(y_i - W_i d_i) \tag{59}$$

which is consistent under the assumptions of Theorem 4.7 (see Prob. 3). Stack the G structural equations as

$$\begin{bmatrix} y_1 \\ y_2 \\ \vdots \\ y_G \end{bmatrix} = \begin{bmatrix} W_1 & & & 0 \\ & W_2 & & \\ & & \ddots & \\ 0 & & & W_G \end{bmatrix} \begin{bmatrix} \delta_1 \\ \delta_2 \\ \vdots \\ \delta_G \end{bmatrix} + \begin{bmatrix} \epsilon_1 \\ \epsilon_2 \\ \vdots \\ \epsilon_G \end{bmatrix} \tag{60}$$

or more compactly as

$$y = W\delta + \epsilon \tag{61}$$

Recall that one derivation of the method of 2SLS for the ith equation is to premultiply the equation by X' and apply GLS to the resulting equation. Similarly, we now premultiply each row of (60) by X' and apply GLS to the resulting system

$$\begin{bmatrix} X'y_1 \\ X'y_2 \\ \vdots \\ X'y_G \end{bmatrix} = \begin{bmatrix} X'W_1 & & & 0 \\ & X'W_2 & & \\ & & \ddots & \\ 0 & & & X'W_G \end{bmatrix} \begin{bmatrix} \delta_1 \\ \delta_2 \\ \vdots \\ \delta_G \end{bmatrix} + \begin{bmatrix} X'\epsilon_1 \\ X'\epsilon_2 \\ \vdots \\ X'\epsilon_G \end{bmatrix} \tag{62}$$

To apply GLS to (62) we need to find the covariance matrix of its residual vector and the inverse of the matrix

$$
\begin{bmatrix} X'W_1 & & 0 \\ & X'W_2 & \\ & & \ddots \\ 0 & & X'W_G \end{bmatrix}'
\begin{bmatrix} X'X\sigma_{11} & X'X\sigma_{12} & \cdots & X'X\sigma_{1G} \\ X'X\sigma_{21} & X'X\sigma_{22} & \cdots & X'X\sigma_{2G} \\ \cdots\cdots\cdots\cdots\cdots\cdots\cdots\cdots \\ X'X\sigma_{G1} & X'X\sigma_{G2} & \cdots & X'X\sigma_{GG} \end{bmatrix}^{-1}
\begin{bmatrix} X'W_1 & & 0 \\ & X'W_2 & \\ & & \ddots \\ 0 & & X'W_G \end{bmatrix}
$$

(63)

$$
=
\begin{bmatrix} \sigma^{11} W_1' X(X'X)^{-1} & \sigma^{12} W_1' X(X'X)^{-1} & \cdots & \sigma^{1G} W_1' X(X'X)^{-1} \\ \sigma^{21} W_2' X(X'X)^{-1} & \sigma^{22} W_2' X(X'X)^{-1} & \cdots & \sigma^{2G} W_2' X(X'X)^{-1} \\ \cdots\cdots\cdots\cdots\cdots\cdots\cdots\cdots\cdots\cdots\cdots \\ \sigma^{G1} W_G' X(X'X)^{-1} & \sigma^{G2} W_G' X(X'X)^{-1} & \cdots & \sigma^{GG} W_G' X(X'X)^{-1} \end{bmatrix}
\begin{bmatrix} X'W_1 & & 0 \\ & X'W_2 & \\ & & \ddots \\ 0 & & X'W_G \end{bmatrix}
$$

where σ^{ij} is the ijth element of Σ^{-1}. Letting $\hat{W}_i = X(X'X)^{-1}X'W_i$, we complete the GLS formula to give

$$
\begin{bmatrix} \hat{\delta}_1 \\ \cdot \\ \hat{\delta}_G \end{bmatrix}
=
\begin{bmatrix} \sigma^{11}\hat{W}_1' W_1 & \sigma^{12}\hat{W}_1' W_2 & \cdots & \sigma^{1G}\hat{W}_1' W_G \\ \cdots\cdots\cdots\cdots\cdots\cdots\cdots\cdots\cdots\cdots\cdots \\ \sigma^{G1}\hat{W}_G' W_1 & \sigma^{G2}\hat{W}_G' W_2 & \cdots & \sigma^{GG}\hat{W}_G' W_G \end{bmatrix}^{-1}
\begin{bmatrix} \hat{W}_1' \sum_j \sigma^{1j} y_j \cdots \\ \\ \hat{W}_G' \sum_j \sigma^{Gj} y_j \end{bmatrix}
$$

(64)

Since we do not know Σ, we can use the estimates $S = (s_{ij})$ given by (59) and replace σ^{ij} in (64) by the elements s^{ij} of S^{-1}. The resulting estimator is the 3SLS estimator.

Theorem 5.2 Under the assumptions of Theorem 4.7, the 3SLS estimator $\hat{\delta}$ given by (64) with σ^{ij} replaced by s^{ij} is consistent and $\sqrt{n}(\hat{\delta} - \delta)$ has a limiting distribution which is normal with mean zero and covariance matrix

$$
\operatorname*{plim}_{n\to\infty} \left\{ n^{-1} \begin{bmatrix} \sigma^{11}\hat{W}_1' W_1 & \cdots & \sigma^{1G}\hat{W}_1' W_G \\ \cdots\cdots\cdots\cdots\cdots\cdots\cdots \\ \sigma^{G1}\hat{W}_G' W_1 & \cdots & \sigma^{GG}\hat{W}_G' W_G \end{bmatrix} \right\}^{-1}
$$

where, by definition, $\hat{W}_i = X(X'X)^{-1}X'W_i$,

$$
\operatorname{plim} n^{-1}\hat{W}_i W_j = \operatorname{plim} (n^{-1}W_i' X)(n^{-1}X'X)^{-1}(n^{-1}X'W_j)
$$

The proof of this theorem is left as exercise (see Prob. 4).

To compare the distribution of the 3SLS estimator with that of the 2SLS estimator we observe that 3SLS is an application of GLS to model (62), whereas 2SLS is an application of GLS to each of Eqs. (62) separately. Instead of using the matrix $\Sigma \otimes (X'X)$ for the matrix V in the GLS formula as 3SLS does, the method of 2SLS uses diag $\Sigma \otimes (X'X)$, where diag Σ is a diagonal matrix copying the diagonal elements of Σ. If the predetermined variables X and the explanatory variables W_i were fixed and not random, (62) would be a linear regression model involving fixed independent variables. By the Gauss-Markov theorem, the covariance matrices of the 3SLS estimator and the 2SLS estimator would satisfy the relation

$$
\begin{bmatrix} \sigma^{11}\hat{W}_1'W_1 & \cdots & \sigma^{1G}\hat{W}_1'W_G \\ \cdots\cdots\cdots\cdots\cdots\cdots\cdots\cdots\cdots \\ \sigma^{G1}\hat{W}_G'W_1 & \cdots & \sigma^{GG}\hat{W}_G'W_G \end{bmatrix}^{-1} < \begin{bmatrix} \sigma_{11}(\hat{W}_1'W_1)^{-1} & & \\ & \ddots & 0 \\ 0 & & \sigma_{GG}(\hat{W}_G'W_G)^{-1} \end{bmatrix} \tag{65}
$$

in the sense that the difference of these two matrices is a negative-definite matrix, assuming that Σ is not diagonal. For a diagonal Σ one can easily see from (64) that the 2SLS and 3SLS estimators are identical. Since X and W_i are random, we can only compare the covariance matrices of the limiting distributions of $\sqrt{n}(\hat{\delta} - \delta)$ by 3SLS and $\sqrt{n}(d - \delta)$ by 2SLS. Relation (65) implies

$$
\operatorname*{plim}_{n \to \infty} \left\{ n^{-1} \begin{bmatrix} \sigma^{11}\hat{W}_1'W_1 & \cdots & \sigma^{1G}\hat{W}_1'W_G \\ \cdots\cdots\cdots\cdots\cdots\cdots\cdots\cdots\cdots \\ \sigma^{G1}\hat{W}_G'W_1 & \cdots & \sigma^{GG}\hat{W}_G'W_G \end{bmatrix} \right\}^{-1}
$$

$$
< \operatorname*{plim}_{n \to \infty} \begin{bmatrix} \sigma_{11}(n^{-1}\hat{W}_1'W_1)^{-1} & & \\ & \ddots & 0 \\ 0 & & \sigma_{GG}(n^{-1}\hat{W}_G'W_G)^{-1} \end{bmatrix} \tag{66}
$$

The conclusion is that 3SLS is asymptotically more efficient that 2SLS.

What can one say about the finite sample efficiencies of 2SLS and 3SLS? Of course, relation (66) is not a statement concerning efficiencies in finite samples. Using Monte Carlo experiments, Mikhail (1975) has shown that for several two-equation examples the 2SLS estimators can be more efficient than the 3SLS estimators when the true value of σ_{12} is smaller than .35. This result is reasonable in spite of the fact that the 3SLS estimator is asymptotically more efficient. We know that if $\sigma_{12} = 0$, the two estimators are identical. However, in computing the 3SLS estimator, one substitutes the estimate s^{12} for σ^{12} in Eq. (64). On the other hand, in computing the 2SLS estimator one substitutes 0 for σ^{12}, which happens to be the true value for σ^{12}. In this case, imposing the true value for a certain parameter σ^{12}, as is done in computing 2SLS, will improve the efficiency of the 3SLS estimator. Now consider the case when σ_{12} or σ^{12} is not exactly zero but nearly so. Imposing the almost correct restriction $\sigma^{12} = 0$ rather than estimating it by s^{12} may still lead to an improvement in efficiency. It is interesting to note that for σ_{12} as large as .35, with $\sigma_{11} = \sigma_{12} = 1$, Mikhail (1975) has found the 2SLS estimators to be more efficient in some examples. The moral of this story perhaps applies to the comparison of the relative finite-sample efficiencies of the limited- and full-information estimators. If the covariances of the residuals in different structural equations are not too large, it may be more efficient to assume that they are zero and estimate the individual equations separately by a limited-information method.

*5.5 METHOD OF FULL-INFORMATION MAXIMUM LIKELIHOOD

The method of full-information maximum likelihood (FIML) is to maximize the likelihood function for the model

$$YB' + X\Gamma' = E \tag{67}$$

where Y is an $n \times G$ matrix of endogenous variables, X is an $n \times k$ matrix of predetermined variables, and E is an $n \times G$ matrix of residuals, the ith row $\epsilon_{i.}'$ of E being normal with zero mean and covariance matrix Σ and independent of another row. The density function of the ith row of E is

$$p(\epsilon_{i.}') = (2\pi)^{-G/2} |\Sigma|^{-1/2} \exp\left(-\tfrac{1}{2}\epsilon_{i.}' \Sigma^{-1} \epsilon_{i.}\right) \tag{68}$$

The likelihood function of the model for the ith row $y_{i.}'$ of Y is obtained by the change of variables from $\epsilon_{i.}'$ to $y_{i.}'$. This amounts to replacing $\epsilon_{i.}'$ in (68) by $y_{i.}' B' + x_{i.}' \Gamma'$ and inserting in (68) the jacobian $|B|$, which is the absolute value of the determinant of the matrix of the partial derivatives of $\epsilon_{i.}$ with respect to $y_{i.}'$. The result is

$$p(y_{i.}'; B, \Gamma, \Sigma) = (2\pi)^{-G/2} |B| \cdot |\Sigma|^{-1/2}$$
$$\cdot \exp\left[-\tfrac{1}{2}(y_{i.}' B' + x_{i.}' \Gamma') \Sigma^{-1}(By_{i.} + \Gamma x_{i.}) \right]$$

Since $y_{1.}', \ldots, y_{n.}'$ are independent, the joint-density function of Y is

$$p(Y; B, \Gamma, \Sigma) = (2\pi)^{-nG/2} |B|^n |\Sigma|^{-n/2}$$
$$\cdot \exp\left[-\frac{1}{2} \sum_{i=1}^{n} (y_{i.}' B' + x_{i.}' \Gamma')\Sigma^{-1}(By_{i.} + \Gamma x_{i.}) \right]$$

which is the likelihood function for our problem if Y is treated as given and $B, \Gamma,$ and Σ are treated as variables. Noting that

$$\sum_{i=1}^{n} \operatorname{tr}(y_{i.}' B' + x_{i.}' \Gamma')\Sigma^{-1}(By_{i.} + \Gamma x_{i.})$$
$$= \sum_{i=1}^{n} \operatorname{tr} \Sigma^{-1}(By_{i.} + \Gamma x_{t.})(y_{i.}' B' + x_{i.}' \Gamma')$$
$$= \operatorname{tr} \Sigma^{-1}(BY' + \Gamma X')(YB' + X\Gamma')$$

we write the log-likelihood function, with c denoting a constant, as

$$\log L = c + n \log |B| - \frac{n}{2} \log |\Sigma| - \tfrac{1}{2} \operatorname{tr} \Sigma^{-1}(BY' + \Gamma X')(YB' + X\Gamma') \tag{69}$$

To maximize $\log L$ we set equal to zero the partial derivatives of (69) with respect to Σ^{-1}, B', and Γ'. Using the differentiation rules

$$\frac{\partial \log |A|}{\partial A} = A'^{-1} \qquad \frac{\partial \log |A|}{\partial A^{-1}} = A' \qquad \frac{\partial \operatorname{tr}(AB)}{\partial A} = B' \tag{70}$$

and recalling the differentiation of (25) with respect to Ω_1^{-1}, we obtain

$$\frac{n}{2}\Sigma - \tfrac{1}{2}(BY' + \Gamma X')(YB' + X\Gamma') = 0 \tag{71}$$

$$\frac{\partial \log L}{\partial B'} = nB^{-1} - Y'(YB' + X\Gamma')\Sigma^{-1} \doteq 0 \tag{72}$$

$$\frac{\partial \log L}{\partial \Gamma'} = -X'(YB' + X\Gamma')\Sigma^{-1} \doteq 0 \tag{73}$$

where the sign $\doteq$ denotes the fact that only the derivatives of log L with respect to the unknown elements of B' and Γ' are set equal to zero. Solving (71) for Σ, we obtain the expected result

$$\hat{\Sigma} = n^{-1}(BY' + \Gamma X')(YB' + X\Gamma') \tag{74}$$

Selected elements from (72) give the derivatives of log L with respect to the unknown elements of B. Recall that $\beta_{ii} = -1$ for normalization and many elements of B are specified to be zero and that β_i is a column vector of unknown coefficients in the ith equation selected from the ith column of B'. Let us select from the ith column of B^{-1} those elements which correspond to the unknown elements of β_i and denote this vector by β^i. For example, let B' be a 5×5 matrix and $i = 1$. If only y_1, y_2, and y_5 appear in the first equation, the unknown coefficients in the first equation are β_{12} and β_{15}, with $\beta_{11} = -1$. β_1 is a column vector consisting of β_{12} and β_{15}. β^1 is a column vector consisting of the second and fifth elements of the first column of B^{-1}. Y_1 is an $n \times 2$ matrix consisting of the second and the fifth columns of Y. Using these definitions and Eq. (72), we have

$$\frac{\partial \log L}{\partial \beta_i} = n\beta^i - Y_i'(YB' + X\Gamma')(\text{ith column of } \Sigma^{-1})$$

$$= n\beta^i - Y_i' \sum_j (y_j - Y_j\beta_j - X_j\gamma_j)\sigma^{ji} = 0 \tag{75}$$

$$\frac{\partial \log L}{\partial \gamma_i} = -X_i' \sum_j (y_j - Y_j\beta_j - X_j\gamma_j)\sigma^{ji} = 0 \tag{76}$$

Our objective is to solve Eqs. (75) and (76) for the unknowns β_i and γ_i ($i = 1, \ldots, G$). The solution is the FIML estimator.

As before, let δ_i be a column vector consisting of β_i and γ_i, and let δ consist of $\delta_1, \ldots, \delta_G$. Equations (75) and (76) can be combined to form

$$\begin{bmatrix} \dfrac{\partial \log L}{\partial \delta_1} \\ \vdots \\ \dfrac{\partial \log L}{\partial \delta_G} \end{bmatrix} = \frac{\partial \log L}{\partial \delta} \equiv f(\delta) = 0 \tag{77}$$

To solve the set of nonlinear equations $f(\delta) = 0$, one useful method is the Newton-Raphson method. Essentially, starting with an initial value δ^0, the Newton-Raphson method linearizes $f(\delta)$ about $\delta = \delta^0$

$$f(\delta) = f(\delta^0) + \left(\frac{\partial f}{\partial \delta'}\right)_{\delta^0} (\delta - \delta^0) = 0$$

and solves the resulting equation for δ

$$\delta^1 = \delta^0 - \left(\frac{\partial f}{\partial \delta'}\right)_{\delta^0}^{-1} f(\delta^0) \tag{78}$$

where the subscript δ^0 indicates that the matrix $\partial f / \partial \delta'$ of partial derivatives of the elements of f with respect to the elements of δ is evaluated at δ^0. The Newton-Raphson method is an iterative method using Eq. (78) to solve the set of equations $f(\delta) = 0$. Starting with an initial value δ^0 in each iteration, the method uses (78) to obtain a new value δ^1. The new value δ^1 will serve as the initial value in the next iteration. The process converges if the value of δ^1 obtained from (78) equals the initial value δ^0 used as input.

It is easy to see that if $f(\delta)$ is linear, say $f(\delta) = A\delta + b$, the process converges in one iteration no matter what the initial value δ^0 may be, since

$$\delta^1 = \delta^0 - A^{-1}(A\delta^0 + b) = -A^{-1}b$$

which is the solution of $A\delta + b = 0$. If $f(\delta)$ is nonlinear but δ^0 is close to the solution value, the linear approximation of f is probably reasonably good and the process of convergence is probably quite rapid. If δ^0 is far from the solution value, the next guess δ obtained from Eq. (78) may be quite far from the true solution, perhaps even farther than the original δ^0. This is demonstrated in Fig. 5.1, where δ and $f(\delta)$ are scalars rather than vectors. The solution value for $f(\delta) = 0$ is shown at point P. If we start from a value δ^0 near P and approximate $f(\delta)$ by a linear function, as shown by the solid straight line tangential to $f(\delta)$ at $\delta = \delta^0$, the solution value δ^1 given by Eq. (78) is closer to P than the initial value

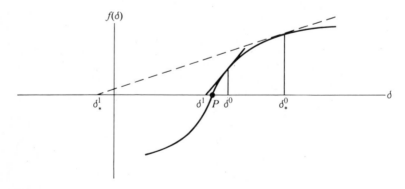

Figure 5.1 Illustration of the Newton-Raphson method.

δ^0 is. If we start from a value δ^0_* quite far from P and approximate $f(\delta)$ by a linear function, as shown by the dashed straight line tangential to $f(\delta)$ at $\delta = \delta^0_*$, the solution value δ^1_* given by Eq. (78) may be even farther from P than δ^0_* is.

To inhibit possibly wide fluctuations in the solution values δ^1 given by Eq. (78) as illustrated in Fig. 5.1 and to speed up convergence it is customary to modify Eq. (78) by a damping factor k and let the new value δ^1 equal only a factor k times the step suggested by Eq. (78). The modified equation is

$$\delta^1 = \delta^0 - k \left(\frac{\partial f}{\partial \delta'}\right)^{-1}_{\delta^0} f(\delta^0) \tag{79}$$

The value of k in each iteration can be determined by evaluating $\log L(\delta^1)$ for different values of k and choosing that value which maximizes $\log L$. The Newton-Raphson method so modified has been found to be useful in computing FIML estimates, as reported in Chow (1968), where analytical expressions of the components of the matrix

$$\frac{\partial f}{\partial \delta'} = \frac{\partial^2 \log L}{\partial \delta \, \partial \delta'} \tag{80}$$

are employed. The inverse of the negative of the above matrix, evaluated at the maximum-likelihood estimate $\hat{\delta}$, can serve as an estimate of the covariance matrix of $\hat{\delta}$. See Sec. 7.6 for analytical expressions of (80).

Rothenberg and Leenders (1964) have proposed a linearized FIML estimator. Employing a consistent estimator δ^* of δ as the initial value δ^0, one computes δ^1 by (78) as the linearized FIML estimator. In other words, this estimator is obtained by taking one step in the Newton-Raphson algorithm starting from a consistent estimator of δ as the initial value. To compare the asymptotic distribution of the linearized FIML estimator with the FIML estimator Rothenberg and Leenders employed the following theorem concerning a linearized maximum-likelihood estimator.

Theorem 5.3 If the consistent estimator θ^* used to compute the linearized maximum-likelihood estimator is such that $n^{1/2}(\theta^* - \theta_0)$ converges in distribution, θ_0 being the true-parameter vector, then the linearized maximum-likelihood estimator has the same asymptotic distribution as the maximum-likelihood estimator, provided that all the partial derivatives of $n^{-1} \log L(\theta)$ up to the third order are continuous functions of θ, are bounded for all values of θ, and have finite probability limits, and that the matrix of the second partials is nonsingular.

PROOF The jth element of the linearized maximum-likelihood estimator θ^1 obtained from the iteration equation (78) is

$$\theta^1_j = \theta^*_j - \sum_i g_{ij} n^{-1} \frac{\partial \log L(\theta^*)}{\partial \theta_i} \tag{81}$$

where g_{ij} is the ijth element of $[n^{-1} \partial^2 \log L(\theta^*)/(\partial\theta \, \partial\theta')]^{-1}$. To express θ_j^1 as a function of the maximum-likelihood estimator $\hat{\theta}$ we observe that $\hat{\theta}$ is obtained by solving

$$n^{-1} \frac{\partial \log L(\hat{\theta})}{\partial \theta} = 0$$

Expanding the ith component in a Taylor series about the consistent estimator θ^*, we have

$$n^{-1} \frac{\partial \log L(\theta^*)}{\partial \theta_i} + n^{-1} \frac{\partial^2 \log L(\theta^*)}{\partial \theta_i \, \partial \theta'} (\hat{\theta} - \theta^*)$$

$$+ \tfrac{1}{2} n^{-1} (\hat{\theta} - \theta^*)' \frac{\partial^3 \log L(\bar{\theta})}{\partial \theta_i \, \partial \theta \, \partial \theta'} (\hat{\theta} - \theta^*) = 0 \quad (82)$$

where $\bar{\theta}$ is between $\hat{\theta}$ and θ^*. Using (82) to substitute for $(n^{-1} \, \partial \log L)/\partial \theta_i$ in (81), we obtain

$$\theta_j^1 = \theta_j^* + (\hat{\theta}_j - \theta_j^*) + \frac{1}{2} \sum_i g_{ij} n^{-1} (\hat{\theta} - \theta^*)' \frac{\partial^3 \log L(\bar{\theta})}{\partial \theta_i \, \partial \theta \, \partial \theta'} (\hat{\theta} - \theta^*)$$

$$= \hat{\theta}_j + \tfrac{1}{2} (\hat{\theta} - \theta^*)' \, 2 \left\{ \sum_i g_{ij} \left(n^{-1} \frac{\partial^3 \log L(\bar{\theta})}{\partial \theta_i \, \partial \theta \, \partial \theta'} \right) \right\} (\hat{\theta} - \theta^*) \quad (83)$$

Because all the partial derivatives of $n^{-1} \log L(\theta)$ up to the third order are assumed to have finite probability limits, the matrix in braces in (83) will have a finite probability limit, to be called A_j say. Taking the probability limit of $n^{1/2}$ times (83), we have

$$\underset{n \to \infty}{\text{plim}} \; n^{1/2} (\theta_j^1 - \hat{\theta}_j) = \tfrac{1}{2} \, \text{tr} \, [A_1 \, \text{plim} \; n^{1/2} (\hat{\theta} - \theta^*)(\hat{\theta} - \theta^*)'] = 0$$

Because plim $(\hat{\theta} - \theta^*)' = 0$ and $n^{1/2}(\hat{\theta} - \theta^*)$ converges in distribution, the probability limit of their product is zero. Given that the difference $\sqrt{n}(\theta^1 - \hat{\theta})$ converges in probability to zero and that $\sqrt{n}(\hat{\theta} - \theta_0)$ converges in distribution to a normal distribution, we conclude that $\sqrt{n}(\theta^1 - \theta_0)$ converges in distribution to the same normal distribution.

Since the assumptions of Theorem 5.3 are valid for FIML estimation of linear simultaneous equations with normal and independent residuals, the linearized FIML estimator suggested by Rothenberg and Leenders will have the same asymptotic distribution as the FIML estimator, provided that a k-class estimator is used for the initial consistent estimator δ^*. Does this mean that once the linearized FIML estimator has been found nothing will be gained by continuing the iterative process by the Newton-Raphson method to compute the FIML estimator? Not necessarily. First, the finite sample distributions are unknown. Second, one might gain some information by iterating. For example, when $k = 1$ is used in formula (79) (as it is in computing the linearized FIML), if the iterative process does not converge, one will suspect that taking the first step may bring the estimate farther from the true maximum than the initial consistent estimate (as illustrated by Fig. 5.1). One might then ask: If the iterative process does not converge, why bother to take one arbitrary step? If the process does converge, why not use the FIML estimate itself?

5.6 METHOD OF INSTRUMENTAL VARIABLES

Recall that 2SLS applied to estimate the ith structural equation is an instrumental-variable (IV) estimator

$$d_i = (\hat{W}'_i \, W_i)^{-1} \hat{W}'_i \, y_i$$

where $\hat{W}_i = X(X'X)^{-1}X'W_i$. If the number n of observations is smaller than the number K of predetermined variables, $X'X$ will be singular and the instrumental variables $\hat{W}_i$ cannot be formed. Instead one may choose a subset of $K_*(<n)$ predetermined variables X_* to form $Y^*_i = X_*(X'_* \, X_*)^{-1}X'_* \, Y_i$ and let the instrumental variables be $W^*_i = (Y^*_i \, X_i)$. W^*_i can replace $\hat{W}_i$ in the above equation to form an IV estimator since it satisfies the two properties stated in Sec. 3.10. We will discuss how the instruments X_* should be selected at the end of Sec. 5.9.

Hausman (1975) has given the following interpretation of the FIML estimator as an instrumental-variable estimator. Postmultiply (71) by $2\Sigma^{-1}$ to obtain

$$nI = (BY' + \Gamma X')(YB' + X\Gamma')\Sigma^{-1}$$

$$nI - BY'(YB' + X\Gamma')\Sigma^{-1} = \Gamma X'(YB' + X\Gamma')\Sigma^{-1}$$

Premultiplication by B^{-1} leads to

$$nB^{-1} - Y'(YB' + X\Gamma')\Sigma^{-1} = -\Pi X'(YB' + X\Gamma')\Sigma^{-1} \tag{84}$$

where $\Pi = -B^{-1}\Gamma$ as usual and $\Pi X'$ will be denoted by $\tilde{Y}'$, which is the estimate of Y' by the reduced form with $\Pi = -B^{-1}\Gamma$ as the coefficient matrix. Substitution of (84) into (72) gives

$$\frac{\partial \log L}{\partial B'} = -\tilde{Y}'(YB' + X\Gamma')\Sigma^{-1} \doteq 0 \tag{85}$$

In place of (75) we have

$$\frac{\partial \log L}{\partial \beta_i} = -\tilde{Y}'_i \sum_j (y_j - Y_j\beta_j - X_j\gamma_j)\sigma^{ji} = 0 \tag{86}$$

Combining Eqs. (86) and (76) and denoting $[\tilde{Y}_i \quad X_i]$ by $\tilde{W}_i$, we can write

$$\frac{\partial \log L}{\partial \delta_i} = -\tilde{W}'_i \sum_j (y_j - W_j\delta_j)\sigma^{ji} = 0 \tag{87}$$

which can be written out in full for $i = 1, \ldots, G$ to yield

$$
\begin{bmatrix}
\sigma^{11}\tilde{W}'_1 W_1 & \sigma^{12}\tilde{W}'_1 W_2 & \cdots & \sigma^{1G}\tilde{W}'_1 W_G \\
\cdots\cdots\cdots\cdots\cdots\cdots\cdots\cdots\cdots\cdots\cdots\cdots\cdots \\
\sigma^{G1}\tilde{W}'_G W_1 & \sigma^{G2}\tilde{W}'_G W_2 & \cdots & \sigma^{GG}\tilde{W}'_G W_G
\end{bmatrix}
\begin{bmatrix}
\delta_1 \\
\cdot \\
\delta_G
\end{bmatrix}
=
\begin{bmatrix}
\tilde{W}'_1 \sum_j \sigma^{j1} y_j \\
\\
\tilde{W}'_G \sum_j \sigma^{jG} y_j
\end{bmatrix}
\tag{88}
$$

The FIML estimator obtained by solving (88) could be interpreted as an instrumental-variable estimator if σ^{ij} and $\tilde{W}'_i$ were known. The model is

$$
y = \begin{bmatrix} y_1 \\ \vdots \\ y_G \end{bmatrix} = \begin{bmatrix} W_1 & & 0 \\ & \ddots & \\ 0 & & W_G \end{bmatrix} \begin{bmatrix} \delta_1 \\ \vdots \\ \delta_G \end{bmatrix} + \begin{bmatrix} \epsilon_1 \\ \vdots \\ \epsilon_G \end{bmatrix} = W\delta + \epsilon
$$

and the matrix of instrumental variables is

$$
\tilde{W}' = \begin{bmatrix}
\sigma^{11}\tilde{W}'_1 & \cdots & \sigma^{1G}\tilde{W}'_1 \\
\cdots\cdots\cdots\cdots\cdots\cdots\cdots \\
\sigma^{G1}\tilde{W}'_G & \cdots & \sigma^{GG}\tilde{W}'_G
\end{bmatrix}
\tag{89}
$$

The instrumental-variable estimator is $(\tilde{W}'W)\tilde{W}'y$.

If one reviews the set of normal equations defining 3SLS, one finds that 3SLS can also be interpreted as an instrumental-variable estimator, the matrix of instruments being

$$
\hat{W}' = \begin{bmatrix}
s^{11}\hat{W}'_1 & \cdots & s^{1G}\hat{W}'_1 \\
\cdots\cdots\cdots\cdots\cdots\cdots\cdots \\
s^{G1}\hat{W}'_1 & \cdots & s^{GG}\hat{W}'_G
\end{bmatrix}
\tag{90}
$$

where
$$
\hat{W}_i = [\hat{Y}_i \quad X_i] = [X(X'X)^{-1}X'Y_i \quad X_i]
$$

The main difference between $\hat{W}_i$ and $\tilde{W}_i$ is that the former use least squares to estimate $\hat{\Pi}$ for $\hat{Y} = X\hat{\Pi}'$ whereas the latter use $-B^{-1}\Gamma$ to estimate $\tilde{\Pi}$ for $\tilde{Y} = X\tilde{\Pi}'$. Since B and Γ are unknown, the instrumental variables $\tilde{W}_i$ are unspecified. Let some consistent estimates β_i^* and γ_i^* of β_i and γ_i be given. We can then estimate $\tilde{\Pi}$ by $\tilde{\Pi}^* = -B^{*-1}\Gamma^*$ and accordingly the variables $\hat{W}_i$ used in (89). The variables σ^{ij} in (89) can be estimated by the inverse of the matrix

$$
n^{-1}(B^*Y' + \Gamma^*X')(YB^{*\prime} + X\Gamma^{*\prime})
$$

An instrumental-variable estimator is now defined using (89), as suggested by Brundy and Jorgenson (1971), Dhrymes (1971), and Lyttkens (1970). If the new instrumental-variable estimates of β_i and γ_i so obtained are used as the initial estimates β_i^* and γ_i^* and the process continues iteratively until convergence, the result is the FIML estimator, since it satisfies Eq. (88) as well as Eq. (71) for Σ. Thus the FIML estimator can be interpreted as an iterative instrumental-variable estimator.

Since plim $(X'X)^{-1}X'Y = \text{plim} (-B^{*-1}\Gamma^{*}) = \Pi$, one can prove that the instrumental-variable estimator just defined has the same asymptotic distribution as the 3SLS estimator (see Prob. 13). Similarly, using Eq. (88), one can show that the instrumental-variable estimator has the same asymptotic distribution as the FIML estimator (see Prob. 14). By Theorem 5.3, the linearized FIML estimator will have the same asymptotic distribution as the above three estimators. The equivalence of asymptotic distributions applies when there are no prior restrictions on the covariance matrix Σ. If there are such restrictions and FIML takes them into account, FIML can be asymptotically more efficient than 3SLS.

★5.7 TREATMENT OF IDENTITIES AND LINEAR RESTRICTIONS

We now consider how the method of FIML should be modified when some equations are identities and when there are linear restrictions on the coefficients. Identities occur frequently in models of simultaneous equations. Let M equations be stochastic and $G - M$ equations be identities. The structural equations can be partitioned as

$$B_{11}y_{t1} + B_{12}y_{t2} + \Gamma_1 x_{t.} = \epsilon_{t.}$$
$$B_{21}y_{t1} + B_{22}y_{t2} + \Gamma_2 x_{t.} = 0 \tag{91}$$

where y_{t1} and $\epsilon_{t.}$ are $M \times 1$. The variables should be so arranged that the remaining variables y_{t2} can be solved by using the second set of equations, i.e.,

$$y_{t2} = -B_{22}^{-1}(B_{21}y_{t1} + \Gamma_2 x_{t.})$$

When y_{t2} is replaced by this solution, the first equation becomes

$$(B_{11} - B_{12}B_{22}^{-1}B_{21})y_{t1} + (\Gamma_1 - B_{12}B_{22}^{-1}\Gamma_2)x_{t.} = \epsilon_{t.}$$

The jacobian in the transformation from the variable $\epsilon_{t.}$ to the variable y_{t1} is the absolute value of the determinant

$$|B_{11} - B_{12}B_{22}^{-1}B_{21}| = |B| \cdot |B_{22}|^{-1}$$

The normal density function for y_{t1} is

$$c|B| \cdot |\Sigma|^{-1/2} \exp\left[-\tfrac{1}{2}(B_{11}y_{t1} + B_{12}y_{t2} + \Gamma_1 x_{t.})'\Sigma^{-1}(B_{11}y_{t1} + B_{12}y_{t2} + \Gamma_1 x_{t.})\right]$$

where c incorporates the known constant $|B_{22}|^{-1}$. The upshot of this demonstration is that when there are identities, the likelihood function applied to the M stochastic equations is the same as before, except that Σ is now $M \times M$. As a consequence, the derivatives of $\log L$ with respect to β_i and γ_i remain the same as given by (75) and (76), except that the summations over j are now from 1 to M.

If there are linear restrictions on the elements of δ (these elements may be coefficients in different structural equations), one must modify the vector $f = (\partial \log L)/\partial \delta$ used in computing the FIML estimate. The modifications required can be seen by considering the restriction

$$\delta_i = c\delta_j + d\delta_k \tag{92}$$

The unknown δ_i will be eliminated, since it is a known linear function of two of the remaining unknowns δ_j and δ_k. The log-likelihood function l will be replaced by a new function l^* of a new set of variables δ^* (having one fewer element than δ), by substituting the right side of (92) for δ_i in l. By (92) and the chain rule of differentiation, the new $f^*(\delta^*) = 0$ will contain the equations

$$\frac{\partial l^*}{\partial \delta_j} = \frac{\partial l}{\partial \delta_j} + \frac{\partial l}{\partial \delta_i} c = 0 \qquad \frac{\partial l^*}{\partial \delta_k} = \frac{\partial l}{\partial \delta_k} + \frac{\partial l}{\partial \delta_i} d = 0$$

where it is understood that the argument δ_i of any derivative of $l = \log L$ is replaced by the right-hand side of (92) [likewise for Eqs. (93) and (94) below]. If $f(\delta)$ has m elements, say, then $f^*(\delta^*)$ and $f(\delta)$ are related by

$$f^*(\delta^*) = Nf(\delta) \tag{93}$$

where N is an $(m - 1) \times m$ matrix which is constructed from the $m \times m$ identity matrix by eliminating its ith row, replacing the zero in the ith position of the jth row by c, and replacing the zero in the ith position of the kth row by d.

By differentiating the elements of $f^*(\delta^*)$ with respect to the remaining $m - 1$ variables one can obtain the new matrix of second partial derivatives

$$\frac{\partial f^*}{\partial \delta^{*\prime}} = N \frac{\partial f}{\partial \delta'} N' \tag{94}$$

Equations (93) and (94) can then be used to modify Eq. (79) in order to perform iterations by Newton's method. If there is a second linear restriction, another matrix, say N^*, can be used to multiply f^* and $\partial f^*/\partial \delta^{*\prime}$ in the same way as N was used in Eqs. (93) and (94) to multiply f and $\partial f/\partial \delta'$. This process can be repeated for any number of linear restrictions. Setting a coefficient equal to a constant c amounts to setting it equal to c times the dummy variable 1 in the list of predetermined variables; similarly, nonhomogeneous linear restrictions can be treated by using this dummy variable.

★5.8 FIML WITH AUTOREGRESSIVE RESIDUALS

Let the model (67) be modified by assuming that its residuals E obey an autoregressive scheme such as

$$E = E_{-1}R_1' + E_{-2}R_2' + U \tag{95}$$

where the G columns of E_{-1} and E_{-2} are the residuals of the G structural equations lagged one and two periods, respectively, R_1 and R_2 are matrices of coefficients of the autoregressive scheme, and the residuals U satisfy the same assumptions originally made for E in the model (67). It will be shown in this section that the method of Sec. 5.7 can be applied to obtain maximum-likelihood estimates of the matrices B, Γ, R_1, and R_2 in this model. To simplify exposition without loss of generality, R_2 will be assumed to be zero.

Since the model lagged one period satisfies

$$Y_{-1}B' + X_{-1}\Gamma' = E_{-1} \tag{96}$$

Eq. (67) minus Eq. (96) postmultiplied by R_1' (with $R_2 = 0$) gives

$$YB' - Y_{-1}B'R_1' + X\Gamma' - X_{-1}\Gamma'R_1' \equiv YB' - Y_{-1}B_1' + X\Gamma' - X_{-1}\Gamma_1' = U \tag{97}$$

The log-likelihood function for this model is, by (69),

$$\log L = c + n \log |B| - \frac{n}{2} \log |\Sigma| - \tfrac{1}{2} \operatorname{tr} (\Sigma^{-1} U'U) \tag{98}$$

where

$$U \equiv YB' - Y_{-1}B'R_1' + X\Gamma' - X_{-1}\Gamma'R_1' \tag{99}$$

with B, Γ, and R_1 treated as unknowns and Y, Y_{-1}, Z, and Z_{-1} treated as given data. The maximization with respect to Σ proceeds as before.

To maximize (98) with respect to these unknowns, consider first the partial maximization with respect to B and Γ, given R_1. From the middle expression of (97) this amounts to maximization with respect to B, Γ, B_1, and Γ_1 subject to the linear restrictions

$$B_1 = R_1 B \qquad \Gamma_1 = R_1 \Gamma \tag{100}$$

This problem can be solved by the method of Sec. 5.7. Now consider the maximization of (98) with respect to R_1, given B and Γ. With B and Γ treated as given, by rearrangement of (97), the model can be written as

$$(YB' + X\Gamma') - (Y_{-1}B' + X_{-1}\Gamma')R_1' = U \tag{101}$$

the terms in parentheses being treated as matrices of observed variables and R_1' being treated as a matrix of coefficients. The likelihood function of the model (101) is that of a standard simultaneous-equation model with identity as the coefficient matrix of the endogenous variables and R_1' as the coefficient matrix of the predetermined variables. The method of Sec. 5.7 can be applied to maximize its likelihood function with respect to the coefficient matrix R_1. If there are no restrictions on R_1, the estimates are simply least-squares estimates (see Prob. 15).

The maximum-likelihood estimates of B, Γ, and R_1 in the model (97) can be obtained as follows. Start with an initial value for R_1, possibly 0, and maximize the likelihood function with respect to B and Γ by the method of Sec. 5.7; take these values of B and Γ as given and maximize the likelihood function with respect to R_1, again by the method of Sec. 5.7; repeat this two-step process until convergence is reached. Convergence will be reached using this process if the method of Sec. 5.7 converges for the problem it is supposed to solve, since the method of this section amounts simply to repeated applications of the method of that section. This two-step iterative procedure has been applied by Chow and Fair (1973) to estimate linear simultaneous equations with autoregressive residuals (see Prob. 20).

5.9 CHOICE OF ESTIMATORS

Since finite-sample distributions of various estimators are difficult to establish and the results are limited to very special cases, Monte Carlo methods have been applied to studying the sampling distributions. Results from Monte Carlo will depend on the particular specifications of the true models assumed in the experiments. Summers (1965) has studied the sampling distributions of the LIML, 2SLS, ordinary least squares, and FIML estimators by Monte Carlo using a model of two structural equations with two different exogenous variables apiece, so that each equation is overidentified.

Among Summers' findings are the following. First, regarding the method of ordinary least squares (OLS), which is known to be inconsistent, the small-sample bias is found to be the largest among the four estimators. Its variance is found to be the smallest. As the mean-square error is the sum of the variance and the square of the bias, OLS sometimes has larger mean-square errors than the other estimators because of the large biases, but in some cases has smaller mean-square errors because of the small variances. Second, concerning FIML, if the model is correctly specified, and if the predetermined variables are not too highly correlated, it is the best estimator according to the criterion of mean-square error. If the predetermined variables are very highly correlated, 2SLS can perform better than FIML and OLS better than LIML. FIML can perform poorly when there are errors in specifying the model, such as omitting a variable. Third, Summers indicates that the steadiest method appears to be 2SLS. In the presence of interdependence of the predetermined variables LIML is so erratic that its use seems risky. Summers has also compared the predictive accuracies of the reduced-form equations, which are derived from the structural equations estimated by the above four methods; 2SLS often performs poorly here while FIML has done somewhat better than the other estimators. OLS as applied to structural equations yields reduced-form equations with poor predictive performance. OLS when applied to the reduced-form equations directly, though ignoring the restrictions imposed by overidentification, does not perform too badly.

In general, the comparison between 2SLS and FIML appears to depend on the seriousness of specification errors, the degree of dependence between the predetermined variables and, as pointed out in Sec. 5.4, the correlations between the random disturbances. FIML would tend to be better for the purpose of estimating the structural parameters when specification errors are small, when the correlations between the predetermined variables are low, and when the correlations between the residuals are high. For the purpose of prediction, misspecification does not seem to affect the performance of FIML adversely, while the performance of 2SLS is often poor, according to Summers' Monte Carlo experiments.

Turning now to the choice of estimators in econometric practice, one notes that LIML was used in the early days by Klein (1950), when he first built his small models of the United States economy and before electronic computers were available to the public. Klein's LIML estimates were computed by an electric desk calculator of approximately 1948 vintage. After the invention of 2SLS, which is computationally simpler, LIML has seldom been used. When Klein and others started to build larger models consisting of well over 100 equations, notably the Brookings Quarterly Econometric Model of the United States, reported in Duesenberry et al. (1965), the method of OLS was used partly because the Brookings model was compiled from submodels of different sectors built by many authors. We have noted that OLS, though inconsistent, may sometimes yield smaller mean-square errors because of its small variance. Since the 1970s, the use of OLS has not been frequent. In the meantime, computer facilities have been improving rapidly and algorithms to compute FIML have been made available. One finds that FIML has been used for models of moderate size, e.g., by Fair (1976). Perhaps the most popular methods have been 2SLS and its variations. When the number of predetermined variables in the system is very large, possibly larger than the number of quarterly time-series observations, it will be inconvenient or impossible to perform the first stage of 2SLS. Kloek and Mennes (1960) have suggested the use of principal components of the predetermined variables, but this does not ease the computational problem in the present case. We have pointed out in Sec. 5.6 that, instead of using 2SLS, one can use an instrumental-variable (IV) estimator where a subset X_* of predetermined variables is used to form the instrumental variables

$$W_i^* = [X_*(X_*' X_*)^{-1} X_*' Y_i \quad X_i]$$

for estimating the ith structural equation.

To select a subset of predetermined variables to serve as explanatory variables in the regression to form W_i^*, Fisher (1965) has suggested rearranging the structural equations to make the matrix B block-triangular

$$B = \begin{bmatrix} B_{11} & & & 0 \\ B_{21} & B_{22} & & \\ & & \ddots & \\ B_{N1} & B_{N2} & \cdots & B_{NN} \end{bmatrix} \tag{102}$$

To select predetermined variables for a regression to form an instrumental variable for a certain endogenous variable, we first consider all variables appearing in the structural equation explaining that variable. These are called *variables of first causal order*. We next consider all variables appearing in the structural equations explaining the endogenous variables of first causal order. These are called *variables of second causal order*. Variables of third or higher causal orders are similarly defined. The variables of the lowest causal orders will be selected first. Variables belonging to orders 1 and 2 are preferred to those belonging to orders 1 and 3. The regression to form an instrumental variable for an endogenous variable in any block will include only predetermined variables in that block or blocks with a lower number because B is block-triangular; variables explaining any endogenous variables can come only from the same block or a lower-numbered block. If the number n of observations is smaller than the number of predetermined variables so ordered, Fisher suggests using $n - 2$ of them to run a regression with 1 degree of freedom. The variable with the smallest insignificant t ratio is first dropped. Fisher recognizes the arbitrary nature of this rule of dropping variables one at a time, not to speak of the problem of choosing the level of significance, which we shall address in Chap. 9. However, this aspect of Fisher's recommendation is minor compared with the usefulness of rearranging the matrix B in block-triangular form and providing causal orders to the variables to be selected in the regression to form each instrumental variable. A full justification of this procedure is found in Fisher (1965); see also Probs. 17 and 18. Chow (1974a) has exploited the diagonality of Σ and the block triangularity of B to develop a family of estimators based on the method of maximum likelihood.

5.10 ESTIMATION OF THE REDUCED FORM

To estimate the coefficient matrix Π of the reduced-form equations one can apply any of the methods previously discussed to estimate the structural parameters B and Γ and use the relation $\Pi = -B^{-1}\Gamma$ to form an estimate of Π. On the other hand, one can simply apply least squares to estimate Π' by $\hat{\Pi}' = (X'X)^{-1}X'Y$. This estimate does not incorporate the overidentifying restrictions imposed on the structural parameters. In other words, no B and Γ exist which satisfy $B\hat{\Pi} = -\Gamma$ and all the identification restrictions imposed upon them. If B and Γ could be uniquely determined by $B\hat{\Pi} = -\Gamma$, all structural equations would be just identified. Because of the failure to incorporate the overidentifying restrictions, $\hat{\Pi}$ has been found by Summers (1965) to perform worse in prediction than the estimate of Π computed from the FIML estimates of B and Γ. In fact the latter estimate of Π is the FIML estimate of Π itself. It is that value of Π which maximizes the likelihood function subject to all the overidentifying restrictions. In general the maximum-likelihood estimate of a function, such as $-B^{-1}\Gamma$, of parameters B and Γ is the function of the maximum-likelihood estimates of B and Γ, as is the case of the function Π. It is interesting to recall that, according to the Monte Carlo experiments of Summers (1965), while 2SLS performs well in estimating B and Γ, it performs poorly in estimating Π for prediction. This result is understandable partly because Π is a nonlinear function of B. For example, an unbiased estimator of B cannot be inverted to form an unbiased estimate of B^{-1}.

We have provided formulas for the covariance matrices of the asymptotic distributions of the various estimators $[\tilde{B} \quad \tilde{\Gamma}]$ of structural parameters presented in this chapter. These covariance matrices can be used to estimate the covariance matrix of the asymptotic distribution of $\tilde{\Pi} = -\tilde{B}^{-1}\tilde{\Gamma}$ using a method suggested by Goldberger, Nagar, and Odeh (1961). We first prove a lemma.

Lemma 5.1 Let $\tilde{\alpha}$ be a consistent estimator of α and let the asymptotic distribution of $\sqrt{n}(\tilde{\alpha} - \alpha)$ be normal with mean zero and covariance matrix

Φ. Let $\pi = \pi(\alpha)$ be a differentiable function of α with $\partial\pi/\partial\alpha' = D$. Define $\tilde{\pi} = \pi(\tilde{\alpha})$. Then the asymptotic distribution of $\sqrt{n}(\tilde{\pi} - \pi)$ is normal with mean zero and covariance matrix $D\Phi D'$.

PROOF Expand $\tilde{\pi}$ about α

$$\tilde{\pi} = \pi(\tilde{\alpha}) = \pi(\alpha) + [D + o(1)](\tilde{\alpha} - \alpha)$$

which implies
$$\sqrt{n}(\tilde{\pi} - \pi) = [D + o(1)]\sqrt{n}(\tilde{\alpha} - \alpha)$$

Since $\sqrt{n}(\tilde{\alpha} - \alpha)$ has a limiting normal distribution with mean zero and covariance matrix Φ and plim $[D + o(1)] = D$, or in fact lim $[D + o(1)] = D$, the conclusion of the lemma follows.

Theorem 5.4 Let $[\tilde{B} \quad \tilde{\Gamma}]$ be a consistent estimator of $[B \quad \Gamma]$, and let α be a column vector composed of the G rows of $[B \quad \Gamma]$, with $\tilde{\alpha}$ similarly defined. (δ was obtained by selecting the unknown elements of α.) Let the asymptotic distribution of $\sqrt{n}(\hat{\alpha} - \alpha)$ be normal with mean zero and covariance matrix Φ. Let π be a column vector composed of the G rows of $\Pi = -B^{-1}\Gamma$, with $\tilde{\pi}$ similarly defined. Then the asymptotic distribution of $\sqrt{n}(\tilde{\pi} - \pi)$ is normal with mean zero and covariance matrix $D\Phi D'$, where

$$D = -B^{-1} \otimes [\Pi' \quad I_K] \tag{103}$$

PROOF This theorem is an immediate consequence of Lemma 5.1 once the matrix D of derivatives of π with respect to α' has been evaluated. Since $\Pi = -B^{-1}\Gamma$, the ijth element of Π, or the jth element of the subvector π_i of π, is

$$\pi_{ij} = -\sum_{m=1}^{G} \beta^{im}\gamma_{mj} \tag{104}$$

where β^{im} is the imth element of B^{-1} and γ_{mj} is the mjth element of Γ. Differentiating (104) with respect to γ_{kl}, we have

$$\frac{\partial\pi_{ij}}{\partial\gamma_{kl}} = \begin{cases} -\beta^{ik} & \text{for } l = j \\ 0 & \text{otherwise} \end{cases}$$

Therefore, the matrix of derivatives of π_i with respect to the vector γ'_k, which is the second component of the kth subvector $[\beta'_k \quad \gamma'_k]$ of α', is

$$\frac{\partial\pi_i}{\partial\gamma'_k} = -\beta^{ik}I_K$$

This proves the second half of Eq. (103).

For the first half we differentiate (104) with respect to β_{kl}

$$\frac{\partial\pi_{ij}}{\partial\beta_{kl}} = -\sum_{m=1}^{G}\frac{\partial\beta^{im}}{\partial\beta_{kl}}\gamma_{mj} = \beta^{ik}\sum_{m=1}^{G}\beta^{lm}\gamma_{mj} = -\beta^{ik}\pi_{lj} \tag{105}$$

where we have applied the differentiation rule

$$\frac{\partial \beta^{im}}{\partial \beta_{kl}} = -\beta^{ik}\beta^{lm} \tag{106}$$

(See Prob. 19 for this differentiation rule.) Equation (105) implies that the matrix of derivatives of π_i with respect to β'_k is

$$\frac{\partial \pi_i}{\partial \beta'_k} = -\beta^{ik}\Pi'$$

This proves the second half of Eq. (103).

The matrix D given by (103) can be consistently estimated by replacing B and Π by $\tilde{B}$ and $\tilde{\Pi}$, respectively. It can be used not only to construct a covariance matrix of $\tilde{\pi}$ but also to estimate the covariance matrix of the vector of errors of forecasts by the reduced form. The reduced form of m future observations is

$$Y_f = X_f \Pi' + V_f \tag{107}$$

where Y_f is $m \times G$. The ith column is $y_{fi} = X_f \pi_i + v_{fi}$. After stacking the G columns of Y_f we have

$$\begin{bmatrix} y_{f1} \\ \vdots \\ y_{fG} \end{bmatrix} = \begin{bmatrix} X_f & & 0 \\ & \ddots & \\ 0 & & X_f \end{bmatrix} \begin{bmatrix} \pi_1 \\ \vdots \\ \pi_G \end{bmatrix} + \begin{bmatrix} v_{f1} \\ \vdots \\ v_{fG} \end{bmatrix}$$

or, more compactly,

$$y_f = (I_G \otimes X_f)\pi + v_f \tag{108}$$

A forecast of y_f is $\tilde{y}_f = (I_G \otimes X_f)\tilde{\pi}$. If X_f can be treated as given, a covariance matrix of the forecasting error $y_f - \tilde{y}_f$ can easily be constructed from the covariance matrices of $\tilde{\pi}$ and v_f. If X_f is stochastic, a solution is given by Feldstein (1971). Of course, instead of using $\tilde{\Pi} = -\tilde{B}^{-1}\tilde{\Gamma}$ to estimate Π, one can use the unrestricted reduced-form estimates $\hat{\Pi}' = (X'X)^{-1}X'Y$. The relative efficiencies of $\hat{\Pi}$ and $\tilde{\Pi}$ are discussed in Dhrymes (1973).

This concludes our discussion of estimation of linear simultaneous equations. The subject has been extensively studied in the econometric literature and it is impossible to cover all important works. A textbook provides tools so that the students can learn by themselves in the future. Even with this principle in mind, one should at least mention the Bayesian estimation methods of Rothenberg (1975), Dreze (1976), and Zellner (1978) and the fixed-point method of Wold, expounded in Mosback and Wold (1970). In selecting material to illustrate how econometric methods are developed, unfortunately some important works have to be omitted. For the estimation of nonlinear simultaneous equations, see Secs. 7.6 to 7.8 and 10.7.

PROBLEMS

1. Show that the k-class estimator is an instrumental-variable estimator.

2. Consider the estimation of the first structural equation by 2SLS and let y_1 and y_2 be included in this equation. One may think of a two-equation system as consisting of a demand and a supply equation explaining price y_1 and quantity y_2. One has the option of normalizing by letting $\beta_{11} = -1$ or $\beta_{12} = -1$. Will the 2SLS estimates be the same in the two cases? Of course, if one lets $\beta_{12} = -1$ or uses y_2 as the dependent variable, after the estimate $\hat{\beta}_{11}$ of β_{11} has been obtained, one should renormalize by dividing all coefficients by $-\hat{\beta}_{11}$ before comparing them with the coefficients obtained by using y_1 as the dependent variable. Explain your answer algebraically. Will the LIML estimates be the same in the two cases? Explain. Insofar as the estimates are different, how should one decide which to use?

3. Show that (59) is a consistent estimator of σ_{ij}.

4. Prove Theorem 5.2. You may use the fact that $n^{-1/2}X'\epsilon_i$ has a limiting normal distribution, as we pointed out in deriving the limiting distribution of the 2SLS estimator.

5. Show that the 3SLS estimator is an instrumental-variable estimator.

6. Show that when each question is just identified, the 2SLS and 3SLS estimators are identical.

7. Show that when the first structural equation is just identified, the method of 2SLS is identical with the method of indirect least squares, which gives an estimate of β_1^0 as the solution of $\hat{\Pi}'_{12}\beta_1^0 = 0$, where $\hat{\Pi}'_{12}$ is the least-squares estimate of Π_{12} using the reduced form for Y_1^0.

8. Show that when the first structural equation is just identified, the method of LIML is identical with the method of indirect least squares defined in Prob. 7.

9. When the first structural equation is underidentified, what happens if one tries to apply the method of indirect least squares as defined in Prob. 7?

10. When the first structural equation is underidentified, what happens if one tries to apply the method of 2SLS? Specifically, what happens in the first stage and in the second stage? Explain your answer.

11. When the first structural equation is underidentified, what happens if one tries to apply the method of LIML by minimizing the variance ratio μ of $\beta_1^{0'}Y_1^{0'}M_1Y_1^0\beta_1^0$ to $\beta_1^{0'}Y_1^{0'}MY_1^0\beta_1^0$? Explain your answer.

12. Prove the differentiation rules (70).

13. Show that the instrumental-variable estimator defined by (88), with $\tilde{W}_i$ and σ^{ij} estimated by using some consistent estimator $[B^* \quad \Gamma^*]$ of $[B \quad \Gamma]$, has the same asymptotic distribution as the 3SLS estimator.

14. Show that the IV-estimator of Prob. 13 has the same asymptotic distribution as the FIML estimator.

15. Maximize (98) where U is defined by (101), with B and Γ treated as given, with respect to Σ^{-1} and R'_1. Show that the resulting estimate of each column of R'_1 is the estimate obtained by applying least squares to each equation (column) of (101).

16. Derive the FIML estimator when the Σ matrix is assumed to be (a) diagonal and (b) block-diagonal.

17. Derive the FIML estimator when the B matrix is triangular (with zeros above the diagonal) and when the Σ matrix is diagonal. Such a system is called *recursive* and was first proposed by Wold.

18. Derive the FIML estimator when the B matrix is block-triangular as given in (102) and when the corresponding Σ matrix is block-diagonal. Such a system is called *block-recursive*.

19. Denoting the imth element of B^{-1} by b^{im}, prove the differentiation rule (106). You may start with the identity $I = BB^{-1}$ and differentiate both sides with respect to β_{kl}.

20. Generalize the method of Sec. 5.8 to the case when the residual E follows a second-order autoregressive process

$$E = E_{-1}R'_1 + E_{-2}R'_2 + U$$

REFERENCES

Anderson, T. W. (1971): *The Statistical Analysis of Time Series*, Wiley, New York.
—— and H. Rubin (1949): "Estimation of the Parameters of a Single Equation in a Complete System of Stochastic Equations," *Ann. Math. Statist.*, **20**: 46–63.
—— and (1950): "The Asymptotic Properties of Estimates of the Parameters of a Single Equation in a Complete System of Stochastic Equations," *Ann. Math. Statist.*, **21**: 570–582.
Basmann, R. L. (1957): "A Generalized Classical Method of Linear Estimation of Coefficients in a Structural Equation," *Econometrica*, **27**: 77–83.
—— (1960): "On Finite Sample Distributions of Generalized Classical Linear Identifiability Test Statistics," *J. Am. Statist. Assoc.* **55**: 650–659.
Brundy, J., and D. W. Jorgenson (1971): "Efficient Estimation of Simultaneous Equation Systems by Instrumental Variables," *Rev. Econo. Statist.*, **53**: 207–224.
Chow, G. C. (1964): "A Comparison of Alternative Estimators for Simultaneous Equations," *Econometrica*, **32**: 532–553.
—— (1968): "Two Methods of Computing Full-Information Maximum Likelihood Estimates in Simultaneous Stochastic Equations," *Int. Econ. Rev.*, **9**: 100–112.
—— (1974a): "A Family of Estimators for Simultaneous Equation Systems," *Int. Econ. Rev.*, **15**: 654–666.
—— (1974b): "Identification and Estimation in Econometric Systems: A Survey," *IEEE Trans. Auto. Control*, **AC-19**: 855–862.
—— and R. C. Fair (1973): "Maximum-Likelihood Estimation of Linear Equations Systems with Auto-regressive Residuals," *Ann. Econ. Soc. Meas.* **2**: 17–28.
Dhrymes, P. J. (1970): *Econometrics*, Harper & Row, New York.
—— (1971): "A Simplified Structural Estimator for Large-Scale Econometric Models," *Aust. J. Statist.*, **13**: 168–175.
—— (1973): "Restricted and Unrestricted Reduced Forms: Asymptotic Distribution and Relative Efficiency," *Econometrica*, **41**: 119–134.
Dreze, J. (1976): "Bayesian Limited Information Analysis of Simultaneous Equations Model," *Econometrica*, **44**: 1045–1075.
Duesenberry, J. S., G. Fromm, L. R. Klein, and E. Kuh (eds.) (1965): *The Brookings Quarterly Econometric Model of the United States*, Rand McNally, Chicago, and North-Holland, Amsterdam.
Fair, R. C. (1976): *A Model of Macroeconomic Activity, Vol. II*, Ballinger (Cambridge, Mass.).
Feldstein, M. S. (1971): "The Error of Forecast in Econometric Models When the Forecast-Period Exogenous Variables are Stochastic," *Econometrica*, **39**: 55–60.
Fisher, F. M. (1965): "Dynamic Structure and Estimation of Economy-Wide Econometric Models," pp. 589–636, in J. S. Duesenberry, G. Fromm, L. R. Klein and E. Kuh (eds.), *The Brookings Quarterly Econometric Model of the United States*, Rand McNally, Chicago.
Goldberger, A. S., A. L. Nagar, and H. S. Odeh (1961): "The Covariance Matrices of Reduced-Form Coefficients and of Forecasts for a Structural Econometric Model," *Econometrica*, **29**: 556–573.
Hausman, J. A. (1975): "An Instrumental-Variable Approach to Full-Information Estimators for Linear and Certain Nonlinear Econometric Models," *Econometrica*, **43**: 727–738.
Klein, L. R. (1950): *Economic Fluctuations in the United States, 1921–1941*, Wiley, New York.
Kloek, T., and L. B. M. Mennes (1960): "Simultaneous Equations Estimation Based on Principal Components of Predetermined Variables," *Econometrica*, **28**: 45–61.
Lyttkens, E. (1970): "Symmetric and Asymmetric Estimation Methods," in E. Mosback and H. Wold (eds.), *Interdependent Systems*, North-Holland, Amsterdam.
Mikhail, W. M. (1975): "A Comparative Monte Carlo Study of the Properties of Econometric Estimators," *J. Am. Statist. Assoc.*, **70**: 94–104.
Mosback, E., and H. Wold (1970): *Interdependent Systems*, North-Holland, Amsterdam.
Richardson, D. H. (1968): "The Exact Distribution of a Structural Coefficient Estimator," *J. Am. Statist. Assoc.*, **63**: 1214–1226.

Rothenberg, T. J. (1975): "Analysis of Simultaneous Equations Models," pp. 405–424, in S. E. Fienberg and A. Zellner (eds.), *Studies in Bayesian Econometrics and Statistics*, North-Holland, Amsterdam.

―――― and C. T. Leenders (1964): "Efficient Estimation of Simultaneous Equation Systems," *Econometrica*, **32**: 57–76.

Summers, R. (1965): "A Capital-Intensive Approach to the Small-Sample Properties of Various Simultaneous-Equation Estimators," *Econometrica*, **33**: 1–41.

Theil, H. (1953): "Repeated Least Squares Applied to Complete Equation Systems," Central Planning Bureau, The Hague, mimeographed.

―――― (1958): *Economic Forecast and Policy*, North-Holland, Amsterdam.

―――― (1971): *Principles of Econometrics*, Wiley, New York.

Zellner, A. (1978): "Estimation of Functions of Population Means and Regression Coefficients Including Structural Coefficients: A Minimum Expected Loss (MELO) Approach," *J. Econometr.* **8**: 125–158.

―――― and H. Theil (1962): "Three-stage Least Squares: Simultaneous Estimation of Simultaneous Equations," *Econometrica*, **30**: 53–78.

SIX

TIME-SERIES ANALYSIS

6.1 TIME-SERIES MODELS

Students of simultaneous-equation models should be interested in models of time series for at least two reasons. First, since models of simultaneous equations are frequently constructed to explain economic relationships through time, the dynamic characteristics of the economic variables generated by such models are of utmost interest. Proponents of systems of simultaneous equations had in mind a major objective, i.e., to explain the dynamic behavior of economic variables through time. The classic monograph 10 of the Cowles Commission at the University of Chicago, edited by Koopmans (1949), was entitled *Statistical Inference in Dynamic Economic Models*. A pioneering attempt to apply the statistical techniques discussed in that monograph to build simple models of the United States economy was made by Klein (1951), and the book was entitled *Economic Fluctuations in the United States*. It is therefore important to develop concepts and methods for studying the dynamic and cyclical characteristics of time series generated by dynamic models. Such concepts are conveniently discussed in connection with models of time series. They form the subjects of Secs. 6.2 to 6.5. For applications of these concepts to the study of dynamic properties of econometric models see Chow (1975, pt. I).

Second, simple time-series models provide an alternative to simultaneous-equation models. Builders of the latter, more complicated models are often asked to show that their models are better than the simpler alternatives. Are the more complicated simultaneous-equation models really better in forecasting, in providing accurate description of the dynamic characteristics of the economy, and/or in the analysis of economic policy? Although space does not allow us to go into these topics in detail, we shall explain what these time-series models are and how they can be constructed, at least in theory. The applications of both types of models to the analysis of economic policy have been treated in Chow (1975, 1981). Even if the complicated models cannot be demonstrated to be superior in the three types of applications above, some econometricians may still argue in their favor in situations where detailed descriptions of the economy are said to be required for policy analysis. For example, if one is interested in studying the effects of changing certain aspects of the social security tax system, the system has to be modeled, but there is still room for debate over whether the tax system should be modeled separately or embedded in a large system of simultaneous equations. This issue of choosing between large and small models will be discussed in Chap. 9. Even if the tax system is modeled separately, it may still take the form of structural simultaneous equations rather than a time-series model to be discussed in this chapter.

To explain the dynamic behavior of an economic variable through time a simple and most useful model is an autoregressive model

$$y_t = a_1 y_{t-1} + a_2 y_{t-2} + \cdots + a_p y_{t-p} + \epsilon_t \tag{1}$$

This model is of order p because y_{t-p} appears in the explanation of y_t. The residuals ϵ_t are assumed to be serially independent, each having zero mean and variance σ^2.

Another model is the moving-average model, taking the form

$$y_t = \epsilon_t + b_1 \epsilon_{t-1} + \cdots + b_q \epsilon_{t-q} \tag{2}$$

This model is of order q. Again, ϵ_t are as specified above. Combining the two types of influences of the past on y_t, one can form an autoregressive moving-average (ARMA) process of orders (p, q)

$$y_t = a_1 y_{t-1} + \cdots + a_p y_{t-p} + \epsilon_t + b_1 \epsilon_{t-1} + \cdots + b_q \epsilon_{t-q} \tag{3}$$

These models can easily be generalized to explain a vector y_t of time series. An ARMA model for a vector y_t is

$$y_t = A_1 y_{t-1} + \cdots + A_p y_{t-p} + \epsilon_t + B_1 \epsilon_{t-1} + \cdots + B_q \epsilon_{t-q} \tag{4}$$

where A_i and B_i are matrices. In a multivariate model, the variable y_{t1} is influenced not only by its own past values but also by the past values of other variables in the system.

For the purpose of mathematical analysis it is often convenient to write (4) as a first-order autoregressive process by redefining the vector time series to be explained, as follows

$$
\begin{bmatrix} y_t \\ y_{t-1} \\ \cdot \\ y_{t-p+1} \\ \epsilon_t \\ \epsilon_{t-1} \\ \cdot \\ \epsilon_{t-q+1} \end{bmatrix} = \begin{bmatrix} A_1 & A_2 & \cdots & A_p & B_1 & B_2 & \cdots & B_q \\ I & 0 & \cdots & 0 & 0 & 0 & \cdots & 0 \\ 0 & \cdots & I & 0 & 0 & 0 & \cdots & 0 \\ 0 & \cdots & 0 & 0 & 0 & 0 & \cdots & 0 \\ 0 & \cdots & 0 & 0 & I & 0 & \cdots & 0 \\ 0 & \cdots & 0 & 0 & 0 & I & 0 \end{bmatrix} \begin{bmatrix} y_{t-1} \\ y_{t-2} \\ \cdot \\ y_{t-p} \\ \epsilon_{t-1} \\ \epsilon_{t-2} \\ \cdot \\ \epsilon_{t-q} \end{bmatrix} + \begin{bmatrix} \epsilon_t \\ 0 \\ \cdot \\ 0 \\ \epsilon_t \\ 0 \\ \cdot \\ 0 \end{bmatrix} \quad (5)
$$

We shall be concerned with studying the dynamic properties of the time series generated by these models and with methods for selecting and estimating them.

Model (5) can be written more compactly as

$$
y_t = A y_{t-1} + b + \epsilon_t
$$

where the vector y_t has been redefined and an intercept b has been added. By taking expectations on both sides we easily see that the mean vector $E y_t \equiv \bar{y}_t$ satisfies

$$
\bar{y}_t = A \bar{y}_{t-1} + b
$$

If the mean is constant through time, we have $\bar{y}_t = \mu$ for all t and

$$
\mu = A\mu + b \qquad \mu = (I - A)^{-1} b
$$

provided $(I - A)^{-1}$ exists. Subtracting the equation for μ from the original model gives

$$
y_t - \bar{y}_t = A(y_{t-1} - \bar{y}_{t-1}) + \epsilon_t
$$

In studying dynamic properties of a linear time-series model, we shall assume that the mean vector has been subtracted from the data and we need only concern ourselves with deviations from the mean.

6.2 DYNAMIC PROPERTIES OF TIME SERIES

Consider first a scalar time series y_t. Its dynamic properties are described by the joint probability distribution of $y_{t-k}, y_{t-k+1}, \ldots, y_t, \ldots y_{t+k}$ for any t and k. For any k, if the joint distribution is independent of t, the process generating the time series is said to be *stationary*. We also say that the time series itself is stationary. The concept of stationarity certainly generalizes to a vector time series. We only need to interpret y_t above as a vector.

Often only the first two moments of the joint distribution are of main concern. If the joint distribution is normal, these two moments completely characterize the distribution. Even when it is not normal, the first two moments still capture some of the most important characteristics. A vector time series y_t is *covariance-stationary* or *weakly stationary* if the first two moments are independent of t. This means that $Ey_t = \mu$ for all t and $E(y_t - \mu)(y_{t-k} - \mu)' = \Gamma_k$ for all t. The matrix Γ_k so defined is the *autocovariance matrix*. Its ijth element

$$\gamma_{ij, k} = E(y_{it} - \mu_i)(y_{j, t-k} - \mu_j) \tag{6}$$

shows the covariance between y_{it} and $y_{j, t-k}$.

How does Γ_k provide important information concerning the dynamic properties of the time series? First, Γ_0 is the covariance matrix of y_t. Its diagonal elements give the variances, and its off-diagonal elements give the covariances of the different components of y_t. The variances measure the degree of economic fluctuations of the time series. The covariances measure the degree of co-movements between time series. Co-movements are considered important in the study of business cycles.

When we speak about a mean or a variance, we may mean one of two things. One is an *ensemble average*. Imagine taking many series of observations, the ith series or realization being $y_{t-k}^i, y_{t-k+1}^i, \ldots, y_t^i, y_{t+1}^i, \ldots y_{t+k}^i$. The ensemble average is

$$\frac{1}{N} \sum_{i=1}^{N} y_t^i$$

The *time average*, obtained by taking only one series or realization but perhaps a very long one, is

$$\frac{1}{2k+1} \sum_{i=-k}^{k} y_{t+i}^1$$

In practice, we observe only one realization of a time series and can compute only the time average. However, these two averages approach the same limit if the time series is covariance-stationary and is *ergodic*. Similarly, the variance can be defined by taking the ensemble average of the squared deviations from the mean using many series of observations or by the time average of the squared deviations from the mean using one very long series. If the covariance-stationary process is ergodic, the two are the same. The processes described in Sec. 6.1, when they satisfy the conditions for covariance stationarity to be presented below, are all ergodic. Therefore, when we speak of means and covariances, we can refer to either concept. When we rely on one long series to estimate the variance of an economic variable through time, we can use the result to measure the degree of possible variations of this variable in one future year, i.e., to measure the variance of the probability distribution of the random variable at a future time.

Returning to the usefulness of Γ_k, we note that its diagonal element

$$\gamma_{ii, k} = E(y_{it} - \mu_i)(y_{i, t-k} - \mu_i)$$

is the covariance between the ith variable at t and at $t - k$; $\gamma_{ii, k}$ is the *auto-*

covariance function (with k as argument) of the time series y_{it}; $\rho_{ii,k} = \gamma_{ii,k}/\gamma_{ii,0}$ is the *autocorrelation function* of the time series y_{it}. If $\rho_{ii,1}$ is large and positive (near 1), successive observations of the time series y_{it} and $y_{i,t-1}$ are highly correlated. The time series tends to be smooth, compared with the case $\rho_{ii,1} = -.9$, say, which tends to create one positive value of the time series followed by a negative value, a positive value, etc. It suggests a short cycle two periods long. The case $\rho_{ii,1} = .9$ suggests long cycles because successive observations tend to be similar. As we shall further elaborate, $\gamma_{ii,k}$ can characterize the cyclical behavior of the time series y_{it}.

An off-diagonal element $\gamma_{ij,k}$ of Γ_k is the covariance between y_{it} and $y_{j,t-k}$. It is called the *cross-covariance function* of k. Similarly, the *cross-correlation function* $\rho_{ij,k}$ is defined as $\gamma_{ij,k}/(\gamma_{ii,0}\gamma_{jj,0})^{1/2}$. If $\gamma_{ij,1}$ is larger than $\gamma_{ij,0}$ and $\gamma_{ij,2}$, this means that $y_{j,t-1}$ is more highly correlated with y_{it} than either y_{jt} or $y_{j,t-2}$. For example, income lagged one quarter may be more highly correlated with consumption than either current income or income lagged two quarters. $\gamma_{ij,k}$ provides information on the lead-lag relations between y_{it} and y_{jt} besides the degrees of association between them.

Box and Jenkins (1970) have suggested using the autocovariance function to select (or "identify" in their terminology) a univariate time-series model from (1) to (3). Using observations on the time series, after first-differencing once or twice to eliminate possible trends from the series, one can compute sample covariances between y_{it} and $y_{i,t-k}$

$$c_{ii,k} = \frac{1}{N-k} \sum_{t=k+1}^{N} y_{it}\, y_{i,t-k} \tag{7}$$

The sample autocorrelations are $r_{ii,k} = c_{ii,k}/c_{ii,0}$. Comparing the sample autocorrelations with the population autocorrelations calculated from a theoretical model, one decides whether the model is appropriate for the data. Therefore, to select or identify a model, one first must know its autocovariance function or autocorrelation function.

6.3 AUTOCOVARIANCE MATRIX OF A LINEAR MODEL

For selecting, or identifying, a time-series model and studying its dynamic properties it is important to derive its autocovariance matrix Γ_k. Since all multivariate ARMA models can be written in the form (5), which can simply be written as

$$y_t = Ay_{t-1} + \epsilon_t \tag{8}$$

by appropriate redefinition of the variables, one need only derive the autocovariance matrix of a first-order vector autoregressive process.

Postmultiply (8) by y'_{t-k} ($k \geq 1$), and take expectations

$$Ey_t y'_{t-k} = AEy_{t-1} y'_{t-k}$$

or
$$\Gamma_k = A\Gamma_{k-1} = A^2\Gamma_{k-2} = A^k\Gamma_0 \tag{9}$$

To find Γ_0, postmultiply (8) by its transpose and take expectations

$$Ey_t y_t' = AEy_{t-1}y_{t-1}'A' + E\epsilon_t\epsilon_t'$$

or
$$\Gamma_0 = A\Gamma_0 A' + \Sigma \qquad (10)$$

Computationally, Γ_0 can be obtained by iterating on (10)

$$\Gamma_0^{(r+1)} = A\Gamma_0^{(r)}A' + \Sigma$$

where $\Gamma_0^{(r)}$ denotes the value of Γ_0 at the rth iteration. A solution for Γ_0 in (10) exists and the iterative process converges if and only if the characteristic roots of the matrix A are all less than 1 in absolute value.

To show this, return to model (8) and write

$$y_t = \epsilon_t + A\epsilon_{t-1} + A^2\epsilon_{t-2} + \cdots \qquad (11)$$

by repeated substitutions for y_{t-j} by $Ay_{t-j-1} + \epsilon_{t-j}$ for $j = 1, 2, \ldots$. The covariance matrix $\Gamma_0 = Ey_t y_t'$ is obtained by taking the expectation of (11) postmultiplied by its transpose and making use of the serial independence of ϵ_t

$$\Gamma_0 = \Sigma + A\Sigma A' + A^2\Sigma A'^2 + \cdots \qquad (12)$$

where $\Sigma = E\epsilon_t\epsilon_t'$. Let B be a matrix whose columns are the right characteristic vectors of A and D be a diagonal matrix consisting of the characteristic roots λ_i of A. We have $AB = BD$ and $A = BDB^{-1}$, assuming that B^{-1} exists. Note that $A^k = BD^kB^{-1}$. Equation (12) can be written

$$\Gamma_0 = \Sigma + BDB^{-1}\Sigma B^{-1}{}'BD' + BD^2B^{-1}\Sigma B^{-1}{}'D^2B' + \cdots$$

$$= BWB' + BDWDB' + BD^2WD^2B' + \cdots$$

$$= B(W + DWD + D^2WD^2 + \cdots)B'$$

$$= B(w_{ij} + w_{ij}\lambda_i\lambda_j + w_{ij}\lambda_i^2\lambda_j^2 + \cdots)B'$$

where we have defined $W = B^{-1}\Sigma B'^{-1}$ and have written out the ijth element of the matrix in parentheses. It can be seen that this matrix, and thus the matrix Γ_0, converges to a limit if and only if all roots of A are less than 1 in absolute value. If this condition is satisfied, we can write out a formula for Γ_0 explicitly

$$\Gamma_0 = B\left[\frac{w_{ij}}{1 - \lambda_i\lambda_j}\right]B' \qquad (13)$$

Equations (12) and (13) are two alternative formulas for computing Γ_0. The former is an infinite sum and is equivalent to iterating with Eq. (10). The latter requires computing the characteristic roots λ_i and the characteristic vectors B of the matrix A.

We have shown that the time series y_t generated by the model (8) is covariance-stationary if and only if the characteristic roots of A are all less than 1 in absolute value. If this condition is satisfied, we can find Γ_0. Given Γ_0, we can use (9) to compute $\Gamma_k = A^k\Gamma_0$. Note that $A^k = BD^kB^{-1}$ will approach the zero matrix as k increases if all roots λ_i are less than 1 in absolute value. It is interesting to note from (9) that each column of Γ_k satisfies the difference equation $\Gamma_k = A\Gamma_{k-1}$ in k corresponding to the difference equation $y_t = Ay_{t-1}$ in t satisfied by model (8) if the disturbance term ϵ_t is absent from (8). This means that the autocovariance function $\gamma_{11,k}$ behaves in a fashion similar to y_{1t} in the deterministic version of the model (8) after ϵ_t has been set equal to zero.

Using the result (9), we can study the behavior of the autocovariance function for the scalar autoregressive model (1). Write (1) as a first-order vector autoregressive process

$$
\begin{bmatrix} y_t \\ y_{t-1} \\ \cdot \\ y_{t-p+1} \end{bmatrix} = \begin{bmatrix} a_1 & a_2 & \cdots & a_p \\ 1 & 0 & \cdots & 0 \\ \multicolumn{4}{c}{\dotfill} \\ 0 & 0 & \cdots & 1 & 0 \end{bmatrix} \begin{bmatrix} y_{t-1} \\ y_{t-2} \\ \cdot \\ y_{t-p} \end{bmatrix} + \begin{bmatrix} \epsilon_t \\ 0 \\ \cdot \\ 0 \end{bmatrix} \tag{14}
$$

According to (9), the autocovariance function γ_k of y_t satisfies

$$
\begin{bmatrix} \gamma_k \\ \gamma_{k-1} \\ \cdot \\ \gamma_{k-p+1} \end{bmatrix} = \begin{bmatrix} a_1 & a_2 & \cdots & a_p \\ 1 & 0 & \cdots & 0 \\ \multicolumn{4}{c}{\dotfill} \\ 0 & 0 & \cdots & 1 & 0 \end{bmatrix} \begin{bmatrix} \gamma_{k-1} \\ \gamma_{k-2} \\ \cdot \\ \gamma_{k-p} \end{bmatrix} \tag{15}
$$

In other words, γ_k satisfies the pth-order univariate difference equation in k

$$
\gamma_k = a_1\gamma_{k-1} + \cdots + a_p\gamma_{k-p} \tag{16}
$$

Write (15) as

$$
\tilde{\gamma}_k = A\tilde{\gamma}_{k-1}
$$

γ_k being the first element of the vector $\tilde{\gamma}_k$. The solution for (15) is then

$$
\tilde{\gamma}_k = A^k\tilde{\gamma}_0 = BD^kB^{-1}\tilde{\gamma}_0 = (b_{ij})D^k(b^{ij})\tilde{\gamma}_0
$$

Its first element accordingly is

$$
\gamma_k = [b_{11} \quad \cdots \quad b_{1p}] \begin{bmatrix} \lambda_1^k & & 0 \\ & \ddots & \\ 0 & & \lambda_p^k \end{bmatrix} \begin{bmatrix} b^1\tilde{\gamma}_0 \\ \vdots \\ b^p\tilde{\gamma}_0 \end{bmatrix}
$$

$$
= (b_{11}b^1\tilde{\gamma}_0)\lambda_1^k + (b_{12}b^2\tilde{\gamma}_0)\lambda_2^k + \cdots + (b_{1p}b^p\tilde{\gamma}_0)\lambda_p^k \tag{17}
$$

where b^i denotes the ith row of B^{-1}. Thus the autocovariance function γ^k is a linear combination of λ_i^k.

Under the condition for covariance stationarity, all λ_i are less than 1 in absolute value. The autocovariance function (17) therefore tends to die down as k increases; i.e., the correlation between y_t and y_{t-k} weakens as k increases. For a first-order univariate time series $y_t = ay_{t-1} + \epsilon_t$ we have $\gamma_k = a\gamma_{k-1} = a^k\gamma_0$. The autocovariance function dies down geometrically as k increases. If $a < 0$, γ_k tends to fluctuate, going from positive to negative, but still dies down geometrically.

In a second- or higher-order autoregressive process, the roots of

$$|A - \lambda I| = \begin{vmatrix} a_1 - \lambda & a_2 & \cdots & a_p \\ 1 & -\lambda & \cdots & 0 \\ & & \cdot & \\ 0 & 0 \cdots & 1 & -\lambda \end{vmatrix}$$

$$= (-1)^p(\lambda^p - a_1\lambda^{p-1} - a_2\lambda^{p-2} - \cdots - a_p\lambda^0) = 0$$

may contain a pair of complex-conjugate roots, say λ_1 and λ_2. That is, the *characteristic equation*

$$\lambda^p - a_1\lambda^{p-1} - a_2\lambda^{p-2} - \cdots - a_p = 0 \tag{18}$$

for the model (1) may contain a pair of roots $\lambda_1 = a + bi$ and $\lambda_2 = a - bi$, $i = \sqrt{-1}$. If λ_1 and λ_2 in (17) are complex conjugate, their coefficients $b_{11}b^1\tilde{\gamma}_0$ and $b_{12}b^2\tilde{\gamma}_0$ will also be complex conjugate because the sum of the first two terms on the last line of (17) is real, as the autocovariance function γ_k is real (see Prob. 9). We write these coefficients as $se^{i\psi}$ and $se^{-i\psi}$ and the two roots as $re^{i\theta}$ and $re^{-i\theta}$ where $r = \sqrt{a^2 + b^2}$ and $\tan\theta = b/a$. Substituting into (17), we have

$$\gamma_k = (se^{i\psi})r^k e^{i\theta k} + (se^{-i\psi})r^k e^{-i\theta k} + \cdots$$

$$= sr^k(e^{i(\theta k + \psi)} + e^{-i(\theta k + \psi)}) + \cdots = 2sr^k \cos(\theta k + \psi) + \cdots \tag{19}$$

Since r, the absolute value or modulo of λ_1 and λ_2, is less than 1, a component of γ_k is a damped cosine function of k, with frequency θ, or with cycle $2\pi/\theta$. To summarize, the autocovariance function of an autoregressive process of order 2 or higher may be a damped oscillating function of the lag k if the matrix A, or the characteristic equation (18) of the process, has a pair of complex-conjugate roots.

We have shown that the autocovariance function γ_k of an autoregressive process is a damped function of k, either monotonically damped or showing damped oscillations in the case of complex roots. What about a moving-average process (2)? Because of the serial independence of ϵ_t, we see that

$$\gamma_k = Ey_t y_{t-k} = \begin{cases} 0 & \text{for } k > q \\ \left(\sum_{j=0}^{q-k} b_j b_{j+k}\right)\sigma^2 & \text{for } q \geq k \geq 0 \end{cases}$$

where $b_0 = 1$ and $b_j = 0$ for $j > q$. That is, the autocovariance function for a moving-average process of order q dies out abruptly at $k = q + 1$.

In order to select or identify a model, Box and Jenkins (1970) also use the partial autocorrelation function between y_t and y_{t-k}, holding the other lag y's constant. If we standardize the variable y_t by division by its standard deviation, the variance of y_t is unity and the partial correlation between y_t and y_{t-k} is simply the (partial) regression coefficient of y_{t-k} in the regression of y_t on y_{t-1}, $\ldots, y_{t-k}, y_{t-k-1}, \ldots$. For the autoregressive model (1), the partial correlations are simply the coefficients a_k. The coefficient terminates abruptly for $k = p + 1$.

The partial autocorrelation coefficients for a moving-average model (2) can be obtained by considering the regression of y_t on $y_{t-1}, y_{t-2}, \ldots, y_{t-m}$, after the variable has been standardized. The vector of partial correlation (or regression) coefficients is obtained by first inverting the correlation matrix of $m\,(>q)$ lagged dependent variables for y_t. For example if the order of the moving-average process is 1 and $m = 4$, the vector of partial correlation coefficients is, by regression theory,

$$
\begin{bmatrix}
\gamma_0 & \gamma_1 & 0 & 0 \\
\gamma_1 & \gamma_0 & \gamma_1 & 0 \\
0 & \gamma_1 & \gamma_0 & \gamma_1 \\
0 & 0 & \gamma_1 & \gamma_0
\end{bmatrix}^{-1}
\begin{bmatrix}
\gamma_1 \\
\gamma_2 \\
\gamma_3 \\
\gamma_4
\end{bmatrix}
$$

These partial autocorrelation coefficients do not die down abruptly for k larger than the order q of the moving-average process.

To summarize, the simple autocorrelation coefficients for an autoregressive process of order p do not die down abruptly but decrease gradually, while for a moving-average process of order q they vanish at k larger than q. The partial autocorrelation coefficients for an autoregressive process of order p terminate abruptly at $k = p + 1$, while for a moving-average process of order q, they do not die down abruptly for k larger than q. For an ARMA (p, q) process, the auto-correlations will die down according to

$$
\rho_k = a_1 \rho_{k-1} + \cdots + a_p \rho_{k-p} \qquad k > q
$$

as can easily be shown by using (5), (9), and (16). The partial autocorrelations will not terminate abruptly but will die out eventually for a stationary process. These and other characteristics of the autocorrelation and the partial autocorrelation functions have been exploited by Box and Jenkins to help select a good model to fit the data.

6.4 SPECTRAL-DENSITY MATRIX OF A LINEAR MODEL

To study the cyclical properties of a time series y_{1t} generated by a multivariate process one can rely on the autocovariance function $\gamma_{11,k}$ or the autocorrelation function $\rho_{11,k} = \gamma_{11,k}/\gamma_{11,0}$. As pointed out in Sec. 6.3, if there is a pair of complex roots $re^{i\theta}$ and $re^{-i\theta}$ in the system, $\gamma_{11,k}$ will contain as a component a damped cosine function $2sr^k \cos(\theta k + \psi)$ which has the same frequency θ as the angle θ of the complex roots. To extract cycles of different frequencies ω in the aucovariance function $\gamma_{11,k}$ one can use the weighted sum

$$
f_{11}(\omega) = \frac{1}{\pi} \sum_{k=-\infty}^{\infty} \gamma_{11,k} \cos \omega k \qquad 0 < \omega < \pi \tag{20}
$$

For a given ω, if the frequency ω in the weighting function $\cos \omega k$ differs from the frequencies of the cyclical components in $\gamma_{11,k}$, the weighted sum $f_{11}(\omega)$ will be small because the product $\gamma_{11,k} \cos \omega k$ may be positive or negative for different k when the frequencies of the two factors do not coincide. On the other hand, if some important cyclical components in $\gamma_{11,k}$ have frequencies close to ω, the weighted sum $f_{11}(\omega)$ will be large. The function $f_{11}(\omega)$ is called the *power spectrum* of the time series y_{1t}. It shows the importance of the cyclical component of frequency ω in the autocovariance function and hence of the time series itself. When the autocorrelation function $\rho_{11,k}$ replaces the autocovariance function $\gamma_{11,k}$ in (20), the result is a *spectral-density function*. That is, the spectral-density function is simply the power spectrum divided by the variance $\gamma_{11,0}$ of y_{1t}. Loosely speaking, one often uses the term "spectral density" to refer to either, without regard to the normalization by $\gamma_{11,0}$.

To extract cycles of different frequencies ω in the cross-covariance function $\gamma_{12,k}$ for the time series y_{1t} and y_{2t} one can consider using the weighted sum

$$\frac{1}{\pi} \sum_{k=-\infty}^{\infty} \gamma_{12,k} \cos(\omega k - \psi)$$

The phase shift ψ is needed because a cyclical component of frequency ω in $\gamma_{12,k}$ may have a phase shift. For example, 3-year cycles ($\omega = 2\pi/3$) in the consumption series y_{1t} may be more highly correlated with 3-year cycles in the income series y_{2t} lagged $\frac{1}{4}$ year than concurrently, producing a peak for this cyclical component of frequency $\omega = 2\pi/3$ in $\gamma_{12,k}$, not at $k = 0$ but at $k = \frac{1}{4}$. It would require a weighting function $\cos(\omega k - \psi)$, with $\psi = \omega k = (2\pi/3)(\frac{1}{4})$, to extract the cyclical component of frequency $\omega = 2\pi/3$ in $\gamma_{12,k}$. To find the appropriate ψ for a given ω, we maximize the above sum with respect to ψ by differentiation.

$$\frac{d}{d\psi}\left[\frac{1}{\pi} \sum_{k=-\infty}^{\infty} \gamma_{12,k}(\cos \omega k \cos \psi + \sin \omega k \sin \psi)\right]$$

$$= -\sin \psi \left(\frac{1}{\pi} \sum_{k=-\infty}^{\infty} \gamma_{12,k} \cos \omega k\right) + \cos \psi \left(\frac{1}{\pi} \sum_{k=1}^{\infty} \gamma_{12,k} \sin \omega k\right) = 0$$

yielding
$$\tan \psi = \frac{q_{12}(\omega)}{c_{12}(\omega)} \tag{21}$$

where
$$c_{12}(\omega) = \frac{1}{\pi} \sum_{k=-\infty}^{\infty} \gamma_{12,k} \cos \omega k \tag{22}$$

is called the *in-phase cross-spectral density* (or cross-spectrum to be more precise) and

$$q_{12}(\omega) = \frac{1}{\pi} \sum_{k=-\infty}^{\infty} \gamma_{12,k} \sin \omega k \tag{23}$$

is called the *out-of-phase cross-spectral density*.

The appropriate phase shift ψ for a given ω and a given pair of time series (y_{1t}, y_{2t}) is

$$\psi_{12}(\omega) = \tan^{-1} \frac{q_{12}(\omega)}{c_{12}(\omega)} \tag{24}$$

The *phase-difference cross-spectral density* $\psi_{12}(\omega)$ indicates that the cyclical component of frequency ω in y_{1t} is most highly correlated with the corresponding component in y_{2t} lagged $k = \psi_{12}(\omega)/\omega$ periods. It thus measures the lead-lag relation between the cyclical components of frequency ω in y_{1t} and y_{2t}.

Having found the appropriate phase shift $\psi_{12}(\omega)$ for a given ω, we can substitute the result for ψ in the weight sum to yield

$$c_{12}(\omega) \cos \psi + q_{12}(\omega) \sin \psi$$

$$= c_{12}(\omega) \frac{c_{12}(\omega)}{[c_{12}^2(\omega) + q_{12}^2(\omega)]^{1/2}} + q_{12}(\omega) \frac{q_{12}(\omega)}{[c_{12}^2(\omega) + q_{12}^2(\omega)]^{-1/2}}$$

$$= [c_{12}^2(\omega) + q_{12}^2(\omega)]^{1/2} \tag{25}$$

which is the *cross-amplitude spectral density*. It measures the strength of the correlation between the ω components of y_{1t} and y_{2t} after an appropriate phase shift.

The above analysis can be achieved more neatly by using the weighted sum

$$f_{12}(\omega) = \frac{1}{\pi} \sum_{k=-\infty}^{\infty} \gamma_{12,k} e^{-i\omega k} = \frac{1}{\pi} \sum_{k=-\infty}^{\infty} \gamma_{12,k}(\cos \omega k - i \sin \omega k) \tag{26}$$

with the complex weighting function $e^{-i\omega k}$. The *cross-spectral density function* $f_{12}(\omega)$ (or cross-power spectrum) for the time series y_{1t} and y_{2t} is a complex function and can be written

$$f_{12}(\omega) = c_{12}(\omega) - iq_{12}(\omega) = |f_{12}(\omega)| e^{-\psi_{12}(\omega)} \tag{27}$$

where $c_{12}(\omega)$, $q_{12}(\omega)$, $\psi_{12}(\omega)$, and the absolute value or modulo $|f_{12}(\omega)|$ have respectively been defined by Eqs. (22) to (25). The spectral-density function (20) can also be defined as

$$f_{11}(\omega) = \frac{1}{\pi} \sum_{k=-\infty}^{\infty} \gamma_{11,k} e^{-i\omega k} = \frac{1}{\pi} \sum_{k=-\infty}^{\infty} \gamma_{11,k} \cos \omega k \tag{28}$$

because $\gamma_{11,k} = \gamma_{11,-k}$ and $\sin \omega k = -\sin(-\omega k)$.

Define the *spectral-density matrix* for a vector time series y_t as

$$F(\omega) = [f_{ij}(\omega)] = \frac{1}{\pi} \sum_{k=-\infty}^{\infty} \Gamma_k e^{-i\omega k}$$

where, as before, Γ_k is the autocovariance matrix. For the time series y_t satisfying a first-order autoregressive process (8), we have, by (9) and (13),

$$\Gamma_k = A^k \Gamma_0 = BD^k \left[\frac{w_{ij}}{1 - \lambda_i \lambda_j} \right] B'$$

We also note, by the definition of $\gamma_{ij,k}$, that $\Gamma_{-k} = \Gamma_k'$. Using these two facts, we evaluate the spectral-density matrix for the linear system (8)

$$F(\omega) = \frac{1}{\pi} \left(\sum_{k=0}^{\infty} \Gamma_k e^{-i\omega k} + \sum_{k=0}^{\infty} \Gamma_{-k} e^{i\omega k} - \Gamma_0 \right)$$

$$= \frac{1}{\pi} B \left(\sum_{k=0}^{\infty} D^k \left[\frac{w_{ij}}{1 - \lambda_i \lambda_j} \right] e^{-i\omega k} + \sum_{k=0}^{\infty} \left[\frac{w_{ij}}{1 - \lambda_i \lambda_j} \right] D^k e^{i\omega k} - \left[\frac{w_{ij}}{1 - \lambda_i \lambda_j} \right] \right) B'$$

The ijth element of the last matrix in parentheses is

$$\frac{w_{ij}}{1 - \lambda_i \lambda_j} \left(\sum_{k=0}^{\infty} \lambda_i^k e^{-i\omega k} + \sum_{k=0}^{\infty} \lambda_j^k e^{i\omega k} - 1 \right)$$

$$= \frac{w_{ij}}{1 - \lambda_i \lambda_j} \left(\frac{1}{1 - \lambda_i e^{-i\omega}} + \frac{1}{1 - \lambda_j e^{i\omega}} - 1 \right)$$

$$= \frac{w_{ij}}{1 - \lambda_i \lambda_j} \frac{1 - \lambda_i \lambda_j}{(1 - \lambda_i e^{-i\omega})(1 - \lambda_j e^{i\omega})}$$

Substituting into the equation above, we obtain

$$F(\omega) = \frac{1}{\pi} B \left[\frac{w_{ij}}{(1 - \lambda_i e^{-i\omega})(1 - \lambda_j e^{i\omega})} \right] B' \tag{29}$$

as the spectral-density matrix for the linear system (8), where the columns of B are the right characteristic vectors of A, $W = (w_{ij}) = B^{-1} \Sigma B'^{-1}$, and λ_i are the characteristic roots of A.

Consider the special case when A in (8) is a scalar a. The system is a first-order univariate autoregressive process. Matrix B becomes 1 and $\lambda_i = a$. The spectral-density matrix is a spectral-density function

$$f(\omega) = \frac{1}{\pi} \frac{\sigma^2}{(1 - ae^{-i\omega})(1 - ae^{i\omega})} = \frac{1}{\pi} \frac{\sigma^2}{(1 + a^2 - 2a \cos \omega)} \tag{30}$$

If $a > 0$, the denominator is an increasing function of ω since $\cos \omega$ is a decreasing function of ω for $0 < \omega < \pi$. The function $f(\omega)$ is therefore a decreasing function of ω. It shows that the low-frequency components of the time series are more important than the high-frequency components. Long cycles dominate short cycles. This shape was termed by Granger (1966) the "typical spectral shape" of an economic time series.

If $a < 0$, the time series tends to oscillate from period to period, as shown by its autocovariance function $\gamma_k = a^k$ ($k > 0$). Its spectral-density function is an increasing function of ω, showing that the high-frequency components are more important than the low-frequency components. Short cycles dominate long cycles, with two-period cycles being the most pronounced, i.e., with the peak of $f(\omega)$ at $\omega = \pi$.

It is possible for a multivariate linear system to generate a spectral-density function which has a peak at ω between 0 and π. For example, a second-order univariate autoregressive process having a pair of complex roots may give rise to such a spectral density (see Prob. 10). Monthly economic time series having seasonal variations will have spectral densities which peak at the seasonal frequencies $\omega = 2\pi/12, 2\pi/6, 2\pi/4, 2\pi/3, 2\pi/2.4$, and $2\pi/2$, corresponding to cycles of 12, 6, etc., months in duration. Nerlove (1964) has estimated spectral-density functions for total United States employment and United States male employment both before and after seasonal adjustment. Before adjustment these series show spectral peaks at the above frequencies, but after adjustment they show some troughs at these frequencies, suggesting possible overadjustment.

★6.5 DECOMPOSITION OF TIME SERIES INTO PERIODIC COMPONENTS

Our discussion has referred to 3-year cycles in consumption and income series and to components of frequencies ω in a time series. This suggests that a time series can be conceived of as a weighted sum of many periodic components. It is possible to decompose a time series into periodic components of cosine and sine functions. We first perform the decomposition for a *set of data* y_{1t} ($t = 1, \ldots, N$), which are simply N *arbitrarily given numbers*. This decomposition will be suggestive to, and enhance the understanding of, a similar decomposition for a theoretical time series. The first decomposition amounts to manipulating sample data. The second is concerned with analyzing population values and should be distinguished from the first.†

Let N arbitrary numbers $y_{11}, y_{12}, \ldots, y_{1N}$ be given. Imagine fitting this set of data by a weighted sum of sine and cosine functions. These functions should have cycle lengths equal to $N, \frac{1}{2}N, \frac{1}{3}N, \ldots, 2$, so that the N points will cover one, two, etc., cycles of the functions. The functions are $\cos \omega_j t$ and $\sin \omega_j t$, where $\omega_j = (2\pi/N)j$ ($j = 1, \ldots, N/2$). For convenience let N be even or $N/2 = n$. For $j = n$ we have $\omega_n = \pi$ and therefore $\sin \omega_n t = 0$. The decomposition is

$$y_{1t} = a_{10} + \sum_{j=1}^{n-1} (a_{1j} \cos \omega_j t + b_{1j} \sin \omega_j t) + a_{1n} \cos \omega_n t \tag{31}$$

The N unknown coefficients a_{1j} and b_{1j} can be determined by performing a least-squares regression of y_{1t} on the explanatory variables $\cos \omega_j t$ ($j = 1, \ldots, n$) and $\sin \omega_j t$ ($j = 1, \ldots, n - 1$).

To obtain the least-squares estimates the sums of squares and cross products of the explanatory variables (measured from their means) are used. Note first that the sum of each variable over t is zero because the positive and negative values of each function cancel out for every cycle and there are an integral number of cycles. Thus

$$\sum_{t=1}^{N} \cos \omega_j t = \sum_{t=1}^{N} \sin \omega_j t = 0 \qquad \begin{matrix} \omega_j = \dfrac{2\pi}{N}j \\ j = 1, \ldots, N/2 \end{matrix} \tag{32}$$

† This section and Sec. 6.6 are modified from Chow (1975), by permission of John Wiley & Sons, Inc.

The explanatory variables have zero mean, and we need to compute their sums of squares and cross products

$$\sum_{t=1}^{N} \cos^2 \omega_j t = \sum_{t=1}^{N} \sin^2 \omega_j t = \frac{N}{2} \qquad j = 1, \ldots, n-1$$

$$\sum_{t=1}^{N} \cos^2 \omega_n t = N \tag{33}$$

$$\sum_{t=1}^{N} (\cos \omega_j t)(\sin \omega_k t) = 0 \qquad j, k = 1, \ldots, n-1$$

$$\sum_{t=1}^{N} (\cos \omega_j t)(\cos \omega_k t) = \sum_{t=1}^{N} (\sin \omega_j t)(\sin \omega_k t) = 0 \qquad j \neq k \tag{34}$$

For the proofs of (33) and (34) consult Probs. 16 and 17. Equations (33) and (34) are important identities. They show that each periodic component $\cos \omega_j t$ or $\sin \omega_j t$ $(j = 1, \ldots, n-1)$ has the same variance and that each component is uncorrelated with any other component.

By the method of least squares the normal equations are

$$\begin{bmatrix} \frac{N}{2} & & & & \mathbf{0} \\ & \frac{N}{2} & & & \\ & & \ddots & & \\ & & & \frac{N}{2} & \\ \mathbf{0} & & & & N \end{bmatrix} \begin{bmatrix} a_{11} \\ b_{11} \\ \vdots \\ b_{1,n-1} \\ a_{1n} \end{bmatrix} = \begin{bmatrix} \sum_t y_{1t} \cos \omega_1 t \\ \sum_t y_{1t} \sin \omega_1 t \\ \vdots \\ \sum_t y_{1t} \sin \omega_{n-1} t \\ \sum_t y_{1t} \cos \pi t \end{bmatrix} \tag{35}$$

Solving these equations and using a well-known formula for the intercept a_{10}, we obtain

$$a_{1j} = \frac{2}{N} \sum_{t=1}^{N} y_{1t} \cos \omega_j t, \qquad b_{1j} = \frac{2}{N} \sum_{t=1}^{N} y_{1t} \sin \omega_j t \qquad j = 1, \ldots, n-1 \tag{36}$$

$$a_{10} = \frac{1}{N} \sum_{t=1}^{N} y_{1t} = \bar{y}_i \qquad a_{1n} = \frac{1}{N} \sum_{t=1}^{N} (-1)^t y_{1t}$$

Because the number of coefficients in (31) equals the number of data points, the equation will fit the observations y_{1t} $(t = 1, \ldots, N)$ exactly, without leaving any residuals. A given set of data has thus been decomposed into a weighted sum of cosine and sine functions that are mutually uncorrelated.

To measure the importance of each periodic component in y_{1t} it seems natural to use the contribution of that component to the sample variance of y_{1t}.

Squaring $y_{1t} - a_{10}$ from (31), summing over t, and using (34) and (33), we have

$$\sum_{t=1}^{N} (y_{1t} - \bar{y}_1)^2 = \sum_{j=1}^{n-1} \left(a_{1j}^2 \sum_{t=1}^{N} \cos^2 \omega_j t + b_{1j}^2 \sum_{t=1}^{N} \sin^2 \omega_j t \right) + a_{1n}^2 \sum_{t=1}^{N} \cos^2 \omega_n t$$

$$= \frac{N}{2} \sum_{j=1}^{n-1} (a_{1j}^2 + b_{1j}^2) + N a_{1n}^2 \tag{37}$$

The contribution of the periodic component of frequency $\omega_j/2\pi$ to the sample variance of y_{1t} is therefore $\frac{1}{2}(a_{1j}^2 + b_{1j}^2)$.

In order to decompose a theoretical time series, we conceive of a time series y_{1t} as *a random function* of t defined by

$$y_{1t} = \sum_{j} [\alpha_1(\omega_j) \cos \omega_j t + \beta_1(\omega_j) \sin \omega_j t] \tag{38}$$

where $\alpha_1(\omega_j)$ and $\beta_1(\omega_j)$ are random variables with zero mean and equal variance $E[\alpha_1^2(\omega_j)] = E[\beta_1^2(\omega_j)]$ for each j and all these random variables are mutually uncorrelated. By introducing randomness in the coefficients $\alpha_1(\omega_j)$ and $\beta_1(\omega_j)$ we attempt to model a stochastic time series. Here ω_j may range over many values between 0 and π, so that there may be many periodic components—even an infinite number of them. What is the contribution of the periodic component of frequency $\omega_j/2\pi$ to the total variance of y_{1t}? To answer this question we decompose the variance of y_{1t}

$$E y_{1t}^2 = E \left\{ \sum_{j} [\alpha_1(\omega_j) \cos \omega_j t + \beta_1(\omega_j) \sin \omega_j t] \right\}^2$$

$$= \sum_{j} \{ [E\alpha_1^2(\omega_j)] \cos^2 \omega_j t + [E\beta_1^2(\omega_j)] \sin^2 \omega_j t \}$$

$$= \sum_{j} [E\alpha_1^2(\omega_j)] = \sum_{j} \text{Var} [\alpha_1(\omega_j)] \tag{39}$$

where use has been made of $E[a_1^2(\omega_j)] = E[\beta_1^2(\omega_j)]$ and the zero correlations of the random coefficients. Thus the total variance of the time series is the sum of the variances of the periodic components. The contribution of the jth component is the common variance of the coefficient of $\cos \omega_j t$ or of $\sin \omega_j t$. Compare this contribution with the contribution given in Eq. (37) by the jth component to the sample variance of an arbitrary set of data. In the latter case we estimated the coefficients a_{1j} and b_{1j}. The common variance of these coefficients can be estimated by $\frac{1}{2}(a_{1j}^2 + b_{1j}^2)$, which is analogous to $E\alpha_1^2(\omega_j)$ of (39).

For the time series (38) let us *redefine the power spectrum $f_{11}(\omega_j)$ as the common variance $E\alpha_1^2(\omega_j)$ of the random coefficient $\alpha_1(\omega_j)$ or $\beta_1(\omega_j)$ or equivalently as the contribution of the random periodic component of frequency $\omega_j/2\pi$ to the total variance of the time series.* In order to make this definition applicable to more general situations we have to allow the variable ω to be continuous. Thus ω_j in (23), even if countably infinite, will have to be replaced by a continuous variable ω. The sum of (23) can indeed be replaced by an appropriate integral such that all covariance-stationary time series can be so represented. This can be done without abandoning the essential structure of the α's and the β's as specified above. We can then speak of a power spectrum or a spectral-density function $f_{11}(\omega)$ for continuous ω between 0 and π. The area $\int_a^b f_{11}(\omega)\, d\omega$ under the spectral-density function between two points a and b measures the contribution of the periodic components with ω between a and b to the total variance of the time series. If the spectral density is normalized, the contribution to total variance is given as a fraction and the total area $\int_0^\pi f_{11}(\omega)\, d\omega$ under the function is equal to 1.

This definition of the spectral-density function enables us to understand the concept in terms of regression theory. As pointed out earlier, we can imagine the decomposition of a time series into many periodic components as the performance of a regression of the time series on many explanatory variables which are cosine and sine functions of time. The variances of the regression coefficients are the spectral densities, but we have to think of an infinite number of explanatory variables and of regression coefficients. These coefficients are also random coefficients.

In order to define a cross-spectral density, let there be another time series defined by

$$y_{2t} = \sum_j [\alpha_2(\omega_j) \cos \omega_j t + \beta_2(\omega_j) \sin \omega_j t] \tag{40}$$

The coefficients $\alpha_2(\omega_j)$ and $\beta_2(\omega_j)$ are also assumed to be random with zero mean, uncorrelated, and with the same variance for each j. In addition, it is specified that

$$E[\alpha_1(\omega_j)\alpha_2(\omega_j)] = E[\beta_1(\omega_j)\beta_2(\omega_j)]$$

$$\tag{41}$$

and $\qquad E[\beta_1(\omega_j)\alpha_2(\omega_j)] = -E[\alpha_1(\omega_j)\beta_2(\omega_j)]$

These are covariances because the means are all zero.

Consider the covariance between the component of frequency $\omega_j/2\pi$ in y_{1t} and the corresponding component in $y_{2,\,t-k}$.

Cov $[\alpha_1(\omega_j) \cos \omega_j t + \beta_1(\omega_j) \sin \omega_j t,\ \alpha_2(\omega_j) \cos (\omega_j t - \omega_j k)$

$\qquad + \beta_2(\omega_j) \sin (\omega_j t - \omega_j k)]$

$= E\{[\alpha_1(\omega_j) \cos \omega_j t + \beta_1(\omega_j) \sin \omega_j t][(\alpha_2 \cos \omega_j t)(\cos \omega_j k)$

$\qquad + (\alpha_2 \sin \omega_j t)(\sin \omega_j k) + (\beta_2 \sin \omega_j t)(\cos \omega_j k) - (\beta_2 \cos \omega_j t)(\sin \omega_j k)]\}$

$= \cos \omega_j k E[(\alpha_1 \cos \omega_j t + \beta_1 \sin \omega_j t)(\alpha_2 \cos \omega_j t + \beta_2 \sin \omega_j t)]$

$\qquad + \sin \omega_j k E[(\alpha_1 \cos \omega_j t + \beta_1 \sin \omega_j t)(\alpha_2 \sin \omega_j t - \beta_2 \cos \omega_j t)] \tag{42}$

Define the *in-phase cross-spectral density* as

$c_{12}(\omega_j) =$ Cov $[\alpha_1(\omega_j) \cos \omega_j t + \beta_1(\omega_j) \sin \omega_j t,\ \alpha_2(\omega_j) \cos \omega_j t + \beta_2(\omega_j) \sin \omega_j t]$

$\qquad = E[\alpha_1(\omega_j)\alpha_2(\omega_j)] = E[\beta_1(\omega_j)\beta_2(\omega_j)] \tag{43}$

where the relations in (41) have been applied. Define the *out-of-phase cross-spectral density* as

$$q_{12}(\omega_j) = \text{Cov} \left[\alpha_1(\omega_j) \cos \omega_j t + \beta_1(\omega_j) \sin \omega_j t, \; \alpha_2(\omega_j) \sin \omega_j t - \beta_2(\omega_j) \cos \omega_j t \right]$$

$$= E[\beta_1(\omega_j)\alpha_2(\omega_j)] = -E[\alpha_1(\omega_j)\beta_2(\omega_j)] \tag{44}$$

The covariance (42) of the two components then becomes, for any ω,

$$\cos \psi c_{12}(\omega) + \sin \psi q_{12}(\omega) \qquad \text{where } \psi = \omega k \tag{45}$$

To find the phase shift ψ that will maximize the covariance (45) we set the derivative equal to zero to obtain

$$\tan \psi_{12}(\omega) = \frac{q_{12}(\omega)}{c_{12}(\omega)} \tag{46}$$

The phase shift $\psi_{12}(\omega)$ so defined shows that the ω component of the second time series leads the ω component of the first time series by $k = \psi_{12}(\omega)/\omega$ time units; $\psi_{12}(\omega)$ is the *phase-difference cross-spectral density*. Once this optimum phase shift is found, the covariance between the ω component of the first series and the appropriately timed ω component of the second series is, by (45) and (46)

$$\sqrt{c_{12}^2(\omega) + q_{12}^2(\omega)} \tag{47}$$

This is the *cross-amplitude spectral density*.

By using (46) and (47) we can define the *cross-spectral density* as the complex function

$$f_{12}(\omega) = \sqrt{c_{12}^2(\omega) + q_{12}^2(\omega)} \, \exp\left[-i\psi_{12}(\omega)\right] = c_{12}(\omega) - iq_{12}(\omega) \tag{48}$$

In sum, the cross-spectral density shows in two parts the magnitude of the covariance between corresponding periodic components in the two time series and their relative lead or lag. For an informal demonstration of the equivalence between this definition of the cross-spectral density and the earlier definition via the cross-covariance function, see Chow (1975, p. 84).

6.6 NOTE ON THE ESTIMATION OF SPECTRAL DENSITIES

The concepts of spectral and cross-spectral densities are useful for studying cyclical properties of econometric models. In addition, and more prevalently, they are useful for extracting cyclical properties of observed economic time series without the intervention of an econometric model. Thus, assuming that certain time series are covariance-stationary, or approximately so, probably after adjustments for trends by fitting trend functions or by taking first differences and the like, we may wish to estimate the spectral and cross-spectral densities directly from the data. This process of estimation is called *spectral analysis* of time-series data. No econometric models in the form of systems of interdependent dynamic equations are needed. The only hypothesis employed is concerned with the form of the trend, if trend is taken out, with the appropriate transformation of variables such as taking logarithms and with the smoothness of the spectral-density function. Little theory is required. Spectral analysis can also be applied, not to economic data directly but to data generated from stochastic simulations of an econometric model estimated from economic data. This will enable us to study certain dynamic properties of the econometric model. Such an undertaking differs from spectral analysis of raw data and also from the analytical derivation of spectral properties from a model as we have done in Sec. 6.4.

Given time-series data for a variable y_{1t} ($t = 1, \ldots, N$), it seems reasonable to use the periodic regression coefficients a_{1j} and b_{1j} of (36) in Sec. 6.5 to estimate the spectral density at ω_j. The spectral density at ω_j is the common variance of the coefficients a_{1j} and b_{1j}. There are $N/2$ of these variances that can be calculated from a sample of size N. Each variance has to cover a range of ω values equal in width to $2\pi/N$ if ω is a continuous variable from 0 to π. Therefore a possible estimate of the spectral density at ω_j is the variance $\frac{1}{2}(a_{1j}^2 + b_{1j}^2)$ divided by the width $2\pi/N$

$$
I(\omega_j) = \frac{1}{2}(a_{1j}^2 + b_{1j}^2)\frac{N}{2\pi}
$$

$$
= \frac{1}{\pi N}\left[\left(\sum_{t=1}^{N} y_{1t} \cos \omega_j t\right)^2 + \left(\sum_{t=1}^{N} y_{1t} \sin \omega_j t\right)^2\right]
$$

$$
= \frac{1}{\pi N}\left\{\sum_{t=1}^{N} y_{1t} y_{1t}(\cos \omega_j t \cos \omega_j t + \sin \omega_j t \sin \omega_j t)\right.
$$

$$
+ \sum_{t=1}^{N-1} y_{1t} y_{1,t+1}[\cos \omega_j t \cos (\omega_j t + \omega_j) + \sin \omega_j t \sin (\omega_j t + \omega_j)]
$$

$$
\left. + \sum_{t=1}^{N-2} y_{1t} y_{1,t+2}[\cos \omega_j t \cos (\omega_j t + 2\omega_j) + \sin \omega_j t \sin (\omega_j t + 2\omega_j)] + \cdots\right\}
$$

$$
= \frac{1}{\pi} \sum_{k=-N+1}^{N-1} c_{11,k} \cos \omega_j k \tag{49}
$$

where, for the third equality sign, we consecutively sum the products of terms with time subscripts differing by 0, 1, 2, ..., $N - 1$, -1, -2, ..., $-N + 1$, and where $c_{11,k}$ is the sample autocovariance

$$
c_{11,k} = c_{11,-k} = \frac{1}{N} \sum_{t=1}^{N-k} y_{1t} y_{1,t+k} \tag{50}
$$

Equation (49) demonstrates that the variance of the ω_j component in regression (31) is the same as the application of a cosine transform to the sample autocovariance $c_{11,k}$. It thus shows the equivalence of the two definitions of spectral density, at least for the sample.

What is the sampling property of the estimate of spectral density given by (49)? If y_{1t} is normally and independently distributed, each regression coefficient a_{1j} and b_{1j} computed by the method of least squares, using (35), will also be normally and independently distributed. Each will have a variance equal to $2/N$ times the variance of y_{1t}, according to least-squares theory. The variables $a_{1j}\sqrt{N/2}$ and $b_{1j}\sqrt{N/2}$ are independently normal and have variance equal to the variance of y_{1t}. The estimate $I(\omega_j)$ in (49) can be written as

$$\left[\left(a_{ij}\sqrt{\frac{N}{2}} \right)^2 + \left(b_{2j}\sqrt{\frac{N}{2}} \right)^2 \right] (2\pi)^{-1}$$

Except for the factor $(2\pi)^{-1}$, it is the sum of the squares of two independent normal random variables with a common variance. Therefore, except for a factor, it is distributed as a χ^2 variable with 2 degrees of freedom. The main point is that, no matter how large the sample size N, the estimate $I(\omega_j)$ for each ω_j will be distributed as a χ^2 random variable with 2 degrees of freedom and thus will not converge to a constant. This means that a consistent estimate of the spectral density cannot be obtained by using $I(\omega_j)$.

In order to obtain a consistent estimate of the spectral density, (49) must be modified by applying a set of weights w_k to the sample autocovariance functions $c_{11,k}$ before performing the cosine transform

$$\hat{f}_{11}(\omega) = \frac{1}{\pi} \sum_{k=-\infty}^{\infty} w_k c_{11,k} \cos \omega k \tag{51}$$

The weighting function w_k is called the *lag window*. Specialists in spectral analysis have proposed various windows and investigated their properties. A simple one is the *Bartlett window*, which for some m smaller than N is

$$w_k = \begin{cases} 1 - \dfrac{|k|}{m} & 0 \le |k| \le m \\ 0 & \text{otherwise} \end{cases} \tag{52}$$

It ignores those sample autocovariances $c_{11,k}$ with lag k larger than m which are computed from fewer and fewer observations as k increases in absolute value. For this particular window the weights w_k are linearly declining with the absolute value of k. Others have proposed windows that are different decreasing functions of $|k|$, but we shall not pursue the subject here. These windows can also be applied to the sample cross-covariance functions before the appropriate cosine and sine transforms are formed for the consistent estimation of cross-spectral densities. This process is termed *cross-spectral analysis*. Computer programs are available to perform spectral analysis and cross-spectral analysis of time-series data; see Anderson (1971) and Bloomfield (1978).

★6.7 ESTIMATION OF ARMA MODELS

First we shall consider maximum-likelihood estimation of a multivariate moving-average MA(q) model of the form

$$y_t = \epsilon_t + B_1\epsilon_{t-1} + \cdots + B_q\epsilon_{t-q} \tag{53}$$

where y_t is $k \times 1$ and ϵ_t are normal and serially independent, having covariance matrix Σ. This topic is treated, among others, by Hillmer and Tiao (1979), on which much of this section is based. A sample of n observations $y_1, \ldots, y_n$ generated by this model can be written as

$$
\begin{bmatrix} y_1 \\ y_2 \\ y_3 \\ \cdot \\ \cdot \\ \cdot \\ y_n \end{bmatrix}
=
\begin{bmatrix}
I & & & & & \mathbf{0} \\
B_1 & I & & & & \\
B_2 & B_1 & I & & & \\
\cdots\cdots\cdots\cdots\cdots & & & & & \\
B_q & B_{q-1} & \cdots & \cdots & I & \\
\cdots\cdots\cdots\cdots\cdots\cdots\cdots & & & & & \\
0 & \cdots & B_q & \cdots & \cdots & \cdots & I
\end{bmatrix}
\begin{bmatrix} \epsilon_1 \\ \epsilon_2 \\ \epsilon_3 \\ \cdot \\ \epsilon_{q+1} \\ \cdot \\ \epsilon_n \end{bmatrix}
$$

$$
+
\begin{bmatrix}
B_q & B_{q-1} & \cdots & B_1 \\
0 & B_q & \cdots & B_2 \\
\cdots\cdots\cdots\cdots\cdots & & & \\
0 & 0 & \cdots & B_q \\
0 & \cdots & \cdots & 0 \\
\cdots\cdots\cdots\cdots\cdots & & & \\
0 & \cdots & \cdots & 0
\end{bmatrix}
\begin{bmatrix} \epsilon_{-q+1} \\ \epsilon_{-q+2} \\ \vdots \\ \epsilon_0 \end{bmatrix}
\tag{54}
$$

or more compactly as

$$y = D\epsilon + C\epsilon_* \tag{55}$$

where D and C are functions of the unknown parameters $B_1, \ldots, B_q$.

To set up the likelihood function we consider the distribution of y as induced by the distribution of ϵ and ϵ_*. Rewrite (55) as

$$
\begin{bmatrix} \epsilon_* \\ \epsilon \end{bmatrix}
=
\begin{bmatrix} I & 0 \\ -D^{-1}C & D^{-1} \end{bmatrix}
\begin{bmatrix} \epsilon_* \\ y \end{bmatrix}
=
\begin{bmatrix} 0 \\ D^{-1} \end{bmatrix} y
-
\begin{bmatrix} -I \\ D^{-1}C \end{bmatrix} \epsilon_* \equiv z - Xb
\tag{56}
$$

where
$$
z = \begin{bmatrix} 0 \\ D^{-1} \end{bmatrix} y \qquad X = \begin{bmatrix} -I \\ D^{-1}C \end{bmatrix} \qquad \epsilon_* = b
\tag{57}
$$

The probability density function of (ϵ_*, ϵ) is normal, with mean zero and covariance matrix $I_{n+q} \otimes \Sigma \equiv \Sigma_{n+q}$; that is,

$$\text{pdf}(\epsilon_*, \epsilon) \propto |I_{n+q} \otimes \Sigma|^{-1/2} \exp\left\{-\tfrac{1}{2}[\epsilon_*' \quad \epsilon]\Sigma_{n+q}^{-1}\begin{bmatrix}\epsilon_* \\ \epsilon\end{bmatrix}\right\}$$

The joint probability density function of $b = \epsilon_*$ and y by the transformation (56) is

$$\text{pdf}(b, y) \propto |\Sigma|^{-(n+q)/2} \exp\left[-\tfrac{1}{2}(z - Xb)'\Sigma_{n+q}^{-1}(z - Xb)\right] \tag{58}$$

where we have noted that the jacobian of the transformation is unity, used the fact that $|A \otimes B| = |A|^m|B|^n$ for an $n \times n$ matrix A and an $m \times m$ matrix B, and written z' for $y'[0 \quad D^{-1'}]$. To find the probability density function of y, we integrate out b. Let $z - Xb = z - X\hat{b} + X\hat{b} - Xb$, where

$$\hat{b} = (X'\Sigma_{n+q}^{-1}X)^{-1}X'\Sigma_{n+q}^{-1}z \tag{59}$$

Using
$$(z - X\hat{b})'\Sigma_{n+q}^{-1}(z - X\hat{b}) = z'\Sigma_{n+q}^{-1}z - \hat{b}'X'\Sigma_{n+q}^{-1}X\hat{b}$$

we can write the exponent of (58) as

$$\tfrac{1}{2}[z'\Sigma_{n+q}^{-1}z - \hat{b}'X'\Sigma_{n+q}^{-1}X\hat{b} + (b - \hat{b})'X'\Sigma_{n+q}^{-1}X(b - \hat{b})]$$

On integrating out b, we employ the multivariate normal density with the normalization constant $|X'\Sigma_{n+q}^{-1}X|^{1/2}$ and obtain the marginal density of z, which implies the likelihood function

$$L(B, \Sigma \mid z) \propto |\Sigma|^{-(n+q)/2}|X'\Sigma_{n+q}^{-1}X|^{-1/2} \exp\left[-\tfrac{1}{2}(z'\Sigma_{n+q}^{-1}z - \hat{b}'X'\Sigma_{n+q}^{-1}X\hat{b})\right] \tag{60}$$

Using definition (57) for z and X, we can rewrite the likelihood function (60) in terms of the original variables y. Since

$$z'\Sigma_{n+q}^{-1}z = y'[0 \quad D^{-1'}]\begin{bmatrix}\Sigma_q^{-1} & 0 \\ 0 & \Sigma_n^{-1}\end{bmatrix}\begin{bmatrix}0 \\ D^{-1}\end{bmatrix}y = y'D^{-1'}\Sigma_n^{-1}D^{-1}y$$

$$X'\Sigma_{n+q}^{-1}X = [-I \quad C'D^{-1'}]\begin{bmatrix}\Sigma_q^{-1} & 0 \\ 0 & \Sigma_n^{-1}\end{bmatrix}\begin{bmatrix}-I \\ D^{-1}C\end{bmatrix}$$

$$= \Sigma_q^{-1} + C'D^{-1'}\Sigma_n^{-1}D^{-1}C \equiv A_{n,q} \equiv A \tag{61}$$

and $\qquad \hat{\epsilon}_* \equiv \hat{b} = (X'\Sigma_{n+q}^{-1}X)^{-1}X'\Sigma_{n+q}^{-1}z = A^{-1}C'D^{-1'}\Sigma_n^{-1}D^{-1}y \tag{62}$

the likelihood function becomes

$$L(B, \Sigma \mid y) \propto |\Sigma|^{-(n+q)/2}|A|^{-1/2} \exp\left[-\tfrac{1}{2}(y'D^{-1'}\Sigma_n^{-1}D^{-1}y - \hat{\epsilon}_*'A\hat{\epsilon}_*)\right] \tag{63}$$

Often (63) is approximated by setting $\hat{\epsilon}_* = 0$ and ignoring the factor

$$|\Sigma|^{-q/2}|A|^{-1/2}$$

to yield

$$L(B, \Sigma \mid y) \propto |\Sigma|^{-n/2} \exp\left(-\tfrac{1}{2}y'D^{-1'}\Sigma_n^{-1}D^{-1}y\right) \tag{64}$$

as is done in Wilson (1973). The right-hand side of (64) is proportional to $\text{pdf}(y \mid \epsilon_* = 0)$.

We now turn to the ARMA (p, q) model

$$y_t = A_1 y_{t-1} + \cdots + A_p y_{t-p} + \epsilon_t + B_1 \epsilon_{t-1} + \cdots + B_q \epsilon_{t-q}$$

or

$$
\begin{bmatrix}
I & & & & & \\
-A_1 & I & & & \mathbf{0} & \\
-A_2 & -A_1 & I & & & \\
\cdots\cdots\cdots\cdots\cdots\cdots\cdots\cdots & & & & \\
-A_p & -A_{p-1} & \cdots & \cdots & I & \\
\cdots\cdots\cdots\cdots\cdots\cdots\cdots\cdots\cdots\cdots & & & & \\
0 & \cdots & -A_p & \cdots & \cdots & I
\end{bmatrix}
\begin{bmatrix}
y_1 \\ y_2 \\ y_3 \\ \cdot \\ y_{p+1} \\ \cdot \\ y_n
\end{bmatrix}
$$

$$
=
\begin{bmatrix}
I & & & & & \\
B_1 & I & & & \mathbf{0} & \\
B_2 & B_1 & I & & & \\
\cdots\cdots\cdots\cdots\cdots\cdots\cdots & & & & \\
B_q & B_{q-1} & \cdots & \cdots & I & \\
\cdots\cdots\cdots\cdots\cdots\cdots\cdots\cdots & & & & \\
0 & \cdots & B_q & \cdots & \cdots & I
\end{bmatrix}
\begin{bmatrix}
\epsilon_1 \\ \epsilon_2 \\ \epsilon_3 \\ \cdot \\ \epsilon_{q+1} \\ \cdot \\ \epsilon_n
\end{bmatrix}
$$

$$
+
\begin{bmatrix}
B_q & B_{q-1} & \cdots & B_1 \\
0 & B_q & \cdots & B_2 \\
\cdots\cdots\cdots\cdots\cdots\cdots & & & \\
0 & 0 & \cdots & B_q \\
0 & \cdots & \cdots & 0 \\
\cdots\cdots\cdots\cdots\cdots\cdots & & & \\
0 & \cdots & \cdots & 0
\end{bmatrix}
\begin{bmatrix}
\epsilon_{-q+1} \\ \epsilon_{-q+2} \\ \vdots \\ \epsilon_0
\end{bmatrix}
+
\begin{bmatrix}
A_p & A_{p-1} & \cdots & A_1 \\
0 & A_p & \cdots & A_2 \\
\cdots\cdots\cdots\cdots\cdots\cdots & & & \\
0 & 0 & \cdots & A_p \\
0 & \cdots & \cdots & 0 \\
\cdots\cdots\cdots\cdots\cdots\cdots & & & \\
0 & \cdots & \cdots & 0
\end{bmatrix}
\begin{bmatrix}
y_{-p+1} \\ y_{-p+2} \\ \vdots \\ y_0
\end{bmatrix}
\quad (65)
$$

Consider first the case of $p = q$. Let $\tilde{y}_1$ denote the vector consisting of $y_1, \ldots,$ y_p and $\tilde{y}_2$ denote the vector consisting of $y_{p+1}, \ldots, y_n$. Let $\tilde{\epsilon}_1$ and $\tilde{\epsilon}_2$ be similarly defined. We can rewrite (65) in this special case as

$$
\begin{bmatrix} F_A & 0 \\ -C_A & D_A \end{bmatrix}
\begin{bmatrix} \tilde{y}_1 \\ \tilde{y}_2 \end{bmatrix}
=
\begin{bmatrix} F_B & 0 \\ C_B & D_B \end{bmatrix}
\begin{bmatrix} \tilde{\epsilon}_1 \\ \tilde{\epsilon}_2 \end{bmatrix}
+
\begin{bmatrix} v \\ 0 \end{bmatrix}
\quad (66)
$$

where we have defined the sum of the last two terms of (65) as $(v' \, 0)'$. Note that the matrices C_A, C_B, D_A, and D_B have the same structures as the matrices C and D defined in (55). Let $w_1 = F_A \tilde{y}_1$ and $w_2 = D_A \tilde{y}_2 - C_A \tilde{y}_1$. We are interested in the joint density function of w_1 and w_2.

Write the joint density of w_1 and w_2 as

$$\text{pdf}(w_1, w_2) = p(w_2) p(w_1 \mid w_2)$$

By (66), $w_2 = D_B \tilde{\epsilon}_2 + C_B \tilde{\epsilon}_1$ has the same form as (55). Thus w_2 consists of $n - q$ observations from a moving-average q-order process. The likelihood function based on these observations is, according to (63),

$$L_1(A, B, \Sigma \mid y) \propto |\Sigma|^{-n/2} |A_{n-p, p}|^{-1/2}$$

$$\cdot \exp \left[- \tfrac{1}{2}(w_2' D_B^{-1'} \Sigma_{n-p}^{-1} D_B^{-1} w_2 - \hat{\epsilon}_1' A_{n-p, p} \hat{\epsilon}_1) \right] \qquad (67)$$

where, as in (62),

$$\hat{\epsilon}_1 = A_{n-p, p}^{-1} C_B' D_B^{-1'} \Sigma_{n-p}^{-1} D_B^{-1} w_2$$

Hillmer and Tiao (1979) have shown that the likelihood based on w_1 and w_2 can be closely approximated by (67) when n is large because $p(w_2)$ dominates $p(w_1 \mid w_2)$. In effect, when the sample size is large, one can compute the likelihood function (67) by using the residuals u_t from the ARMA model

$$y_t - A_1 y_{t-1} - \cdots - A_p y_{t-p} = \epsilon_t + B_1 \epsilon_{t-1} + \cdots + B_q \epsilon_{t-q} \equiv u_t \qquad (68)$$

beginning with $t = p + 1$. Equation (68) corresponds to the bottom part of Eq. (66). The vector w_2 consists of $u_{p+1}, u_{p+2}, \ldots, u_n$.

The approximate likelihood function (67) is applicable to the general ARMA (p, q) model for $p \geq q$. One simply sets $B_{q+1} = 0, \ldots, B_p = 0$. For $p < q$ we follow the decomposition of the model as in (66), where $\tilde{y}_1$ consists of $y_1, \ldots, y_q$, with the understanding that $A_{p+1}, \ldots, A_q$ in the matrix are set equal to zero. Now w_1 is further decomposed into w_{1p} and w_{1*}, and we form a likelihood function based on (w_{1*}, w_2). It is a likelihood function for a moving-average q-order process with $n - p$ observations.

A further approximation to the likelihood function is obtained by setting $\hat{\epsilon}_1 = 0$ in (67) and ignoring the factor $|\Sigma|^{-p/2} |A_{n-p, p}|^{-1/2}$, yielding

$$L_0 \propto |\Sigma|^{-(n-p)/2} \exp \left(- \tfrac{1}{2} w_2' D_B^{-1'} \Sigma_{n-p}^{-1} D_B^{-1} w_2 \right) \qquad (69)$$

as proposed by Wilson (1973).

Another approximation to maximum likelihood is the method of minimum distance, suggested by Malinvaud (1970). This method minimizes the sum

$$\sum_{t=p+1}^{n} e_t' S^{-1} e_t \qquad (70)$$

where $\qquad e_t = y_t - A_1 y_{t-1} - \cdots - A_p y_{t-p} - B_1 e_{t-1} - \cdots - B_q e_{t-q} \qquad (71)$

with initial conditions $e_p = e_{p-1} = \cdots - e_{p+1-q} = 0$ and

$$S = (n - p)^{-1} \sum_{t=p+1}^{n} e_t^0 e_t^{0'} \qquad (72)$$

e_t^0 being some initial value of e_t. The iterations proceed as follows. To begin, we let S be the identity matrix and minimize (70) with respect to the unknown parameters $A_1, \ldots, A_p, B_1, \ldots, B_q$. Having done this, we use (71) to compute e_t as the e_t^0 to be used in (72) for computing S. Given S, we minimize (70) again with respect to $A_1, \ldots, A_p, B_1, \ldots, B_q$. The process continues. This method ignores the estimation of $\epsilon_p, \epsilon_{p-1}, \ldots, \epsilon_{p+q-1}$ by setting them equal to zero. A discussion of the method of minimum distance as applied to the estimation of a system of nonlinear regression equations appears in Sec. 7.2

6.8 BOX–JENKINS TECHNIQUES

One of the most influential books in statistics appearing in the 1970s was Box and Jenkins (1970). They advocate the use of simple ARMA models and related models to analyze time-series data, summarize certain useful techniques to help specify (in their terminology, identify) the orders of a model and to estimate its parameters, and suggest certain ways of checking the appropriateness of the model for final adoption. They consider model building as an iterative process which can be divided into three stages: identification, estimation, and diagnostic checking.

At the stage of identification, the autogressive order p and the moving-average order q in a univariate ARMA model will be chosen. Box and Jenkins deal with a more general model called an *autoregressive integrated moving-average process* (ARIMA). If the original series is x_t, appropriate differencing yields a series

$$y_t = (1 - L)^d x_t \qquad (73)$$

where L is the lag operator, $Lx_t = x_{t-1}$. For $d = 1$, $y_t = x_t - x_{t-1} = \Delta x_t$. For $d = 2$, $y_t = \Delta x_t - \Delta x_{t-1}$. The differencing operations are used to produce a covariance-stationary time series y_t. If x_t contains a polynomial trend of order d, then the trend can be removed by the differencing operation $(1 - L)^d$. If y_t satisfies an ARMA (p, q) process

$$a(L)y_t = b(L)\epsilon_t \qquad (74)$$

where $a(L)$ and $b(L)$ are polynomials in the lag operator L, then the original series x_t satisfies an ARIMA (p, d, q) process

$$a(L)(1 - L)^d x_t = b(L)\epsilon_t \qquad (75)$$

Besides p and q, the order d for the differencing operations must be determined in the identification stage. Seasonal series are analyzed by using additional seasonal differencing, the operation being $(1 - L^s)^D$. For monthly series, $s = 12$ and $(1 - L^s)x_t = x_t - x_{t-12}$ is an example of seasonal differencing with $D = 1$. We shall not comment on seasonal differencing further; the interested reader should see Box and Jenkins (1976).

If a series x_t shows strong trends, differencing once or twice will often produce a series y_t which is approximately covariance-stationary. To determine the autoregressive order p and the moving-average order q, the sample auto-correlation function and the sample partial autocorrelation function are used. As pointed out at the end of Sec. 6.3, the characteristics of these two functions can reveal the orders of an ARMA (p, q) process. A model is then tentatively selected for estimation.

In the estimation stage, point estimates of the coefficients can be obtained by the method of maximum likehood or approximations thereof. Associated standard errors will also be provided, suggesting which coefficients could be dropped.

In the stage of diagnostic checking, additional autoregressive and moving-average variables can be added to the model and their statistical significance can be examined. One useful tool for this purpose, not suggested by Box and Jenkins, is to use the information criterion (Secs. 9.6, 9.9, and 9.10), which can help decide whether additional variables should be included in the model. One should also examine the residuals and see whether they appear to be random. The auto-correlation and partial autocorrelation functions of the residuals can reveal whether they can be explained by an ARMA process. If they are well fitted by an autoregressive process, one should increase the order p of the original ARMA process. If they are well fitted by a moving-average process, one should increase the order q of the original ARMA process. After the model has been respecified, it will be reestimated and diagnostic checks will be applied again until the coefficients are reasonably significant and the residuals are approximately random.

For an extension of the Box-Jenkins identification techniques to multivariate time series, see Granger and Newbold (1977) and Tiao and Box (1981). For other approaches to determination of the orders of a time-series model, see Ozaki (1977), who uses the information criterion, and Hannan and Quinn (1979).

★6.9 DEFINITION AND TESTS OF CAUSALITY

A favorite saying in regression analysis is that regression can measure the degrees of association between variables but cannot confirm causation. Causation is an important concept in economics and in science in general. Causal relations are often difficult to define, and different definitions have been offered. Once a certain definition has been accepted, there is the difficult problem of identifying a causal relation in empirical work. One useful definition of causation in econometrics has been suggested by Granger (1969). The Granger definition exploits time-series relationships to identify causality. By this definition, X *causes* Y, given an information set A_t which includes at least (X_t, Y_t), *if* Y_t *can be predicted better by using past* X_t *than by not using it.*

Let $\bar{A}_t = \{A_s | s \leq t - 1\}$ denote the information set which includes A_s for all past s up to and including $t - 1$. The following three definitions can be introduced:

1. X causes Y if $\sigma^2(Y_t | \bar{A}_t) < \sigma^2(Y_t | \bar{A}_t - X_t)$, where $\sigma^2(Y_t | \bar{A}_t)$ is the variance of Y_t about the best predictor by $\bar{A}_t$.
2. X causes Y instantaneously if $\sigma^2(Y_t | \bar{A}_t, X_t) < \sigma^2(Y_t | \bar{A}_t)$.
3. Feedback exists between X and Y if X causes Y and Y causes X.

In order to define causality in a bivariate time-series model involving X_t and Y_t we make two simplifying assumptions. First, the set A_t includes X_t and Y_t only, and not a third variable. Second, there exist transformations T_x and T_y such that

$x_t = T_x X_t$ and $y_t = T_y Y_t$ are a pair of linear, covariance-stationary time series not including any deterministic components, and that x_t and y_t preserve the causality relationship of X_t and Y_t. Examples of such transormations are ordinary or seasonal differencing, log transform, and the Box–Cox transform $(X_t^\lambda - 1)\lambda^{-1}$. As discussed in the survey paper of Pierce and Haugh (1977), causality can be defined by using any of the following representations of the time-series model for x_t and y_t.

Representation 1 Consider the autoregressive representation

$$\Pi(L)\begin{bmatrix} x_t \\ y_t \end{bmatrix} = \begin{bmatrix} \pi_{11}(L) & \pi_{12}(L) \\ \pi_{21}(L) & \pi_{22}(L) \end{bmatrix}\begin{bmatrix} x_t \\ y_t \end{bmatrix} = \begin{bmatrix} a_t \\ b_t \end{bmatrix} \tag{76}$$

where the elements $\pi_{ij}(L)$ of the 2×2 matrix $\Pi(L)$ are (possibly infinite) polynomials in the lag operator L and $[a_t \quad b_t]$ is a serially independent random vector with mean zero and covariance matrix Σ. Since the model (76) is unaffected when both sides are premultiplied by a nonsingular transformation, we have the option of reparameterizing it to make Σ diagonal. By Granger's definition, if y_t does not cause x_t, $\pi_{12}(L) = 0$, which implies $\pi_{11}(L)x_t = a_t$. Thus *lagged y's cannot add to the predictive accuracy of x_t, given past x_t*, as we have stated before.

Representation 2 The moving-average representation of the model (76) is

$$\begin{bmatrix} x_t \\ y_t \end{bmatrix} = [\Pi(L)]^{-1}\begin{bmatrix} a_t \\ b_t \end{bmatrix} = \begin{bmatrix} \psi_{11}(L) & \psi_{12}(L) \\ \psi_{21}(L) & \psi_{22}(L) \end{bmatrix}\begin{bmatrix} a_t \\ b_t \end{bmatrix} \tag{77}$$

$\pi_{12}(L) = 0$ is equivalent to $\psi_{12}(L) = 0$. If $\psi_{12}(L) = 0$, we have from (77)

$$x_t = \psi_{11}(L)a_t$$

or

$$\psi_{11}^{-1}(L)x_t = a_t \tag{78}$$

Identifying $\psi_{11}^{-1}(L)$ with $\pi_{11}(L)$, we note that lagged y's cannot add to the predictive accuracy of x_t, given past x_t. If $\pi_{12}(L) = 0$, we have $\pi_{11}(L)x_t = a_t$, which implies $x_t = \pi_{11}^{-1}(L)a_t$ and hence x_t is not a function of b_t or $\psi_{12}(L) = 0$. Using (77) and (78), we can write

$$y_t = \psi_{21}(L)a_t + \psi_{22}(L)b_t = \psi_{21}(L)\psi_{11}^{-1}(L)x_t + \psi_{22}(L)b_t \equiv V(L)x_t + f_t \tag{79}$$

By Granger's definition, if y_t does not cause x_t, $\psi_{12}(L) = 0$. It implies (79), which in turn implies that the residuals f_t in the regression of y_t on all current and past x_t are uncorrelated with future x_t or that *future x_t has no effect on y_t, given current and past x_t*.

Representation 3 We consider the representation of (76) by two univariate processes for x_t and y_t. Evaluating $[\Pi(L)]^{-1}$ by

$$[\Pi(L)]^{-1} = |\Pi(L)|^{-1}\begin{bmatrix} \pi_{22}(L) & -\pi_{12}(L) \\ -\pi_{21}(L) & \pi_{11}(L) \end{bmatrix} \tag{80}$$

where $|\Pi(L)|$ is the determinant of $\Pi(L)$, we can write (77) as

$$|\Pi(L)|\,x_t = \pi_{22}(L)a_t - \pi_{12}(L)b_t$$

$$|\Pi(L)|\,y_t = -\pi_{21}(L)a_t + \pi_{11}(L)b_t \tag{81}$$

If we define the following equivalent model which consists of two univariate models

$$\begin{bmatrix} F(L) & 0 \\ 0 & G(L) \end{bmatrix}\begin{bmatrix} x_t \\ y_t \end{bmatrix} = \begin{bmatrix} u_t \\ v_t \end{bmatrix} \tag{82}$$

its residuals u_t and v_t must be related to the original residuals a_t and b_t by

$$\begin{bmatrix} a_t \\ b_t \end{bmatrix} = \begin{bmatrix} \pi_{11}(L) & \pi_{12}(L) \\ \pi_{21}(L) & \pi_{22}(L) \end{bmatrix}\begin{bmatrix} x_t \\ y_t \end{bmatrix} = \begin{bmatrix} \pi_{11}(L) & \pi_{12}(L) \\ \pi_{21}(L) & \pi_{22}(L) \end{bmatrix}\begin{bmatrix} F(L) & 0 \\ 0 & G(L) \end{bmatrix}^{-1}\begin{bmatrix} u_t \\ v_t \end{bmatrix}$$

$$\equiv \begin{bmatrix} \alpha(L) & \beta(L) \\ \gamma(L) & \delta(L) \end{bmatrix}\begin{bmatrix} u_t \\ v_t \end{bmatrix} \tag{83}$$

where $\alpha(L)$, $\beta(L)$, $\gamma(L)$, and $\delta(L)$ are defined by the line above. Analysis of (83) will reveal causality patterns concerning x_t and y_t because u_t and v_t according to (82) are respectively the components of x_t and y_t that cannot be predicted their own past histories.

To see the usefulness of the time series u_t and v_t in detecting causality consider the case where x_t causes y_t but not vice versa. In this case, we have the regression model (79). When (79) is substituted for y_t in the second of Eqs. (82), we have, using also the first of Eqs. (82),

$$v_t = G(L)y_t = G(L)V(L)x_t + G(L)f_t$$

$$= G(L)V(L)F(L)^{-1}u_t + G(L)f_t \equiv v(L)u_t + f_t^* \tag{84}$$

Thus, in the time-series model (84) relating v_t and u_t, the polynomial $v(L)$ is one-sided if and only if the polynomial $V(L)$ in (79) is. Therefore, causality can be detected by examining the coefficients in the regression of v_t on past, current, and future u_t in the same way that it can be detected by regressing y_t on past, current, and future x_t. Similarly, when y_t causes x_t but not vice versa, we have the regression model analogous to (79)

$$x_t = W(L)y_t + g_t \tag{85}$$

which together with (82), implies

$$u_t = F(L)x_t = F(L)W(L)y_t + F(L)g_t$$

$$= F(L)W(L)G(L)^{-1}v_t + F(L)g_t \equiv \omega(L)v_t + g_t^* \tag{86}$$

Causality can be detected by regressing x_t on past, current, and future y_t using (85), as well as by regressing u_t on v_s using (86).

Define $\rho_{uv}(k)$ as the correlation coefficient between u_{t-k} and v_t. Let the polynomial $v(L)$ in (84) be $\sum_k v_k L^k$ and similarly $\omega(L) = \sum_k \omega_k L^k$ in (86). Because the explanatory variables u_{t-k} in (84) are serially uncorrelated, the regression coefficients v_k equal the covariances between v_t and u_{t-k} divided by the variance of u_t

$$v_k = \frac{\text{Cov}(u_{t-k}, v_t)}{\sigma_u^2} = \frac{\rho_{uv}(k)\sigma_v}{\sigma_u} \tag{87}$$

Similarly, the regression coefficients ω_k in (86) are given by

$$\omega_k = \frac{\text{Cov}(v_{t-k}, u_t)}{\sigma_v^2} = \frac{\rho_{uv}(-k)\sigma_u}{\sigma_v} \tag{88}$$

Therefore the cross-correlation function $\rho_{uv}(k)$ completely characterizes the causality relations between x_t and y_t in both directions.

Pierce and Haugh (1977) have used the different representations above to indicate that causality relations can be characterized in many equivalent ways. For example, by their theorem 4.1, *instantaneous causality* exists if and only if the following equivalent conditions hold:

$\rho_{uv}(0) \neq 0.$
$v_0 \neq 0.$
$\omega_0 \neq 0.$
Σ and the 2×2 matrix consisting of the coefficients α_0, β_0, γ_0, and δ_0 of $L^0 = 1$
   in the polynomials $\alpha(L)$, $\beta(L)$, $\gamma(L)$, and $\delta(L)$ in (83) cannot both be diagonal.
At least one of $\pi_{12,0}$, $\pi_{21,0}$, and σ_{12} is nonzero.

By their theorem 4.2, y_t *does not cause* x_t if and only if

$\psi_{12}(L)$ can be chosen to be zero.
In a regression of y_t on all past, current, and future x_t, the coefficients of future x_t
   are zero.
$\beta(L)$ is zero or a constant.
$\pi_{12}(L)$ is zero if Σ is normalized to be diagonal.
$\rho_{uv}(k) = 0$ for $k < 0$, where $\rho_{uv}(k) = \text{Corr}(u_{t-k}, v_t)$.

By their theorem 4.3, y_t *does not cause* x_t *at all* (instantaneous causality being ruled out) given diagonal Σ if and only if

$\psi_{12}(L) = 0$, $\psi_{21,0} = 0.$
$\rho_{uv}(k) = 0$ for $k \leq 0.$
In a regression of y_t on all past, current, and future x_t the coefficients of current
   and future x_t are zero.
$\beta(L) = 0$, $\gamma_0 = 0.$
$\pi_{12}(L) = 0$, $\pi_{21,0} = 0.$
The conditions of theorem 4.2 are met and those of theorem 4.1 are not.

After reviewing the different representations of the time-series model for x_t

and y_t above, the reader will be able to prove most of the assertions in the three theorems cited as exercises and will consider the remaining assertions at least reasonable. These theorems are presented to familiarize the reader with the different time-series representations and to indicate that, because of the existence of so many equivalent definitions, the empirical testing of a given causality relation is difficult. With this background, we present several statistical tests.

Autoregressive Using the autoregressive representation (76), one can test the assertion that y_t does not cause x_t by testing its implication $\pi_{12}(L) = 0$ or $\pi_{11}(L)x_t = a_t$. Hence, one can regress x_t on its own past and on past y_t and test whether y_t causes x_t by testing whether the coefficients of the lagged y's are zero. The test is based on Granger (1969). Equivalently, one can compare $\hat{\sigma}_a^2$ and $\hat{\sigma}_u^2$. These two variances are equal if $\pi_{12}(L) = 0$; otherwise $\hat{\sigma}_a^2$ will be smaller than $\hat{\sigma}_u^2$.

Univariate Using the univariate representation (82), one first constructs the series u_t and v_t as residuals in the univariate time-series models of x_t and y_t, respectively. Box–Jenkins techniques can be used to fit the time-series models of x_t and y_t and thus to construct u_t and v_t. Let

$$u_t = -\sum_{j>0} \alpha_j u_{t-j} - \sum_{j>0} \beta_j v_{t-j} + a_t$$

$$(89)$$

and
$$v_t = -\sum_{j>0} \delta_j v_{t-j} - \sum_{j>0} \gamma_j u_{t-j} + b_t$$

To test whether there is causality from y to x (or from v to u) one writes the first of Eqs. (89) as

$$u_t = \alpha^{-1}(L)\beta(L)v_t + \alpha^{-1}(L)a_t \equiv \tilde{\omega}(L)v_t + \tilde{g}_t \qquad (90)$$

where $\tilde{\omega}(L)$ is one-sided, having coefficients $\tilde{\omega}_j$ ($j \geq 0$). The coefficients $\tilde{\omega}_j$ will be estimated. One then tests whether they are significantly different from zero. This test was used by Granger (1973).

As we have pointed out in (88), ω_k is a monotone function of $\rho_{uv}(-k)$. Hence we can equivalently test the null hypothesis that all $\rho_{uv}(k)$ are zero by using the sample analog

$$r_{uv}(k) = \text{Corr}\,(u_{t-k}, v_t)$$

Under the null hypothesis that x and y are not causally related, $r_{uv}(k)$ are asymptotically independently and normally distributed with mean zero and standard deviation $n^{-1/2}$, as Haugh (1976) has shown. Using m correlations $r_{uv}(k_i) \equiv r(k_i)$ ($i = 1, \ldots, m$), one can employ the statistic

$$n \sum_{i=1}^{m} r^2(k_i)$$

which will be asymptotically distributed as $\chi^2(m)$ under the null hypothesis. A limitation of this approach is that if some $r(k)$ are excluded from the sum, it can hardly detect those nonzero $\rho(k)$ which correspond to these $r(k)$.

Moving average Using the moving-average representation (77), which implies (79), one can find out whether y causes x by regressing y_t on past, current, and future x_t and testing the significance of the coefficients of future x_t. This is the test of Sims (1972). Before testing, Sims used the transformation $P(L) = (1 - .75L)^2$ to transform x_t and y_t to $x_t^* = P(L)x_t$ and $y_t^* = P(L)y_t$, respectively. The purpose of using these transformed variables is to get rid of the serial correlations in the residual f_t of (79). Sims (1972) regressed GNP on current and eight past money stock M1 as well as four future M1. The $F(4, 60)$ statistic for testing the null hypothesis that the four coefficients of future M1 are zero is .36, leading to accepting the null hypothesis or the conclusion that GNP does not cause the money stock. When M1 was regressed on current and eight past GNP as well as four future GNP, the $F(4, 60)$ statistic for testing the null hypothesis that the four coefficients of future GNP are zero is 4.29. The null hypothesis was rejected, i.e., one rejects the conclusion that M1 does not cause GNP. The monetarists were pleased with this conclusion.

The reader should note that the statistical tests of causality are subject to many pitfalls, as partly revealed by a study of Pierce (1977) on the relationships, and the lack thereof, between economic time series, with special reference to money and interest rates. The difficulties in interpreting the results of tests of causality can come from at least three sources:

1. In studying the causal relations between two series using a bivariate time-series model, one has ignored the possible influences of other time series. The information set A_t used to define Granger causality is restricted to information concerning the two series X_t and Y_t of interest and omits all information about other related time series.
2. The processes of differencing, detrending, and Box–Jenkins "prewhitening" (to get u_t and v_t in place of x_t and y_t) may sometimes distort the causal relationships between the original series.
3. The sampling distributions of various statistics used are often ascertained by asymptotic theory. The asymptotic distributions may not be accurate enough in small samples in the context of time-series analysis.

Some of these problems are still being investigated.

PROBLEMS

1. Plot the mean function $\bar{y}_t$ of the time series $y_t = .9y_{t-1} + 1 + \epsilon_t$, given that the variance of ϵ_t is $\frac{1}{2}$ and given $y_0 = 10$. What is the stationary value for the mean? When will this stationary value be a good approximation to the mean?

2. Plot the stationary autocorrelation function for the time series $y_t = ay_{t-1} + \epsilon_t$, given that the variance of ϵ_t is 1, for $a = .8$, $a = .2$, $a = 0$, $a = -.2$, and $a = -.8$. Comment on the differences.

3. Let y_t satisfy the second-order stochastic difference equation

$$y_t = .9y_{t-1} - .8y_{t-2} + \epsilon_t$$

where ϵ has mean 0, variance 1, and is uncorrelated with ϵ_s for $t \neq s$. Find the autocorrelation function of y, in the steady state. Plot this function for $k = 0, \pm 1, \pm 2, \ldots$ and other selected values.

4. Express the autocorrelation function of the time series in Prob. 3 in terms of the characteristic roots and as a modified cosine function of the lag k.

5. What is your estimate of the approximate length of cycles for the time series specified in Prob. 3 using the angle of the pair of complex roots?

6. Compare the behavior of the time series

$$y_t = .99y_{t-1} - .99y_{t-2} + \epsilon_t$$

with the time series specified in Prob. 3 in terms of (a) the autocorrelation function and (b) the length of cycles in terms of the angle of the roots.

7. Construct a time series which will have longer cycles than that of Prob. 3. Check your answer.

8. Find the autocovariance matrix of the system

$$\begin{bmatrix} y_{1t} \\ y_{2t} \end{bmatrix} = \begin{bmatrix} 1 & -1.62 \\ 1 & -.80 \end{bmatrix} \begin{bmatrix} y_{1,t-1} \\ y_{2,t-1} \end{bmatrix} + \begin{bmatrix} \epsilon_{1t} \\ \epsilon_{2t} \end{bmatrix}$$

where the covariance matrix of ϵ_{1t} and ϵ_{2t} is assumed to be the identity matrix.

9. Show that the coefficients $b_{11} b^1 \bar{y}_0$ and $b_{12} b^2 \bar{y}_0$ of (17) are complex conjugate if λ_1 and λ_2 are complex conjugate. Observe that b_{11} and b_{12} are complex conjugate because the first two columns of B corresponding to a pair of complex roots λ_1 and λ_2 are complex conjugate. Why? Observe also that the rows b^1 and b^2 are complex conjugate because they are the left characteristic vectors of A corresponding to a pair of complex conjugate roots. Why? The products of two pairs of complex conjugate numbers are complex conjugate.

10. Provide a numerical example of a second-order (univariate) autoregressive process of which the spectral-density function has a peak at $\hat{\omega}$ between 0 and π. Use a process with a pair of complex roots $re^{i\theta}$ and $re^{-i\theta}$. Compare $\hat{\omega}$ with θ.

11. Plot the spectral densities of the time series $y_t = ay_{t-1} + \epsilon_t$, for $a = .8, .2, .0, -.2$, and $-.8$.

12. Find and plot the spectral densities of the time series

$$y_t = .9y_{t-1} - .8y_{t-2} + \epsilon_t$$

13. Consider y_t and y_{t-1} as two separate time series that satisfy a first-order system of stochastic difference equations obtained by transforming the equation $y_t = .9y_{t-1} - .8y_{t-2} + \epsilon_t$ into first order. Plot the cross-spectral-density function for these two time series. Comment on your answer.

14. Find and plot the spectral-density function of y_{2t} as defined by Prob. 8.

15. Calculate two values at $\omega = 0$ and $\omega = \pi/2$ for the phase-difference spectral-density function and the cross-amplitude spectral-density function of the two time series defined by Prob. 8.

16. Prove Eq. (33). *Hint:* You may write

$$\cos \omega_j t = \tfrac{1}{2}(e^{i\omega_j t} + e^{-i\omega_j t}) \qquad \sin \omega_j t = -\frac{i}{2}(e^{i\omega_j t} - e^{-i\omega_j t})$$

Use (32). Once it is shown that either sum is equal to $N/2$, the other sum can be evaluated by using $\sin^2 \omega_j t + \cos^2 \omega_j t = 1$.

17. Prove (34). *Hint:* See the hint in Prob. 16.

18. Obtain a quarterly series of real GNP in recent years consisting of an even number N (≥ 40) of observations. Use a computer to decompose the series into cosine and sine functions as in (31). Plot the contribution of each periodic component to the sample variance of the series.

19. Fit the model $y_t = ay_{t-1} + \epsilon_t$ to the data obtained in Prob. 18 if you have done that problem.

20. Show that the covariance between y_{1t} and $y_{2,t-k}$ defined by (38) and (40) equals

$$\sum_j E[\alpha_1(\omega_j)\alpha_2(\omega_j)] \cos \omega_j k + \sum_j E[\beta_1(\omega_j)\alpha_2(\omega_j)] \sin \omega_j k$$

21. Find an economic time series of your choice and fit an ARMA model using the methodology of Box-Jenkins.

22. Write a critical essay to discuss the main issues concerning tests of causality based on Pierce (1977) and the Comments on that paper in the *Journal of the American Statistical Association*, March 1977.

REFERENCES

Anderson, T. W. (1971): *The Statistical Analysis of Time-Series*, Wiley, New York.

Bloomfield, P. (1978): *Fourier Analysis of Time Series: An Introduction*, Wiley, New York.

Box, G., and J. M. Jenkins (1970, 1976): *Time-Series Analysis: Forecasting and Control*, Holden-Day, San Francisco.

Chow, G. C. (1975): *Analysis and Control of Dynamic Economic Systems*, Wiley, New York.

—— (1981): *Econometric Analysis by Control Methods*, Wiley, New York.

Granger, C. W. J. (1966): "The Typical Spectral Shape of an Economic Variable," *Econometrica*, **34**, 150–161.

—— (1969): "Investigating Causal Relations by Econometric Models and Cross-Spectral Methods," *Econometrica*, **37**: 428–438.

—— (1973): "Causality, Model Building and Control: Some Comments," *Nottingham Univ. Math. Dep., Nottingham Forecasting Proj., Note 13.*

—— and P. Newbold (1977): *Forecasting Economic Time Series*, Academic, New York.

Hannan, E. J. (1970): *Multiple Time Series*, Wiley, New York.

—— and B. G. Quinn (1979): "The Determination of the Order of an AutoRegression," *J. Royal Statist. Soc.*, **B41**: 190–195.

Haugh, L. D. (1976): "Checking the Independence of Two Covariance-Stationary Time Series: A Univariate Residual Cross-Correlation Approach," *J. Am. Statist. Assoc.*, **71**: 378–385.

Hillmer, S. C., and G. C. Tiao (1979): "Likelihood Function of Stationary Multiple Autoregressive Moving Average Models," *J. Am. Statist. Assoc.*, **74**: 652–660.

Klein, L. R. (1950): *Economic Fluctuations in the United States, 1921–1941,* Wiley, New York.

Koopmans, T. C. (ed.) (1950): *Statistical Inference in Dynamic Economic Models*, Wiley, New York.

Malinvaud, E. (1970): *Statistical Methods of Econometrics*, North-Holland, Amsterdam.

Nerlove, M. (1964): "Spectral Analysis of Seasonal Adjustment Procedures," *Econometrica*, **32**, 241–286.

Ozaki, T. (1977): "On the Order Determination of ARIMA Models," *Appl. Statist.*, **26**: 290–301.

Pierce, D. A. (1977): "Relationships—and the Lack Thereof—Between Economic Time Series, with Special Reference to Money and Interest Rates," *J. Am. Statist. Assoc.*, **72**: 11–21.

—— and L. D. Haugh (1977): "Causality in Temporal Systems: Characterizations and a Survey," *J. Econometr.*, **5**: 265–294.

Sims, C. A. (1972): "Money, Income, and Causality," *Am. Econ. Rev.*, **62**: 540–552.

Tiao, G. C., and G. E. P. Box (1981): "Modeling Multiple Time Series with Applications," *J. Am. Statist. Assoc.*, **76**: 802–816.

Wilson, G. T. (1973): "The Estimation of Parameters in Multivariate Time-Series Models," *J. R. Statist. Soc.*, **B35**: 76–85.

SEVEN

NONLINEAR MODELS

7.1 INTRODUCTION

A linear regression model specifies

$$y_t = \beta_1 x_{t1} + \cdots + \beta_k x_{tk} + \epsilon_t$$

The regression function is linear in both the variables x_{tj} and the coefficients β_j. If the second explanatory variable x_{t2} happens to be x_{t1}^2 or $\log x_{t1}$ and the explanatory variables are treated as fixed, the least-squares estimation of β_j proceeds as usual and nothing is affected. Therefore, for the purpose of estimating the unknown parameters β_j and $\sigma^2 = E\epsilon_t^2$, a nonlinear regression model refers to a model having a regression function which is nonlinear in the unknown coefficient vector β. If the regression function is linear in β, the normal equation for the least-squares estimate b

$$(X'X)b = X'y$$

is linear and least-squares theory applies, although the elements x_{tj} of X may be nonlinear functions of some explanatory variables. A favorite example in econometrics is to define y and some x's as logarithms of the relevant economic variables.

A nonlinear regression is exemplified by

$$y_t = \beta_1 e^{\beta_2 x_t} + \epsilon_t \tag{1}$$

If ϵ_t were multiplicative rather than additive, one could obtain a linear model by taking logarithms of (1). Applying the method of least squares (or equivalently maximum likelihood if the ϵ_t are normal), we minimize

$$\frac{1}{2}\sum_t (y_t - \beta_1 e^{\beta_2 x_t})^2$$

and obtain the following normal equations for β_1 and β_2:

$$\sum_t (y_t - \beta_1 e^{\beta_2 x_t})e^{\beta_2 x_t} = \sum_t y_t e^{\beta_2 x_t} - \beta_1 \sum_t e^{2\beta_2 x_t} = 0 \tag{2}$$

$$\sum_t (y_t - \beta_1 e^{\beta_2 x_t})e^{\beta_2 x_t}x_t = \sum_t y_t x_t e^{\beta_2 x_t} - \beta_1 \sum_t x_t e^{2\beta_2 x_t} = 0 \tag{3}$$

These are nonlinear equations in β_1 and β_2. In this example, the regression function $\beta_1 e^{\beta_2 x}$ is nonlinear in the parameters β_1 and β_2. As a result the normal equations for estimating β_1 and β_2 are also nonlinear functions. We shall present methods for solving such nonlinear equations and study the distribution of the resulting estimators.

In econometrics three kinds of nonlinear models have been found useful, among others. The first is a univariate nonlinear regression model with an additive disturbance

$$y_t = g(x_t, \theta) + \epsilon_t \qquad t = 1, \ldots, n \tag{4}$$

where x_t is a K-component vector denoting the tth observation on K explanatory variables, θ is a k-component vector of parameters, g is a nonlinear function, and the residual ϵ_t is independent and identically distributed with mean zero and variance σ^2. Equation (1) provides an example. The second is a G-variate nonlinear regression model with additive disturbances. The ith regression equation is

$$y_{ti} = g_i(x_t, \theta) + \epsilon_{ti} \qquad \begin{matrix} t = 1, \ldots, n \\ i = 1, \ldots, G \end{matrix} \tag{5}$$

There are G of these regression equations explaining G dependent variables y_{t1}, $\ldots, y_{tG}$. The ith regression function g_i may not include all explanatory variables in x_t and all parameters in θ as arguments, but there is no loss in allowing all elements of x_t and of θ to be included. If we let $y_{t.}$ denote the vector of G dependent variables and g denote the vector of G regression functions, we can write (5) as

$$y_{t.} = g(x_{t.}, \theta) + \epsilon_{t.} \tag{6}$$

The vector x_t in (5) is now written as $x_{t.}$ for consistency in notation with $y_{t.}$. The residual vector $\epsilon_{t.}$ is assumed to be independent and identically distributed, having mean zero and covariance matrix Ω. The third model is a system of nonlinear simultaneous equations with additive disturbances. The ith structural equation is

$$\phi_i(y_{t.}, x_{t.}; \theta_i) = \epsilon_{ti} \qquad i = 1, \ldots, G \tag{7}$$

In econometric practice it often happens that in equation i the ith endogenous variable y_{ti} is an explicit function of other endogenous variables in $y_{t.}$ and predetermined variables $x_{t.}$; θ_i is a vector of parameters in equation i. Denoting by ϕ the vector of G functions $\phi_1, \ldots, \phi_G$, we can write model (7) as

$$\phi(y_{t.}, x_{t.}, \theta) = \epsilon_{t.} \tag{8}$$

The residual vector $\epsilon_{t.}$ is assumed to be independently and identically distributed, having mean zero and covariance matrix Σ. Equation (4) is a generalization of the multiple linear regression model to the nonlinear case. Equation (5) is a generalization of a system of linear regression equations. Equation (7) is a generalization of a system of linear simultaneous equations.

In this chapter we first present a general treatment of the estimation of nonlinear models by two methods. One is an extension of the method of generalized least squares, to be presented in Secs. 7.2 and 7.3. Section 7.2 presents the method of GLS or minimum distance of Malinvaud (1970a) for estimating model (5). Section 7.3 gives a closer approximation to the distribution of the least-squares estimator for the nonlinear regression model using the results of Gallant (1973). The second method is maximum likelihood, presented in Sec. 7.4. Computation methods will be treated in Sec. 7.5. Section 7.6 is concerned with the estimation of nonlinear simultaneous equations by the method of FIML, and Sec. 7.7 deals with the method of instrumental variables for estimating nonlinear simultaneous equations, while Sec. 7.8 presents the methods of nonlinear 2SLS and 3SLS. Section 7.9 deals with models of markets in disequilibrium. Finally, Sec. 7.10 studies certain aspects of dynamic properties of nonlinear simultaneous equations including the computation of various multipliers.

7.2 METHOD OF GLS OR MINIMUM DISTANCE

Following our treatment of the linear regression model in Chaps. 1 and 2, we present the method of least squares before presenting the method of maximum likelihood. The former does not specify that the residuals be normal, and it is of interest to study the sampling distribution of the least-squares estimator without the normality assumption.

To extend the method of GLS to model (5) or (6) let us imagine what we would do if the regression functions g_i were linear and (5) became a system of linear regression equations. We would apply the method of GLS, as discussed in Sec. 3.1, after stacking up the G equations for $y_1, \ldots, y_G$, where y_i denotes a column vector of the n observations $y_{1i}, \ldots, y_{ni}$; see Eq. (19) of Chap. 3. To apply GLS to estimate a linear regression model

$$y = X\beta + \epsilon$$

is to minimize

$$(y - X\beta)'V^{-1}(y - X\beta) \equiv \epsilon'V^{-1}\epsilon$$

with respect to β, where V is (proportional to) the covariance matrix of ϵ. If y is composed of $y_1, \ldots, y_G$, as in the model of a system of G linear regression equations, the matrix V is given by Eq. (20) of Chap. 3, namely, $V = \Omega \otimes I_n$, where $\Omega = \text{Cov } \epsilon_t$. Applying the rule $(A \otimes B)^{-1} = A^{-1} \otimes B^{-1}$, we have

$$V^{-1} = \Omega^{-1} \otimes I = \begin{bmatrix} \omega^{11}I & \omega^{12}I & \cdots & \omega^{1G}I \\ \cdots\cdots\cdots\cdots\cdots\cdots\cdots\cdots \\ \omega^{G1}I & \omega^{G2}I & \cdots & \omega^{GG}I \end{bmatrix}$$

where ω^{ij} is the ijth element of Ω^{-1}. When this matrix for V^{-1} is used, the method of GLS amounts to minimizing

$$\epsilon'V^{-1}\epsilon = \sum_{i,j}^{G} \omega^{ij}\epsilon_i'\epsilon_j = \sum_{i,j}^{G} \omega^{ij} \sum_{t}^{n} \epsilon_{ti}\epsilon_{tj}$$

$$= \sum_{t}^{n} \sum_{i,j}^{G} \omega^{ij}\epsilon_{ti}\epsilon_{tj} = \sum_{t}^{n} \epsilon_{t.}'\Omega^{-1}\epsilon_{t.} \tag{9}$$

where $\epsilon_{t.} = y_{t.} - g(x_{t.}, \theta)$, according to model (6). Therefore, it is quite natural to extend the method of GLS to the system (6) of nonlinear regression equations by minimizing (9). The *method of minimum distance* of Malinvaud (1970a) for model (6) is to minimize

$$L_n(S_n, \theta) = \frac{1}{2n} \sum_{t=1}^{n} [y_{t.} - g(x_{t.}, \theta)]'S_n[y_{t.} - g(x_{t.}, \theta)] \tag{10}$$

for some positive-definite $G \times G$ matrix S_n. "Miminum distance" means exactly the same thing as "least squares." The sum of squares of the deviations $y - g(x)$ is the square of the distance from y to $g(x)$ (see Fig. 2.1).

The minimum-distance estimator is in fact an extension of GLS to nonlinear models. To study its sampling distribution it is convenient to define a linearized model based on (6). We first study the sampling distribution of a minimum-distance estimator for the linearized model. Later we shall show that the minimum-distance estimator for the original model (6) has the same asymptotic distribution. Much of this material can be found in Malinvaud (1970a, chap. 9), except for the proof of consistency in Theorem 7.1. Let us denote $g_i(x_t, \theta)$ by $g_{ti}(\theta)$ and linearize it about the true-parameter vector θ_0. The variables x_t are regarded as fixed

$$g_{ti}(\theta) \approx g_{ti}(\theta_0) + \frac{\partial g_{ti}(\theta_0)}{\partial\theta'} (\theta - \theta_0) = g_{ti}(\theta_0) + z_{ti}'(\theta - \theta_0)$$

where z_{ti}' denotes the row vector of the derivatives of g_{ti} with respect to the elements of θ', evaluated at θ_0. This linearization is carried out for all equations i ($i = 1, \ldots, G$). The vector function $g_{t.} = g(x_{t.}, \theta)$ is linearized as

$$g_{t.}(\theta) \approx g_{t.}(\theta_0) + \frac{\partial g_{t.}(\theta_0)}{\partial\theta'} (\theta - \theta_0) = g_{t.}(\theta_0) + Z_t(\theta - \theta_0)$$

where Z_t is a $G \times k$ matrix having z_{ti}' as its ith row. The linearized model derived from (6) is

$$y_{t.} = g_{t.}(\theta_0) + Z_t(\theta - \theta_0) + \epsilon_{t.} \tag{11}$$

Let the method of minimum distance be applied to the linearized model (11); i.e., let $\bar{\theta}(S_n)$ be that value of θ which minimizes

$$\frac{1}{2n} \sum_{t=1}^{n} [y_{t.} - g_{t.}(\theta_0) - Z_t(\theta - \theta_0)]' S_n [y_{t.} - g_{t.}(\theta_0) - Z_t(\theta - \theta_0)] \tag{12}$$

It is recognized that the estimator $\bar{\theta}$ cannot be calculated in practice since the derivatives in Z_t are functions of the unknown parameter θ_0. We are using $\bar{\theta}$ as a theoretical device in order to study the asymptotic distribution of the minimum-distance estimator $\hat{\theta}(S_n)$ for the original model (6). Differentiating (12) with respect to θ, we obtain

$$-n^{-1} \sum_{t=1}^{n} Z_t' S_n [y_{t.} - g_{t.}(\theta_0) - Z_t(\theta - \theta_0)] = 0 \tag{13}$$

implying

$$n^{-1} \sum_{t=1}^{n} Z_t' S_n Z_t (\bar{\theta} - \theta_0) - n^{-1} \sum_{t=1}^{n} Z_t' S_n [y_{t.} - g_{t.}(\theta_0)] = 0 \tag{14}$$

To study the asymptotic distribution of $\bar{\theta}$ we consider $\sqrt{n}(\bar{\theta} - \theta_0)$ as a solution of Eq. (14)

$$\sqrt{n}(\bar{\theta} - \theta_0) = \left(n^{-1} \sum_{t=1}^{n} Z_t' S_n Z_t \right)^{-1} n^{-1/2} \sum_{t=1}^{n} Z_t' S_n [y_{t.} - g_{t.}(\theta_0)] \tag{15}$$

We assume (i) that for any symmetric positive-definite matrix S of order k the matrix

$$M_n(S) = n^{-1} \sum_{t=1}^{n} Z_t' S Z_t$$

converges to a positive-definite matrix $M(S)$ as n approaches infinity and (ii) that the matrix S_n used to define the minimum-distance estimator converges in probability to a positive-definite matrix S. Under assumption (ii)

$$n^{-1} \sum_{t=1}^{n} Z_t' (S_n - S) Z_t$$

converges in probability to zero provided (iii) that the derivatives of $g_{t.}(\theta)$ in Z_t are bounded. In other words, $M_n(S_n)$ has the same probability limit as $M_n(S)$. Under assumption (i) this probability limit is $M(S)$.

The sum

$$n^{-1/2} \sum_{t=1}^{n} Z_t' S [y_{t.} - g_{t.}(\theta_0)] \tag{16}$$

of independent random vectors will have a normal limiting distribution by the central limit theorem. Since $y_{t.} - g_{t.}(\theta_0)$ has mean zero and covariance matrix Ω, this normal distribution will have mean zero and covariance matrix

$$n^{-1} \sum_{t=1}^{n} Z_t' S\Omega S Z_t$$

which approaches $M(S\Omega S)$ as the limit by assumption (i). By assumption (ii)

$$n^{-1/2} \sum_{t=1}^{n} Z_t'(S_n - S)[y_{t.} - g_{t.}(\theta_0)]$$

converges in probability to zero, or

$$n^{-1/2} \sum_{t=1}^{n} Z_t' S_n[y_{t.} - g_{t.}(\theta_0)]$$

will converge to the same limiting distribution as (16). Using this result and the result that $M_n(S_n)$ converges in probability to $M(S)$, we can use (15) to prove the following lemma.

Lemma 7.1 Under the assumption that (i) $M_n(S) = n^{-1} \sum_{t=1}^{n} Z_t' S Z_t$ converges to a positive-definite matrix $M(S)$, (ii) S_n converges in probability to a positive-definite matrix S, and (iii) the first derivatives of $g_{ti}(\theta)$ with respect to θ are bounded, $\sqrt{n}(\bar{\theta} - \theta_0)$, where $\bar{\theta}$ is the minimum-distance estimator $\bar{\theta}(S_n)$ for the linearized model (11), has a limiting normal distribution with mean zero and covariance matrix

$$[M(S)]^{-1} M(S\Omega S)[M(S)]^{-1}$$

We now apply the method of minimum distance to the original model (6) by minimizing (10). Differentiation of (10) yields

$$\frac{\partial L_n(S_n, \hat{\theta})}{\partial \theta} = -n^{-1} \sum_{t=1}^{n} \frac{\partial g_{t.}(\hat{\theta})'}{\partial \theta} S_n[y_{t.} - g_{t.}(\hat{\theta})] = 0 \tag{17}$$

The minimum-distance estimator $\hat{\theta}$ is obtained by solving the nonlinear equation (17). To study the consistency of $\hat{\theta}$, we examine the derivative of $L_n(S_n, \theta)$ evaluated at the true θ_0, recalling the definition of $Z_t = \partial g_{t.}(\theta_0)/\partial \theta'$,

$$\frac{\partial L_n(S_n, \theta_0)}{\partial \theta} = -n^{-1} \sum_{t=1}^{n} Z_t' S_n[y_{t.} - g_{t.}(\theta_0)] \tag{18}$$

In the paragraph preceding Lemma 7.1 we showed that $n^{1/2}$ times (18) has a limiting normal distribution with mean zero and covariance matrix $M(S\Omega S)$. This means that (18) itself will converge in probability to zero.

Now examine the matrix of second derivatives of $L_n(S_n, \theta)$ evaluated at θ_0

$$\frac{\partial^2 L_n(S_n, \theta_0)}{\partial\theta \, \partial\theta'} = n^{-1} \sum_{t=1}^{n} Z'_t S_n Z_t - n^{-1} \sum_{t=1}^{n} \left\{ \begin{array}{c} [y_t - g_t(\theta_0)]' S_n \dfrac{\partial^2 g_t(\theta_0)}{\partial\theta_1 \, \partial\theta'} \\ \vdots \\ [y_t - g_t(\theta_0)]' S_n \dfrac{\partial^2 g_t(\theta_0)}{\partial\theta_k \, \partial\theta'} \end{array} \right\} \tag{19}$$

In (19), $\partial^2 g_t(\theta_0)/(\partial\theta_1 \, \partial\theta')$ is a $G \times k$ matrix of the partial derivatives of the G elements of $\partial g_t(\theta)/\partial\theta_1$ with respect to the k elements of θ'. The matrix in braces is $k \times k$; we have displayed its first and kth rows. By assumptions (i) to (iii) of Lemma 7.1 we have shown that the first term on the right-hand side of (19) converges in probability to a positive-definite matrix $M(S)$. If we strengthen assumption (iii) to state that the first and second derivatives of $g_t(\theta) = g(x_t, \theta)$ are bounded, we observe that each row of the second term on the right-hand side of (19) is a sample mean of n independent row vectors which have mean zero, since $[y_t - g_t(\theta_0)]'$ has mean zero for all $t = 1, \ldots, n$. By the law of large numbers, the second term converges in probability to zero. Hence (19) converges in probability to a positive-definite matrix $M(S)$.

Having shown that the probability limit of (18) is zero and that the probability limit of (19) is a positive-definite matrix, we conclude that the probability limit of $L_n(S_n, \theta)$ reaches a minimum at $\theta = \theta_0$. In other words, for n sufficiently large and for a vector $\delta > 0$, we have

$$L_n(S_n, \theta_0) < L_n(S_n, \theta_0 \pm \delta)$$

with probability higher than $1 - \epsilon$, however small ϵ may be. With this high probability, $L_n(S_n, \theta)$ will be smaller at $\theta = \theta_0$ than at $\theta = \theta_0 \pm \delta$. Hence the function $L_n(S_n, \theta)$ will have a local minimum within $\theta_0 \pm \delta$. With this high probability, then, a minimum-distance estimator $\hat{\theta}$ which minimizes $L_n(S_n, \theta)$ locally by solving (17) will fall within $\theta_0 \pm \delta$. This means that a root $\hat{\theta}$ of (17) converges in probability to θ_0 or that $\hat{\theta}$ is a consistent estimator of θ. We record this result and derive the asymptotic distribution of $\hat{\theta}$ in the following theorem. Malinvaud (1970a, p. 331; 1970b) discusses sufficient conditions for the $\hat{\theta}$ which maximizes (10) globally to be consistent.

Theorem 7.1 Under the assumption that (i) $M_n(S) = n^{-1} \sum_{t=1}^{n} Z'_t S Z_t$ converges to a positive-definite matrix $M(S)$, (ii) S_n converges in probability to a positive-definite matrix S, and (iii) the derivatives up to the third order of $g_t(\theta)$ with respect to θ are bounded, a minimum-distance estimator $\hat{\theta}$ which satisfies (17) is consistent. For this estimator $\hat{\theta}$, $\sqrt{n}(\hat{\theta} - \theta_0)$ has a limiting normal distribution with mean zero and covariance matrix

$$[M(S)]^{-1} M(S\Omega S)[M(S)]^{-1}$$

PROOF We have already established consistency. To derive the asymptotic distribution of $\sqrt{n}(\hat{\theta} - \theta_0)$ we expand $\partial L_n(S_n, \hat{\theta})/\partial\theta$ given by (17) in a second-order Taylor series about θ_0, using the derivatives given in (18) and (19)

$$\frac{\partial L_n(S_n, \hat{\theta})}{\partial\theta} = \frac{\partial L_n(S_n, \theta_0)}{\partial\theta} + \frac{\partial^2 L_n(S_n, \theta_0)}{\partial\theta\,\partial\theta'}(\hat{\theta} - \theta_0)$$

$$+ \frac{1}{2}\begin{bmatrix} (\hat{\theta} - \theta_0)'B_1 \\ \vdots \\ (\hat{\theta} - \theta_0)'B_k \end{bmatrix}(\hat{\theta} - \theta_0) \tag{20}$$

where
$$B_i = \frac{\partial^3 L_n(S_n, \theta^*)}{\partial\theta\,\partial\theta'\,\partial\theta_i} \quad \text{and} \quad \hat{\theta} \le \theta^* \le \theta_0$$

Given assumption (iii) that the third derivatives B_i of $L_n(S_n, \theta)$ are bounded and the fact that $\hat{\theta}$ is consistent, the matrix in brackets in the last term of (20) converges in probability to a zero matrix, indicated by $o(1)$.

The minimum-distance estimator $\hat{\theta}$ is obtained by setting (20) equal to zero, i.e., by solving

$$\frac{\partial L_n(S_n, \theta_0)}{\partial\theta} + \left[\frac{\partial^2 L_n(S_n, \theta_0)}{\partial\theta\,\partial\theta'} + o(1)\right](\hat{\theta} - \theta_0) = 0$$

The solution for $\sqrt{n}(\hat{\theta} - \theta_0)$ is

$$\sqrt{n}(\hat{\theta} - \theta_0) = \left[\frac{\partial^2 L_n(S_n, \theta_0)}{\partial\theta\,\partial\theta'} + o(1)\right]^{-1}$$

$$\cdot n^{-1/2}\sum_{t=1}^{n} Z_t' S_n[y_{t.} - g_{t.}(\theta_0)] \tag{21}$$

where (18) has been used for $\partial L_n(S_n, \theta_0)/\partial\theta$. Comparing (21) and (15), we find that their right-hand sides are identical except for the matrices to be inverted. From the discussion following Eq. (19) we know that the matrix to be inverted in (21) converges in probability to $M(S)$. Since the matrix to be inverted in (15) also converges to $M(S)$, we conclude that $\sqrt{n}(\hat{\theta} - \theta_0)$ and $\sqrt{n}(\bar{\theta} - \theta_0)$ have the same limiting distribution, and complete the proof of Theorem 7.1.

How should the matrix S_n be selected to construct the minimum-distance estimator? Appealing to the Gauss-Markov theorem for the GLS estimator as applied to the linearized model (11), one should use the inverse of covariance matrix Ω of $\epsilon_{t.}$ for S_n to obtain the minimum covariance matrix of the asymptotic distribution of $\sqrt{n}(\hat{\theta} - \theta_0)$ if Ω were known. With Ω^{-1} used for S_n, the covariance matrix of the asymptotic distribution of $\sqrt{n}(\hat{\theta} - \theta_0)$ is, by Theorem 7.1,

$$[M(\Omega^{-1})]^{-1}M(\Omega^{-1}\Omega\Omega^{-1})[M(\Omega^{-1})]^{-1} = [M(\Omega^{-1})]^{-1} \tag{22}$$

When Ω is unknown, one can use for S_n a consistent estimator $\hat{\Omega}$ of Ω, thus satisfying assumption (ii) of Theorem 7.1 that S_n converges in probability to a positive-definite matrix S, in this case Ω. According to Theorem 7.1, (22) will still be the covariance matrix of the asymptotic distribution of $\sqrt{n}(\hat{\theta} - \theta_0)$. Malinvaud (1970$a$) has suggested using the sample residuals $e_{t.} = y_{t.} - g_{t.}(\theta^1)$ to construct a consistent estimator $\hat{\Omega}$ of Ω, where θ^1 is a consistent estimator of θ. A consistent estimator θ^1 can be obtained by the method of minimum distance, with $S_n = I$. Given θ^1, we compute the sample residuals $e_{t.}$ and form a consistent estimate of Ω by

$$\hat{\Omega} = \frac{1}{n} \sum_{t=1}^{n} e_{t.} e_{t.}'. \tag{23}$$

Using $\hat{\Omega}$ for S_n, we get an asymptotically efficient estimator $\hat{\theta}$ of θ by the method of minimum distance. The new estimate $\hat{\theta}$ could be used to form a new set of sample residuals $y_{t.} - g_{t.}(\hat{\theta})$ and a new estimate of Ω computed, but the asymptotic efficiency of $\hat{\theta}$ will not be improved by further iterations because, by Theorem 7.1, the covariance matrix of $\sqrt{n}(\hat{\theta} - \theta_0)$ remains the same as long as S_n converges to Ω in probability.

7.3 NONLINEAR REGRESSION

An asymptotically efficient estimator for θ in model (5) has been found using the method of GLS or minimum distance. Since the univariate regression model (4) is a special case of model (5), the above theory applies, the matrix Ω being reduced to a scalar $\sigma^2 = E\epsilon_t^2$. For model (4) the expression L_n in (10) to be minimized is reduced to

$$L_n(\theta) = \frac{1}{2n} \sum_{t=1}^{n} [y_t - g(x_t, \theta)]^2 \tag{24}$$

The method of GLS or minimum distance is reduced to the method of least squares. Because of the wide applicability of the nonlinear regression model (4), it may be of interest to see whether one can find a closer approximation to the distribution of the least-squares estimator than that given in Theorem 7.1. The answer is yes. Essentially, if we are willing to introduce the assumption that the residuals ϵ_t in (4) are normal, and if we treat the least-squares estimator as applying to the linearized model derived from (4), we can use the standard t and F distributions to test hypotheses about, and construct confidence intervals for, the elements of θ as we do in linear regression models. The results are contained in Gallant (1973); a good exposition for the practitioner can be found in Gallant (1975a).

To adopt the vector notation used in linear regression theory let the n observations of model (4) be written as

$$y = g(\theta) + \epsilon \tag{25}$$

where y is an $n \times 1$ vector consisting of $y_1, \ldots, y_n$; $g(\theta)$ is an $n \times 1$ vector consisting of $g(x_1, \theta), \ldots, g(x_n, \theta)$; and the elements ϵ_t of ϵ are assumed to be independent and normal, each having mean zero and variance σ^2. The linearized model derived from (25) is

$$y = g(\theta_0) + \frac{\partial g(\theta_0)}{\partial \theta'} (\theta - \theta_0) + \epsilon \tag{26}$$

Let Z denote the $n \times k$ matrix $\partial g(\theta_0)/\partial \theta'$ of the derivatives of the n elements of $g(\theta)$ with respect to the k elements of θ', evaluated at θ_0. Let y^* denote $y - g(\theta_0) + Z\theta_0$; then (26) becomes

$$y^* = Z\theta + \epsilon \tag{27}$$

The least-squares estimator $\hat{\theta}$ minimizes $[y - g(\theta)]'[y - g(\theta)]$. To estimate σ^2 we use

$$s^2 = (n - k)^{-1}[y - g(\hat{\theta})]'[y - g(\hat{\theta})] \tag{28}$$

as in the linear model. By appealing to the linearized model (27) as a good approximation to the original model (25) we have the approximate relations

$$\hat{\theta} \approx \theta_0 + (Z'Z)^{-1}Z'\epsilon \tag{29}$$

$$s^2 \approx (n - k)^{-1}\epsilon'[I - Z(Z'Z)^{-1}Z']\epsilon \tag{30}$$

By Theorem 7.1, $\hat{\theta}$ is asymptotically normal with mean θ_0 and covariance matrix $(Z'Z)^{-1}\sigma^2$, as the reader can easily check. This result agrees with the approximate relation (29) for $\hat{\theta}$. By the approximate relation (30) for s^2, one expects $(n - k)s^2/\sigma^2$ to be independent of $\hat{\theta}$ and asymptotically distributed as $\chi^2(n - k)$. Since $Z = \partial g(\theta_0)/\partial \theta'$ is unknown, we approximate it by $\hat{Z} = \partial g(\hat{\theta})/\partial \theta'$. The matrix $(Z'Z)^{-1}$ is accordingly approximated by

$$\hat{C} = (\hat{Z}'\hat{Z})^{-1} = (\hat{c}_{ij}) \tag{31}$$

To test the hypothesis $\theta_i = \theta_{io}$, we use the ratio

$$\frac{\hat{\theta}_i - \theta_{io}}{\sqrt{\hat{c}_{ii}}\, s}$$

which is approximately distributed as $t(n - k)$. Gallant (1975a, p. 75) illustrates how well the $t(n - k)$ distribution, with $n = 30$ and $k = 4$, approximates the distribution of the above ratio for the model with

$$g(\theta) = \theta_1 x_1 + \theta_2 x_2 + \theta_4 e^{\theta_3 x_3}$$

As expected, the $t(26)$ approximations for $\hat{\theta}_1$, $\hat{\theta}_2$, and $\hat{\theta}_4$ are fairly good, but the t approximation for $\hat{\theta}_3$ is not as good. While the one-tail t probabilities are .0005, .0050, .0250, .0500, and .1000, they are respectively .0000, .0018, .0140, .0358, and .0866 for the ratio implying $\hat{\theta}_3$; they are respectively .0010, .0048, .0270, .0522, and .1026 for $\hat{\theta}_1$. Similarly, to test the linear hypothesis $R\theta = r$, where R is $m \times k$, we apply the method of Sec. 2.4 for the normal linear regression model and use a statistic analogous to (26) of Chap. 2, namely,

$$(R\hat{\theta} - r)'[R(\hat{Z}'\hat{Z})^{-1}R']^{-1}(R\hat{\theta} - r)/ms^2 \tag{32}$$

which is approximately distributed as $F(m, n - k)$.

In deriving his analytical results, Gallant made the following assumptions. First, x_t are chosen either by random sampling from a distribution which has finite first moment or from a (possibly disproportionate) replication of a fixed set of vectors. Second, $g(x, \theta)$ is continuous in its arguments x and θ, having continuous first and second derivatives with respect to θ. Third,

$$\lim_{n \to \infty} \frac{1}{n} \sum_{t=1}^{n} [g(x_t, \theta) - g(x_t, \theta_0)]^2$$

has a unique minimum at θ_0, where x_t are treated as fixed. Furthermore

$$\lim_{n \to \infty} \frac{1}{n} Z'Z = \lim_{n \to \infty} \frac{1}{n} \frac{\partial g'(\theta_0)}{\partial \theta} \frac{\partial g(\theta_0)}{\partial \theta'}$$

is nonsingular. If we treat x_t as fixed, these assumptions are similar to the assumptions introduced to prove Theorem 7.1 for the multivariate nonlinear regression model. The reader is referred to Gallant (1975a, b) for more detailed treatment of nonlinear regression, including alternative tests of hypotheses about θ.

7.4 METHOD OF MAXIMUM LIKELIHOOD

The method of maximum likelihood is applicable to nonlinear models. If one reviews the proofs of consistency and asymptotic normality of the maximum-likelihood estimator given for Theorem 1.4, one finds that the model is not required to be linear. As long as the observations are independent and the four assumptions of Theorem 1.4 hold, a maximum-likelihood estimator $\hat{\theta}$ for θ which satisfies the likelihood equation $\partial \log L/\partial \theta = 0$ is consistent and has an asymptotic distribution which is normal with mean zero and covariance matrix equal to the inverse of

$$-E \frac{\partial^2 \log L(y; \theta_0)}{\partial \theta \, \partial \theta'} \tag{33}$$

where $L(y; \theta_0)$ denotes the likelihood function evaluated at $\theta = \theta_0$. In practice (33) is approximated by

$$\frac{\partial^2 \log L(y; \hat{\theta})}{\partial \theta \, \partial \theta'} \tag{34}$$

The maximum-likelihood estimator $\hat{\theta}$ is asymptotically efficient because the co-variance matrix given by the inverse of (33) reaches the Cramer-Rao bound.

If we are willing to introduce the assumption that $\epsilon_{t.}$ in model (6) is normal, we can apply the method of maximum likelihood to estimate this model. The log-likelihood function is

$$\log L = c - \frac{n}{2} \log |\Omega| - \frac{1}{2} \sum_{t=1}^{n} [y_{t.} - g(x_{t.}, \theta)]' \Omega^{-1} [y_{t.} - g(x_{t.}, \theta)] \qquad (35)$$

Differentiation with respect to Ω^{-1} yields

$$\frac{n}{2} \Omega - \frac{1}{2} \sum_{t=1}^{n} [y_{t.} - g(x_{t.}, \theta)][y_{t.} - g(x_{t.}, \theta)]' = 0 \qquad (36)$$

as we have shown in differentiating (25) of Chap. 5. Thus the maximum-likelihood estimator of Ω is

$$\hat{\Omega} = \frac{1}{n} \sum_{t=1}^{n} [y_{t.} - g(x_{t.}, \theta)][y_{t.} - g(x_{t.}, \theta)]' \qquad (37)$$

Given Ω, the maximum-likelihood estimator $\hat{\theta}$ of θ is obtained by maximizing the last term of (35). Thus the maximum-likelihood estimator for this model is a minimum-distance estimator. In fact the iterative procedure suggested in the last paragraph of Sec. 7.2 for simultaneously obtaining the minimum-distance estimator $\hat{\theta}$ and the matrix $\hat{\Omega}$ defining the distance is an iterative procedure for computing the maximum-likelihood estimators $\hat{\theta}$ and $\hat{\Omega}$ which maximize the likelihood function (35). We have pointed out that as long as $\hat{\Omega}$ is consistent, solving for $\hat{\theta}$ once without further iterations will be asymptotically efficient. The same point was made in Chap. 5, when we discussed the various approximations to the FIML estimator for linear simultaneous equations. As the reader may have observed, the proofs of consistency and asymptotic normality of the minimum-distance estimator in Sec. 7.2 are similar to the proofs of these properties for the maximum-likelihood estimator in Sec. 1.11.

For model (6) the maximum-likelihood estimator under the normality assumption for $\epsilon_{t.}$ is identical with an iterative minimum-distance estimator and has the same asymptotic distribution as a minimum-distance estimator using a consistent $\hat{\Omega}$. From the viewpoint of asymptotic distribution theory, it is not necessary to use the normality assumption and the associated maximum-likelihood procedure. However, the maximum-likelihood method is more general; it is applicable to other models than (6), e.g., simultaneous-equation models, models with multiplicative rather than additive disturbances, models with nonnormal disturbances, and models for markets in disequilibrium. It is therefore important to be able to carry out the maximization of a given likelihood function and compute the associated matrix (33) or (34) for estimating the covariance matrix of the resulting maximum-likelihood estimator. These two important tasks involved in applying the method of maximum likelihood belong to the subject of numerical methods of maximization, to which we now turn.

7.5 NUMERICAL METHODS OF MAXIMIZATION

Much progress in estimating nonlinear models in econometrics using the method of maximum likelihood has resulted from the works of Goldfeld and Quandt (1972, 1976). Quandt (1982a) provides an excellent survey of computational problems and methods in econometrics. This section has drawn from the above works, to which the reader may refer.

To maximize a function $L(\theta)$ which has continuous first and second derivatives with respect to the vector θ of m elements we can set its first derivative equal to zero

$$\frac{\partial L(\theta)}{\partial \theta} \equiv f(\theta) = 0 \tag{38}$$

At any point θ the gradient or vector of first derivatives $f(\theta)$ provides much information concerning where one should move to reach a maximum. For example, for $m = 2$, if $f(\theta) = (2, -1)'$, this means that increasing θ_1 by a small amount ϵ will increase $L(\theta)$ by 2ϵ and decreasing θ_2 by ϵ will increase $L(\theta)$ by ϵ. It sounds like a good idea to increase θ_1 and reduce θ_2 in order to get a higher value for $L(\theta)$, but by how much remains to be investigated. Many algorithms to maximize $L(\theta)$ are based on the gradient $f(\theta)$ and are called gradient algorithms.

An algorithm specifies how one should move from a point θ^0 to the next point θ^1. A *gradient algorithm* takes the form

$$\theta^1 = \theta^0 + k^0 H^0 f(\theta^0) \tag{39}$$

where $f(\theta^0)$ is the gradient evaluated at θ^0, k^0 is a scalar, and H^0 is a matrix to be specified; k^0 gives the step size, and $H^0 f(\theta^0)$ is the search direction.

The *method of steepest ascent* specifies $H^0 = I$. One way to choose the step size k^0 is to approximate $L(\theta)$ by a quadratic function and find k^0 to maximize $L(\theta^1)$. Thus let

$$L(\theta^1) = L(\theta^0) + \frac{\partial L(\theta^0)}{\partial \theta'} (\theta^1 - \theta^0) + \tfrac{1}{2}(\theta^1 - \theta^0)' \frac{\partial^2 L(\theta^0)}{\partial \theta \, \partial \theta'} (\theta^1 - \theta^0) \tag{40}$$

Substituting $kf(\theta^0)$ for $\theta^1 - \theta^0$ and $f(\theta^0)'$ for $\partial L(\theta^0)/\partial \theta'$, we have

$$L(\theta') = L(\theta^0) + kf(\theta^0)'f(\theta^0) + \tfrac{1}{2}k^2 f(\theta^0)' \frac{\partial f(\theta^0)}{\partial \theta'} f(\theta^0)$$

Minimization with respect to k gives

$$k^0 = -f(\theta^0)'f(\theta^0) \left[f(\theta^0)' \frac{\partial f(\theta^0)}{\partial \theta'} f(\theta^0) \right]^{-1}$$

This k^0 may be expensive to compute since it requires the matrix $\partial f(\theta^0)/\partial \theta'$ of second partials of L with respect to θ. If we are willing to compute this matrix, we can choose the Newton-Raphson method.

The *Newton-Raphson method* specifies $H^0 = -[\partial f(\theta^0)/\partial \theta']^{-1}$. It was presented in Eq. (78) of Chap. 5 when we discussed FIML for linear simultaneous equations. We pointed out that if $f(\theta)$ is linear [or $L(\theta)$ is quadratic], the Newton-Raphson method using $k = 1$ converges in one iteration; i.e., starting from any θ^0,

$$\theta^1 = \theta^0 - \left[\frac{\partial f(\theta^0)}{\partial \theta'} \right]^{-1} f(\theta^0)$$

gives the maximum of $L(\theta)$. We also pointed out that insofar as $L(\theta)$ is not quadratic, it would be wise to choose the step size k^0 different from 1. The following rule for choosing k has been found useful in practice. When $k = 1$, if the value of L is larger than in the previous iteration, try $k = 1.25, (1.25)^2,$ ..., until the value of L decreases. If L is not larger when $k = 1$ but the algorithm has not converged according to some prescribed criterion, try $k = 0.8, -0.8,$ $(0.8)^2, -(0.8)^2, \ldots$, hoping to find a larger L than in the previous iteration. If this fails, the algorithm breaks down. If it succeeds, continue with the above sequence (either positive or negative) until the value of L decreases. The final k value is chosen by quadratic interpolation of L as a function of k using the last three points and finding k to maximize this quadratic function. This method of choosing k in connection with the Newton-Raphson method has been found to work well in practice by Chow (1968) and Chow and Fair (1973), among others.

The *Gauss-Newton method* is an approximation to the Newton-Raphson method in that when the matrix of second derivatives of L is computed, the second derivatives of the function $g(x_{t.}, \theta)$ specifying the nonlinear model are ignored. Referring to Eq. (19), we see that the matrix of second derivatives of L consists of two terms. The second term involves the second partials of $g(x_{t.}, \theta)$ with respect to θ. If the function g is not too far from being linear in θ, ignoring this term is justified. Furthermore, the second term of (19) has been shown to converge in probability to a zero matrix because the residuals $y_{t.} - g(x_{t.}, \theta)$ have zero expectations. The Gauss-Newton method would employ the first term $n^{-1} \sum_{t=1}^{n} Z_t' S_n Z_t$ alone to approximate $\partial^2 L/(\partial\theta \, \partial\theta')$. Essentially, this approximation amounts to using a linear approximation for $g(x_{t.}, \theta)$ in the function (10) to be minimized or in the likelihood function to be maximized (see Probs. 6 and 7).

The *method of scoring* is another variation of the Newton-Raphson method applied to computing maximum-likelihood estimates. By the proof of the Cramer-Rao inequality, we have, from Eq. (49) of Chap. 1,

$$E \left[\frac{\partial \log L(y_{t.}, \theta)}{\partial \theta} \frac{\partial \log L(y_{t.}, \theta)}{\partial \theta'} \right] = -E \frac{\partial^2 \log L(y_{t.}, \theta)}{\partial \theta \, \partial \theta'} \tag{41}$$

where $L(y_{t.}, \theta)$ is the likelihood function for the tth observation $y_{t.}$. The Newton-Raphson method for maximizing the average log likelihood $1/n \sum_{t=1}^{n} \log L(y_{t.}, \theta)$ uses as H^0 the inverse of the matrix

$$-\frac{1}{n} \sum_{t=1}^{n} \frac{\partial^2 \log L(y_{t.}, \theta)}{\partial \theta \, \partial \theta'} \tag{42}$$

This matrix is the sample analog of (41). The method of scoring uses (41) for H^0 instead. Sometimes the expectation on the right-hand side of (41) can be evaluated. Sometimes the expectation on the left-hand side is approximated by the sample analog

$$\frac{1}{n} \sum_{t=1}^{n} \frac{\partial \log L(y_{t.}, \theta)}{\partial \theta} \frac{\partial \log L(y_{t.}, \theta)}{\partial \theta'} \tag{43}$$

as done by Berndt et al. (1974). Using (43) one avoids evaluating the second partials of the function to be maximized by using only its first partials.

The *method of quadratic hill-climbing*, proposed by Goldfeld, Quandt, and Trotter (1966), is yet another modification of the Newton-Raphson method. When θ^0 is far from the maximizing value, the matrix $\partial f(\theta^0)/\partial \theta'$ of second partials may not be negative definite. Taking a small step in the Newton-Raphson direction may lead one downhill rather than uphill. To ensure the negative definiteness of $-H^0$ the method of quadratic hill climbing uses for $-H^0$ in (39)

$$\left[\frac{\partial f(\theta^0)}{\partial \theta'} - \alpha I \right]^{-1} \tag{44}$$

where the scalar α is chosen to maximize $L(\theta)$ in a spherical region centered at θ^0, that is, bounded by $(\theta - \theta^0)'(\theta - \theta^0) = r_\alpha$, under the assumption that $L(\theta)$ is quadratic in that region. The method requires computing the characteristic roots of the matrix $\partial f(\theta^0)/\partial \theta'$.

All the methods described above require the use of the gradient $f(\theta) = \partial L/\partial \theta$ or the vector of first derivatives. These derivatives can be evaluated analytically or numerically. In the latter case, one can approximate $\partial f_i/\partial \theta_j$ by

$$\frac{f_i(\theta_1, \ldots, \theta_j + \epsilon_j, \ldots, \theta_m) - f_i(\theta_1, \ldots, \theta_j - \epsilon_j, \ldots, \theta_m)}{2\epsilon_j} \tag{45}$$

where ϵ_j is chosen as the maximum of .001 and $.001\theta_j$, for instance. The derivatives $\partial f/\partial \theta'$ can be used to form H^0 in a Newton-Raphson algorithm or to compute the matrix (34) for estimating the covariance matrix of $\hat{\theta}$.

The *conjugate-gradient method*, despite its name, does not require the use of first derivatives. It evaluates the function $L(\theta)$ to be maximized along mutually conjugate directions, beginning at a point θ^0. For a quadratic function

$$L(\theta) = \theta'A\theta + b'\theta + c$$

two direction vectors d_1 and d_2 are conjugate if $d_1'Ad_2 = 0$. When $A = I_m$, the m columns of the identity matrix I_m are conjugate direction vectors. Let $d_1^0, \ldots, d_m^0$ be m linearly independent direction vectors. Starting from θ^0, one can search along the directions d_i^0 $(i = 1, \ldots, m)$ sequentially, each time going along one direction d_i^0. One begins by searching along d_1^0, that is, by choosing a scalar λ_1 to

$$\max_{\lambda_1} L(\theta^0 + \lambda_1 d_1^0)$$

Having chosen $\hat{\lambda}_1$, one next chooses a scalar λ_2 to

$$\max_{\lambda_2} L(\theta^0 + \hat{\lambda}_1 d_1^0 + \lambda_2 d_2^0)$$

and so forth. Having searched along all m directions, let

$$\bar{\theta}^0 = \theta^0 + \sum_{i=1}^{m} \hat{\lambda}_i d_i^0 \equiv \theta^0 + \delta$$

The following step is to

$$\max_{k} L(\bar{\theta}^0 + k\delta)$$

and set $\theta^1 = \bar{\theta}^0 + \hat{k}\delta$. To start with, let d_i^0 be the coordinate directions, i.e., the m column vectors of the identity matrix I_m. The directions for the next iteration are $d_1^1 = d_2^0$, $d_2^1 = d_3^0, \ldots, d_m^1 = \delta$. In the second iteration treat these d_i^1 $(i = 1, \ldots, m)$ as we treated the d_i^0 $(i = 1, \ldots, m)$ in the first iteration, and so forth. The above method is due to Powell (1964).

Many other algorithms are available. Computer software and hardware to maximize a function of many variables have been advancing rapidly. In an econometrics text one must give the basic ideas underlying the most important algorithms and explain how they work without burdening the reader with mathematical theorems justifying them. Interested readers should refer to Goldfeld and Quandt (1972, chap. 1) and Quandt (1982a). A useful computer package GQOPT which includes several algorithms has been assembled and prepared by Goldfeld and Quandt for optimization and is available from the Econometric Research Program at Princeton University.

★7.6 FIML FOR NONLINEAR SIMULTANEOUS EQUATIONS

This section is concerned with the estimation of the nonlinear simultaneous-equation model (7) by FIML using the Newton-Raphson and related algorithms. It is based on Chow (1973), (1974). The log-likelihood function is set up and differentiated twice with respect to the unknown parameters. The Newton-Raphson method is then applied to compute the FIML estimates iteratively. The section illustrates the kind of derivatives and the nature of the computational steps involved when the Newton-Raphson method is used to solve a fairly complicated problem.

Let the tth observation on the ith structural equation be

$$\phi_i(y_{t.}, x_{t.}; \theta_i) = \epsilon_{ti} \qquad \begin{array}{l} i = 1, \ldots, G \\ t = 1, \ldots, n \end{array} \qquad (46)$$

where θ_i is a column vector of k_i unknown parameters in the ith equation and ϵ_{ti} $(i = 1, \ldots, G)$ are G-variate normal with mean zero and covariance matrix $\Sigma =$

(σ_{ij}) and serially independent. Denote by $\phi_{ti}(\theta_i)$ the function $\phi_i(y_{t.}, x_{t.}; \theta_i)$, and by $\phi_{t.}$ the column vector consisting of $\phi_{t1}, \ldots, \phi_{tG}$. The density function for $\epsilon_{t.}$ is

$$(2\pi)^{-G/2}|\Sigma|^{-1/2} \exp\left(-\tfrac{1}{2}\epsilon'_{t.}\Sigma^{-1}\epsilon_{t.}\right)$$

The density function for $y_{t.}$ is

$$(2\pi)^{-G/2}|\Sigma|^{-1/2}\left|\frac{\partial\phi_{t.}}{\partial y'_{t.}}\right| \exp\left(-\tfrac{1}{2}\phi'_{t.}\Sigma^{-1}\phi_{t.}\right)$$

where the jacobian will be written as

$$\left|\frac{\partial\phi_{t.}}{\partial y'_{t.}}\right| = |B_t| = |\beta_{ij,t}| = \left|\frac{\partial\phi_{ti}}{\partial y_{tj}}\right| \tag{47}$$

to exhibit the analogy with the model of linear simultaneous equations.

The log-likelihood function based on $y_{1.}, \ldots, y_{n.}$ is therefore

$$\log L = \frac{nG}{2}\log 2\pi - \frac{n}{2}\log|\Sigma|$$

$$+ \sum_{t=1}^{n}\log|B_t| - \frac{1}{2}\sum_{t=1}^{n}\phi'_{t.}\Sigma^{-1}\phi_{t.} \tag{48}$$

Differentiating with respect to Σ^{-1} and solving the resulting equation, we get, as in the linear case, with $\Phi = (\phi_{tj}) = (\phi_1 \ \cdots \ \phi_G)$ denoting the $n \times G$ matrix of structural functions,

$$\hat{\Sigma} = n^{-1}\Phi'\Phi \equiv S = (s_{ij}) = (n^{-1}\phi'_i\phi_j) \tag{49}$$

Substituting (49) for Σ in (48), we obtain the logarithmic concentrated likelihood function

$$L^* = \text{const} - \frac{n}{2}\log|S| + \sum_{t=1}^{n}\log|B_t| \tag{50}$$

To maximize the log-likelihood function, one differentiates (50) with respect to the column vector θ_i

$$\frac{\partial L^*}{\partial\theta_i} = -\frac{n}{2}\sum_{g<h}\frac{\partial\log|S|}{\partial s_{gh}}\frac{\partial s_{gh}}{\partial\theta_i} + \sum_t\sum_{g,h}\frac{\partial\log|B_t|}{\partial\beta_{gh,t}}\frac{\partial\beta_{gh,t}}{\partial\theta_i} \tag{51}$$

Note that

$$\frac{\partial\log|S|}{\partial s_{gh}} = 2s^{hg} = 2 \times hg\text{th element of } S^{-1} \qquad g \neq h$$

$$\frac{\partial s_{gh}}{\partial\theta_i} = \begin{cases} 0 & i \neq g,h \\ \dfrac{1}{n}\left[\dfrac{\partial\phi_{1i}}{\partial\theta_i}\cdots\dfrac{\partial\phi_{ni}}{\partial\theta_i}\right]\phi_h = \dfrac{1}{n}Z'_i\phi_h & i = g \neq h \end{cases} \tag{52}$$

where we have denoted by Z_i' the $k_i \times n$ matrix of the derivatives of the n elements of ϕ_i with respect to the k_i elements of θ_i. Similarly,

$$\frac{\partial \log |B_t|}{\partial \beta_{gh,t}} = \beta_t^{hg} = hg\text{th element of } B_t^{-1}$$

$$\frac{\partial \beta_{gh,t}}{\partial \theta_i} = \left\{ \begin{array}{ll} 0 & i \neq g \\ \dfrac{\partial^2 \phi_{ti}}{\partial \theta_i \, \partial y_{th}} & i = g \end{array} \right\} \tag{53}$$

Using (52) and (53), we rewrite (51) as

$$\frac{\partial L^*}{\partial \theta_i} = -\sum_h s^{hi} Z_i' \phi_h + \sum_t \sum_h \beta_t^{hi} \frac{\partial^2 \phi_{ti}}{\partial \theta_i \, \partial y_{th}} = 0 \qquad (i = 1, \ldots, G) \tag{54}$$

These equations will be solved for the unknowns $\theta_1, \ldots, \theta_G$, to obtain the maximum-likelihood estimates.

As the reader of Sec. 7.5 will realize, there are different algorithms utilizing the gradient (54) to maximize L^*. We first consider the Newton-Raphson method, which requires the matrix of second partials of L^*. To obtain this matrix we differentiate (54) with respect to the row vector θ_j' ($j = 1, \ldots, G$). This will be done separately for the two components of (54). Only interested and patient readers should go through all derivations to Eq. (61). For the first component

$$\frac{\partial}{\partial \theta_j'} \left(-\sum_h s^{hi} Z_i' \phi_h \right) = -\sum_h s^{hi} Z_i' \frac{\partial \phi_h}{\partial \theta_j'} - \sum_h Z_i' \phi_h \frac{\partial s^{hi}}{\partial \theta_j'}$$

$$-\sum_h s^{hi} \sum_t \phi_{th} \frac{\partial \phi_{ti}}{\partial \theta_i \, \partial \theta_j'} \tag{55}$$

The only term in (55) that requires further evaluation is the row vector

$$\frac{\partial s^{hi}}{\partial \theta_j'} = \sum_{m,r} \frac{\partial s^{hi}}{\partial s_{mr}} \frac{\partial s_{mr}}{\partial \theta_j'} \tag{56}$$

On account of (52) and the fact that

$$\frac{\partial s^{hi}}{\partial s_{mr}} = -s^{hm} s^{ri}$$

which can be proved by doing Prob. 19 of Chap. 5, (56) can be written as

$$\frac{\partial s^{hi}}{\partial \theta_j'} = \frac{1}{n} \sum_r \frac{\partial s^{hi}}{\partial s_{jr}} \phi_r' Z_j + \frac{1}{n} \sum_{m \neq j} \frac{\partial s^{hi}}{\partial s_{mj}} \phi_m' Z_j$$

$$= -\frac{1}{n} \sum_r (s^{hj} s^{ri} + s^{hr} s^{ji}) \phi_r' Z_j \tag{57}$$

Using (57) and (52), we rewrite (55) finally as

$$\frac{\partial}{\partial \theta'_j}\left(-\sum_h s^{hi} Z'_i \phi_h\right) = -s^{ji} Z'_j Z_j + \frac{1}{n} Z'_i$$

$$\cdot \sum_{h,r} \phi_h(s^{hj}s^{ri} + s^{hr}s^{ji})\phi'_r Z_j$$

$$-\sum_t \frac{\partial^2 \phi_{ti}}{\partial \theta_i \, \partial \theta'_j} \sum_h s^{hi}\phi_{th} \qquad (58)$$

The differentiation of the second component of (54) can be similarly performed

$$\frac{\partial}{\partial \theta'_j}\left(\sum_t \sum_h \beta_t^{hi} \frac{\partial^2 \phi_{ti}}{\partial \theta_i \, \partial y_{th}}\right) = \sum_t \sum_h \left(\beta_t^{hi} \frac{\partial^3 \phi_{ti}}{\partial \theta_i \, \partial \theta'_j \, \partial y_{th}} + \frac{\partial^2 \phi_{ti}}{\partial \theta_i \, \partial y_{th}} \frac{\partial \beta_t^{hi}}{\partial \theta'_j}\right) \qquad (59)$$

Analogous to (56), on account of (53), is

$$\frac{\partial \beta_t^{hi}}{\partial \theta'_j} = \sum_{m,r} \frac{\partial \beta_t^{hi}}{\partial \beta_{mr,t}} \frac{\partial \beta_{mr,t}}{\partial \theta'_j} = \sum_r (-\beta_t^{hj}\beta_t^{ri}) \frac{\partial^2 \phi_{tj}}{\partial \theta'_j \, \partial y_{tr}} \qquad (60)$$

so that (59) becomes

$$\frac{\partial}{\partial \theta'_j}\left(\sum_t \sum_h \beta_t^{hi} \frac{\partial^2 \phi_{ti}}{\partial \theta_i \, \partial y_{th}}\right)$$

$$= \sum_t \sum_h \left[\beta_t^{hi} \frac{\partial^3 \phi_{ti}}{\partial \theta_i \, \partial \theta'_j \, \partial y_{th}} - \frac{\partial^2 \phi_{ti}}{\partial \theta_i \, \partial y_{th}} \sum_r (\beta_t^{hj}\beta_t^{ri}) \frac{\partial^2 \phi_{tj}}{\partial \theta'_j \, \partial y_{tr}}\right] \qquad (61)$$

To summarize, the Newton-Raphson method iterates by the formula

$$\theta^1 - \theta^0 = -k \left(\frac{\partial^2 L^*}{\partial \theta \, \partial \theta'}\right)^{-1} \frac{\partial L^*}{\partial \theta} \qquad (62)$$

where the ith subvector of $\partial L^*/\partial \theta$ is given by (54) and the ijth submatrix of $\partial^2 L^*/\partial \theta \, \partial \theta'$ is given by the sum of (58) and (61). Note that

$$\frac{\partial^2 \phi_{ti}}{\partial \theta_i \, \partial \theta'_j} = 0 \qquad \text{for } i \neq j$$

Hence, for $i \neq j$, the third term of (58) and the first term of (61) are zero.

The computations can be performed as follows. Given the data y_{ti} ($i = 1, \ldots, G$; $t = 1, \ldots, n$), and x_{ti} ($i = 1, \ldots, K$; $t = 1, \ldots, n$), and given the values for θ_{ij} ($i = 1, \ldots, G$; $j = 1, \ldots, k_i$) in the rth iteration, compute

1. ϕ_{ti} as given by (46) ($i = 1, \ldots, G$; $t = 1, \ldots, n$)
2. s_{gh} by $n^{-1}\phi'_g\phi_h$ and s^{hg} by S^{-1} ($g,h = 1, \ldots, G$)
3. $\beta_{gh,t} = \dfrac{\partial \phi_{tg}}{\partial y_{th}}$ and β_t^{hg} by B_t^{-1} ($g,h = 1, \ldots, G$; $t = 1, \ldots, n$)
4. $z_{ti} = \dfrac{\partial \phi_{ti}}{\partial \theta_i}$, the tth column of Z'_i ($i = 1, \ldots, G$; $t = 1, \ldots, n$)

5. $\dfrac{\partial^2 \phi_{ti}}{\partial \theta_i \, \partial y_{th}}$, a column vector $(i,h = 1, \ldots, G; t = 1, \ldots, n)$

6. $\dfrac{\partial L^*}{\partial \theta}$ by (54) and the preceding results

7. $\dfrac{\partial^2 \phi_{ti}}{\partial \theta_i \, \partial \theta_i'}$, a $k_i \times k_i$ matrix $(i = 1, \ldots, G; t = 1, \ldots, n)$

8. $\dfrac{\partial^3 \phi_{ti}}{\partial \theta_i \, \partial \theta_i' \, \partial y_{th}}$, a $k_i \times k_i$ matrix $(i,h = 1, \ldots, G; t = 1, \ldots, n)$

9. $\dfrac{\partial^2 L^*}{\partial \theta \, \partial \theta'}$ as the sum of (58) and (61)

10. $\theta^{r+1} - \theta^r$ by the right-hand side of (62), where the step size k can be determined by the rule given in Sec. 7.5 in describing the Newton-Raphson method

The above calculations can be accomplished by evaluating, either analytically or numerically, the first derivatives of steps 3 and 4, the second derivatives of steps 5 and 7, and the third derivatives of step 8. Analytical derivatives are available in many computer facilities.

Instead of the Newton-Raphson method, one may choose the Gauss-Newton method or the method of scoring. The applications of these methods to the present case are left as exercises (see Probs. 9 and 10). One may also choose an algorithm, e.g., in GQOPT, which requires the computation of $\partial L^*/\partial \theta$ only. In this case, only steps 1 to 6 need be executed. If the model is not too large, one might even forgo the above analysis and the evaluation of $\partial L^*/\partial \theta$ and try an algorithm which does not require computing the gradient. Such an approach is referred to by some econometricians as "using brute force." One need only specify the likelihood function to be maximized and write a FORTRAN subroutine to evaluate this function. The initial trial value θ^0 has to be given. The computer will do the rest, including the search for a maximum and the computation of the second partials at the maximum to be used to estimate the covariance matrix of $\hat{\theta}$. If one algorithm fails to converge, try another.

The method of maximum likelihood can be modified to provide a robust estimator for nonlinear simultaneous equations. We pointed out in Sec. 3.4 that a robust estimator can be interpreted as iterative weighted least squares. Since the method of maximum likelihood as applied to a simultaneous-equation system can also be viewed as a generalization of least squares in the sense to be specified below, the two ideas can be combined to form a robust estimator for simultaneous equations. Specifically, for a column vector ϕ of residuals, a weighted sum of squares takes the form $\phi' W' W \phi$, where W is a diagonal weighting matrix consisting of $w_1, \ldots, w_n$ in the diagonal. When there are columns of residuals ϕ_g and ϕ_h (for equations g and h), the sum of squares or cross products should accordingly be changed to $\phi_g' W_g W_h \phi_h$, with W_g and W_h again denoting diagonal weighting matrices. The method of maximum likelihood amounts to minimizing a generalized variance $|\Sigma|$ of the residuals subject to some normalization rules introduced by the jacobian $|B_t|$. A natural combination of these two ideas is to maximize the function (50) with the elements of S changed to the weighted sum of squares or cross products, i.e., to maximize

$$L^0 = \text{const} - \frac{n}{2} \log |S^*| + \sum_{t=1}^{n} \log |B_t| \tag{63}$$

where

$$S^* = (s_{gh}^*) = \left(\frac{1}{n} \phi_g' W_g W_h \phi_h\right)$$

By using the results (54), (58), and (61) the gradient and the matrix of second partials of (63) can be simply stated. Since the derivatives of $\sum_t \log |B_t|$ are already given in (54) and (61), only the derivatives of $-(n/2) \log |S^*|$ will be recorded

$$\frac{\partial}{\partial \theta_i} \left(-\frac{n}{2} \log |S^*|\right) = Z_i' W_i \sum_{h=1}^{G} s^{*hi} W_h \phi_h \tag{64}$$

$$\frac{\partial^2}{\partial \theta_i\, \partial \theta_j'} \left(-\frac{n}{2} \log |S^*|\right) = -s^{*ji} Z_i' W_i W_j Z_j$$

$$+ \frac{1}{n} Z_i' W_i \sum_{h=1}^{G} W_h \phi_h \sum_n (s^{*hj} s^{*ni} + s^{*hn} s^{*ji}) \phi_n' W_n W_j Z_j$$

$$- \delta_{ij} \sum_{h=1}^{G} s^{hi} \sum_t \phi_{th} \frac{\partial^2 \phi_{ti}}{\partial \theta_i\, \partial \theta_i'} w_{ti} w_{th} \tag{65}$$

where $\delta_{ij} = 1$ for $i = j$ and $\delta_{ij} = 0$ for $i \neq j$. Fair (1974) has successfully applied a robust estimator which maximizes (63) to a system of nonlinear simultaneous equations.

7.7 METHOD OF INSTRUMENTAL VARIABLES

Amemiya (1977) has provided an instrumental-variable interpretation of the FIML estimator, much as Hausman did for the linear case, discussed in Sec. 5.6. Amemiya interprets the second term of the gradient (54) as

$$\sum_t \sum_h \beta_t^{hi} \frac{\partial^2 \phi_{ti}}{\partial \theta_i\, \partial y_{th}} = \sum_t \sum_h \frac{\partial y_{th}}{\partial \epsilon_{ti}} \frac{\partial^2 \phi_{ti}}{\partial \theta_i\, \partial y_{th}} = \sum_t \frac{\partial^2 \phi_{ti}}{\partial \theta_i\, \partial \epsilon_{ti}} = \sum_t \frac{\partial z_{ti}}{\partial \epsilon_{ti}} \tag{66}$$

where, in the last step, $z_{ti} = \partial \phi_{ti}/\partial \theta_i$ has been defined as a vector of k_i derivatives of $\phi_{ti} = \phi_i(y_{t.}, x_{t.}; \theta_i)$ with respect to θ_i, as in Eq. (52).

The gradient (54) can now be written as

$$\frac{\partial L^*}{\partial \theta_i} = \sum_{t=1}^{n} \frac{\partial z_{ti}}{\partial \epsilon_{ti}} - Z_i' \phi \begin{bmatrix} s^{1i} \\ \vdots \\ s^{Gi} \end{bmatrix} = 0 \tag{67}$$

recalling that $\phi = [\phi_1 \quad \cdots \quad \phi_G]$. It is interesting to compare the first-order condition (67) with the first-order condition for the model of linear simultaneous equations given by (75) of Chap. 5, which is

$$\frac{\partial \log L}{\partial \beta_i} = n\beta^i - Y_i'(YB' + X\Gamma') \begin{bmatrix} s^{1i} \\ \vdots \\ s^{Gi} \end{bmatrix} = 0 \tag{68}$$

For the linear model, the jacobian is $|B|$, and β^i in (68) denotes the ith column of B^{-1}. The corresponding term in (67) is the inverse $\partial z_{ti}/\partial \epsilon_{ti}$ of the derivative of ϵ_{ti} with respect to the variables z_{ti}. Every other term in (67) also matches exactly with the corresponding term in (68).

Recall that in the linear case (68) [or (75) of Chap. 5] can be rewritten as (86) of Chap. 5, namely,

$$\frac{\partial \log L}{\partial \beta_i} = -\tilde{Y}_i'(YB' + X\Gamma') \begin{bmatrix} s^{1i} \\ \vdots \\ s^{Gi} \end{bmatrix} = 0 \tag{69}$$

where $\tilde{Y}_i$ is a matrix of selected columns from

$$\tilde{Y} = X\Pi' = Y - V = Y - (YB' + X\Gamma')B'^{-1}$$

to include all endogenous variables in equation i except y_i, whose coefficient β_{ii} has been normalized to equal -1. Accordingly,

$$\tilde{Y}_i' = Y_i' - B_i^{-1}(BY' + \Gamma X') \tag{70}$$

with B_i^{-1} denoting a matrix composed of the rows of B^{-1} which correspond to the variables in Y_i. Substituting (70) for $\tilde{Y}_i'$ in (69), one gets (68)

$$\frac{\partial \log L}{\partial \beta_i} = -Y_i'(YB' + X\Gamma') \begin{bmatrix} s^{1i} \\ \vdots \\ s^{Gi} \end{bmatrix} + B_i^{-1}(BY' + \Gamma X')(YB' + X\Gamma') \begin{bmatrix} s^{1i} \\ \vdots \\ s^{Gi} \end{bmatrix}$$

$$= -Y_i'(YB' + X\Gamma') \begin{bmatrix} s^{1i} \\ \vdots \\ s^{Gi} \end{bmatrix} + n\beta^i$$

where $(BY' + \Gamma X')(YB' + X\Gamma') = nS$.

By analogy to (70) Amemiya defines the instrumental variables $\tilde{Z}_i$ for the nonlinear simultaneous-equation model as

$$\tilde{Z}_i = Z_i - n^{-1} \sum_t \frac{\partial z_{ti}}{\partial \epsilon_t'} \phi' \tag{71}$$

where $\partial z_{ti}/\partial \epsilon_{t.}'$ is a $k_i \times G_i$ matrix of the derivatives. Substituting (71) for $\tilde{Z}_i'$ in

$$\frac{\partial L^*}{\partial \theta_i} = -\tilde{Z}_i' \phi \begin{bmatrix} s^{1i} \\ \vdots \\ s^{Gi} \end{bmatrix} = -\tilde{Z}_i' \sum_{j=1}^{G} s^{ji} \phi_j = 0 \tag{72}$$

and noting that $\phi'\phi = nS$ gives back (67).

To complete the analogy with the linear case, we combine (69) with Eq. (76) of Chap. 5 for $(\partial \log L)/\partial \gamma_i$ and denote $[\tilde{Y}_i \ X_i]$ by $\tilde{W}_i$ and $[\beta_i' \ \gamma_i']$ by δ_i, to write

$$\frac{\partial \log L}{\partial \delta_i} = -\tilde{W}_i'(YB' + X\Gamma') \begin{bmatrix} s^{1i} \\ \vdots \\ s^{Gi} \end{bmatrix} = -\tilde{W}_i' \sum_{j=1}^{G} s^{ji}(-y_j + W_j \delta_j) = 0 \tag{73}$$

which corresponds to (72); see Eqs. (87) and (88) of Chap. 5. In the nonlinear case, the normal equations (72) for all G equations can be combined to form

$$\begin{bmatrix} s^{11}\tilde{Z}_1' & s^{12}\tilde{Z}_1' & \cdots & s^{1G}\tilde{Z}_1' \\ \cdots\cdots\cdots\cdots\cdots\cdots\cdots\cdots\cdots \\ s^{G1}\tilde{Z}_G' & s^{G2}\tilde{Z}_G' & \cdots & s^{GG}\tilde{Z}_G' \end{bmatrix} \begin{bmatrix} \phi_1 \\ \cdot \\ \phi_G \end{bmatrix} = 0$$

$$= \begin{bmatrix} \tilde{Z}_1' & & 0 \\ & \cdot & \\ 0 & & \tilde{Z}_G' \end{bmatrix} \begin{bmatrix} s^{11}I & \cdots & s^{1G}I \\ \vdots & & \vdots \\ s^{G1}I & \cdots & s^{GG}I \end{bmatrix} \begin{bmatrix} \phi_1 \\ \cdot \\ \phi_G \end{bmatrix} = \tilde{Z}'(S^{-1} \otimes I)\phi \tag{74}$$

To solve Eq. (74) iteratively, one may consider linearizing $\phi(\theta)$ about some initial value θ^0. Let the ith structural equation $\phi_i(\theta_i)$ be linearized as

$$\phi_i(\theta_i) = \phi_i(\theta_i^0) + \frac{\partial \phi_i(\theta_i^0)}{\partial \theta_i'}(\theta_i - \theta_i^0) = \phi_i(\theta_i^0) + Z_i(\theta_i - \theta_i^0) \tag{75}$$

Combine all G equations to form

$$\phi(\theta) = \phi(\theta^0) + Z(\theta - \theta^0) \tag{76}$$

and substitute into (74) to yield

$$\tilde{Z}'(S^{-1} \otimes I)\phi(\theta^0) + \tilde{Z}'(S^{-1} \otimes I)Z(\theta - \theta^0) = 0 \tag{77}$$

The solution of (77) is

$$\theta^1 - \theta^0 = -[\tilde{Z}'(S^{-1} \otimes I)Z]^{-1}\tilde{Z}'(S^{-1} \otimes I)\phi(\theta^0) \tag{78}$$

Equation (78) can be used to define an iterative method to compute the FIML estimator for nonlinear simultaneous equations. Given θ^0, it shows how the next value θ^1 can be completed, and the process can proceed iteratively. Note, however, that despite their apparently simple appearance, the matrices $\tilde{Z}_i$ are by no means easy to compute. The computational complexity can be appreciated by reexamining Eqs. (71) and (66). Furthermore, a pretty-looking iteration equation may or may not have good convergence properties. How good the iterative method defined by (78) is remains to be investigated.

Equation (78) also provides an instrumental-variable interpretation to the FIML estimator. The matrix of instrumental variables is $\tilde{Z}'(S^{-1} \otimes I)$. To study the asymptotic distribution of the FIML estimator $\hat{\theta}$ using this interpretation one linearizes $\phi(\hat{\theta})$ about the true θ_0 and writes, analogous to (78),

$$\sqrt{n}(\hat{\theta} - \theta_0) = -[n^{-1}\tilde{Z}'(S^{-1} \otimes I)Z]^{-1}n^{-1/2}\tilde{Z}'(S^{-1} \otimes I)\epsilon \tag{79}$$

where the derivatives of Z and $\tilde{Z}$ are evaluated at the true θ_0 rather than at the initial value θ^0 for the iteration equation (78). If the matrix in brackets in (79) converges in probability to a nonsingular matrix, one can apply the central limit theorem to the remaining vector $n^{-1/2}\tilde{Z}'(S^{-1} \otimes I)\epsilon$ to establish the asymptotic normality of (79). Furthermore, the asymptotic distribution remains the same whether S is a consistent estimate of Σ or equals Σ itself.

★7.8 NONLINEAR TWO- AND THREE-STAGE LEAST SQUARES

To estimate one linear structural equation

$$y_i - [Y_i \quad X_i]\begin{bmatrix} \beta_i \\ \gamma_i \end{bmatrix} = y_i - W_i\delta_i = \epsilon_i$$

the 2SLS method minimizes

$$(y_i - W_i\delta_i)'X(X'X)^{-1}X'(y_i - W_i\delta_i) \tag{80}$$

where X is the $n \times K$ matrix of predetermined variables. Setting the derivative of (80) with respect to δ_i equal to zero gives

$$W_i'X(X'X)^{-1}X'(y_i - W_i\delta_i) = \tilde{W}_i'y_i - \tilde{W}_i'W_i\delta_i = 0 \tag{81}$$

which is the normal equation for the 2SLS estimator of δ_i. To estimate a nonlinear structural equation

$$\phi_i(y_{t.}, x_{t.}, \theta_i) = \epsilon_i$$

the method of nonlinear 2SLS suggested by Amemiya (1974) minimizes

$$\phi_i'X(X'X)^{-1}X'\phi_i \tag{82}$$

The resulting estimator is consistent and asymptotically normal under assumptions similar to those used for Theorem 7.1. To estimate the entire system of G linear structural equations

$$\begin{bmatrix} y_1 \\ \vdots \\ y_G \end{bmatrix} - \begin{bmatrix} W_1 & & 0 \\ & \ddots & \\ 0 & & W_G \end{bmatrix}\begin{bmatrix} \delta_1 \\ \vdots \\ \delta_G \end{bmatrix} = y - W\delta = \epsilon$$

the method of 3SLS minimizes

$$(y - W\delta)'[S^{-1} \otimes X(X'X)^{-1}X'](y - W\delta) \tag{83}$$

On differentiating (83) it is easy to show that the resulting equation defines the 3SLS estimator of δ.

Jorgenson and Laffont (1974) propose a nonlinear 3SLS estimator for the entire system of nonlinear structural equations

$$\phi(y_{t.}, x_{t.}, \theta) = \epsilon$$

by minimizing $\qquad \phi(\theta)'[S^{-1} \otimes X(X'X)^{-1}X']\phi(\theta) \tag{84}$

where S is some consistent estimator of Σ. This estimator is consistent and asymptotically normal, as can be shown by arguments similar to the ones given below Eq. (79). Amemiya (1977) generalizes the nonlinear 3SLS estimator by minimizing

$$\phi(\theta)'A\phi(\theta) \tag{85}$$

where A can take one of the three forms

$$A_1 = (S \otimes I)^{-1/2}P_1(P_1'P_1)^{-1}P_1'(S \otimes I)^{-1/2}$$

$$A_2 = P_2[P_2'(S \otimes I)P_2]^{-1}P_2'$$

or $\qquad A_3 = (S \otimes I)^{-1}P_3[P_3'(S \otimes I)^{-1}P_3]^{-1}P_3'(S \otimes I)^{-1}$

with S denoting a consistent estimator of Σ and P_1, P_2, and P_3 denoting matrices of at least asymptotically nonstochastic variables. The asymptotic covariance matrix of this 3SLS estimator is

$$\left[\text{plim } n^{-1} \frac{\partial\phi(\theta_0)'}{\partial\theta} A \frac{\partial\phi(\theta_0)}{\partial\theta'} \right]^{-1} \tag{86}$$

Amemiya shows that it is asymptotically less efficient than the FIML estimator. This result is reasonable because, as (71) demonstrates, for a nonlinear system one cannot create the most suitable instrumental variables by the operation $X(X'X)^{-1}X'$.

Parke (1982) has devised a computer algorithm to compute FIML and 3SLS estimates for nonlinear simultaneous-equation models and demonstrated the efficiency of his algorithm by estimating a 97-equation model of Fair. Hatanaka (1978) has discussed an asymptotically efficient two-step procedure for estimating a certain class of nonlinear systems.

★7.9 MODELS OF MARKETS IN DISEQUILIBRIUM

The method of maximum likelihood has been applied to estimate models of markets in disequilibrium. In its simplest form, such a model is exemplified by

$$D_t = D_t(p_t, x_{t1}) + \epsilon_{t1} = \alpha_1 p_t + \beta_1' x_{t1} + \epsilon_{t1} \tag{87}$$

$$S_t = S_t(p_t, x_{t2}) + \epsilon_{t2} = \alpha_2 p_t + \beta_2' x_{t2} + \epsilon_{t2} \tag{88}$$

and
$$Q_t = \min(D_t, S_t) \tag{89}$$

where D_t and S_t stand for demand and supply, which are not directly observed, and the observed quantity Q_t is the minimum of D_t and S_t, given the price p_t and the vectors x_{t1} and x_{t2} of exogenous variables. One may add a price-adjustment equation

$$p_t = p_{t-1} + \gamma(D_t - S_t) + \epsilon_{t3} \tag{90}$$

Such a model, with $\epsilon_{t3} = 0$, was first estimated by Fair and Jaffee (1972), and there has been a growing literature since. The modest aim of this section is to give a brief introduction to this topic so that readers who choose can pursue it further. Interested readers should consult Quandt (1982b) and Maddala (1980).

Consider the model of Eqs. (87) to (89). Let $p(D_t, S_t)$ be the joint-density function of the unobserved random variables D_t and S_t. Then the density function $h(Q_t)$ of Q_t is

$$h(Q_t) = f(Q_t \mid D_t < S_t) \Pr(D_t < S_t) + f(Q_t \mid D_t \geq S_t) \Pr(D_t \geq S_t) \tag{91}$$

where the conditional density functions are given by

$$f(Q_t \mid D_t < S_t) = \int_{Q_t}^{\infty} p(Q_t, S_t \mid D_t < S_t) \, dS_t$$

$$= [\Pr(D_t < S_t)]^{-1} \int_{Q_t}^{\infty} p(Q_t, S_t) \, dS_t$$

and
$$f(Q_t \mid D_t \geq S_t) = [\Pr(D_t \geq S_t)]^{-1} \int_{Q_t}^{\infty} p(D_t, Q_t) \, dD_t$$

Substituting into (91), we get

$$h(Q_t) = \int_{Q_t}^{\infty} p(Q_t, S_t) \, dS_t + \int_{Q_t}^{\infty} p(D_t, Q_t) \, dD_t \tag{92}$$

Assume that ε_{t1} and ε_{t2} are normal with means zero, variances σ_1^2 and σ_2^2, and covariance zero. Then

$$\int_{Q_t}^{\infty} p(Q_t, S_t) \, dS_t$$

$$= \frac{1}{2\pi\sigma_1\sigma_2} \int_{Q_t}^{\infty} \exp\left[-\frac{(Q_t - \alpha_1 p_t - \beta_1' x_{t1})^2}{2\sigma_1^2} - \frac{(S_t - \alpha_2 p_t - \beta_2' x_{t2})^2}{2\sigma_2^2} \right] dS_t$$

$$= \frac{1}{\sqrt{2\pi}\sigma_1} \exp\left[-\frac{(Q_t - \alpha_1 p_t - \beta_1' x_{t1})^2}{2\sigma_1^2} \right]\left[1 - \Phi\left(\frac{Q_t - \alpha_2 p_t - \beta_2' x_{t2}}{\sigma_2} \right) \right]$$

where $\Phi(z)$ is the cumulative standard normal distribution function

$$\Phi(z) = \int_{-\infty}^{z} \frac{1}{\sqrt{2\pi}} e^{-x^2/2} \, dx$$

A similar expression can be derived for the second integral of (92). The likelihood function is the product $\Pi_t\, h(Q_t)$

$$L = \prod_{t=1}^{n} \left\{ \frac{1}{\sqrt{2\pi}\sigma_1} \exp\left[-\frac{(Q_t - \alpha_1 p_t - \beta_1' x_{t1})^2}{2\sigma_1^2} \right]\left[1 - \Phi\left(\frac{Q_t - \alpha_2 p_t - \beta_2' x_{t2}}{\sigma_2} \right) \right] \right.$$

$$\left. + \frac{1}{\sqrt{2\pi}\sigma_2} \exp\left[-\frac{(Q_t - \alpha_2 p_t - \beta_2' x_{t2})^2}{2\sigma_2^2} \right]\left[1 - \Phi\left(\frac{Q_t - \alpha_1 p_t - \beta_1' x_{t1}}{\sigma_1} \right) \right] \right\}$$

$$(93)$$

(see Prob. 13). There are points on the boundary of the parameter space, with $\sigma_1 = 0$ or $\sigma_2 = 0$, at which the likelihood function (93) becomes unbounded. For example, if α_1 and β_1 are so chosen as to make $Q_s - \alpha_1 p_s - \beta_1' x_{s1} = 0$ for some time period s, and if $Q_t - \alpha_1 p_t - \beta_1' x_{t1} < 0$ for all $t \neq s$, as σ_1 converges to zero,

$$\frac{1}{\sqrt{2\pi}\sigma_1} \exp\left(-\frac{Q_s - \alpha_1 p_s - \beta_1' x_{s1}}{2\sigma_1^2} \right)$$

will approach infinity, and the last term of (93) in square brackets will not be zero for any $t \neq s$ to prevent the likelihood L from becoming infinity. Quandt (1982*b*) discusses this point and the maximum-likelihood estimation of this and more general disequilibrium models.

Before leaving this subject, it may be useful to point out that there is another way to model disequilibrium in the sense of having actual statistical observations deviate from the solution of a set of equilibrium simultaneous stochastic equations. The alternative model does not employ the minimum condition (89) which might prevail when price is fixed institutionally. If price and other economic variables are allowed to adjust toward an equilibrium specified by a set of simultaneous equations, one can choose the following model. To illustrate with a linear system, let

$$By_t^* + \Gamma x_t = \epsilon_t \tag{94}$$

explain the *equilibrium* value y_t^*, rather than the actual y_t as postulated by the standard linear simultaneous-equation model. The reduced-form equation for y_t^* is

$$y_t^* = -B^{-1}\Gamma x_t + B^{-1}\epsilon_t = \Pi x_t + v_t \tag{95}$$

We assume that the vector y_t of observed values of the endogenous variables is given by

$$y_t - y_{t-1} = D(y_t^* - y_{t-1}) \tag{96}$$

where D is a matrix measuring the speeds of adjustments. Certainly, a more complicated adjustment mechanism than (96) can be introduced, e.g., by assuming that $y_t - y_{t-1}$ is a nonlinear (vector) function of $y_t^* - y_{t-1}$, or that the elements of D are functions of other variables, or that terms involving y_{t-k}^* $(k \geq 1)$ should be included. However, for most purposes the simple form (96) will suffice.

In fact, we may often assume that D is a diagonal matrix and that some of its diagonal elements are unity. Substituting the right-hand side of (95) for y_t^* in (96), we write the model as

$$y_t = -DB^{-1}\Gamma x_t + (I - D)y_{t-1} + DB^{-1}\epsilon_t \tag{97}$$

This equation explains the observed values of the endogenous variables, as Eq. (95) explains the desired values y_t^* of the endogenous variables.

The motivation for the above model is that the system of simultaneous equations formulated by the economist determines only the values of the endogenous variables in equilibrium. One cannot automatically assume that these equilibrium or desired values will be directly observed in the market. The reasoning is exactly the same as that introduced to justify the use of partial adjustment to explain one dependent variable in a single equation. In that case, some equation, such as a demand equation for the stock of consumer durables, explains only the desired or equilibrium value. The change in the actual stock observed is then assumed to be a fraction of the difference between the desired stock and the stock existing in the last period. When a vector of desired values for the endogenous variables is determined by a system of simultaneous equations, a generalization of the single-equation model is to assume that the first difference $y_t - y_{t-1}$ of the observed endogenous variables is a linear transformation D of the vector $y_t^* - y_{t-1}$ of differences between the equilibrium values and the actual values of the preceding period. For a discussion of the rationale of this model, see Chow (1977).

If the simultaneous equations explaining the equilibrium y_t^* are linear, as given by (94), one immediately observes that the parameters $\Pi = -B^{-1}\Gamma$ of the reduced form (95) and the matrix D of the adjustment equation (96) can be consistently estimated by applying least squares to the autoregressive equations (97) or

$$y_t = D\Pi x_t + (I - D)y_{t-1} + BD^{-1}\epsilon_t \tag{98}$$

Since the method of least squares provides consistent estimates of the parameter matrices D and $I - D$ in Eq. (98) under the assumption that ϵ_t is serially uncorrelated, one can solve for the parameters D and Π. Given a consistent estimate of Π, one can apply the method of indirect least squares to obtain consistent estimates of the structural parameters B and Γ, using the equation $B\Pi = -\Gamma$. As is well known, if the ith structural equation is overidentified, there will be too many equations (too many columns of Π) to determine the unknown elements in the ith row of $[B \quad \Gamma]$. A consistent estimate of this row is still obtained by arbitrarily selecting just a sufficient number of columns of Π to solve for the unknown coefficients.

Another obvious method is 2SLS. We use the above consistent estimate of Π, say $\hat{\Pi}$, to form

$$\hat{y}_t^* = \hat{\Pi}x_t$$

These "estimated" values of the equilibrium endogenous variables y_t^* are, for large samples, uncorrelated with the disturbance term ϵ_t according to the reduced-form equations (95). We then use these "estimated" values of y_t^* to apply least squares, in the second stage, to an individual structural equation in (94).

The method of 3SLS is also applicable. We simply stack up the regression equations formulated for the application of the second stage of 2SLS as indicated above for all structural equations, and apply generalized least squares to the resulting stacked regression equations, using an estimate of the covariance matrix obtained from the 2SLS regression residuals. If ϵ_t is further assumed to be multivariate normal, one can apply the method of maximum likelihood, but this subject will not be pursued here.

7.10 DYNAMIC PROPERTIES OF NONLINEAR SIMULTANEOUS EQUATIONS

In Sec. 4.10 we studied dynamic properties of linear simultaneous equations including various multipliers measuring the effects of current and lagged exogenous variables on the current endogenous variables. This section treats the dynamic properties of a system of nonlinear simultaneous equations with additive disturbances. In accordance with the common practice of econometric model builders, the ith endogenous variable is assumed to be an explicit function of the other endogenous variables, lagged endogenous variables, and current and lagged exogenous variables. Thus the ith structural equation is written as

$$y_{ti} = \phi_i(y_{t.}, y_{t-1.}, z_{t.}) + \epsilon_{ti} \qquad (i = 1, \ldots, G) \qquad (99)$$

where $y_{t.}$ is a vector of G endogenous variables and $z_{t.}$ is a vector of K exogenous variables. If $y_{t-2.}, \ldots, z_{t-1.}$, etc., appear in the original system, we can introduce identities to get rid of them, as we did in Sec. 4.10. In studying the dynamic properties of a system of equations (99), we assume the parameter vector θ_i of each equation to be known and suppress it from the function ϕ_i. If we allow for the sampling fluctuations of our estimate $\hat{\theta}_i$ of θ_i, the analysis will be more complicated.

The first step in any dynamic analysis is to solve the nonlinear system forward through time, beginning from the first period of interest, called period 1, and assuming the lagged endogenous variables $y_0.$ of the previous period to be given. Since there is no ambiguity, we shall omit the dots in the subscripts of $y_{t.}$, $z_{t.}$, and $\epsilon_{t.}$. Solving the system forward through time is called *simulation* in the econometrics literature. If the ϵ_t are generated by some random process, it is called a *stochastic simulation*. If the ϵ_t are set equal to zero, it is called a *deterministic simulation*. A common method of solving the nonlinear system, the *Gauss-Siedel method*, computes the values of y_{ti}^{r+1} in the $(r+1)$th iteration by the equations

$$y_{t1}^{r+1} = \phi_1(y_{t1}^{r+1}, y_{t2}^r, \ldots, y_{tG}^r; y_{t-1}, z_t) + \epsilon_{t1}$$

$$y_{t2}^{r+1} = \phi_2(y_{t1}^{r+1}, y_{t2}^{r+1}, y_{t3}^r, \ldots, y_{tG}^r; y_{t-1}, z_t) + \epsilon_{t2}$$

$$y_{t3}^{r+1} = \phi_3(y_{t1}^{r+1}, y_{t2}^{r+1}, y_{t3}^{r+1}, \ldots, y_{tG}^r; y_{t-1}, z_t) + \epsilon_{t3} \qquad (100)$$

$$\cdots\cdots\cdots\cdots\cdots\cdots\cdots\cdots\cdots\cdots\cdots\cdots\cdots\cdots$$

$$y_{tG}^{r+1} = \phi_G(y_{t1}^{r+1}, \ldots, y_{t,G-1}^{r+1}, y_{tG}^{r+1}; y_{t-1}, z_t) + \epsilon_{tG}$$

Each function ϕ_i is used to compute y_{ti}^{r+1}, assuming $y_{t1}^{r+1}, \ldots, y_{t,i-1}^{r+1}$ to have been computed before and treating y_{t-1} and z_t as given. Usually, y_{ti} is not an argument of ϕ_i; if it were, we would iterate on y_{ti} until $y_{ti}^{r+1} = \phi_i(\ldots, y_{ti}^{r+1}, \ldots; y_{t-1}, z_t) + \epsilon_{ti}$ was satisfied.

Several characteristics of the Gauss-Siedel method should be noted:

1. The unknowns in each iteration are computed one at a time. Thus y_{t1}^{r+1} is computed first and is used to compute y_{t2}^{r+1}. Both are then used to compute y_{t3}^{r+1}, and so forth. These unknowns are solved one at a time rather than simultaneously, as in the Newton-Raphson method, for instance.
2. Since in nearly all econometric applications, the variable y_{ti} is not an argument of ϕ_i, each y_{ti}^{r+1} is solved simply by evaluating the function ϕ_i.
3. How fast and whether the method converges depends on how the equations are ordered. There are $G!$ ways of ordering the G equations, and some will lead to faster convergence than others.
4. Given any ordering, there is no guarantee that the iterations will converge to a solution.

For example, consider the following two equations for y_1 and y_2, with subscript t omitted,

$$y_1 = 2y_2 + 1$$

$$y_2 = y_1 + 3$$

Starting with $y_1^0 = 0$ and $y_2^0 = 0$, say, the iterations by the Gauss-Siedel method will not converge. In practice, however, when damping factors are introduced to inhibit oscillations and when the ordering and other convergence problems are properly dealt with, the Gauss-Siedel method has been found very useful for solving nonlinear structural equations in econometrics.

Once the system can be solved forward from $t = 1$ to $t = T$, we can linearize the system about the solution path $\bar{y}_t$ obtained by a deterministic simulation in order to study the dynamic properties of the system. Let $\bar{y}_t$ satisfy

$$\bar{y}_{ti} = \phi_i(\bar{y}_t, \bar{y}_{t-1}, z_t^0) \qquad \begin{aligned} i &= 1, \ldots, G \\ t &= 1, \ldots, T \end{aligned} \qquad (101)$$

or, with ϕ denoting the vector function consisting of $\phi_1, \ldots, \phi_G$,

$$\bar{y}_t = \phi(\bar{y}_t, \bar{y}_{t-1}, z_t^0) \qquad (102)$$

where z_t^0 is treated as given. We linearize y_t about $\bar{y}_t$, $\bar{y}_{t-1}$, and z_t^0 using a first-order Taylor series

$$y_t = \phi(y_t, y_{t-1}, z_t) + \epsilon_t$$

$$= \phi(\bar{y}_t, \bar{y}_{t-1}, z_t^0) + \frac{\partial \phi}{\partial y_t'}(y_t - \bar{y}_t) + \frac{\partial \phi}{\partial y_{t-1}'}(y_{t-1} - \bar{y}_{t-1})$$

$$+ \frac{\partial \phi}{\partial z_t'}(z_t - z_t^0) + \epsilon_t$$

$$= \bar{y}_t + B_{1t}(y_t - \bar{y}_t) + B_{2t}(y_{t-1} - \bar{y}_{t-1}) + B_{3t}(z_t - z_t^0) + \epsilon_t \qquad (103)$$

where the matrices B_{it} of derivatives of the vector ϕ with respect to its ith vector arguments are evaluated at $\bar{y}_t$, $\bar{y}_{t-1}$, and z_t^0; (103) is a set of linearized structural equations.

The linearized structural equations (103) can be solved to obtain a set of linearized reduced-form equations

$$y_t - \bar{y}_t = (I - B_{1t})^{-1} B_{2t}(y_{t-1} - \bar{y}_{t-1}) + (I - B_{1t})^{-1} B_{3t}(z_t - z_t^0)$$

$$+ (I - B_{1t})^{-1} \epsilon_t$$

$$= \Pi_{1t}(y_{t-1} - \bar{y}_{t-1}) + \Pi_{0t}(z_t - z_t^0) + v_t \qquad (104)$$

or
$$y_t = \Pi_{1t} y_{t-1} + \Pi_{0t} z_t + \pi_{0t} + v_t \qquad (105)$$

where
$$\pi_{0t} = \bar{y}_t - \Pi_{1t} \bar{y}_{t-1} - \Pi_{0t} z_t^0$$

The linearized final-form equations for our model are obtained by repeated substitutions for the lagged endogenous variables in the linearized reduced form (105)

$$y_t = \Pi_{0t} z_t + \Pi_{1t} \Pi_{0, t-1} z_{t-1} + \Pi_{1t} \Pi_{1, t-1} \Pi_{0, t-2} z_{t-2} + \cdots$$

$$+ \Pi_{1t} \cdots \Pi_{1, 2} \Pi_{0, 1} z_1 + \pi_{0t} + \Pi_{1t} \pi_{0, t-1} + \Pi_{1t} \Pi_{1, t-1} \pi_{0, t-2} + \cdots$$

$$+ \Pi_{1t} \cdots \Pi_{1, 2} \pi_{0, 1} + v_t + \Pi_{1t} v_{t-1} + \Pi_{1t} \Pi_{1, t-1} v_{t-2} + \cdots$$

$$+ \Pi_{1t} \cdots \Pi_{1, 2} v_1 + \Pi_{1t} \cdots \Pi_{1, 1} y_0 \qquad (106)$$

The impact multipliers are given by the matrix Π_{0t}. The delayed multipliers after one period are given by the matrix $\Pi_{1t} \Pi_{0, t-1}$, and so forth. The method proposed above for computing the multipliers for a nonlinear simultaneous-equation model is to obtain a linearized model (103) first and then solve for the linearized reduced form. In the 1970s many practicing econometricians computed the multipliers Π_{0t} by solving the nonlinear systems for y_t many times after perturbing each variable in z_t by a small amount from the given value z_t^0 and evaluating numerically the rates of changes of y_{ti} with respect to z_{tj}. The method we have recommended requires solving the system only once to satisfy (102). We then linearize the system about the solution path $\bar{y}_t$ to obtain the various multipliers as indicated.

If one is willing to approximate a nonlinear system by a linearized system as of a period t which is considered to be representative, one can apply the tools of

Chap. 6 to study the dynamic properties of the linearized system, including the autocovariance matrix and the spectral-density matrix for the measurement of cyclical properties. Dynamic analysis of nonlinear systems is treated in Chow (1975, chap. 6).

PROBLEMS

1. For the model of a system of linear regression equations presented in Sec. 3.1, let y denote a column vector consisting of $y_1., \ldots, y_n.$, where $y_t.$ is a vector of G dependent variables observed in period t ($t = 1, \ldots, n$). Stack the n regression equations for $y_1., \ldots, y_n.$ to form a single regression equation. Apply GLS to estimate the vector β of all regression coefficients. Write out the covariance matrix V of the regression residuals explicitly and using Kronecker products.

2. For model (6) let y denote a column vector consisting of $y_1., \ldots, y_n.$. Stack the n regression equations to form a single regression equation. Write out the covariance matrix V of the regression residuals explicitly and using Kronecker products.

3. For the nonlinear regression model of Sec. 7.3, we have shown in (32) how to test the hypothesis $R\theta = r$ by using the matrix $\hat{C}$ given in (31). Develop a test of the same hypothesis using the analysis of variance as presented in Sec. 2.7.

4. Apply the Newton-Raphson method to estimate model (1). Show the iteration formula.

5. Apply the Gauss-Newton method to estimate model (1). Show the iteration formula.

6. Show that the Gauss-Newton method, when applied to the maximum-likelihood estimation of model (6) with normal $\epsilon_t.$, is equivalent to first linearizing the model and then applying the method of maximum likelihood.

7. Show that, for model (6) with normal $\epsilon_t.$, the estimator of θ obtained by linearization of the model and application of the method of maximum likelihood is, when converging, identical with the estimator obtained by applying the maximum-likelihood method to the original model using a Newton-Raphson algorithm.

8. Explain how the method of scoring can be applied to estimate (a) model (1), (b) model (6), and (c) model (8).

9. Show how the Gauss-Newton method can be used to compute FIML estimate of the nonlinear simultaneous-equation model. In particular, indicate which terms in $(\partial^2 \log L)/(\partial \theta \, \partial \theta')$ should be omitted and why.

10. Show how the method of scoring can be used to compute FIML estimate of the nonlinear simultaneous-equation model. Explain the computational steps clearly.

11. Linearize each equation of the nonlinear simultaneous-equation model. Stack up the G linearized equations. Apply 3SLS to this model. How does the result compare with the nonlinear 3SLS estimator of Jorgenson and Laffont given in Sec. 7.8?

12. Explain concisely why the normal equations for estimating the parameters of *linear* simultaneous equations are *nonlinear*. In Sec. 7.1 we pointed out that applying least squares or maximum likelihood to *linear* regression models will lead to *linear* estimating equations. Why is this not the case for simultaneous-equation models?

13. Derive the likelihood function for the disequilibrium model (87) to (89) if ϵ_{t1} and ϵ_{t2} are jointly normal with means zero, variances σ_1^2 and σ_2^2, and covariance σ_{12}.

14. Linearize the system

$$y_{t1} = 1 + 2e^{-.05y_{t2}}$$

$$y_{t2} = .4e^{.02y_{t1}}$$

about $y_{t1} = 3$ and $y_{t2} = 1$.

15. Find the second-order Taylor expansion of the system of Prob. 14 about $y_{t1} = 3$ and $y_{t2} = 1$.

16. Starting with initial values $y_{t1} = 3$ and $y_{t2} = 1$, solve the system of Prob. 14 (a) by the Gauss-Siedel method and (b) by the Newton-Raphson method, showing each iteration.

REFERENCES

Amemiya, T. (1974): "The Nonlinear Two-Stage Least-Squares Estimator," *J. Econometr.* **2**: 105–110.

—— (1977): "The Maximum-Likelihood and Nonlinear Three-Stage Least-Squares Estimator in the General Nonlinear Simultaneous-Equation Model," *Econometrica*, **45**: 955–968.

Berndt, E. K., B. H. Hall, T. E. Hall, and J. A. Hausman (1974): "Estimation and Inference in Nonlinear Structural Models," *Ann. Econ. Soc. Meas.*, **3**: 653–666.

Chow, G. C. (1968): "Two Methods of Computing Full-Information Maximum Likelihood Estimates in Simultaneous Stochastic Equations," *Int. Econ. Rev.*, **9**: 100–112.

—— (1973): "On the Computation of Full-Information Maximum-Likelihood Estimates for Nonlinear Equations Systems," *Rev. Econ. Statist.*, **55**: 104–109.

—— (1974): "A Family of Estimators for Simultaneous Equation Systems," *Int. Econ. Rev.*, **15**: 654–666.

—— (1975): *Analysis and Control of Dynamic Economic Systems*, Wiley, New York.

—— (1977): "A Reformulation of Simultaneous-Equations Models for Markets in Disequilibrium," *Princeton Univ., Econometr. Res. Prog. Res. Mem.*, 213.

—— and R. C. Fair (1973): "Maximum-Likelihood Estimation of Linear Equations Systems with Auto-Regressive Residuals," *Ann. Econ. Soc. Meas.*, **2**: 17–28.

Fair, R. C. (1974): "On the Robust Estimation of Econometric Models," *Ann. Econ. Soc. Meas.*, **3**: 667–678.

—— and D. Jaffee (1972): "Methods of Estimation for Markets in Disequilibrium," *Econometrica*, **40**: 497–514.

Gallant, A. R. (1973): "Inference for Nonlinear Models," *North Carolina State Univ., Raleigh, N.C.*, Mimeo. Ser. 875.

—— (1975a): "Nonlinear Regression," *Am. Statist.*, **29**: 73–81.

—— (1975b) "Explicit Estimators of Parametric Functions in Nonlinear Regression," *J. Am. Statist. Assoc.*, **75**: 182–193.

Goldfeld, S. M., and R. E. Quandt (1972): *Nonlinear Methods in Econometrics*, North-Holland, Amsterdam.

—— and —— (1976): *Studies in Nonlinear Estimation*, Ballinger, Cambridge, Mass.

——, ——, and H. F. Trotter (1966): "Maximization by Quadratic Hill-Climbing," *Econometrica*, **34**: 541–551.

Hatanaka, M. (1978): "On the Efficient Estimation Methods for the Macro-Economic Models Nonlinear in Variables," *J. Econometrics*, **8**: 323–356.

Jorgenson, D. W., and J. Laffont (1974): "Efficient Estimation of Nonlinear Simultaneous Equations with Additive Disturbances," *Ann. Econ. Soc. Meas.*, **3**: 615–640.

Maddala, G. S. (1980): "Disequilibrium, Self-Selection and Switching Models," *Calif. Inst. Technol. Soc. Sci. Working Pap.* 303.

Malinvaud, E. (1970a): *Statistical Methods of Econometrics*, American Elsevier, New York.

—— (1970b): "The Consistency of Nonlinear Regressions," *Ann. Math. Statist.*, **41**: 956–969.

Parke, W. R. (1982): "An Algorithm for FIML and 3SLS Estimation of Large Nonlinear Models," *Econometrica*, **50**: 81–96.

Powell, M. J. D. (1964): "An Efficient Method for Finding the Minimum of a Function of Several Variables without Calculating Derivatives," *Comp. J.*, **7**: 155–162.

Quandt, R. E. (1982a): "Computational Problems and Methods," in Z. Griliches and M. Intriligator (eds.), *Handbook of Econometrics, vol. II*, North-Holland, Amsterdam.

—— (1982b): "Econometric Disequilibrium Models," *Econometr. Rev.*, **1**: 1–63.

DISCRETE AND LIMITED DEPENDENT VARIABLES

8.1 INTRODUCTION

One of the major developments in econometrics in the 1960s and 1970s was the increasing use of microeconomic data on individual economic units. For example, in the study of consumer durable goods using micro data, an econometrician can study the factors determining whether a family will buy a car in a certain period. The study of the demand for automobiles in the United States cited in Chap. 2 used mainly aggregate data on the total demand for automobiles in the United States. To arrive at such an aggregate demand relationship it is reasonable to assume that desired demand is a continuous variable. Recall that cars of different qualities, as approximately measured by age, are counted as different units, with a current-year model counting as 1 unit, a 1-year-old model counting as .75 unit, etc. The quantity of cars so specified is treated as a continuous variable. Given income, price, and other factors, a family may demand 1.28 cars for use. At any given time the family's ownership of cars may be somewhat more or less than the 1.28 units according to its demand equation, partly because of the transactions costs in trading cars in order to keep the stock of cars exactly at the desired level all the time. There also are delays in changing the stock of cars to reflect the changes in income and other factors. Such a theory has been found to be a reasonable first approximation for explaining aggregate demand behavior.

To explain the demand behavior of individual economic units one may wish to build a model which is capable of explaining the probability that a family of given characteristics will buy a car. Let z_i be a vector of the important characteristics pertaining to family i and to the car which affect the probability in question.

Let $y_i = \beta' z_i$, where β is a vector of unknown coefficients. The probability is assumed to be a function of y_i. Since the probability must lie between 0 and 1, the range of the function of y must be between 0 and 1.

Two of the most popular statistical models explaining the probability of an economic unit's taking a certain action are the probit model and the logit model. The *probit model* assumes that the probability $G(y)$ is given by the cumulative standard normal distribution function

$$G(y) = \Phi(y) = \int_0^y (2\pi)^{-1/2} e^{-s^2/2} \, ds \tag{1}$$

The *logit model* assumes that the probability $G(y)$ is given by the logistic curve

$$G(y) = \frac{1}{1 + e^{-y}} = \frac{e^y}{e^y + 1} \tag{2}$$

Section 8.2 describes probit analysis briefly. Section 8.3 is devoted to logic analysis for the choice of two alternatives (buying a car or not buying). Section 8.4 provides a theoretical basis for discrete-choice models in terms of utility maximization. Section 8.5 is concerned with maximum-likelihood estimation and related statistics for the multinomial logit model, which explains the choice of one among J alternatives. Section 8.6 presents the nested logit model, which is a variation of the multinomial logit model.

Besides the need to construct models for explaining discrete-choice situations, the econometrician using microdata is faced with the problem that the sample selected often excludes certain data points arbitrarily. Two cases are of particular interest. The first was called to our attention by Tobin (1958), when he observed that if $\beta' x_i$ determines the continuous quantity y_i of a commodity to be purchased, this quantity cannot be negative. Thus all observations with a negative y_i are arbitrarily ruled out. *Tobit analysis* is designed to deal with this situation, as discussed in Sec. 8.7. The second case involves models with sample selection bias. It arises when the sample selected arbitrarily excludes observations for which the values of some explanatory variables fall within certain ranges. For example, in a study of consumer behavior, only consumers with incomes below a certain level have been included. Section 8.9 is concerned with models having such selection biases. Section 8.8 deals with the E-M algorithm, a method for computing maximum-likelihood estimates when the original observations are distorted by a certain observation mechanism, e.g., reporting zeros for negative values of the dependent variable in the Tobit model. Although this algorithm is of general interest, it is conveniently presented in connection with the discussion of Tobit analysis.

8.2 PROBIT ANALYSIS

Let z_i denote a vector of characteristics of the ith economic unit and of the object of choice which are explanatory variables for the probability P_1 that the ith unit will choose alternative 1, say buying a car. According to the *probit model*, this probability is

$$P_1(z_i) = \int_{-\infty}^{\beta' z_i} (2\pi)^{-1/2} e^{-s^2/2} \, ds = \Phi(\beta' z_i) \tag{3}$$

where β is a vector of unknown coefficients. Let the sample consist of n economic units. These units are so arranged that the first m of them chose alternative 1 and the remaining $n - m$ units did not choose alternative 1. The likelihood of observing the sample is

$$L = \prod_{i=1}^{m} \Phi(\beta' z_i) \prod_{i=m+1}^{n} [1 - \Phi(\beta' z_i)]$$

The log-likelihood function is

$$\log L = \sum_{i=1}^{m} \log \Phi(\beta' z_i) + \sum_{i=m+1}^{n} \log [1 - \Phi(\beta' z_i)] \tag{4}$$

To apply the method of maximum likelihood to estimate β we differentiate (4) and obtain the first-order condition

$$\frac{\partial \log L}{\partial \beta} = \sum_{i=1}^{m} [\Phi(\beta' z_i)]^{-1} \phi(\beta' z_i) z_i - \sum_{i=1}^{m} [1 - \Phi(\beta' z_i)]^{-1} \phi(\beta' z_i) z_i = 0 \tag{5}$$

where $\phi(x)$ is the standard normal density function

$$\phi(x) = (2\pi)^{-1/2} e^{-x^2/2} = \frac{d\Phi(x)}{dx} \tag{6}$$

To solve the set of nonlinear equations (5) or to maximize $\log L$ one can apply one of the numerical methods discussed in Sec. 7.5. Using the gradient given by (5), one can apply a gradient method for maximizing $\log L$.

8.3 LOGIT ANALYSIS

A model which is often more convenient than the probit model and has gained popularity in econometrics is the *logit model*. It assumes that the probability P_1 for the ith unit having characteristics z_i to choose alternative 1 is given by

$$P_1(z_i) = P_{1i} = \frac{e^{\beta' z_i}}{e^{\beta' z_i} + 1} \tag{7}$$

To manipulate with this model, the following simple identities are useful:

$$e^{\beta' z_i} = P_{1i}(e^{\beta' z_i} + 1) \qquad e^{\beta' z_i} = \frac{P_{1i}}{1 - P_{1i}}$$

$$\log \frac{P_{1i}}{1 - P_{1i}} = \beta' z_i \qquad 1 - P_{1i} = \frac{1}{e^{\beta' z_i} + 1} \tag{8}$$

To form the likelihood of observing the sample, we introduce a dummy variable f_{1i} such that

$$f_{1i} = \begin{cases} 1 & \text{if } i\text{th unit chose alternative 1} \\ 0 & \text{if } i\text{th unit did not choose alternative 1} \end{cases} \tag{9}$$

The likelihood of the sample of n observations is

$$L = \prod_{i=1}^{n} P_{1i}^{f_{1i}}(1 - P_{1i})^{1 - f_{1i}} \tag{10}$$

The log-likelihood function is

$$
\log L = \sum_{i=1}^{n} [f_{1i} \log P_{1i} + (1 - f_{1i}) \log (1 - P_{1i})]
$$

$$
= \sum_{i=1}^{n} \{f_{1i}[\log P_{1i} - \log (1 - P_{1i})] + \log (1 - P_{1i})\}
$$

$$
= \sum_{i=1}^{n} f_{1i} \beta' z_i - \sum_{i=1}^{n} \log (1 + e^{\beta' z_i}) \tag{11}
$$

where the last line has made use of (8).

To obtain the maximum-likelihood estimator of β we differentiate $\log L$

$$\frac{\partial \log L}{\partial \beta} = \sum_{i=1}^{n} f_{1i} z_i - \sum_{i=1}^{n} (1 + e^{\beta' z_i})^{-1} e^{\beta' z_i} z_i = \sum_{i=1}^{n} (f_{1i} - P_{1i}) z_i = 0 \tag{12}$$

$$\frac{\partial^2 \log L}{\partial \beta \, \partial \beta'} = -\sum_{i=1}^{n} z_i \frac{\partial P_{1i}}{\partial \beta'} = -\sum_{i=1}^{n} z_i \frac{e^{\beta' z_i}}{e^{\beta' z_i} + 1} z_i' + \frac{(e^{\beta' z_i})^2}{(e^{\beta' z_i} + 1)^2} z_i'$$

$$= -\sum_{i=1}^{n} z_i P_{1i}(1 - P_{1i}) z_i' \tag{13}$$

If n is greater than or equal to the number of elements of z and if the z's are not collinear, matrix (13) is negative definite. Using (12) and (13), one can apply the Newton-Raphson method of Sec. 7.5 to maximize $\log L$. Given the initial values β^0 of β in each iteration, we use (7) to compute P_{1i}. Then (12) and (13) can be used to compute β' in the following iteration by the Newton-Raphson formula

$$\beta^1 = \beta^0 - k\left(\frac{\partial^2 \log L}{\partial \beta \, \partial \beta'}\right)^{-1} \frac{\partial \log L}{\partial \beta} \tag{14}$$

where k is the step size, discussed in Sec. 7.5.

To start the iteration, one can find an initial estimate β^0 of β by regressing the dummy variable f_{1i} on the explanatory variables z_i. The regression model

$$f_{1i} = \beta' z_i + \epsilon_i \tag{15}$$

is called a *linear probability* model, as it estimates the probability of choosing a given alternative 1 by a linear function of z_i. The problems with this model are that $\beta' z_i$ is not allowed to fall outside the range between 0 and 1 and that a linear function of continuous variables is not a good approximation to the probability of an event. However, this model is good enough for providing an initial estimate β^0 for use in estimating the logit model. The covariance matrix of $\hat{\beta}$ obtained by iterating with Eq. (14) can be estimated by

$$\left(-\frac{\partial^2 \log L}{\partial \beta \, \partial \beta'} \right)^{-1} = \left[\sum_{i=1}^{n} z_i P_{1i}(1 - P_{1i}) z_i' \right]^{-1} \tag{16}$$

where P_{1i} is given by (7) with β replaced by $\hat{\beta}$.

★8.4 UTILITY THEORY FOR DISCRETE-CHOICE MODELS

Much progress in the development and applications of the logit and related models in econometrics has been due to McFadden (1973, 1976, 1978) and Domencich and McFadden (1975), on which our discussion is based. A good survey article on qualitative choice models is Amemiya (1981).

McFadden has provided a utility theory which can serve as a theoretical basis for discrete-choice models. Let x_{ji} be a vector of characteristics of an alternative j to the individual i, such as different attributes of a car, s_i be a vector of characteristics of the ith consumer, e.g., income, education, sex, etc. These characteristics are summarized by a vector $z_{ji} = z_{ji}(x_{ji}, s_i)$. The utility of the ith consumer choosing alternative j ($j = 1, \ldots, J$) is assumed to be

$$u_i = u(z_{ji}) = V(z_{ji}) + \epsilon(z_{ji}) \tag{17}$$

The utility is decomposed into its mean V and a random part ϵ. The utility function (17) is partly an indirect utility function. A direct utility function has as its arguments the quantities and qualities of the goods chosen. The consumer is assumed to maximize the direct utility function subject to budget constraints, arriving at demand functions for the quantities and qualities of goods as functions of the consumer's income and prices. The indirect utility function results from substituting these functions of income and prices for the quantities and qualities of goods in the direct utility function. Since income may enter as an argument of u_i, it is partly an indirect utility function. The literature is not very explicit about how the function u_i itself is derived from utility maximization subject to a budget constraint.

Taking u as our starting point, we can state that the consumer will choose alternative j over all other alternatives when J alternatives are available if $u(z_{ji}) > u(z_{ki})$ for all $k \neq j$ or if

$$\epsilon(z_{ki}) - \epsilon(z_{ji}) < V(z_{ji}) - V(z_{ki}) \qquad \text{for } k \neq j \tag{18}$$

The probability P_{ji} for the jth alternative to be chosen is

$$P_{ji} = \text{Pr}\left[\epsilon(z_{ki}) - \epsilon(z_{ji}) < V_j - V_k \right] \qquad k \neq j \tag{19}$$

where $V_j = V(z_{ji})$, the individual i being understood. We first consider the case of choosing between only two alternatives, or $J = 2$. Letting G be the cumulative distribution function of the difference $\epsilon(z_{2i}) - \epsilon(z_{1i})$, we can write the probability P_1 of choosing alternative 1 as

$$P_1 = \Pr[\epsilon(z_{2i}) - \epsilon(z_{1i}) < V(z_{1i}) - V(z_{2i})] = G[V(z_{1i}) - V(z_{2i})] \tag{20}$$

We shall assume that V is a linear function of z_{ji}

$$V(z_{ji}) = \beta' z_{ji} \tag{21}$$

that $\epsilon(z_{ji}) = \epsilon_j$ is not a function of z_{ji} and that ϵ_1 and ϵ_2 are statistically independent.

If the function G is the cumulative standard normal distribution function Φ, by (20) and (21) we have

$$P_1 = \Phi(\beta' z_{1i} - \beta' z_{2i}) \tag{22}$$

which gives rise to the probit model (3). If G is logistic, we have

$$P_1 = \frac{1}{1 + \exp\left[-(\beta' z_{1i} - \beta' z_{2i})\right]} \tag{23}$$

which gives rise to the logit model (7). One may ask: What probability distributions for ϵ_1 and ϵ_2 do we have to assume to generate the probit and logit models? If ϵ_1 and ϵ_2 are independently normal, their difference is also normal. Then G is a cumulative normal distribution generating the probit model. If ϵ_1 and ϵ_2 are independently *Weibull*, the cumulative distribution G of the difference $\epsilon_2 - \epsilon_1$ will generate a logit model for P_1, using Eq. (20).

A Weibull distribution has only one parameter α. The cumulative Weibull distribution function for ϵ_j is

$$\Pr(\epsilon_j < \epsilon) = \exp\left(-e^{-(\epsilon + \alpha_j)}\right) \tag{24}$$

The density function is

$$\text{pdf}(\epsilon) = e^{-(\epsilon + \alpha_j)} \exp\left(-e^{-(\epsilon + \alpha_j)}\right) \tag{25}$$

The Weibull distribution has the following characteristics. When the parameter $\alpha = 0$, the mode of the density function is zero; the mean is .575, and the variance is 1.622. Compared with a normal density having mean .5 and unit variance, the Weibull density with $\alpha = 0$ is somewhat skew, having a thicker right tail and shorter left tail (see Prob. 1). If ϵ_i has a Weibull distribution with parameter α_i, then for any constant c, $\epsilon_i + c$ has a Weibull distribution with parameter $\alpha_i - c$ (see Prob. 2). Let ϵ_j $(j = 1, \ldots, J)$ have independent Weibull distributions with parameters α_j, then the maximum of ϵ_j will have a Weibull distribution with parameter $-\log \Sigma_{j=1}^J e^{-\alpha_j}$ (see Prob. 3). We also have, for given V_j,

$$\Pr(V_1 + \epsilon_1 > V_2 + \epsilon_2) = \frac{e^{V_1 - \alpha_1}}{e^{V_1 - \alpha_1} + e^{V_2 - \alpha_2}} \tag{26}$$

$$\Pr(V_j + \epsilon_j > V_k + \epsilon_k, k = 1, \ldots, J) = \frac{e^{V_j - \alpha_j}}{\sum_{k=1}^J e^{V_k - \alpha_k}} \tag{27}$$

If we define $V_k = \beta'z_{ki} + \alpha_k$ so that $V_k - \alpha_k = \beta'z_{ki}$ $(k = 1, \ldots, J)$, we can use (19) and (27) to write

$$P_{ji} = \frac{e^{\beta'z_{ji}}}{\sum_{k=1}^{J} e^{\beta'z_{ki}}} \tag{28}$$

which gives the probability that an individual i will choose alternative j among J alternatives according to the *multinomial logit model*. For $J = 2$, (28) is is reduced to

$$P_{1i} = \frac{e^{\beta'z_{1i}}}{e^{\beta'z_{1i}} + e^{\beta'z_{2i}}} = \frac{1}{1 + e^{-\beta'(z_{1i}-z_{2i})}} \tag{29}$$

which agrees with the logit model (7). Note that the characteristics z_{1i} of alternative 1 for individual i in the model (7) are measured relative to the characteristics z_{2i} of alternative 2.

An implication of the multinomial logit model is that

$$\frac{P_{ji}}{P_{ki}} = \frac{e^{V(z_{ji})}}{e^{V(z_{ki})}} \qquad \log \frac{P_{ji}}{P_{ki}} = V(z_{ji}) - V(z_{ki}) \tag{30}$$

Property (30) gives rise to mathematical convenience for the model as it limits the applicability; it asserts that the relative probabilities of choosing between alternatives j and k are unaffected by the existence of a third alternative. For example, if a consumer is choosing between a radio and a black-and-white TV set, the relative probabilities may be .5 and .5, given the consumer's income, the prices, and other characteristics. When a color TV set appears as a third alternative, the relative probabilities may be .3, .1, and .6, changing the ratio of the first two probabilities and violating property (30). This property is known as the *axiom of independence from irrelevant alternatives*. In empirical applications, the multinomial logit model with this property may not be a good approximation to reality and another discrete-choice model may be preferable.

The above property no longer holds if we relax the assumption that the random variables $\epsilon_1, \ldots, \epsilon_J$ are statistically independent Weibull variables. McFadden (1978) has generalized the cumulative distribution function (24) for independent $\epsilon_j (j = 1, \ldots, J)$ to

$$F(\epsilon_1, \ldots, \epsilon_J) = \exp\left[-G(e^{-\epsilon_1}, \ldots, e^{-\epsilon_J})\right] \tag{31}$$

where G is specified to be a nonnegative homogeneous function of degree 1, tending toward $+\infty$ when any of its arguments tends toward $+\infty$. The nth partial derivatives of G are nonnegative for odd n and nonpositive for even n. The class of models derived from (31) with G so specified is called *generalized extreme-value* (GEV) *models*. If G takes the form

$$G(y_1, \ldots, y_J) = \sum_{j=1}^{J} y_j \tag{32}$$

the variables ϵ_j are independent Weibull and the model is multinomial logit with P_{ji} given by (28).

In general, given (31), the marginal distribution with respect to each ϵ_j is a univariate extreme-value distribution

$$F_j(\epsilon_j) = \lim_{\substack{\epsilon k \to \infty \\ k \neq j}} F(\epsilon_1, \ldots, \epsilon_J) = \exp\left(-c_j e^{-\epsilon_j}\right) \tag{33}$$

where $c_j = G(\delta_{j1}, \ldots, \delta_{jJ})$ with $\delta_{ij} = 1$ if $i = j$ and $\delta_{ij} = 0$ otherwise. As before, if the ith economic unit maximizes its utility (17), the probability of choosing the jth alternative is

$$P_j = \frac{e^{V_j} G_j(e^{V_1}, \ldots, e^{V_J})}{G(e^{V_1}, \ldots, e^{V_J})} \tag{34}$$

where G_j is the partial derivative of G with respect to its jth argument.

It may be useful to exhibit two other generalized extreme-value models besides the multinomial logit. The two-level *nested logit model* is derived from the function

$$G(y_1, \ldots, y_J) = \sum_{r=1}^{R} \left(\sum_{k \in B_r} y_k^{1/\rho_r} \right)^{\rho_r} \tag{35}$$

In this model, there are R exhaustive and mutually exclusive subsets of alternatives, B_r denoting the rth subset. The probability P_j of choosing alternative j is the product of the probability of choosing the subset B_s to which j belongs and the probability of choosing the jth alternative within that subset

$$P_j = \frac{e^{V_j/\rho_s}}{\sum_{k \in B_s} e^{V_k/\rho_s}} \frac{e^{\rho_s I_s}}{\sum_{r=1}^{R} e^{\rho_r I_r}} \tag{36}$$

where

$$I_r = \log\left(\sum_{k \in B_r} e^{V_k/\rho_r} \right)$$

A simple *ordered logit model* is derived from the function

$$G(y_1, \ldots, y_J) = \sum_{j=1}^{J+1} (\tfrac{1}{2} y_j^{1/\rho} + \tfrac{1}{2} y_{j-1}^{1/\rho})^\rho \tag{37}$$

where ρ is a constant satisfying $0 < \rho \leq 1$ and $y_0 \equiv y_{J+1} \equiv 0$. This model allows for some covariance between the neighboring ϵ_j and ϵ_{j-1}. For a discussion of this model see Small (1981) and Small and Brownstone (1981). Nested logit models will be discussed in Sec. 8.6.

8.5 MAXIMUM-LIKELIHOOD ESTIMATION OF MULTINOMIAL LOGIT MODELS

Let us apply the method of maximum likelihood to estimate the parameter vector β of a multinomial logit model. The probability for the ith consumer to choose alternative j is

$$P_{ji} = \frac{e^{\beta' z_{ji}}}{\sum_k e^{\beta' z_{ki}}} \tag{38}$$

where z_{ji} is a column vector of characteristics pertaining to alternative j and individual i. Denote by f_{ji} a dummy variable which equals 1 if individual i chooses alternative j and 0 otherwise. In fact, f_{ji} is the observed frequency for individual i to choose alternative j. Let there be n individuals in the sample, and let the ith individual be faced with J_i alternatives. The likelihood of the sample is

$$L = \prod_{i=1}^{n} P_{1i}^{f_{1i}} P_{2i}^{f_{2i}} \cdots P_{J_i i}^{f_{J_i i}}$$

The log-likelihood function is

$$\log L = \sum_{i=1}^{n} \sum_{j=1}^{J_i} f_{ji} \log P_{ji} = \sum_i \sum_j f_{ji} \log \frac{e^{\beta' z_{ji}}}{\sum_k e^{\beta' z_{ki}}}$$

$$= \sum_i \sum_j f_{ji} \beta' z_{ji} - \sum_i \sum_j f_{ji} \log \left(\sum_k e^{\beta' z_{ki}} \right) \tag{39}$$

The log-likelihood function is maximized by differentiation

$$\frac{\partial \log L}{\partial \beta} = \sum_i \sum_j f_{ji} z_{ji} - \sum_i \sum_j f_{ji} \left(\sum_k e^{\beta' z_{ki}} \right)^{-1} \sum_k e^{\beta' z_{ki}} z_{ki}$$

$$= \sum_i \sum_j f_{ji} (z_{ji} - \bar{z}_i) = 0 \tag{40}$$

where

$$\bar{z}_i = \left(\sum_k e^{\beta' z_{ki}} \right)^{-1} \sum_j e^{\beta' z_{ji}} z_{ji} = \sum_{j=1}^{J_i} P_{ji} z_{ji} \tag{41}$$

Using the fact that $\sum_j P_{ji}(z_{ji} - \bar{z}_i) = 0$, we rewrite the first-order condition (40) as

$$\sum_{i=1}^{n} \sum_{j=1}^{J_i} (f_{ji} - P_{ji})(z_{ji} - \bar{z}_i) = 0 \tag{42}$$

To interpret (42) we note that f_{ji} is the observed frequency for the ith individual to choose alternative j and P_{ji} is the predicted frequency using the logit model with z_{ji} as explanatory variables. According to (42), the residuals $f_{ji} - P_{ji}$ should be uncorrelated with the explanatory variables z_{ji}.

To apply the Newton-Raphson method to maximize $\log L$ we find the matrix of its second partial derivatives by differentiating (40) with respect to the row vector β'

$$\frac{\partial^2 \log L}{\partial \beta \, \partial \beta'} = -\sum_i \frac{\partial \bar{z}_i}{\partial \beta'} \sum_j f_{ji} = -\sum_i \frac{\partial \bar{z}_i}{\partial \beta'} = -\sum_i \sum_j z_{ji} \frac{\partial P_{ji}}{\partial \beta'}$$

Since, by (38),

$$
\frac{\partial P_{ji}}{\partial \beta} = \left(\sum_k e^{\beta' z_{ki}} \right)^{-1} e^{\beta' z_{ji}} z_{ji} - \left(\sum_k e^{\beta' z_{ki}} \right)^{-2} e^{\beta' z_{ji}} \sum_k e^{\beta' z_{ki}} z_{ki}
$$

$$
= P_{ji}(z_{ji} - \bar{z}_i) \tag{43}
$$

we substitute (43) into the equation above it to get

$$
\frac{\partial^2 \log L}{\partial \beta\, \partial \beta'} = - \sum_i \sum_j P_{ji} z_{ji} (z_{ji} - \bar{z}_i)' = - \sum_i \sum_j P_{ji}(z_{ji} - \bar{z}_i)(z_{ji} - \bar{z}_i)' \tag{44}
$$

noting that $\sum_j P_{ji}(z_{ji} - \bar{z}_i) = 0$. Corresponding to $X'X$ in regression analysis, the negative of (44) is a matrix of second moments of the explanatory variables z_{ji} weighted by the probabilities P_{ji}. Although (44) appears deceptively simple, both P_{ji} and $\bar{z}_i$ are functions of the unknown parameter β according to (38) and (41). Given an initial estimate β^0 of β, we can compute the associated P_{ji}^0 and $\bar{z}_i^0$ by (38) and (41). By the Newton-Raphson method, the next value β^1 is obtained by the formula

$$
\beta^1 = \beta^0 + \left[\sum_i \sum_j P_{ji}^0 (z_{ji} - \bar{z}_i^0)(z_{ji} - \bar{z}_i^0)' \right]^{-1} \sum_i \sum_j (f_{ji} - P_{ji}^0)(z_{ji} - \bar{z}_i^0) \tag{45}
$$

To measure the goodness of fit of the fitted logit model one can use a statistic corresponding to the estimated residual variance s^2 of a regression function

$$
s^2(\hat{\beta}) = \sum_i \sum_j [f_{ij} - P_{ji}(\hat{\beta})]^2 P_{ji}(\hat{\beta}) \tag{46}
$$

where $\hat{\beta}$ denotes the maximum-likelihood estimate of β. A measure corresponding to R^2 in regression analysis is

$$
R^2 = 1 - \frac{s^2(\hat{\beta})}{s^2(\bar{\beta})} \tag{47}
$$

where $\bar{\beta}$ is a vector of zeros, except for the coefficients of the dummy variables representing the different alternatives. For small samples the measure (47) is known to be biased toward 1 when there are specification errors.

Another measure of goodness of fit for a logistic model is based on the log likelihood

$$
\log L(\beta) = \sum_i \sum_j f_{ji} \log P_{ji}(\beta)
$$

which is a negative quantity since $\log P_{ji} \leq 0$. The log likelihood is small in absolute value, or close to zero, if the observed frequencies f_{ji} are close to the predicted frequencies P_{ji}. When $f_{ji} = 1$, if P_{ji} is close to $1, f_{ji} \log P_{ji}$ will be close to zero. When $f_{ji} = 1$, if P_{ji} is close to zero, $f_{ji} \log P_{ji}$ will be highly negative. To arrive at a measure which is close to 1 when the model fits well, one can use

$$
\rho^2 = 1 - \frac{\log L(\hat{\beta})}{\log L(\bar{\beta})} \tag{48}
$$

where $\bar{\beta}$ is as defined in the last paragraph. Let $\hat{\beta}$ contain k coefficients and $\bar{\beta}$ contain k_1 nonzero coefficients. Then, under the null hypothesis that the additional $k - k_1$ nonzero coefficients in $\hat{\beta}$ are zero, the statistic

$$\frac{[\log L(\bar{\beta}) - \log L(\hat{\beta})]/(k - k_1)}{[\log L(\hat{\beta})]/k} = \frac{\rho^2/(k - k_1)}{(1 - \rho^2)/k} \tag{49}$$

will have approximately an $F(k - k_1, k)$ distribution. Alternatively, one can use the likelihood ratio $\mu = L(\hat{\beta})/L(\bar{\beta})$ where $-2 \log \mu$ is distributed asymptotically as $\chi^2(k - k_1)$ under the null hypothesis.

If the data are grouped, out of n_i individuals with characteristics z_{ji}, r_{ji} individuals have chosen alternative j, with $n_i = \Sigma r_{ji}$. For ungrouped data $n_i = 1$, and $r_{ji} = 1$ if individual i has chosen alternative j and $r_{ji} = 0$ otherwise. For grouped data, r_{ji} are no longer either 1 or 0. According to the logistic model,

$$\log \frac{P_{ji}}{P_{1i}} = \beta'(z_{ji} - z_{1i})$$

This suggests estimating the model by the regression

$$\log \frac{r_{ji} + .5}{r_{1i} + .5} = \hat{\beta}'(z_{ji} - z_{1i}) + \text{residual} \qquad \begin{matrix} i = 1, \dots, I \\ j = 2, \dots, J_i \end{matrix} \tag{50}$$

using data for I groups of individuals having the same characteristics. The .5s in (50) are continuity corrections because the observed frequencies r_{ji} are integers. The estimator $\hat{\beta}$ from (50) by least squares is consistent and has reasonable sampling properties, but if the sample is large and the selection probabilities are distributed very unevenly among the different alternatives, leading to many very small r_{ji}, the method of maximum likelihood yields a better estimator than least squares using grouped data (see Probs. 4 to 6.)

⋆8.6 NESTED LOGIT MODELS

A second important member of the class of generalized extreme-value (GEV) models defined in Sec. 8.4, the *nested logit model*, has a tree structure. For example, in a model with three levels, the J alternatives in level 1 can be grouped into J_2 alternatives in level 2; the J_2 alternatives can in turn be grouped into J_3 alternatives in level 3. Let $P_{j, k, l}$ be the probability for the ith individual to choose alternative j in level 1, which belongs to group k in level 2, group k being a member of group l in level 3. The probability $P_{j, k, l}$ will be determined in three levels. The nested logit model has been used in the choice of transportation mode by Cosslett (1978), the purchase of consumer durables by Brownstone (1980), the demand for energy by Goett (1979), and the decision on trip timing by Small and Brownstone (1981).

In a nested logit model the probability $P_{j, k, l}$ is determined at three levels as

$$P_{j, k, l} = P_1(j \mid k)P_2(k \mid l)P_3(l) \tag{51}$$

where, for the first level, with $B_2(k)$ denoting the kth group in level 2,

$$P_1(j \mid k) = \frac{\exp (V_j/\rho_k)}{\sum_{j \in B_2(k)} \exp (V_j/\rho_k)} \equiv \frac{\exp (V_j/\rho_k)}{\exp I_{2k}} \tag{51a}$$

for the second level

$$P_2(k \mid l) = \frac{\exp (\rho_k I_{2k}/\rho_l)}{\sum_{k \in B_3(l)} \exp (\rho_k I_{2k}/\rho_l)} = \frac{\exp (\rho_k I_{2k}/\rho_l)}{\exp I_{3l}} \tag{51b}$$

and for the third level

$$P_3(l) = \frac{\exp (\rho_l I_{3l})}{\sum_l \exp (\rho_l I_{3l})} \tag{51c}$$

where
$$V_j = \beta' z_{ji} \qquad j = 1, \ldots, J \tag{51d}$$

$$I_{2k} = \log \sum_{j \in B_2(k)} \exp V_j/\rho_k \qquad k = 1, \ldots, J_2 \tag{51e}$$

$$I_{3l} = \log \sum_{k \in B_3(l)} \exp \frac{\rho_k I_{2k}}{\rho_l} \qquad l = 1, \ldots, J_3 \tag{51f}$$

The ρ parameters must lie between 0 and 1, and for k in the second level and l in the third level, $0 < \rho_k/\rho_l \le 1$.

The log-likelihood function is

$$\log L = \sum_{j=1}^{J} \log P_1(j \mid k_j) + \sum_j \log P_2(k_j \mid l_j) + \sum_j \log P_3(l_j)$$

$$= L_1 + L_2 + L_3 \tag{52}$$

In (52) a subscript has been added to k and l to indicate that when we sum over all level 1 alternatives j ($j = 1, \ldots, J$), the level 2 alternative k_j and the level 3 alternative l_j are associated with the level 1 alternative j. To maximize (52) a sequential estimator has been suggested. It has three stages in the present example. In the first stage it estimates β/ρ_k by maximizing $L_1 = \sum_j \log P_1(j \mid k_j)$. These estimates are used to compute I_{2k}. Given I_{2k}, in the second stage it estimates ρ_k/ρ_l by maximizing $L_2 = \sum_j \log P_2(k_j \mid l_j)$. These estimates are used to compute I_{3l}. Given I_{3l}, in the third stage it estimates ρ_l by maximizing $L_3 = \sum_j \log P_3(l_j)$. If the ρ's at any level are constrained to be equal, the log-likelihood function for that stage has the same form as the log likelihood of a multinomial logit model and existing algorithms for the latter model can be applied. This sequential estimator is not efficient because information about choices at higher levels is not used in estimating parameters at a lower level. FIML has also been applied to maximize (52). Because of the computational difficulties of FIML, a linearized FIML estimator as described in Sec. 5.5 has been used in practice. For further discussion of nested logit models, see McFadden (1981) and Small and Brownstone (1981).

8.7 LIMITED DEPENDENT VARIABLES

Tobin (1958, p. 24) introduced the model of limited dependent variables by writing:

> In economic surveys of households, many variables have the following characteristics: The variable has a lower, or upper, limit and takes on the limiting value for a substantial number of respondents. ... As a specific example, many—indeed, most—households would report zero expenditures on automobiles or major household durable goods during any given year. Among those households who made such expenditure, there would be wide variability in amount.

A model to capture such phenomena is

$$y_t = \begin{cases} \beta'x_t + \epsilon_t & \text{if RHS} > 0 \\ 0 & \text{if RHS} \le 0 \end{cases} \tag{53}$$

where RHS stands for the right-hand side of the equation and x_t is a column vector of explanatory variables. If the limiting value is not zero but α_t, we can change the dependent variable from y_t to $y_t^* = y_t - \alpha_t$ and write the model as

$$y_t^* = \begin{cases} [\beta' \quad -1] \begin{bmatrix} x_t \\ \alpha_t \end{bmatrix} + \epsilon_t & \text{if RHS} > 0 \\ \\ 0 & \text{if RHS} \le 0 \end{cases}$$

Thus formulation (53) covers the case of any given limiting values. Tobin (1958) applied maximum likelihood to estimate this model. The subject of maximum-likelihood estimation was further studied by Amemiya (1973). From these references the present section has freely drawn. Model (53) is known as the *Tobit model*.

Given n independent observations, let S observations record a zero value for the dependent variable and $R = n - S$ observations record a nonzero value. A zero value indicates $\epsilon_t \le -\beta'x_t$ or $-\epsilon_t \ge \beta'x_t$. If ϵ_t is assumed to be normal with variance σ^2, the likelihood function is

$$L = \prod_S [1 - F(\beta'x_t; \sigma^2)] \prod_R f(y_t - \beta'x_t; \sigma^2) \tag{54}$$

where

$$F(\beta'x_t; \sigma^2) = \int_{-\infty}^{\beta'x_t} f(z; \sigma^2)\, dz \tag{55}$$

and

$$f(z; \sigma^2) = \frac{1}{\sqrt{2\pi}\,\sigma} e^{-z^2/2\sigma^2} \tag{56}$$

Denoting $F(\beta'x_t; \sigma^2)$ and $f(\beta'x_t; \sigma^2)$ respectively by F_t and f_t, we can write the log-likelihood function as

$$\log L = \sum_S \log (1 - F_t) - \frac{R}{2} \log \sigma^2 - \sum_R \frac{(y_t - \beta'x_t)^2}{2\sigma^2} \tag{57}$$

To differentiate log L we use

$$\frac{\partial F_t}{\partial \beta} = f_t x_t \qquad \frac{\partial f_t}{\partial \beta} = -f_t \frac{\beta' x_t}{\sigma^2} x_t \tag{58}$$

Rewriting F_t as

$$F_t = \int_{-\infty}^{\beta' x_t/\sigma} \frac{1}{\sqrt{2\pi}} e^{-\lambda^2/2} \, d\lambda$$

leads to

$$\frac{\partial F_t}{\partial \sigma^2} = \frac{\partial F_t}{\partial (\beta' x/\sigma)} \frac{\partial (\beta' x_t/\sigma)}{\partial \sigma^2} = \frac{1}{\sqrt{2\pi}} e^{-(\beta' x_t/\sigma)^2/2}(\beta' x_t) \left(\frac{-\sigma^{-3}}{2} \right)$$

$$= -\tfrac{1}{2}\sigma^{-2}(\beta' x_t)f_t \tag{59}$$

$$\frac{\partial f_t}{\partial \sigma^2} = \left(\frac{-\sigma^{-3}}{2} \right) \frac{1}{\sqrt{2\pi}} e^{-(\beta' x_t/\sigma)^2/2} + \frac{1}{\sqrt{2\pi}\,\sigma} e^{-(\beta' x_t/\sigma)^2/2}(\beta' x_t)^2 \frac{\sigma^{-4}}{2}$$

$$= \frac{(\beta' x_t)^2 - \sigma^2}{2\sigma^4} f_t \tag{60}$$

The results of differentiating log L are

$$\frac{\partial \log L}{\partial \beta} = -\sum_S (1 - F_t)^{-1} f_t x_t + \sigma^{-2} \sum_R (y_t - \beta' x_t) x_t = 0 \tag{61}$$

$$\frac{\partial \log L}{\partial \sigma^2} = (2\sigma^2)^{-1} \sum_S (1 - F_t)^{-1}(\beta' x_t)f_t - (2\sigma^2)^{-1}R + \frac{\sigma^{-4}}{2} \sum_R (y_t - \beta' x_t)^2 = 0 \tag{62}$$

$$\frac{\partial^2 \log L}{\partial \beta \, \partial \beta'} = \sum_S (1 - F_t)^{-1} f_t \frac{\beta' x_t}{\sigma^2} x_t x_t' - \sum_S (1 - F_t)^{-2} f_t^2 \, x_t x_t'$$

$$\qquad - \sigma^{-2} \sum_R x_t x_t'$$

$$= -\sum_S (1 - F_t)^{-2} f_t [f_t - \sigma^{-2}(1 - F_t)(\beta' x_t)] x_t x_t'$$

$$\qquad - \sigma^{-2} \sum_R x_t x_t' \tag{63}$$

Equation (62) can be solved for σ^2 as a function of β, yielding

$$\hat{\sigma}^2 = \frac{\sum_R (y_t - \beta' x_t)^2}{R - \sum_S (1 - F_t)^{-1}(\beta' x_t)f_t} \tag{64}$$

Given σ^2, the Newton-Raphson method can be applied to find β, using the derivatives (61) and (63).

Fair (1977) has suggested an iterative least-squares method for estimating σ^2 and β. First, an estimate of σ^2 is obtained as follows. Premultiply (61) by

$(2\sigma^2)^{-1}\beta'$ to get

$$-(2\sigma^2)^{-1}\sum_{S}(1 - F_t)^{-1}(\beta'x_t)f_t + \frac{\sigma^{-4}}{2}\sum_{R}(y_t - \beta'x_t)\beta'x_t = 0$$

Adding this equation to (62) yields

$$-(2\sigma^2)^{-1}R + \frac{\sigma^{-4}}{2}\sum_{R}(y_t - \beta'x_t)y_t$$

or
$$\hat{\sigma}^2 = R^{-1}\sum_{R}(y_t - \beta'x_t)y_t \tag{65}$$

which is neater than (64) for computing $\hat{\sigma}^2$ given β. To compute β given σ^2 Fair suggests multiplying (61) by σ^2 to obtain

$$-\sum_{S}(1 - F_t)^{-1}\sigma^2 f_t x_t + \sum_{R}(y_t - \beta'x_t)x_t = 0 \tag{66}$$

which can be solved for β. Defining

$$y_1 = \begin{bmatrix} y_1 \\ \vdots \\ y_R \end{bmatrix} \quad X_1 = \begin{bmatrix} x_1' \\ \vdots \\ x_R' \end{bmatrix} \quad X_2 = \begin{bmatrix} x_{R+1}' \\ \vdots \\ x_n' \end{bmatrix} \quad v = -\sigma^2 \begin{bmatrix} (1 - F_{R+1})^{-1}f_{R+1} \\ \vdots \\ (1 - F_n)^{-1}f_n \end{bmatrix} \tag{67}$$

we can write (66) as

$$X_2'v + X_1'(Y_1 - X_1\beta) = 0 \tag{68}$$

The solution of (68) is

$$\hat{\beta} = (X_1'X_1)^{-1}(X_1'Y_1 + X_2'v) \tag{69}$$

Equations (69) and (65) specify a two-step iterative method for finding $\hat{\beta}$ and $\hat{\sigma}^2$.

The iterative method of Fair (1977) has the following interesting interpretation. First, the element

$$v_t = -(1 - F_t)^{-1}\sigma^2 f_t$$

of the vector v is the conditional expectation of $\epsilon_t = y_t - \beta'x_t$ given $\beta'x_t + \epsilon_t \le 0$ or $\epsilon_t \le -\beta'x_t$. To see this, we observe that

$$E(\epsilon_t | \epsilon_t \le -\beta'x_t) = [P(\epsilon_t \le -\beta'x_t)]^{-1}\int_{-\infty}^{-\beta'x_t}\frac{1}{\sqrt{2\pi}\,\sigma}ze^{-z^2/2\sigma^2}\,dz \tag{70}$$

Using the integral

$$\int\frac{1}{\sqrt{2\pi}\,\sigma}ze^{-z^2/2\sigma^2}\,dz = -\frac{\sigma^2}{\sqrt{2\pi}\,\sigma}e^{-z^2/2\sigma^2}$$

which can easily be checked by differentiation, we have

$$\int_{-\infty}^{-\beta'x_t}\frac{1}{\sqrt{2\pi}\,\sigma}ze^{-z^2/2\sigma^2}\,dz = -\frac{\sigma^2}{\sqrt{2\pi}\,\sigma}e^{-(\beta'x_t)^2/2\sigma^2} = -\sigma^2 f_t$$

After substitution in (70) the result is

$$E(\epsilon_t | \epsilon_t \leq -\beta' x_t) = -(1 - F_t)^{-1} \sigma^2 f_t = v_t \tag{71}$$

Dempster, Laird, and Rubin (1977) have suggested an *E-M algorithm* to compute a maximum-likelihood estimator for a model involving unobservables. The Tobit model has unobserved values of $\beta' x_t + \epsilon_t$ when it is zero or negative. The E-M algorithm for this problem consists of two steps. The E step replaces the unobserved values in the likelihood function by their conditional expectations, which are certainly functions of the unknown parameters. The M step is to maximize the resulting likelihood function.

In the Tobit model, if $Y'_2 = y_{R+1}, \ldots, y_n$ were not restricted to being zero but were observed as

$$Y_2 = X_2 \beta + \epsilon_2$$

maximization of the likelihood function would yield the familiar normal equation for $\hat{\beta}$

$$(X'_1 X_1 + X'_2 X_2)\beta = X'_1 Y_1 + X'_2 Y_2$$

Since $X_2 \beta + \epsilon_2$ is not observed, we replace it by $X_2 \beta + v$, where $v = E(\epsilon_2 | \epsilon_2 \leq -X_2 \beta)$. Maximizing the resulting likelihood function would yield

$$(X'_1 X_1 + X'_2 X_2)\beta = X'_1 Y_1 + X'_2(X_2 \beta + v) \tag{72}$$

which is identical with (69). Thus Fair's iterative method is an application of the E-M algorithm to computing the maximum-likelihood estimate of β in a Tobit model.

For a proof of consistency and asymptotic normality of the maximum-likelihood estimator of the Tobit model see Amemiya (1973). The proof is adapted to the special form of the likelihood function (54) for the Tobit model.

★8.8 THE E-M ALGORITHM

As we have just illustrated, the E-M algorithm of Dempster, Laird, and Rubin (1977) is a method for computing the maximum-likelihood estimate when some observations y_i are not directly observed. Since this algorithm can better be appreciated from an example than in the abstract, we have chosen to present it here rather than in Sec. 7.5 along with other algorithms.

In a standard estimation problem by maximum likelihood, a random sample $(y_1, \ldots, y_n)$ is given. Each y_i is assumed to have a density $f(y_i | \theta)$. The method of maximum likelihood finds that value of θ which maximizes the likelihood function $\prod_{i=1}^{n} f(y_i | \theta)$. Sometimes not all y_i are observed directly. Let there be an observation equation $z = z(y)$; when y_i is generated, z_i is observed. Usually, the mapping from y_i to z_i is many to one; i.e., many values of y_i will correspond to a single value of z_i. For example, in the Tobit model, we have $y_i = \beta' x_i + \epsilon_i$. The observation function is

$$z_i = \begin{cases} y_i & \text{if } y_i > 0 \\ 0 & \text{if } y_i \leq 0 \end{cases}$$

Given certain values of z_i, we know from the observation function only that y_i belongs to a set $Y(z_i)$. In the Tobit example, given $z_i = 0$, we know only that $y_i \leq 0$. The likelihood of observing the value z is

$$g(z \mid \theta) = \int_{Y(z)} f(y \mid \theta) \, dy \tag{73}$$

In the Tobit example, by (55) and (56),

$$g(z) = \begin{cases} f(z - \beta'x; \sigma^2) = \dfrac{1}{\sqrt{2\pi}\,\sigma} \exp\left[\dfrac{-(z - \beta'x)^2}{2\sigma^2}\right] & \text{if } z > 0 \\ \displaystyle\int_{-\infty}^{0} f(y - \beta'x; \sigma^2) \, dy & \text{if } z \leq 0 \end{cases} \tag{74}$$

Corresponding to the possibly unobserved vector $(y_1, \ldots, y_n) \equiv y'$ is the observed vector $(z_1, \ldots, z_n) \equiv z'$. Let $L(y; \theta) = \prod_{i=1}^{n} f(y_i \mid \theta)$ denote the likelihood function using the original data y. The likelihood function using the data z is

$$L^*(z; \theta) = \prod_{i=1}^{n} g(z_i \mid \theta) = \int_{Y(z_n)} \cdots \int_{Y(z_1)} \prod_i f(y_i \mid \theta) \, dy_1 \ldots dy_n$$

$$\equiv \int_{Y(z)} L(y; \theta) \, dy \tag{75}$$

where the last term is a multiple integral defined by the term above, y denoting a vector and dy denoting $dy_1 \cdots dy_n$. We shall confine our discussion to deriving the E-M algorithm when the original likelihood function belongs to the exponential family

$$L(y; \theta) = b(y)e^{\theta't(y)}[a(\theta)]^{-1} = b(y)h[t(y); \theta] \tag{76}$$

where $t(y)$ is a *sufficient statistic* having the same dimension as the unknown parameter vector θ. *Since (76) can be factored into the product of b(y) and h[t(y); θ], the (vector) function t(y) is a sufficient statistic.* The likelihood function of β in a normal linear regression model belongs to this family, as will be shown. After deriving the E-M algorithm using (76), we shall apply it to estimating the Tobit model as an illustration. See Dempster, Laird, and Rubin (1977) for a discussion of the E-M algorithm when the likelihood function is not restricted to the form of (76).

Substitution of (76) for $L(y; \theta)$ in (75) gives the log likelihood

$$\log L^*(z; \theta) = \log \int_{Y(z)} b(y)e^{\theta't(y)} \, dy - \log a(\theta) \tag{77}$$

Maximizing the log likelihood by differentiation with respect to θ yields

$$\frac{d}{d\theta} \log a(\theta) = \left[\int_{Y(z)} b(y)e^{\theta't(y)} \, dy \right]^{-1} \int_{Y(z)} t(y)b(y)e^{\theta't(y)} \, dy$$

$$= \left[\int_{Y(z)} b(y)e^{\theta't(y)}a(\theta)^{-1} \, dy \right]^{-1} \int_{Y(z)} t(y)b(y)e^{\theta't(y)}a(\theta)^{-1} \, dy$$

$$= E[t(y)\,|\,z,\,\theta] \tag{78}$$

where we have observed that the integral in brackets after the second equality sign is the probability of observing z, and hence the entire expression is the conditional expectation of $t(y)$ given z (and the parameter θ). Thus, the solution to maximizing the log likelihood (77) amounts to setting the conditional expectation $E[t(y)\,|\,z,\,\theta]$ equal to $[d \log a(\theta)]/d\theta$.

On the other hand, if the vector y could be observed completely, one would simply maximize the log-likelihood function based on (76), or

$$\log L(y;\,\theta) = \log b(y) + \theta't(y) - \log a(\theta) \tag{79}$$

Setting to zero the derivative of (79) with respect to θ gives

$$\frac{d}{d\theta} \log a(\theta) = t(y) \tag{80}$$

This suggests that if we replaced $t(y)$ in (79) by $E[t(y)\,|\,z,\,\theta^p]$ for some given θ^p and maximized the resulting expression

$$\log b(y) + \theta'E[t(y)\,|\,z,\,\theta^p] - \log a(\theta) \tag{81}$$

we would obtain the first-order condition

$$\frac{d}{d\theta} \log a(\theta) = E[t(y)\,|\,z,\,\theta^p] \tag{82}$$

which can be solved for θ. If the solution θ^{p+1}, say, equals θ^p, condition (78) for maximizing $\log L^*(z;\,\theta)$ will be satisfied.

The last paragraph essentially describes the E-M algorithm, which is an iterative method for solving Eq. (78). At the pth iteration, the value θ^p of θ is given. The algorithm consists of two steps for computing θ^{p+1} in the next iteration. In the E step, we evaluate $E[t(y)\,|\,z,\,\theta^p]$ on the right-hand side of (78). This is done by evaluating the two integrals in (78). In the M step, we replace $t(y)$ in the log likelihood $\log L(y;\,\theta)$ by $E[t(y)\,|\,z,\,\theta^p]$ and maximize the resulting expression by solving Eq. (82) for θ^{p+1}, that is,

$$\frac{d}{d\theta} \log a(\theta^{p+1}) = E[t(y)\,|\,z,\,\theta^p] \tag{83}$$

Given θ^{p+1}, in the next iteration we execute the same two steps to obtain θ^{p+2}, and so forth. If the process converges, we have shown that the first-order condition (78) for maximizing the log-likelihood function log L^* for our problem will be satisfied. The convergence properties of this algorithm are discussed in Dempster, Laird, and Rubin (1977).

To illustrate the E-M algorithm for a likelihood function (76) belonging to the exponential family consider the problem of estimating β in the Tobit model of Sec. 8.7. We are concerned only with the estimation of β because once β is known, σ^2 can be estimated by (65). Given σ^2, the likelihood function is

$$L(y; \beta) = (2\pi\sigma^2)^{-n/2} \exp\left[\frac{-(y - X\beta)'(y - X\beta)}{2\sigma^2}\right]$$

$$= (2\pi\sigma^2)^{-n/2} \exp\left(\frac{-y'y}{2\sigma^2}\right) \exp\left(\frac{\beta'X'y}{\sigma^2}\right) \exp\left(\frac{-\beta'X'X\beta}{2\sigma^2}\right) \quad (84)$$

where we have written $L(y; \beta)$ in the form of (76), with

$$b(y) = (2\pi\sigma^2)^{-n/2} \exp\left(\frac{-y'y}{2\sigma^2}\right) \quad (85)$$

$$t(y) = \sigma^{-2}X'y \quad (86)$$

and

$$a(\beta) = \exp\left(\frac{\beta'X'X\beta}{2\sigma^2}\right) \quad (87)$$

In this example, with $\sigma^{-2}X'$ treated as given, $t(y)$ is a linear function of y, and

$$E[t(y)\,|\,z, \beta] = \sigma^{-2}X'E[y\,|\,z, \beta]$$

Therefore, the E-M algorithm is simplified to replacing y in the log likelihood by its conditional expectation given z, as we pointed out at the end of Sec. 8.7.

8.9 TRUNCATED SAMPLE

Related to the Tobit model is a model for a truncated sample. Whereas in the Tobit model the dependent variable smaller than a certain limit is not observed, in a truncated sample the observation with a value of the dependent variable smaller or larger than a certain limit is omitted from the sample. Specifically, the model is

$$y_i = x_i'\beta + \epsilon_i \quad \begin{array}{l} \text{if RHS} \le L_i \text{ (observation included)} \\ \text{if RHS} > L_i \text{ (observation excluded)} \end{array} \quad (88)$$

This model has been discussed by Gronau (1974), Heckman (1976), and Hausman and Wise (1977). In the last reference the authors tried to explain annual earnings of a sample of 684 workers by eduction, IQ, age, and other characteristics, but the example excluded all observations with earnings above certain levels. In fact, for families with two, four, six, and eight members, respectively, those having incomes above $3195, $5002, $6615, and $8160 were excluded from the sample.

To set up the likelihood for the sample we note that

$$\text{pdf } (y_i \mid x_i) = \begin{cases} 0 & \text{if } y_i > L_i \\[2mm] \dfrac{f(y_i - x_i'\beta; \sigma^2)}{\Phi[(L_i - x_i'\beta)/\sigma]} & \text{if } y_i \le L_i \end{cases} \tag{89}$$

where f is the normal density function as defined in (56) and Φ, as distinguished from F as defined in (55), is the cumulative *unit* normal distribution, that is, $\Phi(z) = F(z; 1)$, or

$$\Phi\left(\frac{L_i - x_i'\beta}{\sigma}\right) = \int_{-\infty}^{(L_i - x_{i'}\beta)/\sigma} \frac{1}{\sqrt{2\pi}} \exp\left(\frac{-\lambda^2}{2}\right) d\lambda$$

$$= \int_{-\infty}^{L_i} \frac{1}{\sqrt{2\pi}\sigma} \exp - \left[\frac{(y - x_i'\beta)^2}{2\sigma^2}\right] dy$$

giving the probability that $y_i \le L_i$. The likelihood function of the truncated sample of n observations is

$$L = \prod_{i=1}^{n} \frac{f(y_i - x_i'\beta; \sigma^2)}{\Phi[(L_i - x_i'\beta)/\sigma]} \tag{90}$$

The log-likelihood function is

$$\log L = \sum_{i=1}^{n} \log f(y_i - x_i'\beta; \sigma^2) - \sum_{i=1}^{n} \log \Phi\left(\frac{L_i - x_i'\beta}{\sigma}\right)$$

$$= \text{const} - \frac{n}{2} \log \sigma^2 - \sum_{i=1}^{n} \frac{(y_i - x_i'\beta)^2}{2\sigma^2} - \sum_{i=1}^{n} \log \Phi\left(\frac{L_i - x_i'\beta}{\sigma}\right) \tag{91}$$

Denoting the *unit* normal density function by $\phi(z) = f(z; 1)$, we can write the derivative of (91) with respect to β as

$$\frac{\partial \log L}{\partial \beta} = \sigma^{-2} \sum_{i=1}^{n} (y_i - x_i'\beta)x_i - \sum_{i=1}^{n} \frac{\phi[(L_i - x_i'\beta)/\sigma]}{\Phi[(L_i - x_i'\beta)/\sigma]} (-\sigma^{-1}x_i)$$

$$= \sigma^{-2} \sum_{i=1}^{n} \left\{ y_i - x_i'\beta + \frac{\phi[(L_i - x_i'\beta)/\sigma]}{\Phi[(L_i - x_i'\beta)/\sigma]} \sigma \right\} x_i = 0 \tag{92}$$

The following interpretation can be given to (92). If the sample were not truncated and all observations were taken, the first-order condition for maximizing the log likelihood would be

$$\sigma^{-2} \sum_{i=1}^{n} (y_i - x_i'\beta)x_i = 0$$

i.e., the explanatory variables x_i should be uncorrelated with the residuals $y_i - x_i'\beta$. When the sample is truncated, the residual ϵ_i, conditioned on being included, has a negative expectation equal to $-\phi_i\sigma/\Phi_i$, where $\phi_i = \phi[(L_i - x_i'\beta)/\sigma]$ and $\Phi_i = \Phi[(L_i - x_i'\beta)/\sigma]$. The residual ϵ_i is included in the sample only if $x_i'\beta + \epsilon_i \le L_i$ or $\epsilon_i \le L_i - x_i'\beta$. Conditional on being included, the expectation of ϵ_i is $-\phi_i\sigma/\Phi_i$ (see Prob. 11). The adjusted residual obtained by adding $\phi_i\sigma/\Phi_i$

back, i.e.,

$$y_i - x_i'\beta + \frac{\phi[(L_i - x_i')/\sigma]\sigma}{\Phi[(L_i - x_i')/\sigma]} \tag{93}$$

should be uncorrelated with x_i according to (92).

Several methods of estimating the parameters of a linear regression model using a truncated sample can be suggested. One is iterative least squares. The method of ordinary least squares will yield a biased estimator for β because $E(\epsilon \,|\, \text{sample}) \neq 0$. In the usual proof of unbiasedness of the least-squares estimator we have

$$E(b) = E[(X'X)^{-1}X'(X\beta + \epsilon)] = \beta + (X'X)^{-1}X'E(\epsilon \,|\, \text{sample}) \tag{94}$$

where $E(\epsilon \,|\, \text{sample})$ is no longer zero, leading to a bias in the least-squares estimator β. We have found $E(\epsilon_i \,|\, \text{sample}) = -\phi_i \sigma / \Phi_i$. To apply the method of iterative least squares we need to use $(\partial \log L)/\partial \beta$ as given by (92) and

$$\frac{\partial \log L}{\partial \sigma^2} = -\frac{n}{2\sigma^2} + \frac{1}{2\sigma^4} \sum_{i=1}^{n} (y_i - x_i'\beta)^2 + \frac{1}{2} \sum_{i=1}^{n} \frac{\phi_i}{\Phi_i} \frac{L_i - x_i'\beta}{\sigma^3} = 0 \tag{95}$$

The solution of (95) for σ^2 is

$$\hat{\sigma}^2 = n^{-1} \sum_{i=1}^{n} \left[(y_i - x_i'\beta)^2 + \frac{\phi_i}{\Phi_i} \frac{L_i - x_i'\beta}{\sigma} \right] \tag{96}$$

To iterate, given initial values of $\hat{\beta}$ and $\hat{\sigma}^2$, we use (96) to find a new value of $\hat{\sigma}^2$. We then compute $-\phi_i \hat{\sigma}/\Phi_i$ and solve (92) for a new $\hat{\beta}$. The process continues. Note that (92) can be interpreted as resulting from an adjustment to Eq. (94) to get rid of the bias. Replacing $y = X\beta + \epsilon$ in (94) by $y - E(\epsilon \,|\, \text{sample})$, we have

$$\hat{\beta} = (X'X)^{-1}X'(y - E\epsilon)$$

which is the solution of (92).

In addition to the method of iterative least squares one can apply the Newton-Raphson method, the Gauss-Newton method, and the method of scoring to maximize the log-likelihood function (91). The reader may wish to pursue these methods as exercises (see Probs. 12 and 13).

It may be of interest to exhibit the OLS and maximum-likelihood estimates of certain coefficients in the regression of the logarithm of annual earning on selected explanatory variables as reported by Hausman and Wise (1977, p. 927). The truncated sample has 684 observations, the truncation points having been reported earlier:

	Coefficient of					
Method	Education	IQ	Age	Union membership	Training	Illness
OLS	.0095	.0016	−.0030	.0900	.0022	−.0761
Maximum likelihood	.0146	.0061	−.0162	.2463	.0065	−.2259

The comparison shows that the ML estimates, which take the sample selection bias into account, are in general larger in absolute value than the corresponding OLS estimates.

Hausman and Wise (1977) also discuss a simultaneous-equation version of their model. Consider earnings Y as a product of wage rate W and the number of hours worked H. Then

$$\log Y = \log W + \log H$$

The simultaneous-equation model specifies

$$\log W_i = x'_{i1}\delta_1 + \epsilon_{i1}$$
$$\log H_i = (\log W_i)\beta_1 + x'_{i2}\delta_2 + \epsilon_{i2} \tag{97}$$

The first is a wage equation, with x_{i1} denoting a vector of exogenous variables. The second equation explains the number of hours, with β_1 measuring the elasticity of labor supply and x_{i2} denoting a vector of exogenous variables. The reduced form is

$$\log W_i = x'_{i1}\delta_1 + \epsilon_{i1}$$
$$\log H_i = x'_{i1}\beta_1\delta_1 + x'_{i2}\delta_2 + \beta_1\epsilon_{i1} + \epsilon_{i2} \tag{98}$$

where the first structural equation was substituted for $\log W_i$ in the second structural equation to yield the second reduced-form equation. If $\Sigma = (\sigma_{ij})$ is the covariance matrix of the residuals of the two structural equations, the covariance matrix of the reduced-form equations is

$$\Omega = \begin{bmatrix} \omega_{11} & \omega_{12} \\ \omega_{12} & \omega_{22} \end{bmatrix} = \begin{bmatrix} \sigma_{11} & \beta_1\sigma_{11} + \sigma_{12} \\ \beta_1\sigma_{11} + \sigma_{12} & \beta_1^2\sigma_{11} + \sigma_{22} + 2\beta_1\sigma_{12} \end{bmatrix}$$

Since only workers with earnings below L_i were selected, we have

$$\log Y_i = \log W_i + \log H_i \leq \log L_i$$

From the reduced form, the joint probability density function of $\log W_i$ and $\log H_i$ under the assumption of normal residuals is

pdf $(\log W_i, \log H_i)$

$$= \begin{cases} 0 & \text{if } \log W_i + \log H_i > \log L_i \\ \dfrac{g(\log W_i, \log H_i \mid x'_{i1}\delta_1, x'_{i1}\beta_1\delta_1 + x'_{i2}\delta_2; \Omega)}{\Pr(\log W_i + \log H_i \leq \log L_i)} & \text{otherwise} \end{cases} \tag{99}$$

where g denotes a bivariate normal density function. Because the sum $\log W_i + \log H_i$ is normally distributed with mean $x'_{i1}\delta_1 + x'_{i1}\beta_1\delta_1 + x'_{i2}\delta_2$ and variance $\omega_{11} + \omega_{22} + 2\omega_{12}$, we have

$$\Pr(\log W_i + \log H_i \leq \log L_i) = \Phi\left(\frac{\log L_i - x'_{i1}\delta_1 - x'_{i1}\beta_1\delta_1 - x'_{i2}\delta_2}{\sqrt{\omega_{11} + \omega_{22} + 2\omega_{12}}}\right)$$

where Φ is the cumulative standard normal distribution function. The likelihood function is

$$L = \sum_{i=1}^{n} \text{pdf} (\log W_i, \log H_i)$$

Hausman and Wise (1977) carried out the maximization of log L.

Simultaneous-equation models involving truncated samples, discrete dependent variables, and limited dependent variables have been investigated; see Schmidt and Strauss (1975), Heckman (1978), Amemiya (1981), Manski and Mc-Fadden (1981), and Chappell (1982).

PROBLEMS

1. Plot the Weibull density function with $\alpha = 0$.

2. If ϵ has a Weibull distribution with parameter α_i, show that $\epsilon + c$ has a Weibull distribution with parameter $\alpha_i - c$ for any constant c.

3. Let ϵ_1 and ϵ_2 have independent Weibull distributions with parameters α_1 and α_2, respectively. Show that the maximum of ϵ_1 and ϵ_2 has a Weibull distribution with parameter $-\log (e^{-\alpha_1} + e^{-\alpha_2})$.

4. Consider a logit model with two alternatives 1 and 2. Let the individuals be divided into I groups with n_i observations in group i. The explanatory variables z_{ji} for the individuals in group i are not quantified. For example, the individuals may be classified into I groups according to income; the I income groups are designated by 1, 2, ..., I without explicitly recording the level of mean income in each group. Similarly, the characteristics z_{ji} of the alternatives j ($j = 1, 2$) are not quantified. Let P_{1i} be the probability for a person in group i to choose alternative 1 and $P_{2i} = 1 - P_{1i}$ be the probability for a person in group i to choose alternative 2. Let r_{ji} be the number of persons in group i choosing alternative j ($j = 1, 2$), with $n_i = r_{1i} + r_{2i}$. Define

$$\mu_i = \log \frac{P_{2i}}{P_{1i}} \qquad y_i = \log \frac{r_{2i}}{r_{1i}}$$

Show that $\sqrt{n_i}(y_i - \mu_i)$ has a limiting normal distribution with mean zero and variance $1/[P_{2i}(1 - P_{2i})]$.

5. In the model of Prob. 4 if the income level of each group i is recorded, how would you estimate the probabilities P_{ji}? Will you be able to do better than the analysis suggested in Prob. 4? Explain.

6. In the model of Prob. 5 assume in addition that the characteristics of the two alternatives can be measured. For example, in choosing between traveling by plane and by train (for a given route), the travel time and other characteristics of each model of travel are recorded. How would you estimate the probabilities P_{ji}? Will you be able to do better than the analysis of Prob. 5? Explain.

7. For the nested logit model of Sec. 8.6
   (a) write out L_1 of Eq. (52) explicitly and explain how you would maximize it.
   (b) Repeat for L_2.
   (c) Repeat for L_3.

8. Explain why the sequential estimator by maximizing L_1, L_2, and L_3 in (52) in three stages is not the maximum-likelihood estimator.

9. Give an economic example for which the nested logit model is more reasonable than the multinomial logit model and explain why.

10. Set up the log-likelihood function for the Tobit model assuming that all y_t are observed. Replace y_t in this function by its conditional expectation and maximize the resulting log likelihood to show

that the E-M algorithm does generate the maximum-likelihood estimate of the unknown parameter vector.

11. In a truncated sample the observation is included only if $x_i'\beta + \epsilon_i \le L_i$. Find the expectation of ϵ_i given $\epsilon_i \le L_i - x_i'\beta$ using a normal density with variance σ^2 for ϵ_i.

12. Use the Gauss-Newton method to estimate a linear regression model for a truncated sample.

13. Use the method of scoring to estimate a linear regression model for a truncated sample.

REFERENCES

Amemiya, T. (1973): "Regression Analysis When the Dependent Variable Is Truncated Normal," *Econometrica*, **41**: 997–1016.

——— (1981): "Qualitative Response Models: A Survey," *J. Econ. Lit.*, **19**: 1483–1536.

Brownstone, D. (1980): *An Econometric Model of Consumer Durable Choice and Utilization Rate*, Ph.D. dissertation, University of California, Berkeley, Department of Economics.

Chappell, H. W. (1982): "Campaign Contributions and Congressional Voting: A Simultaneous Probit-Tobit Model," *Rev. Econ. Statist.*, **64**: 77–83.

Cosslett, S. (1978): *Efficient Estimation of Discrete-Choice Models from Choice-Based Samples*, Ph.D. dissertation, University of California, Berkeley, Department of Economics.

Dempster, A. P., N. M. Laird, and D. B. Rubin (1977): "Maximum Likelihood from Incomplete Data via the E-M Algorithm," *J. R. Statist. Soc.*, **B39**: 1–22.

Domencich, T., and D. McFadden (1975): *Urban Travel Demand*, North-Holland, Amsterdam.

Fair, R. C. (1977): "A Note on the Computation of the Tobit Estimator," *Econometrica*, **45**: 1723–1728.

Goett, A. (1979): "A Structured Logit Model of Appliance Investment and Fuel Choice," Cambridge Systematics, Inc./West, Berkeley, Calif., mimeographed.

Gronau, R. (1974): "Wage Comparisons: A Selectivity Bias," *J. Polit. Econ.*, **82**: 1119–1143.

Hartley, M. (1977): "On the Calculation of the Maximum-Likelihood Estimator for a Model of Markets in Disequilibrium," mimeo.

Hausman, J., and D. Wise (1977): "Social Experimentation, Truncated Distributions and Efficient Estimation," *Econometrica*, **45**: 919–938.

Heckman, J. (1976): "The Common Structure of Statistical Models of Truncation, Sample Selection and Limited Dependent Variables and a Simple Estimator for Such Models," *Ann. Econ. Soc. Meas.*, **5**: 475–492.

——— (1978): "Dummy Endogenous Variables in a Simultaneous-Equation System," *Econometrica*, **46**: 931–959.

Manski, C. F., and D. McFadden (eds.) (1981): *Structural Analysis of Discrete Data with Econometric Applications*, M.I.T. Press, Cambridge, Mass.

McFadden, D. (1973): "Conditional Logit Analysis of Qualitative Choice Behavior," in P. Zarembka (ed.), *Frontiers in Econometrics*, Academic, New York.

——— (1976): "Quantal Choice Analysis: A Survey," *Ann. Econ. Soc. Meas.*, **5**: 363–390.

——— (1978): "Modelling The Choice of Residential Location," pp. 75–96, in Karlqvist et al. (eds.), *Spatial Interaction Theory and Planning Models*, North-Holland, Amsterdam.

——— (1981): "Econometric Models of Probabilistic Choice," in C. F. Manski and D. McFadden (eds.), *Structural Analysis of Discrete Data with Econometric Applications*, M.I.T. Press, Cambridge, Mass.

Schmidt, P., and R. P. Strauss (1975): "Estimation of Models with Jointly Dependent Qualitative Variables: A Simultaneous Logit Approach," *Econometrica*, **43**: 745–756.

Small, K. (1981): "Ordered Logit: A Discrete Choice Model with Proximate Covariance among Alternatives," *Princeton Univ. Econometr. Res. Prog. Res. Mem.* 292.

——— and D. Brownstone (1981): "Efficient Estimation of Nested Logit Models: An Application to Trip Timing," Princeton University, Department of Economics, mimeographed.

Tobin, J. (1958): "Estimation of Relationships for Limited Dependent Variables," *Econometrica*, **26**: 24–36.

CRITERIA FOR MODEL SELECTION

9.1 INTRODUCTION

All the other chapters in this book are concerned mainly with estimating various models useful in econometrics. This chapter is devoted to the subject of how to select a model. In a sense, the subject of model selection is treated in classical statistics, which deals with the two topics of estimation and testing hypotheses. Testing hypotheses is one way to select a model, and we have discussed hypothesis testing for regression models in Chaps. 1 and 2. However, the subject of model selection is broader than what is usually treated under the heading of the classical tests of hypotheses, as we shall point out.

For expositional convenience, let us consider a linear regression model

$$y = X\beta + \epsilon = X_1\beta_1 + X_2\beta_2 + \epsilon \tag{1}$$

where X_1 is $n \times k_1$, X_2 is $n \times k_2$, and ϵ has covariance matrix $I_n\sigma^2$. The problem may be to select model (1) or the linear model including X_1 alone as the explanatory variables. The classical treatment is to test the null hypothesis $\beta_2 = 0$ using an F ratio, as discussed in Secs. 2.4 and 2.7. The classical test is an incomplete solution to our problem because it leaves the level of significance undetermined. Many practicing econometricians often use 5 percent as the level of significance, but this rule is arbitrary. Other model-selection criteria presented later in this chapter will determine the level of significance appropriate for each problem.

The choice between model (1) and a linear regression model including X_1 alone is a case of *nested hypotheses*. Two hypotheses are said to be *nested* if one hypothesis assumes that the parameter vector lies in a subspace of the parameter space assumed under the other hypothesis. In our example, one hypothesis assumes $\beta_2 = 0$ while the other, more general, hypothesis allows β_2 to be any vector of real numbers; both hypotheses permit β_1 to be any real vector and σ^2 to be any nonnegative real number. Much attention in classical statistics is devoted to testing nested hypotheses. A null hypothesis imposes certain restrictions on the parameter vector θ, while the alternative hypothesis permits θ to take a wider range of values. By contrast, a pair of *nonnested hypotheses* may consist of model (1) and

$$y = Z\gamma + u \tag{2}$$

where Z is an $n \times p$ matrix which includes a different set of explanatory variables from those included in the $n \times k$ matrix X in model (1). There may be some variables common to both Z and X, but neither hypothesis results from restricting the values of the parameter vector permitted by the other hypothesis.

We begin our discussion in Sec. 9.2 by presenting one test for choosing between nonnested linear regression models. Section 9.3 follows by presenting some other tests for more general nonnested models. Section 9.4 deals with the lagrangian multiplier and related tests of statistical hypotheses. Section 9.5 treats the C_p criterion of Mallows (1973) for selecting nested regression models, which provides a solution to the determination of the level of significance. Section 9.6 develops an information criterion and applies it to the selection of regression models. This criterion also specifies a level of significance to be used. Section 9.7 presents the posterior probability criterion for model selection used by some Bayesians. Section 9.8 compares the information criterion and the posterior probability criterion. Section 9.9 provides formulas for the estimation of the information criterion for selecting linear simultaneous-equation models. Section 9.10, which is concerned with the selection between a larger linear econometric model and a smaller one, attempts to answer the question whether a linear econometric model should be decomposed into submodels or should be aggregated to form a smaller model. Section 9.11 deals with some methods for testing and analyzing model specifications.

9.2 A METHOD FOR SELECTING NONNESTED REGRESSION MODELS

Hotelling (1940) posed the following problem. Given a vector y whose n components are normally and independently distributed, and given the corresponding n observations on two sets of explanatory variables X and Z, test the null hypothesis that the standard errors in the regressions of y on X and y on Z are equal. Hotelling provided a solution for the case where X and Z are both univariate. Chow (1980) has generalized Hotelling's solution to the case where X and Z are sets of variates and there may be more than two sets. It will be assumed that X and Z are fixed variates, although our solution can be shown to apply also to random X and Z.

This problem first came to the author's attention while he was studying the factors affecting the demand for total stock and for annual purchase of automobiles in the United States, as reported in Chow (1957). In that study, the questions arose whether automobile stock y was better explained by liquid asset X or income Z and whether annual purchase y was better explained by permanent income X or by another pair of variables Z consisting of current income and lagged stock of automobiles. The approach taken in Chow (1957, p. 65) was to assume each hypothesis in turn as the true hupothesis and to test whether the additional variable or variables suggested by the other hypothesis were statistically significant using a standard F test. With this approach one may find that, given one hypothesis, the additional variables included in the other hypothesis are significant in both cases. If this happens, the procedure adopted fails to indicate which hypothesis has a better predictive power as measured by the standard error of the regression.

When both X and Z are single vectors, there is no loss of generality in rescaling them to make the elements of each sum to 0 and their squares sum to 1. Let the ith elements of these vectors be denoted by x_i and z_i, respectively. Hotelling (1940) transformed these vectors into two orthogonal vectors X^* and Z^*, where the ith element of X^* is

$$x_i^* = \frac{x_i - z_i}{\sqrt{2(1 - r_{xz})}} \qquad i = 1, \ldots, n$$

and the ith element of Z^* is

$$z_i^* = \frac{x_i + z_i}{\sqrt{2(1 + r_{xz})}} \qquad i = 1, \ldots, n$$

with r_{xz} denoting the correlation coefficient between X and Z. To test the hypothesis that the coefficient of X^* in the regression of y on both X^* and Z^* is zero one can apply the standard t test. The t statistic is easily shown to be

$$\frac{r_{yx} - r_{yz}}{s} \sqrt{\frac{\Sigma(y_i - \bar{y})^2}{2(1 - r_{xz})}} = t(n - 3) \tag{3}$$

where s is standard error of the multiple regression. Since this statistic is a monotone transformation of the difference between the sample correlation coefficients r_{yx} and r_{yz}, Hotelling used it to test the null hypothesis that the population correlation coefficients ρ_{yx} and ρ_{yz} are equal.

The test statistic (3) can be derived in another way. We assume, after rescaling, that the vectors X and Z have unit length and that their elements sum to zero. The rescaling does not affect the predictive power of these explanatory variables. In the linear regression of y on both X and Z we can test the null hypothesis that the difference between the two regression coefficients is zero by using a t statistic. This statistic is the same as the one given by (3) (see Prob. 1).

Hotelling also pointed out that when k other variates are present, the equality between the partial correlation coefficients $\rho_{yx.}$ and $\rho_{yz.}$ can be tested by the analogous expression

$$\frac{r_{yx.} - r_{yz.}}{s} \sqrt{\frac{\Sigma(y_{i.} - \bar{y}.)^2}{2(1 - r_{xz.})}} = t(n - 3 - k) \tag{4}$$

where $r_{yx.}$ and $r_{yz.}$ are the sample partial correlation coefficients, $y_{i.}$ is the residual of y_i in the regression on the other k explanatory variables, and s stands for the standard error of the regression of y on all fixed variates (see Prob. 2).

Interpreting Hotelling's solution from the geometric viewpoint will facilitate its generalization to the case of comparing two sets of fixed variates X and Z. The problem will be formulated in the following way, which will be shown to be identical with the original problem. Consider the random vector y in an n-dimensional vector space. The alternative hypothesis is that $E(y)$ lies in the subspace spanned by X and Z, denoted $\{X \quad Z\}$. The null hypothesis is that $E(y)$ is at an equal distance from the space $\{X\}$ spanned by X and the space $\{Z\}$ spanned by Z. We now show that this null hypothesis is equivalent to the null hypothesis that the population standard errors of the regressions of y on X and y on Z are equal.

Lemma 9.1 The population standard errors of the regressions of y on X and y on Z are equal if and only if $E(y)$ is of equidistance from $\{X\}$ and $\{Z\}$.

PROOF The population standard error of the regression of y on X is defined as the minimum of $\sqrt{E \| y - X\alpha_1 \|^2 / n}$ with respect to α_1, where $\| z \|^2$ denotes $z'z$. Differentiating $E \| y - X\alpha_1 \|^2$ with respect to α_1, we have

$$-2X'(Ey) + 2X'X\alpha_1$$

which, when set equal to zero, gives the minimizing α_1,

$$\alpha_1 = (X'X)^{-1}X'(Ey)$$

Thus $X\alpha_1$ is the orthogonal projection of $E(y)$ on the space $\{X\}$. Figure 9.1 shows the geometry. Similarly, the population standard error of the regres-

Figure 9.1 Testing equal predictive power of two regressions.

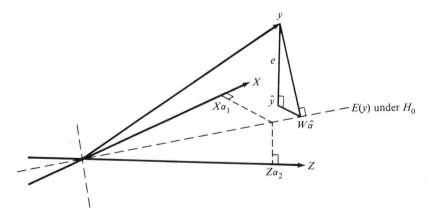

sion of y on Z is defined as $\sqrt{E \| y - Z\alpha_2 \|^2 / n}$, where

$$\alpha_2 = (Z'Z)^{-1} Z'(Ey)$$

and $Z\alpha_2$ is the orthogonal projection of $E(y)$ on $\{Z\}$.

On substituting $(X'X)^{-1} X'(Ey)$ for α_1 in $(1/n)E \| y - X\alpha_1 \|^2$ we find the square of the standard error in the regression of y on X to be

$$\tfrac{1}{n}[E(y'y) - (Ey)'X(X'X)^{-1}X'(Ey)]$$

Similarly the square of the standard error in the regression of y on Z is

$$\tfrac{1}{n}[E(y'y) - (Ey)'Z(Z'Z)^{-1}Z'(Ey)]$$

The expressions $(Ey)'X(X'X)^{-1}X'(Ey)$ and $(Ey)'Z(Z'Z)^{-1}Z'(Ey)$ are respectively the squared lengths $\| X\alpha_1 \|^2$ and $\| Z\alpha_2 \|^2$ of the orthogonal projections of $E(y)$ on $\{X\}$ and on $\{Z\}$. Therefore, the two standard errors are equal if and only if the lengths of the orthogonal projections are equal. But the orthogonal projections have the same length if and only if $E(y)$ is of equal distance from $\{X\}$ and $\{Z\}$.

When X and Z are single vectors, the null hypothesis states that $E(y)$ lies in the union of two lines bisecting the angles between X and Z. By comparing the distances of y from the space under the null hypothesis and from the space $\{X \quad Z\}$ under the alternative hypothesis one can test the null hypothesis stated above using the theory of general linear hypotheses. It can be shown, as suggested in Prob. 3, that the resulting F test is identical with (3). It should be pointed out that because the null space is the union of two lines (as seen in Figure 9.1) and is nonlinear even in this case, the F test is not exact but approximate. The assumption of equality between ρ_{yx} and ρ_{yz} is different from the assumption of equality between $E \| y - X\alpha_1 \|^2$ and $E \| y - Z\alpha_2 \|^2$ because the latter assumption includes $\rho_{yx} = -\rho_{yz}$. We have taken the equality between the standard errors as our null hypothesis.

When X and Z are matrices, we assume that $\{X\}$ and $\{Z\}$ are disjoint. If they are not, we can eliminate the vectors in common and deal with the residuals in the regressions of y and of the remaining two (disjoint) sets of fixed variates on these vectors. Hotelling's second test as given by (4) is a special case of this procedure. Our purpose is to provide a test of the null hypothesis that Ey is at an equal distance from $\{X\}$ and from $\{Z\}$. Let X be an $n \times k_1$ matrix with rank k_1 and Z be an $n \times k_2$ matrix with rank k_2. Let the rank of $[X \quad Z]$ be $k = k_1 + k_2$. Under the alternative hypothesis we estimate Ey by projecting y on $\{X \quad Z\}$, giving

$$y = \hat{y} + e \tag{5}$$

where the estimate $\hat{y}$ of Ey using the least-squares regression on $[X \quad Z]$ is in the space $\{X \quad Z\}$ and e is orthogonal to $\hat{y}$. $\| e \|^2 / \sigma^2$ is distributed as χ^2 $(n - k)$, as shown in Sec. 2.4.

Under the null hypothesis, the mean Ey of y is not only in $\{X \quad Z\}$ but is at an equal distance from $\{X\}$ and $\{Z\}$. This means that Ey satisfies

$$Ey = [X \quad Z]\alpha \tag{6}$$

for some vector α with k elements, and

$$(Ey)'[I - X(X'X)^{-1}X'](Ey) = (Ey)'[I - Z(Z'Z)^{-1}Z'](Ey) \tag{7}$$

Equations (6) and (7) imply

$$\alpha' \begin{bmatrix} X' \\ Z' \end{bmatrix} [X(X'X)^{-1}X' - Z(Z'Z)^{-1}Z'][X \quad Z]\alpha \equiv \alpha'H\alpha = 0 \tag{8}$$

Under the null hypothesis we find α by minimizing the squared distance $\|y - [X \quad Z]\alpha\|^2$ subject to the quadratic constraint (8). If the residuals in the regression of y on X and Z are normal and independent, each having variance σ^2, this estimate of α is identical with the maximum-likelihood estimate subject to constraint (8).

The log-likelihood function L, with W denoting $[X \quad Z]$, is

$$L(y; \alpha, \sigma^2, W) = -\frac{n}{2}\log 2\pi - \frac{n}{2}\log \sigma^2 - \frac{1}{2}\frac{(y - W\alpha)'(y - W\alpha)}{\sigma^2} \tag{9}$$

Introducing a Lagrange multiplier λ_1, we differentiate the lagrangian expression $L + \frac{1}{2}\lambda_1\alpha'H\alpha$ with respect to σ^2 and α_1, obtaining

$$\hat{\sigma}^2 = n^{-1}(y - W\hat{\alpha})'(y - W\hat{\alpha}) \tag{10}$$

$$W'y - W'W\hat{\alpha} + \hat{\sigma}^2\hat{\lambda}_1 H\hat{\alpha} = 0 \tag{11}$$

Equations (8), (10), and (11) can be used to solve for the three unknowns $\hat{\alpha}$, $\hat{\sigma}^2$, and $\hat{\lambda}_1$. Since $\hat{\sigma}^2$ is a function of $\hat{\alpha}$, as given by (10), we can use (8) and (11) to solve for the two unknowns $\hat{\alpha}$ and $\hat{\lambda} = \hat{\sigma}^2\hat{\lambda}_1$. These are the same first-order conditions as those for minimizing the squared distance $\|y - W\alpha\|^2$ subject to $\alpha'H\alpha = 0$, using the lagrangian

$$L^* = (y - W\alpha)'(y - W\alpha) - \lambda\alpha'H\alpha \tag{12}$$

To solve (11) and (8) for α and λ numerically, we linearize these equations about an initial guess $[\alpha^1 \quad \lambda^1]$

$$W'y - W'W\alpha^1 - W'W(\alpha - \alpha^1) + \lambda^1 H\alpha^1 + \lambda^1 H(\alpha - \alpha^1) + H\alpha^1(\lambda - \lambda^1) = 0$$

$$\alpha^{1'}H\alpha^1 + 2\alpha^{1'}H(\alpha - \alpha^1) = 0$$

Combining these equations to form a linear system, we have

$$\begin{bmatrix} W'W - \lambda H & -H\alpha^1 \\ -\alpha^{1'}H & 0 \end{bmatrix} \begin{bmatrix} \alpha - \alpha^1 \\ \lambda - \lambda^1 \end{bmatrix} = \begin{bmatrix} W'y - W'W\alpha^1 + \lambda^1 H\alpha^1 \\ \frac{1}{2}\alpha^{1'}H\alpha^1 \end{bmatrix} \tag{13}$$

which can be used to solve for α and λ iteratively.

The problem of maximizing (9) subject to constraint (8) is an example of maximum-likelihood estimation subject to constraints using lagrange multipliers.

This problem was studied by Aitchison and Silvey (1958) and Silvey (1959). The lagrangian multiplier test of Silvey (1959) will be discussed in Sec. 9.4. If instead of using lagrangian multipliers we use the constraints to eliminate an equal number of unknown parameters and treat the likelihood function as a function of the remaining parameters, the theory of maximum-likelihood estimation applies to the parameters. Subject to suitable mathematical assumptions about the constraints and the likelihood function, the maximum-likelihood estimator is consistent. For the purpose of studying the present problem and motivating the material of Sec. 9.4 we consider the asymptotic distribution of the maximum-likelihood estimator $\hat{\alpha}$ and the associated lagrangian multiplier $\hat{\lambda}$ obtained by maximizing $L^*(\alpha, \lambda)$ given by (12).

As usual, we expand the first-order conditions $\partial L^*(\hat{\alpha}, \hat{\lambda})/\partial \alpha = 0$ and $\partial L^*(\hat{\alpha}, \hat{\lambda})/\partial \lambda = 0$ given by (11) and (8) about the true-parameter vector α_0 (and $\lambda_0 = 0$ under H_0).

$$W'(y - W\alpha_0) - W'W(\hat{\alpha} - \alpha_0) + \hat{\lambda}H\alpha_0 + \hat{\lambda}H(\hat{\alpha} - \alpha_0) = 0$$
$$\alpha_0'H\alpha_0 + 2\alpha_0'H(\hat{\alpha} - \alpha_0) + (\hat{\alpha} - \alpha_0)'H(\hat{\alpha} - \alpha_0) = 0 \tag{14}$$

Given $\alpha_0'H\alpha_0 = 0$, if the true parameters satisfy the constraint (8), we combine these equations to study the joint distribution of $\sqrt{n}(\hat{\alpha} - \alpha_0)$ and $\sqrt{n}\hat{\lambda}$

$$\sqrt{n}\begin{bmatrix} \hat{\alpha} - \alpha_0 \\ \hat{\lambda} \end{bmatrix} = \begin{bmatrix} n^{-1}W'W & -n^{-1}H\alpha_0 - n^{-1}H(\hat{\alpha} - \alpha_0) \\ -n^{-1}\alpha_0'H - \dfrac{n^{-1}}{2}(\hat{\alpha} - \alpha_0)'H & 0 \end{bmatrix}^{-1}$$
$$\cdot n^{-1/2}\begin{bmatrix} W'(y - W\alpha_0) \\ 0 \end{bmatrix} \tag{15}$$

We assume that plim $n^{-1}W'W = Q$, where Q is positive definite. This implies that $n^{-1}H$ has a probability limit, say $\bar{H}$, as can easily be seen by the definition of H given in (8). When this assumption and the consistency of $\hat{\alpha}$ are used, the probability limit of the matrix to be inverted on the right-hand side of (15) is

$$\begin{bmatrix} Q & -\bar{H}\alpha_0 \\ -\alpha_0'\bar{H} & 0 \end{bmatrix} \tag{16}$$

By the central limit theorem, $n^{-1/2}W'(y - W\alpha_0)$ or $n^{-1/2}W'\epsilon$ has a limiting normal distribution with mean zero and covariance matrix $Q\sigma^2$, even if the independent elements of ϵ are not normal. The limiting distribution of $\sqrt{n}(\hat{\alpha} - \alpha_0, \hat{\lambda})$ is therefore normal with mean zero and covariance matrix

$$\begin{bmatrix} Q & -\bar{H}\alpha_0 \\ -\alpha_0'\bar{H} & 0 \end{bmatrix}^{-1}\begin{bmatrix} Q & 0 \\ 0 & 0 \end{bmatrix}\begin{bmatrix} Q & -\bar{H}\alpha_0 \\ -\alpha_0'\bar{H} & 0 \end{bmatrix}^{-1} \tag{17}$$

This discussion is in part a digression to illustrate the joint limiting distribution of the maximum-likelihood estimator and the associated lagrangian multiplier in a problem of maximum-likelihood estimation subject to constraints. Returning to our problem of testing the equal distance of Ey from $\{X\}$ and from

$\{Z\}$, under this null hypothesis we estimate Ey by $W\hat{\alpha}$ obtained by solving the above constrained maximization problem. Geometrically, we are projecting the vector y on the null space given by the quadratic equation (8). The result of this projection yields $W\hat{\alpha}$, which is orthogonal to $y - W\hat{\alpha}$, that is, $\hat{\alpha}'W'(y - W\hat{\alpha}) = 0$, as can be shown by premultiplying (11) by $\hat{\alpha}'$. If both $\hat{\alpha}$ and α_0 satisfy (8) and $\hat{\alpha}$ is near α_0, the neighborhood of the null space near $W\hat{\alpha}$ can be regarded as approximately linear. In other words, one can treat the quadratic constraint (8) approximately as the linear constraint

$$\alpha_0' H\hat{\alpha} = 0 \tag{18}$$

which is the same as the second of Eqs. (14) if the last term $(\hat{\alpha} - \alpha_0)'H(\hat{\alpha} - \alpha_0)$ of the latter equation is disregarded. After replacing constraint (8) by constraint (18) we have reduced our problem to one of testing general linear hypotheses. The null space becomes a vector space of dimension $k - 1$ since it is a subspace of $\{X \quad Z\} = \{W\}$ subject to the linear restriction (18). Under the alternative hypothesis, Ey is estimated by Wb, where $b = (W'W)^{-1}W'y$. In the identity

$$y - W\hat{\alpha} = (y - Wb) + (Wb - W\hat{\alpha}) = e + (Wb - W\hat{\alpha}) \tag{19}$$

e is certainly orthogonal to $Wb - W\hat{\alpha}$ since both Wb and $W\hat{\alpha}$ are in $\{X \quad Z\}$. $y - W\hat{\alpha}$ has $n - (k - 1)$ degrees of freedom if we treat the null space as linear, and e has $n - k$ degrees of freedom as usual. Applying the theory of linear hypotheses to our situation, we have the following theorem.

Theorem 9.1 Under the null hypothesis as stated in Lemma 9.1, the ratio

$$\frac{\|Wb - W\hat{\alpha}\|^2}{\|e\|^2/(n - k)} \tag{20}$$

is approximately distributed as $F(1, n - k)$.

This theorem can be used to test the null hypothesis that the residual variance in the regression of y on X is the same as the residual variance in the regression of y on Z. It is left as an exercise to prove that (20) reduces to Hotelling's test statistic (3) when both X and Z are vectors (see Probs. 3 and 4).

9.3 SOME TESTS OF NONNESTED HYPOTHESES

The previous section provided one test for choosing nontested regression models. The subject of testing nonnested hypotheses is still an important area of research, and many procedures have been suggested. This section mentions several other approaches briefly.

Deaton (1982) presents an interesting approach to nonnested hypotheses. In essence, when there are two nonnested hypotheses explaining the same dependent variable y, this approach takes each hypothesis in turn as the true hypothesis to compute the expectation of the maximum-likelihood estimator of the parameters of the remaining hypothesis and compares this expectation with the maximum-likelihood estimate itself. In comparing two linear regression models with X and Z as alternative explanatory variables, the method amounts to forming an artificially nested regression model with both X and Z as explanatory variables, assuming the true explanatory variables to be X (or Z) alone, and testing the hypothesis that the coefficients of Z (or X) are zero using the standard F statistic. As pointed out in the second paragraph of Sec. 9.2, this method was used in Chow (1957, p. 65) to answer the question whether automobile purchase y was better explained by permanent income X or by a pair of variables Z consisting of current income and the stock of automobiles. Deaton's method can be viewed as a generalization of the above procedure for linear regression models. As we have pointed out, it would fail to make a choice if the additional variables suggested by the alternative hypothesis turned out to be significant in both cases.

Quandt (1974) presents tests of nonnested hypotheses, among which are the following. Let $f_1(y, \theta_1)$ and $f_2(y, \theta_2)$ be two alternative density functions generating the observed vector y. Cox (1961, 1962) and Atkinson (1970) have combined the two competing probability density functions in the model

$$h(y; \theta_1, \theta_2, \lambda) = k f_1(y, \theta_1)^\lambda f_2(y, \theta_2)^{1-\lambda} \qquad (21)$$

The method of maximum likelihood is applied to estimate λ, and the maximum-likelihood estimate is used to choose between the two models. Quandt favors an alternative way of combining the two density functions, namely,

$$h(y; \theta_1, \theta_2, \lambda) = \lambda f_1(y, \theta_1) + (1 - \lambda) f_2(y, \theta_2) \qquad (22)$$

citing three reasons for his preference. First, the probability density function (22) is a convex combination of probability density functions and is intuitively easier to interpret. Second, no normalization constant k is required, as in (21), and the maximization of the likelihood function becomes easier. Third, for a choice between two normal linear regression models, $y = X_1 \beta_1 + \epsilon_1$ and $y = X_2 \beta_2 + \epsilon_2$, all parameters are identifiable, while for (21) one cannot separately identify λ, β_1, β_2, $\sigma_1^2 = E\epsilon_{i1}^2$, and $\sigma_2^2 = E\epsilon_{i2}^2$ (see Prob. 5).

Quandt also points out several difficulties in using (22). First, departure from one hypothesis in a direction not toward the other may yield values of λ outside the (0, 1) interval. This may cause some values of the density given by (22) to become negative. Second, at $\lambda = 0$ or $\lambda = 1$ there is singularity in the likelihood function, and the regularity conditions guaranteeing the asymptotic distribution of the maximum-likelihood estimator of λ may not hold. Third, if f_1 and f_2 are normal, the likelihood function for (22) is unbounded and no proper maximum-likelihood estimates exist. To overcome this difficulty Quandt suggested introducing the assumption $\sigma_1 = \sigma_2$. He has applied the resulting test using the maximum-likelihood estimate of λ in (22) to discriminate between several economic models. If the confidence interval for λ includes neither 1 nor 0, the composite hypothesis should be accepted.

For other approaches to choosing between competing models see Gaver and

Geisel (1974), Pesaran and Deaton (1978), Davidson and MacKinnon (1981), and MacKinnon (1983); see also Secs. 9.5 to 9.7 and 9.11.

9.4 LAGRANGIAN MULTIPLIER AND RELATED TESTS

In Sec. 9.2 we provided an example of maximum-likelihood estimation subject to a constraint and derived the asymptotic distribution of the maximum-likelihood estimator and the associated lagrangian multiplier using Eq. (15), under the assumption that the true parameter satisfies the constraint. The asymptotic distribution in the general case has been studied by Aitchison and Silvey (1958) and Silvey (1959). Let $\log L(y, \theta)$ denote the log likelihood based on the vector y of n independent observations, each having density $f(y_i, \theta)$. Let the constraint be $h(\theta) = 0$, where h is an r-component vector function of the k-dimensional parameter vector θ. Differentiating the lagrangian expression

$$n^{-1} \log L(y, \theta) + \lambda' h(\theta) \tag{23}$$

one obtains the first-order conditions for the maximum-likelihood estimator and λ

$$n^{-1} \frac{\partial \log L(y, \hat{\theta})}{\partial \theta} + H_{\hat{\theta}} \hat{\lambda} = 0 \tag{24}$$

$$h(\hat{\theta}) = 0 \tag{25}$$

where H_θ denotes the $k \times r$ matrix $\partial h'(\theta)/\partial \theta$. The solution of (24) and (25) gives the maximum-likelihood estimator $\hat{\theta}$ and the associated lagrangian multiplier $\hat{\lambda}$.

In order to derive the asymptotic distribution of $\hat{\theta}$ and $\hat{\lambda}$ we first define a vector θ^* which satisfies the restriction $h(\theta^*) = 0$ and to which $\hat{\theta}$ converges stochastically. If the true parameter θ_0 satisfies $h(\theta_0)$, the maximum-likelihood estimator $\hat{\theta}$ converges to θ_0 and θ^* is identical with θ_0. The case $h(\theta_0) \neq 0$ is of interest. If we treat our problem as one of testing the null hypothesis $h(\theta_0) = 0$, we shall be interested in the distribution of $\hat{\theta}$ and $\hat{\lambda}$ when the null hypothesis is *not* true. When $h(\theta_0) \neq 0$, the maximum-likelihood estimator $\hat{\theta}$ subject to the constraint $h(\hat{\theta}) = 0$ will converge stochastically not to θ_0 but to another vector θ^* satisfying $h(\theta^*) = 0$. Define the expected log likelihood of observing y_i as

$$z(\theta) = E_{\theta_0} \log f(y_i, \theta) = \int_{-\infty}^{\infty} [\log f(x, \theta)] f(x, \theta_0) \, dx \tag{26}$$

where the subscript θ_0 of E denotes the fact that the expectation is evaluated using the true parameter θ_0. If θ^* is a vector satisfying $h(\theta^*) = 0$ which maximizes the expected log likelihood $z(\theta)$, we have

$$z(\theta^*) > z(\theta)$$

for all $\theta \neq \theta^*$ satisfying $h(\theta) = 0$. θ^* can be regarded as the parameter of a model $f(\cdot, \theta)$ which best approximates the true model $f(\cdot, \theta_0)$ subject to the constraint

$h(\theta) = 0$. Recalling our proof of the consistency of the maximum-likelihood estimator using inequality (58) of Chap. 1, we now show that a solution $\hat{\theta}$ of (24) and (25) is a consistent estimator of θ^*. If the expectation (26) reaches its maximum at $\theta = \theta^*$ by definition, the sample analog will satisfy the corresponding inequality

$$n^{-1} \sum_{i=1}^{n} \log f(y_i, \theta^*) > n^{-1} \sum_{i=1}^{n} \log f(y_i, \theta^* \pm \delta)$$

for $\delta > 0$ and for sufficiently large n with probability greater than $1 - \epsilon$, however small ϵ may be. This statement is the result of the law of large numbers. With probability greater than $1 - \epsilon$, the function $n^{-1} \sum_i \log f(y_i, \theta)$ will be greater at $\theta = \theta^*$ than at $\theta = \theta^* \pm \delta$. Whenever this happens, this function will have a local maximum within $\theta^* \pm \delta$. In other words, with probability greater than $1 - \epsilon$ a maximum-likelihood estimate $\hat{\theta}$ satisfying (24) and (25) will be within $\theta^* \pm \delta$. Thus this $\hat{\theta}$ converges stochastically to θ^*.

Following the arguments surrounding Eq. (59) of Chap 1, we expand the first term of (24) about θ^* and rewrite (24) as

$$n^{-1} \frac{\partial \log L(y, \theta^*)}{\partial \theta} + \left[n^{-1} \frac{\partial^2 \log L(y, \theta^*)}{\partial \theta \, \partial \theta'} + o(1) \right](\hat{\theta} - \theta^*) + H_{\hat{\theta}} \hat{\lambda} = 0 \quad (27)$$

We also expand (25) about θ^*, assuming the continuity of the first partial derivatives of $h(\theta)$, and rewrite (25) as

$$[H'_{0*} + o(1)](\hat{\theta} - \theta^*) = 0 \tag{28}$$

Since $z(\theta^*)$ is a maximum of $z(\theta)$ for θ satisfying $h(\theta) = 0$, that is, θ^* can be obtained by differentiating the lagrangian $z(\theta) + \lambda h(\theta)$, there exists a lagrangian multiplier λ^* satisfying

$$\frac{\partial z(\theta^*)}{\partial \theta} + H_{\theta*} \lambda^* = 0 \tag{29}$$

Subtracting (29) from (27) and substituting $H_{\theta*} + o(1)$ for $H_{\hat{\theta}}$, we have

$$\left[n^{-1} \frac{\partial \log L(y, \theta^*)}{\partial \theta} - \frac{\partial z(\theta^*)}{\partial \theta} \right] + \left[n^{-1} \frac{\partial^2 \log L(y, \theta^*)}{\partial \theta \, \partial \theta'} + o(1) \right](\hat{\theta} - \theta^*)$$
$$+ [H_{\theta*} + o(1)](\hat{\lambda} - \lambda^*) + (H_{\hat{\theta}} - H_{\theta*})\lambda^* = 0 \quad (30)$$

The last term of (30) can be rewritten by a Taylor expansion of the elements of $H_{\hat{\theta}}$ about θ^*

$$[H_{\hat{\theta}} - H_{\theta*}]\lambda^* = \left[\sum_{i=1}^{r} \lambda_i^* \frac{\partial^2 h_i(\theta^*)}{\partial \theta \, \partial \theta'} + o(1) \right](\hat{\theta} - \theta^*) \tag{31}$$

Substituting (31) into (30) and letting

$$-\hat{B}_{\theta*} = n^{-1} \frac{\partial^2 \log L(y, \theta^*)}{\partial \theta \, \partial \theta'} + \sum_{i=1}^{r} \lambda_i^* \frac{\partial^2 h_i(\theta^*)}{\partial \theta \, \partial \theta'}$$

we obtain

$$[\hat{B}_{\theta*} + o(1)](\hat{\theta} - \theta*) - [H_{\theta*} + o(1)](\hat{\lambda} - \lambda*) = n^{-1} \frac{\partial \log L(y, \theta*)}{\partial \theta} - \frac{\partial z(\theta*)}{\partial \theta}$$

Combining this equation with (28) gives

$$\begin{bmatrix} \hat{B}_{\theta*} + o(1) & -H_{\theta*} + o(1) \\ -H'_{\theta*} + o(1) & 0 \end{bmatrix} \begin{bmatrix} \hat{\theta}* - \theta* \\ \hat{\lambda} - \lambda* \end{bmatrix} = \begin{bmatrix} n^{-1} \dfrac{\partial \log L(y, \theta*)}{\partial \theta} - \dfrac{\partial z(\theta*)}{\partial \theta} \\ 0 \end{bmatrix} \quad (32)$$

where we now write $\hat{\theta}$ as $\hat{\theta}*$ to emphasize that it is an estimate of $\theta*$, or an estimate subject to the restriction $h(\hat{\theta}*) = 0$. The probability limit of the matrix on the left of (32) is

$$\begin{bmatrix} -E \dfrac{\partial^2 \log f(y_i, \theta*)}{\partial \theta \, \partial \theta'} - \displaystyle\sum_{i=1}^{r} \lambda_i^* \dfrac{\partial^2 h_i(\theta*)}{\partial \theta \, \partial \theta'} & -\dfrac{\partial h'(\theta*)}{\partial \theta} \\ -\dfrac{\partial h(\theta*)}{\partial \theta'} & 0 \end{bmatrix} = \begin{bmatrix} B_{\theta*} & -H_{\theta*} \\ -H'_{\theta*} & 0 \end{bmatrix} \quad (33)$$

which we assume to be nonsingular. The inverse of (33) is defined as

$$\begin{bmatrix} P & Q \\ Q' & R \end{bmatrix} = \begin{bmatrix} B_{\theta*} & -H_{\theta*} \\ -H'_{\theta*} & 0 \end{bmatrix}^{-1} \quad (34)$$

where, using the partitioned inverse of (33) and omitting the subscript $\theta*$ in $B_{\theta*}$ and $H_{\theta*}$,

$$P = B^{-1} - B^{-1}H(H'B^{-1}H)^{-1}H'B^{-1}$$
$$Q = -B^{-1}H(H'B^{-1}H)^{-1} \qquad R = -(H'B^{-1}H)^{-1} \quad (35)$$

By the central limit theorem, $\sqrt{n}$ times the vector on the right-hand side of (32) has a normal limiting distribution with mean zero and covariance matrix

$$V_{\theta*} = E_{\theta_0} \frac{\partial \log f(y_i, \theta*)}{\partial \theta} \frac{\partial \log f(y_i, \theta*)}{\partial \theta'} - \frac{\partial z(\theta*)}{\partial \theta} \frac{\partial z(\theta*)}{\partial \theta'} \quad (36)$$

Solving Eq. (32) by using the inverse (34) of the probability limit of the matrix on its left, we derive the asymptotic distribution of $\sqrt{n}(\hat{\theta}* - \theta*, \hat{\lambda} - \lambda*)$ as given by the following lemma (Silvey, 1959).

Lemma 9.2 Let $\hat{\theta}*$ be the maximum-likelihood estimator of θ in the model $f(y_i, \theta)$ subject to the constraint $h(\theta) = 0$, and $\hat{\lambda}$ be the associated lagrangian multiplier. Let $\theta*$ and $\lambda*$ be their probability limits. Under the assumptions of Theorem 1.4 and of the continuity of the first partial derivatives of $h(\theta)$, $\sqrt{n}(\hat{\theta}* - \theta*, \hat{\lambda} - \lambda*)$ will have a normal limiting distribution with mean zero and covariance matrix

$$
\begin{bmatrix} P & Q \\ Q' & R \end{bmatrix} \begin{bmatrix} V_{\theta*} & 0 \\ 0 & 0 \end{bmatrix} \begin{bmatrix} P & Q \\ Q' & R \end{bmatrix} = \begin{bmatrix} PV_{\theta*}P & PV_{\theta*}Q \\ Q'V_{\theta*}P & Q'V_{\theta*}Q \end{bmatrix}
\tag{37}
$$

where the matrices P, Q, and $V_{\theta*}$ are given by (33), (35), and (36).

The asymptotic distribution given by Lemma 9.2 applies whether or not the true θ_0 satisfies the restriction $h(\theta) = 0$. If $h(\theta_0) = 0$, $\theta^* = \theta_0$. By (48) and (49) of Chap. 1 and definition (26), $\partial z(\theta^*)/\partial\theta = 0$ and $\partial^2 z(\theta^*)/(\partial\theta\,\partial\theta')$ is negative definite, implying that $z(\theta)$ reaches its unconstrained maximum at $\theta = \theta^* = \theta_0$. When the constraint $h(\theta^*) = 0$ is automatically satisfied, (29) is replaced by $\partial z(\theta^*)/\partial\theta = 0$ and $\lambda^* = 0$. Using $\partial z(\theta^*)/\partial\theta = 0$, (49) of Chap. 1, and $\lambda^* = 0$, we can write (36) as

$$
V_{\theta*} = E_{\theta*} \frac{\partial \log f(y_i, \theta^*)}{\partial\theta} \frac{\partial \log f(y_i, \theta^*)}{\partial\theta'} = -E \frac{\partial^2 \log f(y_i, \theta^*)}{\partial\theta\,\partial\theta'} = B_{\theta*}
\tag{38}
$$

Given $V_{\theta*} = B_{\theta*}$, the covariance matrix (37) can be simplified as follows. By virtue of (35) and $V_{\theta*} = B_{\theta*} = B$, the covariance matrix (37) becomes

$$
\begin{bmatrix} PBP & PBQ \\ Q'BP & Q'BQ \end{bmatrix} = \begin{bmatrix} P & 0 \\ 0 & -R \end{bmatrix}
\tag{39}
$$

Note that P and R are defined by (35), with $B_{\theta*}$ defined by (38). Thus we have the following corollary.

Corollary 1 Under the assumptions of Lemma 9.2, if the true θ_0 satisfies the constraint $h(\theta_0) = 0$, the random vector $\sqrt{n}(\hat{\theta}^* - \theta_0, \hat{\lambda})$ where $\hat{\theta}^*$ is the maximum-likelihood estimator subject to the constraint and $\hat{\lambda}$ is the associated lagrangian multiplier, has a normal limiting distribution with mean zero and covariance matrix (39), where P and R are defined by (35) and (38).

An example of the asymptotic distribution of $\hat{\theta}^*$ and $\hat{\lambda}$ under the null hypothesis $h(\theta_0) = 0$ was given in Sec. 9.2, with the covariance matrix given by (17). In practice when $\theta^* = \theta_0$ is unknown, P and $-R$ in (39) can be estimated by $\hat{P}$ and $-\hat{R}$, which are computed by replacing $B_{\theta*}$ and $H_{\theta*}$ in (35) by $B_{\hat{\theta}*}$ and $H_{\hat{\theta}*}$.

To test the null hypothesis $h(\theta) = 0$, the *lagrangian multiplier test* employs the statistic $-n\hat{\lambda}'\hat{R}^{-1}\hat{\lambda}$, which is distributed asymptotically as $\chi^2(r)$ because $\sqrt{n}\,\hat{\lambda}$ is distributed asymptotically as r-variate normal with mean zero and covariance matrix $-R$. By (35) and (24), this statistic can be written as a *score* statistic:

$$
n\hat{\lambda}'\hat{H}'\hat{B}^{-1}\hat{H}\hat{\lambda} = \left[\frac{\partial \log L(y, \hat{\theta}^*)}{\partial\theta'}\right]\left[-\frac{\partial^2 \log L(y, \hat{\theta}^*)}{\partial\theta\,\partial\theta'}\right]\left[\frac{\partial \log L(y, \hat{\theta}^*)}{\partial\theta}\right]
$$

Silvey (1959) has considered the asymptotic distributions of two other statistics for testing the same null hypothesis. One is the *likelihood-ratio test*. The statistic used is the likelihood ratio

$$\mu = \frac{L(y, \hat{\theta}^*)}{L(y, \hat{\theta})} \tag{40}$$

where $\hat{\theta}$ is the maximum-likelihood estimator of θ under the alternative hypothesis [without imposing the restriction $h(\hat{\theta}) = 0$] and $\hat{\theta}^*$ is the ML-estimator of θ subject to the restriction. If the null hypothesis is true, μ will tend to be close to 1. If the null hypothesis is not true, μ will tend to be smaller. Under the null hypothesis, $-2 \log \mu = 2 \log \mu^{-1}$ will be distributed asymptotically as $\chi^2(r)$, where r is the number of restrictions in $h(\theta) = 0$. If $-2 \log \mu$ is larger than the critical value given by the $\chi^2(r)$ distribution with a given level of significance, we reject the null hypothesis. The likelihood-ratio test has wide applications in statistics. It requires computing the values of the likelihood function at $\hat{\theta}^*$ and at $\hat{\theta}$. Often the exact distribution of the likelihood ratio under the null hypothesis is known. If not, one can resort to the above χ^2 asymptotic distribution.

A second test is the *Wald test*. Again let $\hat{\theta}$ be the ML-estimate of θ without imposing the restriction. We accept the null hypothesis if $h(\hat{\theta})$ is sufficiently close to zero. The test statistic is

$$W = nh(\hat{\theta})'[\text{Cov } h(\hat{\theta})]^{-1}h(\hat{\theta}) \tag{41}$$

Wald (1943) has shown that this statistic W and $-2 \log \mu$ have the same asymptotic distribution under general conditions. Silvey (1959) has shown that under fairly general assumptions

$$-\text{plim} (2 \log \mu) = \text{plim } W = -\text{plim } n\hat{\lambda}'R^{-1}\hat{\lambda} \tag{42}$$

and that the likelihood-ratio test, the Wald test, and the lagrangian multiplier test are asymptotically equivalent in the sense that their test statistics have the same asymptotic distribution.

To illustrate these three tests let us apply them to test the restriction $h(\beta) = H'\beta - q = 0$, where H' is $r \times k$, in a normal linear regression model $y = X\beta + \epsilon$ with known $\sigma^2 = E\epsilon_i^2$. The log-likelihood function is

$$\log L = -\frac{n}{2} \log 2\pi - \frac{n}{2} \log \sigma^2 - \frac{1}{2\sigma^2} (y - X\beta)'(y - X\beta)$$

Differentiating $n^{-1} \log L + \lambda'(H'\beta - q)/\sigma^2$ with respect to β and λ yields the first-order conditions for $\hat{\beta}^*$ and $\hat{\lambda}$. Using Corollary 1 and some algebra, one can show that

$$-n\hat{\lambda}'\hat{R}^{-1}\hat{\lambda} = \sigma^{-2}(H'b - q)'[H'(X'X)^{-1}H]^{-1}(H'b - q) \tag{43}$$

where b is the unconstrained least-squares estimate of β (see Prob. 6). One can easily show that the Wald test statistic (41) in the present case is also (43) (see Prob. 7). For the likelihood-ratio test we use

$$-2 \log \mu = -2 \log L(\hat{\beta}^*) + 2 \log L(b)$$

$$= \frac{1}{\sigma^2} [(y - X\hat{\beta}^*)'(y - X\hat{\beta}^*) - (y - Xb)'(y - Xb)]$$

which is also equal to (43) (see Prob. 8). Therefore, for this elementary problem, all three tests are identical.

Note, however, that applying the asymptotic χ^2 distribution to any of the above three test statistics is in general not the best approximation possible. For example, if σ^2 is unknown in the above example, replacing σ^2 by s^2 in (43) and approximating the resulting statistic by $\chi^2(r)$ is not the best procedure. We know from Chap. 2 that this statistic, divided by r, has an $F(r, n - k)$ distribution exactly. As another example, to test the nonnested hypothesis of Sec. 9.2 we have recommended the corresponding F test rather than the lagrangian multiplier test. For applications of the lagrangian multiplier test to model specification in econometrics see Breusch and Pagan (1980).

9.5 THE C_p CRITERION

We now turn from significance tests to other criteria for selecting a regression model or a more general econometric model. One defect of the significance tests is that the level of significance must be specified. Other criteria can be used to resolve the problem of choosing the level of significance.

Consider the choice between the regression model

$$Y = X\beta + \epsilon = X_1\beta_1 + X_2\beta_2 + \epsilon \tag{44}$$

and the linear model using X_1 alone as the explanatory variables, where X_1 is $n \times k_1$ and X_2 is $n \times k_2$, ϵ being normal with covariance matrix $I_n\sigma^2$. A standard treatment is to test the null hypothesis $\beta_2 = 0$ using the F ratio, but this does not solve the problem as it begs the question of what level of significance to use. A more satisfactory solution is to choose the model which is estimated to have smaller prediction errors. Specifically, let n future, or out-of-sample, observations be

$$\tilde{Y} = \tilde{X}\beta + \tilde{\epsilon} \tag{45}$$

under the assumption that (44) is the true regression model, and let the model-selection criterion be the expected sum of squared prediction errors. Mallows (1973) has derived a C_p criterion for choosing between the two models.

Using the small model with X_1 alone and denoting the corresponding maximum-likelihood estimate of β by $\hat{\beta}_I$ [consisting of $(X_1'X_1)^{-1}X_1'Y$ and 0], one finds

$$E(\hat{\beta}_I - \beta)(\hat{\beta}_I - \beta)'$$
$$= \begin{bmatrix} (X_1'X_1)^{-1}X_1'X_2\beta_2\beta_2'X_2'X_1(X_1'X_1)^{-1} + (X_1'X_1)^{-1}\sigma^2 & -(X_1'X_1)^{-1}X_1'X_2\beta_2\beta_2' \\ -\beta_2\beta_2'X_2'X_1(X_1'X_1)^{-1} & \beta_2\beta_2' \end{bmatrix}$$
$$\tag{46}$$

(see Prob. 9). Using the estimated small model and thus the predictor $\tilde{X}\hat{\beta}_I$, the expected sum of squared prediction errors is

$$E(\tilde{X}\hat{\beta}_I - \tilde{Y})'(\tilde{X}\hat{\beta}_I - \tilde{Y}) = E(\hat{\beta}_I - \beta)'\tilde{X}'\tilde{X}(\hat{\beta}_I - \beta) + E\tilde{\epsilon}'\tilde{\epsilon}$$

$$= \text{tr}\,[\tilde{X}'\tilde{X}E(\hat{\beta}_I - \beta)(\hat{\beta}_I - \beta)'] + n\sigma^2$$

$$= k_1\sigma^2 + \beta_2' X_2'[I - X_1(X_1'X_1)^{-1}X_1']X_2\beta_2 + n\sigma^2 \quad (47)$$

where the last line made use of (46) and the reasonable assumption that $\tilde{X}'\tilde{X} = X'X$, made to provide a standard for comparing the two models.

Using the large model (44) and denoting the maximum-likelihood estimate of β by $\hat{\beta} = (X'X)^{-1}X'Y$, we have

$$E(\tilde{X}\hat{\beta} - \tilde{Y})'(\tilde{X}\hat{\beta} - \tilde{Y}) = E(\hat{\beta} - \beta)'\tilde{X}'\tilde{X}(\hat{\beta} - \beta) + E\tilde{\epsilon}'\tilde{\epsilon} = (k_1 + k_2)\sigma^2 + n\sigma^2 \quad (48)$$

Comparing (47) and (48), we find that the small model should be used if and only if

$$\beta_2' X_2'[I - X_1(X_1'X_1)^{-1}X_1']X_2\beta_2 \equiv \beta_2' X_{2.1}'X_{2.1}\beta_2 < k_2\sigma^2 \quad (49)$$

where $X_{2.1} = [I - X_1(X_1'X_1)^{-1}X_1']X_2$ denotes the matrix of residuals of the regression of X_2 on X_1.

Since we do not know β_2 and σ^2, we can estimate them for criterion (49). Given that $\hat{\beta}_2$ has mean β_2 and covariance matrix $(X_{2.1}'X_{2.1})^{-1}\sigma^2$, we evaluate the mean of the $\chi^2(k_2)$ variable

$$\frac{E(\hat{\beta}_2 - \beta_2)'(X_{2.1}'X_{2.1})(\hat{\beta}_2 - \beta_2)}{\sigma^2} = \frac{E\hat{\beta}_2' X_{2.1}'X_{2.1}\hat{\beta}_2 - \beta_2' X_{2.1}'X_{2.1}\beta_2}{\sigma^2} = k_2$$
$$(50)$$

or
$$E\hat{\beta}_2' X_{2.1}'X_{2.1}\hat{\beta}_2 = \beta_2' X_{2.1}'X_{2.1}\beta_2 + k_2\sigma^2$$

Selection criterion (49) is equivalent to

$$\beta_2' X_{2.1}'X_{2.1}\beta_2 + k_2\sigma^2 < 2k_2\sigma^2 \quad (51)$$

If the left-hand side of (51) is replaced by the unbiased estimate from (50) and σ^2 on the right-hand side is replaced by the unbiased estimate s^2, we obtain

$$\hat{\beta}_2' X_{2.1}'X_{2.1}\hat{\beta}_2 < 2k_2 s^2 \equiv \frac{2k_2(Y - X\hat{\beta})'(Y - X\hat{\beta})}{n - k_1 - k_2} \quad (52)$$

as the condition for selecting the small model. In the language of testing a hypothesis, this rule amounts to setting the critical value for the F statistic $\hat{\beta}_2'X_{2.1}'X_{2.1}\hat{\beta}_2/k_2 s^2$ under the null hypothesis $\beta_2 = 0$ to 2. We observe from (47) and (48) that omitting the variables X_2 might yield a better model for prediction even when $\beta_2 \neq 0$ because $E(\hat{\beta}_I - \beta)'\tilde{X}'\tilde{X}(\hat{\beta}_I - \beta)$ in (47) might be smaller than $E(\hat{\beta} - \beta)'\tilde{X}'\tilde{X}(\hat{\beta} - \beta)$ in (48). In other words, a misspecified model might lead to better prediction as it reduces the covariance matrix $E(\hat{\beta} - \beta)(\hat{\beta} - \beta)'$ of estimation errors.

The criterion of expected squared prediction error applies to the selection of nonnested regression models. Let the two models have regression functions $X_1\beta_1$ and $X_2\beta_2$, respectively, where X_1 and X_2 are disjointed. Under the assumption that (44) is the true model, we have an expression analogous to (47) for the expected sum of squared prediction errors resulting from using the second model with X_2 alone as the explanatory variables. Comparing these two expressions, we shall select the first model if

$$k_1\sigma^2 + \beta_2' X_{2.1}' X_{2.1}\beta_2 < k_2\sigma^2 + \beta_1' X_{1.2}' X_{1.2}\beta_1 \tag{53}$$

Replacing both sides of (53) by the unbiased estimates from (50) and rearranging terms, we obtain

$$\hat{\beta}_2' X_{2.1}' X_{2.1}\hat{\beta}_2 - \hat{\beta}_1 X_{1.2}' X_{1.2}\hat{\beta}_1 < 2(k_2 - k_1)s^2 \tag{54}$$

as the condition for choosing the first model with X_1 as the explanatory variables. If $k_1 = k_2$, the model with higher R^2 or smaller s^2 will be selected (see Prob. 10).

9.6 THE INFORMATION CRITERION

The information criterion for model selection suggested by Akaike (1973, 1974) can be viewed as an extension of the prediction criterion of Sec. 9.5. Instead of using the expected squared prediction error of a future observation, Akaike has adopted the mean information $E[\log g(\tilde{y}) - \log f(\tilde{y})]$ for discrimination between the density function $g(\cdot)$ of the true model and the density function $f(\cdot)$ of the model used for prediction. In the nested regression example, the log likelihood of the new observation vector $\tilde{Y} = \tilde{X}\beta + \tilde{\epsilon}$ for the true or larger model is

$$\sum_1^n \log g(\tilde{y}_i) = -\frac{n}{2}\log 2\pi - \frac{n}{2}\log \sigma^2 - \frac{1}{2}\frac{(\tilde{Y} - \tilde{X}\beta)'(\tilde{Y} - \tilde{X}\beta)}{\sigma^2} \tag{55}$$

and the log likelihood of $\tilde{Y}$ according to the estimated small model is

$$\sum_1^n \log f(\tilde{y}_i) = -\frac{n}{2}\log 2\pi - \frac{n}{2}\log \hat{\sigma}_I^2 - \frac{1}{2}\frac{(\tilde{Y} - \tilde{X}\hat{\beta}_I)'(\tilde{Y} - \tilde{X}\hat{\beta}_I)}{\hat{\sigma}_I^2} \tag{56}$$

where $\hat{\sigma}_I^2 = (Y - X\hat{\beta}_I)'(Y - X\hat{\beta}_I)/n$. The mean information criterion for given $\hat{\beta}_I$ and $\hat{\sigma}_I$ is

$$E_{\tilde{Y}} \sum_1^n [\log g(\tilde{y}_i) - \log f(\tilde{y}_i)]$$

$$= -\frac{n}{2}(\log \sigma^2 - \log \hat{\sigma}_I^2) - \frac{n}{2} + \frac{1}{2}\frac{E_{\tilde{Y}}(\tilde{Y} - \tilde{X}\hat{\beta}_I)'(\tilde{Y} - \tilde{X}\hat{\beta}_I)}{\hat{\sigma}_I^2} \tag{57}$$

Note that criterion (57) measures the goodness of the estimated model not only by the expected sum of squared prediction errors $E_{\tilde{Y}}(\tilde{Y} - \tilde{X}\hat{\beta}_I)'(\tilde{Y} - \tilde{X}\hat{\beta}_I)$ but also by the difference between $\log \sigma^2$ and $\log \hat{\sigma}_I^2$ due to the error in $\hat{\sigma}_I^2$ as an estimate of the residual variance σ^2 of the regression residual. In general it is better to judge a model $f(\cdot)$ by the expected likelihood ratio $E \log [g(\tilde{y})/f(\tilde{y})]$

than by the expected squared prediction error since the former covers the whole density function while the latter covers only its mean.

In (57) the estimated parameters $\hat{\beta}_I$ and $\hat{\sigma}_I^2$ of the small model are treated as being fixed for the purpose of defining the information measure; only $\tilde{Y}$ is treated as random when the expectation is evaluated. As the next step, one should take the expectation $E_{\hat{\beta}_I, \hat{\sigma}_I^2}$ of (57), treating $\hat{\beta}_I$ and $\hat{\sigma}_I^2$ as random variables, in order to evaluate the estimated model by allowing for the sampling errors of its parameters. Both steps were incorporated in (47) when the expected squared error of prediction was used to evaluate this model. The expectation $E(\cdot)$ in (47) could have been replaced by $E_{\hat{\beta}_I} E_{\tilde{Y}}(\cdot \mid \hat{\beta}_I)$ to make these two steps clear. Having considered the regression example for motivation, we are in a position to develop the information criterion for selecting models in a more general setting.

Given J models represented by the densities $f_1(\cdot \mid \theta_1), \ldots, f_J(\cdot \mid \theta_J)$ for the explanation of a random vector y and given n observations, how should one model be selected as the best? To make our problem manageable, we make two further assumptions. First, there exists a general model $f(\cdot \mid \theta)$ from which all the J competing models can be derived by imposing various restrictions on its parameter vector θ. Second, such a model is the "true" model generating the observations $y_1, \ldots, y_n$. Let it be the first model for convenience. It is recognized that these assumptions are restrictive, as they rule out some important model-selection problems to which the posterior probability criterion of Sec. 9.7 can be applied. However, our framework does encompass the important classical statistical problems of testing the null hypothesis that the parameter vector θ is subject to a set of restrictions and of choosing between several nonnested models provided they can all be derived from restricting the parameters of a more general model.

Let $f(\cdot \mid \theta_0)$ be the true density of y and $f(\cdot \mid \theta)$ be an approximation of $f(\cdot \mid \theta_0)$, where θ is subject to certain restrictions which θ_0 does not satisfy. Following Akaike (1973, 1974), we adopt the Kullback-Leibler information measure, or the expected log-likelihood ratio, to discriminate between the two models using n future independent observations $(\tilde{y}_1, \ldots, \tilde{y}_n) = \tilde{Y}$

$$I_n(\theta_0; \theta) = E \sum_{i=1}^{n} [\log f(\tilde{y}_i \mid \theta_0) - \log f(\tilde{y}_i \mid \theta)] \tag{58}$$

where the expectation is evaluated by the true density $f(\cdot \mid \theta_0)$. As θ is unknown, we assume that n observations $(y_1, \ldots, y_n) = Y$ are available to provide a maximum-likelihood estimate $\hat{\theta}$ of θ subject to the required restrictions. The estimated model $f(\cdot \mid \hat{\theta})$ is to be judged by the expected information

$$E_{\hat{\theta}} I_n(\theta_0; \hat{\theta}) = E_{\hat{\theta}}[E_{\tilde{Y}} \log L(\tilde{Y}; \theta_0) - E_{\tilde{Y}} \log L(\tilde{Y}; \hat{\theta})] \tag{59}$$

where L denotes the likelihood function based on n future observations. Akaike (1973, 1974) has provided an estimate of $E_{\hat{\theta}}[E_{\tilde{Y}} \log L(\tilde{Y}; \hat{\theta})]$ for model selection, since the term $E_{\tilde{Y}} \log L(\tilde{Y}; \theta_0)$, though unknown, is the same for all approximate models. This section proposes an alternative estimate, under the assumption that θ is subject to the known linear restriction $H'\theta + b = 0$. The result will be shown to apply to the case of nonlinear restrictions $h(\theta) = 0$ by making use of the work of Silvey (1959), discussed in Sec. 9.4.

To estimate $E_{\hat{\theta}} E_{\tilde{Y}} \log L(\tilde{Y}; \hat{\theta})$ we first define θ^* as the parameter of the best approximate model which satisfies the restriction $H'\theta^* + b = 0$. Being "best" here means having maximum information, i.e.,

$$E_{\tilde{Y}} \log L(\tilde{Y}; \theta^*) \geq E_{\tilde{Y}} \log L(\tilde{Y}; \theta)$$

To find θ^* we differentiate the lagrangian expression

$$E_{\tilde{Y}} \log L(\tilde{Y}; \theta) - \lambda'(H'\theta + b)$$

assuming that differentiation and the expectation operation can be interchanged, yielding

$$E_{\tilde{Y}} \frac{\partial \log L(\tilde{Y}; \theta^*)}{\partial \theta} - H\lambda = 0 \tag{60}$$

which can be solved with $H'\theta^* + b = 0$ for θ^* and λ^*. In the language of Sawa (1978), θ^* is the pseudo-true parameter of the pseudo-true model $f(\cdot \mid \theta^*)$.

Having defined θ^*, we expand $\log L(\tilde{Y}; \hat{\theta}^*)$ about θ^*

$$\log L(\tilde{Y}; \hat{\theta}^*) = \log L(\tilde{Y}; \theta^*) + \frac{\partial \log L(\tilde{Y}; \theta^*)}{\partial \theta} (\hat{\theta}^* - \theta^*)$$

$$+ \tfrac{1}{2}(\hat{\theta}^* - \theta^*)' \frac{\partial^2 \log L(\tilde{Y}; \theta^*)}{\partial \theta \, \partial \theta'} (\hat{\theta}^* - \theta^*) \tag{61}$$

with $\hat{\theta} = \hat{\theta}^*$ denoting the maximum-likelihood estimate of θ^* or of θ subject to the imposed restriction. The expectations of the three terms on the right-hand side of (61) will be estimated in turn. For the first term

$E_{\hat{\theta}*} E_{\tilde{Y}} \log L(\tilde{Y}; \theta^*)$

$$= E_{\tilde{Y}} \log L(\tilde{Y}; \theta^*) \simeq \log L(Y; \theta^*)$$

$$= \log L(Y; \hat{\theta}^*) + \frac{\partial \log L(Y; \hat{\theta}^*)}{\partial \theta'} (\theta^* - \hat{\theta}^*)$$

$$+ \tfrac{1}{2}(\hat{\theta}^* - \theta^*)' \frac{\partial^2 \log L(Y; \theta^*)}{\partial \theta \, \partial \theta'} (\hat{\theta}^* - \theta^*)$$

$$= \log L(Y; \hat{\theta}^*) + \tfrac{1}{2} \operatorname{tr} \left[\frac{\partial^2 \log L(Y; \theta^*)}{\partial \theta \, \partial \theta'} (\hat{\theta}^* - \theta^*)(\hat{\theta}^* - \theta^*)' \right] \tag{62}$$

The first step of (62) amounts to estimating the expectation $E_{\tilde{Y}} \log L(\tilde{Y}; \theta^*)$ by the sample analog $\log L(Y; \theta^*)$. The second line involves expanding $\log L(Y; \theta^*)$ about $\hat{\theta}^*$; the second term vanishes because $\hat{\theta}^*$ is obtained by maximizing $\log L(Y; \theta)$ subject to $H'\hat{\theta}^* + b = 0$ and thus satisfies

$$\frac{\partial \log L(Y; \hat{\theta}^*)}{\partial \theta} - H\lambda = 0$$

and because $\lambda'H'(\theta^* - \hat{\theta}^*) = 0$. Strictly speaking, the matrix of second partials of $\log L$ should be evaluated at a point between $\hat{\theta}^*$ and θ^* according to the mean-value theorem. We have evaluated it at θ^* by ignoring the remainder term; this matrix eventually will be estimated at $\hat{\theta}^*$, in the same way that the covariance matrix of a maximum-likelihood estimator, when the model is correctly specified, is estimated by the matrix of second partials of $\log L$ evaluated at the maximum-likelihood estimate.

The expectation $E_{\tilde{Y}}$ of the second term on the right-hand side of (61) vanishes because of (60) and $\lambda'H'(\hat{\theta}^* - \theta^*) = 0$. For the third term we have

$$E_{\hat{\theta}*} E_{\tilde{Y}}[\tfrac{1}{2}(\hat{\theta}^* - \theta^*)' \frac{\partial^2 \log L(\tilde{Y}; \theta^*)}{\partial\theta\,\partial\theta} (\hat{\theta}^* - \theta^*)]$$

$$= \frac{1}{2} \operatorname{tr} \left[E_{\tilde{Y}} \frac{\partial^2 \log L(\tilde{Y}; \theta^*)}{\partial\theta\,\partial\theta'} E_{\hat{\theta}*}(\hat{\theta}^* - \theta^*)(\hat{\theta}^* - \theta^*)' \right] \quad (63)$$

Defining
$$J(\theta^*, \theta_0) \equiv -E_{\tilde{Y}} \frac{\partial^2 \log L(\tilde{Y}; \theta^*)}{\partial\theta\,\partial\theta'}$$

where the parameter θ_0 is used to define the distribution of $\tilde{Y}$, we substitute (62) and (63) for the first and third terms on the right-hand side of (61) to obtain

$$E_{\hat{\theta}*} E_{\tilde{Y}} \log L(\tilde{Y}; \hat{\theta}^*) \simeq \log L(Y; \hat{\theta}^*) - \operatorname{tr} [J(\theta^*, \theta_0)E(\hat{\theta}^* - \theta^*)(\hat{\theta}^* - \theta^*)'] \quad (64)$$

In (62) the two matrices inside the brackets have been replaced by their expected values. *(64) is our criterion for selecting a model.*

Formula (64) remains valid for nonlinear restrictions $h(\theta) = 0$ on θ. The only changes in the above derivations are to replace $H'\theta + b$ by $h(\theta)$ and to interpret H as the matrix of partial derivatives of $h(\theta)$, evaluated at $\theta = \theta^*$ for (60) and at $\theta = \hat{\theta}^*$ for the computation of $\hat{\theta}^*$ in (62). The models will be ranked by (64), the one having the highest value being selected. The remaining problem is to provide estimates of $J(\theta^*, \theta_0)$ and $E(\hat{\theta}^* - \theta^*)(\hat{\theta}^* - \theta^*)'$.

To find the distribution of the maximum-likelihood estimator subject to the restrictions $H'\theta^* = -b$ we use the result of Lemma 9.2. The joint distribution of $\hat{\theta}^* - \theta^*$ and the lagrangian multiplier $\hat{\lambda} - \lambda^*$ are asymptotically normal with mean zero and covariance matrix equal to n^{-1} times (37), where $V_{\theta*}$ is given by (36) and P, Q, and R are given by (35). Thus, denoting $L(Y; \theta^*)$ by L^*, we have

$$nV_{\theta*} = E\left[\frac{\partial \log L^*}{\partial\theta} \frac{\partial \log L^*}{\partial\theta'} \right] - \frac{\partial E \log L^*}{\partial\theta} \frac{\partial E \log L^*}{\partial\theta'}$$

and, noting that $B_{\theta*} = n^{-1}J(\theta^*, \theta_0)$,

$$\begin{bmatrix} P & Q \\ Q' & R \end{bmatrix} = \begin{bmatrix} n^{-1}J(\theta^*, \theta) & -H \\ -H' & 0 \end{bmatrix}^{-1}$$

$$= \begin{bmatrix} nJ^{-1} - nJ^{-1}H(H'J^{-1}H)^{-1}H'J^{-1} & -J^{-1}H(H'J^{-1}H)^{-1} \\ -(H'J^{-1}H)^{-1}H'J^{-1} & -n^{-1}(H'J^{-1}H)^{-1} \end{bmatrix}$$

In the important special case when the restrictions consist entirely of zero restrictions on a subset of parameters we write $\theta^* = [\theta_1^* \quad 0]$, $H' = [0 \quad I]$, and

$$J(\theta^*, \theta_0) = \begin{bmatrix} J_{11}(\theta^*, \theta_0) & J_{12}(\theta^*, \theta_0) \\ J_{21}(\theta^*, \theta_0) & J_{22}(\theta^*, \theta_0) \end{bmatrix}$$

The matrix $P_{\theta*}$ above becomes

$$P_{\theta*} = \begin{bmatrix} nJ_{11}^{-1}(\theta^*, \theta_0) & 0 \\ 0 & 0 \end{bmatrix}$$

and the covariance matrix of $\hat{\theta}_1^*$ becomes

$$J_{11}^{-1}(\theta^*, \theta_0)\left(E \frac{\log L^*}{\partial \theta_1} \frac{\log L^*}{\partial \theta_1'} \right) J_{11}^{-1}(\theta^*, \theta_0) \tag{65}$$

since $(\partial E \log L^*)/\partial \theta_1 = 0$ as θ_1^* is obtained by maximizing (differentiating) $E \log L(Y; \theta_1, 0)$ with respect to θ_1. Using this result for the covariance matrix of $\hat{\theta}^*$ in (64), we have the following model-selection criterion in the case of zero restrictions

$$\log L(Y; \hat{\theta}^*) - \text{tr}\left[E\left(\frac{\partial \log L^*}{\partial \theta_1} \frac{\partial \log L^*}{\partial \theta_1'} \right) J_{11}^{-1}(\theta^*, \theta_0) \right] \tag{66}$$

Akaike (1973) was incorrect in claiming that $J_{11}^{-1}(\theta^*, \theta_0)$ is the asymptotic covariance matrix of $\hat{\theta}_1^*$, as we have seen in (65). If this claim were valid, the trace term in (64) would become k, the number of unknown parameters in θ_1, and (64) would become Akaike's information criterion, by which one selects the model having the largest value for the maximum log likelihood minus the number of parameters to be estimated. The claim is false because only when the model is correctly specified, i.e., when $\theta^* = \theta_0$, do we have $J_{11}^{-1}(\theta^*, \theta^*)$ as the asymptotic covariance matrix of $\hat{\theta}^*$. In Sec. 9.4 we clearly distinguished between the distributions of $\hat{\theta}^*$ when $h(\theta_0) \neq 0$ and when $h(\theta_0) = 0$, or when $\theta^* \neq \theta_0$ and when $\theta^* = \theta_0$.

To illustrate the error in approximating the trace of (64) by k, consider the example of a true normal linear regression model for n observations

$$Y = X_1\beta_1^0 + X_2\beta_2^0 + \epsilon = X\beta_0 + \epsilon \qquad \text{Cov } \epsilon = I\sigma_0^2$$

which is being approximated by the smaller model

$$Y = X_1\beta_1^* + \epsilon^*$$

The pseudo-true parameters β_1^* and σ^{*2} can be obtained by maximizing $E_{\tilde{Y}}[\log L(\tilde{Y} \mid \beta_1, 0, \sigma^2)]$ with respect to β_1 and σ^2, where the new observations to be predicted are assumed to satisfy $\tilde{Y} = X\beta_0 + \tilde{\epsilon}$. The results are

$$\beta_1^* = \beta_1^0 + (X_1'X_1)^{-1}X_1'X_2\beta_2^0$$
$$\sigma^{*2} = n^{-1}\beta_2^{0'}X_2'[I - X_1(X_1'X_1)^{-1}X_1']X_2\beta_2^0 + \sigma_0^2 \tag{67}$$

Denoting the partial derivatives of $\log L(Y \mid \beta_1, 0, \sigma^2)$ with respect to β_1 and σ^2

evaluated at β_1^* and σ^{*2} by $\partial \log L^*$, one finds

$$\frac{\partial \log L^*}{\partial \beta_1} = \frac{1}{\sigma^{*2}} X_1'(\tilde{Y} - X_1 \beta_1^*) = \frac{1}{\sigma^{*2}} X_1' \tilde{\epsilon}$$

$$\frac{\partial \log L^*}{\partial \sigma^2} = -\frac{n}{2\sigma^{*2}} + \frac{1}{2\sigma^{*4}} (\tilde{Y} - X_1 \beta_1^*)'(\tilde{Y} - X_1 \beta_1^*)$$

$$= -\frac{n}{2\sigma^{*2}} + \frac{1}{2\sigma^{*4}} (\beta_2^{0'} X_2' M_1 X_2 \beta_2^0 + \tilde{\epsilon}'\tilde{\epsilon} + 2\tilde{\epsilon}' M_1 X_2 \beta_2^0) \qquad (68)$$

where M_1 denotes $I - X_1(X_1'X_1)^{-1}X_1'$. From the last two equations one derives

$$J_{11}(\theta^*, \theta_0) = -E \begin{bmatrix} \dfrac{\partial^2 \log L^*}{\partial \beta_1 \partial \beta_1'} & \dfrac{\partial^2 \log L^*}{\partial \beta_1 \partial \sigma^2} \\[2mm] \dfrac{\partial^2 \log L^*}{\partial \sigma^2 \partial \beta_1'} & \dfrac{\partial^2 \log L^*}{\partial(\sigma^2)^2} \end{bmatrix} = \begin{bmatrix} \dfrac{1}{\sigma^{*2}} X_1'X_1 & 0 \\[2mm] 0 & \dfrac{n}{2\sigma^{*4}} \end{bmatrix}$$

$$E \begin{bmatrix} \dfrac{\partial \log L^*}{\partial \beta_1} \\[2mm] \dfrac{\partial \log L^*}{\partial \sigma^2} \end{bmatrix} \begin{bmatrix} \dfrac{\log L^*}{\partial \beta_1'} & \dfrac{\log L^*}{\partial \sigma^2} \end{bmatrix} = \begin{bmatrix} \dfrac{\sigma_0^2}{\sigma^{*4}} X_1'X_1 & 0 \\[2mm] 0 & \dfrac{n\sigma_0^2(2\sigma^{*2} - \sigma_0^2)}{2\sigma^{*8}} \end{bmatrix} \qquad (69)$$

The derivation of the last equation has made use of the relations $E(\tilde{\epsilon}'\tilde{\epsilon})^2 = (2n + n^2)\sigma_0^4$ and $E\tilde{\epsilon}(\tilde{\epsilon}'\tilde{\epsilon}) = 0$ because the elements $\tilde{\epsilon}_i$ of $\tilde{\epsilon}$ are normal and independent with mean zero.

Using these results for the trace in (64), we get for the approximate model

$$\text{tr} \left\{ E \left(\frac{\partial \log L^*}{\partial \theta_1} \frac{\partial \log L^*}{\partial \theta_1'} \right) [J_{11}(\theta^*, \theta_0)]^{-1} \right\} = \left(\frac{\sigma_0}{\sigma^*} \right)^2 \left[k + 1 - \left(\frac{\sigma_0}{\sigma^*} \right)^2 \right] \qquad (70)$$

where k is the number of parameters (including the elements of β_1^* and σ^{*2}). If the approximate model were true, σ^* would equal σ_0 and the trace term would equal k, as Akaike claims. In general $\sigma^* > \sigma_0$, and the trace term is smaller than k. For example, if the true model contains eight parameters (seven coefficients plus σ_0) and the approximate model contains seven parameters (with the last explanatory variable omitted), and if $(\sigma_0/\sigma^*)^2 = .9$, the difference between the two trace terms to be subtracted from the respective maximum log-likelihood functions is $8 - .9(8 - .9) = 1.61$, compared with $8 - 7 = 1$ by Akaike's formula. Selection rule (64) turns out to favor the small model more than Akaike's rule. The adjustment constant (70) is in agreement with the result of Sawa (1978, theorem 3.2, p. 1280), who has studied the information criterion for the selection of linear regression models in particular. Our formula (64) has more general applicability. Note that to evaluate $E\{[(\partial \log L^*)/\partial \theta_1] (\partial \log L^*)/\partial \theta_1'\}$ and $J_{11}(\theta^*, \theta_0)$, one can specify the true model as the most general of the models to be selected and replace the required parameters θ^* and θ_0 by their maximum-likelihood estimates.

By the information criterion, we choose the larger of the two regression models if its maximum log likelihood adjusted by (70) is greater than the maximum log likelihood of the smaller model similarly adjusted. For the larger model, if it is assumed to be the true model, $\sigma_0 = \sigma^*$ and (70) is simply the number k of parameters in the model. For the smaller model with k_1 parameters, say, the adjustment factor is

$$\left(\frac{\hat{\sigma}_0}{\hat{\sigma}^*}\right)^2 \left[k_1 + 1 - \left(\frac{\hat{\sigma}_0}{\hat{\sigma}^*}\right)^2\right]$$

where $\hat{\sigma}_0^2$ is the estimated standard error of the larger regression and $\hat{\sigma}^{*2}$ is the estimated standard error of the smaller regression model. The larger model will be selected if

$$\log L(Y, \hat{\theta}_0) - \log L(Y, \hat{\theta}^*) > k - \left(\frac{\hat{\sigma}_0}{\hat{\sigma}^*}\right)^2 \left[k_1 + 1 - \left(\frac{\hat{\sigma}_0}{\hat{\sigma}^*}\right)^2\right]$$

For comparison of the regression models, the left-hand side of the above inequality is simply $-n(\log \hat{\sigma}_0 - \log \hat{\sigma}^*)$. Therefore, the larger model will be selected if

$$n \log \left(\frac{\hat{\sigma}^*}{\hat{\sigma}_0}\right) > k - (k_1 + 1)\left(\frac{\hat{\sigma}^*}{\hat{\sigma}_0}\right)^{-2} + \left(\frac{\hat{\sigma}^*}{\hat{\sigma}_0}\right)^{-4} \tag{71}$$

This amounts to a likelihood-ratio test based on the logarithm of the likelihood ratio $\mu = L(y, \hat{\theta}^*)/L(y, \hat{\theta}_0)$. The standard F test for the null hypothesis $\beta_2 = 0$ in the regression model $y = X_1\beta_1 + X_2\beta_2 + \epsilon$ is based on the same likelihood ratio except that the critical point and the level of significance are now determined. Sawa (1978, p. 1283) has tabulated the critical points and the significance levels of the t test for different levels of k and n, k_1 being $k - 1$. For $k = 7$, there are six regression coefficients (in addition to the parameter σ^2) in the larger model; the t test for deciding whether to drop one of the six explanatory variables has critical values 2.264, 1.707, and 1.421, respectively, for $n = 10$, 20, and 500, the corresponding levels of significance being .086, .110, and .156. As n increases, the critical value approaches $\sqrt{2}$. This limit is in agreement with the C_p criterion of Sec. 9.4, which recommends a critical value of 2 for the corresponding F test. Note that the significance levels for $n \geq 20$ are larger than .10 for a two-tail t test or larger than .05 for a one-tail t test. The level of significance approaches .156 for a two-tail t test as n increases. In general, the information criterion is equivalent to a t test for an additional regression coefficient using a critical value which can be larger than 2 when k_1 is large (say 5 or 6) and when n is small.

After presenting this regression example, we should point out the relation between the information criterion and the criterion C_p given in Sec. 9.5. While both criteria are based on the estimated accuracy of a proposed model in predicting future observations, they employ different measures of prediction accuracy. In our regression example, Mallows (1973) would measure the accuracy of future predictions obtained from the smaller model with coefficient vector $\beta^{*\prime} =$

$[\beta_1^*, \quad 0]$ by the expected sum of squared prediction errors

$$E_{\beta^*} E_{\tilde{Y}} \left[\sum_{i=1}^{n} (\tilde{y}_i - x_i \beta^*)^2 \right] \tag{72}$$

By contrast, according to (59), the information criterion measures the goodness of fit of the smaller model to future observations by

$$E_{\theta^*} E_{\tilde{Y}} \left\{ \sum_{i=1}^{n} [\log f(\tilde{y}_i \mid \theta_0) - \log f(\tilde{y}_i \mid \hat{\theta}^*)] \right\} \tag{73}$$

where $f(\cdot \mid \theta_0)$ is the density function of the true model, and the parameter vector θ^* for the smaller model in our regression example consists of $\beta^{*\prime} = [\beta_1^*, \quad 0]$ and σ^{*2}. Thus Mallows (1973) provides an estimate of (72) for the smaller model and compares it with the corresponding estimate for the larger (true) model, with $\hat{\beta}_0$ replacing $\hat{\beta}^*$ in (72). The model having the smaller estimate of expected prediction error so defined will be selected. By the information criterion and the use of formula (66), estimates of (73) will be obtained for the smaller model and the larger (true) model, the latter with $\hat{\theta}_0$ replacing $\hat{\theta}^*$ in (73). The model having the smaller estimate will be selected.

As pointed out at the beginning of this section, the use of the information criterion requires the assumption of a true model from which all competing models can be derived by restrictions on its parameters. Thus we can deal with nonnested models such as regression models using either X_1 or X_2 as possible sets of explanatory variables only if we are willing to assume a more general model including both sets of explanatory variables to be the "true" model for the purpose of statistical analysis.

9.7 THE POSTERIOR-PROBABILITY CRITERION

To state the Jeffreys-Bayes posterior-probability criterion, let $p(M_j)$ be the prior probability for model M_j to be correct and $p(\theta \mid M_j)$ be the prior density for the k_j-dimensional parameter vector θ_j conditioned on M_j being correct. Assume that a random sample of n observations $(y_1, y_2, \ldots, y_n) = Y$ is available. By Bayes' theorem the posterior probability of the jth model's being correct is

$$p(M_j \mid Y) = \frac{p(M_j) p(Y \mid M_j)}{p(Y)} = \frac{p(M_j) p(Y \mid M_j)}{\sum_j p(M_j) p(Y \mid M_j)} \tag{74}$$

where $$p(Y \mid M_j) = \int L_j(Y, \theta) p(\theta \mid M_j) \, d\theta \tag{75}$$

with $L_j(Y, \theta_j)$ denoting the likelihood function for the jth model. Since $p(Y)$ is a common factor for all models, the model with the highest posterior probability of being correct is the one with the maximum value for

$$p(M_j) p(Y \mid M_j) = p(M_j) \int L_j(Y, \theta) p(\theta \mid M_j) \, d\theta$$

If the prior probabilities $p(M_j)$ are equal for the models, the one with the highest $p(Y \mid M_j)$ will be selected.

To evaluate $p(Y \mid M_j)$ for large samples we apply a well-known theorem of Jeffreys (1961, pp. 193ff), cited in Zellner (1971, pp. 31–33), on the posterior density $p(\theta \mid Y, M_j)$ of θ_j given model M_j

$$p(\theta \mid Y, M_j) = \frac{L_j(Y, \theta)p(\theta \mid M_j)}{p(Y \mid M_j)}$$

$$= (2\pi)^{-k_j/2} |S|^{1/2} \exp\left[-\tfrac{1}{2}(\theta - \hat{\theta}_j)'S(\theta - \hat{\theta}_j)\right][1 + 0(n^{-1/2})] \quad (76)$$

where $\hat{\theta}_j$ is the maximum-likelihood estimate of θ_j and the inverse covariance matrix is $S = -[(\partial^2 \log L_j)/(\partial\theta\,\partial\theta')]_{\hat{\theta}} \equiv nR_j$. $O(n^{-1/2})$ refers to a function of order $n^{-1/2}$; that is, the ratio of this function to $n^{-1/2}$ is bounded as $n \to 0$. Thus S is of order n. Equation (76) states that, for large samples, the posterior density of a parameter vector θ in model j is asymptotically normal with mean equal to the maximum-likelihood estimate $\hat{\theta}_j$ and covariance matrix which can be approximated by the inverse of

$$-\frac{\partial^2 \log L_j(Y, \hat{\theta})}{\partial\theta\,\partial\theta'}$$

In classical statistics we would say that, for large samples, the maximum-likelihood estimator $\hat{\theta}_j$ is asymptotically normal with mean equal to the true θ and a covariance matrix which can be approximated by the inverse of the same matrix. This theorem was exemplified by our discussion of Bayesian regression in Sec. 3.5. Evaluating both sides of (76) at $\theta = \hat{\theta}_j$ and taking natural logarithms, we obtain, noting $|S| = |nR_j| = n^{k_j}|R_j|$,

$$\log p(Y \mid M_j) = \log L_j(Y, \hat{\theta}_j) - \frac{k_j}{2}\log n - \tfrac{1}{2}\log |R_j|$$

$$+ \frac{k_j}{2}\log 2\pi + \log p(\hat{\theta}_j \mid M_j) + O(n^{-1/2}) \quad (77)$$

If we retain only the first two terms $\log L_j(Y, \hat{\theta}_j)$ and $-k_j(\tfrac{1}{2}\log n)$ in (77), we obtain the formula of Schwarz (1978) for approximating $\log p(Y \mid M_j)$.

How well can $\log p(Y \mid M_j)$ be approximated by using only the first two terms of (77)? How much will it depend on the prior density $p(\theta \mid M_j)$ of the parameter vector chosen for each model M_j? Bayesian statisticians including Jeffreys (1961), Pratt (1975), and Leamer (1978), among others, have recognized the difficult problem of choosing a prior distribution $p(\theta \mid M_j)$ for the parameters of each model to be used to compute $p(Y \mid M_j)$. The difficulty can be seen from the equation

$$p(Y \mid M_j) = \frac{L_j(Y, \hat{\theta}_j)p(\hat{\theta}_j \mid M_j)}{p(\hat{\theta}_j \mid Y, M_j)}$$

$$\simeq L_j(Y, \hat{\theta}_j)p(\hat{\theta}_j \mid M_j)(2\pi)^{k_j/2}|nR_j|^{-1/2} \quad (78)$$

Observe that, given $L_j(Y, \hat{\theta}_j)$ and $p(\hat{\theta}_j \mid Y, M_j)$, $p(Y \mid M_j)$ is proportional to

$p(\hat{\theta}_j | M_j)$. Thus one can change $p(Y | M_j)$ by a multiplicative factor simply by changing $p(\hat{\theta}_j | M_j)$ by that factor. If one wishes to use a diffuse prior density $p(\theta | M_j)$, many such densities are reasonable but can give very different results. To illustrate, let $p(\theta | M_j)$ in (77) be k_j-variate normal with mean $\hat{\theta}_j$ (just for illustration) and covariance matrix $(\epsilon R_j)^{-1}$. Equation (77) will become

$$\log p(Y | M_j) = \log L_j(Y, \hat{\theta}_j) - \tfrac{1}{2} k_j \log \frac{n}{\epsilon} + O(n^{-1/2}) \tag{79}$$

The adjustment constant suggested by the formula of Schwarz (1978) will be changed from $-\tfrac{1}{2} k_j \log n$ to $-\tfrac{1}{2} k_j \log (n/\epsilon)$. There is no reason why ϵ might not change by a factor of 2 or 3, making Schwarz's formula a poor approximation to $\log p(Y | M_j)$ for finite samples.

9.8 COMPARISON OF THE POSTERIOR-PROBABILITY AND INFORMATION CRITERIA

We begin by criticizing the information criterion from the viewpoint of Bayesian *estimation* theory, as Leamer (1979) has done. Under the assumption stated in Sec. 9.6., the true model is the most general model $f(\cdot | \theta_0)$ with unknown parameter θ_0. In (58) $I(\theta_0; \theta)$ specifies a loss function for the approximate model $f(\cdot | \theta)$. The *risk function* is defined as the expectation of the loss function. Therefore, $E_{\hat{\theta}_i} I(\theta_0; \hat{\theta}_i) = R_i(\theta_0)$ in (59) is the risk function for the estimator $\hat{\theta}_i$ which is subject to the restrictions defining the ith model. Since the risk $R_i(\theta_0)$ depends on the specification of the model, i.e., the estimator, and the unknown θ_0, one cannot select the model (estimator) with minimum risk without knowing θ_0 (see Prob. 15). A Bayesian will specify a prior density for θ_0, take the expectations $E_{\theta_0} R_i(\theta_0)$ $(i = 1, \ldots, J)$, and choose the model i with the smallest expected risk. Instead, the proposal of Sec. 9.6 is to evaluate $R_i(\hat{\theta}_0)$ using the maximum-likelihood estimator $\hat{\theta}_0$ of θ_0. This procedure appears ad hoc from the viewpoint of Bayesian estimation theory. Furthermore, since all Bayesian estimators defined by different prior densities on θ_0 form a complete class of admissible estimators and the above ad hoc procedure is not a Bayesian estimator, it is inadmissible. An admissible estimator is one that cannot be dominated in the sense that there is no other estimator which has smaller risks for all values of the true parameter θ_0. If an estimator can be so dominated, it is inadmissible. The last comment aside, Leamer (1979) was not able to produce an estimator which dominates the information criterion for estimating θ.

A defense of the information criterion against the criticism from Bayesian estimation theory can be made as follows. First, if the risk $R_i(\theta_0)$ is adopted for ranking the ith model or estimator, using a maximum-likelihood estimate $R_i(\hat{\theta}_0)$ of it at least has large-sample justification from the viewpoint of sampling theory. Second, a Bayesian is challenged to provide an alternative procedure for model selection which from the sampling-theory viewpoint will on the average select a better model, as judged by (58), than the information criterion. We consider three Bayesian procedures below.

The first procedure is based on Bayesian estimation theory. Given a prior density on θ_0 and given the loss function $l(\theta_0, \hat{\theta})$, one can find an estimator $\hat{\theta}$ to minimize expected loss $E_{\theta_0} l(\theta_0, \hat{\theta})$, where the expectation is evaluated by the posterior density of θ_0. There are two problems with this procedure: it may not perform well from the sampling viewpoint and it will never recommend imposing zero restrictions on any parameters or dropping any explanatory variables in a regression model unless the prior distribution of θ_0 assigns probability 1 to these restrictions in the first place. Thus this procedure always leads to selecting the largest model in the problem formulated in Sec. 9.6.

To justify dropping variables in statistical practice, two other Bayesian procedures can be mentioned, as discussed in Dickey (1975), for example. One involves introducing a reward for simplicity by subtracting a constant from the loss function $l(\theta_0, \hat{\theta})$ when $\hat{\theta}$ satisfies the restrictions of a small model. The second is a Bayesian procedure for hypothesis testing. Given two hypotheses or models M_1 and M_2, it is required to specify a prior probability $p(M_i)$ for each model to be correct, a prior density $p(\theta_i | M_i)$ of the parameter θ_i for each model M_i, and a utility function $U(d; M)$, where d can take only two values d_i (for the decision to choose M_i) ($i = 1, 2$). If M_1 stands for the general model with parameter $\theta_1 = \theta_0$ and M_2 is obtained by restrictions on θ, the utility function can be written $U(d; \theta)$. The model M_i will be selected if $E_\theta U(d_i, \theta)$ is larger, where the expectation is evaluated by the posterior density of θ. Note that this utility function is different from the loss function used in Bayesian estimation theory, where the argument $\hat{\theta}$ is a continuous variable indicating the parameter estimate. Here d_i is a discrete variable referring to the decision to choose M_i for an unspecified purpose except that $U(d_1, \theta_1) > U(d_2, \theta_1)$ and $U(d_2, \theta_2) > U(d_1, \theta_2)$, where M_2 is the restrictive model with parameter $\theta_2 = \theta^*$. Under the assumptions of a symmetrical utility function, i.e.,

$$U(d_1, \theta_1) = U(d_2, \theta_2) \qquad \text{and} \qquad U(d_2, \theta_1) = U(d_1, \theta_2)$$

this selection procedure amounts to selecting the model with the higher posterior probability $p(M_i | Y)$ of being correct. It further reduces to the selection by $p(Y | M_i)$ when $p(M_1) = p(M_2)$, as discussed in Sec. 9.7.

What can be said about the posterior-probability criterion for model selection? When applied to the choice between two nested models M_1 and M_2, the assumption of a symmetrical utility function becomes unreasonable since $U(d_1, \theta_2)$ depends on how far θ_2 is from θ_1 and $U(d_1, \theta_1)$ cannot reasonably be set equal to $U(d_2, \theta_2)$ for all values of θ_1 and θ_2. More important, the model M_i selected for having a higher value for $E_\theta U(d_i, \theta)$, as evaluated by the posterior density of θ, is not meant to be the model which, when estimated by maximum likelihood using a finite sample, will on the average predict further observations well by the information measure (58). Similarly, neither is the model having a higher $p(Y | M_i)$ meant to be the one which we should estimate for prediction purposes. In our analysis we have already assumed the most general or the largest model to be the true one, and yet imposing restrictions might produce a better model for prediction, given a finite sample.

To put the last point differently, the information criterion maximizes

$$E_{\hat{\theta}} E_{\tilde{Y}} \log L(\tilde{Y}; \hat{\theta}) \tag{80}$$

with the expectation evaluated by the sampling distribution of $\hat{\theta}$, whereas the posterior-probability criterion maximizes

$$\log E_{\theta} L(Y; \theta) = \log \int L(Y; \theta) p(\theta \mid M_j) \, d\theta \tag{81}$$

with the expectation evaluated by the prior density of θ. This comparison brings out the basic difference between the two criteria as they attempt to answer two different questions. The former asks which "model" $f(\cdot \mid \hat{\theta})$ as it is estimated by the given data Y should be used to predict the future $\tilde{Y}$. The latter asks which "model" as defined by $f(\cdot \mid \theta)$ *and* the prior density $p(\theta \mid M)$ is judged by the sample data Y to have the highest probability of being correct. This distinction is not explicitly recognized in the literature. In presenting his estimate of the posterior probability of a model's being correct for large samples Schwarz (1978) stated that he was proposing an alternative formula to Akaike's for solving the same problem. Akaike (1978) asserted that he and Schwarz were trying to solve the same problem and attempted to derive a formula close to his formula by using the posterior-probability criterion. This could be done, for example, by choosing the prior density

$$p(\hat{\theta}_j \mid M_j) = (2\pi)^{-k_j/2} \mid ne^{-2} R_j \mid^{1/2}$$

in (77) to make the entire adjustment factor equal to $-k_j$ instead of $-k_j(\frac{1}{2} \log n)$, but there is no need to justify the information criterion in terms of the posterior-probability criterion, as they are designed to answer different questions.

The above comparison also brings out the difficulty in choosing a robust prior density function $p(\theta \mid M_j)$ for the model-selection problem. The "model" to be judged by the sample data Y using the posterior-probability criterion is precisely defined by this prior density together with the function $f(\cdot \mid \theta)$. Varying the prior density $p(\theta \mid M_j)$ will vary significantly the "model" to be judged. Therefore, it is difficult to avoid choosing a specific prior density for the model-selection problem using the posterior-probability criterion. One might be tempted to resolve this difficulty by using a part Y_1 of the sample $Y = (Y_1 \quad Y_2)$ to obtain a preliminary $p(\theta \mid Y_1, M_j)$ from a diffuse $p(\theta \mid M_j)$ and then using the remaining data Y_2 to judge the "model" now specified by $p(\theta \mid Y_1, M_j)$ together with the function $f(\cdot \mid \theta)$. This suggestion can certainly be carried out, but it will answer the question whether the "model" based on the data Y_1 was good as judged by the data Y_2 and not whether the original model with a diffuse prior was good as judged by Y_1 and Y_2. Nor will it answer the interesting question whether the model estimated by using all the data Y will be good in future predictions.

In conclusion, although the information criterion is subject to criticism from Bayesian estimation theory, it can be justified by sampling theory as it applies maximum likelihood to estimate the risk function $R_i(\theta_0)$. There are three Bayesian answers to the problem of selecting one of several models. First, from Bayesian estimation theory with continuous loss and prior density functions, the largest model will always be selected, implying that explanatory variables should never be dropped from regression analysis. The estimator should take full account of the loss and prior density functions and not be restricted to maximum-likelihood estimation of either the large or the small model, as often done in statistical practice. The second answer justifies the selection of a smaller model by introducing discontinuity in the loss function (extra utility for imposing restrictions) and the third by introducing discontinuities in the prior density function and in the decision variable. If one accepts prediction as the criterion for model building, any of these three answers will have to be evaluated by its ability to produce good predictions. At the present state of knowledge, the information criterion estimated by (64) and (66) is a useful tool for selecting alternative models.

★9.9 ESTIMATION OF THE INFORMATION CRITERION FOR SIMULTANEOUS-EQUATION MODELS

In this section we provide an estimate of the information criterion for the selection of linear simultaneous-equation models, leaving a discussion of its econometric applications to Sec. 9.10. In order to apply our criterion (64) to simultaneous-equation models we must estimate $J(\theta^*, \theta_0)$ and $E(\hat{\theta}^* - \theta^*)(\hat{\theta}^* - \theta^*)'$. The latter matrix is given by (37), or by (65) in the special case of zero restrictions on θ^*. This is our task in the current section. Note that $J(\theta^*, \theta_0)$ can be consistently estimated by its sample analog $-[\partial^2 \log L(Y, \hat{\theta}^*)]/(\partial\theta \; \partial\theta')$. $E(\hat{\theta}^* - \theta^*)(\hat{\theta}^* - \theta^*)'$ can be estimated by Monte Carlo experiments using the larger model with parameter vector $\hat{\theta}$ as the true model. Given these estimates, the information criterion can be applied to the selection of simultaneous-equation models. However, the above estimate of $E(\hat{\theta}^* - \theta^*)(\hat{\theta}^* - \theta^*)'$ is expensive computationally. We shall derive analytical expressions for $J(\theta_1^*, \theta_0)$ and $E(\hat{\theta} - \theta^*)(\hat{\theta} - \theta^*)'$ in this section for linear simultaneous-equation models as we did for linear regression models. Readers not interested in these expressions may skip this section without loss.

Let the true model be

$$YB_0' + X\Gamma_0' = U \qquad EU'U = n\Sigma_0 \equiv nR_0^{-1} \tag{82}$$

where Y is an $n \times G$ matrix of endogenous variables, X is an $n \times K$ matrix of exogenous variables, and selected elements of B_0 and Γ_0 are zero because of the identification restrictions. Let the approximate model be

$$YB^{*'} + X\Gamma^{*'} = U^* \qquad EU^{*'}U^* = n\Sigma^* \equiv nR^{*-1} \tag{83}$$

where the elements of Γ^*, B^*, and Σ^* are subject to additional linear restrictions. The elements of these pseudo-true parameters are obtained by a constrained maximization of

$$E \log L(Y; B, \Gamma, R) = \frac{nG}{2} \log 2\pi + \frac{n}{2} \log |R| + n \log |B|$$

$$- \tfrac{1}{2} \operatorname{tr} [RE(YB' + X\Gamma')'(YB' + X\Gamma')] \qquad (84)$$

where the expectation E is evaluated by assuming that Y is generated by the true model.

To evaluate the matrix $V_{\theta*}$ of (36) we need the derivatives of $\log L(Y; B, \Gamma, R)$ evaluated at B^*, Γ^*, and R^* minus their expectations. The derivatives, with $U^* = YB^{*'} + X\Gamma^{*'} = [u_1^* \; \ldots \; u_g^*]$, are

$$\frac{\partial \log L^*}{\partial \Gamma'} = -X'U^*R^* \qquad (85)$$

$$\frac{\partial \log L^*}{\partial B'} = -Y'U^*R^* + n(B^*)^{-1} \qquad (86)$$

$$\frac{\partial \log L^*}{\partial r_{ij}} = n\sigma_{ij}^* - u_i^{*'}u_j^* \qquad \frac{\partial \log L^*}{\partial r_{ii}} = \tfrac{1}{2}(n\sigma_{ii}^* - u_i^{*'}u_i^*) \qquad (87)$$

Defining the true reduced-form to be

$$Y = -X\Gamma_0' B_0'^{-1} + UB_0'^{-1} \equiv X\Pi_0 + V \qquad EV'V = n\Omega^0 \equiv nB_0^{-1}\Sigma_0 B_0'^{-1} \qquad (88)$$

we can write

$$U^* = YB^{*'} + X\Gamma^{*'} = X(\Pi_0' B^{*'} + \Gamma^{*'}) + VB^{*'} = D + VB^{*'} \qquad (89)$$

where
$$D = EU^* = X(\Pi_0' B^{*'} + \Gamma^{*'}) \qquad (90)$$

Therefore, the derivatives given by (85) and (86) minus their expectations are

$$\frac{\partial \log L^*}{\partial \Gamma'} - E\frac{\partial \log L^*}{\partial \Gamma'} = -X'VB^{*'}R^* \qquad (91)$$

$$\frac{\partial \log L^*}{\partial B'} - E\frac{\partial \log L^*}{\partial B'} = -\Pi_0 X'VB^{*'}R^* - V'DR^* - V'VB^{*'}R^* + n\Omega^0 B^{*'}R^*$$

$$(92)$$

The expectations of (87) are zero.

Since only the unknown elements of B^* and Γ^* are of concern, we denote by β_i and γ_i, respectively, the column vectors consisting of only the unknown elements in the ith rows of B^* and Γ^*. Similarly, Y_i and X_i denote the matrices composed of those columns of Y and X which are associated respectively with the unknown coefficients in β_i and γ_i. Also, we denote $X\Pi_0$ by $\tilde{Y}^0$, $X\Pi^{*'} \equiv -X\Gamma^{*'}B^{*'-1}$ by $\tilde{Y}^*$, and $B^*\Omega^0 B^{*'}$ by W for convenience. Using these notations together with (91) and (92), we derive the required components of $nV_{\theta*}$ as

$$\operatorname{Cov}\left(\frac{\partial \log L^*}{\partial \gamma_i} \frac{\partial \log L^*}{\partial \gamma_j'}\right) = X_i'X_j(r_i^{*'}Wr_j^*) \qquad (93)$$

$$\text{Cov}\left(\frac{\partial \log L^*}{\partial \beta_i} \frac{\partial \log L^*}{\partial \beta_j'}\right) = \tilde{Y}_i^{0'}\tilde{Y}_j^0(r_i^{*'}Wr_j^*) + \Omega_i^{0'}B^{*'}r_j^*\, r_i^{*'}D'\tilde{Y}_j^0$$

$$+ \tilde{Y}_i^{0'}Dr_j^*\, r_i^{*'}B^*\Omega_j^0 + n\Omega_{ij}^0 r_{ij}^* + n\Omega_i^{0'}B^{*'}r_j^*\, r_i^{*'}B^*\Omega_j^0 \quad (94)$$

$$\text{Cov}\left(\frac{\partial \log L^*}{\partial \beta_i} \frac{\partial \log L^*}{\partial \gamma_j'}\right) = \tilde{Y}_i^{0'}X_j(r_i^{*'}Wr_j^*) + \Omega_i^{0'}B^{*'}r_j^*\, r_i^{*'}D'X_j \quad (95)$$

where Ω_i^0 denotes a matrix composed of only those columns of $\Omega^0 = (\omega_{ij}^0)$ which are associated with the unknown elements of β_i^* and Ω_{ij}^0 denotes a matrix extracted from Ω^0 whose rows correspond to the unknown elements of β_i^* and whose columns correspond to the unknown elements of β_j^*. The proof of (94) has made use of the relation, for $V = (v_1 \ldots v_g)$,

$$E(v_1'v_2)(v_3'v_4) = n^2\omega_{12}^0\,\omega_{34}^0 + n\omega_{13}^0\,\omega_{24}^0 + n\omega_{14}^0\,\omega_{23}^0$$

which implies

$$EV'VB^{*'}r_i^*\, r_j^{*'}B^*V'V = n^2\Omega^0 B^{*'}r_i^*\, r_j^{*'}B^*\Omega^0$$

$$+ n\Omega^0 B^{*'}r_j^*\, r_i^{*'}B^*\Omega^0 + n\Omega_{ij}^0(r_i^{*'}B^*\Omega^0 B^{*'}r_j^*)$$

By contrast, the elements of $J(\theta^*, \theta_0)$ as derived from differentiating (85) and (86) are

$$- E\frac{\partial^2 \log L^*}{\partial \gamma_i\, \partial \gamma_j'} = X_i'X_j r_{ij}^* \quad (96)$$

$$- E\frac{\partial^2 \log L^*}{\partial \beta_i\, \partial \beta_j'} = \tilde{Y}_i^{0'}\tilde{Y}_j^0 r_{ij}^* + n\Omega_{ij}^0 r_{ij}^* + n\beta^{j(i)}\beta^{i(j)'} \quad (97)$$

$$- E\frac{\partial^2 \log L^*}{\partial \beta_i\, \partial \gamma_j'} = \tilde{Y}_i^{0'}X_j r_{ij}^* \quad (98)$$

where $\beta^{i(j)}$ denotes a column vector consisting of those elements of the ith row of $(B^{*'})^{-1}$ which correspond to the unknown elements of β_j^*. Note that when $(B^*, \Gamma^*, R^*) = (B_0, \Gamma_0, R^0)$, that is, when the approximate model coincides with the true model, (93) to (95) will reduce to (96) to (98), respectively, as $r_i^{*'}Wr_j^* = r_i^{0'}\Sigma^0 r_j^0$ will become $r_{ij}^0 = r_{ij}^*$ and $D = 0$.

We next derive the expectations involving the derivatives of $\log L$ with respect to r_{ij}. Using (87), we obtain by straightforward manipulations with $B^*\Omega^0 B^{*'} = W = (w_{ij})$,

$$E\left[\frac{\partial \log L^*}{\partial r_{ij}} \frac{\partial \log L^*}{\partial r_{kl}}\right] = n[\sigma_{ik}^* w_{jl} + \sigma_{jk}^* w_{il}$$

$$+ (\sigma_{il}^* - w_{il})w_{jk} + (\sigma_{jl}^* - w_{jl})w_{ik}] \quad (99a)$$

$$E\left[\frac{\partial \log L^*}{\partial r_{ii}} \frac{\partial \log L^*}{\partial r_{kl}}\right] = n[\sigma_{ik}^* w_{il} + (\sigma_{il}^* - w_{il})w_{ik}] \quad (99b)$$

$$E\left[\frac{\partial \log L^*}{\partial r_{ii}} \frac{\partial \log L^*}{\partial r_{kk}}\right] = \frac{n}{2}[\sigma_{ik}^* w_{ik} + (\sigma_{ik}^* - w_{ik})w_{ik}] \quad (99c)$$

and the corresponding expressions

$$- E \frac{\partial^2 \log L^*}{\partial r_{ij} \, \partial r_{kl}} = n(\sigma_{ik}^* \sigma_{jl}^* + \sigma_{jk}^* \sigma_{il}^*) \tag{100a}$$

$$- E \frac{\partial^2 \log L^*}{\partial r_{ii} \, \partial r_{kl}} = n\sigma_{ik}^* \sigma_{il}^* \tag{100b}$$

$$- E \frac{\partial^2 \log L^*}{\partial r_{ii} \, \partial r_{kk}} = \frac{n}{2} \sigma_{ik}^{*2} \tag{100c}$$

Again, when the approximate model coincides with the true model, we have $W = \Sigma^0 = \Sigma^* = \sigma_{ij}^*$, and (99) will be identical with (100).

As can be seen by differentiating (85) and (86), the expectations of $(\partial^2 \log L^*)/(\partial \beta_i \, \partial r_{kl})$ and $(\partial^2 \log L^*)/(\partial \gamma_i \, \partial r_{kl})$ are zero. Therefore, letting α denote a column vector composed of the unknown elements of $\beta_1, \ldots, \beta_g, \gamma_1, \ldots, \gamma_g$, r denote a column vector consisting of $r_{11}, \ldots, r_{1g}, r_{22}, \ldots, r_{2g}, r_{31}, \ldots, r_{gg}$, and θ' denote $[\alpha' \quad r']$, we can write

$$n V_{\theta*} = \mathrm{Cov} \frac{\partial \log L^*}{\partial \theta} \equiv \begin{bmatrix} \mathrm{Cov} \dfrac{\partial \log L^*}{\partial \alpha} & 0 \\ 0 & \mathrm{Cov} \dfrac{\partial \log L^*}{\partial r} \end{bmatrix} \tag{101}$$

where the elements of $\mathrm{Cov} [(\partial \log L^*)/\partial \alpha]$ and $\mathrm{Cov} [(\partial \log L^*)/\partial r]$ are given by (93) to (95) and (99), respectively. These matrices, together with the elements of $J(\theta^*, \theta_0)$ given by (96) to (98) and (100), provide an explicit expression for the asymptotic covariance matrix of $\hat{\theta}^*$ through (37) and also for the adjustment factor $\mathrm{tr} [J(\theta^*, \theta_0) \, \mathrm{Cov} \, \hat{\theta}^*]$ used in our model-selection criterion (64). In actual applications, the parameters of the models (82) and (83) required to evaluate $J(\theta^*, \theta_0)$ and $\mathrm{Cov} \, \hat{\theta}^*$ are unknown but can be estimated by the method of maximum likelihood.

In the important special case when B^*, Γ^*, and Σ^* are obtained by additional zero restrictions on the parameters of the model (82), Σ^* being block diagonal, our model-selection criterion becomes (66) with an adjustment factor equal to

$$\mathrm{tr} \left[\left(\mathrm{Cov} \frac{\partial \log L^*}{\partial \theta_1} \right) J_{11}^{-1}(\theta^*, \theta_0) \right] = \mathrm{tr} \left[\left(\mathrm{Cov} \frac{\partial \log L^*}{\partial \alpha} \right) \left(-E \frac{\partial^2 \log L^*}{\partial \alpha \, \partial \alpha'} \right)^{-1} \right]$$

$$+ \mathrm{tr} \left[\left(\mathrm{Cov} \frac{\partial \log L^*}{\partial r} \right) \left(-E \frac{\partial^2 \log L^*}{\partial r \, \partial r'} \right)^{-1} \right] \tag{102}$$

where the four matrices on the right-hand side are given by (93) to (100).

To appreciate the result (102), consider the special case $B_0 = B^* = I$ and $X_i = X$ $(i = 1, \ldots, G)$, which is a model of G linear regressions. If the approximate model has k_1 explanatory variables, (102) is reduced to

$$k_1 \sum_{i=1}^{G} \frac{r_i^{*\prime} \Sigma^0 r_i^*}{r_{ii}^*} + \text{tr} \left[\left(\text{Cov} \frac{\partial \log L^*}{\partial r} \right) \left(-E \frac{\partial^2 \log L^*}{\partial r \, \partial r'} \right)^{-1} \right] \tag{103}$$

For the case of a multiple regression model, with $G = 1$, (103) is further reduced to

$$k_1 \frac{\sigma_{11}^0}{\sigma_{11}^*} + \frac{\sigma_{11}^0}{\sigma_{11}^*} \left(2 - \frac{\sigma_{11}^0}{\sigma_{11}^*} \right) \tag{104}$$

which is identical with the adjustment factor (70) for regression models, with $k = k_1 + 1$.

9.10 SHOULD A LINEAR ECONOMETRIC MODEL BE DECOMPOSED OR AGGREGATED?

If one accepts the view that the "true" economic world is a very large and interdependent system of simultaneous stochastic equations, as many economists tend to do, one is faced with the almost insurmountable problem of estimating very large systems of simultaneous equations. After making significant contributions to the identification and estimation of simultaneous equations, Koopmans (1950) asked: When is an equation system complete for statistical purposes? He gave very strict statistical conditions which would permit one to specify certain variables as exogenous and/or predetermined for the purpose of explaining the remaining endogenous variables, thus reducing the size of the model for the latter variables. One wonders when, if ever, these strict conditions stated by Koopmans will be met. Liu (1955, 1960), being convinced that the "true" world is a completely interdependent system of simultaneous equations, questioned how one could ever estimate the true parameters even if the sample were infinite; the necessary conditions for identification would not be met since each equation contains almost the same variables. Coming to the rescue, Fisher (1961) argued that if the coefficients of some variables in each structural equation, though not exactly zero, are very small, treating them as zero in order to satisfy the identification condition will lead to only very small inconsistencies in the estimation of the remaining parameters. At the other extreme, Wold (1953) argued that the world is recursive anyway and there is no great statistical difficulty in estimating its parameters.

While we grant that the true economic model may well be a very large and completely interdependent system of simultaneous equations, an econometrician may wish to estimate not the true model but only an approximate model because the sample is finite. One realizes that the conditions stated by Koopmans for defining the exogenous and/or predetermined variables are never met, that the coefficients of many endogenous and exogenous variables in a structural equation are not zero, as Liu pointed out, and that the true model for quarterly economic time series is not strictly recursive in the sense of Wold. Nevertheless, one may not need to raise the question of Fisher: whether by assuming certain structural coefficients to be extremely small the remaining parameters in a true model can be estimated almost consistently. One is seldom in a position to estimate the parameters of the true model because the number of available observations is often smaller than the number of its parameters. One is mainly interested in the parameters θ^* of the approximate models because they are the models relevant for practical purposes. To illustrate, let the true model be

$$-y_{1t} + \theta_1 y_{2t} + \theta_2 x_{1t} + \theta_3 x_{2t} + \cdots + \theta_{100} x_{99,t} = u_{1t}$$

and $\qquad \theta_{101} y_{1t} - y_{2t} - \theta_{102} x_{1t} + \theta_{103} x_{2t} + \cdots + \theta_{200} x_{99,t} = u_{2t}$

where all parameters are small except $\theta_1, \theta_2, \theta_{101}$, and θ_{103}. This model is unidentifiable. Fisher points out that if θ_3 and θ_{102} are extremely small, the remaining parameters can be estimated almost consistently. Our viewpoint is that the approximate model f with $\theta_1, \theta_2, \theta_{101}$, and θ_{103} as the only nonzero coefficients to be estimated may be the best approximation according to the information criterion when, say, 50 observations are available. Although the maximum-likelihood estimators of $\theta_1^*, \theta_2^*, \theta_{101}^*$, and θ_{103}^* will not consistently estimate the true $\theta_1, \theta_2, \theta_{101}$, and θ_{103}, the model f can still be the best approximation for prediction purposes.

Furthermore, Fisher (1961) is concerned with the "cost of approximate specification in simultaneous equation estimation," implying that something is lost by using an approximate model because of the inconsistencies in the estimation of the true parameters. We wish to emphasize the benefits of an approximate specification because specification errors are not necessarily bad. On the right-hand side of criterion (64) the second term tends to increase as sampling errors in estimating θ^* by $\hat{\theta}^*$ increase. The first term $\log L(Y; \hat{\theta}^*)$ tends to decrease as specification errors using $f(y|\theta^*)$ to approximate $g(y)$ increase. Large specification errors from assigning zeros to coefficients may be compensated for by smaller sampling errors and may produce a better model for prediction. Therefore, one may be less concerned about whether an extremely small specification error would obtain if the sample were infinite; instead one is concerned with the total error, due to both specification and sampling, in using an estimated model for forecasting, realizing that the specification error will almost always be present. Even when one knows that a large model is more nearly correctly specified than a small model, the latter can still be selected by the information criterion. It is possible for the true world to be completely interdependent but for a block-recursive model, estimated from a finite sample, to be a better approximation than an estimated simultaneous model. We shall apply the selection criterion of Sec. 9.9 to decide which of the two models to use when one is simultaneous and the other block-recursive or when one is disaggregated and the other aggregated.

First, consider the choice between a simultaneous model

$$[Y_1 \quad Y_2] \begin{bmatrix} B_{11} & B_{12} \\ B_{21} & B_{22} \end{bmatrix}' + X[\Gamma_1' \quad \Gamma_2'] = [U_1 \quad U_2] \tag{105}$$

and a block-recursive model obtained by the restrictions $B_{12} = 0$ and $\Sigma_{12} = (1/n)EU_1'U_2 = 0$. The information criterion (66) and (102) can be applied to choose between them if they are both estimated by the method of FIML. A statistical criterion is thus provided to decide whether a system of simultaneous econometric equations should be decomposed into two recursive blocks. Equivalently, it can be used to decide whether a general or a partial equilibrium model should be selected. The latter model is represented by a block-recursive system which treats y_1 as exogenous in the explanation of y_2.

The second issue is whether one should aggregate across equations. For example, real consumption expenditures y_{t1} and y_{t2} for two commodity groups may satisfy

$$y_{t1} = \theta_1 y_{t3} + \theta_2 y_{t-1,1} + \theta_3 x_{t1} + u_{t1}$$
$$y_{t2} = \theta_4 y_{t3} + \theta_5 y_{t-1,2} + \theta_6 x_{t2} + u_{t2} \tag{106}$$

where y_{3t} may be disposable income and x_{t1} and x_{t2} relative prices. The sum of these equations is

$$y_{t1} + y_{t2} = (\theta_1 + \theta_4)y_{t3} + \theta_2 y_{t-1,1} + \theta_5 y_{t-1,2}$$
$$+ \theta_3 x_{t1} + \theta_6 x_{t2} + (u_{t1} + u_{t2}) \tag{107}$$

Let $y_{t4} = y_{t1} + y_{t2}$ be aggregate consumption, and let $x_{t4} = w_1 x_{t1} + w_2 x_{t2}$ be an aggregate price index with constant weights. An aggregate equation for y_{t4} can be written as

$$y_{t4} = \theta_7 y_{t3} + \theta_2 y_{t-1,4} + \frac{\theta_3}{w_1} x_{t4} + u_{t4} \tag{108}$$

provided that

$$\theta_5 = \theta_2 \quad \text{and} \quad \theta_6 = \theta_3 \frac{w_2}{w_1} \tag{109}$$

This example illustrates that aggregation across equations can be expressed as linear restrictions on the parameters of the disaggregate model. The choice between a disaggregate and an aggregate model can be made by the information criterion. Three cases will be distinguished, depending on the common subset of endogenous variables which both models are supposed to explain or predict.

In the first case one is interested in predicting the individual components y_{t1} and y_{t2} as well as all other endogenous variables in the disaggregate model. One should retain Eqs. (106) for the true model and apply the information criterion to decide whether the restrictions (109) will yield a better approximate model. This is done by estimating the model using the method of maximum likelihood with and without these restrictions. The information criterion for the large model equals the maximum value of its log likelihood minus the number of parameters. For the restricted model it equals the maximum value of the log likelihood minus an adjustment factor equal to tr $[J(\theta^*, \theta_0) \, (\text{Cov } \hat{\theta}^*)]$. Explicit expressions for $J(\theta^*, \theta_0)$ and Cov $\hat{\theta}^*$ were given in Sec. 9.9.

In the second case, one is interested in predicting the aggregate $y_{t4} =$

$y_{t1} + y_{t2}$ and all other endogenous variables in the model. One should then retain Eq. (107) instead of (106) for the true model, treating $\theta_1 + \theta_4$ as one parameter. The approximate model imposes the restrictions (109) on the parameters of this equation.

In the third case, one is interested in predicting the aggregate y_{t4} and a (possibly small) subset of other endogenous variables, including the inflation rate and the unemployment rate, for example. The true model and the approximate model are as defined in the last paragraph. This case differs from the first two cases since only a subset of endogenous variables is of concern. We shall have to consider the reduced-form equations for the subset in question. Two solutions to this model selection problem can be given.

For the first solution the reduced-form equations for each model are estimated by the method of least squares, or maximum likelihood without allowing for the overidentifying restrictions from the structure. Here the two models explaining the common subset of endogenous variables are treated simply as two linear systems of regression equations. If the true model is written to include $y_{t-1,4}$, $y_{t-1,2}$, $x_{t,4}$, and $x_{t,2}$ as its predetermined variables, the approximate model excludes $y_{t-1,2}$ and $x_{t,2}$. To estimate the expected information for the approximate model one can subtract the adjustment constant given by (103) from the maximum likelihood of the reduced form explaining the subset of endogenous variables of interest.

For the second solution the estimates of the reduced-form parameters are derived from the FIML estimates of the parameters of the corresponding structures. The expected information for the approximate model can be estimated by evaluating the two terms given in (64). The first term $\log L(Y; \hat{\theta}^*)$ is the log likelihood of the reduced form for the selected endogenous variables evaluated at $\hat{\theta}^*$, which here denotes the above derived estimates of the reduced-form parameters. The second term equals the trace of the product of $J(\theta^*, \theta_0)$ and Cov $(\hat{\theta}^*)$. $-J(\theta^*, \theta_0)$ is the expectation of the matrix of the second partials of the above log likelihood with respect to the elements of θ^*. Explicit formulas for its elements are given by (96) to (98) and (100). The remaining task is the estimation of Cov $\hat{\theta}^*$. The covariance matrix of the estimates $\hat{\alpha}^*$ and $\hat{r}_{ij}^*$ of the structural parameters, from which the reduced-form parameters $\hat{\theta}^*$ are derived, can be obtained by using the formulas given in Sec. 9.9. Given this covariance matrix, the covariance matrix Cov $\hat{\theta}^*$ of the estimates of the corresponding reduced-form parameters can be estimated by the formula given in Dhrymes (1973, p. 122). This solution is applicable to the choice between any two linear simultaneous-equation models for the purpose of explaining a common subset of endogenous variables provided that one can write down a general model as the true model and express both models by suitable linear restrictions on the parameters of the true model. One of the two models might serve as the true model if they are nested, as in our discussion of aggregation.

It is not difficult, at least in principle, to extend the above method to the case of nonlinear simultaneous equations and of equations estimated by methods other than FIML. Whether the model is linear or not, provided that the estimate

$\hat{\theta}^*$ of θ^* is consistent and satisfies the restriction $H'\hat{\theta}^* = -b$ and that $(\theta^* - \hat{\theta}^*)'$ $[\partial \log L(Y; \hat{\theta}^*)]/\partial\theta$ is approximately zero, our information criterion (64) remains valid, as can be seen by reviewing all the steps used in its derivation. To estimate (64) one can easily evaluate $\log L(Y; \hat{\theta}^*)$ and approximate $J(\theta^*, \theta_0)$ by taking analytical or numerical derivatives for $-[\partial^2 \log L(Y; \hat{\theta}^*)]/(\partial\theta \, \partial\theta')$. The more difficult problem is to estimate the covariance matrix of $\hat{\theta}^*$ when the approximate model is incorrect, i.e., when $\theta_0 \neq \theta^*$. If computational expenses are not an issue, one can always apply Monte Carlo to find the covariance matrix of $\hat{\theta}^*$ under the assumption that the true-parameter vector equals its estimate $\hat{\theta}_0$.

To estimate the covariance matrix of $\hat{\theta}_1^*$ given by (65) for the case of zero restrictions on θ one might be tempted to replace

$$E \left(\frac{\partial \log L^*}{\partial\theta_1} \frac{\partial \log L^*}{\partial\theta_1'} \right) = \text{Cov} \, \frac{\partial \log L^*}{\partial\theta_1} = \sum_{i=1}^{n} \text{Cov} \, \frac{\partial \log f(y_i | \theta_1^*, 0)}{\partial\theta_1}$$

in (65) by

$$\sum_{i=1}^{n} E \left[\frac{\partial \log f(y_i | \theta_1^*, 0)}{\partial\theta_1} \frac{\partial \log f(y_i | \theta_1^*, 0)}{\partial\theta_1'} \right]$$

This procedure is invalid because $E\{\partial \log f(y_i | \theta_1^*, 0)/\partial\theta_1\} \neq 0$, as pointed out in Chow (1981c, pp. 205–206) but overlooked by White (1982, p. 4). Although

$$E \, \frac{\partial \log L(Y; \theta^*)}{\partial\theta_1} = 0$$

where $\theta^{*\prime} = [\theta_1^* \quad 0]'$ is obtained by maximizing $E \log L(Y; \theta_1, 0)$ with respect to θ_1, the individual terms $[\partial \log f(y_i | \theta_1^*, 0)]/\partial\theta_1$ do not have zero expectations. To illustrate this point we can consider a true normal linear regression model with X_1 and X_2 as explanatory variables, while the approximate (misspecified) model uses X_1 alone as explanatory variables. In this example, θ_1^* consists of β_1^* and σ^{*2} as given by (67). It can easily be shown that $[\partial \log f(y_i | \beta_1^*, 0, \sigma^{*2})]/\partial\beta_1$ $(i = 1, \ldots, n)$ do not in general have zero expectation (see Probs. 17 and 18).

9.11 TESTS AND ANALYSIS OF MODEL SPECIFICATIONS

The basic question in econometrics is how to specify a good model for the purpose at hand. We have pointed out in Sec. 1.1 that the specification of a good model is an art. Once a model is specified, however, there are statistical criteria to judge whether the model is bad. Since many models can explain the same set of data about equally well, a given set of data can be used to screen out bad models but not to generate good models, whatever statistical techniques are used. Most of the techniques presented so far in this chapter are concerned with the choice between alternative model specifications—which of two nonnested regression models should be selected, whether a larger or a smaller regression model should be selected, and whether a larger or a smaller simultaneous-equation model should be selected. This section is concerned with methods for testing or analyzing whether a given model specification is acceptable.

One class of specification tests, initiated by Wu (1973) and treated by Hausman (1978), is based on comparing two estimators of a certain parameter vector which are both consistent and asymptotically normal if the model is correctly specified. One estimator $\hat{\gamma}^0$ is asymptotically efficient *if* the model is correctly specified but is inconsistent if the model is incorrectly specified. The second estimator $\hat{\gamma}$ is consistent even if the model is incorrectly specified. In the context of a system of linear simultaneous equations, the 3SLS estimator can serve as $\hat{\gamma}^0$ and the 2SLS estimator can serve as $\hat{\gamma}$. The test makes use of the difference $\hat{q} = \hat{\gamma} - \hat{\gamma}^0$. Let $V(\hat{q})$ be the covariance matrix of the asymptotic distribution of $\sqrt{n}\hat{q}$ and $\hat{V}(\hat{q})$ be a consistent estimate of $V(\hat{q})$. Then

$$n\hat{q}'\hat{V}(\hat{q})^{-1}\hat{q} \tag{110}$$

will have $\chi^2(k)$ as its asymptotic distribution, k being the number of elements in the vector $\hat{q}$, under the null hypothesis that the model is correctly specified, which implies plim $\hat{q} = 0$.

To find the covariance matrix $V(\hat{q})$ Hausman has noted that for $\hat{\gamma}^0$ to be asymptotically efficient, $\hat{\gamma}^0$ and $\hat{q}$ must be uncorrelated asymptotically. If $\hat{\gamma}^0$ and $\hat{q}$ were correlated, with $E\hat{q}(\hat{\gamma}^0 - \gamma)' = C \neq 0$, one could construct an estimator $\hat{\gamma}^0 - rC'\hat{q}$ having a smaller covariance matrix

$$\text{Cov } (\hat{\gamma}^0 - rC'\hat{q}) = \text{Cov } \hat{\gamma}^0 + r^2 C'(\text{Cov } \hat{q})C - 2rC'C \tag{111}$$

For small r, $r^2 C'(\text{Cov } \hat{q})C - 2rC'C$ is negative definite, making (111) smaller than Cov $\hat{\gamma}^0$, a contradiction. Therefore,

$$0 = C = E\hat{q}(\hat{\gamma}^0 - \gamma)' = E\hat{q}(-\hat{q} + \hat{\gamma} - \gamma)' = -E\hat{q}\hat{q}' + E(\hat{\gamma} - \hat{\gamma}^0)(\hat{\gamma} - \gamma)'$$

$$= -E\hat{q}\hat{q}' + E\hat{\gamma}(\hat{\gamma} - \gamma)' - E\hat{\gamma}^0(\hat{q} + \hat{\gamma}^0 - \gamma)'$$

or

$$\text{Cov } \hat{q} = \text{Cov } \hat{\gamma} - \text{Cov } \hat{\gamma}^0 \tag{112}$$

As long as consistent estimates of n Cov $\hat{\gamma}$ and n Cov $\hat{\gamma}^0$ are available, their difference will serve as a consistent estimate of n Cov $\hat{q} = V(\hat{q})$ to be used for the $\chi^2(k)$ statistic (110).

As an application, consider a linear regression model

$$y = X\gamma + \eta \tag{113}$$

for which one wishes to determine whether X is correlated with η, possibly due to errors of observation. Under the null hypothesis plim $n^{-1}X'\eta = 0$ (and $E\eta\eta' = I\sigma^2$), an asymptotically efficient estimator is the least-squares estimator

$$\hat{\gamma}^0 = (X'X)^{-1}X'y \qquad \text{Cov } \hat{\gamma}^0 = (X'X)^{-1}\sigma^2$$

Even if the null hypothesis does not hold, a consistent estimator is the instrumental-variable estimator

$$\hat{\gamma} = (W'X)^{-1}W'y \qquad \text{Cov } \hat{\gamma} = (W'X)^{-1}W'W(X'W)^{-1}\sigma^2$$

where we assume plim $n^{-1}W'X$ to be a nonsingular matrix and plim $n^{-1/2}W'\eta$ to converge in distribution to a k-variate normal distribution with zero mean. Under the null hypothesis σ^2 can be consistently estimated by $s^2 = n^{-1}(y - X\hat{\gamma}^0)'(y - X\hat{\gamma}^0)$. Thus a $\chi^2(k)$ statistic can be constructed to test the null hypothesis, using $\hat{q} = \hat{\gamma} - \hat{\gamma}^0$ and $V(\hat{q}) = n(\text{Cov }\hat{\gamma} - \text{Cov }\hat{\gamma}^0)$. See Wu (1973).

The application of Hausman's test of model specification depends on the existence of an estimator which is consistent even if the model is incorrect. In the above and other examples this means the existence of suitable instrumental variables. Using the instrumental variables, we can write

$$X = W\Gamma + U \tag{114}$$

as the second equation of a simultaneous system consisting of (113) and (114). Given plim $n^{-1}W'\eta = 0$, the null hypothesis plim $n^{-1}X'\eta = 0$ is equivalent to

$$\text{plim } n^{-1}(W\Gamma + U)'\eta = \text{plim } n^{-1}U'\eta = 0$$

Thus the parameter of interest is the covariance matrix $E(n^{-1}U'\eta)$, for any given n. Instead of estimating and testing this (matrix) parameter directly, the Hausman test is based on the (vector) parameter γ, which is not of direct interest as far as the null hypothesis is concerned. Such a parameter is known as a *nuisance parameter*. In the present example, all parameters other than $E(n^{-1}U'\eta)$ are nuisance parameters.

Holly (1982) has characterized the Hausman specification test as the following test based on the difference between two estimates of a vector of nuisance parameters. Let the parameters be divided into α, a vector of parameters of interest, and γ, a vector of nuisance parameters. The classical likelihood approach would consider a null hypothesis H_0: $\alpha = \alpha^0$. Let the sequence of alternative hypotheses be $\alpha_n^0 = \alpha^0 + n^{-1/2}\beta$ for a given vector $\beta \neq 0$. Let $\hat{\gamma}^0$ be the maximum-likelihood estimator subject to the restriction $\alpha = \alpha^0$ and $\hat{\gamma}$ be the maximum-likelihood estimator without imposing the restriction. Then Hausman's test statistic is

$$n(\hat{\gamma} - \hat{\gamma}^0)'[(I_{\gamma\gamma} - I_{\gamma\alpha}I_{\alpha\alpha}^{-1}I_{\alpha\gamma})^{-1} - I_{\gamma\gamma}^{-1}]^{-1}(\hat{\gamma} - \hat{\gamma}^0) \tag{115}$$

where
$$\begin{bmatrix} I_{\alpha\alpha} & I_{\alpha\gamma} \\ I_{\gamma\alpha} & I_{\gamma\gamma} \end{bmatrix} = \text{plim } n^{-1} \left\{ \frac{\partial^2 \log L(Y; \alpha^0, \gamma^0)}{\partial \begin{bmatrix} \alpha \\ \gamma \end{bmatrix} \partial [\alpha' \quad \gamma']} \right\}$$

$L(Y; \alpha^0, \gamma^0)$ being the log-likelihood function evaluated at the true parameters. (When the two estimates to be compared include only a subset of the nuisance parameters in γ, statistic (115) has to be modified, with a generalized inverse replacing the inverse of the expression in square brackets.) The null hypothesis being tested by this statistic is H_0^*: $I_{\gamma\gamma}^{-1}I_{\gamma\alpha}\beta = 0$, with the alternative hypothesis H_1^*: $I_{\gamma\gamma}^{-1}I_{\gamma\alpha}\beta \neq 0$. If the number of nuisance parameters to be tested is greater than or equal to the number of parameters in α, and thus the rank of $I_{\gamma\alpha}$ equals the latter number, H_0^* is equivalent to H_0 and Hausman's test has the same (asymptotic) local power as the likelihood-ratio test. If the number of nuisance parameters to be tested is smaller and the rank of $I_{y\alpha}$ equals this number, the power of the Hausman test may be low against certain alternatives.

The Hausman test applied to the regression example (113) is equivalent to estimating the regression model

$$y = X\gamma + V\alpha + \eta \qquad V = [I - W(W'W)^{-1}W']X$$

and testing the null hypothesis $\alpha = 0$, as shown by Hausman (1978, p. 1259). A related test of the null hypothesis $E(\eta \mid X) = 0$ for the regression model (113) was proposed by Ramsey (1969), with some of its properties discussed by Thursby and Schmidt (1977). Ramsey suggested forming a regression by introducing a matrix Z of additional explanatory variables and test the null hypothesis that the coefficient vector of these variables is zero using an F ratio. The matrix Z may include powers of Xc, where $c = (X'X)^{-1}X'y$, and variables which are suspected of affecting y. Ramsey's RESET test is based on approximating $E(\eta \mid X) = \xi$ in the model (113) by a linear combination $Z\theta$ of the variables in Z. Letting $\hat\theta$ be the least-squares estimate of θ in the regression of y on X and Z, and letting $M_x = I - X(X'X)^{-1}X'$, we have

$$E\hat\theta = (Z'M_x Z)^{-1}Z'M_x \xi$$

$E\hat\theta$ will be nonzero if

$$Z'M_x \xi = Z'\xi - Z'X(X'X)^{-1}X'\xi \neq 0$$

which will be the case if $Z'\xi \neq 0$ or if $Z'X \neq 0$ and $X'\xi \neq 0$. If Z satisfies either of these conditions, $E(\eta \mid X) = \xi \neq 0$ will imply $E\hat\theta \neq 0$, motivating Ramsey's test.

Besides the above formal statistical methods, there are many other formal and informal methods for selecting econometric models. To illustrate the variety of approaches to model selection and evaluation, we quote from Chow and Corsi (1982, pp. 1–2).

> How does one evaluate an econometric model? This is not a simple question to answer.... .
>
> As the following chapters will show, the evaluation of an econometric model can and should be approached in different ways, and the different approaches complement one another. There does not exist a simple way to evaluate an entity as complex as an econometric model. In practice, when the model is specified, its parameters are estimated, passing the tests of correctness in sign and statistical significance at reasonable levels, and the residuals are not obviously correlated, it is often considered a completed model. What can and should be done to evaluate the model consists of a variety of tasks some of which are discussed in this volume. First, one should appeal to economic theory to judge the reasonableness of model specifications. In fact, as the chapters by Klein and Deaton show, economic theory can effectively guide the specification of econometric models. Second, one can compare the model or certain parts of it with alternative formulations, using appropriate statistical criteria for choosing among them. This is a theme of the chapters by Deaton and by Godfrey and Wickens. This theme encompasses the decision as to whether an ARMA structure should be used to model the residuals. Third, one can test whether the exogenous variables used are indeed exogenous and decide how to model accordingly, as discussed in the chapter by Richard.
>
> Fourth, besides the usual significance tests, there are methods to detect unduly influential data points and to limit their undue influence, and methods to pinpoint the parameters and exogenous variables which are most influential in determining the behavior of a model, as

expounded in the chapter by Kuh and Neese. Fifth, methods based on stochastic control theory are also available to uncover the tradeoff relationships implicit in a model, to measure the importance of each policy variable (as a generalization of the multiplier concept), and to perform comparative dynamic analysis for the model when a policy rule or a behavioral relation changes, as pointed out in the chapter by Chow. Sixth, there are tests of the stability of model parameters, as exemplified by the work of Corsi, Pollock and Prakken.

Seventh, one may devise measures of the degree of model misspecification, as Fair has done. Eighth, one can use the accuracy of forecasts to evaluate a model, a topic treated in the chapters by Salmon and Wallis and by Bianchi and Calzolari. Finally, the use of a model for policy analysis and formulation, as exemplified by the work reported by Guillaume, Gauron, Maurice and Milleron will help detect model inadequacies and eventually lead to more reliable econometric models. The above listing is by no means complete, but it does represent a very substantial portion of the tools available for the evaluation of econometric models.

While we have presented a number of statistical methods for selecting econometric models, the above quotation brings home the point that model selection is a complicated matter and that many approaches, formal and informal, can be applied to this problem.

PROBLEMS

1. Show that in a linear regression of y_i on x_i and z_i, with $\sum_i x_i = \sum_i z_i = 0$ and $\sum x_i^2 = \sum z_i^2 = 1$, the test statistic for the null hypothesis of equal regression coefficients of x_i and z_i can be written as (3).

2. Interpret (4) as a test statistic for the equality between two regression coefficients. Show your answer algebraically.

3. In a regression of y on the vectors x and z, let the null hypothesis be that Ey is at an equal distance from the spaces spanned by x and by z. Show that the F test statistic given by (20) for this null hypothesis is the square of (3). Note that in the present case the quadratic constraint (8) becomes the square of a linear constraint.

4. Generalize the test given by (20) for the null hypothesis that the regressions of y on three sets of variables X_1, X_2, and X_3 have equal predictive powers.

5. Set up the composite density function (21) for two competing normal regression models $y = X_1\beta_1 + \epsilon_1$ and $y = X_2\beta_2 + \epsilon_2$ and show why the parameters $\lambda, \beta_1, \beta_2, \sigma_1^2 = E\epsilon_{i1}^2$, and $\sigma_2^2 = E\epsilon_{i2}^2$ cannot be separately identified.

6. Show that (43) is the lagrangian multiplier statistic for the null hypothesis $H'\beta = q$ is a normal regression model $y = X\beta + \epsilon$ with known $\sigma^2 = E\epsilon_i^2$.

7. Show that (43) is the Wald test statistic for the null hypothesis given in Prob. 6.

8. Show that (43) is the likelihood-ratio test statistic for the null hypothesis given in Prob. 6.

9. Write out $\hat{\beta}_I - \beta$ and derive Eq. (46).

10. When the numbers k_1 and k_2 of explanatory variables in two competing regression models are equal, show that the selection criterion (54) amounts to choosing the model with a larger R^2 or a smaller s^2. Comment on this criterion compared with the criterion given by Sec. 9.2.

11. If the true regression model is $Y = X_1\beta_1^0 + X_2\beta_2^0 + \epsilon$, with $E\epsilon_i^2 = \sigma^2$, show that the parameters β_1^* and σ^{*2} of the best approximate model using only X_1 alone are given by (67). By "best" we mean having maximum $E \log L(\tilde{Y} \mid \beta_1, 0, \sigma^2)$ for all β_1 and σ^2.

12. Derive Eq. (68).

13. Derive Eq. (69).

14. Plot the risk function of the C_p criterion for choosing between the normal linear regression model

$y = \beta_1 x_1 + \beta_2 x_2 + \epsilon$ and the smaller model with x_1 as the only explanatory variable, assuming that $E\epsilon_i^2 = 1$ and $X'X = \tilde{X}'\tilde{X} = I$.

15. Plot the risk function of the information criterion (71) for choosing between the normal linear regression model $y = \beta_1 x_1 + \beta_2 x_2 + \epsilon$ and the smaller model with x_1 as the only explanatory variable, assuming $E\epsilon_i^2 = 1$ and $X'X = \tilde{X}'\tilde{X} = I$. An approximate answer will suffice.

16. Find the critical values and the associated levels of significance of the t test for possibly dropping one explanatory variable in a linear regression model with six explanatory variables using the information criterion (71).

17. Using the result of Prob. 11, evaluate the expectation of $[\partial \log f(y_i | \beta_1^*, 0, \sigma^{*2})]/\partial \beta_1$.

18. Using the results of Probs. 11 and 17, find the covariance matrix of $[\partial \log L(Y;\theta^*)]/\partial \beta_1$ and compare it with

$$\sum_{i=1}^{n} E\left[\frac{\log f(y_i | \theta^*)}{\partial \beta_1} \frac{\log f(y_i | \theta^*)}{\partial \beta_1'}\right]$$

This covariance matrix is found in Chow (1981a).

REFERENCES

Aitchison, J., and S. D. Silvey (1958): "Maximum Likelihood Estimation of Parameters Subject to Restraints," *Ann. Math. Statist.*, **28**: 813–828.

Akaike, H. (1973): "Information Theory and an Extension of the Maximum Likelihood Principle," pp. 267–281 in B. N. Petrov and F. Cśaki (eds.), *Proc. 2d Int. Symp. Infor. Theory*, Akademiai Kiadó, Budapest.

—— (1974): "A New Look at the Statistical Model Identification," *IEEE Trans. Autom. Control*, **AC-19**: 716–723.

—— (1978): "A Bayesian Analysis of the Minimum AIC Procedure," *Ann. Inst. Statist. Math.*, **A30**: 9–14.

Atkinson, A. C. (1970): "A Method for Discriminating between Models," *J. R. Statist. Soc.*, **B32**: 323–344.

Breusch, T. S., and A. R. Pagan (1980): "The Lagrange Multiplier Test and Its Applications to Model Specifications in Econometrics," *Rev. Econ. Stud.*, **47**: 239–253.

Chow, G. C. (1957): *Demand for Automobiles in the United States: A Study in Consumer Durables.*, North-Holland, Amsterdam.

—— (1980): "The Selection of Variates for Use in Prediction: A Generalization of Hotelling's Solution," pp. 105–114 in L. R. Klein, M. Nerlove, and S. C. Tsiang (eds.), *Quantitative Econometrics and Development*, Academic, New York.

—— (1981a): "A Comparison of the Information and Posterior Probability Criteria for Model Selection," *J. Econometr.*, **16**: 21–33.

—— (1981b), "Evaluation of Econometric Models by Decomposition and Aggregation," in J. Kmenta and J. Ramsey (eds.), *Methodology of Macro-Economic Models*, North-Holland, Amsterdam.

—— (1981c), "Selection of Econometric Models by the Information Criterion," in E. G. Charatsis (ed.), *Proc. Econometr. Soc. Eur. Meet. 1979*, North-Holland, Amsterdam,

—— and P. Corsi (eds.) (1982): *Evaluating the Reliability of Macro-Economic Models*, Wiley, London.

Cox, D. R. (1961): "Tests of Separate Families of Hypotheses," *Proc. 4th Berkeley Symp. Math. Statist. Probab.*, Berkeley, University of California Press, 105–123.

—— (1962): "Further Results on Tests of Separate Families of Hypotheses," *J. R. Statist. Soc.*, **B24**: 406–424.

Davidson, R., and J. G. MacKinnon (1981): "Several Tests for Model Specification in the Presence of Alternative Hypotheses," *Econometrica*, **49**: 781–793.

Deaton, A. S. (1982): "Model Selection Procedures, or Does the Consumption Function Exist?" chap. 5 in G. C. Chow and P. Corsi (eds.), *Evaluating the Reliability of Macro-Economic Models*, Wiley, London.

Dhrymes, P. J. (1973): "Restricted and Unrestricted Reduced Forms: Asymptotic Distribution and Relative Efficiency," *Econometrica*, **41**: 119–134.

Dickey, J. (1975): "Bayesian Alternatives to the *F*-Test and Least-Squares Estimate in the Normal Linear Model," pp. 515–554 in S. E. Fienberg and A. Zellner (eds.), *Studies in Bayesian Econometrics and Statistics*, North-Holland, Amsterdam.

Fisher, F. M. (1961): "On the Cost of Approximate Specification in Simultaneous-Equation Estimation," *Econometrica*, **29**: 139–170.

Gaver, K. M., and M. S. Geisel (1974): "Discriminating among Alternative Models: Bayesian and Nonbayesian Methods, " pp. 49–77 in P. Zarembka (ed.), *Frontiers in Econometrics*, Academic, New York.

Hausman, J. A. (1978): "Specification Tests in Econometrics," *Econometrica*, **46**: 1251–1272.

Holly, A. (1982): "A Remark on Hausman's Specification Test," *Econometrica*, **50**: 749–759.

Hotelling, H. (1940): "The Selection of Variates for Use in Prediction with Some Comments on the General Problem of Nuisance Parameters," *Ann. Math. Statist.*, **11**: 271–283.

Jeffreys, H. (1961): *Theory of Probability*, 3d. ed., Clarendon, Oxford.

Koopmans, T. C. (1950): "When Is an Equation System Complete for Statistical Purposes?" chap. XVII in T. C. Koopmans (ed.), *Statistical Inference in Dynamic Economic Models*, Wiley, New York.

Leamer, E. (1978): *Specification Searches*, Wiley, New York.

——— (1979): "Information Criterion for Choice Regression Models," *Econometrica*, **47**: 507–510.

Liu, T. C. (1955): "A Simple Forecasting Model for the U. S. Economy," *Int. Monetary Fund Staff Pap.*, 434–466.

——— (1960): "Underidentification, Structural Estimation, and Forecasting," *Econometrica*, **28**: 855–865.

MacKinnon, J. G. (1983): "Model Specification Tests against Nonnested Alternatives." *Econometric Reviews*, **2**.

Mallows, C. L. (1973), "Some Comments on C_p, *Technometrics*, **15**: 661–675.

Pesaran, M. H., and A. S. Deaton (1979): "Testing Non-Nested Non-Linear Regression Models," *Econometrica*, **46**: 677–694.

Pratt, J. W. (1975): "Comments," pp. 71–73 in S. E. Fienberg and A. Zellner (eds.), *Studies in Bayesian Econometrics and Statistics*, North-Holland, Amsterdam.

Quandt, R. E. (1974): "A Comparison of Methods for Testing Nonnested Hypotheses," *Rev. Econ. Statist.*, **56**: 92–99.

Ramsey, J. (1969): "Tests of Specification Errors in Classical Linear Least-Squares Regression Analysis," *J. R. Statist. Soc.*, **B31**: 350–371.

Sawa, T. (1978): "Information Criteria for Discriminating among Alternative Regression Models," *Econometrica*, **46**: 1273–1292.

Schwarz, G. (1978): "Estimating the Dimension of a Model," *Ann. Statist.*, **6**: 461–464.

Silvey, S. D. (1959): "The Lagrangian Multiplier Test," *Ann. Math. Statist.*, **30**: 389–407.

Thursby, J. G., and P. Schmidt (1977): "Some Properties of Tests for Specification Error in a Linear Regression Model," *J. Am. Statist. Assoc.*, **72**: 635–641.

Wald, A. (1943): "Tests of Statistical Hypotheses Concerning Several Parameters When the Number of Observations Is Large," *Trans. Am. Math. Soc.*, **54**: 426–482.

White, H. (1982): "Maximum-Likelihood Estimation of Misspecified Models," *Econometrica*, **50**: 1–25.

Wold, H., and L. Juréen (1953): *Demand Analysis*, Wiley, New York.

Wu, D.-M. (1973): "Alternative Tests of Independence Between Stochastic Regressors and Disturbances," *Econometrica*, **41**: 733–750.

Zellner, A. (1971): *An Introduction to Bayesian Inference in Econometrics*, Wiley, New York.

TEN

MODELS OF TIME-VARYING COEFFICIENTS

10.1 INTRODUCTION

When an econometric model fails to forecast with the degree of accuracy inferred from the standard errors of the random disturbances and of the estimated coefficients, using the forecasting formula (108) of Chap. 5, the econometrician will conclude that the model is unfit for explaining the postsample data. One may argue that the model was adequate during the sample period but the economic structure has changed afterwards, or one may simply admit that the model was inadequate even during the sample period. In either case, a different model is needed for predicting the future. One can specify another model of fixed coefficients, hoping that it will remain valid for future periods. Alternatively, one can model the shifts in the coefficients in a stochastic but well-specified manner. This chapter is devoted to models with changing coefficients. Such models take into account the possibility that the coefficients may be time-dependent and permit the estimation of these coefficients at different times. For the purpose of forecasting, such models might be superior to models with constant coefficients by using the estimates of the most up-to-date coefficients. From the viewpoint of hypothesis testing, a model with changing coefficients serves as a viable alternative to the fixed-coefficient model for the purpose of checking the constancy of the coefficients of the latter model.

Let us first consider a linear regression model with a changing coefficient vector β_t. This model is represented by two equations

$$y_t = x_t \beta_t + \epsilon_t \qquad (t = 1, \ldots, T) \tag{1}$$

and
$$\beta_t = M\beta_{t-1} + \eta_t \qquad (t = 1, \ldots, T) \tag{2}$$

where x_t is a row vector of k fixed explanatory variables, ϵ_t is normally and independently distributed with mean zero and variance σ^2, and η_t is k-variate normal and independent with mean zero and covariance matrix $\sigma^2 P \equiv V$. When $V = 0$ and $M = I$, this model is reduced to the standard normal regression model. We shall be concerned with the estimation and statistical testing of β_t ($t = 1, \ldots, T$), σ^2, V, and M using observations on (y_t, x_t). We are restricting our discussion to the case of fixed x_t. If x_t were to include lagged dependent variables, the log-likelihood function given at the beginning of Sec. 10.4 would no longer be valid since the individual terms would no longer be normal and serially uncorrelated.

Assuming tentatively that σ^2, V, and M are known, we shall consider the problem of estimating β_t using information I_s up to time s. Denote by $E(\beta_t | I_s) \equiv \beta_{t|s}$ the conditional expectation of β_t given I_s. The evaluation of $\beta_{t|t}$ is known as *filtering*. The evaluation of $\beta_{t|s}$ ($s > t$) is called *smoothing*, and the evaluation of $\beta_{t|s}$ ($s < t$) is called *prediction*. In Sec. 10.2, we shall derive the filtered and smoothed estimates of β_t recursively for $t = 1, 2, \ldots$ by the use of a regression of $\beta_1, \ldots, \beta_t$ on $y_1, \ldots, y_s$. The basic results are due to Kalman (1960). Section 10.3 contains an alternative derivation of the same results using the method of Aitken's generalized least squares applied to a regression of $y_1, \ldots, y_s$ on $x_1, \ldots, x_s$ with β_s as the regression coefficient. This exposition is due to Sant (1977). We then study the problem of estimating σ^2, V, and M by the method of maximum likelihood in Sec. 10.4.

In Sec. 10.5 we consider a system of linear regressions with changing coefficients. In Secs. 10.6 and 10.7, respectively, we treat a system of linear and nonlinear simultaneous stochastic equations with changing parameters. Finally in Sec. 10.8 we modify (2) by introducing a mean vector $\bar{\beta}$, thus replacing β_t and β_{t-1} in (2) by $\beta_t - \bar{\beta}$ and $\beta_{t-1} - \bar{\beta}$, respectively, and assuming the characteristic roots of M to be less than 1 in absolute value. When $M = 0$, a random-coefficient regression model results. Section 10.9 states some conditions for the identification of the parameters.

Besides the estimation of parameters, an important problem is to test the null hypothesis $V = 0$. Testing this null hypothesis is equivalent to testing the stability of a set of regression coefficients through time, the model of Eqs. (1) and (2) serving as the alternative hypothesis. This topic is treated in Sec. 10.10. Section 10.11 treats the problem of seasonal adjustment of economic time series using Kalman filtering techniques.

10.2 DERIVATION OF $\beta_{t|s}$ BY RECURSIVE REGRESSION OF β_t ON $y_1, \ldots, y_s$

Given the data $y_1, \ldots, y_t$, we would like to estimate β_t using the model of Eqs. (1) and (2). The task is accomplished by deriving a predictor for β_t as a linear function of $y_1, \ldots, y_t$, that is, a regression of β_t on $y_1, \ldots, y_t$. This regression is derived recursively. We first consider the regression of β_t on y_t, given $y_1, \ldots, y_{t-1}$.

Denote $(y_1, \ldots, y_t)$ by Y_t. By definition, the conditional regression of β_t on y_t is the conditional mean of β_t, given y_t and Y_{t-1}. By regression theory, this regression equals the conditional mean of β_t, given Y_{t-1}, plus a coefficient times the deviation of y_t from its conditional mean, given Y_{t-1}. Thus

$$E(\beta_t \,|\, y_t, \, Y_{t-1}) = E(\beta_t \,|\, Y_{t-1}) + K_t[y_t - E(y_t \,|\, Y_{t-1})] \tag{3}$$

Equation (3) would be a very familiar equation if the conditioning variable Y_{t-1} were absent. The regression relation holds after the conditioning variable Y_{t-1} has been inserted. This regression function is linear in y_t because β_t and y_t are jointly normal as a consequence of the normality of ϵ_t and η_t in the model of Eqs. (1) and (2). K_t is a column vector of regression coefficients. Taking the expectation of y_t from (1) conditioned on Y_{t-1}, we have $y_{t|t-1} \equiv E(y_t \,|\, Y_{t-1}) = x_t \beta_{t|t-1}$. Substituting for $E(y_t \,|\, Y_{t-1})$, we can write (3) as

$$\beta_{t|t} = \beta_{t|t-1} + K_t(y_t - x_t \beta_{t|t-1}) \tag{4}$$

The vector of regression coefficients K_t was originally derived by Kalman (1960). If this vector is known, we can use (4) to update our estimate $\beta_{t|t-1}$ to form $\beta_{t|t}$.

To derive K_t, we recall some results from normal regression theory. From Sec. 1.6 on the multivariate normal distribution, we recall the conditional distribution $g(y_1 \,|\, y_2)$ of a vector y_1 given another vector y_2, as given by equation (30) of Chap. 1. The mean of y_1 is a linear function of y_2. This function is called the *regression function*. The matrix of regression coefficients is

$$\Sigma_{12}\Sigma_{22}^{-1} = [E(y_1 - Ey_1)(y_2 - Ey_2)'][\text{Cov } y_2]^{-1}$$

If there is a third vector y_3 involved and we are interested in the regression of y_1 on y_2 given y_3, the above formula remains valid except that all expectations are conditioned on y_3. For the problem of deriving the Kalman filter let β_t be y_1, y_t be y_2, and Y_{t-1} be y_3. We then have the matrix K_t of regression coefficients in the regression of β_t on y_t, conditioned on Y_{t-1}

$$K_t = [E(\beta_t - \beta_{t|t-1})(y_t - y_{t|t-1})'][\text{Cov } (y_t \,|\, Y_{t-1})]^{-1} \tag{5}$$

Denoting the covariance matrix $\text{Cov } (\beta_t \,|\, Y_{t-1}) = E(\beta_t - \beta_{t|t-1})(\beta_t - \beta_{t|t-1})'$ by $\Sigma_{t|t-1}$ and using

$$y_t - y_{t|t-1} = x_t(\beta_t - \beta_{t|t-1}) + \epsilon_t$$

we have

$$\begin{aligned} E(\beta_t - \beta_{t|t-1})(y_t - y_{t|t-1})' &= E(\beta_t - \beta_{t|t-1})[x_t(\beta_t - \beta_{t|t-1}) + \epsilon_t]' \\ &= \Sigma_{t|t-1} x_t' \end{aligned}$$

and

$$\begin{aligned} \text{Cov } (y_t \,|\, Y_{t-1}) &= E[x_t(\beta_t - \beta_{t|t-1}) + \epsilon_t][x_t(\beta_t - \beta_{t|t-1}) + \epsilon_t]' \\ &= (x_t \Sigma_{t|t-1} x_t' + \sigma^2) \end{aligned}$$

Hence (5) becomes

$$K_t = \Sigma_{t|t-1} x'_t (x_t \Sigma_{t|t-1} x'_t + \sigma^2)^{-1} \tag{6}$$

$\Sigma_{t|t-1}$ can be computed recursively as follows. First, take the conditional expectation of (2)

$$\beta_{t|t-1} = M\beta_{t-1|t-1} \tag{7}$$

subtract (7) from (2), postmultiply the result by its transpose, and take the expectation of the product to obtain

$$\Sigma_{t|t-1} = M\Sigma_{t-1|t-1} M' + V \tag{8}$$

Second, use (4) and (1) to write

$$\beta_t - \beta_{t|t} = \beta_t - \beta_{t|t-1} - K_t[x_t(\beta_t - \beta_{t|t-1}) + \epsilon_t] \tag{9}$$

Taking the expectation of the product of (9) and its transpose and using (6), we obtain

$$\Sigma_{t|t} = \Sigma_{t|t-1} - K_t(x_t \Sigma_{t|t-1} x'_t + \sigma^2)K'_t$$
$$= \Sigma_{t|t-1} - \Sigma_{t|t-1} x'_t(x_t \Sigma_{t|t-1} x'_t + \sigma^2)^{-1} x_t \Sigma_{t|t-1} \tag{10}$$

Equations (8) and (10) can be used to compute $\Sigma_{t|t}$ $(t = 1, 2, ...)$ successively given $\Sigma_{0|0}$, without using the observations y_t $(t = 1, 2, ...)$. Having computed $\Sigma_{t|t-1}$, we can use (6) to compute K_t. Given K_t, (4) and (7) can be used to compute $\beta_{t|t}$ from $\beta_{t-1|t-1}$ if $\beta_{0|0}$ is known. The estimates $\beta_{t|t}$ so obtained are known as *estimates by the Kalman filter*.

Our next topic is *smoothing*, namely, the estimation of β_t using future observations $y_{t+1}, y_{t+2}, ..., y_{t+n}$. We first consider the regression of β_t on y_{t+1}, conditioned on Y_t. Analogous to (4) and (5) are

$$\beta_{t|t+1} = \beta_{t|t} + D_{t|t+1}(y_{t+1} - y_{t+1|t}) \tag{11}$$

and

$$D_{t|t+1} = [E(\beta_t - \beta_{t|t})(y_{t+1} - y_{t+1|t})'][\text{Cov}\,(y_{t+1}\,|\,Y_t)]^{-1} \tag{12}$$

To derive the matrix $D_{t|t+1}$ of regression coefficients we use (1) and (2) to write

$$y_{t+1} - y_{t+1|t} = x_{t+1}\beta_{t+1} + \epsilon_{t+1} - x_{t+1}\beta_{t+1|t}$$
$$= x_{t+1} M\beta_t + x_{t+1}\eta_{t+1} + \epsilon_{t+1} - x_{t+1} M\beta_{t|t}$$

which can be used to evaluate the required expectations in (12) to yield

$$D_{t|t+1} = \Sigma_{t|t} M'x'_{t+1}(x_{t+1}\Sigma_{t+1|t} x'_{t+1} + \sigma^2)^{-1}$$
$$= \Sigma_{t|t} M'\Sigma_{t+1|t}^{-1} K_{t+1} \tag{13}$$

Equations (11) and (13) can be used to evaluate $\beta_{t|t+1}$. With the help of (13) and (4), (11) can be rewritten as

$$\beta_{t|t+1} = \beta_{t|t} + \Sigma_{t|t} M'\Sigma_{t+1|t}^{-1}(\beta_{t+1|t+1} - \beta_{t+1|t}) \tag{14}$$

We have just provided a smoothing formula (14) to evaluate $\beta_{t|t+1}$ in terms of $\beta_{t|t}$, $\beta_{t+1|t+1}$, and $\beta_{t+1|t}$. This formula can be generalized to

$$\beta_{t|t+n} = \beta_{t|t+n-1} + H_t(\beta_{t+1|t+n} - \beta_{t+1|t+n-1})$$

where $$H_t \equiv \Sigma_{t|t} M' \Sigma_{t+1|t}^{-1}$$

$$(15)$$

which will be proved below.

★ Proof of the Smoothing Formulas

The proof of (15), which is not difficult but somewhat tedious, is recorded below because the author cannot find a simpler proof elsewhere. Uninterested readers can skip to formula (25).

To prove (15) by induction, we know it to hold for $n = 1$ and assume it to hold for $n - 1$. This assumption implies, by repeated applications,

$$\beta_{t|t+n-1} = \beta_{t|t+n-2} + H_t(\beta_{t+1|t+n-1} - \beta_{t+1|t+n-2})$$
$$= \beta_{t|t+n-2} + H_t H_{t+1}(\beta_{t+2|t+n-1} - \beta_{t+2|t+n-2})$$
$$= \beta_{t|t+n-2} + H_t H_{t+1} \cdots H_{t+n-2}(\beta_{t+n-1|t+n-1} - \beta_{t+n-1|t+n-2})$$
$$= \beta_{t|t+n-2} + H_t H_{t+1} \cdots H_{t+n-2} K_{t+n-1}'(y_{t+n-1} - y_{t+n-1|t+n-2}) \quad (16)$$

First, consider the regression of β_t on y_{t+n-1}, conditioned on y_{t+n-2}. Analogous to (11) and (12) are

$$\beta_{t|t+n-1} = \beta_{t|t+n-2} + D_{t|t+n-1}(y_{t+n-1} - y_{t+n-1|t+n-2}) \quad (17)$$

and $$D_{t|t+n-1} = [E(\beta_t - \beta_{t|t+n-2})(y_{t+n-1} - y_{t+n-1|t+n-2})']$$
$$\cdot [\text{Cov}(y_{t+n-1} | Y_{t+n-2})]^{-1}$$
$$= H_t H_{t+1} \cdots H_{t+n-2} K_{t+n-1} \quad (18)$$

where the last equality sign results from comparing (16) and (17). Equation (18) gives the regression coefficient $D_{t|t+n-1}$ explicitly and will be useful later. We postmultiply (18) by $\text{Cov}(y_{t+n-1} | Y_{t+n-2})$ to justify the second equality sign of

$$E(\beta_t - \beta_{t|t+n-2})(y_{t+n-1} - y_{t+n-1|t+n-2})'$$
$$= E(\beta_t - \beta_{t|t+n-2})(\beta_{t+n-1} - \beta_{t+n-1|t+n-2})'x'_{t+n-1}$$
$$= H_t H_{t+1} \cdots H_{t+n-2} K_{t+n-1}(x_{t+n-1} \Sigma_{t+n-1|t+n-2} x'_{t+n-1} + \sigma^2)$$
$$= H_t H_{t+1} \cdots H_{t+n-2} \Sigma_{t+n-1|t+n-2} x'_{t+n-1} \quad (19)$$

where (6) has been used for K_{t+n-1}.

Second, having drawn the important implications (18) and (19) from our assumption, we shall find the regression of β_t on y_{t+n}, conditioned on Y_{t+n-1},

$$\beta_{t|t+n} = \beta_{t|t+n-1} + D_{t|t+n}(y_{t+n} - y_{t+n|t+n-1}) \quad (20)$$

To evaluate the vector of regression coefficients $D_{t|t+n}$ we need to find the covariance between $\beta_t - \beta_{t|t+n-1}$ and $y_{t+n} - y_{t+n|t+n-1}$. We use (17) to write

$$\beta_t - \beta_{t|t+n-1} = \beta_t - \beta_{t|t+n-2} - D_{t|t+n-1}(y_{t+n-1} - y_{t+n-1|t+n-2})$$

$$= \beta_t - \beta_{t|t+n-2} - D_{t|t+n-1}$$

$$\cdot [x_{t+n-1}(\beta_{t+n-1} - \beta_{t+n-1|t+n-2}) + \epsilon_{t+n-1}] \qquad (21)$$

and use (1), (2), and (4) to write

$$y_{t+n} - y_{t+n|t+n-1}$$

$$= x_{t+n} M(\beta_{t+n-1} - \beta_{t+n-1|t+n-1}) + x_{t+n}\eta_{t+n} + \epsilon_{t+n}$$

$$= x_{t+n} M[\beta_{t+n-1} - \beta_{t+n-1|t+n-2}$$

$$- K_{t+n-1}(y_{t+n-1} - y_{t+n-1|t+n-2})] + x_{t+n}\eta_{t+n} + \epsilon_{t+n}$$

$$= x_{t+n} M[(I - K_{t+n-1}x_{t+n-1})(\beta_{t+n-1} - \beta_{t+n-1|t+n-2})$$

$$- K_{t+n-1}\epsilon_{t+n-1}] + x_{t+n}\eta_{t+n} + \epsilon_{t+n} \qquad (22)$$

Equations (21) and (22) are used to evaluate the covariance

$$E(\beta_t - \beta_{t|t+n-1})(y_{t+n} - y_{t+n|t+n-1})'$$

$$= E(\beta_t - \beta_{t|t+n-2})(\beta_{t+n-1} - \beta_{t+n-1|t+n-2})'$$

$$\cdot (I - x'_{t+n-1}K'_{t+n-1})M'x'_{t+n}$$

$$- D_{t|t+n-1}[x_{t+n-1}\Sigma_{t+n-1|t+n-2}(I - x'_{t+n-1}K'_{t+n-1})$$

$$- \sigma^2 K'_{t+n-1}]M'x'_{t+n}$$

$$= H_t H_{t+1} \cdots H_{t+n-2} \Sigma_{t+n-1|t+n-1}M'x'_{t+n}$$

$$= H_t H_{t+1} \cdots H_{t+n-1}K_{t+n}(x_{t+n}\Sigma_{t+n|t+n-1}x'_{t+n} + \sigma^2) \qquad (23)$$

where the second equality sign results from using (18), (19), and (10) and the third equality sign is due to (6) and the definition of H_{t+n-1}. Hence, the regression coefficient is

$$D_{t|t+n} = [E(\beta_t - \beta_{t|t+n-1})(y_{t+n} - y_{t+n|t+n-1})'] \text{ Cov } (y_{t+n} | Y_{t+n-1})]^{-1}$$

$$= H_t H_{t+1} \cdots H_{t+n-1}K_{t+n} \qquad (24)$$

which generalizes the coefficient given by (18) from $n-1$ to n. Substituting (24) into (20) yields

$$\beta_{t|t+n} = \beta_{t|t+n-1} + H_t H_{t+1} \cdots H_{t+n-1}(\beta_{t+n|t+n} - \beta_{t+n|t+n-1})$$

$$= \beta_{t|t+n-1} + H_t(\beta_{t+1|t+n} - \beta_{t+1|t+n-1}) \qquad (25)$$

where the last step is due to the third equality sign of (16) with t replaced by $t+1$. Equation (25) completes the proof and provides two alternative formulas for evaluating $\beta_{t|t+n}$; (20) provides a third formula.

To derive the covariance matrix $\Sigma_{t|t+n}$ we use (20) and (23)

$$\begin{aligned}
\Sigma_{t|t+n} &= E(\beta_t - \beta_{t|t+n})(\beta_t - \beta_{t|t+n})' \\
&= E[\beta_t - \beta_{t|t+n-1} - D_{t|t+n}(y_{t+n} - y_{t+n|t+n-1})] \\
&\quad \cdot [\beta_t - \beta_{t|t+n-1} - D_{t|t+n}(y_{t+n} - y_{t+n|t+n-1})]' \\
&= \Sigma_{t|t+n-1} - D_{t|t+n}(x_{t+n}\,\Sigma_{t+n|t+n-1}x'_{t+n} + \sigma^2)D'_{t|t+n}
\end{aligned} \tag{26}$$

By (24), (6), and (10), formula (26) can be written alternatively as

$$\begin{aligned}
\Sigma_{t|t+n} &= \Sigma_{t|t+n-1} - H_t \cdots H_{t+n-1}K_{t+n} \\
&\quad \cdot (x_{t+n}\,\Sigma_{t+n|t+n-1}x'_{t+n} + \sigma^2)K'_{t+n}H'_{t+n-1} \cdots H'_t \\
&= \Sigma_{t|t+n-1} - H_t \cdots H_{t+n-1}\,\Sigma_{t+n|t+n-1}x'_{t+n} \\
&\quad \cdot (x_{t+n}\,\Sigma_{t+n|t+n-1}x'_{t+n} + \sigma^2)^{-1}x_{t+n} \\
&\quad \cdot \Sigma_{t+n|t+n-1}H'_{t+n-1} \cdots H'_t \\
&= \Sigma_{t|t+n-1} + H_t \cdots H_{t+n-1} \\
&\quad \cdot (\Sigma_{t+n|t+n} - \Sigma_{t+n|t+n-1})H'_{t+n-1} \cdots H'_t
\end{aligned} \tag{27}$$

Equations (26) and (27) provide the covariance matrix of the smoothed estimate $\beta_{t|t+n}$ of β_t given the data up to $t + n$. The estimates $\beta_{t|s}$ and $\Sigma_{t|s}$ of this section require knowledge not only of the parameters σ^2, V, and M but also of the initial values $\beta_{0|0}$ and $\Sigma_{0|0}$ at time 0. Section 10.3 will provide a method for estimating $\beta_{0|0}$ and $\Sigma_{0|0}$, and Sec. 10.4 will be concerned with the maximum-likelihood estimation of σ^2, V, and M.

10.3 DERIVATIONS OF $\beta_{t|s}$ BY REGRESSION OF $y_1, \ldots, y_s$ ON $x_1, \ldots, x_s$

Econometricians may find it more appealing to view $\beta_{t|s}$ as a coefficient vector in the regression of $y_1, \ldots, y_s$ on $x_1, \ldots, x_s$. This interpretation was given by Sant (1977) as follows. Applying (2) repeatedly, we have

$$\begin{aligned}
\beta_t &= M\beta_{t-1} + \eta_t = M^2\beta_{t-2} + \eta_t + M\eta_{t-1} \\
&= M^{t-1}\beta_1 + M^{t-2}\eta_2 + \ldots + M\eta_{t-1} + \eta_t
\end{aligned}$$

which can be used to express $\beta_1, \ldots, \beta_{t-1}$ as functions of β_t, provided M^{-1} exists. The observations $y_1, \ldots, y_t$ from (1) thus become

$$\begin{bmatrix} y_1 \\ y_2 \\ \vdots \\ y_{t-1} \\ y_t \end{bmatrix} = \begin{bmatrix} x_1 M^{-t+1} \\ x_2 M^{-t+2} \\ \vdots \\ x_{t-1}M^{-1} \\ x_t \end{bmatrix} \beta_t + \begin{bmatrix} \epsilon_1 \\ \epsilon_2 \\ \vdots \\ \epsilon_{t-1} \\ \epsilon_t \end{bmatrix} - \begin{bmatrix} x_1 M^{-1} & x_1 M^{-2} & \cdots & x_1 M^{-t+1} \\ 0 & x_2 M^{-1} & \cdots & x_2 M^{-t+2} \\ \vdots & \vdots & \ddots & \vdots \\ 0 & 0 & \cdots & x_{t-1}M^{-1} \\ 0 & 0 & \cdots & 0 \end{bmatrix} \begin{bmatrix} \eta_2 \\ \eta_3 \\ \vdots \\ \eta_{t-1} \\ \eta_t \end{bmatrix}$$

$$\tag{28}$$

The filtered estimate $\beta_{t|t}$ is equivalent to the estimate of β_t in the regression model (28) by Aitken's generalized least squares. The covariance matrix of the residuals in this regression is $\sigma^2[I_t + A_t(I_{t-1} \otimes P)A_t']$, where $\sigma^2 P = \text{Cov } \eta_i$ and A_t is the coefficient of $[\eta_2 \quad \eta_3 \quad \cdots \quad \eta_t]'$ in (28).

Similarly, $\beta_{t+s} = M^s\beta_t + M^{s-1}\eta_{t+1} + \cdots + M\eta_{t+s-1} + \eta_{t+s}$ is a function of β_t and observations on y_{t+s} ($s = 1, \ldots, n$) can be used to form a regression model with β_t as the coefficient

$$
\begin{bmatrix} y_{t+1} \\ y_{t+2} \\ \vdots \\ y_{t+n} \end{bmatrix} = \begin{bmatrix} x_{t+1}M \\ x_{t+2}M^2 \\ \vdots \\ x_{t+n}M^n \end{bmatrix} \beta_t + \begin{bmatrix} \epsilon_{t+1} \\ \epsilon_{t+2} \\ \vdots \\ \epsilon_{t+n} \end{bmatrix} - \begin{bmatrix} x_{t+1} & 0 & \cdots & 0 \\ x_{t+2}M & x_{t+2} & \cdots & 0 \\ \vdots & & \ddots & \\ x_{t+n}M^{n-1} & x_{t+n}M^{n-2} & \cdots & x_{t+n} \end{bmatrix} \begin{bmatrix} \eta_{t+1} \\ \eta_{t+2} \\ \vdots \\ \eta_{t+n} \end{bmatrix}
$$

(29)

The smoothed estimate $\beta_{t|t+n}$ is equivalent to the estimate of β_t in a regression model combining (28) and (29) by Aitken's generalized least squares.

A by-product of this interpretation should be noted. Whereas the recursive method of Sec. 10.2 requires the initial values $\beta_{0|0}$ and $\Sigma_{0|0}$, the GLS method of this section provides estimates of $\beta_{k|k}$ and $\Sigma_{k|k}$ by using the first k observations, β_t being a vector of k elements. Applying GLS to (28) for $t = k$ gives

$$
\Sigma_{k|k} = \sigma^2 \left\{ [M'^{-k+1}x_1' \quad M'^{-k+2}x_2' \quad \cdots \quad x_k'] \right.
$$
$$
\left. \cdot [I_k + A_k(I_{k-1} \otimes P)A_k']^{-1} \begin{bmatrix} x_1 M^{-k+1} \\ x_2 M^{-k+2} \\ \vdots \\ x_k \end{bmatrix} \right\}^{-1}
$$

(30)

and

$$
\beta_{k|k} = \sigma^{-2}\Sigma_{k|k}[M'^{-k+1}x_1' \quad M'^{-k+2}x_2' \quad \cdots \quad x_k']
$$
$$
\cdot [I_k + A_k(I_{k+1} \otimes P)A_k']^{-1} \begin{bmatrix} y_1 \\ \vdots \\ y_k \end{bmatrix}
$$

(31)

$\Sigma_{k|k}$ is a function of σ^2, $P = \sigma^{-2}V$, and M; $\beta_{k|k}$ is a function of P and M since $\sigma^{-2}\Sigma_{k|k} = R_k^*$ can be computed from (8) and (10) using these parameters.

10.4 MAXIMUM-LIKELIHOOD ESTIMATION OF σ^2, V, AND M

To form the likelihood function we note that

$$
y_t - y_{t|t-1} = x_t(\beta_t - \beta_{t|t-1}) + \epsilon_t = y_t - x_t\beta_{t|t-1}
$$

is normal and serially uncorrelated. $\beta_t - \beta_{t|t-1}$ is the residual in the regression of β_t on $y_{t-1}, y_{t-2}, \ldots$ and is therefore uncorrelated with $y_{t-1} - y_{t-1|t-2}$. Hence,

$y_t - y_{t|t-1}$ is uncorrelated with $y_{t-1} - y_{t-1|t-2}$. The log-likelihood function based on observations $(y_1, \ldots, y_T)$ is

$$\log L = \text{const} - \frac{1}{2} \sum_{t=k+1}^{T} \log (x_t \Sigma_{t|t-1} x_t' + \sigma^2) - \frac{1}{2} \sum_{t=k+1}^{T} \frac{(y_t - x_t \beta_{t|t-1})^2}{x_t \Sigma_{t|t-1} x_t' + \sigma^2}$$

The first k observations are used to compute $\beta_{k|k}$ and $\Sigma_{k|k}$ by (30) and (31) as functions of σ^2, V, and M. Hence the data $\beta_{t|t-1}$ and $\Sigma_{t|t-1}$ $(t = k + 1, \ldots, T)$ required to evaluate $\log L$ are functions of σ^2, V, and M, as given by the Kalman filtering equations (8), (10), (7), (4), and (6).

To maximize $\log L$ with respect to σ^2, we define $P \equiv \sigma^{-2} V$, $R_t \equiv \sigma^{-2} \Sigma_{t|t-1}$, and $u_t \equiv (y_t - x_t \beta_{t|t-1})/(x_t R_t x_t' + 1)^{1/2}$. The log-likelihood function can be rewritten as

$$\log L = \text{const} - \tfrac{1}{2}(T - k) \log \sigma^2 - \tfrac{1}{2} \sum_{t=k+1}^{T} \log (x_t R_t x_t' + 1) - \frac{1}{2\sigma^2} \sum_{t=k+1}^{T} u_t^2 \quad (32)$$

On maximizing (32) with respect to σ^2 we obtain

$$\hat{\sigma}^2 = \frac{1}{T - k} \sum_{t=k+1}^{T} u_t^2 \quad (33)$$

After the elimination of σ^2 the concentrated likelihood function is

$$\log L^* = \text{const} - \tfrac{1}{2}(T - k) \log \left[\sum_{t=k+1}^{T} \frac{(y_t - x_t \beta_{t|t-1})^2}{x_t R_t x_t' + 1} \right]$$

$$- \tfrac{1}{2} \sum_{t=k+1}^{T} \log (x_t R_t x_t' + 1) \quad (34)$$

where, by (8) and (10),

$$R_t = M R_{t-1}[I - x_{t-1}'(x_{t-1} R_{t-1} x_{t-1}' + 1)^{-1} x_{t-1} R_{t-1}]M' + P$$
$$(t = k + 2, \ldots, T) \quad (35)$$

and, by (7), (4), and (6)

$$\beta_{t|t-1} = M[\beta_{t-1|t-2} + R_{t-1} x_{t-1}'(x_{t-1} R_{t-1} x_{t-1}' + 1)^{-1}$$
$$\cdot (y_{t-1} - x_{t-1}\beta_{t-1|t-2})] \quad t = k + 2, \ldots, T \quad (36)$$

The initial conditions are

$$R_{k+1} = \sigma^{-2} M \Sigma_{k|k} M' + P \quad (37)$$

and
$$\beta_{k+1|k} = M \beta_{k|k} \quad (38)$$

with $\Sigma_{k|k}$ and $\beta_{k|k}$ given by (30) and (31). One would have to rely on a numerical method to maximize (34) with respect to the unknown parameters in P and M, P being symmetric and positive semidefinite. Garbade (1977) gives an example.

An alternative expression of the likelihood function can be obtained by using the normal regression model (28) for $t = T$, that is,

$$y = Z\beta + \epsilon - A\eta \qquad (39)$$

where
$$y = \begin{bmatrix} y_1 \\ y_2 \\ \vdots \\ y_T \end{bmatrix} \quad z = \begin{bmatrix} x_1 M^{-T+1} \\ x_2 M^{T+2} \\ \vdots \\ x_T \end{bmatrix} \quad \epsilon = \begin{bmatrix} \epsilon_1 \\ \epsilon_2 \\ \vdots \\ \epsilon_T \end{bmatrix} \quad \eta = \begin{bmatrix} \eta_2 \\ \eta_3 \\ \vdots \\ \eta_T \end{bmatrix}$$

$\beta = \beta_T$ and $A = A_T$ as defined by the last coefficient matrix of (28) for $t = T$. The log-likelihood function of this model is

$$\log L = \text{const} - \tfrac{1}{2} \log |\sigma^2 I_T| - \tfrac{1}{2} \log |Q| - \frac{\tfrac{1}{2}(y - Z\beta)'Q^{-1}(y - Z\beta)}{\sigma^2} \qquad (40)$$

where
$$Q = I_T + A(I_{T-1} \otimes P)A' \qquad (41)$$

Maximization of (40) with respect to σ^2 yields

$$\hat{\sigma}^2 = \frac{1}{T}(y - Z\beta)'Q^{-1}(y - Z\beta) \qquad (42)$$

Maximization of (40) with respect to β yields

$$\hat{\beta} = (Z'Q^{-1}Z)^{-1}Z'Q^{-1}y \qquad (43)$$

Differentiating (40) with respect to the unknown elements $p_{ij} = p_{ji}$ of P gives

$$\frac{\partial \log L}{\partial p_{ij}} = -\text{tr}\left(Q^{-1}\frac{\partial Q}{\partial p_{ij}}\right) - \sigma^2(y - Z\beta)'\frac{\partial Q^{-1}}{\partial p_{ij}}(y - Z\beta) \qquad (44)$$

To evaluate $\partial Q^{-1}/\partial p_{ij}$ we differentiate both sides of $QQ^{-1} = I$ with respect to p_{ij} to get

$$\frac{\partial Q^{-1}}{\partial p_{ij}} = -Q^{-1}\frac{\partial Q}{\partial p_{ij}}Q^{-1} \qquad (45)$$

Using the definition (41) for Q, we have

$$\frac{\partial Q}{\partial p_{ij}} = A(I_{T-1} \otimes E_{ij})A' \qquad (46)$$

where E_{ij} is an elementary $k \times k$ matrix with all zero elements except the ijth and jith elements, which equal unity. Substituting (42), (43), (45), and (46) into (44) gives

$$\frac{\partial \log L}{\partial p_{ij}} = -\text{tr}\left[Q^{-1}A(I_{T-1} \otimes E_{ij})A'\right]$$

$$+ \left(\frac{1}{T}y'N'Q^{-1}y\right)^{-1}y'N'Q^{-1}A(I_{T-1} \otimes E_{ij})A'Q^{-1}Ny \qquad (47)$$

where N denotes $I - Z(Z'Q^{-1}Z)^{-1}Z'Q^{-1}$. Equation (47) is useful for maximizing (40) when a numerical method requiring analytical first derivatives is applied. Furthermore, in econometric applications M is frequently assumed to be an indentity matrix and P to be diagonal. In this important special case, after the substitution of (42) and (43), the only unknown parameters in (40) are $p_{11} \cdots p_{kk}$. One can start with zero as the initial value for each p_{ii} and increase its value if $(\partial \log L)/\partial p_{ii}$ as evaluated by (47) is positive, using a gradient method of Sec. 7.5.

For the general case, we substitute (42) and (43) for σ^2 and β in (40) to yield

$$\log L^* = \text{const} - \tfrac{1}{2} \log |\sigma^2 Q| = \text{const} - \tfrac{1}{2} \log |y'N'Q^{-1}y|$$

Numerical methods can be applied to maximize $\log L^*$ with respect to the unknown parameters in P and M. For a discussion of conditions for the identifiability of these parameters and the asymptotic distribution of the maximum-likelihood estimator, see Sec. 10.9.

★10.5 SYSTEM OF LINEAR REGRESSIONS WITH TIME-VARYING COEFFICIENTS

A generalization of the regression model of Eqs. (1) and (2) is a system of m linear regressions with time-varying coefficients

$$\begin{bmatrix} y_{1t} \\ \vdots \\ y_{mt} \end{bmatrix} = \begin{bmatrix} x_{1t} & & 0 \\ & \ddots & \\ 0 & & x_{mt} \end{bmatrix} \begin{bmatrix} \beta_{1t} \\ \vdots \\ \beta_{mt} \end{bmatrix} + \begin{bmatrix} \epsilon_1 \\ \vdots \\ \epsilon_{mt} \end{bmatrix} \qquad t = 1, \ldots, T \tag{48}$$

$$\begin{bmatrix} \beta_{1t} \\ \vdots \\ \beta_{mt} \end{bmatrix} = \begin{bmatrix} M_1 & & 0 \\ & \ddots & \\ 0 & & M_m \end{bmatrix} \begin{bmatrix} \beta_{1, t-1} \\ \vdots \\ \beta_{m, t-1} \end{bmatrix} + \begin{bmatrix} \eta_{1t} \\ \vdots \\ \eta_{mt} \end{bmatrix} \qquad t = 1, \ldots, T \tag{49}$$

where x_{jt} is a row vector of k_j explanatory variables and $[\epsilon_{1t} \ \cdots \ \epsilon_{mt}]$ is m-variate normal and independent with mean zero and covariance matrix $\Sigma = (\sigma_{ij})$. This Σ, without subscript, should be distinguished from $\Sigma_{t|s} = \text{Cov}(\beta_t | Y_s)$ in (8); η_{jt} is k_j-variate normal and independent with mean zero and covariance matrix $V_j = \sigma_{jj} P_j$, being independent of η_{it} for $i \neq j$. If σ_{ij} were zero for $i \neq j$, the m regression models would be treated separately, each by the methods previously presented. When $\sigma_{ij} \neq 0$, efficiency in estimating β_{jt} can be gained by combining the m regressions into a system.

If we write (48) and (49) more compactly as

$$y'_{.t} = X_t \beta_{.t} + \epsilon_{.t} \tag{50}$$
$$\beta_{.t} = M\beta_{.t-1} + \eta_{.t} \tag{51}$$
$$t = 1, \ldots, T$$

the filtering and smoothing equations of Sec. 10.2 remain entirely valid for this model, with σ^2, V_1, ..., V_m, and M treated as given. The derivations are the same as in Sec. 10.2, with the scalar y_t replaced by the column vector y'_t, the row vector x_t by the $m \times (\Sigma_j k_j)$ matrix X_t, and the variance σ^2 by the covariance matrix Σ of the vector $\epsilon_{.t}$. K_t in (6) becomes a $(\Sigma_j k_j) \times m$ matrix.

For the estimation of Σ, V_1, ..., V_m, and M, we write the T observations on the jth regression model with coefficient $\beta_{jT} = \beta_j$ in the notation of (39) as

$$y_j = Z_j \beta_j + \epsilon_j - A_j \eta_j \tag{52}$$

where the residual vector $\epsilon_j - A_j \eta_j$ has covariance matrix $\sigma_{jj} Q_j$, with

$$Q_j = I_T + A_j (I_{T-1} \otimes P_j) A'_j \tag{53}$$

Combining the m regression models, we have

$$\begin{bmatrix} y_1 \\ \vdots \\ y_m \end{bmatrix} = \begin{bmatrix} Z_1 & & 0 \\ & \ddots & \\ 0 & & Z_m \end{bmatrix} \begin{bmatrix} \beta_1 \\ \vdots \\ \beta_m \end{bmatrix} + \begin{bmatrix} \epsilon_1 \\ \vdots \\ \epsilon_m \end{bmatrix} - \begin{bmatrix} A_1 \eta_1 \\ \vdots \\ A_m \eta_m \end{bmatrix} \tag{54}$$

where the residual vector has covariance matrix

$$\Phi = \begin{bmatrix} \sigma_{11} Q_1 & \sigma_{12} I & \cdots & \sigma_{1m} I \\ \sigma_{12} I & \sigma_{22} Q_2 & \cdots & \sigma_{2m} I \\ \multicolumn{4}{c}{\dotfill} \\ \sigma_{1m} I & \sigma_{2m} I & \cdots & \sigma_{mm} Q_m \end{bmatrix}$$

$$\Phi^{-1} = \begin{bmatrix} \sigma^{11} Q_1^{-1} & \sigma^{12} I & \cdots & \sigma^{1m} I \\ \sigma^{12} I & \sigma^{22} Q_2^{-1} & \cdots & \sigma^{2m} I \\ \multicolumn{4}{c}{\dotfill} \\ \sigma^{1m} I & \sigma^{2m} I & \cdots & \sigma^{mm} Q_m^{-1} \end{bmatrix} \tag{55}$$

σ^{ij} denoting the ijth element of Σ^{-1}.

The log-likelihood function for model (54) is

$$\log L = \text{const} - \tfrac{1}{2} \log |\Phi| - \tfrac{1}{2} \sum_{i=1}^{m} (y_1 - Z_i \beta_i)' Q^{-1} (y_i - Z_i \beta_i) \sigma^{ii}$$

$$- \sum_{i<j}^{m} (y_i - Z_i \beta_i)'(y_j - Z_j \beta_j) \sigma^{ij} \tag{56}$$

Observing that

$$\frac{\partial \log |\Phi|}{\partial \sigma^{ii}} = -\frac{\partial \log |\Phi^{-1}|}{\partial \sigma^{ii}} = -\text{tr}\left(\Phi \frac{\partial \Phi^{-1}}{\partial \sigma^{ii}}\right) = -T \sigma_{ii}$$

and

$$\frac{\partial \log |\Phi|}{\partial \sigma^{ij}} = -2 \, \text{tr}\left(\Phi \frac{\partial \Phi^{-1}}{\partial \sigma^{ij}}\right) = -2T \sigma_{ij} \qquad \begin{array}{c} \sigma_{ij} = \sigma_{ji} \\ i \neq j \end{array}$$

we differentiate (56) with respect to σ^{ii} and σ^{ij} to obtain

$$\hat{\sigma}_{ii} = \frac{1}{T} (y_i - Z_i \beta_i)' Q_i^{-1} (y_i - Z_i \beta_i) \tag{57}$$

and

$$\hat{\sigma}_{ij} = \frac{1}{T} (y_i - Z_i \beta_i)'(y_j - Z_j \beta_j) \qquad i \neq j \tag{58}$$

Equation (57) is identical with (42) and shows that $\hat{\sigma}_{ii}$ can be obtained from the residuals $y_i - Z_i \beta_i$ of only the ith regression if the parameters P_i and M_i are known. Equation (58) shows that σ_{ij} $(i \neq j)$ is the sample covariance of the residuals in the ith and jth regressions and is independent of P_i and P_j.

Differentiating (56) with respect to β_i gives

$$\frac{\partial \log L}{\partial \beta_i} = \sigma^{ii} Z_i' Q_i^{-1}(y_i - Z_i \beta_i) + Z_i' \sum_{j \neq i}^{m} \sigma^{ij}(y_j - Z_j \beta_j) = 0$$

Combining the above equations for $i = 1, \ldots, m$, we have

$$\begin{bmatrix} \sigma^{11} Z_1' Q_1^{-1} Z_1 & \sigma^{12} Z_1' Z_2 & \cdots & \sigma^{1m} Z_1' Z_m \\ \cdots\cdots\cdots\cdots\cdots\cdots\cdots\cdots\cdots\cdots\cdots\cdots \\ \sigma^{m1} Z_m' Z_1 & \sigma^{m2} Z_m' Z_2 & \cdots & \sigma^{mm} Z_m' Q_m^{-1} Z_m \end{bmatrix} \begin{bmatrix} \beta_1 \\ . \\ \beta_m \end{bmatrix}$$

$$= \begin{bmatrix} Z_1' \left(\sigma^{11} Q_1^{-1} y_1 + \sum_{j \neq 1} \sigma^{ij} y_j \right) \\ \\ Z_m' \left(\sigma^{mm} Q_m^{-1} y_m + \sum_{j \neq m} \sigma^{mj} y_j \right) \end{bmatrix} \tag{59}$$

Differentiating (56) with respect to the ijth element $p_{k,ij}$ of P_k yields

$$\frac{\partial \log L}{\partial p_{k,ij}} = -\text{tr} \left(\Phi^{-1} \frac{\partial \Phi}{\partial p_{k,ij}} \right) - (y_k - Z_k \beta_k)' \frac{\partial Q_k^{-1}}{\partial p_{k,ij}} (y_k - Z_k \beta_k)$$

$$= -\text{tr} \left(\sigma^{kk} \sigma_{kk} Q_k^{-1} \frac{\partial Q_k}{\partial p_{k,ij}} \right)$$

$$+ (y_k - Z_k \beta_k)' Q_k^{-1} \frac{\partial Q_k}{\partial p_{k,ij}} Q_k^{-1}(y_k - Z_k \beta_k)$$

$$= -\sigma^{kk} \sigma_{kk} \, \text{tr} \left[Q_k^{-1} A_k (I_{T-1} \otimes E_{ij}) A_k' \right]$$

$$+ (y_k - Z_k \beta_k)' Q_k^{-1} A_k (I_{T-1} \otimes E_{ij}) A_k' Q_k^{-1}(y_k - Z_k \beta_k) \tag{60}$$

The maximization of log L with respect to P_k $(k = 1, \ldots, m)$ can proceed iteratively as follows. First consider the important case with $M_1, \ldots, M_m$ given. Starting with $P_k = 0$ for all k, which implies $Q_k = I_T$, solve (57) to (59) for $\hat{\sigma}_{ij}$ and

$\hat{\beta}_i$ (all i, j) as a standard problem of estimating a system of linear regressions. Use (60) to find the gradient of log L with respect to the unknown elements $p_{k,ij}$ and apply a gradient method to maximize log L with $\hat{\sigma}_{ij}$ and $\hat{\beta}_i$ (all i, j) treated as fixed. By (56), log L equals const $-\frac{1}{2}\log|\Phi|$, where σ_{ij} is replaced by $\hat{\sigma}_{ij}$. Having revised $p_{k,ij}$, solve (57) to (59) again for $\hat{\sigma}_{ij}$ and $\hat{\beta}_i$, and so forth. In practice, the computational burden is not as heavy as it appears because only a small number of equations k will contain time-varying coefficients and for those equations P_k are often assumed to be diagonal with a few unknown $p_{k,ij}$.

The computational problem becomes more difficult in the general case with unknown elements in M_k. We shall still treat σ_{ij} and β_i (all i, j) separately from the unknown parameters in M_k and P_k ($k = 1, \ldots, m$). Given the latter, (57) to (59) will be used to estimate $\hat{\sigma}_{ij}$ and $\hat{\beta}_i$. Given $\hat{\sigma}_{ij}$, we maximize log $L =$ const $-\frac{1}{2}\log|\Phi|$ with respect to the unknown parameters in M_k and P_k by some numerical method.

For both the special and the general case an approximate solution to the problem of maximum likelihood is to ignore the interdependence of the m regressions due to the covariances σ_{ij} and to treat the estimation of P_k and M_k separately for each regression k by the method of Sec. 10.4. This approximation is appealing because, without pooling the m regressions, the GLS estimate of β_k for each regression k is still consistent; so are the associated estimates of the unknown elements of P_k and M_k. They correspond to the estimates of the parameters of one structural equation in a system of simultaneous equations by a limited-information method such as 2SLS. Having so obtained the estimates of P_k and M_k, one can pool the regression equations to estimate σ_{ij} and β_i by (57) to (59). Or, as a further approximation, treat the estimates of σ_{ij} as given and use (59) alone to reestimate β_i ($i = 1, \ldots, m$). This procedure corresponds to 3SLS where the estimates of the covariance matrix of the residuals are obtained by 2SLS.

The above discussion has concentrated on the estimation of $\beta_k \equiv \beta_{kT}$ for the last period and the associated covariance matrices Σ and P_k. Given estimates of Σ and P_k and the initial values $\beta_{k:\tau|\tau}$ and $\Sigma_{k:\tau|\tau}$ as obtained by (59) using τ observations, we can apply the filtering and smoothing algorithms to (50) and (51) to estimate $\beta_{k:t|t}$ and $\beta_{k:t|T}$ for $t > \tau$.

★10.6 SYSTEM OF LINEAR SIMULTANEOUS EQUATIONS

Let the tth observation of a system of m linear simultaneous equations with time-varying coefficients be written as

$$y_{.t}B_t + x_{.t}\Gamma_t = -\epsilon'_{.t} \qquad t = 1, \ldots, T \tag{61}$$

where $y_{.t} = [y_{1t} \cdots y_{mt}]$ is a row vector of m endogenous variables, $x_{.t}$ is a row vector of K exogenous variables, and the diagonal elements $\beta_{ii,t}$ of B_t are normalized to -1. (Note that B and Γ are the transposes of the B and Γ matrices defined in Chaps. 4 and 5.) The reduced form of (61) is

$$y_{.t} = -x_{.t}\Gamma_t B_t^{-1} - \epsilon'_{.t}B_t^{-1} \equiv x_{.t}\Pi_t + u'_{.t} \qquad t = 1, \ldots, T \qquad (62)$$

where we have defined Π_t as $-\Gamma_t B_t^{-1}$ and $u'_{.t}$ as $-\epsilon'_{.t}B_t^{-1}$. The jth structural equation can be written as

$$y_{jt} = y^*_{jt}\beta_{jt} + x^*_{jt}\gamma_{jt} + \epsilon_{jt} \equiv z^*_{jt}\delta_{jt} + \epsilon_{jt} \qquad (63)$$

where y^*_{jt} is a row vector of endogenous variables appearing in equation j, other than y_{jt}; β_{jt} is a column vector of unknown coefficients in equation j composed of selected elements from the jth column $\beta_{.jt}$ of B_t; and similarly for x^*_{jt} and γ_{jt}. We have also defined z^*_{jt} as $[y^*_{jt} \ x^*_{jt}]$ and δ'_{jt} as $[\beta'_{jt} \ \gamma'_{jt}]$.

Corresponding to (48) and (49) are

$$\begin{bmatrix} y_{1t} \\ \vdots \\ y_{mt} \end{bmatrix} = \begin{bmatrix} z^*_{1t} & & 0 \\ & \ddots & \\ 0 & & z^*_{mt} \end{bmatrix} \begin{bmatrix} \delta_{1t} \\ \vdots \\ \delta_{mt} \end{bmatrix} + \begin{bmatrix} \epsilon_{1t} \\ \vdots \\ \epsilon_{mt} \end{bmatrix} \qquad t = 1, \ldots, T \qquad (64)$$

$$\begin{bmatrix} \delta_{1t} \\ \vdots \\ \delta_{mt} \end{bmatrix} = \begin{bmatrix} M_1 & & 0 \\ & \ddots & \\ 0 & & M_m \end{bmatrix} \begin{bmatrix} \delta_{1,t-1} \\ \vdots \\ \delta_{m,t-1} \end{bmatrix} + \begin{bmatrix} \eta_{1t} \\ \vdots \\ \eta_{mt} \end{bmatrix} \qquad t = 1, \ldots, T \qquad (65)$$

as we are making similar assumptions about the evolution of δ_{jt}. However, the techniques of Sec. 10.5 cannot be applied directly to (64) and (65) because (64), unlike (48) or (1), is a nonlinear function of the random coefficient vector $\delta_t = [\delta'_{1t} \cdots \delta'_{mt}]$. The y^*_{jt} component of z^*_{jt} is itself a nonlinear function of $[\beta'_{1t} \cdots \beta'_{mt}]$, as seen from the reduced form (62). In order to apply the techniques of Sec. 10.5 it is proposed to approximate the right-hand side of (62) by a linear function of δ_t and $\epsilon_{.t}$. This approach amounts to treating a regression problem involving a nonlinear model $y = f(x, \beta, \epsilon)$ by approximating f by a linear function of β and ϵ. In the control engineering literature, the resulting estimation method is known as an *extended Kalman filter*.

We shall linearize the right-hand side of (62) about $\delta^0_t = \delta_{t|t-1}$. First we linearize Π_t about δ^0_t and define

$$\Pi^0_t = -(\Gamma_{t|t-1})(B_{t|t-1})^{-1} = [\pi^0_{1t} \cdots \pi^0_{mt}] \qquad (66)$$

The jth column of Π_t is $\pi_{jt} = -\Gamma_t \beta^{.j}_t$, where $\beta^{.j}_t$ denotes the jth column of B_t^{-1}. The linear approximation of π_{jt} is

$$\pi_{jt} \approx \pi^0_{jt} + \left(\frac{\partial \pi_{jt}}{\partial \delta'_t}\right)_0 (\delta_t - \delta_{t|t-1}) \qquad (67)$$

where the subscript 0 indicates that the matrix $\partial \pi_{jt}/\partial \delta'_t$ is evaluated at $\delta^0_t = \delta_{t|t-1}$. To evaluate the matrix $\partial \pi_{jt}/\partial \delta'_t$ we note that, using Eq. (106) of Chap. 5,

$$\frac{\partial \pi_{jt}}{\partial \beta_{ik,t}} = -\Gamma_t \frac{\partial \beta^{.j}_i}{\partial \beta_{ik,t}} = \Gamma_t \beta^{.i}_t \beta^{kj}_t$$

or, with $\beta_{.k,t}$ denoting the kth column of B_t,

$$\frac{\partial \pi_{jt}}{\partial \beta'_{.k,t}} = \Gamma_t B_t^{-1} \beta_t^{kj} = -\Pi_t \beta_t^{kj} \tag{68}$$

and

$$\frac{\partial \pi_{jt}}{\partial \gamma_{ik,t}} = -\frac{\partial \Gamma_t}{\partial \gamma_{ik,t}} \beta_t^{.j} = -\begin{bmatrix} 0 \\ \vdots \\ \beta_t^{kj} \\ \vdots \\ 0 \end{bmatrix} \quad (\beta_t^{kj} \text{ in } i\text{th row})$$

or, with $\gamma_{.k,t}$ denoting the kth column of Γ_t,

$$\frac{\partial \pi_{jt}}{\partial \gamma'_{.k,t}} = -I_K \beta_t^{kj} \tag{69}$$

Hence the matrix $(\partial \pi_{jt}/\partial \delta'_t)_0$ of (67) can be evaluated by (68) and (69) with Π_t replaced by Π_t^0 and B_t^{-1} replaced by $B_t^{0-1} = B_{t|t-1}^{-1}$. Similarly, approximating $-\epsilon'_{.t} B_t^{-1}$ by a linear function of $\epsilon_{.t}$ and $[\beta_{1t} \cdots \beta_{mt}]$ about $\epsilon_{.t} = 0$ and $[\beta_{1t} \cdots \beta_{mt}] = [\beta_{1t|t-1} \cdots \beta_{mt|t-1}]$ yields $-\epsilon'_{.t} B_{t|t-1}^{-1}$. Combining this result with (67) and denoting $x_{.t} \pi_{jt}^0$ by y_{jt}^0, we can write the linearized version of (the transpose of) (62) as

$$\begin{bmatrix} y_{1t} \\ \vdots \\ y_{mt} \end{bmatrix} = \begin{bmatrix} y_{1t}^0 \\ \vdots \\ y_{mt}^0 \end{bmatrix} + \begin{bmatrix} x_{.t} \left(\dfrac{\partial \pi_{1t}}{\partial \delta'_t} \right)_0 \\ \vdots \\ x_{.t} \left(\dfrac{\partial \pi_{mt}}{\partial \delta'_t} \right)_0 \end{bmatrix} (\delta_t - \delta_{t|t-1}) - B_{t|t-1}^{'-1} \epsilon_{.t} \tag{70}$$

or more compactly as

$$y'_{.t} = y_{.t}^{0'} + W_t^0 (\delta_t - \delta_{t|t-1}) - B_{t|t-1}^{'-1} \epsilon_{.t} \tag{71}$$

where the jth row of W_t^0 is, by (68) and (69),

$$x_{.t} \frac{\partial \pi_{jt}}{\partial \delta'_t} = -\{ [y_{1t}^{*0} \quad x_{1t}^*] \beta_{t|t-1}^{1j} \quad \cdots \quad [y_{mt}^{*0} \quad x_{mt}^*] \beta_{t|t-1}^{mj} \}$$
$$= -[z_{1t}^{*0} \beta_{t|t-1}^{1j} \quad \cdots \quad z_{mt}^{*0} \beta_{t|t-1}^{mj}] \tag{72}$$

with y_{it}^{*0} denoting a row vector composed of those elements of $y_{.t}^0 = x_{.t} \Pi_t^0$ which correspond to β_{it}.

The linearized model (71) will replace (48) or (50) for the purpose of deriving filtering equations. For the model of Eqs. (71) and (65), the derivations are exactly the same as in Sec. 10.5 or 10.2 with $\Sigma = E\epsilon_{.t}\epsilon'_{.t}$, $V_i = E\eta_{it}\eta'_{it}$ $(i = 1, \ldots, m)$, and M_i $(i = 1, \ldots, m)$ treated as given. From the linear model (71) one finds the conditional expectation $y'_{.t|t-1}$ to be $y_{.t}^{0'}$. Repeating the derivations from (4) to (10) one finds

$$\delta_{t|t} = \delta_{t|t-1} + K_t(y'_{.t} - y'_{.t|t-1}) \tag{73}$$

and, denoting $E(\delta_t - \delta_{t|t-1})(\delta_t - \delta_{t|t-1})'$ by $\Sigma_{t|t-1}$, etc.,

$$K_t = \Sigma_{t|t-1} W_t^{0\prime}(W_t^0 \Sigma_{t|t-1} W_t^{0\prime} + B_{t|t-1}^{\prime -1} S B_{t|t-1}^{-1})^{-1} \tag{74}$$

Corresponding to (8), (10), and (7) are respectively

$$\Sigma_{t|t-1} = M \Sigma_{t-1|t-1} M' + V \tag{75}$$

where M is the coefficient matrix of (65) and V the covariance matrix of its residual $\eta_t' = [\eta_{1t}' \quad \cdots \quad \eta_{mt}']$,

$$\Sigma_{t|t} = \Sigma_{t|t-1} - K_t(W_t^0 \Sigma_{t|t-1} W_t^{0\prime} + B_{t|t-1}^{\prime -1} S B_{t|t-1}^{-1})K_t' \tag{76}$$

and

$$\delta_{t|t-1} = M \delta_{t|t-1} \tag{77}$$

An alternative way of estimating $\delta_{T|T}$ given Σ, V_i, and M_i is to form a regression model analogous to (28) using (71) for $y_{.t}'$ ($t = 1, \ldots, T$) and denoting $y_{.t}' - y_{.t}^{0\prime} + W_t^0 \delta_{t|t-1}$ by $\tilde{y}_{.t}'$

$$
\begin{bmatrix} \tilde{y}_{.1}' \\ \tilde{y}_{.2}' \\ \vdots \\ \tilde{y}_{.T-1}' \\ \tilde{y}_{.T}' \end{bmatrix}
=
\begin{bmatrix} W_1^0 M^{-T+1} \\ W_2^0 M^{-T+2} \\ \vdots \\ W_{T-1}^0 M^{-1} \\ M_T^0 \end{bmatrix}
\delta_T -
\begin{bmatrix} B_1^{0\prime-1}\epsilon_{.1} \\ B_2^{0\prime-1}\epsilon_{.2} \\ \vdots \\ B_{T-1}^{0\prime-1}\epsilon_{.T-1} \\ B_T^{0\prime-1}\epsilon_{.T} \end{bmatrix}
$$

$$
-
\begin{bmatrix} W_1^0 M^{-1} & W_1^0 M^{-2} & \cdots & W_1^0 M^{-T+1} \\ & W_2^0 M^{-1} & \cdots & W_2^0 M^{-T+2} \\ & & \ddots & \\ \mathbf{0} & & & W_{T-1}^0 M^{-1} \\ & & & 0 \end{bmatrix}
\begin{bmatrix} \eta_2 \\ \eta_3 \\ \vdots \\ \eta_{T-1} \\ \eta_T \end{bmatrix}
\tag{78}
$$

The covariance matrix of the residual vector of (78) has an ijth block

$$\delta_{ij} B_i^{0\prime-1} \Sigma B_i^{0-1} + W_i^0 \sum_{t=\max(i,j)}^{T-1} M^{-(t-i+1)} V M'^{-(t-j+1)} W_j^{0\prime} \tag{79}$$

where δ_{ij} is the Kronecker delta. Aitken's generalized least squares can be applied to estimate δ_T once the coefficients W_t^0 and B_t^0 of the linearized model (71) have been evaluated. One can choose an initial guess δ_T^0 for $\delta_{T|T}$ and the associated $\delta_t^0 = M^{-(T-t)}\delta_T^0$ ($t = 1, \ldots, T$). These initial values permit the evaluation of W_t^0, B_t^0, $y_{.t}^0 = -x_{.t}\Gamma_t^0 B_t^{0-1}$, and $\delta_{t|t-1} = \delta_t^0$. Equation (78) will be treated as a linear regression model to estimate $\delta_{T|T}$. The resulting estimate will be used to form a new initial guess δ_T^0, and the process continues iteratively.

In order to estimate the unknown parameters in Σ, V_i ($i = 1, \ldots, m$), and M_i ($i = 1, \ldots, m$) (78) can be used to form a likelihood function. However, unlike the situation with truly constant coefficients W_t^0 and B_t^0, the evaluation of the likelihood function requires iterative solution of $\delta_{T|T}$, as described in the last paragraph. Hence the computational problem involved in maximizing the likelihood function is more burdensome than for a truly linear (in contrast with a linearized) model. This problem deserves further study. Furthermore, the normal likelihood function is only an approximation because the residuals of the linearized model (78) are not normal; $B_t^{0'-1}\epsilon_{.t}$ is not normal since the coefficient matrix $B_t^{0'-1} = B_{t|t-1}^{'-1}$ is not constant but a function of random variables via the Kalman filter. Therefore, the sampling distribution of the resulting estimates is difficult to establish.

★ 10.7 SYSTEM OF NONLINEAR SIMULTANEOUS EQUATIONS

Let the tth observation of a system of m nonlinear simultaneous equations with time-varying parameters be written as

$$y_{.t}' = \Phi(y_{.t}, x_{.t}, \delta_t) + \epsilon_{.t} \qquad t = 1, \ldots, T \qquad (80)$$

where Φ is a vector function of m components and

$$\delta_t = M\delta_{t-1} + \eta_t \qquad t = 1, \ldots, T \qquad (81)$$

which is identical with (65). Like the reduced form (62) for a system of linear structural equations, (80) is a nonlinear function of the parameter vector δ_t. The approach to be adopted, similar to the one used in Sec. 10.6, amounts to linearizing the nonlinear observation equation (80) about some δ_t^0 and the associated $y_{.t}^0$, defined by

$$y_{.t}^{0'} = \Phi(y_{.t}^0, x_{.t}, \delta_t^0)$$

Given δ_t^0 and $x_{.t}$, $y_{.t}^0$ can be computed by the Gauss-Seidel method, for example.

Linearizing Φ in (80) about δ_t^0 and $y_{.t}^0$, we have

$$y_{.t}' = y_{.t}^{0'} + \left(\frac{\partial\Phi}{\partial y_{.t}}\right)_0 (y_{.t}' - y_{.t}^{0'}) + \left(\frac{\partial\Phi}{\partial\delta_t'}\right)_0 (\delta_t - \delta_t^0) + \epsilon_{.t}$$

where, as in Sec. 10.6, the zero subscript indicates that the matrix of partial derivatives of Φ is evaluated at $y_{.t}^0$ and δ_t^0. Solving for $y_{.t}'$, we get

$$y_{.t}' = y_{.t}^{0'} + \left[I - \left(\frac{\partial\Phi}{\partial y_{.t}}\right)_0\right]^{-1} \left(\frac{\partial\Phi}{\partial\delta_t'}\right)_0 (\delta_t - \delta_t^0) + \left[I - \left(\frac{\partial\Phi}{\partial y_{.t}}\right)_0\right]^{-1} \epsilon_{.t}$$

$$\equiv y_{.t}^0 + W_t^0(\delta_t - \delta_t^0) + R_t\epsilon_{.t} \qquad (82)$$

which replaces the linearized observation equation (71). The treatment of the model of Eqs. (82) and (81) is the same as in Sec. 10.6. The computational problem is only slightly more difficult because the linearization to achieve (82) requires the evaluation of the partial derivatives $(\partial\Phi/\partial y_{.t})_0$ and $(\partial\Phi/\partial\delta_t')_0$ whereas the linearization to obtain (71) requires only matrix inversion. These partial derivatives can be evaluated numerically, and their evaluation is computationally much simpler than the maximization of the likelihood function for the linearized model with respect to the parameters Σ, V_i ($i = 1, \ldots, m$), and M_i ($i = 1, \ldots, m$), as discussed at the end of Sec. 10.6.

10.8 MODEL WITH STATIONARY COEFFICIENTS

An alternative specification to (1) and (2) is

$$y_t = x_t \beta_t + \epsilon_t \tag{83}$$

$$\beta_t - \bar{\beta} = M(\beta_{t-1} - \bar{\beta}) + \eta_t \tag{84}$$

where all characteristic roots of M are assumed to be less than 1 in absolute value. In stochastic equilibrium β_t will have mean $\bar{\beta}$ and a covariance matrix Γ satisfying, according to Eq. (10) of Chap. 6,

$$\Gamma = M\Gamma M' + V$$

where, as before, V is the covariance matrix of η_t. In the special case with $M = 0$, the model of Eqs. (83) and (84) becomes a linear regression model with random coefficients.

Although the model of Eqs. (83) and (84) differs from that of (1) and (2) mainly by the introduction of the parameter vector $\bar{\beta}$, it can be rewritten in the same form as (1) and (2), so that our results in Sec. 10.2 are applicable here as well. Defining $\beta_t^* = \beta_t - \bar{\beta}$ and $\bar{\beta}_t = \bar{\beta}$ for all t, we write (83) and (84) as

$$y_t = [x_t \quad x_t] \begin{bmatrix} \bar{\beta}_t \\ \beta_t^* \end{bmatrix} + \epsilon_t \tag{85}$$

$$\begin{bmatrix} \bar{\beta}_t \\ \beta_t^* \end{bmatrix} = \begin{bmatrix} I & 0 \\ 0 & M \end{bmatrix} \begin{bmatrix} \bar{\beta}_{t-1} \\ \beta_{t-1}^* \end{bmatrix} \begin{bmatrix} 0 \\ \eta_t \end{bmatrix} \tag{86}$$

which is a special case of (1) and (2). In most applications, not all components of β_t in (84) are random. If only a subvector $\tilde{\beta}_t$ of β_t consisting of k_1 elements, say, is random, (85) and (86) will become

$$y_t = [x_t \quad \tilde{x}_t] \begin{bmatrix} \bar{\beta}_t \\ \tilde{\beta}_t^* \end{bmatrix} + \epsilon_t \tag{87}$$

$$\begin{bmatrix} \bar{\beta}_t \\ \tilde{\beta}_t^* \end{bmatrix} = \begin{bmatrix} I & 0 \\ 0 & M \end{bmatrix} \begin{bmatrix} \bar{\beta}_{t-1} \\ \tilde{\beta}_{t-1}^* \end{bmatrix} + \begin{bmatrix} 0 \\ \eta_t \end{bmatrix} \tag{88}$$

Since the model of Eqs. (87) and (88) is a special case of the model of Eqs. (1) and (2), all the filtering and smoothing equations of Sec. 10.2 and the log-likelihood functions (32) and (34) are applicable to this model. However, the estimation problem for this model deserves special treatment. Because the roots of M are less than 1 in absolute value and the process generating $\tilde{\beta}_t^*$ is covariance-stationary, one may choose to estimate this model by assuming that the $\tilde{\beta}_t^*$ process starts in a stochastic equilibrium, rather than assuming a fixed but unknown initial value $\tilde{\beta}_1^*$ in period 1. The latter assumption was made in (28), where we used the relation

$$\tilde{\beta}_t^* = M\tilde{\beta}_{t-1}^* + \eta_t = M^{t-1}\tilde{\beta}_1^* + \eta_t + M\eta_{t-1} + \cdots + M^{t-2}\eta_2$$

and treated $\tilde{\beta}_1^*$ as fixed. In estimating the model (87) and (88) one can treat $\tilde{\beta}_1^*$ as random, with mean zero and covariance matrix Γ_0 satisfying

$$\Gamma_0 = M\Gamma_0 M' + V \tag{89}$$

The autocovariance matrix for the $\tilde{\beta}_t^*$ process is

$$\Gamma_s = E\tilde{\beta}_t^* \tilde{\beta}_{t-s}^{*\prime} = M^s\Gamma_0 = \Gamma'_{-s} \qquad \begin{matrix} s \geq 0 \\ t \geq 1 \end{matrix} \tag{90}$$

If $\tilde{\beta}_1^*$ is regarded as fixed, instead of (89) and (90), the covariance matrix of $\tilde{\beta}_t^*$ and $\tilde{\beta}_{t-s}^{*\prime}$ is

$$E(\tilde{\beta}_t^* - M^{t-1}\tilde{\beta}_1^*)(\tilde{\beta}_{t-s}^* - M^{t-s-1}\tilde{\beta}_1^*)'$$

$$= E(\eta_t + M\eta_{t-1} + \cdots + M^{t-2}\eta_2)(\eta_{t-s} + M\eta_{t-s-1} + \cdots + M^{t-s-2}\eta_2)$$

$$= \sum_{i=0}^{t-s-2} M^{s+i}VM'^i \qquad \begin{matrix} s \geq 0 \\ t \geq 1 \end{matrix} \tag{91}$$

The difference in the treatment of $\tilde{\beta}_1^*$ has implications for estimation. When $\tilde{\beta}_1^*$ is regarded as fixed, all inferences are conditional on this assumption. When $\tilde{\beta}_1^*$ is regarded as a random drawing from a distribution with mean zero and covariance matrix Γ_0 as specified by (89), the inferences are no longer conditional. Furthermore, to provide the initial estimates $\beta_{k|k}$ and $\Sigma_{k|k}$ to start up the Kalman filtering equations for the evaluation of the log-likelihood functions (32) and (34) the two assumptions lead to different procedures. For fixed $\tilde{\beta}_1^*$ we regard (87) as a special case of (1). Therefore, the number of initial observations required to perform a generalized least-squares regression equals the number of elements in $\bar{\beta}_t$ and $\tilde{\beta}_t^*$, or $k + k_1$, say. Equations (30) and (31) are applied to these $k + k_1$ observations, and the analysis proceeds as before. For random $\tilde{\beta}_1^*$, (87) can be written as

$$y_t = x_t\bar{\beta} + (\tilde{x}_t\tilde{\beta}_t^* + \epsilon_t) = x_t\bar{\beta} + u_t \tag{92}$$

The term in parentheses or u_t is treated as a serially correlated residual satisfying

$$Eu_t u'_{t-s} = \tilde{x}_t\Gamma_s\tilde{x}'_{t-s} + \delta_{t,t-s}\sigma^2 \tag{93}$$

where Γ_s is defined by (90) and $\delta_{t,t-s}$ is the Kronecker delta. Therefore, given (93), only k initial observations are required to obtain a GLS estimate $\bar{\beta}_{k|k}$ of $\bar{\beta}$ and its covariance matrix. Writing the first k observations of (92) as

$$y = X\bar{\beta} + u \tag{94}$$

where X is assumed to be a nonsingular $k \times k$ matrix and $Euu' = W$ is given by

(93), we have

$$\bar{\beta}_{k|k} = (X'W^{-1}X)^{-1}X'W^{-1}y = X^{-1}y \tag{95}$$

$$\text{Cov}\,(\bar{\beta}_{k|k} - \bar{\beta}) = (X'W^{-1}X)^{-1} = X^{-1}WX'^{-1} \tag{96}$$

For $\tilde{\beta}_k^*$ in equilibrium, we set its mean equal to zero and its covariance matrix to Γ_0, that is,

$$\tilde{\beta}_{k|k}^* = 0 \qquad \text{Cov}\,(\tilde{\beta}_k^* - \tilde{\beta}_{k|k}^*) = \Gamma_0 \tag{97}$$

The covariance of $\bar{\beta}_{k|k} - \bar{\beta}$ and $\tilde{\beta}_k^* - \tilde{\beta}_{k|k}^*$ is, by (95), (94), (92), and (90),

$$E(\bar{\beta}_{k|k} - \bar{\beta})\tilde{\beta}_k^{*\prime} = EX^{-1}u\tilde{\beta}_k^{*\prime} = X^{-1}\begin{bmatrix} \tilde{x}_1\Gamma_{k-1}' \\ \vdots \\ \tilde{x}_k\Gamma_0' \end{bmatrix} \tag{98}$$

Equations (95) to (98) provide the components of $\beta_{k|k}$ and $\Sigma_{k|k}$ to be used for the evaluation of the log-likelihood functions (32) and (34). They are to be contrasted with (30) and (31) for fixed β_1^*, which would require $k + k_1$ initial observations.

Once the likelihood function (34) can be evaluated, a numerical method can be applied to maximize it with respect to the unknown parameters in $V = \sigma^2 P$ and M. The computations will be simplified when P and M are diagonal, being diag $\{p_i\}$ and diag $\{m_i\}$, respectively. Equations (89) and (90) would become

$$\gamma_{ii,\,0} = E\beta_{it}^{*2} = \frac{\sigma^2 p_i}{1 - m_i^2} \tag{99}$$

and

$$\gamma_{ii,\,s} = E\beta_{it}^*\beta_{i,\,t-s}^* = m_i^s\gamma_{ii,\,0} \qquad i = 1, \ldots, k_1 \tag{100}$$

and $E\beta_{it}^*\beta_{j,\,t-s}^* = 0$ for $i \neq j$ and for all s. Accordingly, the matrix Γ_s used in (93) is a diagonal matrix with elements given by (99) and (100). As an alternative to using the likelihood function (34) one can form a likelihood function using the regression model (94) for all T observations, as was done by using the model (39) in Sec. 10.4.

For further discussion of the stationary-coefficient regression model see Rosenberg (1973a), Cooley and Prescott (1976), Harvey and Phillips (1982), and Pagan (1980). The exposition of this section has drawn from Harvey and Phillips (1982). For a survey of the random-coefficient model, see Swamy (1971, 1974). Swamy and Tinsley (1980) generalize the model of Eqs. (83) and (84) by replacing $\bar{\beta}$ by $\bar{B}z_t$, where z_t is a vector of fixed variables. Kelejian (1974) treats linear simultaneous-equation models with random parameters.

★10.9 IDENTIFIABILITY OF PARAMETERS

Pagan (1980) studies identifiability conditions for the parameters of a regression model with stationary parameters. His model is

$$y_t = x_t\bar{\beta} + x_t\beta_t^* + \epsilon_t = x_t\bar{\beta} + u_t \tag{101}$$

$$\beta_t^* = \beta_t - \bar{\beta} = A^{-1}(L)e_t \tag{102}$$

where $A(L)$ is a ratio of polynomials of orders p and q in the lag operator L and e_t is normal, independent, and identically distributed, so that β_t^* follows an ARMA (p, q) process. Since an ARMA process can be written as a first-order autoregressive process, as

$$\beta_t^* = A_1 \beta_{t-1}^* + A_2 \beta_{t-2}^* + e_t + A_3 e_{t-1}$$

for example can be written as

$$\begin{bmatrix} \beta_t^* \\ \beta_{t-1}^* \\ e_t \end{bmatrix} = \begin{bmatrix} A_1 & A_2 & A_3 \\ I & 0 & 0 \\ 0 & 0 & 0 \end{bmatrix} \begin{bmatrix} \beta_{t-1}^* \\ \beta_{t-2}^* \\ e_{t-1} \end{bmatrix} + \begin{bmatrix} e_t \\ 0 \\ e_t \end{bmatrix}$$

or

$$\tilde{\beta}_t^* = M \tilde{\beta}_{t-1}^* + \eta_t$$

the model of Eqs. (101) and (102) is formally identical with our model (87) and (88), $\tilde{x}_t$ in (87) denoting $[x_t \quad 0 \quad 0]$ in the above example. The parameters of (101) and (102) consist of $\bar{\beta}$, $\sigma^2 = \text{Var } \epsilon_t$, and all the parameters in the ARMA (p, q) process for β_t^*. By "identification" Pagan means asymptotic local parametric identification, i.e., the nonsingularity of $\lim_{T \to \infty} T^{-1} I(\theta^0)$, where I is the information matrix, under certain regularity conditions. Pagan has provided two sets of sufficient conditions for the identifiability of $\bar{\beta}$ and of all parameters, respectively.

First, under the assumptions (i) that the ARMA (p, q) process generating $\beta_t^* = \beta_t - \bar{\beta}$ is stationary and obeys the identification conditions set out in Hannan (1968), (ii) that x_t has an upper bound for all elements t, and (iii) that $\lim_{T \to \infty} T^{-1} X'X$ is positive definite, $\bar{\beta}$ is identifiable.

To state the second set of sufficient conditions, let Γ_j denote $E\beta_t^* \beta_{t-j}^{*\prime}$ as in Sec. 10.8 and observe that if all Γ_j are known, the parameters of the ARMA (p, q) process (102) can be determined by these covariance matrices. Let a subset of all Γ_j $(j \in \psi)$ be sufficient to determine the parameters of (102) uniquely. Then, if 0 is not in the set ψ, that is, if Γ_0 is not required to determine the parameters of (102) a set of sufficient conditions for the identification of all parameters in (101) and (102) consists of (i) to (iii) and (iv), the nonsingularity of

$$R_k = \lim_{T \to \infty} T^{-1} \sum_t x_{t-k}' x_{t-k} \otimes x_t' x_t \qquad \text{for all } k \in \psi$$

To motivate the condition (iv) recall that

$$Eu_t u_{t-k} = x_t \Gamma_k x_{t-k}' + \delta_{t, t-k} \sigma^2 = (x_{t-k} \otimes x_t) \text{ vec } \Gamma_k + \delta_{t, t-k} \sigma^2 \qquad (103)$$

Thus vec Γ_k is a vector of coefficients in the regression of $u_t u_{t-k}$ on $x_{t-k} \otimes x_t$. TR_k is the cross-product matrix of the explanatory variables in this regression. If it is nonsingular, the elements of Γ_k can be consistently estimated, but the knowledge of Γ_k $(k \in \psi)$ is sufficient to identify the parameters of the model (102). If (102) is a first-order autoregressive process $\beta_t^* = M \beta_{t-1}^* + \eta_t$ with diagonal M

and $V = E\eta_t \eta_t'$, $\Gamma_k = (\gamma_{ij,k})$ is diagonal and

$$Eu_t u_{t-k} = \sum_j x_{jt} x_{j,t-k} \gamma_{jj,k} \qquad k > 0$$

Assumption (iv) in this case states that the matrix with $\lim_{T \to \infty} T^{-1} \sum_t (x_{it} x_{jt} x_{i,t-k} x_{j,t-k})$ as its ijth element must be nonsingular. If Γ_0 is in the set of Γ_k required to determine the parameters of (102), (iv) should be modified to include $\lim_{T \to \infty} T^{-1} \sum_t w_t w_t' > 0$, where $w_t = [x_t \otimes x_t, 1]$

Pagan (1980) also shows that if (i) the model is locally asymptotically identified (ii) x_t is uniformly bounded from above and nonstochastic, (iii) the model in state-space form is uniformly completely observable and uniformly completely controllable, (iv) the characteristic roots of M are less than 1 in absolute value, and (v) the true parameter vector θ^0 is an interior point of the permissible parameter space which is a subset of R^s, then the maximum-likelihood estimator of θ^0 is consistent and has a limiting distribution which is normal with a covariance matrix equal to the inverse of the information matrix. If the transition matrix M is given, the conclusion holds for the maximum-likelihood estimator of the remaining parameters with assumption (iv) omitted.

For a regression model with nonstationary coefficients, that is, M having characteristic roots equal to unity, conditions for the identifiability of the parameters remain to be investigated further. Hatanaka and Tanaka (1980) have studied the identifiability conditions under the assumption that β_0 has a known normal prior distribution.

10.10 TESTING CONSTANCY OF REGRESSION COEFFICIENTS

An important question in regression analysis is whether the coefficients for different observations are identical. A test, given in Sec. 2.8, is to divide the observations into two groups and test the null hypothesis of the equality of the entire set or a subset of coefficients in the two regressions using an F statistic. A number of other tests have been suggested for the null hypothesis of constancy of regression coefficients, partly depending on the alternative hypotheses to be compared. A useful alternative hypothesis is that the vector $\tilde{\beta}_t$ of k_1 regression coefficients of interest is generated by the process

$$\tilde{\beta}_t = \tilde{\beta}_{t-1} + \eta_t \tag{104}$$

where η_t is normally and independently distributed with mean zero and a diagonal covariance matrix V. The null hypothesis states that $V = 0$. Several tests of the null hypothesis have been suggested. Because 0 is on the boundary of the parameter space for V, we know the asymptotic distribution of the lagrange multiplier test statistic, but not that of the Wald or likelihood-ratio statistic.

First, by the asymptotic normality of the maximum-likelihood estimator of the elements of V one can use a quadratic form in these elements weighted by the inverse of their covariance matrix (obtained from the information matrix) and approximate its distribution by a χ^2 distribution, but this approximation is crude because it is a special case of the Wald test statistic.

Second is the likelihood-ratio test. Let λ be the ratio of the maximum-likelihood functions under the null and alternative hypotheses. However, the distribution of $-2 \log \lambda$ under the null hypothesis $V = 0$ is not well approximated by a χ^2 distribution because, with the restriction that the maximum-likelihood estimates of the diagonal elements of V be nonnegative, there is a density mass at $\hat{V} = 0$ and, accordingly, the distribution of $-2 \log \lambda$ is more concentrated toward the origin than the χ^2 distribution. Therefore, applying the χ^2 distribution will lead to rejecting the null hypothesis less frequently than the stated level of significance. Garbade (1977) has applied the likelihood-ratio test and studied the sampling distribution of $-2 \log \lambda$ by Monte Carlo experiments. It would be worthwhile to obtain a better approximation to the distribution of the likelihood-ratio test statistic for the present problem when some parameters are subject to inequality constraints along the lines of Chernoff (1954), Moran (1970), and Gourieroux, Holly, and Montfort (1982).

Third is an application of the lagrangian multiplier test of Silvey (1959) or, equivalently, the score test of Rao (1973, p. 417). With $\tilde{\beta}_0$ regarded as fixed, we have

$$\tilde{\beta}_t = \tilde{\beta}_0 + \sum_{s=1}^{t} \eta_s$$

and the regression model is

$$y_t = x_t \beta_t + \epsilon_t = x_t \beta + \epsilon_t + \tilde{x}_t \sum_{1}^{t} \eta_s = x_t \beta + u_t \qquad t = 1, \ldots, T \qquad (105)$$

where β has a subvector $\tilde{\beta}_0$ corresponding to the time-varying coefficients and

$$E u_t^2 = \sigma^2 + t \tilde{x}_t V \tilde{x}_t' \qquad (106)$$

For $V = \text{diag} \{v_{ii}\}$, (106) becomes

$$E u_t^2 = \sigma^2 + t \sum_{i=1}^{k_1} x_{it}^2 v_{ii} \qquad t = 1, \ldots, T \qquad (107)$$

Let $\hat{u}_t$ be the residuals of (105) estimated by OLS. According to a theorem of Breusch and Pagan (1979, p. 1288), the lagrangian multiplier statistic for testing H_0: $v_{ii} = 0$ $(i = 1, \ldots, k_1)$ in (107) equals one-half the explained sum of squares in a regression of $T(\Sigma \hat{u}_t^2)^{-1} \hat{u}_t^2$ on $t x_{it}^2$ $(i = 1, \ldots, k_1)$. This statistic is asymptotically distributed as $\chi^2(k_1)$ when the null hypothesis is true. Although this test is based on the lagrangian multiplier, its null hypothesis is formulated solely on the relations (107) and ignores the relations

$$E u_t u_s = \min (t, s) \sum_{i=1}^{k_1} x_{it} x_{is} v_{ii} \qquad t \neq s$$

for the parameters v_{ii}. Thus the null hypothesis, though implied by $v_{ii} = 0$, is not equivalent to it.

Fourth is a test proposed by Pagan and Tanaka (1979) based on the score-test statistic of Rao (1973), namely, $S = \hat{d}'_1 \hat{I}^{11} \hat{d}_1$, where $\hat{d}_1$ is a vector of first derivatives of the log likelihood with respect to the parameters v_{ii} ($i = 1, \ldots, k_1$) and $\hat{I}^{11}$ is the submatrix of the inverse of the information matrix which corresponds to these parameters, both evaluated at the maximum-likelihood estimates obtained under H_0: $v_{ii} = 0$ ($i = 1, \ldots, k_1$). Pagan and Tanaka showed how the exact distribution of this statistic can be evaluated under H_0 and concluded by Monte Carlo experiments that, unlike the likelihood-ratio test statistic $-2 \log \lambda$, the score-test statistic can be well approximated by the χ^2 distribution.

Fifth is a test suggested by LaMotte and McWhorter (1978). They assume that $V = \sigma_\eta^2 D$, where the diagonal matrix D is known; therefore, in our notation, $\beta_t = \tilde{\beta}_t$, the constant coefficients corresponding to the zero diagonal elements of D. Consider T observations of the regression model (105). The covariance matrix of the vector u of its T residuals is

$$Euu' = I_T \sigma^2 + \sigma_\eta^2 \Phi$$

with the tsth element of Φ equal to $\min(t, s) x_t D x'_s$. Define

$$HH' = I_T - X(X'X)^{-1}X' \qquad \text{and} \qquad H'H = I_{T-k}$$

Let $\lambda_1, \ldots, \lambda_q$ be the distinct characteristic roots of $H'\Phi H$ with multiplicities $r_1, \ldots, r_q$, respectively. Let P_i be a $(T-k) \times r_i$ matrix whose columns are orthonormal characteristic vectors of $H'\Phi H$, and let Q_i be $y'HP_i P'_i H'y$. It can be shown that $(s^2 + \lambda_i \sigma_\eta^2)^{-1} Q_i$ is distributed as $\chi^2(r_i)$. Assume that $\lambda_1 > \lambda_2 > \ldots > \lambda_q$ and partition $(Q_1, \ldots, Q_q)$ into two sets $(Q_1, \ldots, Q_g)$ and $(Q_{g+1}, \ldots, Q_q)$ for some $0 < g < q$. Under the null hypothesis $\sigma_\eta^2 = 0$, LaMotte and McWhorter showed that

$$\frac{\sum_{i=1}^g Q_i / \sum_{i=1}^g r_i}{y'HH'y / (T - k - \sum_{i=1}^g r_i)}$$

will have an F distribution with $\sum_1^g r_i$ and $T - k - \sum_1^g r_i$ degrees of freedom; they also suggested a procedure for selecting the value g to increase the power of the test, although a uniformly most powerful test is not available.

This brief review of several tests of the constancy of regression coefficients, using the model of time-varying coefficients as the alternative, indicates that further research is required to obtain a uniformly most powerful test statistic which has a known distribution in small samples and is also computationally simple.

Two other tests of the temporal stability of regression coefficients were proposed by Brown, Durbin, and Evans (1975). These tests, unlike those above, do not require the explicit formulation of a regression model with time-varying coefficients as an alternative hypothesis. They are based on the one-period-ahead forecasting errors $y_t - x_t b_{t-1}$, where $b_{t-1} = (X'_{t-1} X_{t-1})^{-1} X'_{t-1} Y_t$ is the OLS estimate of the regression coefficient vector using data up to period $t - 1$. These errors are normalized to form the recursive residuals

$$w_t = \frac{y_t - x_t b_{t-1}}{[1 + x_t(X'_{t-1}X_{t-1})^{-1}x'_t]^{1/2}} \qquad t = k+1, \ldots, T \qquad (108)$$

The denominator is the standard deviation of $y_t - x_t b_{t-1}$ divided by σ^2. The ratio (108) therefore has variance σ^2. Successive w_t are independent under the null hypothesis $y_t = x_t \beta + \epsilon_t$. Using these properties of w_t under the null hypothesis, Brown, Durbin, and Evans have suggested two tests of the stability of the regression coefficients.

The first is the *cusum test* using the cumulative sums

$$W_t = \sum_{j=k+1}^{t} \frac{w_j}{s} \qquad t = k+1, \ldots, T \qquad (109)$$

where $s^2 = (Y_T - X_T b_T)'(Y_T - X_T b_T)/(T - k)$. Under the null hypothesis, W_t has an asymptotic distribution which is normal with mean zero and variance $t - k$. If

$$|W_t| > a(T - k)^{1/2} + 2a(t - k)(T - k)^{-1/2}$$

for any t between $k+1$ and T, the null hypothesis is rejected, the scalar a being chosen to set the desired level of significance, with $a = 1.143$ and $a = .948$ for a 1 percent and a 5 percent level, respectively.

The second is the *cusum-of-squares test* using the cumulative sum of squares

$$S_t = \frac{\sum_{j=k+1}^{t} w_j^2}{\sum_{j=k+1}^{T} w_j^2} \qquad t = k+1, \ldots, T \qquad (110)$$

Under the null hypothesis, $1 - S_t$ has a beta distribution with density function

$$f(x) = \frac{(\alpha + \beta + 1)!}{\alpha! \beta!} x^\alpha (1 - x)^\beta \qquad 0 < x < 1$$

where
$$\alpha = -1 + \frac{T - k}{2} \qquad \beta = -1 + \frac{t - k}{2}$$

The mean of this distribution is $(t - k)/(T - k)$. A confidence interval can be constructed for S_t using $[(t - k)/(T - k)] \pm c_0$, where c_0 can be found in table 1 of Brown, Durbin, and Evans (1975) according to the level of confidence desired. If any S_t falls outside this interval, the null hypothesis will be rejected.

10.11 THE ESTIMATION OF SEASONAL COMPONENTS IN ECONOMIC TIME SERIES

Seasonal adjustment of economic time series has been studied extensively in the literature. This section contains a modest suggestion for combining seasonal analysis with the estimation of an econometric model for cyclical fluctuations. Pagan (1975) has pointed out the possibility of applying the filtering and estimation methods for state-space models to the estimation of seasonal and cyclical components in economic time series. The following suggestion is essentially a combination of an econometric model for the cyclical components with the filtering and estimation of the seasonal components formulated in a state-space form.

Assume, first, that the vector y_t of endogenous variables is the sum of cyclical, seasonal, and irregular components, as given by

$$y_t = y_t^c + y_t^s + v_t \qquad (111)$$

and, second, that the cyclical component y_t^c is governed by the model

$$y_t^c = A y_{t-1}^c + C x_t + b + u_t \qquad (112)$$

where x_t is a vector of exogenous variables and u_t is a vector of random disturbances. The exogenous variables may or may not be seasonally adjusted, but this issue does not affect our analysis since the vector x_t, seasonally adjusted or not, is treated as predetermined. Third, an autoregressive seasonal model is assumed for the seasonal component, as illustrated by, but not confined to, the simple scheme

$$y_t^s = B y_{t-12}^s + w_t \qquad (113)$$

where w_t consists of random residuals. Combining Eqs. (112) and (113), we can write the vector z_t of unobserved components in the form

$$z_t = M z_{t-1} + N x_t + \epsilon_t \qquad (114)$$

where z_t includes both y_t^c and y_t^s as its first two subvectors as well as the necessary lagged y_{t-k}^c and y_{t-k}^s to transform the original model (112) of possibly higher order and Eq. (113) of order 12 into first order; the matrix M will depend on the matrices A and B, the matrix N will depend on C and b, the vector x_t will include dummy variables to absorb the intercept b of Eq. (112), and ϵ_t will depend on u_t and w_t. Equation (111) can be rewritten as

$$y_t = [I \quad I \quad 0] z_t + v_t \qquad (115)$$

Thus, Eqs. (114) and (115) correspond to (51) and (50) respectively, the first explaining the unobserved state variables z_t and the second relating the observed y_t to z_t. Given observations on y_t and x_t, the conditional expectations of the unobserved components of z_t can be estimated by the well-known techniques of Kalman filtering and smoothing, provided that the parameters A, C, b, and thus M and N, are known.

In practice, the parameters A, C, and b of the econometric model (112) are unknown. One can employ seasonally adjusted data for y_t^c, obtained by a standard seasonal adjustment procedure, and the standard statistical estimation techniques to obtain estimates of A, C, and b. Using these estimates, one can then compute estimates of the seasonal and cyclical components in z_t by Kalman filtering and smoothing. The new estimates of y_t^c will serve as new data for the reestimation of the econometric model (112). New estimates of the seasonal components y_t^s will result from this process. This approach appears to be worthy of empirical implementation.

PROBLEMS

1. In the linear regression model of Eqs. (1) and (2) with changing coefficients, let β_t be a vector of two coefficients, and let $M = I$, $V = I$, $\sigma^2 = 1$, $\beta_{0|0} = 0$, and $\Sigma_{0|0} = I$. Given $x_1 = [1 \quad 1]$, $x_2 = [1 \quad 2]$, $x_3 = [1 \quad 3]$, $y_1 = 2.3$, $y_2 = 2.6$, and $y_3 = 4.1$, compute $\Sigma_{t|t}$, K_t and $\beta_{t|t}$ for $t = 1, 2, 3$.

2. In Prob. 1, drop the assumption $\sigma^2 = 1$ and let σ^2 be unknown. Find the maximum-likelihood estimate of σ^2.

3. In the regression model of Eqs. (1) and (2) let $M = I$ and $V = 0$. How is the estimate $\beta_{T|T}$ obtained by the Kalman filter related to the estimate by ordinary least squares using all T observations?

4. In the regression model of Eqs. (1) and (2), let $M = I$ and $V = 0$. How are the recursive residuals w_t used by Brown, Durbin, and Evans (1975) related to the residuals u_t used in the likelihood function (32)?

5. Under the null hypothesis $M = I$ and $V = 0$ in the regression model of Eqs. (1) and (2), show that the recursive residuals w_t used by Brown, Durbin, and Evans (1975) are serially uncorrelated.

6. Find the smoothed estimates $\beta_{t|3}$ for $t = 2, 3$ in Prob. 1 and the associated covariance matrices $\Sigma_{t|3}$.

7. Let the prior density of β in a regression model $y_t = x_t \beta + \epsilon_t$ based on data up to $t - 1$ be normal with mean $\hat{\beta}_{t-1}$ and covariance matrix $\hat{\Sigma}_{t-1}$. Find the mean $\hat{\beta}_t$ and covariance matrix $\hat{\Sigma}_t$ of the posterior density of β after the observation (x_t, y_t) is available. You may refer to Eqs. (47) and (48) of Chap. 3. Compare the Bayesian estimates $\hat{\beta}_t$ and $\hat{\Sigma}_t$ with the estimates obtained by Kalman filter. Hint: $(A + BCB')^{-1} = A^{-1} - A^{-1}B(C^{-1} + B'A^{-1}B)^{-1}B'A^{-1}$.

8. Using the model of Eqs. (1) and (2) assuming M, V, and σ^2 to be known, let the prior density of β_{t-1} be normal with mean $\hat{\beta}_{t-1}$ and covariance matrix $\hat{\Sigma}_{t-1}$. Find the prior density of β_t, assuming η_t to be normal. Find the mean $\hat{\beta}_t$ and covariance matrix $\hat{\Sigma}_t$ of the posterior density of β_t after the observation (x_t, y_t) is available. You may refer to Eqs. (47) and (48) of Chap. 3. Compare $\hat{\beta}_t$ and $\hat{\Sigma}_t$ with $\beta_{t|t}$ and $\Sigma_{t|t}$ obtained by the Kalman filter. This problem generalizes the result of Prob. 7.

9. Derive the smoothing equation (14) using the Bayesian approach. This problem is easier after completion of Prob. 8.

10. Prepare a computer program (in a language of your own or the instructor's choice) to perform Kalman filtering. Apply it to a set of economic data using the model of Eqs. (1) and (2), assuming $M = I$, $V = I$, $\beta_{0|0} = b = (X'X)^{-1}X'y$, $\Sigma_{0|0} = (X'X)^{-1}\sigma^2$, and $\sigma^2 = (y - Xb)'(y - Xb)/(T - k)$, where T is the number of observations and k is the number of regression coefficients.

11. Using the data of Prob. 10, estimate $\Sigma_{k|k}$ and $\beta_{k|k}$ for the model of Eqs. (1) and (2) assuming $M = I$, $V = I$, and $\sigma^2 = (y - Xb)'(y - Xb)/(T - k)$, with $\beta_{0|0}$ treated as fixed but unknown. Using the computer program of Prob. 10, estimate $\beta_{t|t}$ and $\Sigma_{t|t}$ for $t = k + 1, \ldots, T$.

12. Modify Prob. 11 by assuming σ^2 to be unknown and plot the log-likelihood function as a function of σ^2. Letting $V = \alpha I$, evaluate the log-likelihood function as a function of σ^2 and α. Find the maximum-likelihood estimates of σ^2 and α approximately.

13. Do Prob. 11 using the model of Eqs. (83) and (84) and treating $\beta_{0|0}$ as random, with M changed to $.9I$.

14. Modify Prob. 13 by assuming σ^2 to be unknown and plot the log-likelihood function as a function of σ^2. Letting $V = \alpha I$, evaluate the log-likelihood function as a function of σ^2 and α. Find the maximum-likelihood estimates of σ^2 and α approximately.

15. For the model of Sec. 10.6 assume that $M_i = I$ and $\eta_{it} = 0$ ($i = 1, \ldots, m$), that is, the model to be a linear simultaneous-equation model with constant coefficients. Is the estimate $\delta_{T|T}$ of the vector of structural coefficients recommended in Sec. 10.6 using T observations the same as the FIML estimate of Chap. 5? Explain your answer.

16. Apply the two tests of Brown, Durbin, and Evans (1975) for model stability to the data of Prob. 10. Compare the results with the results of Prob. 12 if you have done it.

REFERENCES

Arora, S. S. (1973): "Error Components Regression Model and Their Applications," *Ann. Econ. Soc. Meas.*, **2**: 451–462.

Belsley, D. A. (1973a): "On the Determination of Systematic Parameter Variation in the Linear Regression Model," *Ann. Econ. Soc. Meas.*, **2**: 487–494.

—— (1973b): "A Test for Systematic Variation in Regression Coefficients," *Ann. Econ. Soc. Meas.*, **2**: 495–500.

—— (1973c): "The Applicability of the Kalman Filter in the Determination of Systematic Parameter Variation," *Ann. Econ. Soc. Meas.*, **2**: 531–534.

——, and E. Kuh (1973): "Time-Varying Parameter Structures: An Overview," *Ann. Econ. Soc. Meas.*, **2**: 375–380.

Breusch, T. S., and A. R. Pagan (1979): "A Simple Test for Heteroscedasticity and Random Coefficient Variation," *Econometrica*, **47**: 1287–1294.

Brown, R. L., J. Durbin, and J. M. Evans (1975): "Techniques for Testing the Constancy of Regression Relationships over Time, with Comments," *J. R. Statist. Soc.*, **B37**: 149–192.

Chernoff, H. (1954): "On the Distribution of the Likelihood Ratio," *Ann. Math. Statist.*, **25**: 573–578.

Chow, G. C. (1960): "Tests of Equality between Sets of Coefficients in Two Linear Regressions," *Econometrica*, **28**: 591–605.

—— (1975): *Analysis and Control of Dynamic Economic Systems*, Wiley, New York.

—— (1978): "Comments on 'A Time Series Analysis of Seasonality in Econometric Models' by Charles Plosser," pp. 398–401 in A. Zellner (ed.), *Seasonal Analysis of Economic Time Series*, U.S. Department of Commerce, Bureau of the Census, Economic Research Report ER-1.

—— (1981): *Econometrica Analysis by Control Methods*, Wiley, New York.

Cooley, T. F., and E. Prescott (1973): "An Adaptive Regression Model," *Int. Econ. Rev.*, **14**: 364–371.

—— and E. Prescott, (1973c): "Tests of an Adaptive Regression Model," *Rev. Econ. Statist.*, **55**: 248–256.

—— and —— (1973b): "Varying Parameter Regression: A Theory and Some Applications," *Ann. Econ. Soc. Meas.*, **2**: 463–474.

—— and —— (1976): "Estimation in the Presence of Stochastic Parameter Variation," *Econometrica*, **44**: 167–183.

——, B. Rosenberg, and K. Wall (1977): "A Note on Optimal Smoothing for Time-Varying Coefficient Problems," *Ann. Econ. Soc. Meas.*, **6**: 453–456.

Cooper, J. P. (1973): "Time-Varying Regression Coefficients: A Mixed Estimation Approach and Operational Limitations on the General Markov Structure," *Ann. Econ. Soc. Meas.*, **2**: 525–530.

Duncan, D. B., and S. D. Horn (1972): "Linear Dynamic Recursive Estimation from the Viewpoint of Regression Analysis," *J. Am. Statist. Assoc.*, **67**: 815–821.

Engle, R. F. (1978): "Estimating Structural Models of Seasonality," pp. 281–297 in A. Zellner (ed.), *Seasonal Analysis of Economic Time Series*, U.S. Department of Commerce, Bureau of the Census, Economic Research Report ER-1.

Garbade, K. (1977): "Two Methods for Examining the Stability of Regression Coefficients," *J. Am. Statist. Assoc.*, **72**: 54–63.

Goldfeld, S. M., and R. E. Quandt (1973): "The Estimation of Structural Shifts by Switching Regressions," *Ann. Econ. Soc. Meas.*, **2**: 475–486.

Gourieroux, C., A. Holly, and A. Montfort, (1982): "Likelihood Ratio Test, Wald Test and Kühn-Tucker Test in Linear Models with Inequality Constraints on the Regression Parameters," *Econometrica*, **50**, 63–80.

Hannan, E. J. (1968): "The Identification of Vector Mixed Autoregressive-Moving Average Systems," *Biometrika*, **56**: 223–225.

Harvey, A. C. (1978): "The Estimation of Time-Varying Parameters from Panel Data," *Ann. INSEE,* **30-31**: 203–226.

—— and P. Collier (1977): "Testing for Functional Misspecification in Regression Analysis," *J. Econometr.,* **6**: 103–120.

—— and G. D. A. Phillips (1976): "The Maximum Likelihood Estimation of Autoregressive-Moving Average Models by Kalman Filtering," *Univ. Kent (Canterbury), Working Pap.* 3, SSRS-Supported Project on Testing for Specification Error in Econometric Models.

—— and —— (1979): "Maximum Likelihood Estimation of Regression Models with Autoregressive-Moving Average Disturbances," *Biometrika,* **66**: 49–58.

—— and —— (1982): "The Estimation of Regression Models with Time-Varying Parameters," in M. Deistler, E. Fürst, and G. Schwödiauer (eds.), *Games, Economic Dynamics, and Time Series Analysis,* Physica-Verlag, Cambridge, Mass.

Hatanaka, M. (1980): "A Note on the Applicability of the Kalman Filter to Regression Models with Some Parameters Time-Varying and Others Invarying," *Aust. J. Statist.,* **22**: 298–306.

—— and K. Tanaka, (1980): "On the Estimability of the Covariance Matrix in the Random Walk Representing the Time-Changing Parameters of the Regression Models," *Osaka Univ. Fac. Econ., Discuss. Pap.* 28.

Ho, Y. C., and R. C. K. Lee (1964): "A Bayesian Approach to Problems in Stochastic Estimation and Control," *IEEE Trans. Autom. Control,* **AC-9**: 333–339.

Kalman, R. E. (1960): "A New Approach to Linear Filtering and Prediction Problems," *Trans. ASME Ser. D, J. Basic Eng.,* **82**: 35–45.

Kelejian, H. H., (1974): "Random Parameters in Simultaneous Equation Framework: Identification and Estimation," *Econometrica,* **42**: 517–527.

LaMotte, L. R., and McWhorter, A., Jr. (1978): "An Exact Test for the Presence of Random Walk Coefficients in a Linear Regression Model," *J. Am. Statist. Assoc.,* **73**: 816–820.

Ljung, L. (1979): "Asymptotic Behavior of the Extended Kalman Filter as a Parameter Estimator for Linear Systems," *IEEE Trans. Autom. Control,* **AC-24**: 36–50.

Mehra, R. K. (1970): "On the Identification of Variances and Adaptive Kalman Filtering," *IEEE Trans. Auto. Control,* **AC-15**: 175–184.

—— (1971): "Identification of Stochastic Linear Dynamic Systems Using Kalman Filter Representation," *AIAA J.,* **9**: 28–31.

—— (1979): "Kalman Filters and Their Applications to Forecasting," in *TIMS Studies in the Management Sciences,* North-Holland, Amsterdam, 75–94.

Moran, P. A. P. (1970): "On Asymptotically Optimal Tests of Composite Hypotheses," *Biometrika,* **57**: 47–55.

Pagan, A. R. (1975): "A Note on the Extraction of Components from Time Series," *Econometrica,* **43**: 163–168.

—— (1978): "A Unified Approach to Estimation and Inference for Stochastically Varying Coefficient Regression Models," *Cent. Op. Res. Econometr., Louvain-la-Neuve, CORE Discuss. Pap.* 7814.

—— (1980): "Some Identification and Estimation Results for Regression Models with Stochastically Varying Coefficients," *J. Econometr.,* **13**: 341–363.

—— and K. Tanaka (1979): "A Further Test for Assessing the Stability of Regression Coefficients," *Aust. Nat. Univ., Canberra,* unpublished manuscript.

Phillips, G. D. A., and A. C. Harvey (1974): "A Simple Test for Serial Correlation in Regression Analysis," *J. Am. Statist. Assoc.,* **69**: 935–939.

Poirier, D. (1976): *The Econometrics of Structural Change,* North-Holland, Amsterdam.

Rao, C. R. (1973): *Linear Statistical Inference and Its Applications,* 2d ed., Wiley, New York.

Rosenberg, B. (1972): "Estimation of Stationary Stochastic Regression Parameters Reexamined," *J. Am. Statist. Ass.,* **67**: 650–654.

—— (1973): "A Survey of Stochastic Parameter Regression," *Ann. Econ. Soc. Meas.,* **2**: 381–398.

—— (1973b): "The Analysis of a Cross Section of Time Series by Stochastically Convergent Parameter Regression," *Ann. Econ. Soc. Meas.,* **2**: 399–428.

—— (1977): "Estimation Error Covariance in Regression with Sequentially Varying Parameters," *Ann. Econ. Soc. Meas.,* **6**: 457–462.

Sage, A. P. (1968): *Optimum Systems Control*, pp. 265–275, Prentice-Hall, Englewood Cliffs, N.J.

Sant, D. (1977): "Generalized Least Squares Applied to Time-Varying Parameter Models," *Ann. Econ. Soc. Meas.*, **6**: 301–314.

Sarris, A. H. (1973): "A Bayesian Approach to Estimation of Time-Varying Regression Coefficients," *Ann. Econ. Soc. Meas.*, **2**: 501–524.

Schweder, T. (1976): "Some Optimal Methods to Detect Structural Shifts or Outliers in Regression," *J. Am. Statis. Assoc.*, **71**: 491–501.

Schweppe, F. C. (1965): "Evaluation of Likelihood Functions for Gaussian Signals," *IEEE Trans. Inform. Theory*, **11**: 61–70.

Silvey, S. D. (1959): "The Lagrangian Multiplier Test," *Ann. Math. Statis.*, **30**: 389–407.

Swamy, P. A. V. B. (1971): '*Statistical Inference in Random Coefficient Regression Models*, Springer Verlag, New York.

——— (1973): "Criteria, Constraints and Multicollinearity in Random Coefficient Regression Models," *Ann. Econ. Soc. Meas.*, **2**: 429–450.

——— (1974): "Linear Models with Random Coefficients," pp. 143–168 in P. Zarembka (ed.), *Frontiers in Econometrics*, Academic, NewYork.

——— (1979): "Relative Efficiencies of Some Simple Bayes Estimators of Coefficients in a Dynamic Equation with Serially Correlated Errors, II," *J. Econometr.*, **7**: 245–258.

——— and J. S. Mehta (1975): "Bayesian and Non-Bayesian Analysis of Switching Regressions and of Random Coefficient Regression Models," *J. Am. Statist. Assoc.*, **70**: 593–602.

——— and P. Tinsley (1980): "Linear Prediction and Estimation Methods for Regression Models with Stationary Stochastic Coefficients," *J. Econometr.*, **12**: 103–142.

Taylor, L. (1970): "The Existence of Optimal Distributed Lags," *Rev. Econ. Stud.*, **37**: 95–106.

Tesfatsion, L. (1978): "A New Approach to Filtering and Adaptive Control," *J. Optimization Theory Appl.*, **25**: 247–261.

——— (1979): "Direct Updating of Intertemporal Criterion Functions for a Class of Adaptive Control Problems," *IEEE Trans. Systems, Man, Cybernet.*, **SMC-9**: 143–151.

Wall, K. (1976): "Time-Varying Models in Econometrics: Identifiability and Estimation," unpublished manuscript.

Zellner, A. (1970): "Estimation of Regression Relationships Containing Unobservable Variables," *Int. Econ. Rev.*, **11**: 441–454.

ELEVEN

MODELS UNDER RATIONAL EXPECTATIONS

11.1 THE ASSUMPTION OF RATIONAL EXPECTATIONS

It is generally agreed that the behavior of economic agents depends on what they think the values of certain crucial economic variables will be. In deciding on how much land to be used for the cultivation of a particular crop the farmer will have to form an estimate of what the future price of that crop will be relative to the prices of other crops the land can produce. In deciding on the amount of capital investment, the business manager will have to form estimates of future profits to be derived from the investment, and thus estimates of future revenues and costs. An economist wishing to explain economic behavior will have to formulate a hypothesis on how the expectations are formed.

One hypothesis capable of explaining some economic data is

$$y_t^e - y_{t-1}^e = \beta(y_{t-1} - y_{t-1}^e) \tag{1}$$

where y_t is the economic variable in question and y_t^e is the expected value of this variable at time t, presumably based on the information available to the economic agents up to the end of period $t - 1$. This hypothesis asserts that expectations change from period $t - 1$ to period t by a fraction β of the discrepancy between the actual observation at $t - 1$ and the expected value at $t - 1$. This hypothesis, known as the *hypothesis of adaptive expectations*, was first used by Cagan (1956) in his work to explain hyperinflation by expected price change. It was used by Friedman (1957) to specify expected income, which is an important variable for explaining total consumption through time. After repeated substitutions for y_{t-k}^e hypothesis (1) implies

$$y_t^e = \beta y_{t-1} + (1 - \beta)y_{t-1}^e = \beta y_{t-1} + (1 - \beta)\beta y_{t-2} + (1 - \beta)^2 \beta y_{t-3} + \ldots \tag{2}$$

which shows that y_t^e is a weighted average of past y_{t-k} ($k = 1, 2, \ldots$) with geometrically declining weights. The hypothesis of Eqs. (1) and (2) has found wide applications in economics.

To the extent that the formula (2) works empirically, one may ask why it works. Is there an underlying model which generates the time series y_t and for which the formula (2) provides an optimal forecast of y_t? Muth (1960) found the following answer to this question. Let the underlying model for y_t be

$$y_t = \epsilon_t + \beta \sum_{i=1}^{\infty} \epsilon_{t-i} = y_{t-1} + \epsilon_t - (1 - \beta)\epsilon_{t-1} \tag{3}$$

where ϵ_t are independently and identically distributed and where the second equation is obtained by subtracting $y_{t-1} = \epsilon_{t-1} + \beta \sum_{i=2}^{\infty} \epsilon_{t-i}$ from the first. Given model (3), the conditional expectation $y_t^e = E(y_t | I_{t-1}) \equiv y_{t|t-1}$ given information I_{t-1} up to $t - 1$ satisfies, on taking conditional expectations on both sides of (3),

$$y_{t|t-1} = y_{t-1} - (1 - \beta)\epsilon_{t-1} = \beta y_{t-1} + (1 - \beta)(y_{t-1} - \epsilon_{t-1})$$

$$= \beta y_{t-1} + (1 - \beta)y_{t-1|t-2} \tag{4}$$

Identifying $y_{t|t-1}$ with y_t^e and $y_{t-1|t-2}$ with y_{t-1}^e, we find that (4) gives the same mechanism for the formation of expectations as (1).

In the above example the expectations of economic agents are assumed to be the same as the mathematical expectations of the corresponding economic variables generated by an econometric model. This is known as the *assumption of rational expectations*. In order to explain how expectations of economic agents are formed under this assumption, one must first formulate an econometric model and then derive the conditional expectations from the model, as in the above example. Model (3) was somewhat ad hoc. In general, it would be better to formulate the underlying model used to derive the conditional expectations by appealing to economic theory. Furthermore, the model itself may include expectation variables.

Such a model was indeed used in the classic paper of Muth (1961), which coined the term *rational expectations*. Muth (1961) explained the expected price p_t^e of a product by postulating a demand equation and a supply equation for the product and assuming market equilibrium at demand equal to supply:

$$C_t = -\beta p_t \qquad \text{demand}$$

$$P_t = \gamma p_t^e + u_t \qquad \text{supply}$$

$$P_t = C_t \qquad \text{market equilibrium}$$

where p_t denotes price, C_t denotes consumption, P_t is production, u_t is a random disturbance, and $p_t^e = p_{t|t-1}$. This simple model sets an example of simultaneous-equation models where expectations enter. Under the assumption of rational expectations, the expected price variable p_t^e is the same as the conditional expectation $p_{t|t-1}$ generated from the model. The approach of formulating an econometric model incorporating expectation variables in order to explain the formation of expectations has an additional virtue. It will explain all other endogenous variables in the model as well as the formation of expectations in a unified manner.

Another example using this approach is a macroeconomic model of Taylor (1979) to explain the percentage deviation y of real output from potential output and the rate of inflation π

$$y_t = \beta_1 y_{t-1} + \beta_2 y_{t-2} + \beta_3 (m_t - p_t) + \beta_4 (m_{t-1} - p_{t-1}) + \beta_5 \pi_{t|t-1}$$
$$+ \eta_t + \theta_1 \epsilon_{t-1} \tag{5}$$
$$\pi_t = \pi_{t-1} + \gamma y_{t|t-1} + \epsilon_t + \theta_2 \epsilon_{t-1}$$

where m is the logarithm of money supply, p is the logarithm of the price level, and η and ϵ are serially uncorrelated shocks to aggregate demand and inflation, respectively. The first equation represents the influence of money supply on aggregate demand, and the second represents the influence of expected aggregate demand on inflation. Note the two expectation variables $\pi_{t|t-1}$ and $y_{t|t-1}$.

As of the end of the 1970s, the expectations of economic variables in many econometric models were assumed to be linear functions of the past values of the variables themselves, as in Eq. (2). For example, expected price was assumed to be weighted average of past prices. If the expected price so calculated turns out to be very different from the mathematical expectation of the price variable generated by an econometric model, period after period, one may wonder why economic agents are so foolish as to ignore the structural relations of the econometric model in forming their expectations. The assumption of rational expectations is precisely to let the econometric model itself generate the expectation variables required. Econometricians insisting on using an additional distributed-lag equation to explain an expectation variable may argue that such a relation works empirically. It is not our task here to engage in a philosophical debate on this issue but to present statistical methods for estimating econometric models involving expectation variables under the assumption of rational expectations.

Section 11.2 points out that, under the assumption of rational expectations, there are multiple solutions to linear simultaneous equations if expectations of future endogenous variables enter. Section 11.3 proposes a resolution to the problem of multiple solutions in linear rational-expectation models. Section 11.4 comments on the solution proposed by Blanchard and Kahn (1980). Section 11.5 treats the problem of estimating linear models which do not include expectations of future variables, while Sec. 11.6 deals with estimation with the presence of these expectation variables.

11.2 THE PROBLEM OF MULTIPLE SOLUTIONS

The basic strategy adopted in estimating an econometric model involving expectation variables is to eliminate the expectation variables first and treat an equivalent model involving only directly observable variables. If the model is linear and includes expectations of only current endogenous variables but not of future endogenous variables, it is very simple to eliminate the expectation variables. Let the model be

$$By_t + A_1 y_{t-1} + A_2 y_{t-2} + B_0 y_{t|t-1} + \Gamma z_t = u_t \tag{6}$$

where u_t is a vector of serially uncorrelated disturbances and z_t is a vector of exogenous variables known at the end of $t-1$; that is, $z_{t|t-1} = z_t$. Taking the conditional expectations of (6), we have

$$By_{t|t-1} + A_1 y_{t-1} + A_2 y_{t-2} + B_0 y_{t|t-1} + \Gamma z_t = 0 \tag{7}$$

and, solving (7) for $y_{t|t-1}$, we have

$$y_{t|t-1} = -(B + B_0)^{-1}(A_1 y_{t-1} + A_2 y_{t-2} + \Gamma z_t) \tag{8}$$

When (8) is substituted for $y_{t|t-1}$ in (6), we obtain

$$By_t + [I - B_0(B + B_0)^{-1}](A_1 y_{t-1} + A_2 y_{t-2} + \Gamma z_t)$$
$$= By_t + B(B + B_0)^{-1}(A_1 y_{t-1} + A_2 y_{t-2} + \Gamma z_t) = u_t \tag{9}$$

which is a model involving only observable variables, the expectation variables $y_{t|t-1}$ having been eliminated. We call Eq. (9) a *solution* to the model (6).

However, if expectations of future endogenous variables enter into the model, the above solution procedure will not work (see Prob. 1). An example of an econometric model employing the expectations of future endogenous variables is given by Sargent and Wallace (1975). This model, called an *ad hoc model* by its authors, consists of the following equations

Aggregate supply schedule:

$$y_t = a_1 k_{t-1} + a_2(p_t - p_{t|t-1}) + u_{1t} \qquad \begin{matrix} a_1 > 0 \\ a_2 > 0 \end{matrix}$$

Aggregate demand schedule or IS curve:

$$y_t = b_1 k_{t-1} + b_2[r_t - (p_{t+1|t-1} - p_{t|t-1})] + b_3 Z_t + u_{2t} \qquad \begin{matrix} b_1 > 0 \\ b_2 < 0 \end{matrix}$$

Portfolio balance or LM schedule:

$$m_t = p_t + c_1 y_t + c_2 r_t + u_{3t} \qquad \begin{matrix} c_1 > 0 \\ c_2 < 0 \end{matrix}$$

Determination of productive capacity:

$$k_t = d_1 k_{t-1} + d_2[r_t - (p_{t+1|t-1} - p_{t|t-1})] + d_3 Z_t + u_{4t} \qquad d_2 < 0$$

Evolution of the exogenous variables:

$$Z_t = \sum_{j=1}^{q} \rho_j Z_{t-j} + \xi_t \qquad u_{it} = \sum_{j=1}^{q} \rho_{ij} u_{i,t-j} + \xi_{i,t}$$

In this model y_t, p_t, and m_t are the natural logarithms of output, the price level, and the money supply, respectively; r_t is the nominal rate of interest (not its logarithm); k_{t-1} is a measure of productive capacity, such as the logarithm of the stock of capital or labor or some linear combination of the logarithms of those stocks at the end of period $t - 1$; and Z_t is a vector of exogenous variables. For such models, there exist multiple solutions, as illustrated by the following example.

Consider a simple model for a scalar y_t

$$y_{t+1|t-1} + by_t + d + z_t = u_t \qquad (10)$$

where z_t is an exogenous variable and u_t is a serially uncorrelated disturbance. Let the solution take the form

$$y_t = c + r_0 u_t + r_1 u_{t-1} + \cdots + k_0 z_t + k_1 z_{t-1} + \cdots \qquad (11)$$

where the sums are infinite. Taking conditional expectations of the terms in (10) given the information I_{t-1} up to the end of $t - 1$, with $z_{t|t-1} = z_t$, and subtracting the result from (10), we have

$$by_t - by_{t|t-1} = u_t \qquad y_t - y_{t|t-1} = b^{-1} u_t$$

Performing the same operations on (11) gives $y_t - y_{t|t-1} = r_0 u_t$, implying $r_0 = b^{-1}$.

Advancing the time subscripts of (11) by 1 yields

$$y_{t+1} = c + b^{-1} u_{t+1} + r_1 u_t + r_2 u_{t-1} + \cdots + k_0 z_{t+1} + k_1 z_t + k_2 z_{t-1} + \cdots$$

and taking expectations given I_{t-1} gives

$$y_{t+1|t-1} = c + r_2 u_{t-1} + k_0 z_{t+1|t-1} + k_1 z_t + k_2 z_{t-1} + \cdots$$

The difference of these two equations is

$$y_{t+1} - y_{t+1|t-1} = b^{-1} u_{t+1} + r_1 u_t + k_0(z_{t+1} - z_{t+1|t-1}) \qquad (12)$$

where $z_{t+1} - z_{t+1|t-1}$ is the error in forecasting z_{t+1} one-period ahead, to be denoted by e_{t+1}.

Using (12) to substitute for $y_{t+1|t-1}$ in (10), we obtain the model

$$y_{t+1} + by_t + d + z_t = b^{-1} u_{t+1} + (1 + r_1)u_t + k_0 e_{t+1} \qquad (13)$$

which no longer involves any expectation variables. To show that model (13) implies the original model (10), we take expectations of (13) given I_{t-1},

$$y_{t+1|t-1} + by_{t|t-1} + d + z_t = 0 \qquad (14)$$

We also take expectations of (13) given I_t, noting $e_{t+1|t} = e_{t+1}$, and subtract the result from (13) to yield

$$y_{t+1} - y_{t+1|t} = b^{-1} u_{t+1} \qquad y_t - y_{t|t-1} = b^{-1} u_t$$

When $y_{t|t-1}$ in (14) is replaced by $y_t - b^{-1} u_t$, the original model (10) results.

Equation (13) is a dynamic model explaining y_{t+1}, which is consistent with the original model (10) but does not utilize any expectation variables. It has two more parameters r_1 and k_0 than the original model. If only model (10) is given, one is free to choose the values of these parameters and thus produce many stochastic models in the form of (13) which are consistent with the specification (10). In other words, model (10) has multiple solutions which are generated by different values of the parameters r_1 and k_0 in (13). Taylor (1977) has employed an extra parameter to characterize the existence of multiple solutions to a linear stochastic model explaining a scalar dependent variable y_t by its future expectation. In the next section, we will extend the method of Eqs. (11) to (13) to replace a multivariate linear model involving expectations of future endogenous variables by a series of models which are free of these expectation variables.

11.3 SOLUTION TO LINEAR EXPECTATIONS MODELS

Let the reduced form of a system of linear simultaneous equations be written as

$$B^{-1}(By_t + A_1 y_{t-1} + \cdots + A_p y_{t-p} + B_0 y_{t|t-1} + B_1 y_{t+1|t-1} + \cdots$$
$$+ B_q y_{t+q|t-1} + \Gamma z_t) = B^{-1} u_t = v_t \quad (15)$$

where y_t is a vector of G endogenous variables, z_t is a vector of K exogenous variables, u_t is a vector of normal and serially uncorrelated random disturbances, and $y_{t+i|t-1}$ is the expectation of y_{t+i} conditional on information up to the end of period $t - 1$, such information including $y_{t-1}, y_{t-2}, \ldots, u_{t-1}, u_{t-2}, \ldots$, and z_t, $z_{t-1}, \ldots$. Note that z_t is treated as given when the model is solved to explain y_t. This treatment of z_t appears to be in accord with econometric practice and is accepted, for example, by Shiller (1978, p. 27) in reviewing the literature of rational expectations. It also accords with the convention adopted in dynamic models in areas other than economics, where z_{t-1} instead of z_t is used in a model explaining y_t.

Assume that (15) is consistent with the following model

$$y_t = R_0 v_t + R_1 v_{t-1} + R_2 v_{t-2} + \cdots + K_0 z_t + K_1 z_{t-1} + K_2 z_{t-2} + \cdots \quad (16)$$

This assumption is justified because any linear model explaining y_t by y_{t-1}, y_{t-2}, $\ldots, z_t, z_{t-1}, \ldots$, and v_t can be put in this form after repeated substitutions for the lagged y's. Recall how the final form of an econometric model is derived from its reduced form as it was demonstrated in Eq. (58) of Chap. 4. Taking expectations of (15) given I_{t-1} and subtracting the result from (15), we have $y_t - y_{t|t-1} = v_t$. Similar operations on Eq. (16) yield $y_t - y_{t|t-1} = R_0 v_t$, implying $R_0 = I$.

We will find the relation between $y_{t+m|t-1}$ and y_{t+m} as follows. Advancing the time subscripts in (16) by m,

$$y_{t+m} = v_{t+m} + R_1 v_{t+m-1} + R_2 v_{t+m-2} + \cdots$$
$$+ K_0 z_{t+m} + K_1 z_{t+m-1} + K_2 z_{t+m-2} + \cdots$$

and taking conditional expectations of the result given I_{t-1},

$$y_{t+m|t-1} = R_{m+1}v_{t-1} + R_{m+2}v_{t-2} + \cdots + K_0 z_{t+m|t-1} + K_1 z_{t+m-1|t-1} + \cdots$$
$$+ K_m z_t + K_{m+1}z_{t-1} + \cdots$$

we can subtract the two equations to obtain

$$y_{t+m} - y_{t+m|t-1} = v_{t+m} + R_1 v_{t+m-1} + \cdots$$
$$+ R_m v_t + K_0 e_{t+m} + \cdots + K_{m-1}e_{t+1} \qquad (17)$$

where $e_{t+j} = z_{t+j} - z_{t+j|t-1}$. Equation (17) can be employed to replace all expectations $y_{t+m|t-1}$ ($m = 0, 1, \ldots, q$) in model (15) by the directly observed y_{t+m} minus a linear combination of v_{t+m-k} ($k = 0, \ldots, m$) and e_{t+m-k} ($k = 0, \ldots, m-1$). If $B^{-1}B_q$ is nonsingular, the resulting model can explain the dynamic evolution of the entire vector y_{t+q}. This model is free of expectation variables, and can be shown to be consistent with model (15) by the method to treat Eq. (19) below. It does employ the additional parameters $R_1, \ldots, R_q$ and $K_0, \ldots, K_{q-1}$ which characterize the multiple solutions to (15).

However, frequently in practice the matrix $B^{-1}B_q$ is singular because some elements of $y_{t+q|t-1}$ are absent from model (15). The matrix B_q will have columns of zeros corresponding to these elements. Let $y_{t+q|t-1}^a$ be a vector consisting of the g_1 nonzero elements of $y_{t+q|t-1}$ and reorder the elements of y_t to write

$$B_q y_{t+q|t-1} = (B_q^a \quad 0)y_{t+q|t-1} = B_q^a y_{t+q|t-1}^a$$

We will consider the reduced-form equations for y_t^a, which are the first g_1 equations of (15). Denoting the first g_1 rows of B^{-1} by B_a^{-1}, we write these reduced-form equations as

$$B_a^{-1}(By_t + A_1 y_{t-1} + \cdots + A_p y_{t-p} + B_0 y_{t|t-1} + \cdots$$
$$+ B_q^a y_{t+q|t-1}^a + \Gamma z_t) = B_a^{-1}u_t \equiv v_t^a \qquad (18)$$

where $B_a^{-1}By_t = y_t^a$. Our strategy is to find a model free of expectation variables to replace (18) for explaining y_t^a, a second model to explain another subvector y_t^b of y_t which represents variables appearing in $y_{t+q-1|t-1}$ but not in $y_{t+q|t-1}$, and so forth.

To explain y_{t+q}^a, we use (17) to replace all expectation variables in (18) to yield the model

$$B_a^{-1}[B_q^a y_{t+q}^a + \cdots + B_1 y_{t+1} + (B_0 + B)y_t + A_1 y_{t-1} + \cdots + A_p y_{t-p} + \Gamma z_t]$$
$$= B_a^{-1}B_q(K_0 e_{t+q} + \cdots + K_{q-1}e_{t+1}) + \cdots + B_a^{-1}B_1(K_0 e_{t+1})$$
$$+ B_a^{-1}B_q(v_{t+q} + R_1 v_{t+q-1} + \cdots + R_q v_t) + \cdots$$
$$+ B_a^{-1}B_1(v_{t+1} + R_1 v_t) + B_a^{-1}B_0 v_t + v_t^a$$
$$= N_q e_{t+q} + \cdots + N_1 e_{t+1} + B_a^{-1}B_q^a v_{t+q}^a + C_{q-1}v_{t+q-1} + \cdots + C_0 v_t \qquad (19)$$

where the matrices C_j ($j = 0, \ldots, q-1$) are $g_1 \times G$ and are defined by the line above. We will assume that $B_a^{-1}B_q^a$ is nonsingular. If this is not the case, we can rearrange the equations of (19) to make it so. For example, B_q^a may be a 10×2 matrix with all zeros except for the two elements in its first row. If any row of B_{q-1}^a other than the first row is nonzero, we can use it to replace the corresponding zero row of B_q^a, making $B_a^{-1}B_q^a$ nonsingular. This is done by advancing the time subscripts of the corresponding equation by 1. If no such row from B_{q-1}^a can be found, we will try to select a nonzero row from B_{q-2}^a other than the first and advance the time subscripts of the corresponding equation by 2, and so forth. Premultiplying (19) by $(B_a^{-1}B_q^a)^{-1}$ we will have a model explaining y_{t+q}^a. (Shifting equations cannot make B_q nonsingular if, e.g., all elements of B_q^a are nonzero.)

To show that (19) is consistent with (18), we take expectations of (19) given I_{t-1}, yielding

$$B_a^{-1}[B_q^a y_{t+q|t-1}^a + \cdots + B_1 y_{t+1|t-1} + (B_0 + B)y_{t|t-1}$$
$$+ A_1 y_{t-1} + \cdots + A_p y_{t-p} + \Gamma z_t] = 0 \quad (20)$$

We also take expectations of (19) given I_{t+q-1} and subtract the result from (19) to obtain

$$B_a^{-1}B_q^a(y_{t+q}^a - y_{t+q|t+q-1}^a) = B_a^{-1}B_q^a v_{t+q}^a$$

which implies $y_t^a - y_{t|t-1}^a = v_t^a$. Replacing $B_a^{-1}By_{t|t-1} = y_{t|t-1}^a$ in (20) by $y_t^a - v_t^a$, we derive the reduced form (18).

Model (19) can now be used to explain y_t^a. It is free of all expectation variables, but employs additional parameters. We will call it a solution to the reduced-form equations for y_t^a because it is a stochastic model describing how y_t^a evolves. To specify (19) completely, we have to specify $e_{t+m} = z_{t+m} - z_{t+m|t+m-2}$ ($m = 1, \ldots, q$). In practice, z_t is assumed to be governed by some stochastic process independent of u_t and y_{t-k} ($k \geq 0$) and $z_{t|t-2}$ is assumed to be a linear function of $z_{t-1}, \ldots, z_{t-s}$. The latter assumption is justified if z_t is governed by an autoregressive process of order s. If z_t obeys an ARMA process, it will be assumed that the expectation $z_{t|t-2}$ is formed by s lagged values of z_t because economic agents only possess so much information. In any case, we assume that the modelling of the z_t process has been completed and $e_{t+1}, \ldots, e_{t+q}$ will be treated as observable variables. With this understanding, *the solution (19) to the reduced-form equations for y_t^a is obtained by (i) replacing all expectation variables by their actual values (dropping "$|t-1$" in the subscripts), and (ii) replacing the residual v_t^a by $B_a^{-1}B_q^a v_{t+q}^a + C_{q-1}v_{t+q-1} + \cdots + C_0 v_t$, plus a linear function $N_q e_{t+q} + \cdots + N_1 e_{t+1}$ of the one-period-ahead prediction errors $e_{t+1}, \ldots, e_{t+q}$ of the z_t process.* An alternative to this treatment of z_t is to specify an AR model for z_t and combine it with model (15). The vector y_t^* of endogenous variables in the combined model will include both y_t and z_t. Using this combined model, we can delete the terms involving z_t in (15) and (18), and the terms involving z_t, $e_{t+1}, \ldots, e_{t+q}$ in (19). In the following discussion, we will retain $z_t, e_{t+1}, \ldots, e_{t+q}$.

The solution (19) will be used to express $y_{t+i|t-1}^a$ ($0 \leq i \leq q$) as functions of actual variables. To demonstrate the algebra involved, we let $p = 1$ and $q = 2$ in the following derivations. Denoting by y_t^b the vector of all other variables whose expectations appear in (15), we solve Eq. (19) for y_{t+2}^a, yielding

$$
\begin{aligned}
y_{t+2}^a &= -(B_a^{-1}B_2^a)^{-1}B_a^{-1}[B_1 y_{t+1} + (B + B_0)y_t + A_1 y_{t-1} + \Gamma z_t] \\
&\quad + (B_a^{-1}B_2^a)^{-1}(N_2 e_{t+2} + N_1 e_{t+1}) \\
&\quad + v_{t+2}^a + (B_a^{-1}B_2^a)^{-1}(C_1 v_{t+1} + C_0 v_t) \\
&\equiv G_1 y_{t+1}^b + G_2 y_t^b + G_3 y_{t-1} + G_4 y_{t+1}^a + G_5 y_t^a + G_6 z_t \\
&\quad + N_2^a e_{t+2} + N_1^a e_{t+1} + v_{t+2}^a + C_1^a v_{t+1} + C_0^a v_t \\
&\equiv g^a(y_{t+1}^b, y_t^b, y_{t-1}, y_{t+1}^a, y_t^a, z_t) \\
&\quad + N_2^a e_{t+2} + N_1^a e_{t+1} + v_{t+2}^a + C_1^a v_{t+1} + C_0^a v_t
\end{aligned}
\tag{21}
$$

where the coefficients G_i ($i = 1, \ldots, 6$), N_i^a ($i = 1, 2$), and C_i^a ($i = 0, 1$) are defined by the line above and g^a stands for the linear function defined in the line above.

By taking conditional expectations of (21) we can evaluate $y_{t|t-1}^a$, $y_{t+1|t-1}^a$, and $y_{t+2|t-1}^a$ successively

$$
\begin{aligned}
y_{t|t-1}^a &= G_1 y_{t-1}^b + G_2 y_{t-2}^b + G_3 y_{t-3} + G_4 y_{t-1}^a + G_5 y_{t-2}^a + G_6 z_{t-2} \\
&\quad + N_2^a e_t + N_1^a e_{t-1} + C_1^a v_{t-1} + C_0^a v_{t-2} \\
&= g^a(y_{t-1}^b, y_{t-2}^b, y_{t-3}, y_{t-1}^a, y_{t-2}^a, z_{t-2}) \\
&\quad + N_2^a e_t + N_1^a e_{t-1} + C_1^a v_{t-1} + C_0^a v_{t-2}
\end{aligned}
\tag{22}
$$

$$
\begin{aligned}
y_{t+1|t-1}^a &= G_1 y_{t|t-1}^b + G_2 y_{t-1}^b + G_3 y_{t-2} + G_4 y_{t|t-1}^a + G_5 y_{t-1}^a \\
&\quad + G_6 z_{t-1} + N_1^a e_t + C_0^a v_{t-1} \\
&= g^a(y_{t|t-1}^b, y_{t-1}^b, y_{t-2}, y_{t|t-1}^a, y_{t-1}^a, z_{t-1}) + N_1^a e_t + C_0^a v_{t-1} \\
&= F_{11} y_{t|t-1}^b + F_{12} y_{t-1} + F_{13} y_{t-2} + F_{14} y_{t-3} + F_{15} z_{t-1} \\
&\quad + F_{16} z_{t-2} + F_{17} e_t + F_{18} e_{t-1} + F_{19} v_{t-1} + F_{1,10} v_{t-2} \\
&\equiv f_1^a(y_{t|t-1}^b, y_{t-1}, y_{t-2}, y_{t-3}, z_{t-1}, z_{t-2}, e_t, e_{t-1}) + F_{19} v_{t-1} + F_{1,10} v_{t-2}
\end{aligned}
\tag{23}
$$

where the coefficients F_{1i} ($i = 1, \ldots, 10$) are obtained by substituting (22) for $y_{t|t-1}^a$ in the line above, and the function f_1^a is defined by the line above; and

$$
\begin{aligned}
y_{t+2|t-1}^a &= G_1 y_{t+1|t-1}^b + G_2 y_{t|t-1}^b + G_3 y_{t-1} + G_4 y_{t+1|t-1}^a + G_5 y_{t|t-1}^a + G_6 z_t \\
&= F_{21} y_{t+1|t-1}^b + F_{22} y_{t|t-1}^b + F_{23} y_{t-1} + F_{24} y_{t-2} + F_{25} y_{t-3} + F_{26} z_t \\
&\quad + F_{27} z_{t-1} + F_{28} z_{t-2} + F_{29} e_t + F_{2,10} e_{t-1} + F_{2,11} v_{t-1} + F_{2,12} v_{t-2} \\
&\equiv f_2^a(y_{t+1|t-1}^b, y_{t|t-1}^b, y_{t-1}, y_{t-2}, y_{t-3}, z_t, z_{t-1}, z_{t-2}, e_t, e_{t-1}) \\
&\quad + F_{2,11} v_{t-1} + F_{2,12} v_{t-2}
\end{aligned}
\tag{24}
$$

where the coefficients $F_{2i}(i = 1, \ldots, 12)$ are obtained by substituting (22) and (23) respectively for $y^a_{t|t-1}$ and $y^a_{t+1|t-1}$ in the line above and the function f^a_2 is defined by the preceding line. If y^b_t is null or if all expectation variables are included in $y^a_{t+q} = y^a_{t+2}$, our problem is solved. Equations (22) to (24) will have converted all expectations variables into observables.

Let all elements of y^b_t appear in $y_{t+q-1|t-1}$, that is, in the first argument of g^a. We need to find a model to convert all $y^b_{t+i|t-1}$ into observables. To do so we substitute (22) to (24) for $y^a_{t|t-1}$, $y^a_{t+1|t-1}$, and $y^a_{t+2|t-1}$ in the structural equations of model (15) and obtain a model

$$F(By_t, y_{t-1}, y_{t-2}, y_{t-3}, z_t, z_{t-1}, z_{t-2}, e_t, e_{t-1}, v_{t-1}, v_{t-2}, y^b_{t|t-1},$$
$$\cdot \tilde{B}^b_1 y_{t+1|t-1}) = u_t \quad (25)$$

which involves only the expectations $y^b_{t+i|t-1}$ $(0 \leq i \leq q - 1)$. In this function F we know the structural coefficient matrix of y_t to be B, and we designate the coefficient matrix of $y^b_{t+1|t-1}$ by $\tilde{B}^b_1$. The reduced form for y^b_t is derived from premultiplying (25) by B_b^{-1}, where $B_b^{-1}By_t = y^b_t$.

Applying the method of solution (19), we can write the solution to this reduced form by replacing the expectations by the actual variables and adding an appropriate residual

$$B_b^{-1}F(By_t, y_{t-1}, y_{t-2}, y_{t-3}, z_t, z_{t-1}, z_{t-2}, e_t, e_{t-1}, v_{t-1}, v_{t-2}, y^b_t, \tilde{B}^b_1 y^b_{t+1})$$
$$= \tilde{N}^b_1 e_{t+1} + (B_b^{-1} \tilde{B}^b_1) v^b_{t+1} + \tilde{C}^b_0 v_t \quad (26)$$

where $v^b_t = B_b^{-1} u_t$. Equation (26) can be solved for y^b_{t+1}, yielding

$$y^b_{t+1} = g^b(y^a_t, y^b_t, y_{t-1}, y_{t-2}, y_{t-3}, z_t, z_{t-1}, z_{t-2}, e_t, e_{t-1}, v_{t-1}, v_{t-2})$$
$$+ N^b_1 e_{t+1} + v^b_{t+1} + C^b_0 v_t \quad (27)$$

where g^b stands for the linear function obtained by solving (26) for y^b_{t+1}. Equation (27) can be used to evaluate $y^b_{t|t-1}$ and $y^b_{t+1|t-1}$ successively

$$y^b_{t|t-1} = g^b(y^a_{t-1}, y^b_{t-1}, y_{t-2}, y_{t-3}, y_{t-4}, z_{t-1}, z_{t-2}, z_{t-3}, e_{t-1}, e_{t-2}, v_{t-2}, v_{t-3})$$
$$+ N^b_1 e_t + C^b_0 v_{t-1} \quad (28)$$

$$y^b_{t+1|t-1} = g^b(y^a_{t|t-1}, y^b_{t|t-1}, y_{t-1}, y_{t-2}, y_{t-3}, z_t, z_{t-1}, z_{t-2}, e_t, e_{t-1}, v_{t-1}, v_{t-2})$$
$$= f^b_1(y_{t-1}, y_{t-2}, y_{t-3}, y_{t-4}, z_t, z_{t-1}, z_{t-2}, z_{t-3}, e_t, e_{t-1}, e_{t-2}, v_{t-1}, v_{t-2},$$
$$v_{t-3}) \quad (29)$$

where the function f^b_1 is obtained by substituting (22) for $y^a_{t|t-1}$ and (28) for $y^b_{t|t-1}$ in the preceding line.

If only a subset of the elements of y^b_t appears in $y_{t+q-1|t-1}$, or the first argument of g^a, while the remaining elements appear in $y_{t+q-2|t-1}$, or the second argument of g^a, solution (26) would apply only to the former variables, which form the last argument of the function F in (25) and (26). The next to the last argument of F in (25) and (26) would include both sets of variables, now re-designated y^b_t and y^c_t, respectively, y^c_t being those variables which appear in

$y_{t+q-2|t-1}$ but not in $y_{t+q-1|t-1}$ or $y_{t+q|t-1}$. Beginning with model (25), with its last two arguments so reinterpreted, we could provide a solution for y_t^b having a moving-average residual of order $q - 1$, as in (26). This solution would be used in the same way that Eq. (21) was used, to replace the variables $y_{t+i|t-1}^b$ in (25) and to yield a solution for y_t^c having a moving-average residual of order $q - 2$. In the exposition hereafter, we shall assume that y_t^a and y_t^b include all expectation variables and that the remaining variables y_t^c are directly observable.

To complete the construction of a model consistent with (15) but involving no expectation variables, we combine Eq. (21) for y_t^a, Eq. (27) for y_t^b and the reduced-form equations for y_t^c, in which expectation variables are replaced by using the first two equations. By this model we can compute $y_{t|t-1}^b$ and $y_{t+1|t-1}^b$ using (28) and (29). The results can be used to compute $y_{t+1|t-1}^a$ and $y_{t+2|t-1}^a$ using (23) and (24).

In the special case with $q = 0$, y_t^a will be a subvector consisting of all endogenous variables appearing in $y_{t|t-1}$, having a reduced form

$$B_a^{-1}(By_t + A_1 y_{t-1} + \cdots + A_p y_{t-p} + B_0^a y_{t-1}^a + \Gamma z_t) = B_a^{-1} u_t = v_t^a$$

The solution to this reduced-form equation is

$$(I + B_a^{-1} B_0^a) y_t^a + B_a^{-1}(A_1 y_{t-1} + \ldots + A_p y_{t-p} + \Gamma z_t) = (I + B_a^{-1} B_0^a) v_t^a \quad (30)$$

which can be used to compute $y_{t|t-1}^a$ in terms of the actual variables. In the special case with $y_t^a = y_t$ and $B_0^a = B_0$, the solution (30) coincides with (9) after the latter has been premultiplied by $(I + B^{-1} B_0) B^{-1}$.

There is another way to resolve the multiple-solution problem in rational-expectation models. One may argue that when multiple solutions exist, the econometrician has not completed the job of specifying a complete model. Take model (10) for example. Just to say that y_t depends on what people expect its value will be in $t + 1$ and on other factors is not a complete theory until one specifies how the expectation $y_{t+1|t-1}$ is formed. From this point of view, simply postulating rational expectations is not sufficient to complete the theory. The econometrician using model (10) should go back to the drawing board and specify something more about the expectation variable until a unique solution is obtained. If the econometrician does not wish to specify the model further, our proposal is to complete the model by introducing additional parameters and to estimate the values of these parameters empirically.

*11.4 THE SOLUTION OF BLANCHARD AND KAHN

One method to find a solution to the univariate model (10) consists of two steps. First, construct a difference equation for $y_{t+i|t-1}$ by advancing the time subscripts of (10) by i and taking expectations conditioned on information I_{t-1}, using $E[E(y_{t+i+1} | I_{t+i-1}) | I_{t-1}] = E(y_{t+i+1} | I_{t-1})$:

$$y_{t+i+1|t-1} + by_{t+i|t-1} + d + z_{t+i|t-1} = 0 \qquad i \geq 0 \quad (31)$$

Second, solve the resulting difference equation for $i = 1$ by repeated substitutions forward. The *forward solution* for $y_{t+1|t-1}$ is

$$
\begin{aligned}
y_{t+1|t-1} &= -b^{-1}(d + z_{t+1|t-1} + y_{t+2|t-1}) \\
&= -b^{-1}(d + z_{t+1|t-1}) + (-b^{-1})^2(d + z_{t+2|t-1}) + \cdots \\
&= -b^{-1}\sum_{h=0}^{\infty}(-b^{-1})^h z_{t+1+h|t-1} - d(1+b)^{-1} \qquad (31a)
\end{aligned}
$$

(31a) can be substituted into (10) to form a solution for y_t.

$$
by_t + db(1+b)^{-1} + z_t = u_t + b^{-1}\sum_{h=0}^{\infty}(-b^{-1})^h z_{t+1+h|t-1} \qquad (31b)
$$

Given a covariance stationary z_t process, this solution works if and only if $|-b^{-1}| < 1$, or when the difference equation (31) has an explosive root $|-b| > 1$. Otherwise, the infinite series will not converge. Our solution (13) does not depend on this condition. Using solution (31b) to form $y_{t+1} + by_t$, one can show that it is a special case of (13) with $r_1 = 0$. Multiple solutions can be constructed by adding an explosive term $c_t(-b)^{t+1}$ to (31a). The augmented solution satisfies the difference equation (31) for $i = 1$ because $c_t(-b)^{t+2} + bc_t(-b)^{t+1} = 0$. This explosive term was exploited by Flood and Garber (1980) and Burmeister and Wall (1983) to model explosive price expectations or bubbles in hyperinflations where price depends on future expected prices. Gourieroux, Laffont, and Montfort (1982) described the set of all solutions of (10). Blanchard and Kahn (1980) tried to generalize solution (31a) to the multivariate case by using canonical variables.

To explain the approach of Blanchard and Kahn and to conform to their notation, let the model explaining y_{t+1} be written as

$$
y_{t+1} = A_0 y_t + A_1 y_{t-1} + A_2 y_{t-2} + B_1 y_{t+1|t} + B_2 y_{t+2|t} + B_3 y_{t+3|t} + \Gamma_0 z_t \qquad (32)
$$

which can be rewritten as

$$
\begin{bmatrix} y_{t-1} \\ y_t \\ y_{t+1} \\ \hline y_{t+2|t} \\ y_{t+2|t} \\ y_{t+3|t} \end{bmatrix}
=
\begin{bmatrix}
0 & I & 0 & 0 & 0 & 0 \\
0 & 0 & I & 0 & 0 & 0 \\
0 & 0 & 0 & I & 0 & 0 \\
\hline
0 & 0 & 0 & 0 & 0 & I \\
0 & 0 & 0 & 0 & 0 & I \\
-B_3^{-1}A_2 & -B_3^{-1}A_1 & -B_3^{-1}A_0 & B_3^{-1} & -B_3^{-1}B_1 & -B_3^{-1}B_2
\end{bmatrix}
\begin{bmatrix} y_{t-2} \\ y_{t-1} \\ y_t \\ \hline y_{t+1} \\ y_{t+1|t} \\ y_{t+2|t} \end{bmatrix}
+
\begin{bmatrix} 0 \\ 0 \\ 0 \\ \hline 0 \\ 0 \\ \Gamma_0 \end{bmatrix} z_t
$$

$$
(33)
$$

The assumption that B_3^{-1} exists is quite restrictive, but it can be weakened (see Prob. 2). Defining

$$
x_t = \begin{bmatrix} y_{t-2} \\ y_{t-1} \\ y_t \end{bmatrix} \qquad \text{and} \qquad p_t = \begin{bmatrix} y_{t+1} \\ y_{t+1|t} \\ y_{t+2|t} \end{bmatrix}
$$

we can rewrite (33) as

$$\begin{bmatrix} x_{t+1} \\ p_{t+1|t} \end{bmatrix} = A \begin{bmatrix} x_t \\ p_t \end{bmatrix} + \Gamma z_t \qquad (34)$$

This model does *not* fit into the Blanchard-Kahn framework because x_t does not satisfy their definition of predetermined variables; that is, $x_{t+1|t} = x_{t+1}$. In the above model $y_{t+1|t} \neq y_{t+1}$. To satisfy the Blanchard-Kahn requirement, we must drop y_{t+1} in (32) and deal with a linear model involving only y_t, y_{t-1}, y_{t-2}, $\ldots$, $y_{t+1|t}$, $y_{t+2|t}$, $y_{t+3|t}$, $\ldots$ without y_{t+1} itself.

To solve model (32) we redefine a vector of predetermined variables to be $x_{t|t} = x_t$; that is, x_t is given information at time t. (Blanchard and Kahn defined x_{t+1} to be given information at time t.) Introduce canonical variables Y_t and Q_t which satisfy

$$\begin{bmatrix} x_t \\ p_t \end{bmatrix} = B \begin{bmatrix} Y_t \\ Q_t \end{bmatrix} \qquad A = BJB^{-1} = C^{-1} \begin{bmatrix} J_1 & 0 \\ 0 & J_2 \end{bmatrix} C \qquad (35)$$

where the diagonal matrix J_1 consists of all stable roots of A and J_2 consists of all roots greater than 1 in absolute value. Replace t in (34) by $t + i$, take expectations given I_t and premultiply by C, with C_{ij} denoting submatrices of C,

$$Q_{t+i+1|t} = J_2 Q_{t+i|t} + [C_{21} \quad C_{22}]\Gamma z_{t+i|t}$$

Therefore $Q_{t|t}$ can be obtained by repeated substitutions for future $Q_{t+i|t}$ ($i \geq 0$) in

$$Q_{t|t} = J_2^{-1} Q_{t+1|t} - J_2^{-1}[C_{21} \quad C_{22}]\Gamma z_{t|t}$$

as we have obtained the forward solution (3/a). Letting $Q_t = Q_{t|t}$ so obtained, we have the result [Blanchard-Kahn's equation (A4)]

$$Q_t = - \sum_{i=0}^{\infty} J_2^{-i-1}[C_{21} \quad C_{22}]\Gamma z_{t+i|t} \qquad (35a)$$

Assuming the number of unstable roots of A to equal the number of elements in p_t or the number of stable roots of A to equal the number of predetermined variables in x_t, we can write

$$C_{21}x_t + C_{22}p_t = Q_t \qquad (36)$$

where C_{22} is square. Furthermore, the first part of the model (34) can be written as

$$x_{t+1} = A_{11}x_t + A_{12}p_t + \gamma_1 z_t \qquad (37)$$

Given Q_t from (35a) we can solve (36) and (37) for x_{t+1} and then for p_{t+1}. Solving (36) for p_t, we have

$$p_t = -C_{22}^{-1} C_{21}x_t + C_{22}^{-1} Q_t \qquad (38)$$

Substituting (38) into (37) gives

$$x_{t+1} = (A_{11} - A_{12} C_{22}^{-1} C_{21})x_t + A_{12} C_{22}^{-1} Q_t + \gamma_1 z_t$$
$$= B_{11} J_1 B_{11}^{-1} x_t + A_{12} C_{22}^{-1} Q_t + \gamma_1 z_t \tag{39}$$

which is the Blanchard-Kahn solution, where

$$A_{11} - A_{12} C_{22}^{-1} C_{21} = B_{11} J_1 B_{11}^{-1} \qquad A_{12} = B_{11} J_1 C_{12} + B_{12} J_2 C_{22}$$

by the definitions of A, B, C, J_1, and J_2. Using (39) for x_{t+1}, one easily finds p_{t+1} by (38).

In summary, by assuming the number of unstable roots to equal the number of elements in p_t and by adopting the solution (35a) for the canonical variables associated with the unstable roots, a unique solution (39) is found. If the number of unstable roots is larger, (36) cannot be solved for p_t since there are more equations than unknowns. Thus no solution exists. If the number of unstable roots is smaller, (36) has multiple solutions since there are fewer equations than unknowns. Thus the problem of multiple solutions remains.

11.5 ESTIMATION OF LINEAR MODELS WITHOUT EXPECTATIONS OF FUTURE VARIABLES

When expectations of future endogenous variables are absent from model (6), the solution is given by Eq. (9). We now consider the estimation of (6) using full-information and limited-information methods. The discussion of this section draws from Taylor (1979) and Wallis (1980).

Assume that the vector u_t in (6) is normal and serially uncorrelated with covariance matrix Σ. A likelihood function based on n observations from the solution (9) can be formulated. This likelihood function can be maximized with respect to the unknown parameters of (6), according to the method of FIML. Denote by δ the vector of unknown coefficients in the matrices B, A_1, A_2, B_0, and Γ in model (6). Denote by x_t the vector consisting of all the variables in (9), namely, y_t, y_{t-1}, y_{t-2}, and z_t. Equation (9) can be written as

$$A(\delta)x_t = u_t$$

The concentrated log-likelihood function, obtained after maximization with respect to Σ, is

$$n \log |B| - \frac{n}{2} \log |A(\delta)X'X A'(\delta)|$$

where X is an $n \times s$ matrix consisting of n observations on the elements of y_t, y_{t-1}, y_{t-2}, and z_t. A numerical method can be applied to maximize the log likelihood with respect to δ.

Wallis (1980) recommends the following gradient method based on the work of Sargan (1972). Differentiating the log likelihood with respect to the ith element

δ_i of δ gives

$$n \operatorname{tr}\left[(B')^{-1}\frac{\partial B}{\partial \delta_i}\right] - n \operatorname{tr}\left[n^{-1}\hat{\Sigma}^{-1}(\delta)A(\delta)X'X\frac{\partial A'}{\partial \delta_i}\right] = 0$$

where
$$\hat{\Sigma}(\delta) = n^{-1}A(\delta)X'XA'(\delta)$$

Let $\tilde{Y}$ be the estimated value of Y using model (9); that is, $\tilde{Y}$ satisfies

$$B\tilde{Y}' + B(B + B_0)^{-1}(A_1 Y'_{-1} + A_2 Y'_{-2} + \Gamma Z') = 0$$

Also let $\tilde{X} = (\tilde{Y}, Y_{-1}, Y_{-2}, Z)$. By the instrumental-variable interpretation of the method of FIML given in Sec. 11.5 the above gradient of the log likelihood can be rewritten as

$$-n \operatorname{tr}\left[n^{-1}\hat{\Sigma}^{-1}(\delta)A(\delta)X'\tilde{X}\frac{\partial A'}{\partial \delta_i}\right] = 0$$

Numerical or analytical derivatives for $\partial A'/\partial \delta_i$ can be obtained, and a gradient method can be applied to maximize the likelihood, yielding FIML estimates.

Turning to a limited-information method to estimate the parameters of one structural equation in (6), we observe that (9) gives the following solution for y_t

$$y_t = -(B + B_0)^{-1}(A_1 y_{t-1} + A_2 y_{t-2} + \Gamma z_t) + B^{-1}u_t$$
$$\equiv P_1 y_{t-1} + P_2 y_{t-2} + P_3 z_t + v_t \tag{40}$$

The conditional expectation of (40) given information up to $t-1$ is the same as Eq. (8). The coefficients P_1, P_2, and P_3 in (40) can be estimated consistently by the method of least squares. Denote these estimates by $\hat{P}_1$, $\hat{P}_2$, and $\hat{P}_3$, respectively. By (8) or (40)

$$\hat{y}_{t|t-1} = \hat{P}_1 y_{t-1} + \hat{P}_2 y_{t-3} + \hat{P}_3 z_t$$

is a consistent estimate of $y_{t|t-1}$. The estimation of $\hat{y}_{t|t-1}$ corresponds to the first stage of the method of 2SLS for estimating the parameters in one structural equation in a system of simultaneous equations.

In the second stage of the method of 2SLS for estimating the ith equation in model (6) one replaces not only the endogenous variables y_{jt} by the estimates $\hat{y}_{jt}$ obtained from regressions on the predetermined variables in the system; one also replaces the expectation variables $y_{k, t|t-1}$ with the estimates $\hat{y}_{k, t|t-1}$ obtained above. The estimates $\hat{y}_{k, t|t-1}$ of the expectation variables are uncorrelated with the residuals u_t in the limit since it is a property of the method of least squares that the estimated regression function

$$\hat{P}_1 Y'_{-1} + \hat{P}_2 Y'_{-2} + \hat{P}_3 Z'$$

of the model (40) be uncorrelated with the estimated residuals and, in the limit, with the true residuals $B^{-1}u_t$. Therefore, the method of 2SLS as modified above for estimating one structural equation of (6) is consistent.

Wallis (1980) discusses conditions for identification of the structural parameters of model (6) without making the assumption $z_{t|t-1} = z_t$, as we do in this chapter. Accordingly, $z_{t|t-1}$ would appear as a predetermined variable in Eq. (40). A stochastic model for z_t would have to be formulated and estimated in order to estimate the variable $z_{t|t-1}$ (see Prob. 7). Wallis (1980) also suggests that the hypothesis of rational expectations can be tested by comparing the constrained estimates of the coefficients P_1, P_2, and P_3 in (40), which are functions of the structural parameters B, B_0, A_1, A_2, and Γ, with the unconstrained least-squares estimates. A likelihood-ratio test based on the two models, restricted and unrestricted, can be constructed for this purpose.

11.6 ESTIMATION OF LINEAR MODELS WITH FUTURE EXPECTATIONS

As in the previous section, we first consider FIML estimation of the parameters of (15) when $q \geq 1$. The solution method of Sec. 11.3 is used to convert model (15) into three submodels involving no expectation variables, namely (21) for y_t^a, (27) for y_t^b (assuming only two sets of expectation variables in model (15)), and a third submodel for the remaining variables, say y_t^c, obtained by using (22) to (24), (28), and (29) to replace the expectation variables in the reduced-form equations for y_t^c. For $q = 2$ and $p = 1$ we write these three submodels as

$$y_t^a = G_1 y_{t-1}^b + G_2 y_{t-2}^b + G_3 y_{t-3} + G_4 y_{t-1}^a + G_5 y_{t-2}^a + G_6 z_{t-2}$$
$$+ N_2^a e_t + N_1^a e_{t-1} + v_t^a + C_1^a v_{t-1} + C_0^a v_{t-2} \tag{41}$$

which is identical with (21) with $t + 2$ replaced by t

$$y_t^b = F_1 y_{t-1}^a + F_2 y_{t-1}^b + F_3 y_{t-2} + F_4 y_{t-3} + F_5 y_{t-4} + F_6 z_{t-1} + F_7 z_{t-2}$$
$$+ F_8 z_{t-3} + F_9 e_{t-1} + F_{10} e_{t-2} + F_{11} v_{t-2} + F_{12} v_{t-3} + N_1^b e_t$$
$$+ v_t^b + C_0^b v_{t-1} \tag{42}$$

which is identical with (27) with the coefficients F_i written out explicitly, and

$$y_t^c = H_1 y_{t-1} + H_2 y_{t-2} + H_3 y_{t-3} + H_4 y_{t-4} + H_5 z_t + H_6 z_{t-1} + H_7 z_{t-2}$$
$$+ H_8 z_{t-3} + H_9 e_t + H_{10} e_{t-1} + H_{11} e_{t-2} + H_{12} v_{t-1}$$
$$+ H_{13} v_{t-2} + H_{14} v_{t-3} + v_t^c \tag{43}$$

which results from substituting (22) to (24), (28), and (29) for the expectation variables in the reduced-form equations for y_t^c. Note that the coefficients G_i, F_i, and H_i in these three equations are known functions of the parameters of (15), and of N_1^a, N_2^a, and N_1^b, to be denoted by a vector δ. Furthermore, the coefficients F_9 to F_{12} in (42) are functions also of N_2^a, N_1^a, C_1^a, and C_0^a in (41) on account of the substitution of (22) and (23) for $y_{t|t-1}^a$ and $y_{t+1|t-1}^a$ in (15) to form (25) and (27). Similarly, the coefficients H_9 to H_{14} are functions also of N_2^a, N_1^a, C_1^a, and C_0^a, whereas the coefficients H_9 and H_{12} are functions also of N_1^b and C_0^b.

The model of Eqs. (41) to (43) can be written as

$$y_t = A(\delta)x_t + w_t \tag{44}$$

where y_t is a column vector consisting of y_t^a, y_t^b, and y_t^c; x_t is a vector consisting of $y_{t-1}, \ldots, y_{t-4}, z_{t-1}, \ldots, z_{t-3}$ and e_t, e_{t-1}, e_{t-2}; and w_t satisfies

$$w_t = v_t + \begin{bmatrix} C_1^a \\ C_0^b \\ H_{12} \end{bmatrix} v_{t-1} + \begin{bmatrix} C_0^a \\ F_{11} \\ H_{13} \end{bmatrix} v_{t-2} + \begin{bmatrix} 0 \\ F_{12} \\ H_{14} \end{bmatrix} v_{t-3}$$

$$\equiv v_t + \theta_1 v_{t-1} + \theta_2 v_{t-2} + \theta_3 v_{t-3} \tag{45}$$

with v_t consisting of subvectors v_t^a, v_t^b, and v_t^c. Let the covariance matrix of v_t be $\Omega = B^{-1}\Sigma B^{-1\prime}$. The autocovariance matrix $Ew_t w'_{t-k}$ of w_t can be derived from (45) as a function of $\Omega, \theta_1, \theta_2$, and θ_3. The n observations of the model (44) can be written as

$$Y = XA'(\delta) + W$$

where Y is $n \times g$. If we stack the columns of the matrix Y into a vector y, stack the columns of W into a vector w, and denote the columns of $A'(\delta)$ by a_i, the above system can be written as

$$y = \begin{bmatrix} X & & & \\ & X & & 0 \\ & & \ddots & \\ 0 & & & X \end{bmatrix} \begin{bmatrix} a_1 \\ a_2 \\ \vdots \\ a_g \end{bmatrix} + w \tag{46}$$

The covariance matrix V of w can be derived from the autocovariance matrix $Ew_t w'_{t-k}$ and is a function of $\Omega, \theta_1, \theta_2$, and θ_3. Given $\delta, C_1^a, C_0^a, C_0^b$, and Σ, and hence given $\theta_1, \theta_2, \theta_3$ and $\Omega = B^{-1}\Sigma B^{-1\prime}$, the covariance matrix V can be computed. The log-likelihood function of the model of Eqs. (44) and (45) is

$$\log L = -\tfrac{1}{2}|V| - \tfrac{1}{2} w'V^{-1}w \tag{47}$$

In principle, this function can be maximized numerically with respect to the unknown parameters δ (including N_1^a, N_2^a, and N_1^b) and Σ of the structural equations (15) and the free parameters C_1^a, C_0^a, and C_0^b introduced to solve the problem of multiple solutions.

An approximation to the above FIML estimates can be obtained by minimizing the expression

$$\sum_{t=1}^{n} v_t' \Omega^{-1} v_t \tag{48}$$

where $\Omega = Evv_t' = B^{-1}\Sigma B^{-1\prime}$ and v_t is defined by (45) and (44) as

$$v_t = w_t - \theta_1 v_{t-1} - \theta_2 v_{t-2} - \theta_3 v_{t-3}$$

$$= y_t - A(\delta)x_t - \theta_1 v_{t-1} - \theta_2 v_{t-2} - \theta_3 v_{t-3} \tag{49}$$

To start the computation of v_1 in (48), we set v_{-1}, v_{-2}, and v_{-3} equal to their expected value zero. Expression (48) can be minimized with respect to δ, Σ, C_1^a, C_0^a, and C_0^b using a numerical method. It is easier to evaluate than the log likelihood of (47) since there is no need to compute $|V|$ and V^{-1}, which are of order ng.

The computations using (48) can be simplified somewhat by replacing the covariance matrix Ω by an estimate

$$\hat{\Omega} = \frac{1}{n} \sum_{t=1}^{n} \hat{v}_t \hat{v}_t'$$

where $\hat{v}_t$ is given by the last line of (49) with the values of the parameters $\delta, \theta_1, \theta_2$, and θ_3 given by the previous iteration. That is, given the values of $\delta, \theta_1, \theta_2$, and θ_3, we compute $\hat{v}_t$ $(t = 1, \ldots, n)$ and $\hat{\Omega}$. Treating $\hat{\Omega}$ as given, we minimize $\Sigma_t v_t' \hat{\Omega}^{-1} v_t$ with respect to δ, θ_1, θ_2, and θ_3 using a numerical method. We then recompute $\hat{v}_t$ and $\hat{\Omega}$ using the new values of the parameters and iterate until convergence. This procedure separates Σ from the rest of the parameters. Having estimated Ω and δ (and thus B), one can estimate Σ using the relation $\Sigma = B\Omega B'$. The procedure was suggested by Malinvaud (1970) as a minimum-distance estimator and was used by Taylor (1979) to estimate model (5) under rational expectations; see Sec. 7.2 for a description and Eq. (70) of Chap. 6 for an application to estimating linear ARMA models. If the total number of parameters is not too large, say below 100, the above modified method of maximum-likelihood estimation using brute force can be recommended.

For simultaneous-equation models under rational expectations the solution submodels for y_t^a, y_t^b, and y_t^c correspond to the reduced-form equations of the traditional models. The parameters of these submodels, like the parameters of the reduced-form equations, are functions of the structural parameters. To obtain maximum-likelihood estimates of the structural parameters one can set up the likelihood function for the reduced form or the solution submodels and maximize it with respect to the parameters of the structure using a numerical method.

When the number of structural parameters is very large, it may be computationally more convenient to set up the likelihood function for the structural equations (15) and maximize it iteratively in two steps as follows. The likelihood function of (15) is as given in Eq. (69) of Chap. 5 except that the expectation variables themselves should be interpreted as functions of the structural parameters as well as the parameters of the moving-average residuals of (21) and (27), via Eqs. (22) to (24), (28), and (29). In principle, one can substitute the right-hand side of (22) to (24), etc., for these expectation variables in the likelihood function and maximize it accordingly. However, since efficient algorithms have already been devised for maximum-likelihood estimation of (15) with the expectation variables treated as given, e.g., by Chow and Fair (1973), it may be desirable to divide our task into two steps. First, treating the values of the functions $y_{t+i|t-1}^a$ and $y_{t+i|t-1}^b$ as fixed tentatively, use an existing algorithm for traditional simultaneous-equation models to estimate the parameters of (15). Second, recompute the values of the functions $y_{t+i|t-1}^a$ and $y_{t+i|t-1}^b$ using revised estimates of the parameters of (15) and of the moving-average residuals in (21) and (27) or in (41) and (42).

The second step is executed in the following manner. Form the coefficients of the autoregressive processes in (21) and (27) using the revised structural parameters and maximize the likelihood function for (21) and (27) with respect only to the moving-average parameters. Given the parameters of (21) and (27), evaluate $y^a_{t+i|t-1}$ and $y^b_{t+i|t-1}$ using (22) to (24), (28), and (29). This two-step procedure can be iterated. If it converges, the result is a set of maximum-likelihood estimates at least in the sense of satisfying the first-order conditions for maximizing the likelihood function which are imposed in each of the two steps.

To economize on computations and still obtain consistent estimates of the structural parameters of (15) one can devise a limited-information method. This is done by revising the second step above by finding consistent estimates of the parameters of (21) and (27), using maximum likelihood for example, without imposing the nonlinear restrictions on their autoregressive parameters as derived from the structure. These estimates are used to evaluate $y^a_{t+i|t-1}$ and $y^b_{t+i|t-1}$. Given the values of the expectations variables, the method of 2SLS, for example, can be applied to estimate the parameters of (15). To show that the method of 2SLS provides consistent estimates of the structural parameters in the present case we need only show that the reduced-form parameters in the first stage of 2SLS are consistently estimated. If the "composite" predetermined variables $y^a_{y+i|t-1}$ and $y^b_{t+i|t-1}$ in the reduced form are formed by the true parameters of (21) and (27), they are uncorrelated with the residuals v_t of the reduced form and the method of least squares in the first stage is consistent. But consistent estimates of the matrix coefficients of (21) and (27) are also uncorrelated with the residuals v_t in the limit. Hence, the predetermined variables $y^a_{t+i|t-1}$ and $y^b_{t+i|t-1}$ formed by using these estimated coefficients are also uncorrelated with the reduced-form residuals in the limit, which implies consistency of the least-squares estimates of the reduced-form coefficients. In essence, when one applies an existing method such as 2SLS to estimate the parameters of (15) under rational expectations, the additional complication lies in having to estimate (21) and (27) consistently in order to form the predetermined variables $y^a_{t+i|t-1}$ and $y^b_{t+i|t-1}$.

The estimation of model (41) to (43) may be computationally expensive, but it is the model that generates the vector y_t without using expectations variables. It provides a unique solution to model (15) which has multiple solutions. If one does not care to provide a unique solution to (15) and is concerned only with the parameters of (15), one need not estimate the moving-average parameters of (41) to (43). To find consistent estimates of the parameters of the structural equations in (15), one can apply the following method of instrumental variables described in McCallum (1976a).

As in the construction of (16), we assume that y_t can be explained linearly by a set of variables including $y_{t-1}, y_{t-2}, \ldots, z_t, z_{t-1}, \ldots,$ and v_t. This implies that $y_{t+m|t-1}$ is a linear function of $y_{t-1}, y_{t-2}, \ldots, z_t, z_{t-1}, \ldots,$ since $z_{t+j|t-1}$ $(j = 1, \ldots, m)$ are functions of $z_t, z_{t-1}, \ldots$. The difference $y_{t+m} - y_{t+m|t-1}$ is a linear function of $v_{t+m}, \ldots, v_t, e_{t+m}, \ldots, e_{t+1}$ as given by (17) where $e_{t+j} = z_{t+j} - z_{t+j|t-1}$. Call this linear function η_{t+m}. We can thus rewrite (17) as

$$y_{t+m|t-1} = y_{t+m} - \eta_{t+m} \qquad (m = 0, 1, \ldots, q) \qquad (50)$$

where η_{t+m} is uncorrelated with $y_{t-1}, y_{t-2}, \ldots, z_t, z_{t-1}, \ldots$. Let n observations of the ith structural equation be written as

$$y_i = Y_i \beta_i + Y_{i+|t-1} \beta_i^* + X_i \gamma_i + \epsilon_i \qquad (51)$$

where the symbols are as defined in Eq. (11) of Chap. 5 except for $Y_{i+|t-1}$, which consists of expectations of future endogenous variables (in different periods) included in the ith equation, with coefficient vector β_i^*. Using (50) to replace these expectations variables $Y_{i+|t-1}$ in (51) by the actual values Y_{i+} minus the residuals η_{i+}, we have

$$y_i = Y_i \beta_i + Y_{i+} \beta_i^* + X_i \gamma_i + (\epsilon_i - \eta_{i+} \beta_i^*) \qquad (52)$$

To form a matrix of instrumental variables for $(Y_i \quad Y_{i+})$, we regress $(Y_i \quad Y_{i+})$ on a set of variables Z_i selected from $y_{t-1}, y_{t-2}, \ldots, z_t, z_{t-1}, \ldots$, and obtain the estimated values

$$(\hat{Y}_i \quad \hat{Y}_{i+}) = Z_i (Z_i' Z_i)^{-1} Z_i' (Y_i \quad Y_{i+}) \qquad (53)$$

The instrumental-variable estimator of β_i, β_i^*, and γ_i is

$$[(\hat{Y}_i \quad Y_{i+} \quad X_i)'(Y_i \quad Y_{i+} \quad X_i)]^{-1}(\hat{Y}_i \quad \hat{Y}_{i+} \quad X_i)' y_i \qquad (54)$$

This estimator is consistent because the matrix $(\hat{Y}_i \quad \hat{Y}_{i+})$ of instrumental variables is uncorrelated with the residual $\epsilon_i - \eta_{i+} \beta_i^*$ in the limit, i.e.,

$$\operatorname*{plim}_{n \to \infty} n^{-1} (\hat{Y}_i \quad \hat{Y}_{i+})'(\epsilon_i - \eta_{i+} \beta_i^*) = 0$$

This method of instrumental variables can be applied to each structural equation to estimate all the parameters of (15). However, if one is interested in obtaining a unique solution to (15), one still needs to estimate the model (41)–(43), or (44)–(45). Using the above estimates of the structural parameters for δ in (44), one can estimate the moving-average parameters in (44)–(45) by the method of maximum likelihood or minimum distance for this purpose.

In this chapter a unique solution to (15) is found by introducing as additional variables the moving-average residuals and the one-period-ahead forecast errors e_{t+j} for the exogenous variables z_{t+j}. Some exogenous variables may be difficult to model. A practical strategy is to model certain important exogenous variables and inbed them in the vector y_t and test the hypothesis that in solution (19) the forecast errors e_{t+j} for the remaining exogenous variables have zero coefficients. Accepting this hypothesis will permit one not to model these exogenous variables and lead to a simpler model.

PROBLEMS

1. Let $B_1 y_{t+1|t-1}$ be added to the left-hand side of (6). Explain why the procedure from (7) to (9) fails to eliminate $y_{t+1|t-1}$.

2. In Eq. (32) if B_3 is singular having columns of zeros and $B_3 y_{t+3|t} = B_3^a y_{t+3|t}^a$, how should Eq. (33) be modified? Assume $B_2 = (B_2^a \quad B_2^b)$, B_2^a having full column rank.

3. Prove that the forward solution (3/b) to the univariate model (10) is a special case of solution (13) with $r_1 = 0$. Use (3/b) to form $y_{t+1} + by_t$.

4. If the residual vector u_t in (15) satisfies $u_t = Ru_{t-1} + \epsilon_t$, where ϵ_t is serially uncorrelated, provide a solution to the reduced-form equation (18).

5. If the residual vector u_t in (15) satisfies $u_t = Ru_{t-1} + \epsilon_t$, where ϵ_t is serially uncorrelated, how should the full- and limited-information estimation methods of Sec. 10.5 be modified?

6. If the residual vector u_t in (15) satisfies $u_t = Ru_{t-1} + \epsilon_t$, where ϵ_t is serially uncorrelated, how should the instrumental-variable estimation method of Sec. 10.5 be modified?

7. Derive a set of conditions for identification of the structural parameters of (6) following the lines of Wallis (1980, pp. 62–64) by assuming $z_{t|t-1} = z_t$. Compare these conditions with those of Wallis, who did not assume $z_{t|t-1} = z_t$.

8. In Eq. (10) let z_t follow $z_t = \phi z_{t-1} + \epsilon_t$ and ϵ_t be uncorrelated with u_t. Find a solution to model (10) by combining it with this equation for z_t in a bivariate model. Compare the solution with (13).

9. Derive (13) by the method of undetermined coefficients: Use (11) to evaluate the left-hand side and right-hand side of (10) and equate coefficients on both sides to find the coefficients of (11) as functions of b and d. Let $z_{t+1|t-1}$ be $\delta_0 z_t + \delta_1 z_{t-1} + \cdots$.

10. Describe carefully how you can estimate model (5) of Taylor (1979) by FIML.

11. Describe carefully how you can estimate model (5) of Taylor (1979) by a limited-information method.

12. Using the method of Sec. 11.3, solve the model of Sargent and Wallace (1975) given in Sec. 11.2.

13. Describe carefully how you can estimate the model of Sargent and Wallace (1975) given in Sec. 11.2 (a) by FIML and (b) by a limited-information method.

REFERENCES

Aoki, M., and M. Canzoneri (1979): "Reduced Forms of Rational Expectations Models," *Q. J. Econ.*, **93**: 59–72.

Blanchard, O. J., and C. M. Kahn (1980): "The Solution of Linear Difference Models under Rational Expectations," *Econometrica*, **38**: 1305–1311.

Burmeister, E., and K. Wall (1983): "Kalman Filtering Estimation of Unobserved Rational Expectations with an Application to German Hyperinflation," *J. Econometr.*, **11**.

Cagan, P. (1956): "The Monetary Dynamics of Hyper-Inflation," in M. Friedman (ed.), *Studies in the Quantity Theory of Money*, University of Chicago Press, Chicago.

Chow, G. C. (1981): "Solution and Estimation of Simultaneous Equations under Rational Expectations," *Princeton Univ., Econometr. Res. Prog. Res. Mem.* 291.

――― and R. C. Fair (1973): "Maximum Likelihood Estimation of Linear Equations Systems with Auto-Regressive Residuals," *Ann. Econ. Soc. Meas.*, **2**: 17–28.

Flood, R. P., and P. M. Garber (1980): "Market Fundamentals versus Price-Level Bubbles: The First Tests," *J. Pol. Econ.*, **88**: 745–770.

Friedman, M. (1957): *A Theory of the Consumption Function*, Princeton University Press, Princeton, N.J.

Gourieroux, C., J. J. Laffont, and A. Montfort (1982): "Rational Expectations in Dynamic Linear Models," *Econometrica*, **50**: 409–425.

McCallum, B. T. (1976): "Rational Expectations and the Natural Rate Hypothesis: Some Consistent Estimates," *Econometrica*, **44**: 43–52.

――― (1976): "Rational Expectations and the Estimation of Econometric Models: An Alternative Procedure," *Int. Econ. Rev.*, **17**: 484–490.

Malinvaud, E. (1970): *Statistical Methods of Econometrics*, North-Holland, Rotterdam.

Muth, J. F. (1960): "Optimal Properties of Exponentially Weighted Forecasts," *J. Am. Statist. Assoc.*, **55**: 299–306.

—— (1961): "Rational Expectations and the Theory of Price Movements," *Econometrica*, **29**: 315–335.

—— (1981): "Estimation of Economic Relationships Containing Latent Expectations Variables," chap. 17 in R. E. Lucas, Jr., and T. J. Sargent (eds.), *Rational Expectations and Econometric Practice*, University of Minnesota Press, Minneapolis.

Sargan, J. D. (1972): "The Identification and Estimation of Sets of Simultaneous Stochastic Equations," London School of Econ., Mimeo.

Sargent, T. J., and N. Wallace (1975): "'Rational' Expectations, the Optimal Monetary Instrument, and the Optimal Money Supply Rule," *J. Polit. Econ.*, **83**: 241–254.

Shiller, R. (1978): "Rational Expectations and the Dynamic Structure of Macroeconomic Models: A Critical Review," *J. Monetary Econ.*, **4**: 1–44.

Taylor, J. B. (1977): "Conditions for Unique Solutions in Stochastic Macroeconomic Models with Rational Expectations," *Econometrica*, **45**: 1377–1385.

—— (1979): "Estimation and Control of a Macroeconomic Model with Rational Expectations," *Econometrica*, **47**: 1267–1286.

Wallis, K. F. (1980): "Econometric Implications of the Rational Expectations Hypothesis," *Econometrica*, **48**: 49–73.

TWELVE

MODELS OF OPTIMIZING AGENTS

12.1 INTRODUCTION AND PREVIEW

It is worth emphasizing that econometric models ought to be formulated according to economic theory. The model of simultaneous equations owes its popularity to the fact that economic theory often takes the form of a system of simultaneous equations. The Walrasian general equilibrium model is a system of simultaneous equations. So is the Marshallian model of demand and supply, not to mention the Keynesian model of macroeconomics, which has provided the theoretical basis for many macroeconometric models since the 1950s. Keynesian macroeconomic theory, however, has constantly been subjected to challenges and revisions by economists who wished to find theoretical bases for the basic postulates of Keynes. Thus the consumption function, the investment function, and the liquidity-preference relation have all been the subject of serious theoretical inquiries. Economists have sought to provide a microeconomic foundation for macroeconomics.

Microeconomic theory is based mainly on the assumption that economic agents behave as if they were to maximize some objective function subject to the constraint of their environment. Actions of consumers and of firms are so explained. Consumption functions, demand functions for money and other assets, investment equations, and demand equations for inputs can be so derived. For example, to derive a demand equation for labor as an input an econometrician assumes that firms maximize profits, or minimize costs, subject to the constraint of a production function. The demand equation for input so derived can be estimated econometrically (see Prob. 1). It may serve as one equation in a system of simultaneous equations. Other equations in the system can also be derived by the assumption of maximizing behavior.

To go one step further, the theory of maximizing behavior not only provides behavioral equations (demand functions for inputs) for econometric models but also pinpoints the economic environment (demand functions for outputs) and the objective function (cost function, production function) which the econometrician needs to take into account in the modeling process. Obviously, the parameters of the behavioral equations are related to the parameters of the economic environment and of the objective function since the former are derived from the latter through optimization. If the latter parameters remain unchanged, the parameters of the behavioral equations will also remain unchanged; and knowledge of the behavioral equations alone will suffice in obtaining forecasts of the endogenous variables. However, if the parameters of the economic environment or of the objective function change, the parameters of the behavioral equations will change accordingly. Knowledge of the former parameters can be used to derive the parameters of the behavior equations, which can then be employed to provide economic forecasts.

The last point was made when we drew the important distinction between structural equations and reduced-form equations in simultaneous-equation models. The reduced-form equations are derived from the structural equations. If the parameters of the structural equations remain unchanged, the parameters of the reduced-form equations will also remain unchanged. Estimation of the reduced-form equations will suffice for prediction purposes, but if the structural parameters change, knowledge of the structural parameters is required to rederive the reduced-form parameters for prediction purposes. For example, in a simple Keynesian model involving a linear consumption function

$$C = \beta_0 + \beta_1(1 - \tau)Y$$

$$Y = C + I + G$$

where I and G are treated as exogenous and τ is the tax rate, the reduced-form equation for Y is

$$Y = \frac{\beta_0}{1 - \beta_1(1 - \tau)} + \frac{1}{1 - \beta_1(1 - \tau)} I + \frac{1}{1 - \beta_1(1 - \tau)} G$$

This shows clearly that the reduced-form parameters are functions of the structural parameters and that knowledge of the structural parameters β_0 and β_1 is required for predicting Y if the tax rate τ changes. In the context of models based explicitly on maximizing behavior, the parameters of the environment facing economic agents and of their objective function are structural parameters. The parameters of the behavioral equations derived from maximization are reduced-form parameters. Marschak (1953) pointed out the importance of estimating structural parameters in models of simultaneous equations, and Lucas (1976) emphasized this point in the context of models of optimizing agents.

In this chapter we shall be concerned with the derivation of behavioral equations of economic agents who face an economic environment described by a linear stochastic model and whose objective function is quadratic. The choice of a linear stochastic model and a quadratic objective function is based on econometric convenience, because the behavioral equation so derived will be linear. We shall be concerned with methods for estimating the parameters of the environment, of the objective function, and of the resulting behavioral equations. Models involving one set of economic agents will be extended to include two sets of agents facing each other in the context of a dynamic game. Lucas and Sargent (1981) provide a good introductory exposition of models of optimizing agents, which they refer to as *rational expectations models*. We have used a different, and perhaps more descriptive term in order to distinguish the models of this chapter from those of the preceding chapter. Historically speaking, when Muth (1961) introduced the term "rational expectations," he did not formulate an optimization model to derive the demand and supply equations. Many econometricians today may employ the assumption of rational expectations in the context of models of simultaneous equations, as discussed in the last chapter, without adopting the optimal control framework used in this chapter.

To summarize the material in this chapter, let us assume that the economic agents are confronted with an environment to be described by a linear system (1) with a stochastic disturbance u_t and that their objective or loss function is given by a quadratic function (2). Two economic examples are given in Sec. 12.5. The agents are assumed to solve a stochastic optimal control problem, namely, deriving their optimal decision rule (3) for the control variables x_t by minimizing the expectation of the loss function (2) subject to constraint (1). If the model describing the environment is *linear* (with an additive stochastic disturbance u_t) and the loss function is *quadratic*, then the optimal decision rule is that the vector x_t of control variables is a *linear* function of the vector y_{t-1} of past endogenous and control variables. Section 12.2 will provide a mathematical derivation of the optimal control rule (3).

By observing time-series data on y_t and x_t the econometrician's task is to estimate the parameters of the functions (1) to (3). The task is essentially to estimate the parameters of (1) and (2), from which parameters of (3) can be derived by solving the optimal control problem. From the viewpoint of estimation one cannot estimate the parameters of (1) to (3) freely, since the parameters of (3) are functions of the parameters of (1) and (2). Section 12.3 solves the estimation problem by applying the method of maximum likelihood subject to the above constraints on the parameters. Section 12.4 presents a solution by applying least squares twice. This method of 2SLS is to be distinguished from the 2SLS method used in Chap. 5 to estimate the parameters of simultaneous equations.

While we have derived the optimal control rule in Sec. 12.2 by the method of dynamic programming, others, notably Sargent (1979) and Hansen and Sargent (1980), have presented an alternative "classical" method (Sec. 12.6) to derive the optimal control rule. The relative advantages and disadvantages of the two methods are still subjects of research. Current opinions differ. The following discussion may not be entirely objective because of the author's background. In about 1967 or 1968, he tried to apply the classical method using canonical factorization of generating functions to solve optimal control problems in macroeconomics but did not find it convenient to use. Later, the formulas for the optimal control rule presented in Sec. 12.2 were derived by the use of lagrangian multipliers in Chow (1970) and by the method of dynamic programming in Chow (1973). In the 1970s most people working on stochastic control preferred the method of dynamic programming to the classical method. In the late 1970s and early 1980s interest in the classical method revived. Sections 12.6 and 12.7 may help the reader form an initial opinion on the subject. Perhaps, for certain types of models, one method is more convenient and for other types the alternative method is more convenient. Further research is needed to settle this issue.

The assumptions underlying the use of the above type of optimization models in econometrics will be discussed in Sec. 12.8. One should also point out that the problem of aggregation needs more vigorous treatment. Given a model of the optimization behavior for a firm, how is the behavior of a group of firms to be derived? For example, assuming the parameters of the environment (1) to apply to all firms, x_t denoting either the sum or the mean of the (vector) control variables of all firms, must one further assume that the parameters of the objective function (2) are the same for all firms in order to justify using an aggregate linear decision rule in the form of (3)? The answer is probably no, and the problem of aggregation deserves to be further studied. Furthermore, how restrictive is the assumption of a quadratic loss function, and how sensitive to this assumption are the results?

A model of a dynamic game is introduced in Sec. 12.9 to study the optimization behavior of two sets of economic agents. Equation (64) represents the environment facing two sets of agents (players 1 and 2) with control variables x_{1t} and x_{2t}, respectively. Given their objective functions (65), they will derive their optimal decision rules (66) under two alternative solution concepts for the game. One is the solution with player 2 (the government, for example) as the dominant player. Player 1 (the private sector) will take the decision rule of player 2 as given when solving its optimal control problem. Deriving the decision rule of player 1 in terms of the decision rule of player 2 provides a solution to the problem of econometric policy evaluation raised by Lucas (1976). As Lucas points out, to the extent that a government decision rule forms a part of the environment (1) facing the private economic agents who are assumed to solve an optimization problem to derive their decision rules, the decision rules will change when the policy of the government changes. Section 12.10 shows how the private sector will change its decision rules in response to changes in government policy.

The government, anticipating the reactions of the private sector to its policy, can choose a policy to maximize its objective function. This solves the problem of designing an optimal policy for the government which incorporates the private sector's reaction, as pointed out in Sec. 12.10. In order for this solution to be stable, however, the private sector must trust the government, or the announced policy rule of the government must be credible. Otherwise, people in the private sector could put themselves in bad situations and wait for the government to save them. This issue was raised by Kydland and Prescott (1977). The solution given in Sec. 12.10 avoids this issue by assuming the credibility of the government. Without this assumption one can resolve this issue by modifying the solution algorithm of dynamic programming, as Chow (1981, chap. 15) shows.

Given the solutions of the decision rules of the two players with player 2 as the dominant player, the econometrician can estimate the parameters of the dynamic-game model using time-series observations, as will be discussed in Sec. 12.11. In Sec. 12.12 we employ a second solution concept, that of a Nash equilibrium, to derive the decision rules of the two players and present an iterative method to estimate the parameters of the model. For the estimation of nonlinear models when the private sector takes the decision rule of the government sector as given, see Chow (1981, chap. 16).

12.2 DERIVING AN OPTIMAL FEEDBACK CONTROL EQUATION

Let the environment facing the economic decision makers be represented by a linear system

$$y_t = A_t y_{t-1} + C_t x_t + b_t + u_t \tag{1}$$

where y_t is a vector of p state variables, x_t is a vector of q control variables, A_t, C_t, and b_t are matrices of known constants, and u_t is a random vector that is serially independent and identically distributed. It is understood that state variables have been introduced to eliminate $y_{t-2}, y_{t-3}, \ldots, x_{t-1}, x_{t-2}, \ldots$ from the system, and to incorporate x_t as a subvector of y_t so that the loss function (2) below need not have x_t as an argument. For example, if there are 50 endogenous variables in the original system and the model includes a variable $y_{6,t-2}$, an identity $y_{51,t} = y_{6,t-1}$ can be introduced. Given this identity, $y_{6,t-2}$ can be written as $y_{51,t-1}$ and the second-order lag disappears. If $y_{6,t-3}$ is present, another identity $y_{52,t} = y_{51,t-1}$ can be used and $y_{6,t-3}$ can be written as $y_{52,t-1}$. Let there be 40 identities of this type to rid the system of second- and higher-order lagged endogenous variables. If $x_{1,t-1}$ and $x_{1,t-2}$ are present, we can define $y_{91,t} = x_{1,t-1}$ and write $x_{1,t-2}$ as $y_{91,t-1}$, and so forth. Let there be 10 identities of this type. We then define $y_{101,t} = x_{1t}$, $y_{102,t} = x_{2t}$ to incorporate x_t as a subvector of y_t.

It is assumed that the objective or loss function measuring the preference of the decision makers is quadratic

$$W = \sum_{t=1}^{T} (y_t - a_t)' K_t (y_t - a_t) \tag{2}$$

where K_t is a given symmetric positive-semidefinite weighting matrix and a_t is a vector of targets. The optimal control problem is to find strategies for x_t in order to minimize expected loss. The solution to this problem takes the form of a linear feedback control equation

$$x_t = G_t y_{t-1} + g_t \qquad t = 1, \ldots, T \tag{3}$$

The matrices G_t are obtained by solving the pair of matrix equations

$$G_t = -(C_t' H_t C_t)^{-1} C_t' H_t A_t \tag{4}$$

$$H_{t-1} = K_{t-1} + (A_t + C_t G_t)' H_t (A_t + C_t G_t) \tag{5}$$

backward in time ($t = T, T - 1, \ldots, 1$) with initial condition $H_T = K_T$. The vectors g_t are obtained by solving

$$g_t = -(C_t' H_t C_t)^{-1} C_t'(H_t b_t - h_t) \tag{6}$$

$$h_{t-1} = K_{t-1} a_{t-1} - (A_t + C_t G_t)'(H_t b_t - h_t) \tag{7}$$

backward in time ($t = T, T - 1, \ldots, 1$) with initial condition $h_T = K_T a_T$.

To derive the above solution one can use the method of dynamic programming. First, we find the optimal policy for the last period T, given all the information up to (the end of) period $T - 1$. Denote by V_T the expectation, conditioned on information up to $T - 1$, of the loss for period T, which is a function of the policy x_T

$$V_T = E_{T-1}(y_T - a_T)' K_T(y_T - a_T) = E_{T-1}(y_T' H_T y_T - 2y_T' h_T + c_T) \tag{8}$$

where we have set $K_T = H_T$, $K_T a_T = h_T$, and $c_T = a_T' K_T a_T$. Substituting $A_T y_{T-1} + C_T x_T + b_T + u_T$ for y_T in (8) and minimizing V_T with respect to x_T by differentiation, we find the optimal policy for the last period

$$\hat{x}_T = G_T y_{T-1} + g_T \tag{9}$$

where
$$G_T = -(C_T' H_T C_T)^{-1}(C_T' H_T A_T) \tag{10}$$

and
$$g_T = -(C_T' H_T C_T)^{-1} C_T'(H_T b_T - h_T). \tag{11}$$

The minimum expected loss for the last period is obtained by substituting for x_T in V_T,

$$\begin{aligned}
\hat{V}_T = {} & y_{T-1}'(A_T + C_T G_T)' H_T(A_T + C_T G_T)y_{T-1} \\
& + 2y_{T-1}'(A_T + C_T G_T)'(H_T b_T - h_T) + (b_T + C_T g_T)' H_T(b_T + C_T g_T) \\
& - 2(b_T + C_T g_T)' h_T + c_T + E_{T-1} u_T' H_T u_T
\end{aligned} \tag{12}$$

To obtain the optimal policies for the last two periods, we observe that $\hat{x}_T$ is already found that would yield the minimum loss $\hat{V}_T$, and that, by the principle of optimality of dynamic programming, we need only find x_{T-1} to minimize

$$\begin{aligned}
V_{T-1} &= E_{T-2}[(y_{T-1} - a_{T-1})' K_{T-1}(y_{T-1} - a_{T-1}) + \hat{V}_T] \\
&= E_{T-2}(y_{T-1}' H_{T-1} y_{T-1}' - 2y_{T-1}' h_{T-1} + c_{T-1})
\end{aligned} \tag{13}$$

where, using the expression (12) for $\hat{V}_T$, we have defined

$$H_{T-1} = K_{T-1} + (A_T + C_T G_T)' H_T(A_T + C_T G_T) \tag{14}$$

$$h_{T-1} = K_{T-1} a_{T-1} - (A_T + C_T G_T)'(H_T b_T - h_T) \tag{15}$$

$$\begin{aligned}
c_{T-1} = {} & a_{T-1}' K_{T-1} a_{T-1} + (b_T + C_T g_T)' H_T(b_T + C_T g_T) \\
& - 2(b_T + C_T g_T)' h_T + c_T + E_{T-1} u_T' H_T u_T
\end{aligned} \tag{16}$$

Because the second line of (13) is identical with the last expression of (8) with T replaced by $T - 1$, the solution for $\hat{x}_{T-1}$ is identical with (9) with T replaced by $T - 1$, where G_{T-1} and g_{T-1} are defined by (10) and (11), respectively, with a similar change in time subscripts. Accordingly, $\hat{V}_{T-1}$ will be given by (12) with the subscripts T replaced by $T - 1$.

When we attempt to solve the problem for the last three periods, we observe that $\hat{x}_T$ and $\hat{x}_{T-1}$ have been found that would yield the minimum expected loss $\hat{V}_{T-1}$ for the last two periods and that, by the principle of optimality, we need only minimize

$$V_{T-2} = E_{T-3}[(y_{T-2} - a_{T-2})'K_{T-2}(y_{T-2} - a_{T-2}) + \hat{V}_{T-1}]$$

with respect to x_{T-2}, and so forth. At the end of this process, we find $\hat{x}_1 = G_1 y_0 + g_1$ as the optimal policy for the first period, and the associated minimum expected loss $\hat{V}_1$ for *all* periods (or from period 1 onward). Computationally, we solve (10) and (14) with t replacing T for G_t and H_t backward in time, for $t = T, T - 1, \ldots, 1$. We then solve (11) and (15) with t replacing T for g_t and h_t backward in time, for $t = T, T - 1, \ldots, 1$. Finally, solution of (16) with t replacing T backward in time yields c_1, which is used to evaluate $\hat{V}_1$ given by (12), with 1 replacing T.

The above solution can be used to find optimal macroeconomic policy for the government if (1) is regarded as an econometric model and (2) is the preference function for the government which controls the variable x_t. This important topic in econometrics is discussed only briefly below because it is treated fairly extensively in Chow (1975, 1981). Alternatively (1) may represent the economic environment facing some economic decision makers in the private sector (business firms or consumers) and (2) their objective function. Equation (3) would be the optimal investment function, demand function for inputs, or consumption function. The method of optimal control is used to derive the behavioral equations for the decision makers because they are assumed to maximize a multi-period objective function subject to the constraint of a stochastic environment, with a random disturbance u_t present in Eq. (1).

In the application of this chapter, the parameters A_t, C_t, and b_t of model (1) will be assumed to be time-invariant, with the time subscript t omitted. The parameters of the objective function (2) will be assumed to satisfy $K_t = \beta^t K$ and $a_t = a$, where β is a (scalar) discount factor. The parameters G_t and g_t of the optimal feedback control equation (3) will be assumed to be time-invariant; i.e., both Eqs. (4) and (5) and Eqs. (6) and (7) are assumed to reach a steady state when they are solved backward in time. These equations become the algebraic equations

$$(C'HC)G + C'HA = 0 \tag{17}$$

$$H - K - \beta(A + CG)'H(A + CG) = 0 \tag{18}$$

$$(C'HC)g + C'(Hb - h) = 0 \tag{19}$$

$$[I - \beta(A + CG)']h - Ka + (A + CG)'Hb = 0 \tag{20}$$

When the equation pair (17) and (18) is solved numerically, it is computationally convenient to use (18) to iterate. That is, one first sets $H = K$ and solves (17) for G. One then computes H in the next iteration as $K + \beta(A + CG)'H(A + CG)$, and so forth. Unless the largest characteristic root of $A + CG$ is very close to unity, this iterative procedure converges rapidly. Of course, if a root of $A + CG$ is greater than 1 in absolute value, the procedure will not converge and no steady-state solution exists for Eqs. (4) and (5). Having computed G and H, one can solve the linear equation (20) for h and then the linear equation (19) for the intercept g in the optimal feedback control equation.

We have shown how the optimal behavioral equation (3) of a maximizing economic agent can be derived from the parameters of the linear stochastic model (1) describing his environment and the parameters of his objective function (2). The main problem of this chapter is to estimate the parameters of (1) and (2) using time-series data on (y_t, x_t) $(t = 1, \ldots, n)$.

★12.3 METHOD OF MAXIMUM LIKELIHOOD

For the purpose of estimation, let us write out explicitly a higher-order system describing the stochastic environment (1) as

$$y_t = A_1 y_{t-1} + \cdots + A_m y_{t-m} + A_{m+1} x_{t-1} + \cdots + A_{m+r} x_{t-r} + C_0 x_t$$
$$+ b + u_t \tag{21}$$

where the residual vector u_t is normal and serially uncorrelated, with covariance matrix Σ. Model (21) can be written as the following first-order system to agree with the notation of (1)

$$
\begin{bmatrix} y_t \\ y_{t-1} \\ \cdot \\ y_{t-m+1} \\ x_t \\ x_{t-1} \\ \cdot \\ x_{t-r+1} \\ \Delta x_t \\ \Delta x_{t-1} \end{bmatrix}
=
\begin{bmatrix}
A_1 & \cdots & A_{m-1} & A_m & A_{m+1} & A_{m+2} & \cdots & A_{m+r} & 0 & 0 \\
I & \cdots & 0 & 0 & 0 & 0 & \cdots & 0 & 0 & 0 \\
\multicolumn{10}{c}{\cdots\cdots\cdots\cdots\cdots\cdots\cdots\cdots\cdots\cdots} \\
0 & \cdots & I & 0 & 0 & 0 & \cdots & 0 & 0 & 0 \\
0 & \cdots & 0 & 0 & 0 & 0 & \cdots & 0 & 0 & 0 \\
0 & \cdots & 0 & 0 & I & 0 & \cdots & 0 & 0 & 0 \\
\multicolumn{10}{c}{\cdots\cdots\cdots\cdots\cdots\cdots\cdots\cdots\cdots\cdots} \\
0 & \cdots & 0 & 0 & 0 & 0 & \cdots & I & 0 & 0 \\
0 & \cdots & 0 & 0 & -I & 0 & \cdots & 0 & 0 & 0 \\
0 & \cdots & 0 & 0 & I & -I & \cdots & 0 & 0 & 0
\end{bmatrix}
\begin{bmatrix} y_{t-1} \\ y_{t-2} \\ \cdot \\ y_{t-m} \\ x_{t-1} \\ x_{t-2} \\ \cdot \\ x_{t-r} \\ \Delta x_{t-1} \\ \Delta x_{t-2} \end{bmatrix}
$$
$$
+ \begin{bmatrix} C_0 \\ 0 \\ \cdot \\ 0 \\ I \\ 0 \\ \cdot \\ 0 \\ I \\ 0 \end{bmatrix} x_t
+ \begin{bmatrix} b \\ 0 \\ \cdot \\ 0 \\ 0 \\ 0 \\ \cdot \\ 0 \\ 0 \\ 0 \end{bmatrix}
+ \begin{bmatrix} u_t \\ 0 \\ \cdot \\ 0 \\ 0 \\ 0 \\ \cdot \\ 0 \\ 0 \\ 0 \end{bmatrix} \tag{22}
$$

In the vector of state variables on the left-hand side, x_t is included because it may be an argument in the objective function; $x_{t-1}, \ldots, x_{t-r+1}$ are included so that only the current x_t appears as control variable; and Δx_t and Δx_{t-1} are included in case they are used as arguments in the objective function.

From (22) we can write the optimal feedback control equation as

$$x_t = G_1 y_{t-1} + \cdots + G_m y_{t-m} + G_{m+1} x_{t-1} + \cdots + G_{m+r} x_{t-r} + 0\, \Delta x_{t-1}$$

$$+ 0\, \Delta x_{t-2} + g + v_t \tag{23}$$

Provided that the state variables include x_t and x_{t-1}, the coefficients of Δx_t and Δx_{t-1} are zero because $G = -(C'HC)^{-1} C'HA$ and the last two columns of matrix A in (22) are zero. For the purpose of estimation we introduce a random residual v_t in (23) which is due to errors in the execution of the optimal policy or to omitted variables and assume that v_t is normal, serially uncorrelated, and uncorrelated with u_t in (21), having a covariance matrix Θ. (If v_t is correlated with u_t, one can easily modify the likelihood function below; see Prob. 3.)

Let n observations of (21) be available, let Y be a $n \times g$ matrix of the g dependent variables, and let Y_{-1} be an $n \times g$ matrix of the lagged values of Y, etc. Then model (21) can be written as

$$Y' = BZ' + C_0 X' + bw' + U' \tag{24}$$

where
$$\underset{g \times s}{B} = [A_1 \quad \cdots \quad A_m \quad A_{m+1} \quad \cdots \quad A_{m+r}]$$

$$\underset{n \times s}{Z} = [Y_{-1} \quad \cdots \quad Y_{-m} \quad X_{-1} \quad \cdots \quad X_{-r}] \tag{25}$$

and w is a column of n ones. Model (23) can be written as

$$X' = \tilde{G} Z' + g w' + V' \tag{26}$$

where
$$\underset{g \times s}{\tilde{G}} = [G_1 \quad \cdots \quad G_m \quad G_{m+1} \quad \cdots \quad G_{m+r}] \qquad G = [\tilde{G} \quad 0 \quad 0] \tag{27}$$

In this setup the variables x_{t-1} and x_{t-2} are assumed to be present in (21) and (24), with the matrix Z in (25) including X_{-1} and X_{-2}. If these variables are in fact absent, the restrictions $A_{m+1} = 0$ and $A_{m+2} = 0$ must be imposed in estimation.

To estimate the parameters of (24) and the parameters K, a, and β in the objective function we maximize the log-likelihood function of (24) and (26) subject to the constraints (17) to (20). The lagrangian expression is

$$L = \text{const} - \frac{n}{2} \log |\Sigma| - \frac{n}{2} \log |\Theta|$$

$$- \tfrac{1}{2} \operatorname{tr} [\Sigma^{-1}(Y' - BZ' - C_0 X' - bw')(Y - ZB' - XC'_0 - wb')]$$

$$- \tfrac{1}{2} \operatorname{tr} [\Theta^{-1}(X' - \tilde{G}Z' - gw')(X - Z\tilde{G}' - wg')] - \operatorname{tr} [\Omega(C'HC\tilde{G} + C'H\tilde{A})]$$

$$- \tfrac{1}{2} \operatorname{tr} \{\Phi[H - K - \beta(A + CG)'H(A + CG)]\} - \omega'[C'HCg + C'(Hb - h)]$$

$$- \phi'\{[I - \beta(A + CG)']h - Ka + \beta(A + CG)'Hb\} \tag{28}$$

where $\tilde{A}$ $(p \times k)$ is the coefficient matrix A in (22) with the last two columns deleted, Ω $(k \times g)$ and Φ $(p \times p)$ are matrices of lagrangian multipliers and ω and ϕ are vectors of lagrangian multipliers. Φ is symmetric because the constraint (18) is symmetric. The parameters to be estimated are B, C_0, b, and Σ of (24), G, g, and Θ of (26), and K and a of the objective function.

Let us first find estimating equations for the covariance matrices Σ and Θ. Using the differentiation rules $\partial \log |A|/\partial A = A^{-1\prime}$ and $\partial \, \text{tr} \, (AB)/\partial A = B'$, we differentiate L with respect to the elements of Σ^{-1} and Θ^{-1} to obtain

$$n\Sigma - (Y' - BZ' - C_0 X' - bw')(Y - ZB' - XC_0' - wb') = 0 \tag{29}$$

$$n\Theta - (X' - \tilde{G}Z' - gw')(X - Z\tilde{G}' - wg') = 0 \tag{30}$$

Thus, as usual, when the coefficients of (24) and (26) have been estimated, the covariance matrices of the residuals can be estimated by the observed sums of squares and cross products of the sample residuals.

We next turn to the estimation of the target vector a and the intercepts b and g. Denote by K^* the $d \times p$ matrix consisting of the nonzero rows of K which correspond to the d target variables. Denote by a^* the vector consisting of the unknown elements of a which correspond to the d target variables. Differentiation of L with respect to h and a^* gives

$$\frac{\partial L}{\partial h} = C\omega - [I - \beta(A + CG)]\phi = 0 \tag{31}$$

$$\frac{\partial L}{\partial a^*} = K^*\phi = 0 \tag{32}$$

Equations (31) and (32) are $p + d$ linear equations in the $p + q$ unknowns in ϕ and ω. If the number d of target variables equals or exceeds the number q of instruments [as we shall assume to make (3) a unique solution of the economic agent's optimization problem], both lagrangian multipliers ϕ and ω will be zero provided that the $(p + d) \times (p + q)$ matrix of the coefficients of (31) and (32)

$$\begin{bmatrix} C & -[I - \beta(A + CG)] \\ 0 & K^* \end{bmatrix}$$

is of rank $p + q$. The solution $\phi = 0$ and $\omega = 0$ from (31) and (32) simplifies many of the remaining equations obtained by differentiating L.

Given $\phi = 0$ and $\omega = 0$, differentiation of L with respect to b' and g' gives

$$\frac{\partial L}{\partial b'} = w'(Y - ZB' - XC_0' - wb')\Sigma^{-1} = 0 \tag{33}$$

$$\frac{\partial L}{\partial g'} = w'(X - Z\tilde{G}' - wg')\Theta^{-1} = 0 \tag{34}$$

The vector w being a column of ones, the intercepts b and g are obtained by the familiar equations

$$b = \bar{y} - B\bar{z} - C_0\bar{x} \tag{33a}$$

$$g = \bar{x} - \tilde{G}\bar{z} \tag{34a}$$

where the bar denotes sample mean; that is, $\bar{y} = n^{-1}Y'w$.

When all coefficients are known, Eqs. (19) and (20) can be solved for h and a. Solving (20) for h, substituting the result in (19), and denoting $A + CG$ by R, we obtain

$$C'[I - \beta R']Ka = C'HCg + C'[I - \beta(I - \beta R')^{-1}R']Hb \tag{35}$$

Because C' is $q \times p$, this is a system of q linear equations for the d unknowns in a. If the number d of target variables equals the number q of control variables, the solution for a is unique. If $d > q$, the solution for a is not unique. This result is reasonable because the observable behavior of the economic agents that is relevant for the estimation of a consists of a $q \times 1$ vector g in the optimal feedback control equation. If a has more elements than g, it cannot be estimated uniquely.

To estimate the remaining parameters, we again differentiate L, using the partitions

$$C'H \overset{p \times k}{\tilde{A}} = [C_0' \quad C_*'] \begin{bmatrix} \overset{p \times g}{H_1} & \overset{p \times (p-g)}{H_2} \end{bmatrix} \begin{bmatrix} \overset{g \times k}{B} \\ A_* \end{bmatrix} \qquad \Phi = \begin{bmatrix} \overset{k \times p}{\Phi_1} \\ \Phi_2 \end{bmatrix} \tag{36}$$

The results are

$$\frac{\partial L}{\partial B'} = Z'(Y - ZB' - XC_0' - wb')\Sigma^{-1} - \Omega C'H_1 + \beta\Phi_1(A + CG)'H_1 = 0 \tag{37}$$

$$\frac{\partial L}{\partial C_0'} = X'(Y - ZB' - XC_0' - wb')\Sigma^{-1} - \Omega'(\tilde{A} + C\tilde{G})'H_1 - \tilde{G}\Omega C'H_1$$

$$+ \beta G\Phi(A + CG)'H_1 = 0 \tag{38}$$

$$\frac{\partial L}{\partial G'} = Z'(X - Z\tilde{G}' - wg')\Theta^{-1} - \Omega C'HC + \beta\Phi_1(A + CG)'HC = 0 \tag{39}$$

$$\frac{\partial L}{\partial H} = -(\tilde{A} + C\tilde{G})\Omega C' - C\Omega'(\tilde{A} + C\tilde{G})' - \Phi + \beta(A + CG)\Phi(A + CG)' = 0 \tag{40}$$

$$\frac{\partial L}{\partial k_{ii}} = \phi_{ii} = 0 \qquad \frac{\partial L}{\partial k_{ij}} = 2\phi_{ij} = 0 \qquad (i \neq j) \tag{41}$$

In equation (41), k_{ij} and ϕ_{ij} denote respectively the ijth element of K and Φ, both being symmetric matrices. We differentiate L with respect only to the unknown elements of K.

Tentatively treating the unknown k_{ij} and β as given, we use the following iterative method to solve for B, C_0, G, H, Ω, and Φ. Start with initial estimates of

(B, C_0), Σ, and Θ. In the first iteration the method of least squares can be applied to (24) and (26) to obtain these estimates. Each iteration consists of seven steps:

1. Given (B, C_0), and thus (A, C), solve Eqs. (17) and (18) for G and H.
2. Given $\tilde{G}$, compute g by (34a) and Θ by (30).
3. Solve (39) for Ω, namely,

$$\Omega = Z'(X - Z\tilde{G}' - wg')\Theta^{-1}(C'HC)^{-1}$$

noting that the last term of (39) vanishes on account of (17).
4. Solve (40) for Φ by iterating with

$$\Phi = \beta(A + CG)\Phi(A + CG)' - (\tilde{A} + C\tilde{G})\Omega C' - C\Omega'(\tilde{A} + C\tilde{G})'$$

5. Solve (37) for B

$$B = \{(Y' - C_0 X' - bw')Z + \Sigma H_1'[\beta(A + CG)\Phi_1' - C\Omega']\}(Z'Z)^{-1}$$

6. Solve (38) for C_0

$$C_0 = \{(Y' - BZ' - bw')X + \Sigma H_1'[-(\tilde{A} + C\tilde{G})\Omega - C\Omega'\tilde{G}'$$
$$+ \beta(A + CG)\Phi'G']\}(X'X)^{-1}$$

7. Compute b by (33a) and Σ by (29).

This iterative method assumes that k_{ij} and β are given. To maximize L with respect to these parameters one can apply a numerical method. Note that $\partial L/\partial k_{ij}$ is given by (41) and

$$\frac{\partial L}{\partial \beta} = \tfrac{1}{2} \, \text{tr} \, [\Phi(A + CG)'H(A + CG)] \qquad (42)$$

Thus a gradient method using the above derivatives can conveniently be applied. This solves the problem of maximum-likelihood estimation using explicitly the first-order conditions of maximizing a lagrangian expression for the constrained likelihood function.

A second approach to the method of maximum likelihood is to regard the concentrated log-likelihood function, obtained by substitution of (29) and (30) for Σ and Θ, i.e.,

$$-\frac{n}{2} \log \left| \frac{1}{n} (Y' - BZ' - C_0 X' - bw')(Y - ZB' - XC_0' - wb') \right|$$

$$-\frac{n}{2} \log \left| \frac{1}{2} (X' - \tilde{G}Z' - gw')(X - Z\tilde{G}' - wg') \right| \qquad (43)$$

as a function of the parameters of (24) and the objective function and to maximize this function with respect to these parameters directly by a numerical method. $(\tilde{G}, g)$ in the above log likelihood is a function of B, C_0, b, K, a, and β through the solution of Eqs. (17) to (20). A computer program can be written to evaluate the log likelihood as a function of these parameters. A numerical method can be applied for maximization, as discussed in Sec. 7.5.

12.4 METHOD OF TWO-STAGE LEAST SQUARES

Besides maximum likelihood, there is a family of consistent estimators for estimating the parameters of (2). It is based on the observation that the least-squares estimator $\hat{G}$ of the coefficients G obtained by regressing X on Z in (26) is consistent and that if G is the solution to the optimal control problem, it should satisfy Eqs. (17) and (18). The problem is analogous to the estimation of structural parameters $[B \quad \Gamma]$ in a system of linear simultaneous equations

$$By_t + \Gamma x_t = \epsilon_t$$

by the use of the least-squares estimate $\hat{\Pi}$ of the matrix of reduced-form coefficients $\Pi = -B^{-1}\Gamma$. $\hat{\Pi}$ is a consistent estimate of Π, and if the model is correct, Π satisfies $B\Pi = -\Gamma$, which corresponds to (17) and (18) in the present problem. Therefore, if we solve (17) and (18) for H, K, and β (the structural parameters) using the least-squares estimate $\hat{G}$ for G and consistent estimates $\hat{A}$ and $\hat{C}$ for A and C, we shall obtain consistent estimates of the former parameters just as we shall obtain consistent estimates of B and Γ by solving $B\hat{\Pi} = -\Gamma$.

As the first step of this method we obtain least-squares estimates $\hat{G}$ of G and $(\hat{A} \quad \hat{C})$ of $(A \quad C)$ by using regression equations (26) and (24) respectively. Having obtained $\hat{G}$ and $(\hat{A} \quad \hat{C})$, we find H, K, and β to satisfy Eqs. (17) and (18), but, as in the case of overidentified structural equations, there may be more equations than unknowns. Defining $R = (r_{ij}) = \hat{A} + \hat{C}\hat{G}$, we write these equations as

$$C'HR = 0 \tag{44}$$

$$K = H - \beta R'HR \tag{45}$$

Let H be a symmetric $p \times p$ matrix with elements h_{ij}, and let C be a $p \times q$ matrix with elements c_{ij}. These two equations respectively imply

$$\sum_{i,j}^{p} c_{im} r_{jl} h_{ij} = 0 \qquad \begin{matrix} m = 1, \ldots, q \\ l = 1, \ldots, p \end{matrix} \tag{46}$$

and

$$h_{ml} - \beta \sum_{i,j}^{p} r_{im} r_{jl} h_{ij} = 0 \qquad \text{if } k_{ml} = 0 \tag{47}$$

These are linear equations in $h_{ij} = h_{ji}$. Let h be the column vector consisting of the $p(p + 1)/2$ elements h_{ij} ($i = 1, \ldots, p; j \geq i$). Write (46) and (47) as a system of linear equations in h

$$Qh = 0 \tag{48}$$

Exact, over- or underidentification occurs accordingly as the rank of Q is equal to, larger than, or smaller than $[p(p + 1)/2] - 1$. In the overidentified case there will be more equations than unknowns in (48); the elements on its right-hand side cannot all vanish. In a method corresponding to that of indirect least squares for simultaneous equations, one can suggest discarding extra equations in (48) and solving the remaining $p(p + 1)/2$ homogeneous linear equations, which are made nonhomogeneous by a normalization $h_{11} = 1$. This method is still consistent, but it discards useful information. In a method corresponding to that of 2SLS, according to the interpretation of Chow (1964), we normalize by setting $h_{11} = 1$ (or any $h_{ii} = 1$), partition Q and h' respectively as $[q_1 \quad Q_2]$ and $[1 \quad h_2']$ to write (48) as

$$q_1 + Q_2 h_2 = 0 \tag{49}$$

and estimate h_2 by $\hat{h}_2 = -(Q_2' Q_2)^{-1} Q_2' q_1$ using the method of least squares in the second stage.

In a method corresponding to that of LIML, according to the interpretation of Chow (1964), we normalize symmetrically by setting $h'h = \text{const}$ and find h to minimize $h'Q'Qh$ subject to this normalization constraint. The minimizing h is the characteristic vector associated with the smallest characteristic root of $Q'Q$. Unlike the method of 2SLS, this method yields a vector estimate of h which is invariant with respect to the choice of the variable for normalization. However, if the order of Q is very large, the symmetric normalization is not recommended, as it is computationally expensive. If β is unknown, one must find a scalar to minimize the appropriate sum of squares $h_2' Q_2' Q_2 h_2$ or $h'Q'Qh$, but this is an easy problem. Having obtained h and β, we use the remaining equations of (45), other than (47), to compute the nonzero elements of K. Given H, $\hat{A}$, and $\hat{C}$, we can obtain a new estimate $G_{(2)}$ of G by using (17). Having estimated G, g, A, C, b, and H consistently, we can use (35) to estimate a.

If the estimates of H, K, β, and a by the method of this section are not accepted as final, they can serve as initial estimates to be used in the (more expensive) maximization of the likelihood function by the method of Sec. 12.3. The consistent estimates of this section can be recommended if the method of Sec. 12.3 is considered too expensive.

12.5 TWO ECONOMIC EXAMPLES

This section gives two examples of a maximizing economic agent facing a linear stochastic environment and having a quadratic objective function. The first, by Sargent (1979) and Hansen and Sargent (1980), deals with demand for an input. A competitive firm's environment is described by two linear stochastic processes, one for a random shock to technology y_{1t}

$$y_{1t} = \alpha_1 y_{1, t-1} + \cdots + \alpha_q y_{1, t-q} + u_{1t}$$

and a second for the real wage (or factor rental) y_{2t}

$$\begin{bmatrix} y_{2t} \\ \vdots \\ y_{pt} \end{bmatrix} = B_1 \begin{bmatrix} y_{2,t-1} \\ \vdots \\ y_{p,t-1} \end{bmatrix} + \cdots + B_r \begin{bmatrix} y_{2,t-r} \\ \vdots \\ y_{p,t-r} \end{bmatrix} + \begin{bmatrix} u_{2t} \\ \vdots \\ u_{pt} \end{bmatrix}$$

These processes are assumed to be jointly covariance-stationary.

The firm wishes to maximize its expected present value

$$V = E_0 \sum_{t=0}^{\infty} \beta^t \left[(\gamma_0 + y_{1,t} - y_{2,t})x_t - \frac{\gamma_1}{2} x_t^2 - \frac{\delta}{2} (x_t - x_{t-1})^2 \right]$$

with respect to the quantity x_t of factor input. The objective function is quadratic in the state variables y_{1t} and y_{2t} and the control variables x_t. Note that the state variables are not functions of the control variable.

It is straightforward to write the processes generating the two state variables y_{1t} and y_{2t} as a first-order system, say

$$\tilde{y}_t = A_1 \tilde{y}_{t-1} + \tilde{u}_t$$

Since both x_t and Δx_t enter the objective function, we incorporate them in the vector of state variables, and write the system as

$$\begin{bmatrix} \tilde{y}_t \\ x_t \\ \Delta x_t \end{bmatrix} = \begin{bmatrix} A_1 & 0 & 0 \\ 0 & 0 & 0 \\ 0 & -I & 0 \end{bmatrix} \begin{bmatrix} \tilde{y}_{t-1} \\ x_{t-1} \\ \Delta x_{t-1} \end{bmatrix} + \begin{bmatrix} 0 \\ I \\ I \end{bmatrix} x_t + \begin{bmatrix} \tilde{u}_t \\ 0 \\ 0 \end{bmatrix} \tag{50}$$

where all I's are simply 1's in this example but are so written for possible generalization to a vector x_t. Equation (50) is a special case of (1) with

$$A_t = A = \begin{bmatrix} A_1 & 0 & 0 \\ 0 & 0 & 0 \\ 0 & -I & 0 \end{bmatrix} \qquad C_t = C = \begin{bmatrix} 0 \\ I \\ I \end{bmatrix} \qquad b_t = 0$$

Note the special feature of the matrix C allowing for no effect of x_t on $\tilde{y}_t$. The K_t matrix in the objective function is

$$K_t = \beta^t K = \beta^t \begin{bmatrix} 0 & 0 & \cdots & 0 & -1 & 0 \\ 0 & 0 & \cdots & 0 & 1 & 0 \\ \hdotsfor{6} \\ 0 & 0 & \cdots & 0 & -\gamma_0 & 0 \\ -1 & 1 & \cdots & -\gamma_0 & \gamma_1 & 0 \\ 0 & 0 & \cdots & 0 & 0 & \delta \end{bmatrix}$$

where, to accommodate the product $\gamma_0 x_t$ in V, we introduce a variable y_{st} as the last element of the vector $\tilde{y}_t$ and let $y_{st} = y_{s, t-1}$ with initial condition $y_{s0} = 1$.

The second example, due to Blanchard (1983), is concerned with the determination of the inventory x_t of the automobile industry in the United States. The state variables are the sales of automobiles y_{1t} and y_{2t} to other countries and to the United States, respectively. They are assumed to follow fourth-order autoregressive processes. The system governing the state variables is transformed into a first-order system for a vector of eight variables

$$
\begin{bmatrix} y_{1t} \\ y_{2t} \\ \cdot \\ y_{1, t-3} \\ y_{2, t-3} \end{bmatrix} = \begin{bmatrix} a_{11} & a_{12} & \cdots & a_{15} & a_{16} & a_{17} & a_{18} \\ a_{21} & a_{22} & \cdots & a_{25} & a_{26} & a_{27} & a_{28} \\ \cdots\cdots\cdots\cdots\cdots\cdots\cdots\cdots\cdots \\ 0 & 0 & \cdots & 1 & 1 & 0 & 0 \\ 0 & 0 & \cdots & 1 & 1 & 0 & 0 \end{bmatrix} \begin{bmatrix} y_{1, t-1} \\ y_{2, t-1} \\ \cdot \\ y_{1, t-4} \\ y_{2, t-4} \end{bmatrix} + \begin{bmatrix} u_{1t} \\ u_{2t} \\ \cdot \\ 0 \\ 0 \end{bmatrix}
$$

or
$$
\tilde{y}_t = A_1 \tilde{y}_{t-1} + \tilde{u}_t
$$

Production y_{3t} is related to inventory change and sales by the identity

$$
y_{3t} = x_t - x_{t-1} + y_{1t} + y_{2t}
$$

There are three components of cost to be included in the objective function: cost of production, $\frac{1}{2}c(y_{3t} + \epsilon_t)^2$; cost of adjusting production, $\frac{1}{2}k(\Delta y_{3t} + \eta_t)^2$; and cost of deviating from target inventory, $\frac{1}{2}d(x_{t-1} - x_{t-1}^* + u_{t-1})^2$, where $x_{t-1}^* = ay_{2t}$. Using the production identity, we can write the objective function to be minimized as

$$
\frac{1}{2}E_0 \sum_{t=0}^{\infty} \beta^t [c(\Delta x_t + y_{1t} + y_{2t} + \epsilon_t)^2 + k(\Delta x_t - \Delta x_{t-1} + y_{1t} - y_{1, t-1}
$$
$$
+ y_{2t} - y_{2, t-1} + \eta_t)^2 + d(x_{t-1} - ay_{2t} + u_{t-1})^2]
$$

Since the variables ϵ_t, η_t, and u_t are assumed to be random and uncorrelated with y_{1t}, y_{2t}, and x_t, the objective function is quadratic in y_{1t}, y_{2t}, $y_{1, t-1}$, $y_{2, t-1}$, x_{t-1}, Δx_t, and Δx_{t-1}.

Blanchard prefers to formulate his model as explaining y_{t+1} by y_t and x_t or explaining y_t by y_{t-1} and x_{t-1} (not x_t). Thus, combining x_t, x_{t-1}, Δx_t, and Δx_{t-1} with $\tilde{y}_{t+1}$ to form a new vector of state variables, we have

$$
\begin{bmatrix} \tilde{y}_{t+1} \\ x_t \\ x_{t-1} \\ \Delta x_t \\ \Delta x_{t-1} \end{bmatrix} = \begin{bmatrix} A_1 & 0 & 0 & 0 & 0 \\ 0 & 0 & 0 & 0 & 0 \\ 0 & I & 0 & 0 & 0 \\ 0 & -I & 0 & 0 & 0 \\ 0 & I & -I & 0 & 0 \end{bmatrix} \begin{bmatrix} \tilde{y}_t \\ x_{t-1} \\ x_{t-2} \\ \Delta x_{t-1} \\ \Delta x_{t-2} \end{bmatrix} + \begin{bmatrix} 0 \\ I \\ 0 \\ I \\ 0 \end{bmatrix} x_t + \begin{bmatrix} \tilde{u}_t \\ 0 \\ 0 \\ 0 \\ 0 \end{bmatrix} \quad (51)
$$

Compare (51) with (22). In fact model (51) has motivated the introduction of the variables x_{t-1} and Δx_{t-1} into the vector of state variables in (22). The variables in the feedback control equations are $\tilde{y}_t$ (not $\tilde{y}_{t-1}$), x_{t-1}, and x_{t-2}. Δx_{t-1} and Δx_{t-2} are absent or have zero coefficients, as shown in the last part of Eq. (27).

For this model, the K matrix is 12×12, as $\tilde{y}_{t+1}$ is an 8×1 vector consisting of $y_{1,t+1}, y_{2,t+1}, y_{1t}, y_{2t}, \ldots, y_{1,t-2}, y_{2,t-2}$. The elements of the K matrix are obtained from the objective function. Corresponding to the 12 state variables, the nonzero elements are given in the following symmetric matrix:

	y_{1t}	y_{2t}	$y_{1,t-1}$	$y_{2,t-1}$	$y_{1,t-2}$	$y_{2,t-2}$	x_t	x_{t-1}	Δx_t	Δx_{t-1}
	3	4	5	6	7	8	9	10	11	12
3	$c+k$	$c+k$	$-k$	$-k$	$\cdot$	$\cdot$	$\cdot$	$\cdot$	$c+k$	$-k$
4		$c+k+da^2$	$-k$	$-k$	$\cdot$	$\cdot$	$\cdot$	$-ad$	$c+k$	$-k$
5			k	k	$\cdot$	$\cdot$	$\cdot$	$\cdot$	$-k$	k
6				k	$\cdot$	$\cdot$	$\cdot$	$\cdot$	$-k$	k
7					$\cdot$	$\cdot$	$\cdot$	$\cdot$	$\cdot$	$\cdot$
8						$\cdot$	$\cdot$	$\cdot$	$\cdot$	$\cdot$
9							$\cdot$	$\cdot$	$\cdot$	$\cdot$
10								d	$\cdot$	$\cdot$
11									$c+k$	$-k$
12										k

These elements are subject to the linear restrictions:

$$k_{35} = -k_{55}$$

$$k_{45} = k_{36} = k_{46} = k_{3,12} = k_{4,12} = k_{5,11} = k_{6,11} = k_{11,12} = -k_{55}$$

$$k_{56} = k_{66} = k_{5,12} = k_{6,12} = k_{12,12} = k_{55}$$

and
$$k_{34} = k_{3,11} = k_{4,11} = k_{11,11} = k_{33}$$

There is also one nonlinear restriction

$$k_{44} - k_{33} - \frac{k_{4,10}^2}{k_{10,10}} = 0$$

The introduction of linear and nonlinear restrictions on the elements k_{ij} of the K matrix in the objective function would require only minor modifications to the method of maximum-likelihood estimation presented in Sec. 12.3. The essence of that method is to produce the maximum of the log likelihood with respect to all other parameters subject to the appropriate constraints, given k_{ij} and β. It then maximizes the above maximum with respect to k_{ij} and β. If there is a linear restriction, say

$$k_{26} = c_1 k_{11} + c_2 k_{33}$$

and a nonlinear restriction on k_{44} as given above, the variables k_{26} and k_{44} will be eliminated from the vector of unknowns. Numerical maximization will proceed with two fewer unknowns.

If an analytical gradient is used in the numerical maximization procedure, the chain rule of differentiation yields the following derivative of the log likelihood with respect to k_{11} subject to the above linear constraint

$$\frac{\partial L}{\partial k_{11}} = \left(\frac{\partial L}{\partial k_{11}}\right)_{k_{26}} + \frac{\partial L}{\partial k_{26}}\frac{\partial k_{62}}{\partial k_{11}} = \phi_{11} + 2c_1\phi_{26}$$

and, similarly,
$$\frac{\partial L}{\partial k_{33}} = \phi_{33} + 2c_2\,\phi_{26}$$

For the nonlinear restriction, we have

$$\frac{\partial L}{\partial k_{4,\,10}} = 2\phi_{4,\,10} + \phi_{44}\frac{\partial k_{44}}{\partial k_{4,\,10}} = 2\phi_{4,\,10} + 2\phi_{44}\frac{k_{4,\,10}}{k_{10,\,10}}$$

and so forth. These modifications are minor.

12.6 ALTERNATIVE DERIVATION OF THE OPTIMAL RULE

For the examples given in the last section, although not for the general problem of maximizing the expectation of a quadratic function subject to the constraint of a linear stochastic model, there exists a method other than dynamic programming for deriving the optimal decision rule. This method was used by the authors of the two examples (Sargent, 1979; Hansen and Sargent, 1980; Blanchard, 1983) and consists of four main steps.

1. Using the linear model, substitute control variables for the state variables in the objective function, so that the expectation of the objective function depends on the control variables.
2. Maximize the expected objective function with respect to the control variables and obtain a set of first-order conditions for maximum. These first-order conditions take the form of dynamic relations between the expectations of control and state variables, called stochastic Euler equations.
3. By canonical factorization transform the above dynamic relations so that the control variables become a function of their own lagged values and of conditional expectations of future state variables.
4. Using an appropriate forecasting formula and the linear model for the state variables, replace the above conditional expectations by the past (and current, if assumed known) values of the state variables. This is the optimal feedback rule.

We illustrate this method by the example of Hansen and Sargent (1980) given in the last section. The first step is not required in this example because the expected value V is already expressed as a function of the control variable x_t. It is required in the example of Blanchard (1982), where y_{3t} is replaced by $\Delta x_t + y_{1t} + y_{2t}$. This is the step that limits the applicability of this method to general linear quadratic control problems. If the model takes the form

$$y_t = Ay_{t-1} + Cx_t + u_t = Cx_t + u_t + ACx_{t-1} + Au_{t-1} + A^2Cx_{t-2} + \cdots$$

replacement of y_t by x_t, x_{t-1}, etc., would lead to an infinite number of x_{t-k} in the objective function for period t alone. Step 2 will involve an infinite number of unknowns and cannot be carried out.

Returning to the Hansen-Sargent example, we take the second step by differentiating the expected value V, interchanging the operations of differentiation and taking expectations (or differentiating inside the integral sign) to obtain, for $t = 0, 1, 2, \ldots$,

$$\frac{\partial V}{\partial x_t} = E_0\,\beta^t[(\gamma_0 + y_{1t} - y_{2t}) - \gamma_1 x_t - \delta(x_t - x_{t-1}) + \beta\delta(x_{t+1} - x_t)]$$

$$= E_0\,\beta^t E_t(\beta\,\delta x_{t+1} + \phi\,\delta x_t + \delta x_{t-1} + y_{1t} - y_{2t} + \gamma_0) = 0 \qquad (52)$$

where $\phi = -[(\gamma_1/\delta) + (1 + \beta)]$ and E_t is added on account of $E_0(\cdot) = E_0\,E_t(\cdot)$. The first-order conditions are obtained by setting $E_t(\cdot)$ in (52) equal to zero for all t, that is,

$$E_t[\beta x_{t+1} + \phi x_t + x_{t-1} + \delta^{-1}(y_{1t} - y_{2t} + \gamma_0)]$$
$$= \beta E_t x_{t+1} + \phi x_t + x_{t-1} + \delta^{-1}(y_{1t} - y_{2t} + \gamma_0) = 0 \quad (53)$$

Third, in order to get rid of $E_t x_{t+1}$ in the optimal feedback control equation for x_t, which can depend on past but not future x's, we write

$$\beta x_{t+1} + \phi x_t + x_{t-1} = (\beta z^{-1} + \phi + z)x_t$$

where z is the lag operator, with $zx_t = x_{t-1}$ and $z^{-1}x_t = x_{t+1}$. Note $E_t(z^{-j}E_t x_t) = E_t(E_{t+j}x_{t+j}) = E_t(z^{-j}x_t)$ or $E_t z^{-j}E_t(\cdot) = E_t z^{-j}(\cdot)$. If we can factor the polynomial

$$\beta z^{-1} + \phi + z = \beta(z^{-1} - \rho_2)(1 - \rho_1 z) = \beta(z^{-1} - \rho_1 - \rho_2 + \rho_1\rho_2 z)$$

into the product of two polynomials, the first involving (nonnegative) powers of z^{-1} and the second involving (nonnegative) powers of z, we can apply the operator $E_t[\beta(z^{-1} - \rho_2)]^{-1}$ to (53) to get rid of x_{t+1} (or x_{t+k}, $k > 0$, in the general case), using $E_t[\beta(z^{-1} - \rho_2)]^{-1} \cdot E_t[\beta(z^{-1} - \rho_2)](\cdot) = E_t[\beta(z^{-1} - \rho_2)]^{-1} [\beta(z^{-1} - \rho_2)](\cdot) = E_t(\cdot)$.

In the current example, ρ_1 and ρ_2 are found by equating coefficients. The results are $\beta\rho_1\rho_2 = 1$ or $\rho_2 = (\beta\rho_1)^{-1}$ and $\beta(\rho_1 + \rho_2) = -\phi$; ρ_1 is the smaller root of the equation $\beta\rho_1 + \rho_1^{-1} + \phi = 0$. Now we multiply (or premultiply in the matrix case) the expression inside the brackets in (53) by

$$[\beta(z^{-1} - \rho_2)]^{-1} = \beta^{-1}[-\rho_2(1 - \rho_2^{-1}z^{-1})]^{-1}$$
$$= -\rho_1(1 + \lambda z^{-1} + \lambda^2 z^{-2} + \lambda^3 z^{-3} + \cdots)$$

where we have defined $\lambda = \rho_2^{-1} = \beta\rho_1$. Equation (53) then becomes

$$E_t\left[(1 - \rho_1 z)x_t - \rho_1\left(\sum_{j=0}^{\infty}\lambda^j z^{-j}\right)\delta^{-1}(y_{1t} - y_{2t} + \gamma_0)\right] = 0$$

or
$$x_t = \rho_1 x_{t-1} + \frac{\rho_1}{\delta} \sum_{j=0}^{\infty} \lambda^j E_t(y_{1,t+j} - y_{2,t+j} + \gamma_0) \tag{54}$$

We have eliminated $E_t x_{t+1}$ in (53) but inherited the expectations of future state variables in (54).

Fourth, to evaluate the expectations of future state variables in (54) we rely on the model

$$\tilde{y}_t = A_1 \tilde{y}_{t-1} + b_1 + \tilde{u}_t$$

defined for these variables above Eq. (50), and apply the prediction formula

$$E_t \tilde{y}_{t+j} = A_1^j \tilde{y}_t + (b_1 + Ab_1 + \cdots + A^{j-1}b)$$

Substituting this result into (54) gives an optimal feedback control equation. Finally, x_t is a function of past x's and current and past y's. Current y's appear because Hansen and Sargent write their model to explain $\tilde{y}_{t+1}$, and not $\tilde{y}_t$, by x_t, as in (51).

It is partly a matter of opinion whether the method of this section is attractive, in view of the complicated mathematical operations and the difficulty in using the method for the general linear-quadratic control problem. In special cases, the user is able to obtain the coefficient G in the optimal control rule as function of the parameters of (1) and (2) explicitly. The method of dynamic programming presented in Sec. 12.2 solves the general linear-quadratic control problem. The mathematical operations are less complicated. The optimal control rule is easy to compute. Whether the solution for its coefficient G by Eqs. (17) and (18) is explicit or not is perhaps not a matter of great concern in most econometric applications. However, in the special case of the Hansen-Sargent example, an explicit solution can also be obtained from Eqs. (17) and (18), as pointed out in Sec. 12.7 (see also Probs. 6 to 8).

12.7 EXPLICIT SOLUTION FOR THE OPTIMAL RULE

Let the model be given by (50), where x_t may be a vector although the Hansen-Sargent example treats x_t as a scalar. The matrix K_t satisfies

$$K_t = \beta^t K = \beta^t \begin{bmatrix} K_{11} & K_{12} & 0 \\ K'_{12} & K_{22} & 0 \\ 0 & 0 & K_{33} \end{bmatrix}$$

where K_{22} and K_{33} corresponding to x_t and Δx_t are assumed to be diagonal, the former capturing increasing marginal costs of using the inputs x_t in the example on the demand for inputs and the latter measuring the adjustment costs of changes in the inputs. We are concerned with the solution of

$$G = -(C'HC)^{-1}C'HA \tag{17}$$

$$H = K + \beta(A + CG)'H(A + CG) = K + \beta A'H(A + CG) \tag{18}$$

where the second equality sign of (18) is due to (17).

Using (26) and the definitions for A and C, with (symmetric) H partitioned into 3×3 blocks corresponding to K, we can simplify (17) into

$$G = -(H_{22} + H_{23} + H'_{23} + H_{33})^{-1}[(H'_{12} + H'_{13})A_1 \quad -(H_{23} + H_{33}) \quad 0] \qquad (55)$$

Because A' has all zeros in its last row, so does $\beta A'H(A + CG)$. By (18) the last row of H equals the last row of K; that is,

$$H'_{13} = K'_{13} = 0 \qquad H'_{23} = K'_{23} = 0 \qquad H_{33} = K_{33} \qquad (56)$$

Using (56), we simplify (55) further to yield

$$G = -(H_{22} + K_{33})^{-1}[H'_{12}A_1 \quad -K_{33} \quad 0] \qquad (57)$$

We need find only H_{22} and H_{12} to evaluate G. Using (30) and letting $\theta = (H_{22} + K_{33})^{-1}$, we have

$$A'H(A + CG) = \begin{bmatrix} A'_1(H_{11} - H_{12}\theta H'_{12})A_1 & A'_1 H_{12}\theta K_{33} & 0 \\ K_{33}\theta H'_{12} A_1 & K_{33} - K_{33}\theta K_{33} & 0 \\ 0 & 0 & 0 \end{bmatrix} \qquad (58)$$

Equations (58) and (18) imply

$$H_{22} = K_{22} + \beta K_{33} - \beta K_{33}(H_{22} + K_{33})^{-1}K_{33} \qquad (59)$$

$$H_{12} = K_{12} + \beta A'_1 H_{12}(H_{22} + K_{33})^{-1}K_{33} \qquad (60)$$

Because K_{22} and K_{33} are diagonal by assumption, a diagonal H_{22} is a solution of (59) with its ith diagonal element satisfying

$$h_{22,i} = k_{22,i} + \beta k_{33,i} - \beta \frac{k^2_{33,i}}{h_{22,i} + k_{33,i}}$$

or $\qquad h^2_{22,i} - (k_{22,i} + k_{33,i}\beta - k_{33,i})h_{22,i} - k_{22,i}k_{33,i} = 0 \qquad (61)$

which can be solved for $h_{22,i}$. We take the smaller root of the quadratic equation (61) since we wish to make $h_{22,i}$ as small as possible. The dynamic programming solution to the linear-quadratic control problem (see Sec. 12.1) transforms a multiperiod maximization problem into many one-period problems. For each period t, one minimizes the expectation of a quadratic function in y_t involving $y'_t H_t y_t (H_t \geq 0)$. Hence H_{22} should be diagonal with small elements. Having obtained H_{22}, we use (60) to compute $H_{12} = (h_{12,ij})$. Denoting the diagonal matrix $(H_{22} + K_{33})^{-1}K_{33}$ by $D = \text{diag}\{d_i\}$, and the elements of A_1 by a_{ij}, we have

$$h_{12,ij} = k_{12,ij} + \beta \sum_l a_{li} d_l h_{12,lj} \qquad (62)$$

The elements $h_{12,ij}$ in the jth column of H_{12} satisfy a set of linear equations (62). We have thus provided an explicit expression for G as a function of A_1, β, and K by using formulas (57), (61), and (62).

As an illustration for a scalar x_t, consider the example of Hansen and Sargent (1980), where x_t denotes the demand for an input labor. Referring to their objective function, we have $\gamma_1 = K_{22}$ and $\delta = K_{33}$ in our notation, both being scalars.

Equations (59) and (61) are identical for a scalar x_t. They become

$$h_{22}^2 - (\gamma_1 + \delta\beta - \delta)h_{22} - \gamma_1\delta = 0$$

implying

$$h_{22} = \tfrac{1}{2}[(\gamma_1 + \delta\beta - \delta) - \sqrt{(\gamma_1 + \delta\beta - \delta)^2 + 4\gamma_1\delta}]$$

The matrix K_{12} becomes a column vector consisting of the coefficients of the products of x_t and y_{it} in the objective function. Because $H_{22} + K_{33}$ in (60) is the scalar $h_{22} + \delta$, we can write the solution of (60) as

$$H_{12} = [I - \beta\delta(h_{22} + \delta)^{-1}A_1']^{-1}K_{12}$$

The coefficient of x_{t-1} in the optimal feedback control equation (or a demand for labor equation) is $(H_{22} + K_{33})^{-1}K_{33}$ according to (57), or $\delta/(h_{22} + \delta)$. This result agrees with the result of Sec. 12.6. The coefficient ρ_1 is the inverse of the (smaller) root of the quadratic equation

$$\delta\beta - (\gamma_1 + \delta + \delta\beta)z + \delta z^2 = 0$$

Note how easy it is to get the coefficients of the state variables in the feedback control equation. They are simply

$$-(H_{22} + K_{33})^{-1}H_{12}'A_1 \tag{63}$$

according to (57).

The explicit solution of this section breaks down when the matrix C does not have a submatrix of zeros, for then $(C'HC)^{-1}$ can no longer be written $(H_{22} + K_{33})^{-1}$, as in (57), and one cannot solve an equation corresponding to (59) explicitly for the elements of H_{22} even if K_{22} is diagonal.

12.8 THE ASSUMPTIONS OF OPTIMIZATION MODELS

Besides providing practical methods, this chapter so far has pinpointed the problems involved in the estimation of models of optimizing agents. It should be pointed out that even when the problems are overcome, the estimates by the methods presented will not strictly satisfy the assumption of rational expectations.

If the economic agents and the econometrician share the same model (1) and (1) indeed is the true model of the economic environment (two strong assumptions), the optimal policy for maximizing the expectation of the objective function (2), correctly specified by the econometrician (another assumption), is *not* (3) with coefficients given by (17) to (20) because the economic agents do not know (and are not assumed to know) the numerical values of the parameters A, C, and b exactly. Given uncertainty concerning A, C, and b, (17) to (20) no longer specify the parameters of the optimal behavioral equation for the agents to maximize the expectation of (2). In fact, no one knows how to compute the truly optimal behavioral equation. Some perhaps nearly optimal solutions are given in Chow

(1975, chaps. 10 and 11), for example. Equations (17) to (20) only specify the certainty-equivalent solution, which is not optimal when A, C, and b are uncertain. Strictly speaking, a true believer in optimization models should use the optimal behavioral equation which no one knows, or at least the more complicated but more nearly optimal behavioral equation referenced above. Economists who build models other than optimization models have been criticized for their failure to take optimizing behavior into account. The question is how far one should push optimizing behavior in building economic models for multiperiod decisions under uncertainty and where one should stop.

As has been recognized, advocates of optimization models often ignore, or fail to model explicitly, the process of learning by the economic agents about the economic environment (1) and assume, as in the methods of this chapter, that a steady state is always observed for the optimal behavioral equation (3). The modeling of learning will automatically be incorporated if one uses a behavioral equation which is more nearly optimal than the certainty-equivalent strategy by taking into account the uncertainty in the model parameters. Such a behavioral equation incorporates the process of learning, is strictly speaking nonlinear in y_{t-1}, and is time-dependent. The estimation of such models is much more difficult. Again, how far should one push the assumption of optimal behavior? How useful are the models based on approximate solutions (how approximate?) to optimal behavior as exemplified by the methods of this chapter?

12.9 MODEL OF A DYNAMIC GAME

A model of a dynamic game can be constructed by introducing two sets of economic decision makers, so that the model becomes

$$y_t = Ay_{t-1} + C_1 x_{1t} + C_2 x_{2t} + b_t + u_t \tag{64}$$

Each set i of decision makers chooses its control variables x_{it} to maximize an objective function

$$-E_0 \sum_{t=1}^{T} (y_t - a_{it})' K_{it}(y_t - a_{it}) \qquad i = 1, 2 \tag{65}$$

and derives its optimal behavioral equation

$$x_{it} = G_{it} y_{t-1} + g_{it} \qquad i = 1, 2 \tag{66}$$

The econometric problem is to estimate the parameters of (64) and (65). Furthermore, when one decision maker is the government, we are concerned with the evaluation of the effects of government policy changes and the choice of an optimum policy for the government.

To illustrate the application of this model, let x_{1t} be the variables subject to the control of some group of decision makers in the private sector and x_{2t} be the variables subject to the control of the government. If the government adheres to a policy rule, i.e., if G_2 and g_{2t} are given, the environment facing the private decision makers is

$$y_t = (A + C_2 G_2)y_{t-1} + C_1 x_{1t} + (b_t + C_2 g_{2t}) + u_t$$

$$\equiv A_{12} y_{t-1} + C_1 x_{1t} + b_{12.t} + u_t \tag{67}$$

They would maximize their objective function to derive their behavioral equation. As Lucas (1976) has stressed, if the policy rule of the government changes, the behavioral equation of the private decision makers will also change. Therefore, an econometrician should not rely on a stable relation (3) to evaluate the effects of government policy. A correct procedure is to estimate (1) and (2), rather than (1) and (3), and then derive the changes in (3) due to changes in (1). Lucas (1976, p. 20) reminds us that this point had been made by the proponents of structural estimation for simultaneous-equation models and cites Marschak (1953) as having pointed out the change in the reduced-form equations due to a policy change. Another manifestation of this problem occurs when the behavioral equations of the private sector contain expectation variables which are explained by some distributed lag relationships. As government policy changes, the model (1) or (67) will change, and these expectations will also change under rational expectations, making the historical distributed-lag relationships unstable. The solution again is to rederive the expectations using the new structure (1) or (67), as pointed out in Chap. 11.

A model of dynamic games allows for two sets of decision makers whose actions affect each other's environment. In the above example, while the government policy rule $x_{2t} = G_2 y_{t-1} + g_{2t}$ affects the optimal policy of the private sector, the latter's optimal behavioral relation $x_{1t} = G_1 y_{t-1} + g_{1t}$ will also affect the policy rule of the government if it is also assumed to maximize its objective function. We study this dynamic game model in the remainder of the chapter. Section 12.11 deals with the estimation of the parameters of this model under the assumption that player 2 (the government) is the dominant player. Section 12.12 treats the estimation problem when the two players are assumed to be in a noncooperative Nash equilibrium. Section 12.10 sets the stage by treating the topic of government policy evaluation and optimization under the assumption that the government is the dominant player. Again we assume that the optimal reaction coefficient G_{it} in (6) for both players will reach a steady state G_i, that is, the rational-expectation equilibrium. Otherwise, no stable relationships can be estimated.

⋆12.10 POLICY EVALUATION AND OPTIMIZATION UNDER RATIONAL EXPECTATIONS

The critique by Lucas (1976) of econometric policy evaluation is essentially that when the policy of player 2 (the government) is being evaluated, the econometrician should not take the behavioral equation $x_{1t} = G_1 y_{t-1} + g_{1t}$ for the private sector as given. To evaluate the consequences of any government policy rule (G_2, g_{2t}) proper account has to be taken of the optimizing reaction of the private sector since its environment consists of $x_{2t} = G_2 y_{t-1} + g_{2t}$. The private sector derives its optimum behavioral equation $x_{1t} = G_1 y_{t-1} + g_{1t}$ by maximizing its objective function subject to this environment. Linear-quadratic optimal control theory (Sec. 12.2) can be used to find this optimal feedback control equation. The problem of policy evaluation is thus solved.

Turning to policy optimization by the government, we observe that its optimal policy is the strategy of the dominant player in a two-person dynamic game. We shall derive a pair of optimal steady-state strategies (G_1, g_1) and (G_2, g_2) for the two players when the system is in a covariance-stationary equilibrium, assuming that $b_t, a_{1t}, K_{1t}, a_{2t}$, and K_{2t} are all time-invariant, the time subscript t for these variables being omitted in the remainder of this section.

If the dominant player adheres to a feedback control policy $x_{2t} = G_2 y_{t-1} + g_2$, player 1 will face (67) as its environment and adopt the optimal equilibrium strategy $x_{1t} = G_1 y_{t-1} + g_1$, where, by (17) to (20),

$$C_1' H_1 C_1 G_1 + C_1' H_1 (A + C_2 G_2) = 0 \tag{68}$$

$$H_1 - K_1 - (A + C_2 G_2 + C_1 G_1)' H_1 (A + C_2 G_2 + C_1 G_1) = 0 \tag{69}$$

$$C_1' H_1 C_1 g_1 + C_1' [H_1 (b + C_2 g_2) - h_1] = 0 \tag{70}$$

$$[I - (A + C_2 G_2 + C_1 G_1)'] h_1 - K_1 a_1$$
$$- (A + C_2 G_2 + C_1 G_1)' H_1 (b + C_2 g_2) = 0 \tag{71}$$

Given G_2, Eqs. (68) and (69) can be solved to obtain G_1 and H_1. Given g_2 in addition, Eqs. (70) and (71) can be solved to obtain g_1 and h_1. In a covariance-stationary equilibrium, the system will have a mean vector $\bar{y}$ and a covariance matrix $\Gamma = E(y_t - \bar{y})(y_t - \bar{y})'$ which satisfy (see Chap. 6)

$$(I - A - C_1 G_1 - C_2 G_2)\bar{y} - b - C_1 g_1 - C_2 g_2 = 0 \tag{72}$$

$$\Gamma - (A + C_1 G_1 + C_2 G_2)\Gamma(A + C_1 G_1 + C_2 G_2)' - E u_t u_t' = 0 \tag{73}$$

Player 2's problem is to minimize

$$\tfrac{1}{2} E(y_t - a_2)' K_2 (y_t - a_2) = \tfrac{1}{2} \operatorname{tr}(K_2 \Gamma) + \tfrac{1}{2}(\bar{y} - a_2)' K_2 (\bar{y} - a_2)$$

with respect to G_2 and g_2 in its feedback control equation, subject to the constraints (68) to (73). This problem can be solved by forming the lagrangian expression

$$L = \tfrac{1}{2} \operatorname{tr}(K_2 \Gamma) + \tfrac{1}{2}(\bar{y} - a_2)' K_2 (\bar{y} - a_2) - \omega'(70) - \phi'(71) - \lambda'(72)$$
$$- \operatorname{tr}[\Omega(68)] - \tfrac{1}{2} \operatorname{tr}[\Phi(69)] - \tfrac{1}{2} \operatorname{tr}[\Psi(73)]$$

where $\omega, \phi, \lambda, \Omega, \Phi = \Phi'$, and $\Psi = \Psi'$ are vectors and matrices of lagrangian multipliers and, for brevity, the equation number in parentheses denotes the corresponding constraint.

Using the differentiation rule $[\partial \operatorname{tr}(AB)/\partial A = B']$, we obtain the following equations, with R denoting $A + C_1 G_1 + C_2 G_2$,

$$\frac{\partial L}{\partial g_1} = -C_1' H_1 C_1 \omega + C_1' \lambda = 0 \tag{74}$$

$$\frac{\partial L}{\partial h_1} = C_1 \omega - (I - R)\phi = 0 \tag{75}$$

$$\frac{\partial L}{\partial g_2} = -C_2' H_1 C_1 \omega + C_2' H_1 R\phi + C_2' \lambda = 0 \tag{76}$$

$$\frac{\partial L}{\partial \bar{y}} = K_2(\bar{y} - a_2) - (I - R')\lambda = 0 \tag{77}$$

$$\frac{\partial L}{\partial G_1} = C_1'[H_1 C_1 \Omega' + H_1 R\Phi + \Psi R\Gamma + h_1 \phi' + H_1(b + C_2 g_2)\phi' + \lambda \bar{y}'] = 0 \tag{78}$$

$$\frac{\partial L}{\partial G_2} = C_2'[H_1 C_1 \Omega' + H_1 R\Phi + \Psi R\Gamma + h_1 \phi' + H_1(b + C_2 g_2)\phi' + \lambda \bar{y}'] = 0 \tag{79}$$

$$\frac{\partial L}{\partial H_1} = -\Phi + R\Phi R' - C_1 g_1 \omega' C_1' - C_1 \omega g_1' C_1' - (b + C_2 g_2)\omega' C_1'$$
$$- C_1 \omega(b + C_2 g_2)' + (b + C_2 g_2)\phi' R + R'\phi(b + C_2 g_2)' = 0 \tag{80}$$

$$\frac{\partial L}{\partial \Gamma} = K_2 - \Psi + R'\Psi R = 0 \tag{81}$$

To solve these equations we first consider an approximate solution for G_2, G_1, and H_1 in a simpler problem. The problem is the minimization of $\operatorname{tr}(K_2 \Gamma)$ when $b = 0$, $a_1 = 0$, and $a_2 = 0$. The optimal strategies are $x_{1t} = G_1 y_{t-1}$ and $x_{2t} = G_2 y_{t-1}$; constraints (70) to (72) are no longer relevant. One need only solve Eqs. (78) to (81), with $\omega = 0$, $\phi = 0$, $\lambda = 0$, $\bar{y} = 0$, and $g_2 = 0$. Equation (80) becomes $\Phi = R\Phi R'$, which has a solution $\Phi = 0$; (78) implies

$$\Omega' = -(C_1' H_1 C_1)^{-1}(\Psi R\Gamma)$$

which, when substituted into (79), yields

$$C_2'[I - H_1 C_1(C_1' H_1 C_1)^{-1}]\Psi(A + C_1 G_1 + C_2 G_2)\Gamma = 0 \tag{82}$$

Starting with an initial guess for G_2, we solve (68) and (69) for G_1 and H_1. Given G_1, we solve (81) for Ψ. Equation (82), postmultiplied by Γ^{-1}, can be used to compute a new G_2

$$G_2 = \{C_2'[I - H_1 C_1(C_1' H_1 C_1)^{-1}]\Psi C_2\}^{-1}$$
$$\times C_2'[I - H_1 C_1(C_1' H_1 C_1)^{-1}]\Psi(A + C_1 G_1)$$

This iterative process can be continued to find G_2, G_1, and H_1 for the simpler problem.

To solve the original problem we start with the above approximate solution for G_2, G_1, and H_1. Equations (74) to (77) respectively imply, with $P_1 = C_1(C_1'H_1C_1)^{-1}C_1'$,

$$\omega = (C_1'H_1C_1)^{-1}C_1'\lambda \tag{74a}$$

$$\phi = (I - R)^{-1}P_1\lambda \tag{75a}$$

$$C_2'\{I - H_1[I - R(I - R)^{-1}]P_1\}\lambda = 0 \tag{76a}$$

$$\lambda = (I - R')^{-1}K_2(\bar{y} - a_2) \tag{77a}$$

while (77a) and (72) give

$$\lambda = (I - R')^{-1}K_2[(I - R)^{-1}(b + C_1g_1 + C_2g_2) - a_2] \tag{83}$$

Combining (83) with (76a), we get

$$C_2'\{I - H_1[I - R(I - R)^{-1}]P_1\}(I - R')^{-1}K_2$$
$$\cdot [(I - R)^{-1}(b + C_1g_1 + C_2g_2) - a_2] = 0 \tag{84}$$

With G_2, G_1, and H_1 given, Eqs. (84), (70), and (71) can be solved for g_2, g_1, and h_1. Equation (84) is used to express g_2 as a linear function of g_1; Eqs. (70) and (71) become two linear equations in g_1 and h_1. Equations (83), (74a), and (75a) are then used to find λ, ω, and ϕ, while Eq. (72) is used to compute $\bar{y}$.

We now follow the steps of the simpler problem to solve Eqs. (78) to (81). Equation (80) is used to solve for Φ iteratively; that is, $\Phi^{(i+1)} = R\Phi^{(i)}R' + \text{known}$ matrix. Equations (78) and (79) imply

$$\Omega' = -(C_1'H_1C_1)^{-1}C_1'(H_1R\Phi + \Psi R\Gamma + \cdots) \tag{78a}$$

$$C_2'(I - H_1P_1)[H_1R\Phi + \Psi R\Gamma + h_1\phi' + H_1(b + C_2g_2)\phi' + \lambda\bar{y}'] = 0 \tag{79a}$$

Since (73) and (81) can be used to compute Γ and Ψ, respectively, (79a) after being postmultiplied by Γ^{-1} can be solved for G_2 iteratively; i.e.,

$$C_2'(I - H_1P_1)\Psi C_2 G_2 = C_2'(I - H_1P_1)[H_1R\Phi\Gamma^{-1} + \Psi(A + C_1G_1) + \cdots] \tag{82a}$$

where we recall that $R = A + C_1G_1 + C_2G_2$. Having thus obtained a new matrix G_2, we can continue with the iterative process by returning to the beginning of the preceding paragraph.

Mathematically, the solution to the two-person dynamic game formulated above under a Nash (or Cournot) equilibrium is simpler, for each player would treat the other's strategy as given, without being affected by his own strategy. Given (G_2, g_2), player 1 would find (G_1, g_1) by Eqs. (68) to (70), as before. Symmetrically, given (G_1, g_1), player 2 would find (G_2, g_2) by solving an identical set of equations with subscripts 1 and 2 interchanged. A Nash equilibrium is found by solving these two sets of equations.

*12.11 ESTIMATION OF A DYNAMIC GAME MODEL WITH A DOMINANT PLAYER

When x_{2t} in (64) represents the policy instruments of the government and the government is treated as the dominant player, we study the estimation problem in two stages. First, assuming that the government adheres to a policy rule $x_{2t} = G_2 y_{t-1} + g_{2t}$, which is decided upon by whatever means, we shall consider the estimation of the parameters of (64) and (65) for $i = 1$ under the assumption that the private sector behaves optimally. Second, from the above framework we take the next step by assuming that the government is also trying to maximize (65) for $i = 2$ and consider the estimation of the parameters of its objective function as well.

For the first problem, the stochastic environment facing the private sector consists of two equations, (64) and

$$x_{2t} = G_2 y_{t-1} + g_2 \tag{66a}$$

which constitute the model (1) in Secs. 12.3 and 12.4. Two methods were provided to estimate the parameters of (1), now consisting of (64) and (66a), and of (2), now represented by (65) with $i = 1$. The methods are maximum likelihood and a consistent method analogous to 2SLS. The latter method requires consistent estimates of the parameters of (1) and (3); using them, it solves for the parameters of (2) in the second stage of 2SLS.

We now incorporate the assumption that the government also maximizes to obtain its behavioral equation (66a). If we are not interested in estimating the objective function of the government and are willing to assume that the parameters of (64) and (65) remained unchanged for the sample observations, then (66a) is a stable equation and the methods of Secs. 12.3 and 12.4 will suffice, as pointed out in the last paragraph. The new problem is to estimate the objective function of the government as well. From the viewpoint of the maximizing government, the stochastic environment consists of (64) and (65) with $i = 1$, which, together with its own policy (G_2, g_2), determine G_1 and g_1 in (66) as a result of the private sector's maximizing behavior.

Maximum-likelihood estimation of the parameters of (64) and (65) under the assumption that player 2 (the government) is the dominant player can proceed as follows. Adding a residual v_{it} to (66) and assuming a joint normal distribution of u_t, v_{1t}, and v_{2t}, one can easily write down the likelihood function which has the parameters of (64) and (66) as arguments. As a first step, we postpone the estimation of K_2 and a_2 and assume some given values for G_2 and g_2 (which could be the coefficients of a least-squares regression of x_{2t} on y_{t-1}). Given G_2 and g_2, we can express G_1 and g_1 as functions of the parameters of (64) and K_1 and a_1 in (65) through the maximization of the private sector. K_{1t} and a_1 thus replace G_1 and g_1 as arguments in the likelihood function. To reduce the number of parameters, we assume here, as in Sec. 12.3, that $K_{1t} = \beta_1^t K_1$, β_1 being the discount factor for the private sector. Then given G_2 and g_2, we can maximize the likelihood function with respect to the parameters of (64) and K_1, β_1, and a_1. This problem was solved in Sec. 12.3. We now solve the more difficult problem of estimating K_2 and a_2. Given K_1, a_1, K_2, a_2, and the parameters of (64), we can apply the method of Sec. 12.10 to find (G_1, g_1) and (G_2, g_2); thus the likelihood function can be evaluated. A gradient method can in principle be applied to maximize the likelihood with respect to these parameters, but this numerical maximization problem requires further investigation.

★12.12 ESTIMATION OF A DYNAMIC GAME MODEL UNDER NASH EQUILIBRIUM

The estimation problem for a dynamic game model under a Nash equilibrium is simpler. We can apply iterative techniques by considering this estimation problem in two stages. First, assuming tentatively that the government adheres to a policy rule (G_2, g_2), we shall consider the estimation of the parameters of (64) and $K_{1t} = \beta_1^t K_1$ and a_1 under the assumption that the private sector behaves optimally. Our estimation procedure assumes optimal behavior (G_1, g_1) of the private sector, with (G_2, g_2) taken as given. Second, assuming that the private sector adheres to the policy (G_2, g_2) as determined above, we consider the estimation of the parameters of (64) and $K_2 = \beta_2^t K_2$ and $a_2 = \phi_2^t a_2$ under the assumption that the government behaves optimally. Similarly, this estimation procedure assumes optimal behavior (G_2, g_2) of the government, with (G_1, g_1) taken as given. We now go back to step 1 and iterate back and forth until convergence.

As pointed out previously, given (G_2, g_2), the methods of Secs. 12.3 and 12.4 can be used to estimate the parameters of (64), K_1, β_1, a_1, and, accordingly, G_1 and g_1. Similarly, given (G_1, g_1), the same methods can be used to estimate the parameters of (64), K_2, β_2, a_2, and, accordingly, G_2 and g_2. If the method of maximum likelihood is used, we start with some consistent estimates of G_2 and g_2 (as obtained by regressing x_{2t} on y_{t-1}) and maximize the likelihood function with respect to the parameters of (64), K_1, β_1, and a_1, yielding maximum-likelihood estimates of G_1 and g_1 as well. Using these estimates of G_1 and g_1, we again maximize the likelihood function with respect to the parameters of (64), K_2, β_2, and a_2, and so forth until convergence. This procedure amounts to maximizing the likelihood function with respect to two sets of parameters iteratively, i.e., to one set while holding the other set fixed and alternatively.

Equivalently, we can maximize the likelihood subject to two sets of constraints. One set of constraints consists of the four equations (68) to (71), and the second set is identical with subscripts 1 and 2 interchanged. A lagrangian expression can be formed which is to be maximized. Given the parameters of the objective function and the optimal decision rule for player 1, the method of Sec. 12.3 can be used to find the remaining parameters of the model. Given the estimates of the parameters pertaining to player 2 so obtained, one can maximize the likelihood function with respect to the parameters for player 1, and the process proceeds iteratively until convergence.

To propose a simpler and yet consistent method we start with consistent estimates of the parameters of (64) and of (G_2, g_2) and (G_1, g_1), by the method of least squares, for instance. The parameters of (64) and (G_i, g_i) can be used to solve for K_i, β_i, and a_i for $i = 1, 2$ by the method analogous to 2SLS as given in Sec. 12.4. Given the parameters of (64) and K_i, β_i, and a_i $(i = 1, 2)$, one can then find the Nash equilibrium solution for (G_1, g_1) and (G_2, g_2) iteratively, to improve upon the initial, consistent estimates of these parameters. The situation is exactly analogous to the estimation of the reduced-form parameters Π in linear simultaneous stochastic equations. Consistent estimate $\hat{\Pi}$ of Π by least squares can be used to estimate the parameters $[B \quad \Gamma]$ of the structure using the method of two-stage least squares. Given these estimates of $[B \quad \Gamma]$, denoted by $[\hat{B} \quad \hat{\Gamma}]$, we can obtain a new estimate of Π as $-\hat{B}^{-1}\hat{\Gamma}$, to improve upon the initial estimate $\hat{\Pi}$.

This section has treated the estimation of optimization models under the assumption of Nash equilibrium. If player 2 represents the government, the solution concept of having a dominant player as expounded in Sec. 12.11 may be more appropriate.

PROBLEMS

1. Let the price p_t facing a competitive firm satisfy a kth-order autoregressive process. Let the production cost of a firm be $c + d_t x_t$, where the marginal cost d_t follows a qth-order autoregressive process. Let the second component of cost, due to changes in production, equal $b(x_t - x_{t-1})^2$. The firm maximizes expected total discounted future profits. Formulate this optimization problem using a first-order dynamic system to describe the environment of the firm and a quadratic objective function in the notation of (2).

2. Formulate the problem of Lucas and Prescott (1971) as an optimal control problem using a first-order dynamic system to describe the environment of the decision maker and a quadratic objective function in the notation of (2).

3. Assuming that u_t in (21) and v_t in (23) are correlated, modify the method of FIML for estimating the parameters of (21), (23), and the quadratic objective function.

4. If the residual v_t in (23) obeys a first-order autoregressive process $v_t = Rv_{t-1} + \epsilon_t$, where ϵ_t is serially uncorrelated and has covariance matrix V, show how the method of constrained maximum likelihood should be modified.

5. Let the intercept b in (21) be replaced by $B_0 w_t$, where w_t is a vector of exogenous variables not subject to control, which include the dummy variable 1. If a random process is assumed for w_t, show how our framework can be modified for estimating all unknown parameters.

6. Using the method of Sec. 12.6, derive the first-order conditions corresponding to (53) for the model of Blanchard (1983) given in Sec. 12.5.

$$Answer: \quad E_t[B_1(z)x_t - B_2(z)y_{1t} - B_3(z)y_{2t} - \xi_t] = 0$$

where

$$B_1(z) \equiv b_2 kz^{-2} - b[c + 2(b + 1)k]z^{-1} + \{c + (2b + 1)k + b[c + (b + 2)k] + db\}$$
$$- [c + 2(b + 1)k]z + kz^2$$

$$B_2(z) \equiv -b^2 kz^{-2} + b[c + (b + 2)k]z^{-1} - [c + (2b + 1)k] + kz$$

$$B_3(z) \equiv -b^2 kz^{-2} + b[ad + c + (b + 2)k]z^{-1} - [c + (2b + 1)k] + kz$$

$$\xi_t \equiv -db\, u_t - (1 - bz^{-1})(c\epsilon_t + k\eta_t - bk\eta_{t+1})$$

7. Obtain the optimal decision rule for the model of Blanchard (1983) by using the results of Prob. 6 and writing (for $k = 1$)

$$B_1(z) = b^2 z^2 (z^{-1} - \lambda_1)(z^{-1} - \lambda_2)(z^{-1} - \lambda_1^{-1} b^{-1})(z^{-1} - \lambda_2^{-1} b^{-1})$$

i.e., letting λ_1, λ_2, $\lambda_1^{-1} b^{-1}$, and $\lambda_2^{-1} b^{-1}$ be the four roots of the polynomial $B_1(F^{-1}) = 0$ in F, with $F \equiv z^{-1}$.

8. Using the method of Sec. 12.7, obtain the optimal decision rule for the model of Blanchard (1983) given in Sec. 12.5. The matrices A and C defined by (51) can be used to evaluate $C'HC$ and $C'HA$, where H is partitioned into 5×5 submatrices H_{ij}. Use the fact that A' has all zeros in its last two rows to conclude that $H_{4i} = K_{4i}$ and $H_{5i} = K_{5i}$. Write out $G = -(C'HC)^{-1} C'HA \equiv -\theta C'HA$ as a function of A_1, K_{ij}, and several unknown H_{ij}. Follow the steps of (58) to (60).

9. (Livesey, 1980). For $L'L = K$ and assuming L to be $q \times p$, prove

$$|L(xI_p - A)^{-1} C| = \text{const} \, |xI_p - (A + CG)| \cdot |xI_p - A|^{-1}$$

where G is defined by (17) and (18) and x is a scalar. Observe that

$$|I_q - G(xI_p - A)^{-1} C| = |xI_p - A|^{-1} \begin{vmatrix} xI_p - A & C \\ G & I_q \end{vmatrix} = |xI_p - A|^{-1} |xI_p - (A + CG)|$$

using

$$\begin{vmatrix} B_{11} & B_{12} \\ B_{21} & B_{22} \end{vmatrix} = |B_{11}| \cdot |B_{22} - B_{21} B_{11}^{-1} B_{12}|$$

and that

$$|I_q - G(xI_p - A)^{-1} C| = \text{const} \, |L(xI_p - A)^{-1} C|$$

by expanding $(x^{-1} I_p - A' - G'C')H(xI_p - A - CG)$ and premultiplying by $C'(x^{-1} I_p - A')$ and post-multiplying by $(xI_p - A)^{-1} C$, using (17) and (18). Conclude therefore that the roots of $A + CG$ are those of $|L(xI - A)^{-1} C|$. This conclusion fails if the number of target variables (number of nonzero diagonal elements of K) is larger than the number q of control variables, for then K cannot be written as $L'L$, L being $q \times p$.

10. (Livesey, 1980). Write out the characteristic equation $|xI - (A + CG)| = 0$ for the following model of Taylor (1979) under optimal control. The model explains two dependent variables y_t and π_t by

$$(1 - a\beta_1 z - a\beta_2 z^2) y_t = a\beta^5 z\pi_t + a(\beta_3 + \beta_4 z)x_t + \eta_t - a(\beta_5 \theta_2 + \theta_1) z^{-1} \epsilon_t$$

$$(1 - z)\pi_t = \gamma_1 y_t + (1 - \theta_2 z)\epsilon_t - \gamma_1 \eta_t$$

where z is the lag operator, x_t is a control variable, and η_t and ϵ_t are random residuals, the rest being parameters. The optimal feedback rule takes the form

$$x_t = g_1 y_{t-1} + g_2 y_{t-2} + g_3 x_{t-1} + g_4 \pi_{t-1} + g_5 \epsilon_{t-1}$$

where ϵ_{t-1} appears because ϵ_t is treated as a state variable to change the system with ϵ_{t-1} in the residuals into a system with serially uncorrelated residuals. Using these three equations to obtain an equation for y_t alone, show that the latter equation takes the form

$$\{(1 - g_3 z)[1 - a(1 + \beta_1)z + a(\beta_1 - \beta_2)z^2 + a\beta_2 z^3]$$

$$- a(\beta_3 + \beta_4 z)[(g_1 + g_4 \gamma_1)z + (g_2 - g_1)z^2 - g_2 z^3]\} y_t = [\cdot]\eta_t + [\cdot]\epsilon_t$$

Since the system $y_t = (A + CG)y_{t-1}$ can be written as $[I - (A + CG)z]y_t = 0$ or $[xI - (A + CG)]y_t = 0$, where $x = z^{-1}$, one obtains the characteristic equation for the Taylor (1979) model under optimal control as

$$(1 - g_3 x^{-1})[1 - a(1 + \beta_1)x^{-1} + a(\beta_1 - \beta_2)x^{-2} + \cdots - g_2 x^{-3}] = 0$$

11. (Livesey, 1980). (a) Using y_t, y_{t-1}, π_t, x_t, and ϵ_t as state variables, write out the matrices A and C in a first-order system (1) for the Taylor (1979) model.

(b) Given the objective function $E \sum_t [\lambda y_t^2 + (1 - \lambda)\pi_t^2]$, explain why one cannot write $|L(xI - A)^{-1} C| = 0$ where L is 1×5 and $L'L = K$. (I owe this point to A. B. Kennickell.)

REFERENCES

Blanchard, O. J. (1983): "The Production and Inventory Behavior of the American Automobile Industry," *J. Polit. Econ.*, **91**.

Chow, G. C. (1964): "A Comparison of Alternative Estimators for Simultaneous Equations," *Econometrica*, **32**: 532–553.

―――― (1970): "Optimal Stochastic Control of Linear Economic Systems," *J. Money, Credit Banking*, **2**: 291–302.

―――― (1973): "Effect of Uncertainty on Optimal Control Policies," *Int. Econ. Rev.*, **14**: 632–645.

―――― (1975): *Analysis and Control of Dynamic Economic Systems*, Wiley, New York.

―――― (1980): "Estimation of Rational Expectations Models," *J. Econ. Dynam. Control*, **2**: 241–255.

―――― (1981): *Econometric Analysis by Control Methods*, Wiley, New York.

Cruz, J. B., Jr. (1975): "Survey of Nash and Stackelberg Equilibrium Strategies in Dynamic Games," *Ann. Econ. Soc. Meas.*, **4**: 339–344.

Hansen, L. P., and T. J. Sargent (1980): "Formulating and Estimating Dynamic Linear Rational Expectations Models," *J. Econ. Dynam. Control*, **2**: 7–46.

―――― and ―――― (1981): "Linear Rational Expectations Models for Dynamically Interrelated Variables," chap. 8 in R. E. Lucas, Jr., and T. J. Sargent (eds.), *Rational Expectations and Econometric Practice*, vol. 1, University of Minnesota Press, Minneapolis.

Kydland, F. E. (1975): "Non-cooperative and Dominant Player Solutions in Discrete Dynamic Games," *Int. Econ. Rev.*, **16**: 321–335.

―――― and E. C. Prescott (1977): "Rule Rather than Discretion: The Inconsistency of Optimal Plans," *J. Polit. Econ.*, **85**: 473–491.

Livesey, D. A. (1980): "Stabilization Policy: A View from the Complex Plane," *Univ. Penn. Cent. Anal. Res. Econ. Soc. Sci. Working Pap.* 80-09.

Lucas, R. E., Jr. (1967): "Optimal Investment Policy and the Flexible Accelerator," *Int. Econ. Rev.*, **8**: 78–85.

―――― (1976): "Econometric Policy Evaluation: A Critique," in K. Brunner and A. H. Meltzer (eds.), *The Phillips Curve and Labor Markets*, Carnegie-Rochester Conference Series on Public Policy, vol. 1, North-Holland, Amsterdam.

―――― and E. C. Prescott (1971): "Investment under Uncertainty," *Econometrica*, **39**: 659–681; reprinted as chap. 6 in R. E. Lucas, Jr., and T. S. Sargent (eds.), *Rational Expectations and Econometric Practice*, vol. 1, University of Minnesota Press, Minneapolis, 1981.

―――― and T. J. Sargent (1981): "Introduction," pp. xi–xl, in R. E. Lucas, Jr., and T. J. Sargent (eds.), *Rational Expectations and Econometric Practice*, vol. 1, University of Minnesota Press, Minneapolis.

―――― and ―――― (eds.) (1981): *Rational Expectations and Econometric Practice*, University of Minnesota Press, Minneapolis.

Marschak, J. (1953): "Economic Measurements for Policy and Prediction," in W. C. Hood and T. C. Koopmans (eds.), *Studies in Econometric Method, Cowles Comm. Monogr.* 14, Wiley, New York.

Muth, J. F. (1961): "Rational Expectations and the Theory of Price Movements," *Econometrica*, **29**: 315–335.

Salemi, M., and T. J. Sargent (1979): "The Demand for Money during Hyperinflation under Rational Expectations," *Int. Econ. Rev.*, **20**: 741–758.

Sargent, T. J. (1979): *Macroeconomic Theory*, Academic, New York.

Taylor, J. B. (1979): "Estimation and Control of a Macroeconomic Model with Rational Expectations," *Econometrica*, **47**: 1267–1286.

―――― (1981): "Stabilization, Accommodation, and Monetary Rules," *Am. Econ. Rev.*, **71**: 145–149.

TABLES

Table I Cumulative normal distribution

$$\Phi(x) = \int_{-\infty}^{x} \frac{1}{\sqrt{2\pi}} \, e^{-t^2/2} \, dt$$

x	.00	.01	.02	.03	.04	.05	.06	.07	.08	.09
.0	.5000	.5040	.5080	.5120	.5160	.5199	.5239	.5279	.5319	.5359
.1	.5398	.5438	.5478	.5517	.5557	.5596	.5636	.5675	.5714	.5753
.2	.5793	.5832	.5871	.5910	.5948	.5987	.6026	.6064	.6103	.6141
.3	.6179	.6217	.6255	.6293	.6331	.6368	.6406	.6443	.6480	.6517
.4	.6554	.6591	.6628	.6664	.6700	.6736	.6772	.6808	.6844	.6789
.5	.6915	.6950	.6985	.7019	.7054	.7088	.7123	.7157	.7190	.7224
.6	.7257	.7291	.7324	.7357	.7389	.7422	.7454	.7486	.7517	.7549
.7	.7580	.7611	.7642	.7673	.7704	.7734	.7764	.7794	.7823	.7852
.8	.7881	.7910	.7939	.7967	.7995	.8023	.8051	.8078	.8106	.8133
.9	.8159	.8186	.8212	.8238	.8264	.8289	.8315	.8340	.8365	.8389
1.0	.8413	.8438	.8461	.8485	.8508	.8531	.8554	.8577	.8599	.8621
1.1	.8643	.8665	.8686	.8708	.8729	.8749	.8770	.8790	.8810	.8830
1.2	.8849	.8869	.8888	.8907	.8925	.8944	.8962	.8980	.8997	.9015
1.3	.9032	.9049	.9066	.9082	.9099	.9115	.9131	.9147	.9162	.9177
1.4	.9192	.9207	.9222	.9236	.9251	.9265	.9279	.9292	.9306	.9319
1.5	.9332	.9345	.9357	.9370	.9382	.9394	.9406	.9418	.9429	.9441
1.6	.9452	.9463	.9474	.9484	.9495	.9505	.9515	.9525	.9535	.9545
1.7	.9554	.9564	.9573	.9582	.9591	.9599	.9608	.9616	.9625	.9633
1.8	.9641	.9649	.9656	.9664	.9671	.9678	.9686	.9693	.9699	.9706
1.9	.9713	.9719	.9726	.9732	.9738	.9744	.9750	.9756	.9761	.9767
2.0	.9772	.9778	.9783	.9788	.9793	.9798	.9803	.9808	.9812	.9817
2.1	.9821	.9826	.9830	.9834	.9838	.9842	.9846	.9850	.9854	.9857
2.2	.9861	.9864	.9868	.9871	.9875	.9878	.9881	.9884	.9887	.9890
2.3	.9893	.9896	.9898	.9901	.9904	.9906	.9909	.9911	.9913	.9916
2.4	.9918	.9920	.9922	.9925	.9927	.9929	.9931	.9932	.9934	.9936
2.5	.9938	.9940	.9941	.9943	.9945	.9946	.9948	.9949	.9951	.9952
2.6	.9953	.9955	.9956	.9957	.9959	.9960	.9961	.9962	.9963	.9964
2.7	.9965	.9966	.9967	.9968	.9969	.9970	.9971	.9972	.9973	.9974
2.8	.9974	.9975	.9976	.9977	.9977	.9978	.9979	.9979	.9980	.9981
2.9	.9981	.9982	.9982	.9983	.9984	.9984	.9985	.9985	.9986	.9986
3.0	.9987	.9987	.9987	.9988	.9988	.9989	.9989	.9989	.9990	.9990
3.1	.9990	.9991	.9991	.9991	.9992	.9992	.9992	.9992	.9993	.9993
3.2	.9993	.9993	.9994	.9994	.9994	.9994	.9994	.9995	.9995	.9995
3.3	.9995	.9995	.9995	.9996	.9996	.9996	.9996	.9996	.9996	.9997
3.4	.9997	.9997	.9997	.9997	.9997	.9997	.9997	.9997	.9997	.9998

x	1.282	1.645	1.960	2.326	2.576	3.090	3.291	3.891	4.417
$\Phi(x)$	.90	.95	.975	.99	.995	.999	.9995	.99995	.999995
$2[1 - \Phi(x)]$	.20	.10	.05	.02	.01	.002	.001	.0001	.00001

(Reprinted from Mood and Graybill, *Introduction to the Theory of Statistics*, 3d ed., McGraw-Hill Book Company, New York, 1973. By permission of the publishers.)

Table II Percentage points of the chi-square distribution*

$$F(u) = \int_u^\infty \frac{x^{(n-2)/2}e^{-x/2}\,dx}{2^{n/2}\Gamma(n/2)}$$

n \ F	.995	.990	.975	.950	.900	.750	.500	.250	.100	.050	.025	.010	.005
1	$.0^4393$	$.0^3157$	$.0^3982$	$.0^2393$	.0158	.102	.455	1.32	2.71	3.84	5.02	6.63	7.88
2	.0100	.0201	.0506	.103	.211	.575	1.39	2.77	4.61	5.99	7.38	9.21	10.6
3	.0717	.115	.216	.352	.584	1.21	2.37	4.11	6.25	7.81	9.35	11.3	12.8
4	.207	.297	.484	.711	1.06	1.92	3.36	5.39	7.78	9.49	11.1	13.3	14.9
5	.412	.554	.831	1.15	1.61	2.67	4.35	6.63	9.24	11.1	12.8	15.1	16.7
6	.676	.872	1.24	1.64	2.20	3.45	5.35	7.84	10.6	12.6	14.4	16.8	18.5
7	.989	1.24	1.69	2.17	2.83	4.25	6.35	9.04	12.0	14.1	16.0	18.5	20.3
8	1.34	1.65	2.18	2.73	3.49	5.07	7.34	10.2	13.4	15.5	17.5	20.1	22.0
9	1.73	2.09	2.70	3.33	4.17	5.90	8.34	11.4	14.7	16.9	19.0	21.7	23.6
10	2.16	2.56	3.25	3.94	4.87	6.74	9.34	12.5	16.0	18.3	20.5	23.2	25.2
11	2.60	3.05	3.82	4.57	5.58	7.58	10.3	13.7	17.3	19.7	21.9	24.7	26.8
12	3.07	3.57	4.40	5.23	6.30	8.44	11.3	14.8	18.5	21.0	23.3	26.2	28.3
13	3.57	4.11	5.01	5.89	7.04	9.30	12.3	16.0	19.8	22.4	24.7	27.7	29.8
14	4.07	4.66	5.63	6.57	7.79	10.2	13.3	17.1	21.1	23.7	26.1	29.1	31.3
15	4.60	5.23	6.26	7.26	8.55	11.0	14.3	18.2	22.3	25.0	27.5	30.6	32.8
16	5.14	5.81	6.91	7.96	9.31	11.9	15.3	19.4	23.5	26.3	28.8	32.0	34.3
17	5.70	6.41	7.56	8.67	10.1	12.8	16.3	20.5	24.8	27.6	30.2	33.4	35.7
18	6.26	7.01	8.23	9.39	10.9	13.7	17.3	21.6	26.0	28.9	31.5	34.8	37.2
19	6.84	7.63	8.91	10.1	11.7	14.6	18.3	22.7	27.2	30.1	32.9	36.2	38.6
20	7.43	8.26	9.59	10.9	12.4	15.5	19.3	23.8	28.4	31.4	34.2	37.6	40.0
21	8.03	8.90	10.3	11.6	13.2	16.3	20.3	24.9	29.6	32.7	35.5	38.9	41.4
22	8.64	9.54	11.0	12.3	14.0	17.2	21.3	26.0	30.8	33.9	36.8	40.3	42.8
23	9.26	10.2	11.7	13.1	14.8	18.1	22.3	27.1	32.0	35.2	38.1	41.6	44.2
24	9.89	10.9	12.4	13.8	15.7	19.0	23.3	28.2	33.2	36.4	39.4	43.0	45.6
25	10.5	11.5	13.1	14.6	16.5	19.9	24.3	29.3	34.4	37.7	40.6	44.3	46.9
26	11.2	12.2	13.8	15.4	17.3	20.8	25.3	30.4	35.6	38.9	41.9	45.6	48.3
27	11.8	12.9	14.6	16.2	18.1	21.7	26.3	31.5	36.7	40.1	43.2	47.0	49.6
28	12.5	13.6	15.3	16.9	18.9	22.7	27.3	32.6	37.9	41.3	44.5	48.3	51.0
29	13.1	14.3	16.0	17.7	19.8	23.6	28.3	33.7	39.1	42.6	45.7	49.6	52.3
30	13.8	15.0	16.8	18.5	20.6	24.5	29.3	34.8	40.3	43.8	47.0	50.9	53.7

Table III Percentage points of the *t*-distribution*

v	$Q = 0.4$ $2Q = 0.8$	0.25 0.5	0.1 0.2	0.05 0.1	0.025 0.05	0.01 0.02	0.005 0.01
1	0.325	1.000	3.078	6.314	12.706	31.821	63.657
2	.289	0.816	1.886	2.920	4.303	6.965	9.925
3	.277	.765	1.638	2.353	3.182	4.541	5.841
4	.271	.741	1.533	2.132	2.776	3.747	4.604
5	0.267	0.727	1.476	2.015	2.571	3.365	4.032
6	.265	.718	1.440	1.943	2.447	3.143	3.707
7	.263	.711	1.415	1.895	2.365	2.998	3.499
8	.262	.706	1.397	1.860	2.306	2.896	3.355
9	.261	.703	1.383	1.833	2.262	2.821	3.250
10	0.260	0.700	1.372	1.812	2.228	2.764	3.169
11	.260	.697	1.363	1.796	2.201	2.718	3.106
12	.259	.695	1.356	1.782	2.179	2.681	3.055
13	.259	.694	1.350	1.771	2.160	2.650	3.012
14	.258	.692	1.345	1.761	2.145	2.624	2.977
15	0.258	0.691	1.341	1.753	2.131	2.602	2.947
16	.258	.690	1.337	1.746	2.120	2.583	2.921
17	.257	.689	1.333	1.740	2.110	2.567	2.898
18	.257	.688	1.330	1.734	2.101	2.552	2.878
19	.257	.688	1.328	1.729	2.093	2.539	2.861
20	0.257	0.687	1.325	1.725	2.086	2.528	2.845
21	.257	.686	1.323	1.721	2.080	2.518	2.831
22	.256	.686	1.321	1.717	2.074	2.508	2.819
23	.256	.685	1.319	1.714	2.069	2.500	2.807
24	.256	.685	1.318	1.711	2.064	2.492	2.797
25	0.256	0.684	1.316	1.708	2.060	2.485	2.787
26	.256	.684	1.315	1.706	2.056	2.479	2.779
27	.256	.684	1.314	1.703	2.052	2.473	2.771
28	.256	.683	1.313	1.701	2.048	2.467	2.763
29	.256	.683	1.311	1.699	2.045	2.462	2.756
30	0.256	0.683	1.310	1.697	2.042	2.457	2.750
40	.255	.681	1.303	1.684	2.021	2.423	2.704
60	.254	.679	1.296	1.671	2.000	2.390	2.660
120	.254	.677	1.289	1.658	1.980	2.358	2.617
∞	.253	.674	1.282	1.645	1.960	2.326	2.576

* Q is the upper-tail area of the distribution for v degrees of freedom, appropriate for use in a single-tail test. For a two-tail test, $2Q$ must be used. This table is based on Table 12 of *Biometrika Tables for Statisticians*, vol. I, edited by E. S. Pearson and H. O. Hartley (1970). By permission of the Biometrika Trustees.

Table IV Percentage points of the F-distribution*
Upper 10% points

v_2 \ v_1	1	2	3	4	5	6	7	8	9
1	39.86	49.50	53.59	55.83	57.24	58.20	58.91	59.44	59.86
2	8.53	9.00	9.16	9.24	9.29	9.33	9.35	9.37	9.38
3	5.54	5.46	5.39	5.34	5.31	5.28	5.27	5.25	5.24
4	4.54	4.32	4.19	4.11	4.05	4.01	3.98	3.95	3.94
5	4.06	3.78	3.62	3.52	3.45	3.40	3.37	3.34	3.32
6	3.78	3.46	3.29	3.18	3.11	3.05	3.01	2.98	2.96
7	3.59	3.26	3.07	2.96	2.88	2.83	2.78	2.75	2.72
8	3.46	3.11	2.92	2.81	2.73	2.67	2.62	2.59	2.56
9	3.36	3.01	2.81	2.69	2.61	2.55	2.51	2.47	2.44
10	3.29	2.92	2.73	2.61	2.52	2.46	2.41	2.38	2.35
11	3.23	2.86	2.66	2.54	2.45	2.39	2.34	2.30	2.27
12	3.18	2.81	2.61	2.48	2.39	2.33	2.28	2.24	2.21
13	3.14	2.76	2.56	2.43	2.35	2.28	2.23	2.20	2.16
14	3.10	2.73	2.52	2.39	2.31	2.24	2.19	2.15	2.12
15	3.07	2.70	2.49	2.36	2.27	2.21	2.16	2.12	2.09
16	3.05	2.67	2.46	2.33	2.24	2.18	2.13	2.09	2.06
17	3.03	2.64	2.44	2.31	2.22	2.15	2.10	2.06	2.03
18	3.01	2.62	2.42	2.29	2.20	2.13	2.08	2.04	2.00
19	2.99	2.61	2.40	2.27	2.18	2.11	2.06	2.02	1.98
20	2.97	2.59	2.38	2.25	2.16	2.09	2.04	2.00	1.96
21	2.96	2.57	2.36	2.23	2.14	2.08	2.02	1.98	1.95
22	2.95	2.56	2.35	2.22	2.13	2.06	2.01	1.97	1.93
23	2.94	2.55	2.34	2.21	2.11	2.05	1.99	1.95	1.92
24	2.93	2.54	2.33	2.19	2.10	2.04	1.98	1.94	1.91
25	2.92	2.53	2.32	2.18	2.09	2.02	1.97	1.93	1.89
26	2.91	2.52	2.31	2.17	2.08	2.01	1.96	1.92	1.88
27	2.90	2.51	2.30	2.17	2.07	2.00	1.95	1.91	1.87
28	2.89	2.50	2.29	2.16	2.06	2.00	1.94	1.90	1.87
29	2.89	2.50	2.28	2.15	2.06	1.99	1.93	1.89	1.86
30	2.88	2.49	2.28	2.14	2.05	1.98	1.93	1.88	1.85
40	2.84	2.44	2.23	2.09	2.00	1.93	1.87	1.83	1.79
60	2.79	2.39	2.18	2.04	1.95	1.87	1.82	1.77	1.74
120	2.75	2.35	2.13	1.99	1.90	1.82	1.77	1.72	1.68
∞	2.71	2.30	2.08	1.94	1.85	1.77	1.72	1.67	1.63

* $F = \dfrac{s_1^2}{s_2^2} = \dfrac{S_1}{v_1} \bigg/ \dfrac{S_2}{v_2}$, where $s_1^2 = S_1/v_1$ and $s_2^2 = S_2/v_2$ are independent mean squares estimating a common variance σ^2 and based on v_1 and v_2 degrees of freedom, respectively. This table is based on Table 18 of *Biometrica Tables for Statisticians*, vol. I, edited by E. S. Pearson and H. O. Hartley (1970). By permission of the Biometrika Trustees.

10	12	15	20	24	30	40	60	120	∞
60.19	60.71	61.22	61.74	62.00	62.26	62.53	62.79	63.06	63.33
9.39	9.41	9.42	9.44	9.45	9.46	9.47	9.47	9.48	9.49
5.23	5.22	5.20	5.18	5.18	5.17	5.16	5.15	5.14	5.13
3.92	3.90	3.87	3.84	3.83	3.82	3.80	3.79	3.78	3.76
3.30	3.27	3.24	3.21	3.19	3.17	3.16	3.14	3.12	3.10
2.94	2.90	2.87	2.84	2.82	2.80	2.78	2.76	2.74	2.72
2.70	2.67	2.63	2.59	2.58	2.56	2.54	2.51	2.49	2.47
2.54	2.50	2.46	2.42	2.40	2.38	2.36	2.34	2.32	2.29
2.42	2.38	2.34	2.30	2.28	2.25	2.23	2.21	2.18	2.16
2.32	2.28	2.24	2.20	2.18	2.16	2.13	2.11	2.08	2.06
2.25	2.21	2.17	2.12	2.10	2.08	2.05	2.03	2.00	1.97
2.19	2.15	2.10	2.06	2.04	2.01	1.99	1.96	1.93	1.90
2.14	2.10	2.05	2.01	1.98	1.96	1.93	1.90	1.88	1.85
2.10	2.05	2.01	1.96	1.94	1.91	1.89	1.86	1.83	1.80
2.06	2.02	1.97	1.92	1.90	1.87	1.85	1.82	1.79	1.76
2.03	1.99	1.94	1.89	1.87	1.84	1.81	1.78	1.75	1.72
2.00	1.96	1.91	1.86	1.84	1.81	1.78	1.75	1.72	1.69
1.98	1.93	1.89	1.84	1.81	1.78	1.75	1.72	1.69	1.66
1.96	1.91	1.86	1.81	1.79	1.76	1.73	1.70	1.67	1.63
1.94	1.89	1.84	1.79	1.77	1.74	1.71	1.68	1.64	1.61
1.92	1.87	1.83	1.78	1.75	1.72	1.69	1.66	1.62	1.59
1.90	1.86	1.81	1.76	1.73	1.70	1.67	1.64	1.60	1.57
1.89	1.84	1.80	1.74	1.72	1.69	1.66	1.62	1.59	1.55
1.88	1.83	1.78	1.73	1.70	1.67	1.64	1.61	1.57	1.53
1.87	1.82	1.77	1.72	1.69	1.66	1.63	1.59	1.56	1.52
1.86	1.81	1.76	1.71	1.68	1.65	1.61	1.58	1.54	1.50
1.85	1.80	1.75	1.70	1.67	1.64	1.60	1.57	1.53	1.49
1.84	1.79	1.74	1.69	1.66	1.63	1.59	1.56	1.52	1.48
1.83	1.78	1.73	1.68	1.65	1.62	1.58	1.55	1.51	1.47
1.82	1.77	1.72	1.67	1.64	1.61	1.57	1.54	1.50	1.46
1.76	1.71	1.66	1.61	1.57	1.54	1.51	1.47	1.42	1.38
1.71	1.66	1.60	1.54	1.51	1.48	1.44	1.40	1.35	1.29
1.65	1.60	1.55	1.48	1.45	1.41	1.37	1.32	1.26	1.19
1.60	1.55	1.49	1.42	1.38	1.34	1.30	1.24	1.17	1.00

Table IV (continued) Upper 5% points

v_2 \ v_1	1	2	3	4	5	6	7	8	9
1	161.4	199.5	215.7	224.6	230.2	234.0	236.8	238.9	240.5
2	18.51	19.00	19.16	19.25	19.30	19.33	19.35	19.37	19.38
3	10.13	9.55	9.28	9.12	9.01	8.94	8.89	8.85	8.81
4	7.71	6.94	6.59	6.39	6.26	6.16	6.09	6.04	6.00
5	6.61	5.79	5.41	5.19	5.05	4.95	4.88	4.82	4.77
6	5.99	5.14	4.76	4.53	4.39	4.28	4.21	4.15	4.10
7	5.59	4.74	4.35	4.12	3.97	3.87	3.79	3.73	3.68
8	5.32	4.46	4.07	3.84	3.69	3.58	3.50	3.44	3.39
9	5.12	4.26	3.86	3.63	3.48	3.37	3.29	3.23	3.18
10	4.96	4.10	3.71	3.48	3.33	3.22	3.14	3.07	3.02
11	4.84	3.98	3.59	3.36	3.20	3.09	3.01	2.95	2.90
12	4.75	3.89	3.49	3.26	3.11	3.00	2.91	2.85	2.80
13	4.67	3.81	3.41	3.18	3.03	2.92	2.83	2.77	2.71
14	4.60	3.74	3.34	3.11	2.96	2.85	2.76	2.70	2.65
15	4.54	3.68	3.29	3.06	2.90	2.79	2.71	2.64	2.59
16	4.49	3.63	3.24	3.01	2.85	2.74	2.66	2.59	2.54
17	4.45	3.59	3.20	2.96	2.81	2.70	2.61	2.55	2.49
18	4.41	3.55	3.16	2.93	2.77	2.66	2.58	2.51	2.46
19	4.38	3.52	3.13	2.90	2.74	2.63	2.54	2.48	2.42
20	4.35	3.49	3.10	2.87	2.71	2.60	2.51	2.45	2.39
21	4.32	3.47	3.07	2.84	2.68	2.57	2.49	2.42	2.37
22	4.30	3.44	3.05	2.82	2.66	2.55	2.46	2.40	2.34
23	4.28	3.42	3.03	2.80	2.64	2.53	2.44	2.37	2.32
24	4.26	3.40	3.01	2.78	2.62	2.51	2.42	2.36	2.30
25	4.24	3.39	2.99	2.76	2.60	2.49	2.40	2.34	2.28
26	4.23	3.37	2.98	2.74	2.59	2.47	2.39	2.32	2.27
27	4.21	3.35	2.96	2.73	2.57	2.46	2.37	2.31	2.25
28	4.20	3.34	2.95	2.71	2.56	2.45	2.36	2.29	2.24
29	4.18	3.33	2.93	2.70	2.55	2.43	2.35	2.28	2.22
30	4.17	3.32	2.92	2.69	2.53	2.42	2.33	2.27	2.21
40	4.08	3.23	2.84	2.61	2.45	2.34	2.25	2.18	2.12
60	4.00	3.15	2.76	2.53	2.37	2.25	2.17	2.10	2.04
120	3.92	3.07	2.68	2.45	2.29	2.17	2.09	2.02	1.96
∞	3.84	3.00	2.60	2.37	2.21	2.10	2.01	1.94	1.88

10	12	15	20	24	30	40	60	120	∞
241.9	243.9	245.9	248.0	249.1	250.1	251.1	252.2	253.3	254.3
19.40	19.41	19.43	19.45	19.45	19.46	19.47	19.48	19.49	19.50
8.79	8.74	8.70	8.66	8.64	8.62	8.59	8.57	8.55	8.53
5.96	5.91	5.86	5.80	5.77	5.75	5.72	5.69	5.66	5.63
4.74	4.68	4.62	4.56	4.53	4.50	4.46	4.43	4.40	4.36
4.06	4.00	3.94	3.87	3.84	3.81	3.77	3.74	3.70	3.67
3.64	3.57	3.51	3.44	3.41	3.38	3.34	3.30	3.27	3.23
3.35	3.28	3.22	3.15	3.12	3.08	3.04	3.01	2.97	2.93
3.14	3.07	3.01	2.94	2.90	2.86	2.83	2.79	2.75	2.71
2.98	2.91	2.85	2.77	2.74	2.70	2.66	2.62	2.58	2.54
2.85	2.79	2.72	2.65	2.61	2.57	2.53	2.49	2.45	2.40
2.75	2.69	2.62	2.54	2.51	2.47	2.43	2.38	2.34	2.30
2.67	2.60	2.53	2.46	2.42	2.38	2.34	2.30	2.25	2.21
2.60	2.53	2.46	2.39	2.35	2.31	2.27	2.22	2.18	2.13
2.54	2.48	2.40	2.33	2.29	2.25	2.20	2.16	2.11	2.07
2.49	2.42	2.35	2.28	2.24	2.19	2.15	2.11	2.06	2.01
2.45	2.38	2.31	2.23	2.19	2.15	2.10	2.06	2.01	1.96
2.41	2.34	2.27	2.19	2.15	2.11	2.06	2.02	1.97	1.92
2.38	2.31	2.23	2.16	2.11	2.07	2.03	1.98	1.93	1.88
2.35	2.28	2.20	2.12	2.08	2.04	1.99	1.95	1.90	1.84
2.32	2.25	2.18	2.10	2.05	2.01	1.96	1.92	1.87	1.81
2.30	2.23	2.15	2.07	2.03	1.98	1.94	1.89	1.84	1.78
2.27	2.20	2.13	2.05	2.01	1.96	1.91	1.86	1.81	1.76
2.25	2.18	2.11	2.03	1.98	1.94	1.89	1.84	1.79	1.73
2.24	2.16	2.09	2.01	1.96	1.92	1.87	1.82	1.77	1.71
2.22	2.15	2.07	1.99	1.95	1.90	1.85	1.80	1.75	1.69
2.20	2.13	2.06	1.97	1.93	1.88	1.84	1.79	1.73	1.67
2.19	2.12	2.04	1.96	1.91	1.87	1.82	1.77	1.71	1.65
2.18	2.10	2.03	1.94	1.90	1.85	1.81	1.75	1.70	1.64
2.16	2.09	2.01	1.93	1.89	1.84	1.79	1.74	1.68	1.62
2.08	2.00	1.92	1.84	1.79	1.74	1.69	1.64	1.58	1.51
1.99	1.92	1.84	1.75	1.70	1.65	1.59	1.53	1.47	1.39
1.91	1.83	1.75	1.66	1.61	1.55	1.50	1.43	1.35	1.25
1.83	1.75	1.67	1.57	1.52	1.46	1.39	1.32	1.22	1.00

Table IV (continued) Upper 1% points

v_2 \ v_1	1	2	3	4	5	6	7	8	9
1	4052	4999.5	5403	5625	5764	5859	5928	5982	6022
2	98.50	99.00	99.17	99.25	99.30	99.33	99.36	99.37	99.39
3	34.12	30.82	29.46	28.71	28.24	27.91	27.67	27.49	27.35
4	21.20	18.00	16.69	15.98	15.52	15.21	14.98	14.80	14.66
5	16.26	13.27	12.06	11.39	10.97	10.67	10.46	10.29	10.16
6	13.75	10.92	9.78	9.15	8.75	8.47	8.26	8.10	7.98
7	12.25	9.55	8.45	7.85	7.46	7.19	6.99	6.84	6.72
8	11.26	8.65	7.59	7.01	6.63	6.37	6.18	6.03	5.91
9	10.56	8.02	6.99	6.42	6.06	5.80	5.61	5.47	5.35
10	10.04	7.56	6.55	5.99	5.64	5.39	5.20	5.06	4.94
11	9.65	7.21	6.22	5.67	5.32	5.07	4.89	4.74	4.63
12	9.33	6.93	5.95	5.41	5.06	4.82	4.64	4.50	4.39
13	9.07	6.70	5.74	5.21	4.86	4.62	4.44	4.30	4.19
14	8.86	6.51	5.56	5.04	4.69	4.46	4.28	4.14	4.03
15	8.68	6.36	5.42	4.89	4.56	4.32	4.14	4.00	3.89
16	8.53	6.23	5.29	4.77	4.44	4.20	4.03	3.89	3.78
17	8.40	6.11	5.18	4.67	4.34	4.10	3.93	3.79	3.68
18	8.29	6.01	5.09	4.58	4.25	4.01	3.84	3.71	3.60
19	8.18	5.93	5.01	4.50	4.17	3.94	3.77	3.63	3.52
20	8.10	5.85	4.94	4.43	4.10	3.87	3.70	3.56	3.46
21	8.02	5.78	4.87	4.37	4.04	3.81	3.64	3.51	3.40
22	7.95	5.72	4.82	4.31	3.99	3.76	3.59	3.45	3.35
23	7.88	5.66	4.76	4.26	3.94	3.71	3.54	3.41	3.30
24	7.82	5.61	4.72	4.22	3.90	3.67	3.50	3.36	3.26
25	7.77	5.57	4.68	4.18	3.85	3.63	3.46	3.32	3.22
26	7.72	5.53	4.64	4.14	3.82	3.59	3.42	3.29	3.18
27	7.68	5.49	4.60	4.11	3.78	3.56	3.39	3.26	3.15
28	7.64	5.45	4.57	4.07	3.75	3.53	3.36	3.23	3.12
29	7.60	5.42	4.54	4.04	3.73	3.50	3.33	3.20	3.09
30	7.56	5.39	4.51	4.02	3.70	3.47	3.30	3.17	3.07
40	7.31	5.18	4.31	3.83	3.51	3.29	3.12	2.99	2.89
60	7.08	4.98	4.13	3.65	3.34	3.12	2.95	2.82	2.72
120	6.85	4.79	3.95	3.48	3.17	2.96	2.79	2.66	2.56
∞	6.63	4.61	3.78	3.32	3.02	2.80	2.64	2.51	2.41

10	12	15	20	24	30	40	60	120	∞
6056	6106	6157	6209	6235	6261	6287	6313	6339	6366
99.40	99.42	99.43	99.45	99.46	99.47	99.47	99.48	99.49	99.50
27.23	27.05	26.87	26.69	26.60	26.50	26.41	26.32	26.22	26.13
14.55	14.37	14.20	14.02	13.93	13.84	13.75	13.65	13.56	13.46
10.05	9.89	9.72	9.55	9.47	9.38	9.29	9.20	9.11	9.02
7.87	7.72	7.56	7.40	7.31	7.23	7.14	7.06	6.97	6.88
6.62	6.47	6.31	6.16	6.07	5.99	5.91	5.82	5.74	5.65
5.81	5.67	5.52	5.36	5.28	5.20	5.12	5.03	4.95	4.86
5.26	5.11	4.96	4.81	4.73	4.65	4.57	4.48	4.40	4.31
4.85	4.71	4.56	4.41	4.33	4.25	4.17	4.08	4.00	3.91
4.54	4.40	4.25	4.10	4.02	3.94	3.86	3.78	3.69	3.60
4.30	4.16	4.01	3.86	3.78	3.70	3.62	3.54	3.45	3.36
4.10	3.96	3.82	3.66	3.59	3.51	3.43	3.34	3.25	3.17
3.94	3.80	3.66	3.51	3.43	3.35	3.27	3.18	3.09	3.00
3.80	3.67	3.52	3.37	3.29	3.21	3.13	3.05	2.96	2.87
3.69	3.55	3.41	3.26	3.18	3.10	3.02	2.93	2.84	2.75
3.59	3.46	3.31	3.16	3.08	3.00	2.92	2.83	2.75	2.65
3.51	3.37	3.23	3.08	3.00	2.92	2.84	2.75	2.66	2.57
3.43	3.30	3.15	3.00	2.92	2.84	2.76	2.67	2.58	2.49
3.37	3.23	3.09	2.94	2.86	2.78	2.69	2.61	2.52	2.42
3.31	3.17	3.03	2.88	2.80	2.72	2.64	2.55	2.46	2.36
3.26	3.12	2.98	2.83	2.75	2.67	2.58	2.50	2.40	2.31
3.21	3.07	2.93	2.78	2.70	2.62	2.54	2.45	2.35	2.26
3.17	3.03	2.89	2.74	2.66	2.58	2.49	2.40	2.31	2.21
3.13	2.99	2.85	2.70	2.62	2.54	2.45	2.36	2.27	2.17
3.09	2.96	2.81	2.66	2.58	2.50	2.42	2.33	2.23	2.13
3.06	2.93	2.78	2.63	2.55	2.47	2.38	2.29	2.20	2.10
3.03	2.90	2.75	2.60	2.52	2.44	2.35	2.26	2.17	2.06
3.00	2.87	2.73	2.57	2.49	2.41	2.33	2.23	2.14	2.03
2.98	2.84	2.70	2.55	2.47	2.39	2.30	2.21	2.11	2.01
2.80	2.66	2.52	2.37	2.29	2.20	2.11	2.02	1.92	1.80
2.63	2.50	2.35	2.20	2.12	2.03	1.94	1.84	1.73	1.60
2.47	2.34	2.19	2.03	1.95	1.86	1.76	1.66	1.53	1.38
2.32	2.18	2.04	1.88	1.79	1.70	1.59	1.47	1.32	1.00

Table V Durbin-Watson statistic d. Significance points of d_L and d_U: 5%*

n	$k' = 1$		$k' = 2$		$k' = 3$		$k' = 4$		$k' = 5$	
	d_L	d_U	d_L	d_U	d_L	d_U	d_L	d_U	d_L	d_U
15	1.08	1.36	0.95	1.54	0.82	1.75	0.69	1.97	0.56	2.21
16	1.10	1.37	0.98	1.54	0.86	1.73	0.74	1.93	0.62	2.15
17	1.13	1.38	1.02	1.54	0.90	1.71	0.78	1.90	0.67	2.10
18	1.16	1.39	1.05	1.53	0.93	1.69	0.82	1.87	0.71	2.06
19	1.18	1.40	1.08	1.53	0.97	1.68	0.86	1.85	0.75	2.02
20	1.20	1.41	1.10	1.54	1.00	1.68	0.90	1.83	0.79	1.99
21	1.22	1.42	1.13	1.54	1.03	1.67	0.93	1.81	0.83	1.96
22	1.24	1.43	1.15	1.54	1.05	1.66	0.96	1.80	0.86	1.94
23	1.26	1.44	1.17	1.54	1.08	1.66	0.99	1.79	0.90	1.92
24	1.27	1.45	1.19	1.55	1.10	1.66	1.01	1.78	0.93	1.90
25	1.29	1.45	1.21	1.55	1.12	1.66	1.04	1.77	0.95	1.89
26	1.30	1.46	1.22	1.55	1.14	1.65	1.06	1.76	0.98	1.88
27	1.32	1.47	1.24	1.56	1.16	1.65	1.08	1.76	1.01	1.86
28	1.33	1.48	1.26	1.56	1.18	1.65	1.10	1.75	1.03	1.85
29	1.34	1.48	1.27	1.56	1.20	1.65	1.12	1.74	1.05	1.84
30	1.35	1.49	1.28	1.57	1.21	1.65	1.14	1.74	1.07	1.83
31	1.36	1.50	1.30	1.57	1.23	1.65	1.16	1.74	1.09	1.83
32	1.37	1.50	1.31	1.57	1.24	1.65	1.18	1.73	1.11	1.82
33	1.38	1.51	1.32	1.58	1.26	1.65	1.19	1.73	1.13	1.81
34	1.39	1.51	1.33	1.58	1.27	1.65	1.21	1.73	1.15	1.81
35	1.40	1.52	1.34	1.58	1.28	1.65	1.22	1.73	1.16	1.80
36	1.41	1.52	1.35	1.59	1.29	1.65	1.24	1.73	1.18	1.80
37	1.42	1.53	1.36	1.59	1.31	1.66	1.25	1.72	1.19	1.80
38	1.43	1.54	1.37	1.59	1.32	1.66	1.26	1.72	1.21	1.79
39	1.43	1.54	1.38	1.60	1.33	1.66	1.27	1.72	1.22	1.79
40	1.44	1.54	1.39	1.60	1.34	1.66	1.29	1.72	1.23	1.79
45	1.48	1.57	1.43	1.62	1.38	1.67	1.34	1.72	1.29	1.78
50	1.50	1.59	1.46	1.63	1.42	1.67	1.38	1.72	1.34	1.77
55	1.53	1.60	1.49	1.64	1.45	1.68	1.41	1.72	1.38	1.77
60	1.55	1.62	1.51	1.65	1.48	1.69	1.44	1.73	1.41	1.77
65	1.57	1.63	1.54	1.66	1.50	1.70	1.47	1.73	1.44	1.77
70	1.58	1.64	1.55	1.67	1.52	1.70	1.49	1.74	1.46	1.77
75	1.60	1.65	1.57	1.68	1.54	1.71	1.51	1.74	1.49	1.77
80	1.61	1.66	1.59	1.69	1.56	1.72	1.53	1.74	1.51	1.77
85	1.62	1.67	1.60	1.70	1.57	1.72	1.55	1.75	1.52	1.77
90	1.63	1.68	1.61	1.70	1.59	1.73	1.57	1.75	1.54	1.78
95	1.64	1.69	1.62	1.71	1.60	1.73	1.58	1.75	1.56	1.78
100	1.65	1.59	1.63	1.72	1.61	1.74	1.59	1.76	1.57	1.78

n = number of observations.
k' = number of explanatory variables.

* This Table is reproduced from *Biometrika*, vol. 41, pp. 173 and 175, 1951, with the permission of the Biometrika Trustees.

Table V (continued) **Significance points of** d_L **and** d_U: 1%

n	$k' = 1$		$k' = 2$		$k' = 3$		$k' = 4$		$k' = 5$	
	d_L	d_U	d_L	d_U	d_L	d_U	d_L	d_U	d_L	d_U
15	0.81	1.07	0.70	1.25	0.59	1.46	0.49	1.70	0.39	1.96
16	0.84	1.09	0.74	1.25	0.63	1.44	0.53	1.66	0.44	1.90
17	0.87	1.10	0.77	1.25	0.67	1.43	0.57	1.63	0.48	1.85
18	0.90	1.12	0.80	1.26	0.71	1.42	0.61	1.60	0.52	1.80
19	0.93	1.13	0.83	1.26	0.74	1.41	0.65	1.58	0.56	1.77
20	0.95	1.15	0.86	1.27	0.77	1.41	0.68	1.57	0.60	1.74
21	0.97	1.16	0.89	1.27	0.80	1.41	0.72	1.55	0.63	1.71
22	1.00	1.17	0.91	1.28	0.83	1.40	0.75	1.54	0.66	1.69
23	1.02	1.19	0.94	1.29	0.86	1.40	0.77	1.53	0.70	1.67
24	1.04	1.20	0.96	1.30	0.88	1.41	0.80	1.53	0.72	1.66
25	1.05	1.21	0.98	1.30	0.90	1.41	0.83	1.52	0.75	1.65
26	1.07	1.22	1.00	1.31	0.93	1.41	0.85	1.52	0.78	1.64
27	1.09	1.23	1.02	1.32	0.95	1.41	0.88	1.51	0.81	1.63
28	1.10	1.24	1.04	1.32	0.97	1.41	0.90	1.51	0.83	1.62
29	1.12	1.25	1.05	1.33	0.99	1.42	0.92	1.51	.085	1.61
30	1.13	1.26	1.07	1.34	1.01	1.42	0.94	1.51	0.88	1.61
31	1.15	1.27	1.08	1.34	1.02	1.42	0.96	1.51	0.90	1.60
32	1.16	1.28	1.10	1.35	1.04	1.43	0.98	1.51	0.92	1.60
33	1.17	1.29	1.11	1.36	1.05	1.43	1.00	1.51	0.94	1.59
34	1.18	1.30	1.13	1.36	1.07	1.43	1.01	1.51	0.95	1.59
35	1.19	1.31	1.14	1.37	1.08	1.44	1.03	1.51	0.97	1.59
36	1.21	1.32	1.15	1.38	1.10	1.44	1.04	1.51	0.99	1.59
37	1.22	1.32	1.16	1.38	1.11	1.45	1.06	1.51	1.00	1.59
38	1.23	1.33	1.18	1.39	1.12	1.45	1.07	1.52	1.02	1.58
39	1.24	1.34	1.19	1.39	1.14	1.45	1.09	1.52	1.03	1.58
40	1.25	1.34	1.20	1.40	1.15	1.46	1.10	1.52	1.05	1.58
45	1.29	1.38	1.24	1.42	1.20	1.48	1.16	1.53	1.11	1.58
50	1.32	1.40	1.28	1.45	1.24	1.49	1.20	1.54	1.16	1.59
55	1.36	1.43	1.32	1.47	1.28	1.51	1.25	1.55	1.21	1.59
60	1.38	1.45	1.35	1.48	1.32	1.52	1.28	1.56	1.25	1.60
65	1.41	1.47	1.38	1.50	1.35	1.53	1.31	1.57	1.28	1.61
70	1.43	1.49	1.40	1.52	1.37	1.55	1.34	1.58	1.31	1.61
75	1.45	1.50	1.42	1.53	1.39	1.56	1.37	1.59	1.34	1.62
80	1.47	1.52	1.44	1.54	1.42	1.57	1.39	1.60	1.36	1.62
85	1.48	1.53	1.46	1.55	1.43	1.58	1.41	1.60	1.39	1.63
90	1.50	1.54	1.47	1.56	1.45	1.59	1.43	1.61	1.41	1.64
95	1.51	1.55	1.49	1.57	1.47	1.60	1.45	1.62	1.42	1.64
100	1.52	1.56	1.50	1.58	1.48	1.60	1.46	1.63	1.44	1.65

INDEX

INDEX

Abrahamse, A. P. J., 88, 109
Adaptive expectation, 103, 351
Additive disturbance, 221, 231, 240
Adjustment mechanism, 246, 247
Aggregation, 49, 376
Aggregation and specification of
    model, 309–313
Aitchison, J., 282, 286, 318
Aitken's generalized least squares, 78,
    327
Akaike, H., 293, 294, 297, 298, 304, 318
Algorithm, 232
Almon, S., 104, 109
Amemiya, T., 240, 241, 243–245, 252,
    257, 265, 268, 275, 276
Analysis of variance, 60, 63, 64
Anderson, T. W., 75, 157, 163, 164,
    186, 206, 219
Andrews, D. F., 89, 90, 109
Angle between dependent vector and
    explanatory vector, 42
Aoki, M., 371
a priori restrictions, 154, 164,
    177–179, 182
Arora, S. S., 348
Asymptotic distribution, 156, 166,
    168, 169, 174, 177, 182, 183,
    224–227, 230, 231, 243, 244
  of approximate GLS estimator, 82
  of FIML estimator, 174, 177, 243
  of GLS estimator, 81–84
  of instrumental-variable estimator,
    176

Asymptotic distribution (*Cont.*):
  of k-class estimator, 166, 167
  of least-squares estimator, 72–73
  of linearized FIML estimator, 174,
    177
  of maximum-likelihood estimator,
    230, 231
  of minimum-distance estimator,
    224–227
  of nonlinear 3SLS, 244
  of nonlinear 2SLS, 243
  of three-stage least squares
    estimator, 168, 169, 177
  of 2SLS estimator, 156, 157, 166,
    169
Asymptotic normality, 22
Asymptotically efficient, 27
Asymptotically normal, 22
Atkinson, A. C., 285, 318
Autocorrelation function, 79
Autocovariance function, 79
Automobiles:
  demand for, 47, 57, 64
  desired stock of, 47
  elasticities of demand for, 57
  forecasting demand for, 65
  price of, 54
  purchase of, 54
  stock of, 54
Autoregressive (AR) model, 189
  first-order, 79
Autoregressive moving average
    (ARMA) model, 189

Autoregressive moving average
process, 104
Autoregressive residuals, 178–180
Axiom of independence from
irrelevant alternatives, 259

Bain, A. D., 30, 37, 87
Baldwin, K. F., 98, 110
Basmann, R. L., 155, 164, 186
Bayes theorem, 91
Bayesian, 96
Bayesian approach, distinction of, 91
Bayesian estimation, 90–96, 184
Bayesian method, 90
Behavioral equations, 374, 375, 380,
394, 396, 397, 400
Belsley, D. A., 90, 101, 109
Berndt, E. K., 233, 252
Best linear unbiased, 5
Best unbiased, 24
Bias, 180, 254
Blanchard, O. J., 353, 362, 371, 388,
390, 402–404
Block-recursive systems, 185
Block-triangular *B* matrix, 181, 182
Bloomfield, P., 206, 219
BLUE (best linear unbiased
estimator), 40, 78
BLUS (best linear unbiased scalar)
residuals, 87–88
Boot, J., 152
Box, G. E. P., 192, 195, 211, 212, 219
Box-Jenkins approach to time series,
211–212
Breusch, T. S., 291, 318, 343, 348
Brookings Quarterly Econometric
Model of the United States, 181
Brown, R. L., 344, 345, 348
Brownstone, D., 260, 263, 264, 276
Brundy, I., 176, 186
Brute force, 239
Burmeister, E., 362, 371

Cagan, P., 351, 371

Canonical factorization, 375, 390,
391
Canzoneri, M., 371
Causal order, 181
Causality:
Granger's definition of, 212
tests of, 216–217
Central limit theorem, 6, 16, 18–22
Lindeberg-Feller, 21, 22, 157
Certainty-equivalent solution, 395
Chappell, H. W., 275, 276
Characteristic equation, 195
Characteristic function, 19
of multivariate normal vector, 20
of random variable, 19
of random vector, 19
Characteristic roots, 162, 165, 166,
195, 234
Characteristic vectors, 162, 166
Chebyschev's inequality, 17
Chernoff, H., 343, 348
Choice of estimators, 180–182
Chow, G. C., 37, 65, 75, 88, 103, 107,
109, 126, 129, 139, 152, 173, 180,
182, 186, 188, 189, 204, 219, 233,
235, 247, 251, 252, 278, 279, 285,
316, 318, 348, 368, 371, 376, 377,
379, 386, 394, 404
Classical method of optimal control,
375, 390–392
Coefficient:
multiple correlation, 43, 70
partial correlation, 56, 69–71
Collier, P., 348
Comparison of 3SLS with 2SLS,
168–169
Computers:
demand for, 27, 29, 35
price of, 31, 34
quantity of, 31, 34
Concentrated log-likelihood function,
236, 328, 364, 384
Conditional density, 9, 245
of multivariate normal distribution,
10
Conditional mean, 12

Confidence interval, 6
  for β if σ^2 is known, 43
Conjugate gradient method, 234–235
Consistency, 18, 156, 166, 168,
    225–227, 230, 243, 244
  of estimator for σ^2, 73
  of k-class estimator, 166
  of maximum-likelihood estimator,
    230
  of minimum-distance estimator,
    225–227
  of nonlinear 2SLS, 243
  of three-stage least squares, 168
  of two-stage least squares, 156
Consumption function, 126
  theory of, 15
Convergence:
  in distribution, 16, 19
  in probability, 16–18
  with probability 1 (almost surely),
    17
Cooley, T. F., 340, 348
Cooper, J. P., 348
Coordinate directions, 235
Correlation, serial, 79, 88
Correlation coefficient, 12, 69
  multiple, 43, 70
  partial, 56, 69–71
Corsi, P., 316, 318
Cosslett, S., 263, 276
Covariance matrix, 12, 39
  of least-squares estimate, 39, 40
Covariance-stationary time series, 79
Cox, D. R., 285, 318
Cramer, H., 37
Cramer-Rao bound, 230
Cramer-Rao inequality, 22–24, 72,
    78, 233
Critical value of a statistic, 5
Cross-section regression, 15
Cross-spectral density, 197, 198, 203,
    204
Cruz, J. B., Jr., 404
Cumulative standard normal
    distribution function, 245, 254,
    258, 275

Cumulative unit normal distribution,
    272
Cumulative Weibull distribution
    function, 258

Damping factors, 249
Davidson, R., 286, 318
Deaton, A. S., 284, 286, 316, 318, 319
Degree of freedom, 7
Delayed multipliers, 250
Demand:
  for automobiles, 47–58
  for computers, 27–35
  for money, 129, 140
Dempster, A. P., 268, 269, 271, 272,
    276
Density:
  conditional, 11, 12
  conditional normal, 94
  diffuse prior, 95
  gamma, 93, 94, 96
  informative prior, 95
  joint, 9
  marginal, 9, 13
  posterior, 91
  prior, 91
Desired stock, 47
Deterministic simulation, 248
Dhrymes, P. J., 109, 152, 176, 184,
    186, 319
Diagonalizing a matrix, 43, 44
Dickey, J., 303, 319
Differentiation rules for vector, 39
Direct utility function, 257
Discrete-choice models, 254–264
Disequilibrium, 222, 231, 245–248
Distribution:
  asymptotic, 25–27
  χ^2, 6
  F, 7
  in large samples, 18–19
  multivariate normal, 8–14
  sampling, 4, 16
  standard normal, 20
  Student's t, 7

Disturbance term, 3
Domencich, T., 257, 276
Dominant player, 396, 400–402
Drèze, J., 184, 186
Duesenberry, J. S., 181, 186
Dummy variable, 34, 61, 62
Duncan, D. B., 348
Durbin, J., 85, 97, 109, 344, 345, 348
Durbin-Watson statistic, 35, 85, 108
Dynamic game, 376, 396–402
Dynamic programming, 375–379, 393
Dynamic properties, 222, 248–251

Econometric policy evaluation, 374,
    376, 396–399
Econometrics:
    definition of, 1
    method of, 2
Economic environment, 374, 375,
    377, 379, 380, 386, 394, 396, 397,
    400
Efficiency, 22
    of least-squares estimator, 24
EM algorithm, 254, 268–271
Endogenous variables, 112, 154, 155,
    157, 164, 179, 181, 182, 221, 222,
    241, 246–248, 250
Engle, R. F., 348
Ensemble average, 191
"Equilibrium" simultaneous
    stochastic equations, 246, 247
Equivalent units, 53
Errors:
    measurement of, 15
    of observations, 14–16, 105–107
    standard, 34
Estimate, 4
    point estimate of σ^2, 5
Estimation:
    for β and σ^2, 39
    interval, 6–7
    mixed, 97
    point, 3–5
    of rational expectations models,
        364–370, 380, 385, 400–402

Estimation (*Cont.*):
    subject to constraints, 282–284
    time-series, 207–211
Estimator:
    best linear unbiased, 5
    consistent (GLS), 80
    consistent for σ^2, 73
    GLS, 78
    linear, 5
    maximum-likelihood, 25–27
    minimum distance, 210, 211, 368
    property of least-squares, 42
    ridge, 97, 98
    robust, 88, 90, 239–240
    Stein, 101, 102
    unbiased, 5
    unbiased for β, 39
Evans, J. M., 344, 345, 348
Exogenous variables, 112, 153, 156,
    245, 248, 274
Expectation formation, 351–352
Expectations, mathematical, 3
Expected loss function, 102
Explained part of a dependent
    variable, 41
Explicit solution of optimal rule,
    390–394
Exponential family, 269, 271

F distribution, 7, 60, 228, 230, 289
F statistic for testing general linear
    restriction, 60
Fair, R. C., 180, 181, 186, 233, 240,
    245, 252, 266–268, 276, 368, 371
Feldstein, M. S., 184, 186
Feller, W., 21, 37, 157
Filtering, 321
Final form:
    of linear model, 145–151
    of nonlinear model, 250
Finite samples, 166, 169, 174
Fisher, F. M., 152, 181, 182, 186, 309,
    310, 319
Fisher, R. A., 37, 75
Fixed-point method, 184

Flood, R. P., 362, 371
Forecasting, 62
Friedman, M., 15, 37, 53, 75, 351, 371
Fromm, G., 181, 186
Full-information estimation, 153,
    163, 167
Full-information maximum
    likelihood (FIML),170–180, 222,
    235, 240, 243, 264, 364, 367–369
  with autoregressive residuals,
    178–180
  as instrumental variable estimator,
    175–176, 240
  for nonlinear simultaneous
    equations, 222, 235–240, 242

Gale, D., 124, 152
Gallant, A. R., 222, 228–230, 252
Garbade, K., 328, 343, 348
Garber, P. M., 362, 371
Gauss-Markov theorem, 40, 168,
    227
Gauss-Newton method, 233, 239, 273
Gauss-Siedel method, 248, 249
Gaver, K. M., 285, 319
Geary, R., 107, 109
Geisel, M. S., 286, 319
Generalized extreme value models,
    259, 260, 263–264
Generalized inverse, 100
Generalized least squares, 167, 168,
    222–228
Godfrey, L. G., 85, 109, 316
Goett, A., 263, 276
Goldberger, A. S., 97, 110, 182, 186
Goldfeld, S. M., 85, 110, 232, 234,
    235, 252, 348
Gompertz curve, 28–30, 35, 36
Gompertz rate of growth, 29
Goodness of fit, 262
Gourieroux, C., 343, 348, 362, 371
Gradient, 232, 234, 240, 255
Gradient algorithm, 232–234
Gradient methods, 255, 332, 264
Granger, C. W. J., 212, 216, 219

Granger causality, 212
Gronau, R., 271, 276

Haavelmo, T., 114, 152
Hall, B. H., 234, 252
Hall, T. E., 234, 252
Hannan, E. J., 212, 219, 348
Hansen, L. P., 375, 386, 390–393,
    404
Hartley, M., 276
Harvey, A. C., 340, 349
Hatanaka, M., 244, 252, 342, 349
Haugh, L. D., 212, 215, 219
Hausman, J., 175, 186, 234, 240, 252,
    271, 273, 275, 276, 314, 316, 319
Heckman, J., 271, 275, 276
Heteroscedasticity, 78
  existence of, 84
  test for, 85
Hicks, J. R., 126, 152
Hicksian discussion, 141
Hillmer, S. C., 207, 210, 219
Ho, Y. C., 349
Hoerl, A. E., 97, 110
Holly, A., 315, 319, 343, 348
Hood, W. C., 114, 152
Horn, S. D., 348
Hotelling, H., 56, 76, 278, 279,
    319
Hsiao, C., 125, 152
Huber, P. J., 89, 110
Hypotheses:
  alternative, 6
  nested, 277
  nonnested, 278
  null, 6
  testing, 6–7
    about β with σ^2 unknown, 45

Idempotent matrix, 43
Identifiability:
  of coefficients, 124
  of linear combination, 124
Identifiable parameters, 117

Identification, 114, 154, 164, 182
    asymptotic local parametric, 341
    Box-Jenkins definition of, 192, 195,
        211
    of rational expectations models,
        365
    time-varying coefficients, 342
Identified, just (or exactly), 118
Identities, 177
Impact multipliers, 250
Independently and identically
    distributed residuals, 18
Indirect least squares, 247
Indirect utility function, 257
Information, prior, 90
Information matrix, 24
    Fisher's, 23, 24
Inner product, 7
Instrumental variable estimator, 107,
    156, 175, 369
Instrumental variables, 107, 156, 175,
    176, 222, 240–243, 245, 369
Intriligator, M. D., 127
Investment function, 127
Iteration, 172, 174, 176, 178, 180, 228,
    231, 234, 235, 238, 239, 242, 243,
    248, 249, 256, 257, 262, 266, 267,
    270, 273, 383–384, 399, 401
Iterative least squares, 266, 267, 273
Iterative weighted least squares, 239

Jaffee, D., 245, 252
Jeffreys, H., 301, 319
Jenkins, J. M., 192, 195, 211, 219
Johnston, J., 76, 152
Joint density function, 158, 170, 245
Joint normal density, 12
Jorgenson, D. W., 104, 110, 176, 186,
    244, 252
Juréen, L., 319

k-class estimator, 164–167
Kahn, C. M., 353, 362, 371
Kalman, R. E., 321, 322, 349

Kalman filter, 321–323
    extended, 334
    GLS interpretation, 327
Kelejian, H. H., 340, 349
Kennard, R. W., 98, 110
Keynes, J. M., 126, 152
Klein, L. R., 181, 186, 188, 316
Kloek, T., 181, 186
Kmenta, J., 97, 98, 110
Koerts, J., 88, 109
Koopmans, T. C., 114, 152, 188, 309,
    319
Koyck, L. M., 102, 110
Koyck transform, 102
Kronecker product, 81
Kuh, E., 90, 101, 109, 181, 186, 348
Kullback-Leibler information
    measure, 294
Kydland, F. E., 376, 404

Laffont, J., 244, 252, 362, 371
Lag, rational distributed, 104
Lag operator, 104, 391
Lag structure, 129
Lagged endogenous variables, 157,
    248, 250
Lagged exogenous variables, 248
Lagrangian multipliers, 376
Laird, N. M., 128, 129, 269, 271,
    276
LaMotte, L. R., 344, 349
Law of large numbers, weak, 18
Leamer, E. E., 301, 302, 319
Learning in optimal control, 395
Least squares:
    method of, 4
    residual vector, 86
Least variance ratio estimator, 164
Lee, R. C. K., 349
Leenders, C. T., 173, 174, 187
Likelihood function, 158, 170, 179,
    230, 231, 233, 235, 236, 239, 246,
    255, 256, 261, 262, 264, 265, 268,
    269, 271, 272, 275, 364, 367, 381
Limited dependent variable, 265–268

Limited information estimation,
153–167, 169, 180–182, 365, 369
Limited information maximum
likelihood (LIML), 157, 165,
166, 180, 181, 333, 365, 369, 386
as *k*-class estimator, 165, 166
Lin, A., 97, 98, 109, 110
Lindeberg condition, 21, 37
Lindeberg-Feller central limit
theorem, 21, 22, 157
Lindley, D. V., 105–110
Linear probability model, 256
Linear regression model, 3, 38, 220,
222, 228
Linear restriction on regression
coefficients, 58
Linear restrictions, 177–179, 389
Linear simultaneous stochastic
equations, 153, 174, 241, 373,
374, 385
Linear stochastic model, 374, 377,
386, 392, 395
Linearized FIML estimator, 173, 177
Linearized maximum-likelihood
estimator, 173
Linearized model, 223, 224, 228, 229,
242, 243, 250
Liu, T. C., 125, 126, 152, 309, 319
Livesey, D. A., 403, 404
Ljung, L., 349
Log concentrated likelihood function,
236, 384
Log-likelihood functions, 158, 170,
179, 231, 233, 236, 255, 256, 261,
262, 264, 265, 269, 271, 272, 381
Logistic curve, 28, 254, 258
Logistic hypothesis, 35
Logistic rate of growth, 29
Logit model, 254–256, 258–264
Loss function, 377
Lucas, R. E., Jr., 374, 375, 396, 402,
404
Lyttkens, E., 176, 186

McCallum, B. T., 369, 371

McFadden, D., 257, 259, 264, 275,
276
MacKinnon, J. G., 286, 313
McWorther, A., Jr., 344, 349
Maddala, G. S., 76, 152, 245, 252
Malinvaud, E., 76, 152, 210, 219, 222,
223, 228, 252, 368, 371
Mallows, C. L., 278, 291, 299, 300,
319
Manski, C. F., 275, 276
Marginal density, 9
of multivariate normal distribution,
13
Marschak, J., 116, 135, 152, 174, 396,
404
Marshallian model, 373
Matrix:
characteristic root (eigenvalue), 44
characteristic roots, 44, 148, 162
characteristic vector (eigenvector),
44, 148, 162
diagonalize, 44
diagonalize simultaneously, 162
differentiation rule (for the trace),
88
generalized inverse, 100
idempotent, 43
Kronecker product, 81
positive semidefinite, 24
principal components of, 99–101
product, 8
quadratic form, 8, 46
trace, 41
transpose, 7
Maximum likelihood, 157–166,
170–182, 222, 230, 231, 235–240,
243, 245, 246, 248, 254, 256,
260–265, 268, 270, 273, 380–384,
386, 400, 401
Maximum-likelihood estimator,
25–27
Mean, conditional, 12
Mean-squared error, 5, 180
Mehra, R. K., 349
Mehta, J. S., 350
Mennes, L. B. M., 181, 186

Mikhail, W. M., 169, 186
Minimum condition, 245, 246
Minimum distance estimator, 210, 222–228, 368
Modigliani, F., 126, 152
Moments:
  population, 80
  sample, 80
Monte Carlo methods, 169, 180, 182
Montfort, A., 343, 348, 362, 371
Moran, P. A. P., 343, 349
Mosback, E., 184, 186
Moving average (MA) model, 189
Multicollinearity, 98
Multinomial logit model, 254, 259–264
Multiple linear regression, 38
Multiple solutions to rational expectations models, 353
Multipliers, 147, 222, 250
  delayed, 147
  impact, 147
  interim, 147
  intermediate-run, 147
  short-run, 147
  total or long-run, 147
Multivariate nonlinear regression model, 221
Multivariate normal density function, 8, 10
Munroe, M. E., 37
Muth, J. F., 352, 371

Nagar, A. L., 182, 186
Nash equilibrium, 377, 396, 399, 401
Nerlove, M., 85, 110, 199, 219
Nested logit model, 254, 260, 263–264
Newbold, P., 212, 219
Newton-Raphson method, 172–174, 178, 232–235, 237–239, 249, 259, 261, 262, 266, 273
Nonlinear models, 220, 334, 337
Nonlinear regression model, 220, 228–230

Nonlinear simultaneous equations, 221, 231, 240, 321, 337
Nonlinear three-stage least squares, 222, 244, 245
Nonlinear two-stage least squares, 222, 243
Normal distribution, 8
Normal equations, 4, 221, 242, 243, 268
Normality assumption, detect the violation of, 86
Normalization, 113, 154, 163, 166, 386
Nuisance parameter, 315
Null hypothesis on linear restriction, 46
Numerical methods of maximization, 232–235

Objective function, 373, 375, 377, 387, 389, 392, 395, 397
Observationally equivalent structures, 117, 119
Odeh, H. S., 182, 186
Optimal control, 377–380, 386, 390–399
Optimal feedback control equation, 377–381, 391, 392, 395, 397, 400
Order condition, 118
Ordered logit model, 260
Ordinary least squares, 180, 181, 220, 221, 228, 229, 239, 247, 273
Orthogonal matrix, 44
Orthogonal projection, 42
Overidentified structural equation, 118
Ozaki, T., 212, 219

Pagan, A. R., 291, 318, 340, 342–345, 348, 349
Parke, W. R., 245, 252
Partial equilibrium model, 111
Partitioned inverse, 11
Permanent consumption, 15

Permanent income, 15, 53, 54, 64
Pesaran, M. H., 286, 319
Phillips, G. D. A., 340, 349
Pierce, D. A., 212, 215, 217, 219
Poirier, D., 349
Positive semidefinite covariance
    matrix, 23, 24
Powell, M. J. D., 235, 252
Pratt, J. W., 301, 319
Precision matrix, 93
Predetermined variables, 153,
    155–157, 164, 168, 170, 178–182,
    222, 243
Prediction, 321
Prediction error, 64
Predictor:
  least-squares, 62
  unbiased, 62
Prescott, E. C., 340, 348, 376, 402,
    404
Price-adjustment equation, 245
Principal components, 99–101, 181
Principle of optimality, 378, 379
Probability density function, 158,
    170, 236, 245, 272, 285
Probit model, 254, 255, 258

Quadratic form, 9
  of m-variate normal variables, 46
Quadratic hill-climbing, 234
Quadratic interpolation, 233
Quadratic objective function, 375,
    377, 386, 387, 389, 392, 395
Quandt, R. E., 85, 110, 232, 234, 235,
    245, 246, 252, 285, 319, 348
Quinn, B. G., 212, 219

Raiffa, H., 110
Ramsey, J., 316, 319
Random coefficient regression model,
    321, 338, 342
Random disturbance, 7
Rank condition, 118
Rao, C. R., 37, 343, 344, 349

Rational expectations models, 353,
    375, 395–400
  estimation, 364–370, 380, 385, 400
  forward solution, 362
  identification, 365
  multiple solutions, 353, 356
Reduced form, 113, 147, 154, 155,
    157, 180, 182–184, 246, 247,
    250, 276, 374, 385, 396
Reduced-form coefficients, matrix of,
    113
Reduced-form equation, 113
Regression:
  cross-section, 15
  multiple linear, 7
  simple linear, 3
  slope of, 12
  timer-series, 15
Regression coefficients:
  matrix of, 12
  ratio between, 36
Regression function, 3, 12
Reiersøl, O., 107, 110
Residual, unexplained part of, 41
Restricted regression, residual of, 60
Richardson, D. H., 167, 186
Richmond, J., 122, 152
Ridge estimator, 97, 98
Risk function, 102, 302
Robust estimation, 89
Robust estimator, 88–90, 239, 240
Rosenberg, B., 340, 348, 349
Rothenberg, T. J., 152, 173, 174, 184,
    187
Rubin, D. B., 268, 269, 271, 276
Rubin, H., 163, 164, 186

Sage, A. P., 350
Salemi, M., 404
Sample mean, 18
Sample residuals, 228
Sample selection bias, 254
Samuelson, P. A., 126, 152
Sant, D., 321, 326, 350
Sargan, J. D., 107, 110, 364, 372

Sargent, T. J., 354, 372, 375, 386, 390–393, 404
Sarris, A. H., 350
Savage, L. J., 90, 110
Sawa, T., 298, 319
Schlaifer, R., 110
Schmidt, P., 110, 275, 276, 319
Schwarz, G., 301, 304, 319
Schweder, T., 350
Schweppe, F. C., 350
Score form of Lagrange multiplier test, 289
Scoring, 233, 239, 273
Search direction, 232
Seasonal components, 345–347
Seemingly unrelated regression equations, 81
Selection criteria:
  Bayesian, 300–305
  information criterion, (AIC), 293–300, 302, 303, 305–309
  Mallow's C_p, 291–293, 299, 300
  posterior probability criterion, 300–305
Serial correlation, 79, 88, 178–180
Shiller, R. J., 105, 110, 356, 372
Silvey, S. D., 101, 110, 283, 286, 288–290, 318, 319, 343, 350
Sims, C. A., 125, 152, 217, 219
Simulation, 248
Simultaneous equation model with multiplicative disturbances, 231
Simultaneous stochastic equations:
  linear, 111, 113
  nonlinear, 235–244
Singular matrix, 98
  nearly, 98, 101
Small, K., 260, 263, 264, 276
Smoothing, 321, 323–326
Specification errors, 180, 262
Specification tests, 314–316
Spectral density, 196, 251
Spectral theory, 196, 206
  cross-amplitude spectral density, 198, 204

Spectral theory (*Cont.*):
  cross-spectral density, 197, 198, 203, 204
  estimation, 204–206
  in-phase cross-spectral density, 197, 203
  lag window, 206
  out-of-phase cross-spectral density, 197, 204
  phase-difference cross-spectral density, 198, 204
  power spectrum, 197, 202, 203
  spectral density, 197, 198, 203, 204
Standard error, 34
  of regression coefficient, 46
Standard normal density function, 255
Stationarity, 190, 194, 363
Statistic, 6
Steady state, 193, 379, 395–397
Steepest ascent method, 232
Stein, C. M., 101, 110
Stein estimator, 101, 102
Step size, 232, 256
Stochastic simulation, 248
Stock-adjustment model, 103
Strauss, R. P., 275, 276
Structural coefficients, 153, 155
Structural equations, 112, 113, 154, 164, 165, 167, 168, 180–182, 235, 242–244, 248, 250, 274, 374, 385
Structure, 112
Sufficient statistic, 269
Summers, R., 180, 182, 187
Swamy, P. A. V. B., 340, 350

t distribution, 7, 228, 229
  k-variate, 95
t test, 35
Tanaka, K., 342, 344, 349
Targets, 377, 382
Taylor, J. B., 353, 364, 368, 372, 403, 404
Taylor, L., 350

Taylor, W. E., 105, 110
Taylor series, 250
Tesfatsion, L., 351
Test(s):
  cusum, 345
  cusum-of-squares, 345
  Hausman's specification, 314, 316
  Lagrange multiplier, 286–290, 343
  likelihood ratio, 289, 290, 343
  of nonnested hypotheses, 278, 284,
    286
  Ramsey's reset, 316
  score, 343, 344
  Wald, 290, 343
Test variable, 48
Testing equality among regression
  coefficients, 60–62
Testing general linear hypothesis,
  58–60
Testing hypotheses, 6–7
  about β with σ^2 unknown, 45
Theil, H., 76, 82, 87, 88, 97, 110, 152,
  155, 164, 167, 187
Three-stage least squares (3SLS),
  167–169, 176, 244, 248
  as generalized least squares, 168
  as instrumental variable estimator,
    176
Thursby, J. G., 319
Tiao, G. C., 207, 210, 212, 219
Time-series analysis, 188–219
  autocorrelation function, 79, 192
  autocovariance function, 79,
    191–192
  autocovariance matrix, 191, 192
  covariance stationary, 79, 191
  cross-correlation function, 192
  cross-covariance function, 192
  ensemble average, 191
  ergodic, 192
  frequency approach, 196–206
  partial autocorrelation function,
    195
  specification (identification), 192,
    195, 211

Time-series analysis (*Cont.*):
  spectral theory, 196–206
  stationary, 190, 194
  time average, 191
  time-domain estimation, 207–212
  weakly stationary, 191
Time-series observations, 79
Time-varying coefficients model,
  320–346
Tinbergen, J., 114–152
Tinsley, P., 340, 350
Tobin, J., 254, 265, 276
Tobit model, 254, 265, 268, 269, 271
Trace, 41
Transformation of model with
  autocorrelated residuals, 83
Transpose, 7
Tree structure, 363
Trotter, H. F., 234, 252
Truncated sample, 271–275
Turvey, R., 140, 152
Two-stage least squares (2SLS), 115,
  153–157, 164, 166–168, 180–182,
  243, 247, 248, 333, 365, 369, 385,
  386, 400, 402
  as generalized least squares, 155
  as instrumental variables estimator,
    156
  as k-class estimator, 164, 165

Uncertainty, decisions under, 395
Uncorrelated residual vector, 42
Underidentified structural equation,
  118
Unexplained part of residual, 41
Unidentifiable parameters, 115
Unit normal density function, 272
U.S. economy, model of, 131, 138,
  142
Univariate extreme-value
  distribution, 260
Univariate nonlinear regression
  model with additive disturbance,
  221

Univariate normal density function, 9
Utility maximization, 254, 257–260

Variables:
  dependent, 3
  endogenous (*see* Endogenous
    variables)
  exogenous (*see* Exogenous
    variables)
  explanatory, 3, 7
  of first causal order, 181
  independent, 7
  predetermined (*see* Predetermined
    variables)
  of second causal order, 181
Variance, smallest, 5
Vector autoregressive moving average
  (VARMA) model, 189

Wald, A., 26, 37, 290, 319

Wall, K., 348, 350, 362, 391
Wallace, N., 354, 372
Wallis, K. F., 85, 110, 364–366,
  372
Walrasian model, 373
Watson, G. S., 85, 109
Weibull distribution, 258
Weighted sum of squares, 239
Weighting matrix in optimal control,
  377, 387, 389
Weik, M. H., Jr., 31, 37
Welsch, R. E., 90, 101, 109
White, H., 86, 110, 313, 319
Wilson, G. T., 208, 210, 219
Wise, D., 271, 273, 275, 276
Wold, H., 184–186, 309, 319
Working, E. J., 115, 152
Wu, D.-M., 314, 315, 319

Zellner, A., 81, 83, 91, 110, 167, 184,
  187, 319, 350